Autodesk® Revit Fundamentals

ASCENT – Center for Technical Knowledge®

SDC Publications
P.O. Box 1334
Mission KS 66222
913-262-2664
www.SDCpublications.com
Publisher: Stephen Schroff

Copyright © 2021 ASCENT – Center for Technical Knowledge®, a division of Rand Worldwide™

All rights reserved. No part of this manual may be reproduced in any form by any photographic, electronic, mechanical or other means, or used in any information storage and retrieval system, without prior written permission of the publisher, SDC Publications.

Examination Copies
Books received as examination copies are for review purposes only and may not be made available for student use. Resale of examination copies is prohibited.

Electronic Files
Any electronic files associated with this book are licensed to the original user only. These files may not be transferred to any other party.

Trademarks
The following are registered trademarks or trademarks of Autodesk, Inc., and/or its subsidiaries and/or affiliates in the USA and other countries: 123D, 3ds Max, Algor, Alias, AliasStudio, ATC, AutoCAD LT, AutoCAD, Autodesk, the Autodesk logo, Autodesk 123D, Autodesk Homestyler, Autodesk Inventor, Autodesk MapGuide, Autodesk Streamline, AutoLISP, AutoSketch, AutoSnap, AutoTrack, Backburner, Backdraft, Beast, BIM 360, Burn, Buzzsaw, CADmep, CAiCE, CAMduct, CFdesign, Civil 3D, Cleaner, Combustion, Communication Specification, Constructware, Content Explorer, Creative Bridge, Dancing Baby (image), DesignCenter, DesignKids, DesignStudio, Discreet, DWF, DWG, DWG (design/logo), DWG Extreme, DWG TrueConvert, DWG TrueView, DWGX, DXF, Ecotect, ESTmep, Evolver, FABmep, Face Robot, FBX, Fempro, Fire, Flame, Flare, Flint, FMDesktop, ForceEffect, FormIt, Freewheel, Fusion 360, Glue, Green Building Studio, Heidi, Homestyler, HumanIK, i-drop, ImageModeler, Incinerator, Inferno, InfraWorks, Instructables, Instructables (stylized robot design/logo), Inventor LT, Inventor, Kynapse, Kynogon, LandXplorer, Lustre, MatchMover, Maya, Maya LT, Mechanical Desktop, MIMI, Mockup 360, Moldflow Plastics Advisers, Moldflow Plastics Insight, Moldflow, Moondust, MotionBuilder, Movimento, MPA (design/logo), MPA, MPI (design/logo), MPX (design/logo), MPX, Mudbox, Navisworks, ObjectARX, ObjectDBX, Opticore, Pipeplus, Pixlr, Pixlr-o-matic, Productstream, RasterDWG, RealDWG, ReCap, Remote, Revit LT, Revit, RiverCAD, Robot, Scaleform, Showcase, ShowMotion, Sim 360, SketchBook, Smoke, Socialcam, Softimage, Sparks, SteeringWheels, Stitcher, Stone, StormNET, TinkerBox, ToolClip, Topobase, Toxik, TrustedDWG, T-Splines, ViewCube, Visual LISP, Visual, VRED, Wire, Wiretap, WiretapCentral, XSI.
All other brand names, product names, or trademarks belong to their respective holders.

ISBN-13: 978-1-63057-431-4
ISBN-10: 1-63057-431-7

Printed and bound in the United States of America.

Contents

Preface ix

In This Guide xiii

Practice Files xv

Chapter 1: Introduction to BIM and Autodesk Revit 1-1

    1.1 **BIM and Autodesk Revit** 1-2
            Workflow and BIM 1-3
            Revit Terms 1-4
            Revit and Construction Documents 1-5

    1.2 **Overview of the Interface** 1-6

    1.3 **Starting Projects** 1-22
            Opening Projects 1-23
            Starting New Projects 1-25
            Saving Projects 1-26

    1.4 **Viewing Commands** 1-29
            Zooming and Panning 1-29
            Viewing in 3D 1-31
            Visual Styles 1-36

    Practice 1a Open and Review a Project 1-38

    Chapter Review Questions 1-46

    Command Summary 1-48

Chapter 2: Basic Sketching and Modify Tools 2-1

    2.1 **Using General Sketching Tools** 2-2
            Draw Tools 2-2
            Drawing Aids 2-5
            Reference Planes 2-8

    2.2 **Editing Elements** 2-10
            Selecting Multiple Elements 2-13
            Filtering Selection Sets 2-15

Practice 2a Sketch and Edit Elements	**2-17**
2.3 Working with Basic Modify Tools	**2-24**
Moving and Copying Elements	2-24
Rotating Elements	2-26
Mirroring Elements	2-28
Creating Linear and Radial Arrays	2-29
Practice 2b Work with Basic Modify Tools	**2-33**
2.4 Working with Additional Modify Tools	**2-41**
Aligning Elements	2-41
Splitting Linear Elements	2-42
Trimming and Extending	2-43
Offsetting Elements	2-45
Practice 2c Work with Additional Modify Tools	**2-47**
Chapter Review Questions	**2-51**
Command Summary	**2-55**
Chapter 3: Starting Structural Projects	**3-1**
3.1 Linking and Importing CAD Files	**3-2**
Introduction to Worksharing	3-7
Practice 3a Start a CAD-Based Structural Project	**3-8**
3.2 Linking in Revit Models	**3-11**
Managing Links	3-14
Practice 3b Start a Structural Project	**3-16**
3.3 Setting Up Levels	**3-19**
Modifying Levels	3-21
Creating Plan Views	3-24
3.4 Copying and Monitoring Elements	**3-25**
Practice 3c Copy and Monitor Elements	**3-29**
3.5 Coordinating Linked Models	**3-35**
Practice 3d Coordinate Linked Models	**3-39**
Chapter Review Questions	**3-42**
Command Summary	**3-44**
Chapter 4: Working with Views	**4-1**
4.1 Modifying the View Display	**4-2**
View Control Bar	4-2
View Properties	4-3
Hiding and Overriding Graphics	4-6
Temporarily Hide/Isolate	4-11
Using View Templates	4-13
Project Browser Organization	4-14

| 4.2 | Duplicating Views | 4-17 |
| Duplication Types | 4-17 |

Practice 4a Duplicate Views and Set the View Display 4-20

4.3	Adding Callout Views	4-23
Working with Crop Regions	4-27
Plan Regions	4-28

Practice 4b Add Callout Views 4-31

4.4	Creating Elevations and Sections	4-33
Elevations	4-34
Sections	4-36
Modifying Elevations and Sections	4-37
3D Section Views	4-41

Practice 4c Create Elevations and Sections 4-45

Chapter Review Questions 4-52

Command Summary 4-55

Chapter 5: Grids and Structural Columns 5-1

| 5.1 | Adding Grid Lines | 5-2 |
| Modifying Grid Lines | 5-5 |

Practice 5a Add Grid Lines 5-8

| 5.2 | Loading Components | 5-13 |

5.3	Placing Structural Columns	5-16
Modifying Columns	5-18
Loading Structural Content	5-19
Purging Unused Elements	5-22

Practice 5b Place Structural Columns 5-23

Chapter Review Questions 5-25

Command Summary 5-26

Chapter 6: Foundations 6-1

6.1	Modeling Walls	6-2
Modifying Walls	6-10
Wall Joins	6-13
Wall Openings	6-14

| 6.2 | Adding Wall Footings | 6-16 |
| Wall Profiles and Footings | 6-18 |

Practice 6a Model Walls and Wall Footings 6-21

| 6.3 | Creating Piers and Pilasters | 6-26 |

Practice 6b Create Piers and Pilasters 6-28

© 2021, ASCENT - Center for Technical Knowledge®

6.4 Adding Isolated Footings 6-31
    Working with Custom Families 6-33

Practice 6c Add Isolated Footings 6-35

Chapter Review Questions 6-42

Command Summary 6-44

Chapter 7: Structural Framing 7-1

7.1 Modeling Structural Framing 7-2
    Beam Systems 7-4
    Adding Bracing 7-8
    Cross Bracing Settings 7-9

Practice 7a Model Structural Framing 7-11

7.2 Modifying Structural Framing 7-20
    Sloping and Offsetting Beams 7-22
    Adding Beam Cantilevers and Cutbacks 7-24
    Changing the Cutback 7-25
    Changing Justifications 7-27
    Attaching a Column to a Beam 7-30
    Applying Beam Coping 7-31
    Editing Beam Joins 7-32

Practice 7b Modify Structural Framing 7-34

7.3 Adding Trusses 7-38
    Attaching Trusses to Roofs 7-39
    Setting Framing Types in Trusses 7-40

Practice 7c Add Trusses 7-42

Chapter Review Questions 7-48

Command Summary 7-50

Chapter 8: Adding Structural Slabs 8-1

8.1 Modeling Structural Slabs 8-2
    Modifying Slabs 8-6
    Slab Edges 8-8
    Joining Geometry 8-9

Practice 8a Model Structural Slabs 8-10

8.2 Creating Shaft Openings 8-19

Practice 8b Create Shaft Openings 8-21

Chapter Review Questions 8-25

Command Summary 8-27

Contents

Chapter 9: Structural Reinforcement 9-1

    9.1 Structural Reinforcement 9-2
        Setting the Rebar Cover Depth 9-3
        Reinforcement Settings 9-5
        Rebar Visibility 9-10

    9.2 Adding Rebar 9-11
        Sketching Rebar Shapes 9-18
        Multi-planar Rebar 9-19
        Free-Form Rebar 9-21

    9.3 Modifying Rebar 9-23
        3D Rebar Shapes 9-28
        Rebar Coupler 9-31

    Practice 9a Add Rebar 9-33

    9.4 Reinforcing Walls, Floors, and Slabs 9-41
        Area Reinforcement 9-42
        Path Reinforcement 9-45
        Fabric Reinforcement 9-47
        Modifying Area, Path, and Fabric Reinforcement 9-53

    Practice 9b Reinforce Structural Elements 9-56

    Chapter Review Questions 9-66

    Command Summary 9-69

Chapter 10: Structural Analysis 10-1

    10.1 Preparing Projects for Structural Analysis 10-2
        Structural Settings 10-3

    10.2 Viewing Analytical Models 10-13
        Graphic Overrides for Analytical Model Categories 10-16

    Practice 10a Analytical Settings and Views 10-19

    10.3 Adjusting Analytical Models 10-24
        Analytical Justifications 10-25
        Analytical Properties 10-26
        Manually Adjusting the Analytical Model 10-28
        Creating Analytical Links 10-31

    10.4 Placing Loads 10-33
        Boundary Conditions 10-33
        Adding Loads 10-35

    Practice 10b Place Loads 10-39

    Chapter Review Questions 10-48

    Command Summary 10-51

Chapter 11: Creating Construction Documents 11-1

11.1 Setting Up Sheets 11-2
Sheet (Title Block) Properties 11-4

11.2 Placing and Modifying Views on Sheets 11-5

Practice 11a Create Construction Documents 11-12

11.3 Printing Sheets 11-19
Printing Options 11-19
Export Views and Sheets to PDF 11-23

Chapter Review Questions 11-24

Command Summary 11-26

Chapter 12: Annotating Construction Documents 12-1

12.1 Working with Dimensions 12-2
Modifying Dimensions 12-5
Setting Constraints 12-9
Multi-Rebar Annotation 12-14

Practice 12a Work with Dimensions 12-17

12.2 Working with Text 12-22
Editing Text 12-25
Spell Checking 12-29
Creating Text Types 12-29

Practice 12b Work with Text 12-31

12.3 Adding Tags 12-37
Tagging in 3D Views 12-45
Beam Annotations 12-46

12.4 Adding Detail Lines and Symbols 12-49
Using Symbols 12-50
Structural Specific Symbols 12-50

Practice 12c Add Tags and Symbols 12-54

12.5 Creating Legends 12-58

Practice 12d Create Legends 12-61

Chapter Review Questions 12-66

Command Summary 12-68

Chapter 13: Creating Details 13-1

13.1 Setting Up Detail Views 13-2
Referencing a Drafting View 13-5
Saving Drafting Views 13-6

13.2 Adding Detail Components 13-9
Detail Components 13-9
Repeating Details 13-12

13.3 Annotating Details 13-13
Creating Filled Regions 13-13
Adding Detail Tags 13-16

Practice 13a Create a Detail Based on a Section Callout 13-19

Practice 13b Create a Bracing Detail 13-27

Practice 13c Additional Details 13-30

Chapter Review Questions 13-33

Command Summary 13-35

Chapter 14: Scheduling 14-1

14.1 Structural Schedules 14-2

14.2 Graphical Column Schedules 14-3
Modifying Graphical Column Schedules 14-4

Practice 14a Create a Graphical Column Schedule 14-7

14.3 Working with Schedules 14-10
Modifying Schedules 14-11
Modifying a Schedule on a Sheet 14-13
Split a Schedule Across Multiple Sheets 14-14

Practice 14b Work with Schedules 14-16

Chapter Review Questions 14-23

Command Summary 14-24

Appendix A: Introduction to Worksharing A-1

A.1 Introduction to Worksharing A-2
Worksharing Definitions A-2
Saving a Worksharing Project A-6

Command Summary A-8

Appendix B: Additional Tools B-1

B.1 Selection Sets B-2

B.2 Placing Slanted Structural Columns B-5

B.3 Editing Wall Joins B-8

B.4 Creating Slab Types B-10

B.5 Creating Rebar Types B-12

B.6 Editing Plan and Section Profiles B-14

B.7 Working with Guide Grids on Sheets B-16

B.8	**Revision Tracking**	**B-18**
	Issuing Revisions	B-23
B.9	**Annotating Dependent Views**	**B-24**
	Annotating Views	B-25
B.10	**Importing and Exporting Schedules**	**B-28**
B.11	**Creating Building Component Schedules**	**B-30**
	Schedule Properties	B-39
	Material Takeoff Schedules	B-39
B.12	**Creating a Repeating Detail**	**B-41**
Command Summary		**B-43**

Appendix C: Project - Concrete Structure C-1

C.1	Start a Structural Project	C-2
C.2	Create Foundation Elements	C-6
C.3	Frame a Concrete Structure	C-9

Index **Index-1**

Preface

To take full advantage of Building Information Modeling, the *Autodesk® Revit® 2022: Fundamentals for Structure* guide has been designed to teach the concepts and principles of creating 3D parametric models of structural buildings from engineering design through construction documentation.

This guide is intended to introduce you to the user interface and the basic building components of the software that makes Autodesk® Revit® a powerful and flexible structural modeling tool. The goal is to familiarize you with the tools required to create, modify, analyze, and document a parametric model. The examples and practices are designed to take you through the basics of a full structural project, from linking in an architectural model to construction documents.

Topics Covered

- Introduction to the Autodesk Revit software
- Basic drawing and editing tools
- Setting up levels and grids
- Working with views
- Starting a structural project based on a linked architectural model
- Adding structural columns and walls
- Adding foundations and structural slabs
- Structural reinforcement
- Beams, trusses, and framing systems
- Analytical models and placing loads
- Project practices to reinforce learning
- Construction documents
- Annotating construction documents
- Detailing and scheduling

Prerequisites

- Access to the 2022.0 version of the software, to ensure compatibility with this guide. Future software updates that are released by Autodesk may include changes that are not reflected in this guide. The practices and files included with this guide might not be compatible with prior versions (e.g., 2021).

- This guide introduces the fundamental skills in learning how to use the Autodesk Revit software, with a focus on the structural tools. It is highly recommended that students have experience and knowledge in structural engineering and its terminology.

Note on Software Setup

This guide assumes a standard installation of the software using the default preferences during installation. Lectures and practices use the standard software templates and default options for the Content Libraries.

Students and Educators Can Access Free Autodesk Software and Resources

Autodesk challenges you to get started with free educational licenses for professional software and creativity apps used by millions of architects, engineers, designers, and hobbyists today. Bring Autodesk software into your classroom, studio, or workshop to learn, teach, and explore real-world design challenges the way professionals do.

Get started today - register at the Autodesk Education Community and download one of the many Autodesk software applications available.

Visit www.autodesk.com/education/home/

Note: Free products are subject to the terms and conditions of the end-user license and services agreement that accompanies the software. The software is for personal use for education purposes and is not intended for classroom or lab use.

Lead Contributor: Cherisse Biddulph

Cherisse is an Autodesk Certified Professional for Revit, as well as an Autodesk Certified Instructor. She brings over 18 years of industry, teaching, and technical support experience to her role as a Learning Content Developer with ASCENT. With a passion for design and architecture, she received her Associates of Applied Science in Drafting and Design and has worked in the industry assisting firms with their CAD management and software implementation needs as they modernize to a Building Information Modeling (BIM) design environment. Although her main passion is the Revit design product, she is also proficient in AutoCAD, Autodesk BIM 360, and Autodesk Navisworks. Today, Cherisse continues to expand her knowledge in the ever-evolving AEC industry and the software used to support it.

Cherisse Biddulph has been the Lead Contributor for *Autodesk Revit: Fundamentals for Structure* since 2020.

In This Guide

The following highlights the key features of this guide.

Feature	Description
Practice Files	The Practice Files page includes a link to the practice files and instructions on how to download and install them. The practice files are required to complete the practices in this guide.
Chapters	A chapter consists of the following - Learning Objectives, Instructional Content, Practices, Chapter Review Questions, and Command Summary. • **Learning Objectives** define the skills you can acquire by learning the content provided in the chapter. • **Instructional Content**, which begins right after Learning Objectives, refers to the descriptive and procedural information related to various topics. Each main topic introduces a product feature, discusses various aspects of that feature, and provides step-by-step procedures on how to use that feature. Where relevant, examples, figures, helpful hints, and notes are provided. • **Practice** for a topic follows the instructional content. Practices enable you to use the software to perform a hands-on review of a topic. It is required that you download the practice files (using the link found on the Practice Files page) prior to starting the first practice. • **Chapter Review Questions**, located close to the end of a chapter, enable you to test your knowledge of the key concepts discussed in the chapter. • **Command Summary** concludes a chapter. It contains a list of the software commands that are used throughout the chapter and provides information on where the command can be found in the software.
Appendices	Appendices provide additional information to the main course content. It could be in the form of instructional content, practices, tables, projects, or skills assessment.

Practice Files

To download the practice files for this guide, use the following steps:

1. Type the URL *exactly as shown below* into the address bar of your Internet browser, to access the Course File Download page.

   www.SDCpublications.com/downloads/978-1-63057-431-1

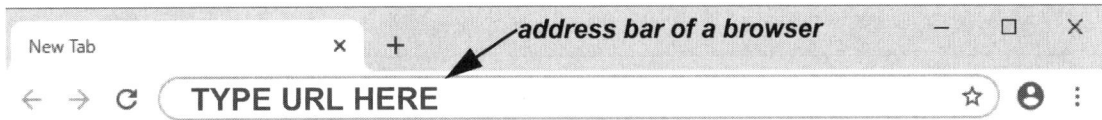

2. On the Course File Download page, click the **DOWNLOAD File** button to download the .ZIP file that contains the practice files.

3. Once the download is complete, unzip the file and extract its contents.

   The recommended practice files folder location is:
   C:\Revit 2022 Fundamentals for Structure Practice Files

   Note: It is recommended that you do not change the location of the practice files folder. Doing so may cause errors when completing the practices.

Chapter 1

Introduction to BIM and Autodesk Revit

Building Information Modeling (BIM) and the Autodesk® Revit® software work hand in hand to help you create smart 3D models that are useful at all stages in the building process. Understanding the software interface and terminology enhances your ability to create and navigate around in the various views of the model.

Learning Objectives in This Chapter

- Describe the concept of Building Information Modeling in conjunction with applying Revit.
- Navigate the graphic user interface, including the ribbon (where most of the tools are found), the Properties palette (where you make modifications to element information), and the Project Browser (where you can open various views of the model).
- Open existing projects and start new projects using templates.
- Use viewing commands to navigate around the model in 2D and 3D views.

1.1 BIM and Autodesk Revit

Building Information Modeling (BIM) is an approach to the entire building life cycle, including design, construction, and facilities management. The BIM process supports the ability to coordinate, update, and share design data with team members across disciplines.

Revit is a model authoring software. It enables you to create complete 3D building models (as shown on the left in Figure 1–1) that provide considerable information, reported through construction documents, and it enables you to share these models with other programs for more extensive analysis.

Figure 1–1

Revit is a Parametric Building Modeler software.

- *Parametric:* A relationship is established between building elements: when one element changes, all other related elements and/or geometry are modified as well. For example, when you place a door in a wall, the door removes part of the wall and stays inside that wall if it moves.

- *Building:* The software is designed for working with buildings and the surrounding landscape, as opposed to gears or highways.

- *Modeler:* A project is built in a single file based on the 3D building model, as shown on the left in Figure 1–1. All views, such as plans (as shown on the right in Figure 1–1), elevations, sections, details, construction documents, and reports, are generated based on the model.

- It is important that everyone who is collaborating on a project works in the same version and build of the software.

Introduction to BIM and Autodesk Revit

Workflow and BIM

BIM has changed the process of how a building is planned, budgeted, designed, constructed, and (in some cases) operated and maintained.

In the traditional design process, construction documents are created independently, typically including plans, sections, elevations, details, and notes. Sometimes, a separate 3D model is created in addition to these documents. Changes made in one document, such as the addition of a light fixture in a plan, have to be coordinated with the rest of the documents and schedules in the set, as shown in Figure 1–2.

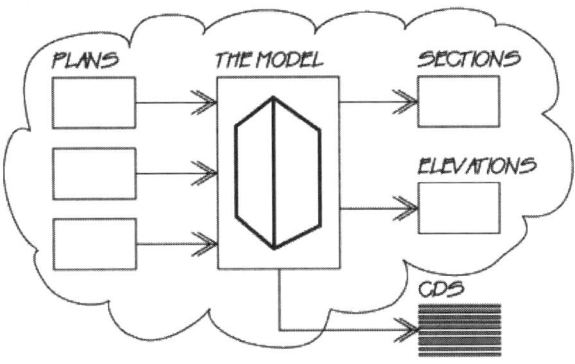

Figure 1–2

In BIM, the design process revolves around the model, as shown in Figure 1–3. Plans, elevations, and sections are simply 2D versions of the 3D model, while schedules are reports of the information stored in the model. Changes made in one view automatically update in all views and related schedules. Even construction documents update automatically with callout tags in sync with the sheet numbers. This is called bidirectional associativity.

By creating complete models and associated views of those models, Revit takes much of the tediousness out of producing a building design.

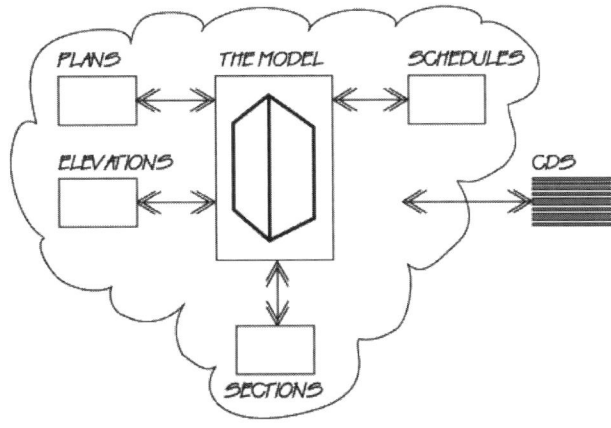

Figure 1–3

Revit Terms

When working in Revit, it is important to know the typical terms used to describe items. Views and reports display information about the elements that form a project. There are three types of elements: model, datum, and view-specific, as shown in Figure 1–4 and described below.

Figure 1–4

Views	Views enable you to display and manipulate the model. For example, you can view and work in floor plans, ceiling plans, elevations, sections, schedules, and 3D views. You can change a design from any view. All views are stored in the project.
Reports	Reports, including schedules, gather information from the building model element that can be presented in the construction documents or used for analysis.
Model Elements	Model elements include all parts of a building, such as structural walls, floors, roofs, ceilings, doors, windows, plumbing fixtures, lighting fixtures, mechanical equipment, columns, beams, furniture, casework, plants, etc. • *Host* elements support other categories of elements, such as structural walls. • *Hosted* elements must be attached to a host element. For example, a door must be placed on a (host) wall. • Standalone elements do not require hosts.
Datum Elements	Datum elements define the project context, such as the levels for the floors, grids, and reference planes.

Introduction to BIM and Autodesk Revit

View-specific Elements	View-specific elements only display in the view in which they are placed. The view scale controls their size. These include annotation elements such as dimensions, text, tags, and symbols, as well as detail elements such as detail lines, filled regions, and 2D detail components.

The software includes tools for architectural, mechanical, electrical, plumbing, and structural design.

- Revit elements are "smart": the software recognizes them as walls, columns, plants, ducts, lighting fixtures, etc. This means that the information stored in their properties automatically updates in schedules, which ensures that views and reports are coordinated across an entire project and are generated from a single model.

Revit and Construction Documents

In a traditional workflow, the most time-consuming part of the project is the construction documents. With BIM, the base views of those documents (i.e., plans, elevations, sections, and schedules) are produced automatically and update as the model is updated, saving hours of work. The views are then placed on sheets that form the construction document set.

For example, a floor plan is duplicated. Then, in the new view, all but the required categories of elements are hidden or set to halftone and annotations are added. The plan is then placed on a sheet, as shown in Figure 1–5.

Figure 1–5

- Work can continue on a view and is automatically updated on the sheet.
- Annotating views in the preliminary design phase is often not required. You might be able to wait until you are further along in the project.

1.2 Overview of the Interface

The Autodesk Revit interface is designed for intuitive and efficient access to commands and views. It includes the ribbon, Quick Access Toolbar, Navigation Bar, and Status Bar, which are common to most of the Autodesk® software. It also includes tools that are specific to the Autodesk Revit software, including the Properties palette, Project Browser, and View Control Bar. Revit includes access to tools for architectural, mechanical, electrical, plumbing, and structural design but can be altered by using the customized workspace. Setting up a customized workspace tailors your Revit environment to your specific discipline. A breakdown of the Revit interface is shown in Figure 1–6.

Figure 1–6

1. Home Screen	7. File Tab
2. Quick Access Toolbar	8. Properties Palette
3. View Tabs	9. Project Browser
4. Options Bar	10. View Control Bar
5. Ribbon	11. Status Bar
6. Navigation Bar	

Introduction to BIM and Autodesk Revit

1. The Home Screen

When you first open the Autodesk Revit software, the **Home** screen displays with recently used projects and families, as shown in Figure 1–7.

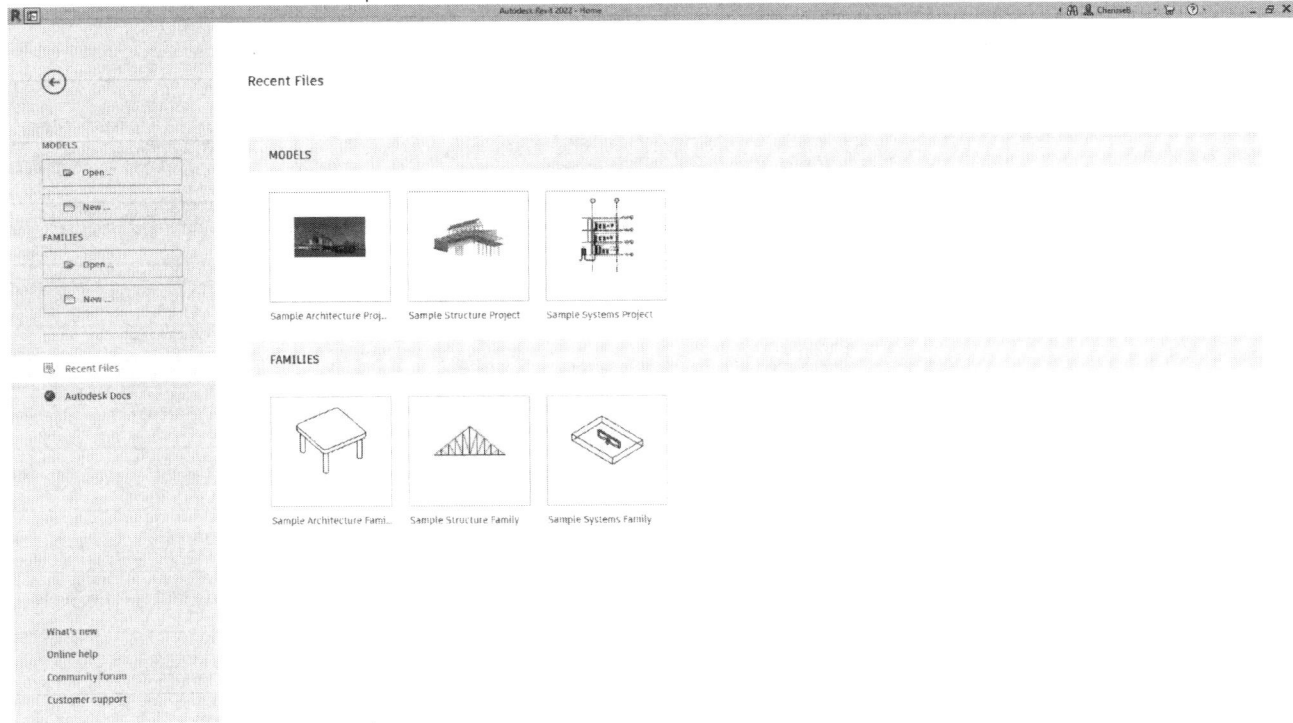

Figure 1–7

- From the Home screen, you can select the picture of a recently opened project or use one of the options on the left to open or start a new project using the default templates.

- In the Quick Access Toolbar, click (Home) to return to the screen.

- On the Home screen, click (Back) to return to the active model.

- Press <Ctrl>+<D> to toggle between the Home screen and the active model.

2. Quick Access Toolbar

The Quick Access Toolbar (shown in Figure 1–8) includes commonly used commands, such as **Home, Open, Save, Undo, Redo,** and **Print**. It also includes frequently used annotation tools, including measuring tools, **Aligned Dimension, Tag by Category,** and **Text**. Viewing tools, including several different 3D views and **Sections**, are also easily accessed here.

Figure 1–8

Hint: Customizing the Quick Access Toolbar

Right-click on the Quick Access Toolbar to change the docked location of the toolbar to be above or below the ribbon, or to add, relocate, or remove tools on the toolbar. You can also right-click on a tool in the ribbon and select **Add to Quick Access Toolbar**, as shown in Figure 1–9.

Figure 1–9

The top toolbar also hosts the InfoCenter (as shown in Figure 1–10), which includes the Autodesk sign-in, access to the Autodesk App Store, and Help options. A search field, shown in Figure 1–11, is also available to find help on the web.

Figure 1–10

Click here to expand or collapse the search field

Figure 1–11

Introduction to BIM and Autodesk Revit

3. View Tabs

Each view of a project opens in its own tab and can be pulled out of the application window and moved to another monitor. Each view displays a Navigation Bar (for quick access to viewing tools), the View Control Bar, and elevation markers, as shown in Figure 1–12.

In 3D views, you can also use the ViewCube to rotate the view.

- To close a tab, click the **X** that displays when you hover over the tab, as shown in Figure 1–12.

Figure 1–12

- Click on the tab to switch between views. You can also:
    - Press <Ctrl>+<Tab>.
    - Select the view in the Project Browser.
    - In the Quick Access Toolbar or *View* tab>Windows panel, expand (Switch Windows) and select the view from the list.

- Expand the drop-down list at the far end of the tabs, as shown in Figure 1–13, and select a view.

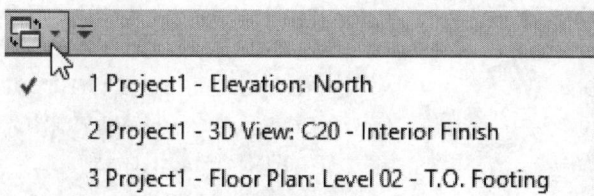

Figure 1–13

- To close all open views except the current view, in the Quick Access Toolbar or *View* tab>Windows panel, click (Close Inactive Views). If you have multiple projects open, one view of each project remains open. If you have dragged a view to another monitor, that view will need to be manually closed by clicking the **X** in the upper-right corner.

- You can switch between tabbed and tiled views from the *View* tab>Windows panel by clicking (Tab Views) or (Tile Views).

- Drag the edge of tiled views to resize them. The other views resize to match.

- Elevation markers are included in plan views to indicate the four exterior views that are defined in the default template. For more information on elevations, see *4.4 Creating Elevations and Sections*.

4. Options Bar

The Options Bar displays options that are related to the selected command or element. For example, when the **Rotate** command is active, the Options Bar displays options for rotating the selected elements, as shown at the top in Figure 1–14. When the **Place Dimensions** command is active, the Options Bar displays dimension-related options, as shown at the bottom in Figure 1–14.

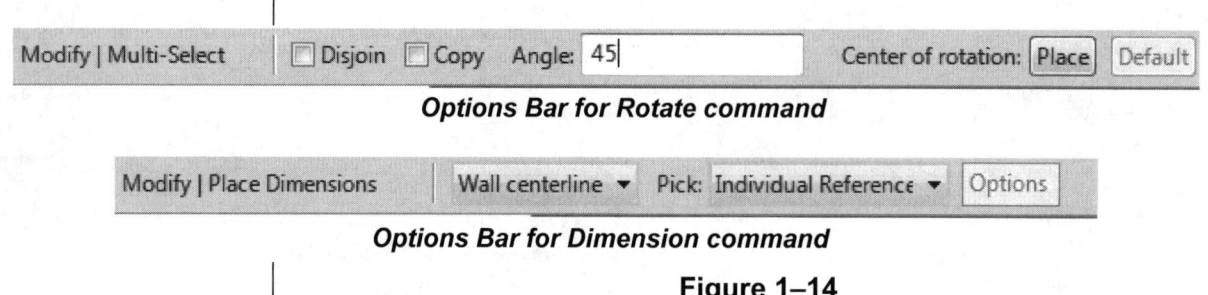

Options Bar for Rotate command

Options Bar for Dimension command

Figure 1–14

5. Ribbon

The ribbon contains tools in a series of tabs and panels, as shown in Figure 1–15. Selecting a tab displays a group of related panels. The panels contain a variety of tools, grouped by task.

Figure 1–15

When you start a command that creates new elements or you select an element, the ribbon displays the *Modify* contextual tab. This contains general editing commands and command specific tools, as shown in Figure 1–16.

Figure 1–16

- When you hover over a tool on the ribbon, tooltips display the tool's name and a short description. If you continue hovering over the tool, a graphic displays (and sometimes a video), as shown in Figure 1–17.

Figure 1–17

- Many commands have shortcut keys. For example, type **AL** for **Align** or **MV** for **Move**. The shortcuts are listed next to the name of the command in the tooltips. Do not press <Enter> when typing shortcuts.

- To arrange the order in which the ribbon tabs are displayed, select the tab, hold <Ctrl>, and drag it to a new location. The location is remembered when you restart the software.

- Any panel can be dragged by its title into the view window to become a floating panel. Click the **Return Panels to Ribbon** button (as shown in Figure 1–18) to reposition the panel in the ribbon.

Figure 1–18

- When you are finished working with a tool, you typically default back to the **Modify** command. To end a command, use one of the following methods:

    - In any tab on the ribbon, click (Modify).
    - Press <Esc> once or twice to revert to **Modify**.
    - Right-click and select **Cancel...** once or twice.
    - Start another command.

6. Navigation Bar

The Navigation Bar enables you to access the 2D and Full Navigation (3D views) Wheel to navigate the view, as well as the Zoom in Region viewing commands, as shown in Figure 1–19.

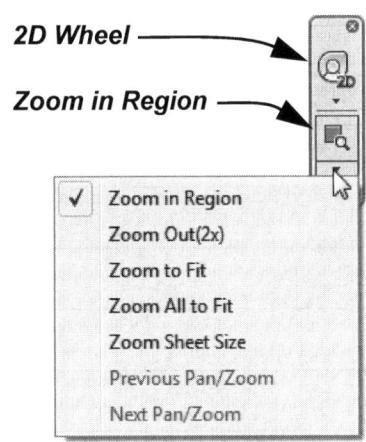

Figure 1–19

7. File Tab

The *File* tab of the ribbon provides access to file commands, settings, and documents, as shown in Figure 1–20. Hover the cursor over a command to display a list of additional tools.

If you click the primary icon, rather than the arrow, it starts the default command.

Figure 1–20

- To display a list of recently used documents, click (Recent Documents). The documents can be reordered using the drop-down list, as shown in Figure 1–21.

Figure 1–21

Click (Pin) next to a document name to keep it available.

- To display a list of open documents and views, click (Open Documents). The list displays the documents and views that are open, as shown in Figure 1–22.

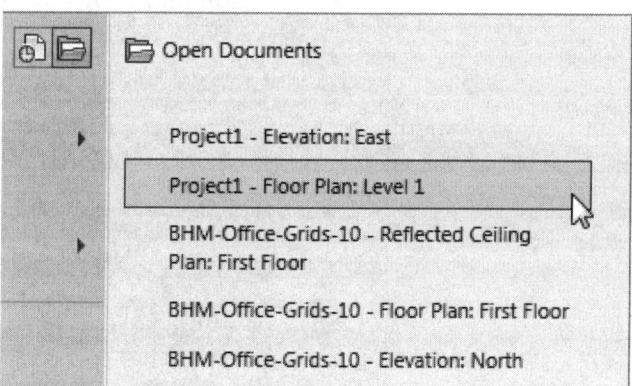

Figure 1–22

You can use the Open Documents list to change between views.

- Click (Close) to close the current project.

- At the bottom of the menu, click **Options** to open the Options dialog box or click **Exit Revit** to exit the software.

Introduction to BIM and Autodesk Revit

8. Properties Palette

The Properties palette contains several parts, as shown in Figure 1–23. The Type Selector, which can be found at the top, enables you to choose the size or style of the element you are adding or modifying. The options available on the palette enable you to make changes to information (parameters). There are two types of properties:

- **Instance Properties** are set for the individual element(s) you are creating or modifying.

- **Type Properties** control options for all elements of the same type. If you modify these parameter values, all elements of the selected type change.

The Properties palette is usually kept open while working on a project to easily permit changes at any time. If it does not display, in the *Modify* tab>Properties panel, click (Properties) or type **PP**. Alternatively, you can right-click in the view and select **Properties**.

Some parameters are only available when you are editing an element. They are grayed out when unavailable.

Figure 1–23

- Options for the current view display if the **Modify** command is active, but you have not selected an element.

- If a command or element is selected, the options for the associated element display.

- You can save the changes either by moving the cursor off of the palette, by pressing <Enter>, or by clicking **Apply**.

- When you start a command or select an element, you can set the element type in the Type Selector, as shown in Figure 1–24.

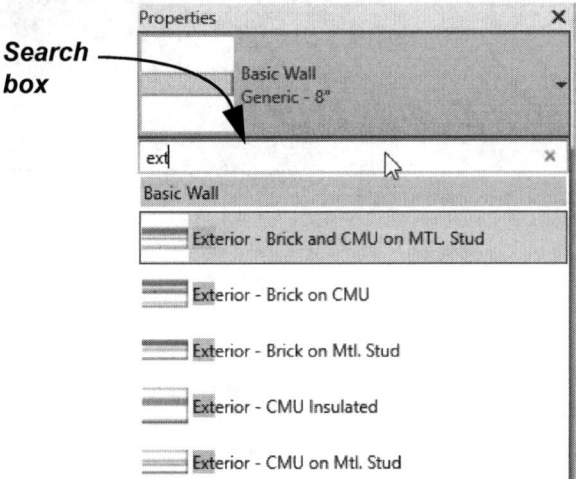

Figure 1–24

- When multiple elements are selected, you can filter the type of elements that display using the drop-down list, as shown in Figure 1–25.

You can limit what shows in the drop-down list by typing in the search box.

The Properties palette can be placed on a second monitor, or floated, resized, and docked on top of the Project Browser or other dockable palettes, as shown in Figure 1–26. Click the tab to display its associated palette.

Figure 1–25

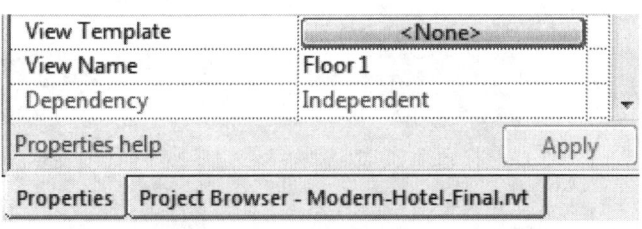

Figure 1–26

Introduction to BIM and Autodesk Revit

9. Project Browser

The Project Browser lists all views of the model in which you can work (as shown in Figure 1–27) and any additional views that you create, such as floor plans, ceiling plans, 3D views, elevations, sections, etc. It also includes schedules, legends, sheets (for plotting), lists of families by category, groups, and Revit links.

The Project Browser displays the name of the active project.

Figure 1–27

- To display the views associated with a view type (e.g., floor plans, ceiling plans, etc.), click ⊞ (Expand) next to the section name. To hide the views in the section, click ⊟ (Collapse). You can also expand and collapse sets using the shortcut menu, as shown in Figure 1–28.

Figure 1–28

- To open a view, double-click on the view name or right-click and select **Open**.

- To rename a view, slowly click twice on the view name and the text highlights so you can change it, as shown in Figure 1–29. You can also right-click on a view name and select **Rename...** or press <F2>.

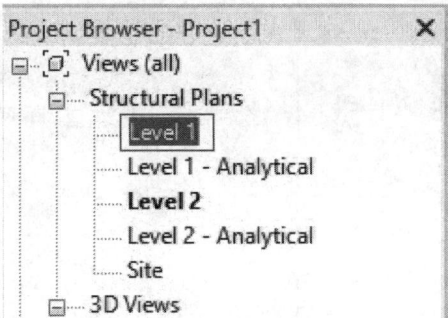

Figure 1–29

- If you no longer require a view, you can delete it. Right-click on its name in the Project Browser and select **Delete**.

- The Project Browser can be customized by changing the **Browser Organization** or its location within the application. The Project Browser can be floated, resized, or docked on top of the Properties palette.

How To: Search the Project Browser

1. In the Project Browser, right-click on the top-level view and select **Search...**, as shown in Figure 1–30.

Figure 1–30

2. In the Search in Project Browser dialog box, type the words that you want to find (as shown in Figure 1–31) and click **Next**.
3. In the Project Browser, the first instance of that search highlights, as shown in Figure 1–32.

Figure 1–31

Figure 1–32

4. Continue using **Next** and **Previous** to move through the list.
5. Click **Close** when you are done.

10. View Control Bar

The View Control Bar (shown in Figure 1–33) displays at the bottom of each view window. It controls aspects of that view, such as the scale and detail level. It also includes tools that display parts of the view and hide or isolate elements in the view.

Figure 1–33

- The number of options in the View Control Bar change when you are in a 3D view, as shown in Figure 1–34.

Figure 1–34

Tool	Tooltip	Description
1/8" = 1'-0"	View Scale	Sets the scale of individual views.
	Detail Level	Sets the detail level of a view.
	Visual Style	Controls which graphic style representation is used for the view.
	Sun Path On/Off	Controls the visibility of the sun's path.
	Shadows On/Off	Controls elements' shadow visibility in a view.
	Show/Hide Rendering Dialog	Available in 3D only. Shows or hides the rendering dialog box.
	Crop View	Define the crop boundaries for a view.
	Show/Hide Crop Region	Displays the crop region in a view.
	Unlocked/Locked 3D Views	Locks a 3D view's orientation.
	Temporary Hide/Isolate	Temporarily isolates/hides by category or element.
	Reveal Hidden Elements	Shows hidden elements or unhides them in the active view.
	Worksharing Display	Available when worksharing is enabled. Controls display settings.
	Temporary View Properties	Enables, applies, or restores view properties, and displays recent templates and applies them.
	Show or Hide the Analytical Model	Only used for structural and MEP to display the analytical information.
	Highlight Displacement Sets	Used to highlight displacement sets (also known as exploded views).
	Reveal Constraints	Used to temporarily view the dimension and alignment constraints in the active view.
	Preview Visibility	Available in the Family Editor only. Controls the visibility of the preview.

11. Status Bar

The Status Bar provides information about the current process, such as the next step for a command, as shown in Figure 1–35.

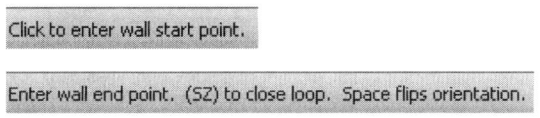

Figure 1–35

Other options in the Status Bar are related to worksets and design options (advanced tools), as well as selection methods and filters.

Hint: Shortcut Menus

Shortcut menus help you to work smoothly and efficiently by enabling you to quickly access required commands. These menus provide access to basic viewing commands, recently used commands, and the available browsers, as shown in Figure 1–36. Additional options vary depending on the element or command that you are using.

Figure 1–36

1.3 Starting Projects

File operations to open existing files, create new files from a template, and save files in Revit are found in the *File* tab, as shown in Figure 1–37.

Figure 1–37

There are three main file formats:

- **Project files (.rvt):** These are where you do the majority of your work in the building model by adding elements, creating views, annotating views, and setting up printable sheets. They are initially based on template files.

- **Family files (.rfa):** These are separate components that can be inserted in a project. They include elements that can stand alone (e.g., a table or piece of mechanical equipment) or are items that are hosted in other elements (e.g., a door in a wall or a lighting fixture in a ceiling). Title block and annotation symbol files are special types of family files.

- **Template files (.rte and .rft):** These are the base files for any new project or family. Project templates (**.rte**) hold standard information and settings for creating new project files. The software includes several templates for various types of projects. You can also create custom templates. Family templates (**.rft**) include base information for creating families. Template files are usually saved as a new file.

Introduction to BIM and Autodesk Revit

Opening Projects

To open an existing project, in the Quick Access Toolbar or *File* tab, click (Open), or press <Ctrl>+<O>. The Open dialog box opens, and you can navigate to the required folder and select a project file. An example of the Open dialog box is shown in Figure 1–38.

Figure 1–38

- The software release version of the currently selected project displays below the preview. Do not open a drawing that should remain in an earlier version, as you cannot save back to previous versions.

Note: It is important that everyone working on a project uses the same software version (e.g., 2022) and is on the same updated version (e.g., 2022.1). While your software may be able to open files created in its earlier versions, it will not be able to open files created in versions newer than the one you are using currently. For example, if you are working in Revit 2021, you cannot open a model created in Revit 2022.

- When you open a file created in an earlier version, the Model Upgrade dialog box (shown in Figure 1–39) indicates the release of a file and the release to which it will be upgraded. If needed, you can cancel the upgrade before it completes.

Figure 1–39

Hint: Opening Workset-Related Files

Worksets are used when the project becomes large enough for multiple people to work on it at the same time. At this point, a central model with multiple worksets (such as element interiors, building shell, and site) that are used by the project team members is created.

When you open a workset-related file, it creates a new local file on your computer, as shown in Figure 1–40. Do not work in the main central model.

Figure 1–40

- For more information about opening and saving workset-related files, see *Appendix A: Introduction to Worksharing.*

- When you click on a central model showing on the Home screen, a local copy of the file is created.

- For more information on establishing and using worksets, refer to the ASCENT guide *Autodesk Revit: Collaboration Tools.*

Starting New Projects

New projects are based on a template file. The template file includes preset levels, views, and some families, such as wall styles and text styles. Check with your BIM manager about which template you need to use for your projects. Your company might have more than one based on the types of building that you are designing.

How To: Start a New Project

1. In the *File* tab, expand (New) and click (Project) (as shown in Figure 1–41), or press <Ctrl>+<N>.

Figure 1–41

2. In the New Project dialog box (shown in Figure 1–42), select the template that you want to use and click **OK**.

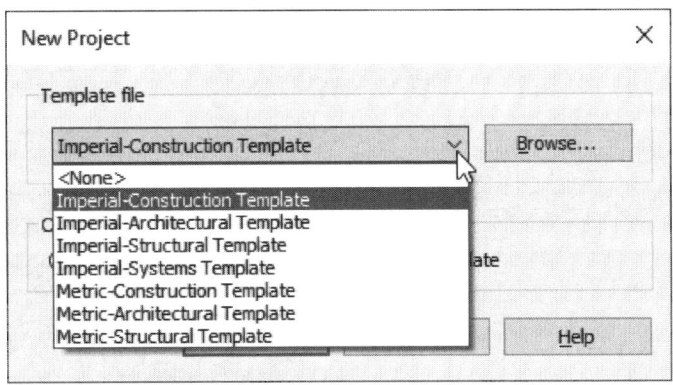

Figure 1–42

The list of Template files is set in the Options dialog box in the File Locations tab. It might vary depending on the installed product and company standards.

You can select from a list of templates if they have been set up by your BIM manager.

- You can add ☐ (New) to the Quick Access Toolbar. At the end of the Quick Access Toolbar, click ▼ (Customize Quick Access Toolbar) and select **New**, as shown in Figure 1–43.

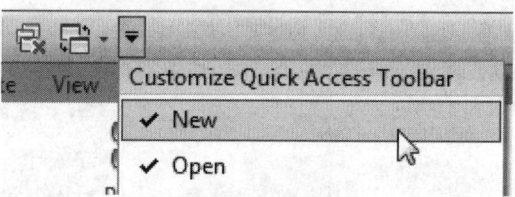

Figure 1–43

Saving Projects

It is important to save your projects frequently. In the Quick Access Toolbar or *File* tab, click 💾 (Save), or press <Ctrl>+<S> to save your project. If the project has not yet been saved, the Save As dialog box opens, where you can specify a file location and name.

- To save an existing project with a new name, in the *File* tab, expand 💾 (Save As) and click 📄 (Project).

- If you have not saved in a certain amount of time, the software will notify you with the Project Not Saved Recently alert box, as shown in Figure 1–44. Select **Save the project**. If you want to set reminder intervals or not save at this time, select one of the other two options shown in Figure 1–44.

Figure 1–44

- You can set the *Save reminder interval* to **15** or **30 minutes**, **One**, **Two**, or **Four hours**, or to have **No reminders** display. In the *File* tab, click **Options** to open the Options dialog box. Select **General** and set the interval as shown in Figure 1–45.

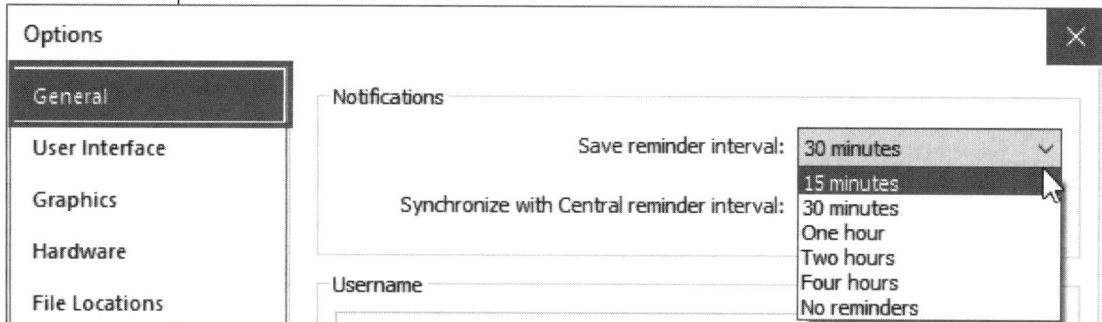

Figure 1–45

Saving Backup Copies

By default, the software saves a backup copy of a project file when you save the project. Backup copies are numbered incrementally (e.g., **My Project.0001.rvt**, **My Project.0002.rvt**, etc.) and are saved in the same folder as the original file. In the Save As dialog box, click **Options...** to control how many backup copies are saved. The default number is three backups. If you exceed this number, the software deletes the oldest backup file.

> **Hint: Saving Workshared Projects**
>
> If you use worksets in your project, you need to save the project locally and to the central model. It is recommended to save the local file frequently, just like any other file, and to save to the central model every hour or so by synchronizing with the central model.
>
> To synchronize your changes with the central model, in the Quick Access Toolbar, expand (Synchronize and Modify Settings) and click (Synchronize Now). After you save to the central model, save the file locally again.
>
> At the end of the day, or when you are finished with the current session, in the Quick Access Toolbar, expand (Synchronize and Modify Settings) and click (Synchronize and Modify Settings) to relinquish the files you have been working on to the central model.
>
> - The maximum number of backups for workset-enabled files is set to 20 by default.
>
> - Note: Workshared files do not have the same backup files as non-workshared files.

1.4 Viewing Commands

Viewing commands are crucial to working efficiently in most drawing and modeling programs, and Revit is no exception. Once in a view, you can use the Zoom controls to navigate in it. You can zoom in and out and pan in any view. There are also special tools for viewing in 3D.

Zooming and Panning

Using the Mouse to Zoom and Pan

Use the mouse wheel (shown in Figure 1–46) as the main method of moving around the models.

Figure 1–46

- Scroll the wheel on the mouse up to zoom in and down to zoom out.
- Hold the wheel and move the mouse to pan.
- Double-click on the wheel to zoom to the extents of the view.
- In a 3D view, hold <Shift> and the mouse wheel and move the mouse to rotate around the model.
- When you save a model and exit the software, the pan and zoom location of each view is remembered. This is especially important for complex models.

Zoom Controls

A number of additional zoom methods enable you to control the screen display. **Zoom** and **Pan** can be performed at any time while using other commands.

- You can access the **Zoom** commands in the Navigation Bar in the upper-right corner of the view (as shown in Figure 1–47). You can also access them from most shortcut menus and by typing the shortcut commands.

*(2D Wheel) provides cursor-specific access to **Zoom** and **Pan**.*

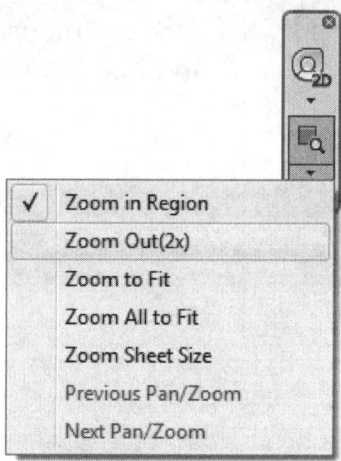

Figure 1–47

Zoom Commands

	Command	Description
	Zoom in Region (ZR)	Zooms in to a region that you define. Drag the cursor or select two points to define the rectangular area you want to zoom in to. This is the default command.
	Zoom Out(2x) (ZO)	Zooms out to half the current magnification around the center of the elements.
	Zoom to Fit (ZF or ZE)	Zooms out so that the entire contents of the project display on the screen in the current view.
	Zoom All to Fit (ZA)	Zooms out so that the entire contents of the project display on the screen in all open views.
	Zoom Sheet Size (ZS)	Zooms in or out in relation to the sheet size.
N/A	**Previous Pan/Zoom (ZP)**	Steps back one **Zoom** command.
N/A	**Next Pan/Zoom**	Steps forward one **Zoom** command if you have used **Previous Pan/Zoom**.

Viewing in 3D

Even if you started a project entirely in plan views, you can quickly create 3D views of the model, as shown in Figure 1–48. There are two types of 3D views: isometric views created by the **Default 3D View** command and perspective views created by the **Camera** command.

Figure 1–48

Working in 3D views helps you visualize the project and position some of the elements correctly. You can create and modify elements in both isometric and perspective 3D views, just as you can in plan views.

- Once you have created a 3D view, you can save it and easily return to it.

How To: Create and Save a 3D Isometric View

1. In the Quick Access Toolbar or *View* tab>Create panel, click (Default 3D View). The default 3D southeast isometric view opens, as shown in Figure 1–49.

You can spin the view to a different angle using the mouse wheel or the middle button of a three-button mouse. Hold <Shift> as you press the wheel or middle button and drag the cursor.

Figure 1–49

2. Modify the view to display the building from other directions.
3. In the Project Browser, slowly click twice on the **{3D}** view or right-click and select **Rename...**.
4. The name is placed in a text box with the original name highlighted, as shown in Figure 1–50. Type a new name in the text box, as shown in Figure 1–51.

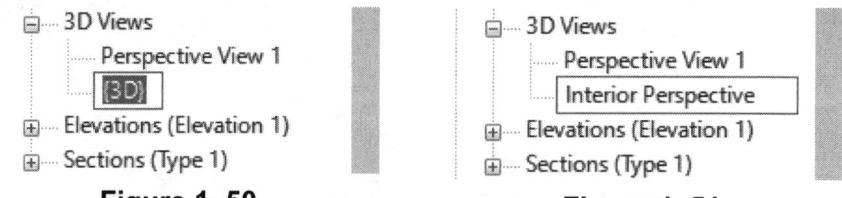

Figure 1–50   Figure 1–51

All types of views can be renamed.

- When changes to the default 3D view are saved and you start another default 3D view, it displays the southeast isometric view once again. If you modified the default 3D view but did not save it with a new name, the **Default 3D View** command opens the view in the last orientation you specified.

Introduction to BIM and Autodesk Revit

How To: Create a Perspective View

1. Switch to a floor plan view.
2. In the Quick Access Toolbar or *View* tab>Create panel, expand (Default 3D View) and click (Camera).
3. Place the camera on the view.
4. Point the camera in the direction in which you want it to shoot by placing the target on the view, as shown in Figure 1–52.

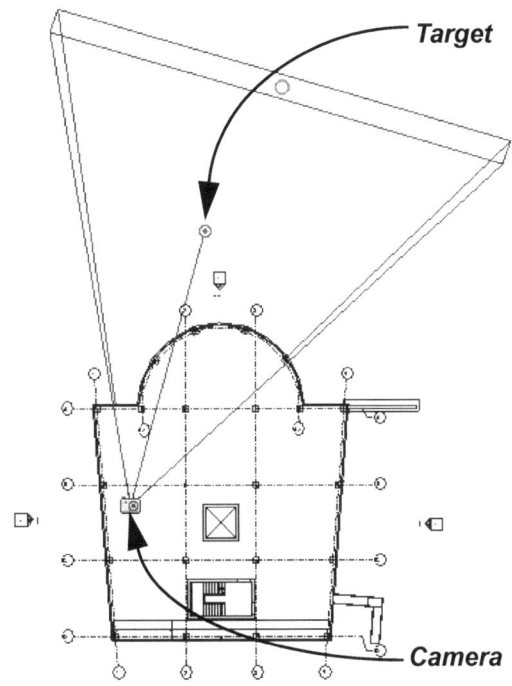

Figure 1–52

5. A new view is displayed, as shown in Figure 1–53.

Figure 1–53

Use the round controls to modify the display size of the view and press <Shift> + the mouse wheel to change the view.

6. In the Properties palette, scroll down and adjust the *Eye Elevation* and *Target Elevation* as needed.

- If the view becomes distorted, reset the target so that it is centered in the boundary of the view (called the crop region).

  In the *Modify | Cameras* tab>Camera panel, click (Reset Target).

- You can further modify a view by adding shadows, as shown in Figure 1–54. In the View Control Bar, toggle (Shadows Off) and (Shadows On). Shadows display in any model view, not just in the 3D views. To set up the sun location, expand (Sun Path Off) and select **Sun Settings...**. Select (Sun Path On) to see the visual location of the sun.

Figure 1–54

Hint: Using the ViewCube

The ViewCube provides visual clues as to where you are in a 3D view. It helps you move around the model with quick access to specific views (such as top, front, and right), as well as corner and directional views, as shown in Figure 1–55.

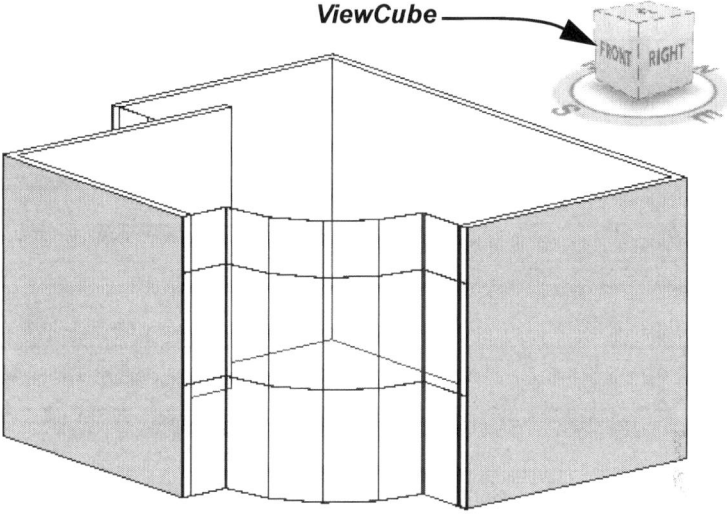

Figure 1–55

Move the cursor over any face of the ViewCube to highlight it. Once a face is highlighted, you can select it to reorient the model. You can also click and drag the ViewCube to rotate the box, which rotates the model.

- (Home) displays when you roll the cursor over the ViewCube. Click it to return to the view defined as **Home**. To change the Home view, set the view as you want it, right-click on the ViewCube, and select **Set Current View as Home**.

- The ViewCube is available in isometric and perspective views.

- You can switch between Perspective and Isometric mode by right-clicking on the ViewCube and selecting either **Perspective** or **Orthographic**.

Visual Styles

Any view can have a visual style applied. The **Visual Style** options found in the View Control Bar (shown in Figure 1–56) specify the shading of the building model. These options apply to plan, elevation, section, and 3D views.

Figure 1–56

- (Wireframe) displays the lines and edges that make up elements, but hides the surfaces. This can be useful when you are dealing with complex intersections.

- (Hidden Line) displays the lines, edges, and surfaces of the elements, but it does not display any colors. This is the most common visual style to use while working on a design.

- (Shaded) and (Consistent Colors) give you a sense of the materials, including transparent glass. An example that uses Consistent Colors is shown in Figure 1–57.

Figure 1–57

Introduction to BIM and Autodesk Revit

- (Realistic) displays what is shown when you render the view, including Rich Photorealistic Content (RPC) components and artificial lights. It takes a lot of computer power to execute this visual style. Therefore, it is better to use the other visual styles most of the time as you are working.

> **Hint: Rendering**
>
> Rendering is a powerful tool that enables you to display a photorealistic view of the model you are working on, such as the example shown in Figure 1–58. This can be used to help clients and designers understand a building's design in better detail.
>
>
>
> Figure 1–58
>
> - In the View Control Bar, click (Show Rendering Dialog) to set up the options. **Show Rendering Dialog** is only available in 3D views.

Practice 1a: Open and Review a Project

Practice Objectives

- Navigate the graphic user interface.
- Manipulate 2D and 3D views by zooming and panning.
- Create 3D isometric and perspective views.
- Set the visual style of a view.

In this practice, you will open a project file and view each of the various areas in the interface. You will investigate elements, commands, and their options. You will also open views through the Project Browser and view the model in 3D, as shown in Figure 1–59.

Figure 1–59

- This is a version of the main project you will work on throughout this guide.

Introduction to BIM and Autodesk Revit

Task 1 - Explore the interface.

1. In the *File* tab, expand (Open) and click (Project).

   - If you are on the Home page, click **Open...** in the *MODELS* area of the sidebar.

2. In the Open dialog box, navigate to the practice files folder and select **Structural-Suites.rvt**.

3. Click **Open**. The 3D view of the building opens in the view window.

4. In the Project Browser, double-click on the **Structural Plans: 00 GROUND FLOOR** view. It opens a plan with the *Visual Style* set to **Wireframe** so that the footings and foundation walls display, although there is a slab over them.

5. In the View Control Bar, change the *Visual Style* to **Hidden Line**. The lines that are hidden in the view display as dashed lines, as shown in Figure 1–60.

Figure 1–60

If the Project Browser and Properties palette are docked over each other, use the Project Browser tab at the bottom to display it.

6. In the Project Browser, double-click on the **Structural Plans: T.O. FOOTING** view. The strip footings and spread footings display as continuous lines because they are not obscured by a slab, as shown in Figure 1–61.

Figure 1–61

7. Zoom in on one corner of the building. The foundation walls are in-filled with the appropriate concrete hatch, as shown in Figure 1–62.

Figure 1–62

8. Double-click the mouse wheel or type **ZE** to zoom to the extents of the view. (**ZA** zooms to the extents of all of the opened view windows.) Find the section marker that extends vertically along the model, as shown in Figure 1–63.

Figure 1–63

9. Double-click on the section head to open the **NORTH-SOUTH SECTION** view.

10. In the Project Browser, navigate to the *Sections (Building Section)* category. The **NORTH-SOUTH SECTION** view name is bold. You can navigate through your model by double-clicking on the element in the Project Browser or by using the graphical view elements in the model.

11. In the section view, zoom in on the area in which the callout has been placed, as shown in Figure 1–64. Double-click on the callout-head to open the **TYPICAL EDGE DETAIL** view.

Figure 1–64

12. In the **TYPICAL EDGE DETAIL** view, select the floor, as shown in Figure 1–65.

Figure 1–65

13. This is a full 3D floor element. You can edit it using the standard modify tool and the concrete floor-specific tools found in the *Modify | Floors* contextual tab, as shown in Figure 1–66.

Figure 1–66

14. The Properties palette displays the instance parameters for the element, as shown in Figure 1–67.

Any changes made here are applied to the selected element only.

Figure 1–67

Any changes made to the element here are applied to all of its other instances in the project.

15. In Properties, click (Edit Type) to access the *Type Parameters* in the Type Properties dialog box, as shown in Figure 1–68.

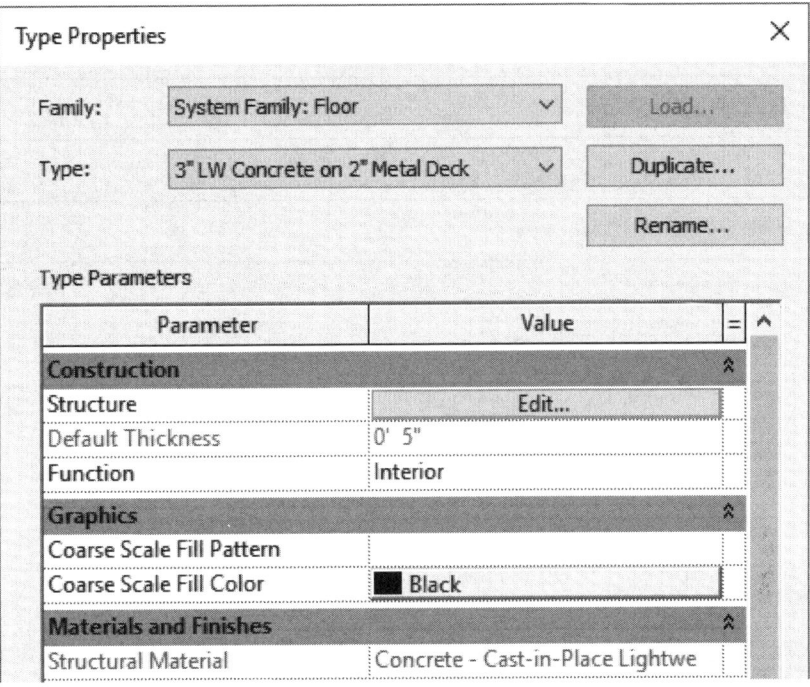

Figure 1–68

16. Click **Cancel** to close the Type Properties dialog box.

17. End the command using one of the following methods:

    - In any tab on the ribbon, click (Modify).
    - Press <Esc> once or twice to revert to **Modify**.
    - Right-click and select **Cancel...** once or twice.
    - Start another command.

18. Select one of the bolted connections. This is a detail component (2D element). The *Modify | Detail Items* contextual tab displays the modifying options specific to this element, as shown in Figure 1–69.

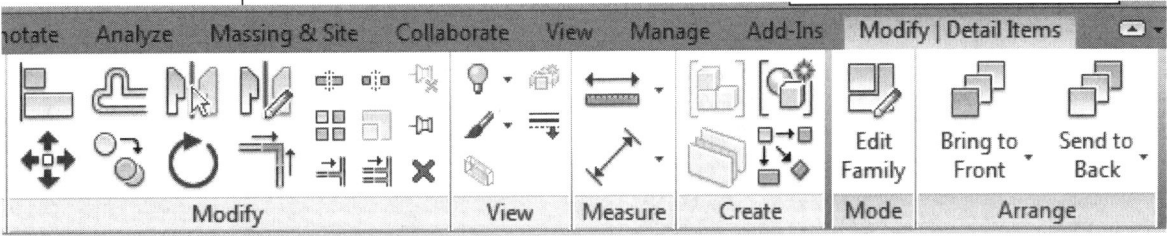

Figure 1–69

19. Press <Esc> to clear the selection.

Task 2 - Work with multiple views and 3D views.

1. At the top of the view, click each tab to switch between the open views.

2. In the *View* tab>Windows panel, click ▯ (Tile Views). All of the open views are tiled. Type **ZA** (for Zoom All) to zoom out to the extents of each view, as shown in Figure 1–70.

Figure 1–70

3. Click inside the 3D view to make it active.

4. In the *View* tab>Windows panel, click ▯ (Tab Views). The views return to the tabs and the 3D view is first in the group.

5. In the Quick Access Toolbar, click ▯ (Close Inactive Windows) so that only the current window remains open.

6. Using the mouse wheel, zoom in on the building.

7. Press and hold <Shift> and then press and hold the wheel on the mouse. Move the mouse to dynamically view the 3D model. You can also navigate in 3D using the ViewCube in the upper-right corner of the view.

8. Expand the *File* tab and click (Close) to exit the project. Do not save changes.

Chapter Review Questions

1. When you create a project in the Autodesk Revit software, do you work in 3D or 2D?

    a. You work in 2D in plan views and in 3D in non-plan views.

    b. You work in 3D almost all of the time, even when you are using what looks like a flat view.

    c. You work in 2D or 3D depending on how you toggle the 2D/3D control.

    d. You work in 2D in plan and section views and in 3D in isometric views.

2. What is the purpose of the Project Browser?

    a. It enables you to browse through the building project, similar to a walk through.

    b. It is the interface for managing all of the files that are required to create the complete architectural model of the building.

    c. It manages multiple Autodesk Revit projects as an alternative to using Windows Explorer.

    d. It is used to access and manage the views of the project.

3. Where do you change the visual style?

    a. Ribbon

    b. View Control Bar

    c. Options Bar

    d. Properties Palette

4. What is the difference between Type Properties and Properties?

    a. Properties stores parameters that apply to the selected individual element(s). Type Properties stores parameters that impact every element of the same type in the project.

    b. Properties stores the location parameters of an element. Type Properties stores the size and identity parameters of an element.

    c. Properties only stores parameters of the view. Type Properties stores parameters of model components.

5. When you start a new project, how do you specify the base information in the new file?

   a. Transfer the base information from an existing project.

   b. Select the right template for the task.

   c. The Autodesk Revit software automatically extracts the base information from imported or linked file(s).

6. What is the main difference between a view made using (Default 3D View) and a view made using (Camera)?

   a. Use **Default 3D View** for exterior views and **Camera** for interiors.

   b. **Default 3D View** creates a static image and a **Camera** view is live and always updated.

   c. **Default 3D View** is isometric and a **Camera** view is perspective.

   d. **Default 3D View** is used for the overall building and a **Camera** view is used for looking in tight spaces.

Command Summary

Button	Command	Location
General Tools		
	Home	• Quick Access Toolbar • Shortcut: <Ctrl>+<D>
	Modify	• Ribbon: All tabs>Select panel • Shortcut: MD
	New	• *File* tab • Shortcut: <Ctrl>+<N>
	Open	• Quick Access Toolbar • *File* tab • Shortcut: <Ctrl>+<O>
	Open Documents	• *File* tab
	Properties	• Ribbon: *Modify* tab>Properties panel • Shortcut: PP
	Recent Documents	• *File* tab
	Save	• Quick Access Toolbar • *File* tab • Shortcut: <Ctrl>+<S>
	Synchronize and Modify Settings	• Quick Access Toolbar
	Synchronize Now	• Quick Access Toolbar: expand Synchronize and Modify Settings
	Type Properties	• Ribbon: *Modify* tab>Properties panel • Properties palette
Viewing Tools		
	Camera	• Quick Access Toolbar: expand Default 3D View • Ribbon: *View* tab>Create panel> expand Default 3D View
	Close Inactive Views	• Quick Access Toolbar • Ribbon: *View* tab>Windows panel
	Default 3D View	• Quick Access Toolbar • Ribbon: *View* tab>Create panel
	Home	• ViewCube
N/A	Next Pan/Zoom	• Navigation Bar • Shortcut Menu

Introduction to BIM and Autodesk Revit

	Previous Pan/Zoom	• Navigation Bar
N/A		• Shortcut Menu
		• Shortcut: ZP
	Shadows On/Off	• View Control Bar
	Show Rendering Dialog/Render	• View Control Bar
		• Ribbon: *View* tab>Graphics panel
		• Shortcut: RR
	Switch Windows	• Quick Access Toolbar
		• Ribbon: *View* tab>Windows panel
	Tab Views	• Ribbon: *View* tab>Windows panel
		• Shortcut: TW
	Tile Views	• Ribbon: *View* tab>Windows panel
		• Shortcut: WT
	Zoom All to Fit	• Navigation Bar
		• Shortcut: ZA
	Zoom in Region	• Navigation Bar
		• Shortcut Menu
		• Shortcut: ZR
	Zoom Out(2x)	• Navigation Bar
		• Shortcut Menu
		• Shortcut: ZO
	Zoom Sheet Size	• Navigation Bar
		• Shortcut: ZS
	Zoom to Fit	• Navigation Bar
		• Shortcut Menu
		• Shortcut: ZF, ZE
Visual Styles		
	Consistent Colors	• View Control Bar
	Hidden Line	• View Control Bar
		• Shortcut: HL
	Realistic	• View Control Bar
	Shaded	• View Control Bar
		• Shortcut: SD
	Wireframe	• View Control Bar
		• Shortcut: WF

2.1 Using General Sketching Tools

When you start a command, the contextual tab on the ribbon, the Options Bar, and the Properties palette (as shown in Figure 2–1) enable you to set up features for each new element you are placing in the project. As you are working, several features called *drawing aids* display, as shown in Figure 2–1. They help you to create designs quickly and accurately.

Figure 2–1

- In Autodesk Revit, you are most frequently creating 3D model elements rather than 2D sketches. These tools work with both 3D and 2D elements in the software.

Draw Tools

Many linear elements (such as walls, beams, ducts, pipes, and conduits) are modeled using the tools on the contextual tab in the Draw panel. Other elements (such as floors, ceilings, roofs, and slabs) have boundaries that are sketched using many of the same tools. Draw tools are also used when you create details or schematic drawings.

Two methods are available:

- *Draw* the element using a geometric form.
- *Pick* an existing element (such as a line, face, or wall) as the basis for the new element's geometry and position.

The exact tools vary according to the element being modeled.

Basic Sketching and Modify Tools

How To: Create Linear Elements

1. Start the command you want to use.
2. In the contextual tab>Draw panel (shown in Figure 2–2), select a drawing tool.

Figure 2–2

You can change from one Draw tool shape to another in the middle of a command.

3. Select points to define the elements or watch the Status Bar, in the lower-left corner, for hints on what to do.
4. Finish the command using one of the standard methods:

   - Click ▸ (Modify).
   - Press <Esc> twice.
   - Start another command.

Draw Options

When you are in Drawing mode, several options display in the Options Bar, as shown in Figure 2–3.

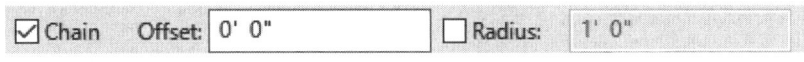

Figure 2–3

Different options display according to the type of element that is selected or the command that is active.

- **Chain:** Controls how many segments are created in one process. If this option is not selected, the **Line** and **Arc** tools only create one segment at a time. If it is selected, you can continue adding segments until you press <Esc> or select the command again.

- **Offset:** Enables you to enter values so you can create linear elements at a specified distance from the selected points or element.

- **Radius:** Enables you to enter values when using a radial tool or to add a radius to the corners of linear elements as you sketch them.

Draw Tools

	Tool	Description
	Line	Draws a straight line defined by the first and last points. If **Chain** is enabled, you can continue selecting end points for multiple segments.
	Rectangle	Draws a rectangle defined by two opposing corner points. You can adjust the dimensions after selecting both points.
	Inscribed Polygon	Draws a polygon inscribed in a hypothetical circle, with the number of sides specified in the Options Bar.
	Circumscribed Polygon	Draws a polygon circumscribed around a hypothetical circle, with the number of sides specified in the Options Bar.
	Circle	Draws a circle defined by a center point and radius.
	Start-End-Radius Arc	Draws a curve defined by a start, end, and radius of the arc. The outside dimension shown is the included angle of the arc. The inside dimension is the radius.
	Center-ends Arc	Draws a curve defined by a center, radius, and included angle. The selected point of the radius also defines the start point of the arc.
	Tangent End Arc	Draws a curve tangent to another element. Select an end point for the first point, but do not select the intersection of two or more elements. Then, select a second point based on the included angle of the arc.
	Fillet Arc	Draws a curve defined by two other elements and a radius. Because it is difficult to select the correct radius by clicking, this command automatically moves to edit mode. Select the dimension and then modify the radius of the fillet.
	Spline	Draws a spline curve based on selected points (sketches, model, and detail lines only). The curve does not actually touch the points.
	Ellipse	Draws an ellipse from a primary and secondary axis (walls, sketches, model, and detail lines only).
	Partial Ellipse	Draws only one side of the ellipse, like an arc (sketches, model, and detail lines only). A partial ellipse also has a primary and secondary axis.

Basic Sketching and Modify Tools

Pick Tools

	Pick Lines	Use this option to select existing linear elements in the project. This is useful when you start the project from an imported 2D drawing.
	Pick Face	Use this option to select the face of a 3D massing element (walls and 3D views only).
	Pick Walls	Use this option to select an existing wall in the project to be the basis for a new sketch line (floors, ceilings, etc.).

Drawing Aids

As soon as you start sketching or placing elements, three drawing aids display, as shown in Figure 2–4:

- Alignment line
- Temporary dimensions
- Snaps

These aids are available with most modeling and many modification commands.

Figure 2–4

Alignment lines display as soon as you select your first point. They help keep lines horizontal, vertical, or at a specified angle. They also line up with the implied intersections of walls and other elements.

- Hold <Shift> to force the alignments to be orthogonal (90° angles only).

Temporary dimensions display to help place elements at the correct length, angle, and location.

- You can type in a value or move the cursor until you see the dimension you want, or you can place the element and then modify the value as needed.

- The length and angle increments shown vary depending on how far in or out the view is zoomed.

- For imperial measurements (feet and inches), the software uses a default of feet. For example, when you type **4** and press <Enter>, it assumes **4'-0"**. For a distance such as **4'-6"**, you can type any of the following: **4'-6"**, **4'6**, **4-6**, or **4 6** (the numbers separated by a space). To indicate distances less than one foot, type the inch mark (") after the distance, or enter **0**, a space, and then the distance.

> **Hint: Temporary Dimensions and Permanent Dimensions**
>
> Temporary dimensions disappear as soon as you finish adding elements. If you want to make them permanent, select the dimension symbol (⊢⊣), as shown in Figure 2–5.
>
>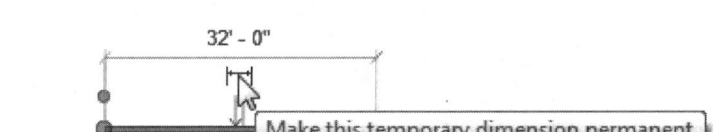
>
> Figure 2–5

Snaps are key points that help you reference existing elements to exact points when modeling, as shown in Figure 2–6.

Figure 2–6

- When you move the cursor over an element, the snap symbol displays. Each snap location type displays with a different symbol.

Basic Sketching and Modify Tools

Hint: Snap Settings and Overrides

In the *Manage* tab>Settings panel, click (Snaps) to open the Snaps dialog box (shown in Figure 2–7), which enables you to set which snap points are active and set the dimension increments displayed for temporary dimensions (both linear and angular).

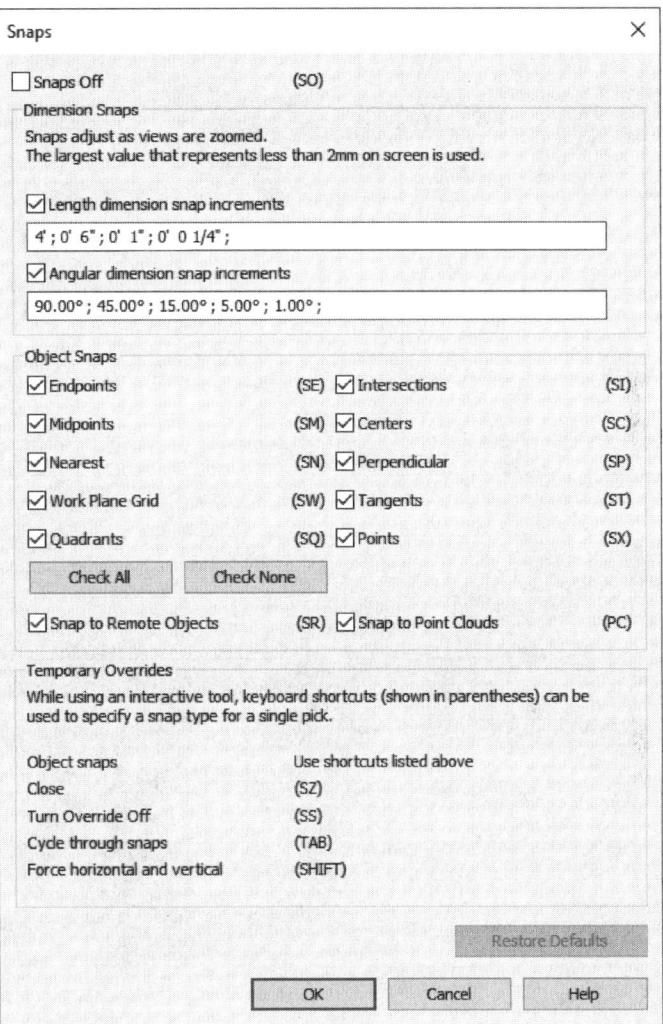

Figure 2–7

- Keyboard shortcuts for each snap can be used to override the automatic snapping. Temporary overrides only affect a single pick, but can be very helpful when there are snaps nearby other than the one you want to use.

Reference Planes

As you develop designs in the Autodesk Revit software, there are times when you need lines to help you define certain locations. You can sketch reference planes (displayed as dashed green lines) and snap to them whenever you need to line up elements. For the example shown in Figure 2–8, the elevator is placed using a reference plane.

Reference planes do not display in 3D views.

- To insert a reference plane, in the *Architecture*, *Structure*, or *Systems* tab>Work Plane panel, click (Reference Plane) or type **RP**.

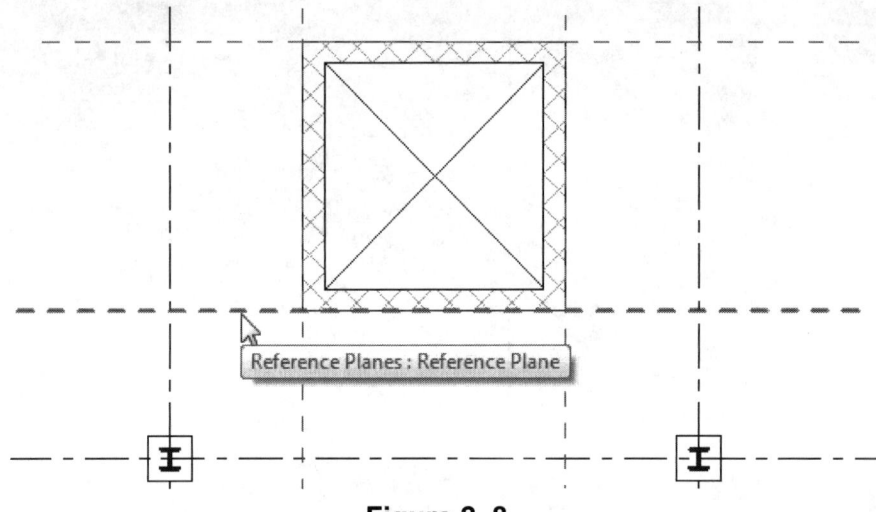

Figure 2–8

- Reference planes display in associated views because they are infinite planes and not just lines.

- You can name reference planes by clicking **<Click to name>** and typing in the text box, as shown in Figure 2–9.

Figure 2–9

- If you sketch a reference plane in sketch mode (used with floors and similar elements), it does not display once the sketch is finished.

- Reference planes can have different line styles if they have been defined in the project. In Properties, select a style from the *Subcategory* list.

Hint: Model Line vs. Detail Line

While most of the elements that you create are representations of actual building elements, there are times you may need to add lines to clarify the design intent. These can be either detail lines, as shown in Figure 2–10, or model lines. Detail lines are also useful as references because they are only reflected in the view in which you sketch them.

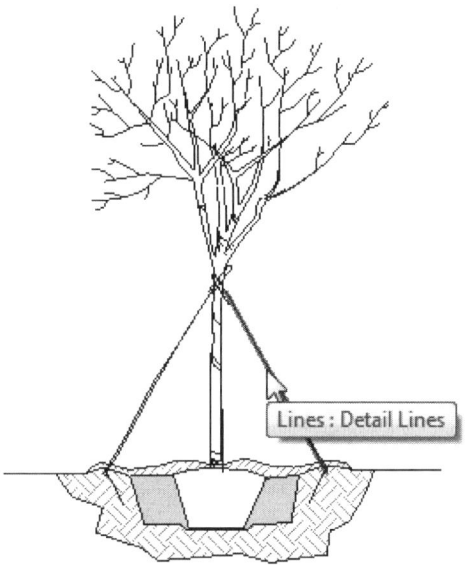

Figure 2–10

- A model line (*Architecture* or *Structure* tab>Model panel> (Model Line)) functions as a 3D element and displays in all views.

- A detail line (*Annotate* tab>Detail panel> (Detail Line)) is strictly a 2D element that only displays in the view in which it is drawn.

- In the *Modify* contextual tab, shown in Figure 2–11, select a Line Style and then the Draw tool that you want to use to draw the model or detail line.

Figure 2–11

2.2 Editing Elements

Building design projects typically involve extensive changes to the model. The Autodesk Revit software was designed to make such changes quickly and efficiently. You can change an element using the following methods, as shown in Figure 2–12:

- Type Selector enables you to specify a different type. This is frequently used to change the size and/or style of the elements.

- Properties enables you to modify the information (parameters) associated with the selected elements.

- The contextual tab in the ribbon contains the Modify commands and element-specific tools.

- Temporary dimensions enable you to change the element's dimensions or position.

- Controls enable you to drag, flip, lock, and rotate the element.

- Shape handles enable you to drag elements to modify their height or length.

Figure 2–12

- To delete an element, select it and press <Delete>, right-click and select **Delete**, or in the Modify panel, click ✖ (Delete).

Working with Controls and Shape Handles

When you select an element, various controls and shape handles display depending on the element and view. For example, in plan view you can use controls to drag the ends of a wall and change its orientation. You can also drag the wall ends in a 3D view, and you can use the arrow shape handles to change the height of the wall, as shown in Figure 2–13.

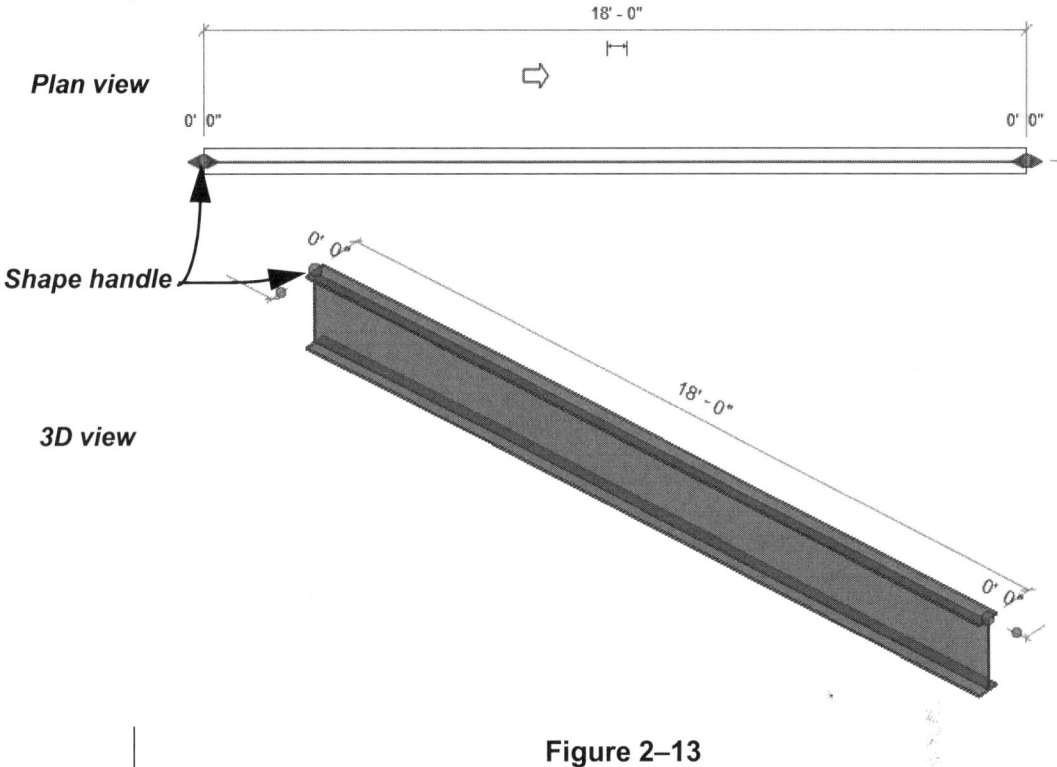

Figure 2–13

- If you hover the cursor over the control or shape handle, a tooltip displays showing its function.

Hint: Editing Temporary Dimensions

Temporary dimensions automatically link to the closest wall. To change this, drag the *Witness Line* control, as shown in Figure 2–14, to connect to a new reference. You can also click on the control to toggle between justifications in the wall.

Before - connected to wall

After - connected to grid line

Figure 2–14

- The new location of a temporary dimension for an element is remembered as long as you are in the same session of the software.

Selecting Multiple Elements

- Once you have selected at least one element, hold <Ctrl> and select another item to add it to a selection set.

- To remove an element from a selection set, hold <Shift> and select the element.

- If you click and drag the cursor to *window* around elements, you have two selection options, as shown in Figure 2–15. If you drag from left to right, you only select the elements completely inside the window. If you drag from right to left, you select elements both inside and crossing the window.

Window: left to right   **Crossing: right to left**

Figure 2–15

- If several elements are on or near each other, hover your cursor over an edge and press <Tab> to cycle through them before you click. If there are elements that might be linked to each other, such as walls that are connected, pressing <Tab> selects the chain of elements.

- Press <Ctrl>+<Left Arrow> to reselect the previous selection set. You can also right-click in the view window with nothing selected and select **Select Previous**.

- To select all elements of a specific type, right-click on an element and select **Select All Instances>Visible in View** or **In Entire Project**, as shown in Figure 2–16. For example, if you select a column of a specific size and use this command, only the columns of the same size are selected.

Figure 2–16

- You can save selections and use them again. For more information, see *B.1 Selection Sets*.

Hint: Measuring Tools

When modifying a model, it is useful to know the distance between elements. This can be done with temporary dimensions or, more frequently, by using the measuring tools found in the Quick Access Toolbar or in the *Modify* tab> Measure panel, as shown in Figure 2–17.

Figure 2–17

- (Measure Between Two References): Select two elements and the measurement displays.

- (Measure Along An Element): Select the edge of a linear element and the total length displays. Use <Tab> to highlight other elements and then click to measure along all of them, as shown in Figure 2–18.

Figure 2–18

- References include any snap point, wall lines, or other parts of elements (such as door center lines).

Basic Sketching and Modify Tools

Filtering Selection Sets

When multiple element categories are selected, the *Multi-Select* contextual tab opens in the ribbon. This gives you access to all of the Modify tools and the Filter command. The **Filter** command enables you to specify the types of elements to select. For example, you might only want to select columns, as shown in Figure 2–19.

Figure 2–19

How To: Filter a Selection Set

1. Select everything in the area.
2. In the *Modify | Multi-Select* tab>Selection panel, or in the Status Bar, click ▼ (Filter). The Filter dialog box opens, as shown in Figure 2–20.

The Filter dialog box displays all types of elements in the original selection.

Figure 2–20

© 2021, ASCENT - Center for Technical Knowledge®

3. Click **Check None** to clear all of the options or **Check All** to select all of the options. You can also select or clear individual categories as needed.
4. Click **OK**. The selection set is now limited to the elements you specified.

- The number of elements selected displays on the right end of the Status Bar and in Properties.

> **Hint: Selection Options**
>
> You can control how the software selects specific elements in a project by toggling selection options on and off in the Status Bar, as shown in Figure 2–21. Alternatively, in any tab on the ribbon that has the Modify command, expand the Select panel's title and select the option.
>
>
>
> Figure 2–21
>
> - **Select links:** When toggled on, you can select linked CAD drawings or Autodesk Revit models. When it is toggled off, you cannot select them when using Modify or Move.
>
> - **Select underlay elements:** When toggled on, you can select underlay elements. When toggled off, you cannot select them when using Modify or Move.
>
> - **Select pinned elements:** When toggled on, you can select pinned elements. When toggled off, you cannot select them when using Modify or Move.
>
> - **Select elements by face:** When toggled on, you can select elements (such as the floors or walls in an elevation) by selecting the interior face or selecting an edge. When toggled off, you can only select elements by selecting an edge.
>
> - **Drag elements on selection:** When toggled on, you can hover over an element, select it, and drag it to a new location. When toggled off, the crossing or box select mode starts when you press and drag, even if you are on top of an element. Once elements have been selected, they can still be dragged to a new location.

Practice 2a | Sketch and Edit Elements

Practice Objective

- Use modify tools and drawing aids.

In this practice, you will use a variety of ways to select elements, use the Filter dialog box to only select one type of element, select only elements of one type in the view, and use the Type Selector to change the type. You will then modify element locations using temporary dimensions, as shown in Figure 2–22.

Figure 2–22

Task 1 - Select elements.

1. Open **Structural-Select.rvt** from the practice files folder.

2. The file should automatically open to the **Structural Plans: Level 1** view.

3. Create a selection window around the building by selecting a point just outside the upper-left corner of the building and, while continuing to hold the left mouse button, drag the mouse toward the lower-right corner and click to select the second point, as shown in Figure 2–23.

Figure 2–23

4. All of the elements inside the window are selected and those outside the window are not selected. Press <Esc>.

5. Select the building again, but this time use a crossing window by selecting a point just outside the upper-right corner of the building and, while continuing to hold the left mouse button, drag the mouse toward the lower-left corner, as shown in Figure 2–24. All of the elements inside and touching the window are selected.

Basic Sketching and Modify Tools

Figure 2–24

6. In the Status Bar, click (Filter).

7. In the Filter dialog box, shown in Figure 2–25, review the selected element categories.

The numbers here and in the next steps might be slightly different depending on your selection.

Category:	Count:
☑ Array	1
☑ Grids	9
☑ Model Groups	4
☑ Railings	2
☑ Ramps	1
☑ Rectangular Straight Wall Opening	2
☑ Shaft Openings	2
☑ Slab Edges	1
☑ Stairs	1
☑ Structural Area Reinforcement	1
☑ Structural Columns	34
☑ Structural Foundations	33
☑ Structural Rebar	11
☑ Walls	15

Total Selected Items: 117

Figure 2–25

8. Click **Check None**.

9. Select only the **Structural Columns** category and click **OK**.

10. The total number of structural columns in the selection set displays in the Status Bar, as shown in Figure 2–26.

Figure 2–26

11. In Properties, the display indicates that multiple families are selected.

12. Click in an empty space in the view to clear the selection.

13. Zoom in on the lower-left corner of the building and select one structural column, as shown in Figure 2–27.

Figure 2–27

14. In the Type Selector, the column name and type are displayed, as shown in Figure 2–28.

Figure 2–28

15. In the view, right-click, expand **Select All Instances**, and select **Visible in View**, as shown in Figure 2–29.

Basic Sketching and Modify Tools

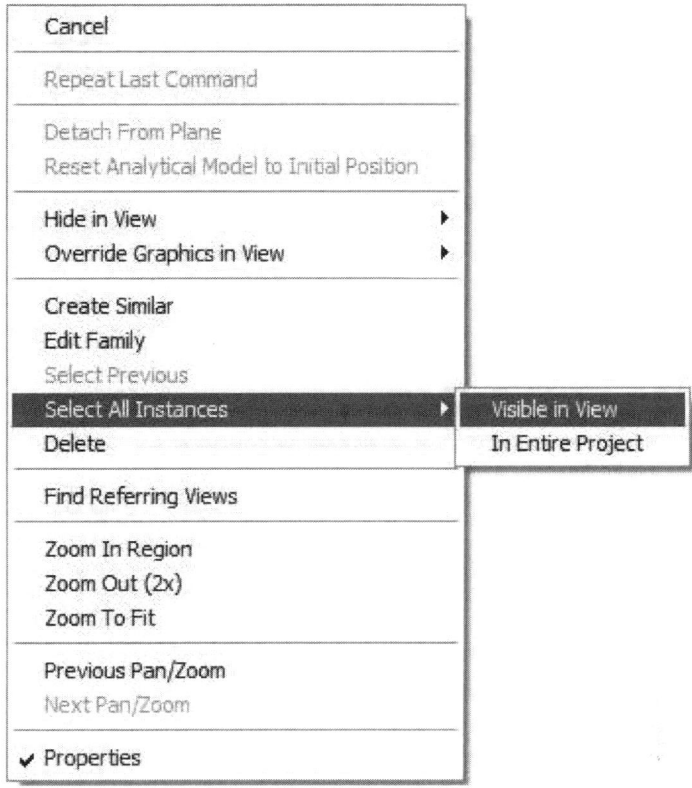

Figure 2–29

16. The total number of this type of column displays in the Status Bar beside the Filter and in Properties.

17. In the Type Selector, select **W-Wide Flange-Column: W12x40**, as shown in Figure 2–30.

Figure 2–30

18. The view regenerates and the selected columns are updated to the new type. Press <Esc> to release the selection set.

Task 2 - Use temporary dimensions.

1. Zoom out to see the entire building.

2. Select grid line **C**.

3. If the temporary dimensions are not displayed, in the Options Bar, click **Activate Dimensions**.

4. The temporary dimensions are automatically connected to the closest structural elements.

5. Use the **Move Witness Line** controls on the temporary dimensions and move them to the nearest grid lines, as shown in Figure 2–31.

Figure 2–31

6. Click ⌐⌐ (Make this temporary dimension line permanent).

7. Click in an empty space in the view to release the selection. The new dimensions are now part of the view.

8. Select grid line **C** again.

9. Click **Activate Dimensions**, if needed.

10. Select the lower dimension text and change it to **24'-0"**, as shown in Figure 2–32. Press <Enter>.

Figure 2–32

- The model regenerates and the percentage of completion is displayed in the Status Bar, as shown in Figure 2–33. This change is being made to the grid line and throughout the model, wherever elements touch the grid line.

Figure 2–33

11. Save and close the project.

2.3 Working with Basic Modify Tools

The basic modifying tools, **Move**, **Copy**, **Rotate**, **Mirror**, and **Array**, can be used with individual elements or any selection of elements. They are found in the Modify panel (shown in Figure 2–34), in the *Modify* tab, and in contextual tabs.

Figure 2–34

- For these modify commands, you can either select the elements and start the command, or start the command, select the elements, and press <Enter> to finish the selection and move to the next step in the command.

Moving and Copying Elements

The **Move** and **Copy** commands enable you to select the element(s) and move or copy them from one place to another. You can use alignment lines, temporary dimensions, and snaps to help place the elements, as shown in Figure 2–35.

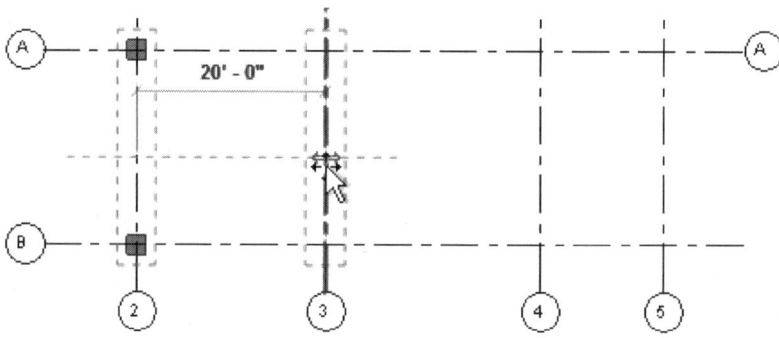

Figure 2–35

How To: Move or Copy Elements

1. Select the elements you want to move or copy.
2. In the Modify panel, click (Move) or (Copy). Alternatively, you can type **MV** for Move and **CO** for Copy. A boundary box displays around the selected elements.
3. Select a start point on or near the element.
4. Select a second point. Use alignment lines and temporary dimensions to help place the elements.

Basic Sketching and Modify Tools

5. When you are finished, you can start another modify command using the elements that remain selected, or click (Modify) to end the command.

- You can drag elements to new locations without starting the **Move** command. Holding <Ctrl> and dragging copies the element. This is quick, but not very precise.

Move/Copy Elements Options

The **Move** and **Copy** commands have several options that display in the Options Bar, as shown in Figure 2–36.

Figure 2–36

Constrain	Restricts the movement of the cursor to horizontal or vertical, or along the axis of an item that is at an angle. This keeps you from selecting a point at an angle by mistake. **Constrain** is off by default.
Disjoin (Move only)	Breaks any connections between the elements being moved and other elements. If **Disjoin** is on, the elements move separately. If it is off, the connected elements also move or stretch. **Disjoin** is off by default.
Multiple (Copy only)	Enables you to make multiple copies of one selection.

- These commands only work in the current view, not between views or projects. To copy between views or projects, in the *Modify* tab>Clipboard panel, click (Copy to Clipboard), (Cut to the Clipboard), or (Paste from Clipboard).

> **Hint: Pinning Elements**
>
> If you do not want elements to be moved, you can pin them in place, as shown in Figure 2–37. Select the elements and in the *Modify* tab>Modify panel, click (Pin) or type the shortcut **PN**. Pinned elements can be copied, but not moved. If you try to delete a pinned element, a warning dialog displays reminding you that you must unpin the element before the command can be started.
>
> Figure 2–37
>
> Select the element and click (Unpin) or type the shortcut **UP** to unpin the element.

Rotating Elements

The **Rotate** command enables you to rotate selected elements around a center point or origin, as shown in Figure 2–38. You can use alignment lines, temporary dimensions, and snaps to help specify the center of rotation and the angle. You can also create copies of the element as it is being rotated.

Figure 2–38

Basic Sketching and Modify Tools

How To: Rotate Elements

1. Select the element(s) you want to rotate.
2. In the Modify panel, click ○ (Rotate) or type the shortcut **RO**.
3. The center of rotation is automatically set to the center of the element or group of elements, as shown on the left in Figure 2–39. To change the center of rotation, as shown on the right in Figure 2–39, use the following:

    - Drag the ○ (Center of Rotation) control to a new point.
    - In the Options Bar, next to **Center of rotation**, click **Place** and use snaps to move it to a new location.
    - Press <Spacebar> to select the center of rotation and click to move it to a new location.

*To start the **Rotate** command with a prompt to select the center of rotation, select the elements first and type R3.*

Figure 2–39

4. In the Options Bar, specify if you want to make a copy (select **Copy**), type an angle in the *Angle* field (shown in Figure 2–40), and press <Enter>. You can also specify the angle on screen using temporary dimensions.

Figure 2–40

5. The rotated element(s) remain highlighted, enabling you to start another command using the same selection, or click ▷ (Modify) to finish.

- The **Disjoin** option breaks any connections between the elements being rotated and other elements. If **Disjoin** is on (selected), the elements rotate separately. If it is off (cleared), the connected elements also move or stretch, as shown in Figure 2–41. **Disjoin** is toggled off by default.

Figure 2–41

Mirroring Elements

The **Mirror** command enables you to mirror elements about an axis defined by a selected element, as shown in Figure 2–42, or by selected points.

Figure 2–42

How To: Mirror Elements

1. Select the element(s) to mirror.
2. In the Modify panel, select the method you want to use:

    - Click (Mirror - Pick Axis) or type the shortcut **MM**. This prompts you to select an element as the **Axis of Reflection** (mirror line).

    - Click (Mirror - Draw Axis) or type the shortcut **DM**. This prompts you to select two points to define the axis about which the elements mirror.

3. The new mirrored element(s) remain highlighted, enabling you to start another command, or click (Modify) to finish.

- By default, the original elements that were mirrored remain. To delete the original elements, clear the **Copy** option in the Options Bar.

Basic Sketching and Modify Tools

> **Hint: Scale**
>
> The Autodesk Revit software is designed with full-size elements. Therefore, not much should be scaled. For example, scaling a wall increases its length but does not impact the width, which is set by the wall type. However, you can use ▯ (Scale) in reference planes, images, and imported files from other programs.

Creating Linear and Radial Arrays

A linear array creates a straight line pattern of elements, while a radial array creates a circular pattern around a center point.

The **Array** command creates multiple copies of selected elements in a linear or radial pattern, as shown in Figure 2–43. For example, you can array a row of columns to create a row of evenly spaced columns on a grid line, or array a row of parking spaces. The arrayed elements can be grouped or placed as separate elements.

Figure 2–43

How To: Create a Linear Array

1. Select the element(s) to array.
2. In the Modify panel, click ▯ (Array) or type the shortcut **AR**.
3. In the Options Bar, click ▯ (Linear).
4. Specify the other options as needed.
5. Select a start point and an end point to set the spacing and direction of the array. The array is displayed.

6. If **Group And Associate** is selected, you are prompted again for the number of items, as shown in Figure 2–44. Type a new number or click on the screen to finish the command.

Figure 2–44

- To make a linear array in two directions, you need to array one direction first, select the arrayed elements, and then array them again in the other direction.

Array Options

In the Options Bar, set up the array options for **Linear Array** (top of Figure 2–45) or **Radial Array** (bottom of Figure 2–45).

Figure 2–45

Group And Associate	Creates an array group element out of all arrayed elements. The group can be selected by selecting any elements in the group.
Number	Specifies how many instances you want in the array.
Move To:	**2nd** specifies the distance or angle between the center points of the two elements. **Last** specifies the overall distance or angle of the entire array.
Constrain	Restricts the direction of the array to only vertical or horizontal (Linear only).
Angle	Specifies the angle (Radial only).
Center of rotation	Specifies a location for the origin about which the elements rotate (Radial only).

Basic Sketching and Modify Tools

How To: Create a Radial Array

1. Select the element(s) to array.
2. In the Modify panel, click (Array).
3. In the Options Bar, click (Radial).
4. Drag (Center of Rotation) or use **Place** to move the center of rotation to the appropriate location, as shown in Figure 2–46.

*Remember to set the **Center of Rotation** control first, before specifying the angle.*

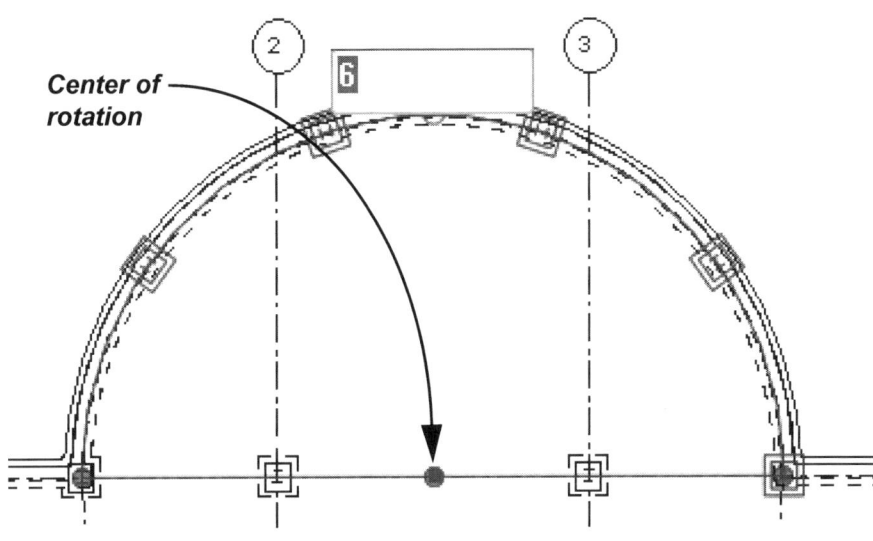

Figure 2–46

5. In the Options Bar, type an angle and press <Enter>, or specify the rotation angle by selecting points on the screen.
6. Specify the other options as needed.

Modifying Array Groups

When you select an element in an array that has been grouped, you can change the number of instances in the array, as shown in Figure 2–47. For radial arrays, you can also modify the distance to the center.

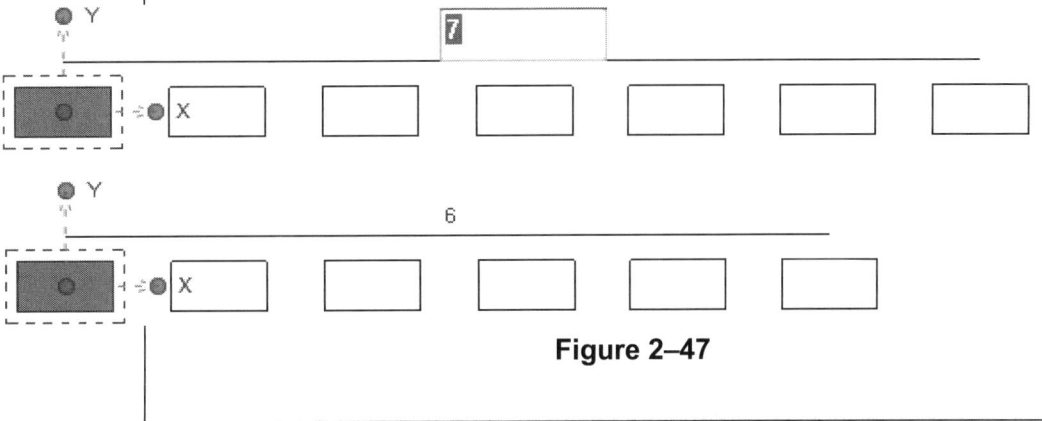

Figure 2–47

- Dashed lines surround the elements in a group, and the XY control lets you move the origin point of the group.

If you move one of the elements in the array group, the other elements move in response based on the distance and/or angle, as shown in Figure 2–48.

Figure 2–48

- To remove the array constraint on the group, select all of the elements in the array group and, in the *Modify* contextual tab>Group panel, click (Ungroup).

- If you select an individual element in an array and click (Ungroup), the element you selected is removed from the array, while the rest of the elements remain in the array group.

- You can use (Filter) to ensure that you are selecting only **Model Groups**.

Practice 2b

Work with Basic Modify Tools

Practice Objective

- Use basic modify tools, such as Move, Copy, Rotate, and Array.

In this practice, you will use **Move** and **Copy** to create grid lines with columns using existing elements in a project. You will then rotate one of the grid lines and the columns along that grid line and mirror the new grid lines to create the opposite part of the building. Finally, you will array a set of columns around an arc and create a grid line of the array, as shown in Figure 2–49.

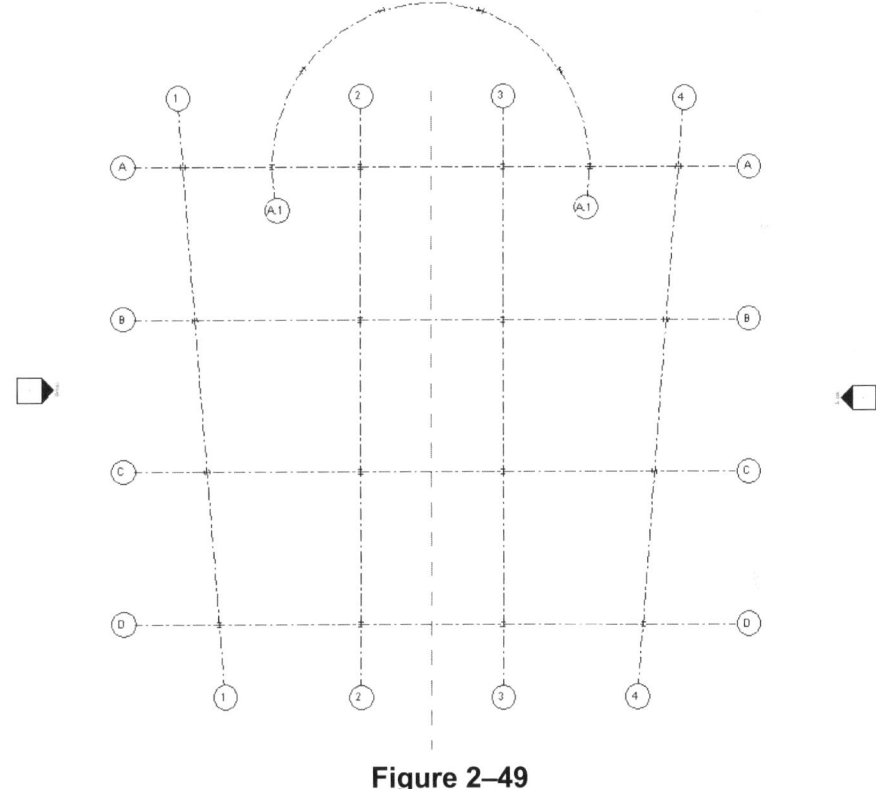

Figure 2–49

Task 1 - Move and copy elements.

1. Open **Structural-Editing.rvt** from the practice files folder.

2. The file should automatically open to the **Structural Plans: Level 2** view.

3. Select grid line **A** and the structural column that is at the intersection. (**Hint:** Hold <Ctrl> to select more than one element.)

4. In the *Modify | Multi-Select* tab>Modify panel, click (Copy).

5. In the Options Bar, select **Multiple**, as shown in Figure 2–50.

Figure 2–50

6. Pick a point anywhere along grid line **A** for the start point.

7. Move the cursor down below grid line **A** and type **24**. Create two more copies that are **24'-0"** apart for a total of four horizontal grid lines.

8. Click (Modify) to end the Copy command.

9. Select grid line **1** and the four columns along grid line **1**. Copy the elements to the right at a distance of **24'-0"** until you have a total of four vertical grid lines with the associated columns.

   Click (Modify) to end the command.

10. Click twice inside each grid bubble and renumber the grid lines as shown in Figure 2–51.

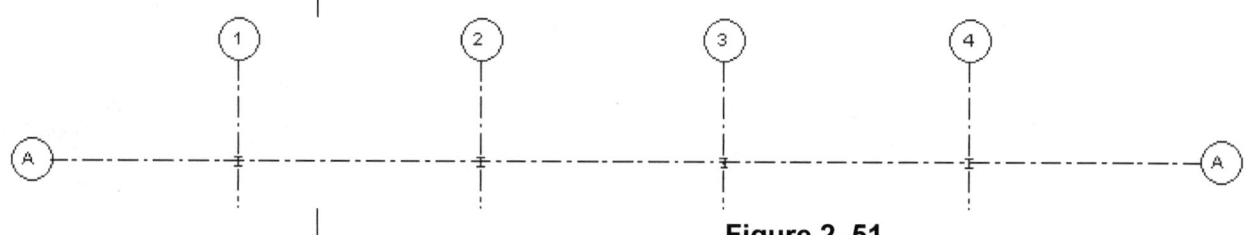

Figure 2–51

11. Zoom in on the column at grid intersection **A1**.

12. Select the column (but not the grid line). In the *Modify* tab> Modify panel, click (Move) and move the column **6'-0"** to the left, as shown in Figure 2–52.

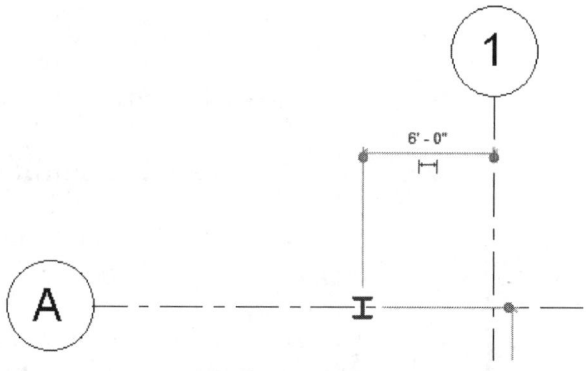

Figure 2–52

13. Click (Modify).

14. Save the project.

Basic Sketching and Modify Tools

Task 2 - Rotate elements.

1. Select grid line **1**.

2. In the *Modify | Grids* tab>Modify panel, click ⟳ (Rotate).

3. Move the center of rotation by going to the Options Bar and clicking **Place**. Select the midpoint of column **D1** as the center of rotation.

4. Specify the first ray of rotation by clicking on the **A1** grid intersection.

5. Specify the second ray of rotation to finish the rotation by selecting the midpoint of the column you moved **6'** to the left of grid line **1** earlier, as shown in Figure 2–53.

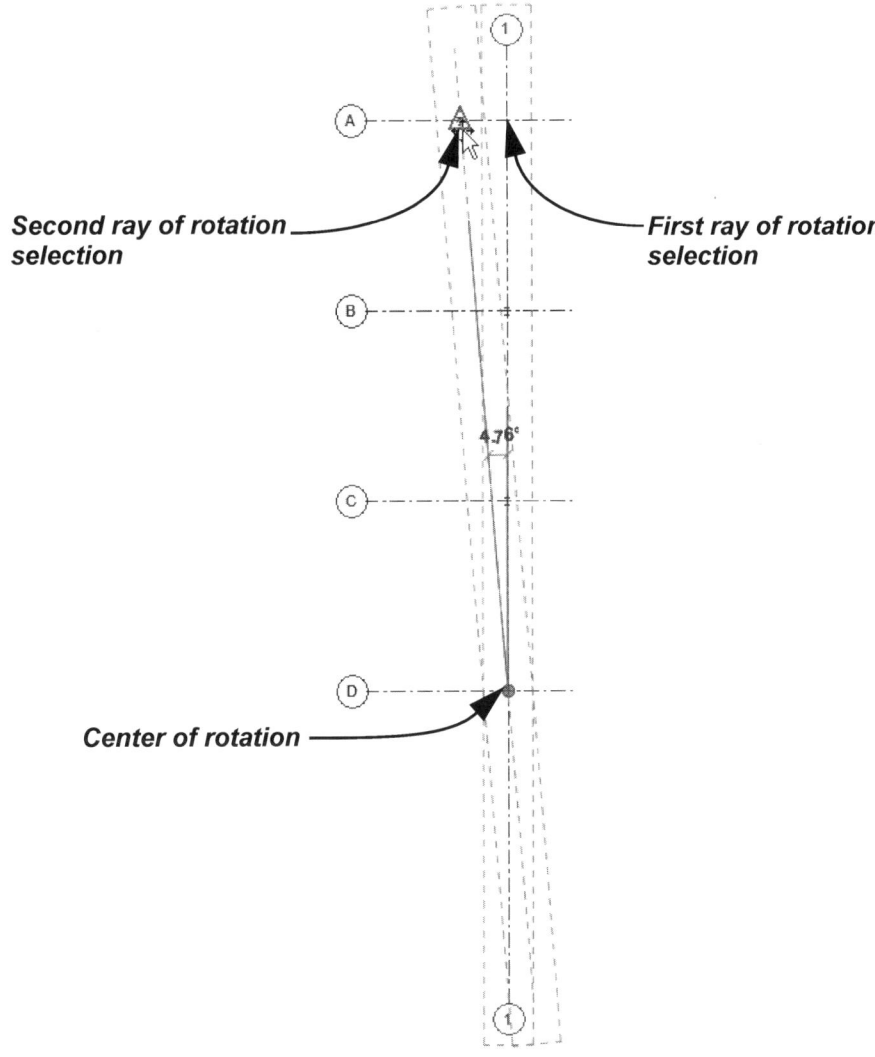

Figure 2–53

Task 3 - Rotate columns to match grid line.

1. Zoom in on the **A1** grid intersection. Select the column at the **A1** intersection.

2. Click ○ (Rotate). Keep the center point in the current location, which is the center of the column.

3. For the first ray of rotation, select a point to the right along grid line **A**, as shown in Figure 2–54.

Figure 2–54

4. For the second ray of rotation, select a point along grid line **1**, as shown on the left in Figure 2–55. The column is now rotated perpendicular to the angle of grid line **1**, as shown on the right in Figure 2–55.

Figure 2–55

5. Repeat the process for the rest of the columns along grid line **1**.

6. Click ▷ (Modify).

7. Save the project.

Basic Sketching and Modify Tools

Task 4 - Mirror elements.

1. Delete grid line **4** and its columns. You are going to mirror grid line **1** and its columns to this location.

2. In the *Structure* tab>Work Plane panel, click (Ref Plane).

3. In the *Modify | Place Reference Plane* tab>Draw panel, click (Line).

4. Draw a vertical line between grid line **2** and grid line **3** and use temporary dimensions to set the distances from each grid line to **12'-0"**, as shown in Figure 2–56. When finished, click (Modify) to end the command.

Figure 2–56

5. Select grid line **1** and all of the columns on the grid line. (To select multiple elements, draw a window around the group or hold <Ctrl> as you select.)

6. In the *Modify | Multi-Select* tab>Modify panel, click (Pick Mirror Axis).

7. Select the vertical reference plane that you created earlier, as shown in Figure 2–57. Grid line **1** and all of its columns are mirrored about the selected reference plane. If the new grid line is not automatically renumbered, select the bubble and rename it to **4**.

Figure 2–57

8. Click (Modify).

9. Save the project.

Task 5 - Array elements.

1. Select the column at grid intersection **A3**. Click (Copy) and copy this column to the right by **15'-0"**. The new copied column is now the current selected column.

2. In the *Modify | Structural Columns* tab>Modify panel, click (Array).

3. A warning dialog box opens. This issue will be corrected in later steps. Click **OK**.

4. In the Options Bar, click (Radial). Select **Group And Associate**, set the *Number* to **8**, and set *Move to:* to **Last**.

5. Relocate the center of the array by dragging to the intersection of the vertical reference plane, as shown in Figure 2–58.

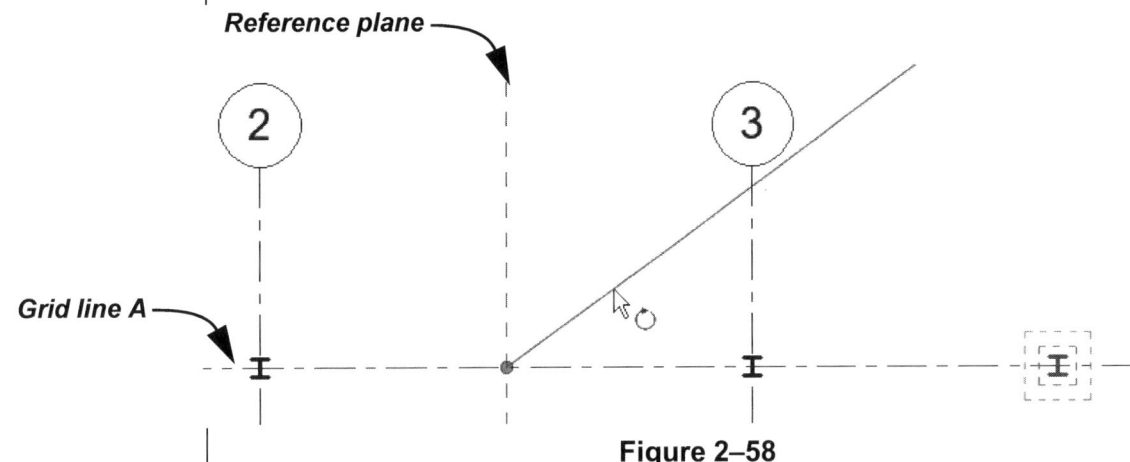

Figure 2–58

6. In the Options Bar, set the *Angle* to **180** and press <Enter>. The new columns display along the arc. The number of array is displayed at the top of the arc, allowing for further modifications to the number of arrayed items, as shown in Figure 2–59.

Figure 2–59

7. Change the number to **6** and the array updates.

8. Click in an empty space in the view to release the selection and end the Array command.

9. Draw a grid line for the new array of columns by going to the *Structure* tab>Datum panel and clicking ⌗ (Grid).

10. In the Draw panel, click (Pick Lines).

11. Move the cursor over the area of the array. When your cursor is over the arc, it will highlight, as shown in Figure 2–60. Select it to create the grid line.

Figure 2–60

12. Click (Modify).

13. The new grid bubbles are on top of the columns. Drag the grid bubbles down past the columns and rename the new grid line **A.1**, as shown in Figure 2–61.

Figure 2–61

14. Save and close the project.

Basic Sketching and Modify Tools

2.4 Working with Additional Modify Tools

As you work on a project, some additional tools found in the *Modify* tab>Modify panel (shown in Figure 2–62) can help you with placing, modifying, and constraining elements. **Align** can be used with a variety of elements, while **Split Element**, **Trim/Extend**, and **Offset** can only be used with linear elements.

Figure 2–62

Aligning Elements

The **Align** command enables you to line up one element with another, as shown in Figure 2–63. Most Autodesk Revit elements can be aligned. For example, you can line up the tops of windows with the top of a door, or line up furniture with a wall.

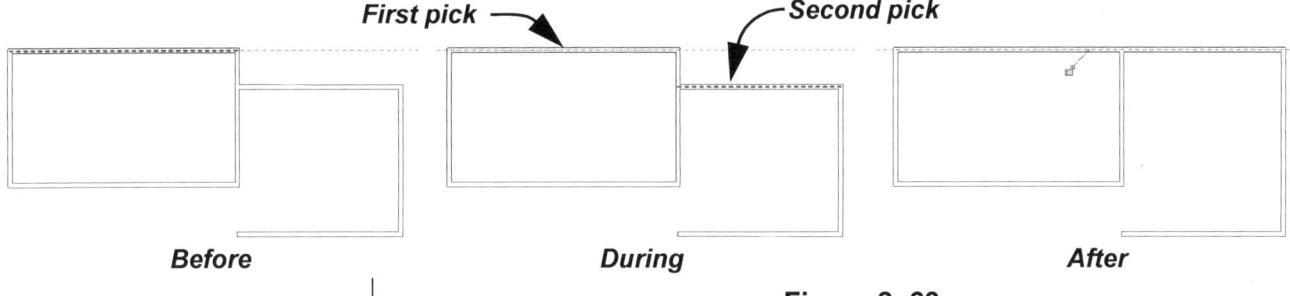

Figure 2–63

How To: Align Elements

1. In the *Modify* tab>Modify panel, click (Align) or type the shortcut **AL**.
2. Select a line or point on the element that is going to remain stationary. For walls, press <Tab> to select the correct wall face.
3. Select a line or point on the element to be aligned. The second element moves into alignment with the first one.

- The **Align** command works in all model views, including parallel and perspective 3D views.

© 2021, ASCENT - Center for Technical Knowledge®

- You can lock alignments so that the elements move together if either one is moved. Once you have created the alignment, a padlock is displayed. Click on the padlock to lock it, as shown in Figure 2–64.

Locking elements enlarges the size of the project file, so use this option carefully.

Figure 2–64

- In the Options Bar, select **Multiple Alignment** to select multiple elements to align with the first element. You can also hold <Ctrl> to select multiple elements to align.

- For walls, you can specify if you want the command to prefer **Wall centerlines**, **Wall faces**, **Center of core**, or **Faces of core**, as shown in Figure 2–65. The core refers to the structural members of a wall as opposed to facing materials, such as sheet rock.

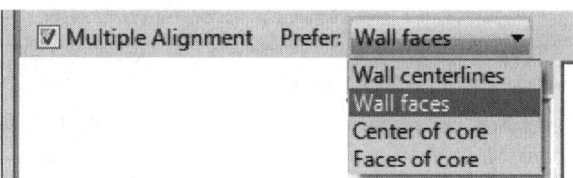

Figure 2–65

Splitting Linear Elements

The **Split Element** command enables you to break a linear element at a specific point. You can use alignment lines, snaps, and temporary dimensions to help place the split point. After you have split the linear element, you can use other editing commands to modify the two parts, or change the type of one part, as shown with walls in Figure 2–66. You can split walls in plan, elevation, or 3D views.

Figure 2–66

Basic Sketching and Modify Tools

- The **Split with Gap** command only works when splitting walls.

How To: Split Linear Elements

1. In the *Modify* tab>Modify panel, click (Split Element) or type the shortcut **SL**.
2. In the Options Bar, select or clear the **Delete Inner Segment** option.
3. Move the cursor to the point you want to split and select the point.
4. Repeat for any additional split locations.
5. Modify the elements that were split, as needed.

- The **Delete Inner Segment** option is used when you select two split points along a linear element. When the option is selected, the segment between the two split points is automatically removed.

- An additional option, (Split with Gap), splits the linear element at the point you select, as shown in Figure 2–67, but also creates a *Joint Gap* that is specified in the Options Bar.

Split

Split with Gap

Figure 2–67

Trimming and Extending

This command is typically used with structural precast walls.

There are three trim/extend methods that you can use with linear elements: **Trim/Extend to Corner**, **Trim/Extend Single Element**, and **Trim/Extend Multiple Elements**.

- When selecting elements to trim, click the part of the element that you want to keep. The opposite part of the line is then trimmed.

How To: Trim/Extend to Corner

1. In the *Modify* tab>Modify panel, click (Trim/Extend to Corner) or type the shortcut **TR**.
2. Select the first linear element on the side you want to keep.

3. Select the second linear element on the side you want to keep, as shown in Figure 2–68.

Figure 2–68

How To: Trim/Extend a Single Element

1. In the *Modify* tab>Modify panel, click (Trim/Extend Single Element).
2. Select the cutting or boundary edge.
3. Select the linear element to be trimmed or extended, as shown in Figure 2–69.

Figure 2–69

How To: Trim/Extend Multiple Elements

1. In the *Modify* tab>Modify panel, click (Trim/Extend Multiple Elements).
2. Select the cutting or boundary edge.

Basic Sketching and Modify Tools

3. Select the linear elements that you want to trim or extend by selecting one at a time, or by using a crossing window (as shown in Figure 2–70). For trimming, select the side you want to keep.

Figure 2–70

- You can click in an empty space in the view to clear the selection and select another cutting edge or boundary.

Offsetting Elements

The **Offset** command is an easy way of creating parallel copies of linear elements at a specified distance, as shown in Figure 2–71. Walls, beams, braces, and lines are among the elements that can be offset.

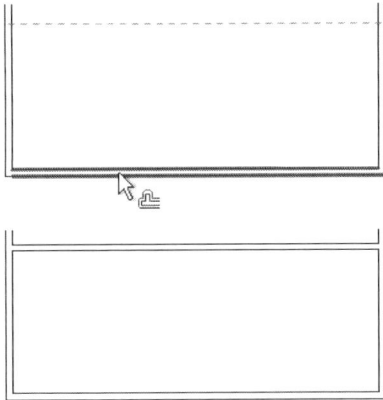

Figure 2–71

- If you offset a wall that has a door or window embedded in it, the elements are copied with the offset wall.

The offset distance can be set by typing the distance (**Numerical** method), as shown in Figure 2–72, or by selecting points on the screen (**Graphical** method).

Figure 2–72

How To: Offset Using the Numerical Method

1. In the *Modify* tab>Modify panel, click ⌐ (Offset) or type the shortcut **OF**.
2. In the Options Bar, select the **Numerical** option.
3. In the Options Bar, type the required distance in the *Offset* field.
4. Move the cursor over the element you want to offset. A dashed line previews the offset location. Move the cursor to flip the sides, as needed.
5. Click to create the offset.
6. Repeat Steps 4 and 5 to offset other elements by the same distance.

- With the **Numerical** option, you can select multiple connected linear elements for offsetting. Hover the cursor over an element and press <Tab> until the other related elements are highlighted. Select the element to offset all of the elements at the same time.

*The **Copy** option (which is on by default) makes a copy of the element being offset. If this option is not selected, the **Offset** command moves the element the set offset distance.*

How To: Offset Using the Graphical Method

1. In the *Modify* tab>Modify panel, click ⌐ (Offset) or type the shortcut **OF**.
2. In the Options Bar, select **Graphical**.
3. Select the linear element to offset.
4. Select two points that define the distance of the offset and which side to apply it. You can type an override in the temporary dimension for the second point.

- Most linear elements connected at a corner automatically trim or extend to meet at the offset distance, as shown in Figure 2–73.

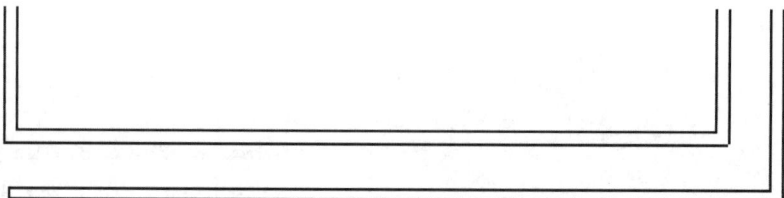

Figure 2–73

Practice 2c Work with Additional Modify Tools

Practice Objective

- Align, Split, Trim/Extend, and Offset elements.

In this practice, you will use **Split** and **Trim** to clean up existing walls in a project. You will then offset the entire foundation from the centerline, as shown in Figure 2–74, where it can support an architectural brick facade.

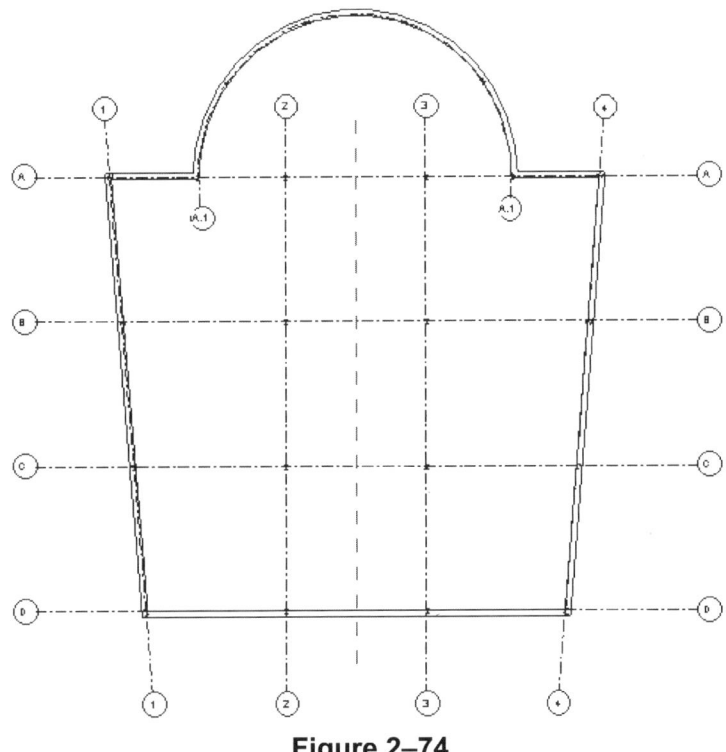

Figure 2–74

Task 1 - Split and trim elements.

1. Open **Structural-Modify.rvt** from the practice files folder.

2. The file should automatically open to the **Structural Plans: Level 2** view.

3. Select the horizontal foundation wall on grid line **A**. In the Modify | Walls tab>Modify panel, click (Split Element).

4. Select the intersection of the reference plane and grid line **A**, between grid lines **2** and **3**, as shown in Figure 2–75.

Figure 2–75

5. Click (Modify) to end the command.

6. Connect the arc foundation wall on grid line **A.1** with the foundation wall on grid line **A** by going to the *Modify* tab>Modify panel and clicking (Trim/Extend to Corner).

7. Select the horizontal wall along grid line **A** on the left side of the arc, as shown in Figure 2–76.

  - Remember to select the side of the wall that you want to keep.

Figure 2–76

8. Select the arc wall. The walls are trimmed and joined together and the excess wall is deleted (the before and after are shown in Figure 2–77).

  - If the Reset analytical model warning opens, close it.

Basic Sketching and Modify Tools

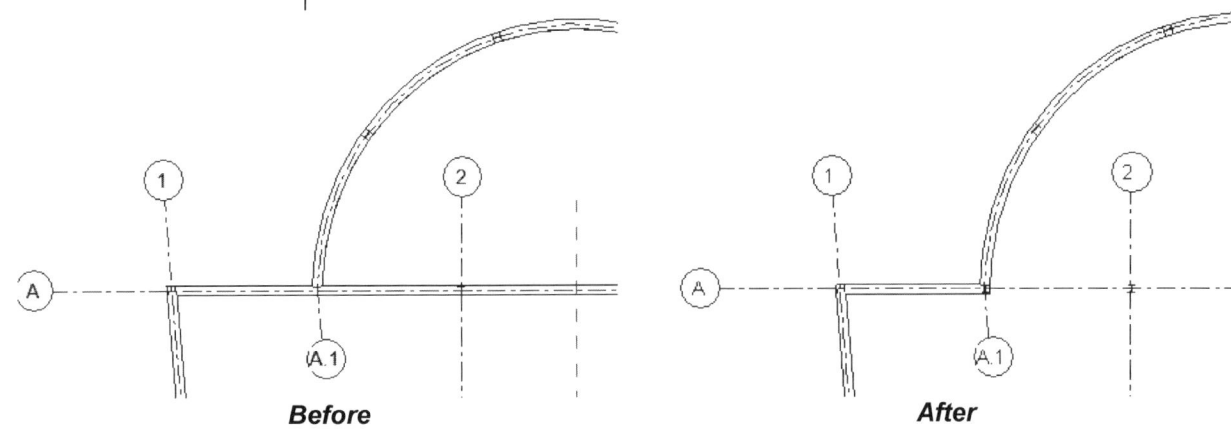

Before　　　　　　　　　　　　　　**After**

Figure 2–77

9. Repeat the process on the other side.

Task 2 - Offset foundation walls.

1. Offset all of the foundation walls by going to the *Modify* tab>Edit panel and clicking ⌐ (Offset).

2. In the Options Bar, select **Numerical**, set the *Offset* to **4"**, and clear the **Copy** option, as shown in Figure 2–78.

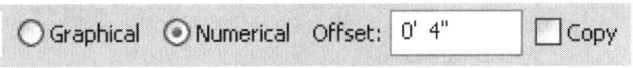

Figure 2–78

3. Hover the cursor over one of the foundation walls but do not select the wall. The blue alignment line should display on the inside of the wall and above the grid line, as shown in Figure 2–79.

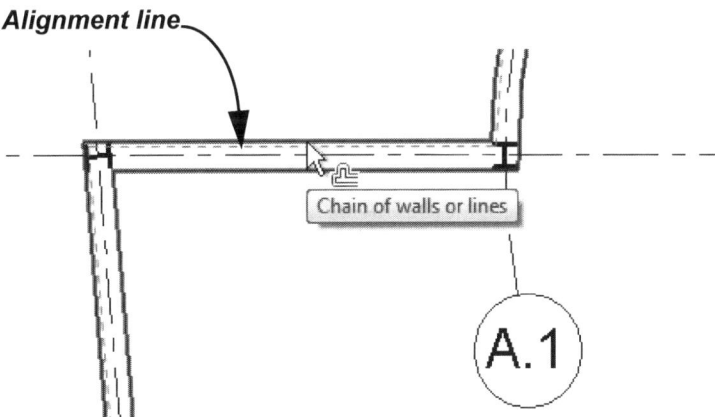

Figure 2–79

4. Press <Tab> until all of the foundation walls are highlighted, meaning they are all selected, and click to offset the walls 4", as shown in Figure 2–80.

Figure 2–80

5. Press <Esc> to finish the command.
6. Save and close the model.

Chapter Review Questions

1. What is the purpose of an alignment line?
   a. Displays when the new element you are placing or modeling is aligned with the grid system.
   b. Indicates that the new element you are placing or modeling is aligned with an existing element.
   c. Displays when the new element you are placing or modeling is aligned with a selected tracking point.
   d. Indicates that the new element is aligned with true north rather than project north.

2. Temporary dimensions snap to the nearest perpendicular element.
   a. True
   b. False

3. How do you select all the doors of various sizes, but no other elements in a view?
   a. In the Project Browser, select the *Door* category.
   b. Select one door, right-click, and select **Select All Instances>Visible in View**.
   c. Select all of the elements in the view and use (Filter) to clear the other categories.
   d. Select one door and click (Select Multiple) in the ribbon.

4. What are the two methods for starting commands such as **Move**, **Copy**, **Rotate**, **Mirror**, and **Array**?
   a. Start the command from the *Modify* tab and select the element.
   b. Select the element, then start the command from the *Modify* tab.
   c. Select the element, right-click, and select the command from the list.

5. Where do you change the type for an existing structural column selected in a view, as shown in Figure 2–81?

Figure 2–81

a. In the *Modify | Walls* tab>Properties panel, click (Type Properties) and select a new wall type in the dialog box.

b. In the Options Bar, click **Change Element Type**.

c. Select the dynamic control next to the selected wall and select a new type in the drop-down list.

d. In Properties, select a new type in the Type Selector drop-down list.

Basic Sketching and Modify Tools

6. Both ⟳ (Rotate) and ▦ (Array) with 🔄 (Radial) have a center of rotation that defaults to the center of the element or group of elements you have selected. How do you move the center of rotation to another point, as shown in Figure 2–82? (Select all that apply.)

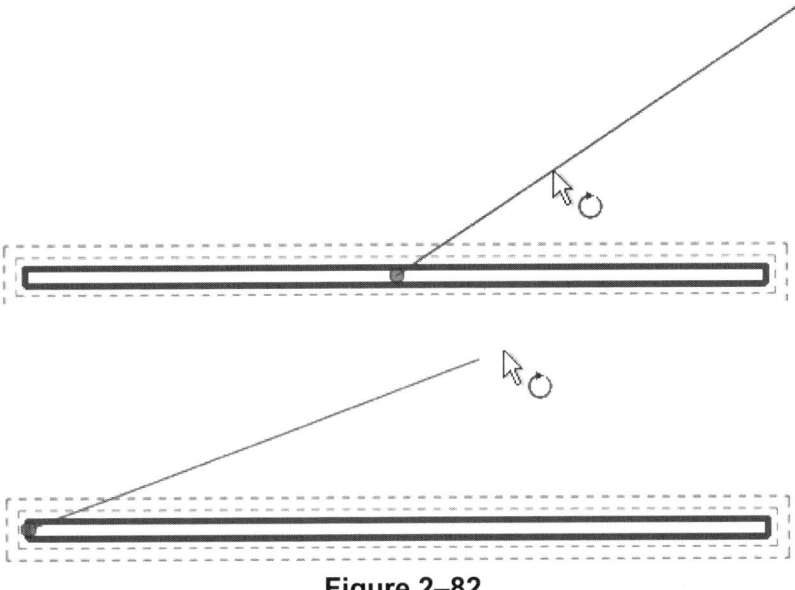

Figure 2–82

   a. Select the center of rotation and drag it to a new location.
   b. In the Options Bar, click **Place** and select the new point.
   c. In the *Modify* tab>Placement panel, click ⊙ (Center) and select the new point.
   d. Right-click and select **Snap Overrides>Centers** and select the new point.

7. Which command would you use to remove a part or a segment of a wall?

   a. ✥ (Split Element)
   b. 📐 (Wall Joins)
   c. ⌗ (Cut Geometry)
   d. 🔨 (Demolish)

8. Which of the following are ways in which you can create additional parallel walls, as shown in Figure 2–83? (Select all that apply.)

Figure 2–83

   a. Use the **Trim/Extend Multiple Elements** tool.
   b. Use the **Offset** tool in the *Modify* tab.
   c. Select an existing wall, hold <Ctrl>, and drag the wall to a new location.
   d. Use the **Align** command with an offset.

9. Which command do you use if you want two walls that are not touching to come together, as shown in Figure 2–84?

Figure 2–84

   a. (Edit Wall Joins)
   b. (Trim/Extend to Corner)
   c. (Join Geometry)
   d. (Edit Profile)

Command Summary

Button	Command	Location
Draw Tools		
	Center-ends Arc	• **Ribbon:** *Modify	(various linear elements)* tab>Draw panel
	Circle	• **Ribbon:** *Modify	(various linear elements)* tab>Draw panel
	Circumscribed Polygon	• **Ribbon:** *Modify	(various linear elements)* tab>Draw panel
	Ellipse	• **Ribbon:** *Modify	Place Lines, Place Detail Lines, and various boundary sketches* tab>Draw panel
	Ellipse Arc	• **Ribbon:** *Modify	Place Lines, Place Detail Lines, and various boundary sketches* tab>Draw panel
	Fillet Arc	• **Ribbon:** *Modify	(various linear elements)* tab>Draw panel
	Inscribed Polygon	• **Ribbon:** *Modify	(various linear elements)* tab>Draw panel
	Line	• **Ribbon:** *Modify	(various linear elements)* tab>Draw panel
	Pick Faces	• **Ribbon:** *Modify	Place Wall* tab>Draw panel
	Pick Lines	• **Ribbon:** *Modify	(various linear elements)* tab>Draw panel
	Pick Walls	• **Ribbon:** *Modify	(various boundary sketches)* tab>Draw panel
	Rectangle	• **Ribbon:** *Modify	(various linear elements)* tab>Draw panel
	Spline	• **Ribbon:** *Modify	Place Lines, Place Detail Lines, and various boundary sketches* tab>Draw panel
	Start-End-Radius Arc	• **Ribbon:** *Modify	(various linear elements)* tab>Draw panel
	Tangent End Arc	• **Ribbon:** *Modify	(various linear elements)* tab>Draw panel
Modify Tools		
	Align	• **Ribbon:** *Modify* tab>Modify panel • **Shortcut:** AL
	Array	• **Ribbon:** *Modify* tab>Modify panel • **Shortcut:** AR
	Copy	• **Ribbon:** *Modify* tab>Modify panel • **Shortcut:** CO

	Copy to Clipboard	• **Ribbon:** *Modify* tab>Clipboard panel • **Shortcut:** <Ctrl>+<C>
	Delete	• **Ribbon:** *Modify* tab>Modify panel • **Shortcut:** DE
	Mirror - Draw Axis	• **Ribbon:** *Modify* tab>Modify panel • **Shortcut:** DM
	Mirror - Pick Axis	• **Ribbon:** *Modify* tab>Modify panel • **Shortcut:** MM
	Move	• **Ribbon:** *Modify* tab>Modify panel • **Shortcut:** MV
	Offset	• **Ribbon:** *Modify* tab>Modify panel • **Shortcut:** OF
	Paste	• **Ribbon:** *Modify* tab>Clipboard panel • **Shortcut:** <Ctrl>+<V>
	Pin	• **Ribbon:** *Modify* tab>Modify panel • **Shortcut:** PN
	Rotate	• **Ribbon:** *Modify* tab>Modify panel • **Shortcut:** RO, R3
	Scale	• **Ribbon:** *Modify* tab>Modify panel • **Shortcut:** RE
	Split Element	• **Ribbon:** *Modify* tab>Modify panel • **Shortcut:** SL
	Split with Gap	• **Ribbon:** *Modify* tab>Modify panel
	Trim/Extend Multiple Elements	• **Ribbon:** *Modify* tab>Modify panel
	Trim/Extend Single Element	• **Ribbon:** *Modify* tab>Modify panel
	Trim/Extend to Corner	• **Ribbon:** *Modify* tab>Modify panel • **Shortcut:** TR
	Unpin	• **Ribbon:** *Modify* tab>Modify panel • **Shortcut:** UP

Select Tools

	Drag elements on selection	• **Ribbon:** All tabs>expanded Select panel • **Status Bar**
	Filter	• **Ribbon:** *Modify	Multi-Select* tab>Filter panel • **Status Bar**
	Select Elements By Face	• **Ribbon:** All tabs>expanded Select panel • **Status Bar**

Basic Sketching and Modify Tools

	Select Links	• **Ribbon:** All tabs>expanded Select panel • **Status Bar**
	Select Pinned Elements	• **Ribbon:** All tabs>expanded Select panel • **Status Bar**
	Select Underlay Elements	• **Ribbon:** All tabs>expanded Select panel • **Status Bar**
Additional Tools		
	Aligned Dimension	• **Ribbon:** *Modify* tab>Measure panel • Quick Access Toolbar
	Component	• **Ribbon:** *Architecture/Structure/Systems* tab • **Shortcut:** CM
	Detail Line	• **Ribbon:** *Annotate* tab>Detail panel • **Shortcut:** DL
	Model Line	• **Ribbon:** *Architecture* tab>Model panel • **Shortcut:** LI
	Reference Plane	• **Ribbon:** *Architecture/Structure/Systems* tab>Work Plane panel

Chapter 3

Starting Structural Projects

Structural projects typically need to utilize information provided by architects as a base for their designs. This can be a file from either AutoCAD® or Revit® that you will then build the structural model around. Ideally, you should never start your work inside of the architectural model. Instead, you should start from either the Revit structural template or your company's custom template and link the architectural model into your project.

If you link a Revit architectural model into your project, you can use the monitoring and coordinating features to copy/monitor necessary items, such as walls, floors, and grids, from the architectural model into the structural model to help reduce errors in the design process.

Learning Objectives in This Chapter

- Link or import CAD files to use as a basis for developing a design.
- Link Revit models into the project so that you can design the structural project.
- Add levels to define floor-to-floor heights and other vertical references.
- Copy and monitor elements from linked Revit models so that you know when changes have been made.
- Run Coordination Reviews to identify changes between the current project and any linked models.

3.1 Linking and Importing CAD Files

CAD files can be imported or linked into an Autodesk Revit structural project. As an example, a designer might lay out a floor plan using the standard 2D AutoCAD software, and you need to incorporate that information into your structural model. In addition, many renovation projects start with existing 2D drawings. Instead of redrawing from scratch, link or import the CAD file (as shown in Figure 3–1) and trace over it in the Autodesk Revit software.

Figure 3–1

- When you select an imported or linked CAD file, a tooltip displays indicating that it is an Import Symbol.

- CAD file formats that can be imported or linked are AutoCAD® (DWG and DXF), MicroStation (DGN), 3D ACIS modeling kernel (SAT), Trimble SketchUp (SKP), FormIt (AXM), and Rhino Files (3dm). FormIt files can only be imported.

Linking vs. Importing

- **Link:** A connection is maintained with the original file and the link updates if the original file is updated.

- **Import:** No connection is maintained with the original file. It becomes a separate element in the Autodesk Revit model.

Starting Structural Projects

How To: Link or Import a CAD File

1. Open the view into which you want to link or import the file.
   - For a 2D file, this should be a 2D view. For a 3D file, open a 3D view.
2. In the *Insert* tab>Link panel, click (Link CAD), or in the *Insert* tab>Import panel, click (Import CAD).

The dialog boxes for Link CAD Formats and Import CAD Formats are the same.

3. In the Link CAD Formats or Import CAD Formats dialog box (shown in Figure 3–2), select the file that you want to import.
   - Select a file format in the Files of type: drop-down list to limit the files that are displayed.

Figure 3–2

4. Set the other options, as shown in Figure 3–3.

Figure 3–3

5. Click **Open**.

> **Hint: Link or Importing PDFs**
>
> You can link or import a PDF into Autodesk Revit as a raster image. If the PDF contains vector data, you can snap to the elements in the PDF.
>
> - In the *Insert* tab>Import panel, click (PDF).
> - In the *Insert* tab>Link panel, click (Link PDF).

For more information on importing and linking CAD files, see the ASCENT guide Autodesk Revit: Collaboration Tools.

Link and Import Options

Current view only	Determines whether the CAD file is placed in every view or only in the current view. This is especially useful if you are working with a 2D floor plan that you only need to have in one view.
Colors	Specify the color settings. Typical Autodesk Revit projects are mainly black and white. However, other software frequently uses color. You can **Invert** the original colors, **Preserve** them, or change everything to **Black and White**.
Layers/ Levels	Indicates which CAD layers are going to be brought into the model. Select how you want layers/levels to be imported: **All**, **Visible**, or **Specify**. • Layers are in .DWG files, while levels are in .DGN files.
Import units	Select the units of the original file, as required. **Auto-Detect** works in most cases.
Correct lines...	If lines in a CAD file are off axis by less than 0.1 degrees, selecting this option straightens them. It is selected by default.

Positioning	Specify how you want the imported file to be positioned in the current project.
	
	Auto - Center to Center Auto - Center to Center
	Auto - Origin to Internal Origin Auto - Origin to Internal Origin
	Manual - Origin Auto - By Shared Coordinates
	Manual - Center Manual - Origin
	                                  Manual - Center
	
	   Import options *Linking options*
	
	The default position is **Auto - Origin to Internal Origin**.

Place at	Select a level at which to place the imported file. If you selected **Current view only**, this option is grayed out.
Orient to View	Select this option if the view you are working in is set to true north (and is different from project north) so that the CAD file is aligned to true north.

- When a file is positioned **Auto - Origin to Internal Origin**, it is pinned in place and cannot be moved. To move the file, click on the pin to unpin it, as shown in Figure 3–4.

Figure 3–4

Setting an Imported or Linked File to Halftone

To see the difference between the host model elements and the linked or imported file, you can set the linked/imported file to **Halftone**, as shown in Figure 3–5.

Figure 3–5

How To: Set an Element to Halftone

1. Select the imported file.
2. Right-click and select **Override Graphics in View>By Element...**.
3. In the View-Specific Element Graphics dialog box, select **Halftone**, as shown in Figure 3–6.

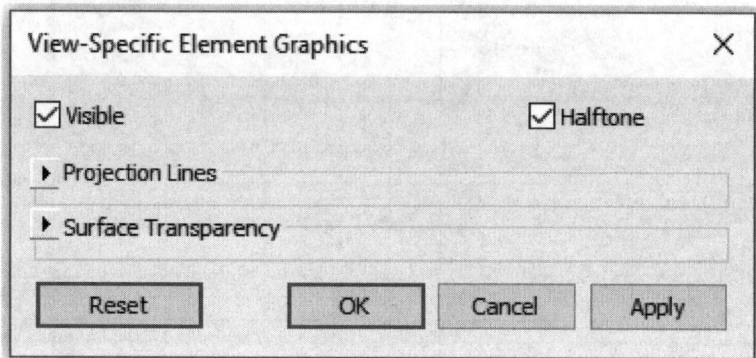

Figure 3–6

4. Click **OK**.

Draw Layer

Linked CAD files are typically in the background of a view. To change this, select the CAD file and, in the Options Bar or in Properties in the *Other* section, change the *Draw Layer* to **Foreground**.

Introduction to Worksharing

When a project becomes too big for one person, it needs to be subdivided so that a team of people working on the same network can work on it. Since Autodesk Revit projects include the entire building model in one file, the file needs to be separated into logical components, as shown in Figure 3–7, without losing the connection to the whole. This process is called *worksharing* and the main components are worksets.

Figure 3–7

- For more information on worksharing, see *Appendix A: Introduction to Worksharing.*

- For more information about establishing and using worksets, refer to the ASCENT guide *Autodesk Revit: Collaboration Tools.*

Practice 3a Start a CAD-Based Structural Project

Practice Objective

- Link a 2D DWG file into a new project.

In this practice, you will link an AutoCAD (.DWG) file as the base floor plan for a project, move elevation markers in the current project to match the footprint of the building, and modify the visibility graphics of the linked file so that it displays in halftone, as shown in Figure 3–8.

Figure 3–8

1. In the *File* tab, click (New).

   - If starting from the Home screen, click **New...** in the *MODELS* area of the sidebar.

2. In the New Project dialog box, select **Imperial-Structural Template** from the Template File drop-down list and click **OK**.

3. In the Project Browser, open the **Structural Plans: Level 1** view. (The default structural template automatically opens in Level 2. You are importing the **Level 1** floor plan from the AutoCAD file and therefore need to open that view).

Starting Structural Projects

4. In the *Insert* tab>Link panel, click (Link CAD).

5. In the Link CAD Formats dialog box, navigate to your practice files *CAD Files* folder and select, but do not open, **First-Floor-Structural-Suites.dwg**.

6. Set or verify the options as follows:
   - Select **Current view only**
   - *Colors:* **Black and White**
   - *Layers:* **All**
   - *Import Units:* **Auto-Detect**
   - *Positioning:* **Auto - Origin to Internal Origin**

7. Click **Open**.

8. Zoom to the extents of the view. (Hint: Type **ZE** or double-click on the mouse wheel.)

9. Move the building elevation markers so that they are on the outside of the imported file, as shown in Figure 3–9. Select both parts of the elevation markers.

Use a window selection to select both parts of the elevation markers.

Figure 3–9

10. Right-click on the linked file (also called an import symbol) and select **Override Graphics in View>By Element**.

11. In the View-Specific Element Graphics dialog box, select **Halftone**, as shown in Figure 3–10.

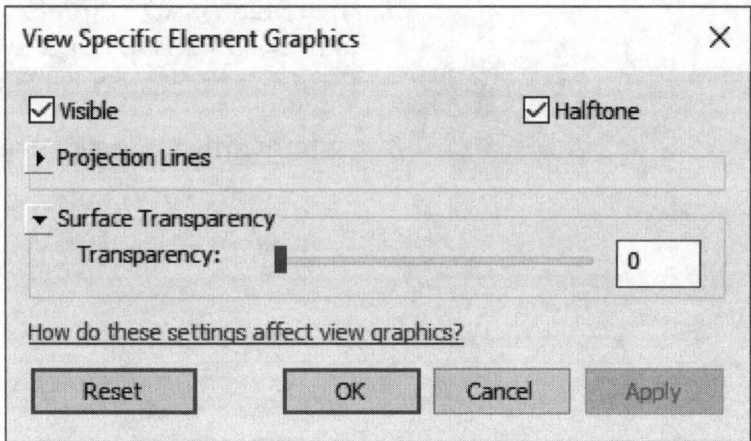

Figure 3–10

12. Click **OK**.

13. Click away from the linked file to release the selection.

14. In the Quick Access Toolbar, click (Default 3D View). No linked file displays because you linked it only into the Level 1 view.

15. Return to the **Structural Plans: Level 1** view.

16. Save the model as **Structural-Suites-CAD.rvt** and close the project.

3.2 Linking in Revit Models

You can link Autodesk Revit architectural or engineering models directly into your structural project. Doing this will make your project the host model because it will be hosting the other linked models. When an architectural or engineering model is linked into the structural project, only structural-related elements, such as floors, columns, and walls, are displayed by default. An example is shown in Figure 3–11.

A linked model automatically updates when the original file is changed.

Architectural model linked into a structural project

Figure 3–11

- You can link multiple Revit models into your project, but each model can only be linked once. If you try to link a model that has already been linked into your project, a warning will appear stating that an instance of this link already exists.

- Architectural, structural, and MEP models created in the Autodesk Revit software can be linked to each other as long as they are from the same release cycle.

- When you use linked models, clashes between disciplines can be detected and information can be passed between disciplines.

- Revit models are always linked. They cannot be imported.

> **Hint: Views and Disciplines**
>
> When using a structural template, most of the views are set to display only structural elements. To display the architectural information (or that of another discipline), change the *Discipline* of the view in Properties.

How To: Add a Linked Model to a Host Project

1. In the *Insert* tab>Link panel, click (Link Revit).
2. In the Import/Link RVT dialog box, select the file that you want to link. Before opening the file, set the *Positioning*, as shown in Figure 3–12.

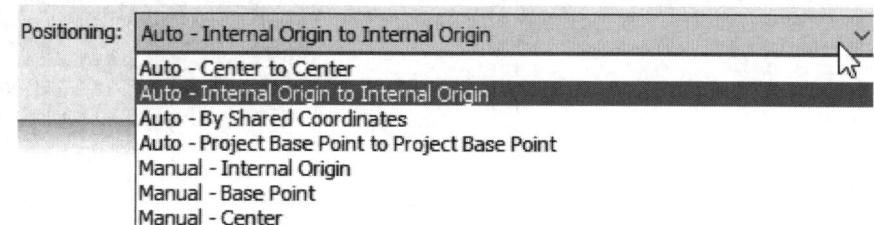

Figure 3–12

3. Click **Open**.
4. Depending on how you decide to position the file, it is automatically placed in the project or you can manually place it with the cursor.

- As the links are loading, do not click on the screen or click any buttons. The more links present in a project, the longer it takes to load.

Multiple Copies of Linked Models

Copied instances of a linked model are typically used when creating a master project with the same building placed in multiple locations, such as a university campus with six identical student residence halls.

- Linked models can be moved, copied, rotated, arrayed, and mirrored. There is only one linked model, and any copies are additional instances of the link.

- Copies are numbered automatically. You can change their names in Properties when the instance is selected.

- When you have placed a link in a project, you can drag and drop additional copies of the link into the project from the Project Browser>**Revit Links** node, as shown in Figure 3–13.

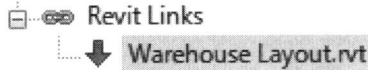

Figure 3–13

Hint: Preventing the Linked Model from Being Moved

Once a linked model is in the correct location, you can lock it in place to ensure that it does not get moved by mistake or toggle options to prevent the linked model from being selected.

- To pin the linked model in place, select it and in the *Modify* tab>Modify panel, click (Pin).

- To prevent pinned elements from being selected, in the Status Bar, click (Select Pinned Elements).

- To toggle off the ability to select links, in the Status Bar, click (Select Links).

If a linked file is moved, you can reposition it to the **Project Base Point** or **Internal Origin**. Right-click on it and select the desired option, as shown in Figure 3–14.

Figure 3–14

Managing Links

The Manage Links dialog box (shown in Figure 3–15) enables you to reload, unload, add, and remove links, and also provides access to set other options. To open the Manage Links dialog box, in the *Insert* tab>Link panel, click (Manage Links), or select the link and in the *Modify | RVT Links* tab>Link panel, click (Manage Links).

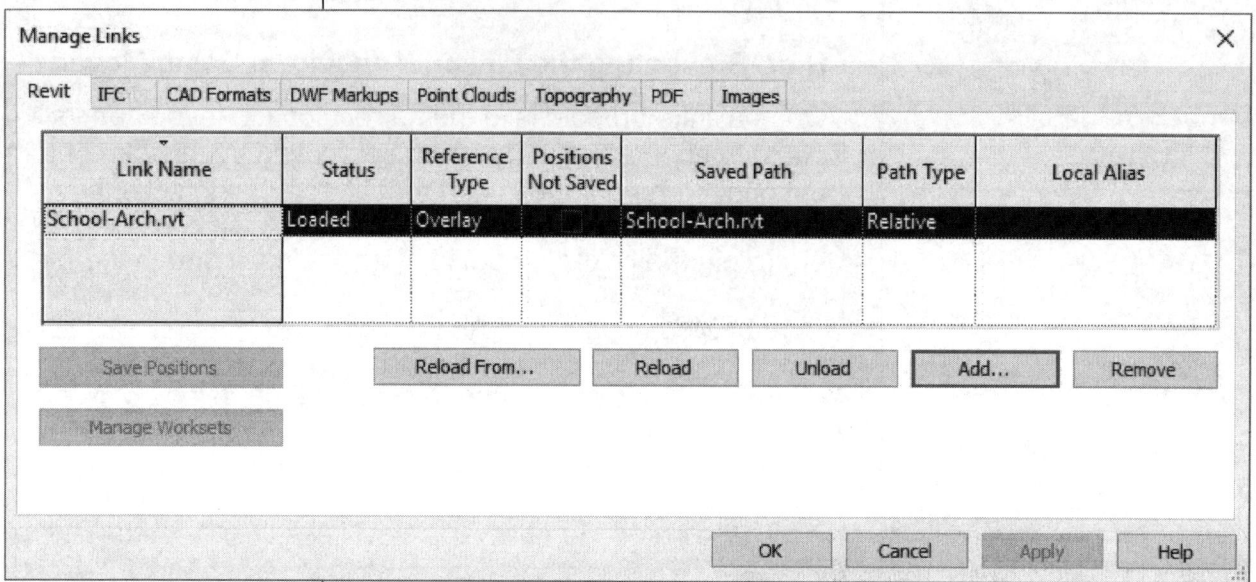

Figure 3–15

The available options include the following:

- **Reload From:** Opens the Add Link dialog box, which enables you to select the file you want to reload. Use this if the linked file location or name has changed.

- **Reload:** Reloads the file without additional prompts.

- **Unload:** Unloads the file so that the link is kept, but the file is not displayed or calculated in the project. Use **Reload** to restore it.

- **Add:** Opens the Import/Link RVT dialog box, which enables you to link additional models into the host project.

- **Remove:** Deletes the link from the file.

Links can be nested into one another. How a link responds when the host project is linked into another project depends on the option shown in the *Reference Type* column.

- **Overlay:** The nested linked model is not referenced in the new host project.

- **Attach:** The nested linked model displays in the new host project.

*Some of these options are also available in the Project Browser. Expand the Revit Links node, right-click on the Revit Link, and select **Reload**, **Unload**, or **Reload From...**.*

Starting Structural Projects

The option shown in the *Path Type* column controls how the location of the link is remembered.

- **Relative**
  - Searches the root folder of the current project.
  - If the file is moved, the software still searches for it.

- **Absolute**
  - Searches only the folder where the file was originally saved.
  - If the original file is moved, the software is not able to find it.

Other options control how the linked file interfaces with worksets and shared positioning.

> **Hint: Visibility Graphics and Linked Files**
>
> When you open the Visibility/Graphic Overrides dialog box (type **VV** or **VG**), you can modify the graphic overrides for Revit links, as shown in Figure 3–16. This can help you clean up the view or assign a view to build on.
>
>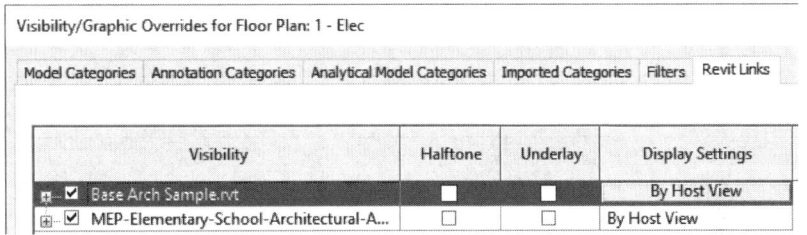
>
> Figure 3–16
>
> The *Display Settings* include:
>
> - **By Host View:** The display of the Revit link is based on the view properties of the current view in the host model.
>
> - **By Linked View:** The appearance of the Revit link is based on the view properties of the selected linked view and ignores the view properties of the current view.
>
> - **Custom:** You can override all of the graphical elements.

Practice 3b

Start a Structural Project

Practice Objectives

- Start a new project from a template.
- Link an architectural model into a structural project.

In this practice, you will link an architectural Revit model into a new structural project and pin the linked model into place. You will then change view properties to a coordination view that shows both the structural and architectural features, as shown in Figure 3–17.

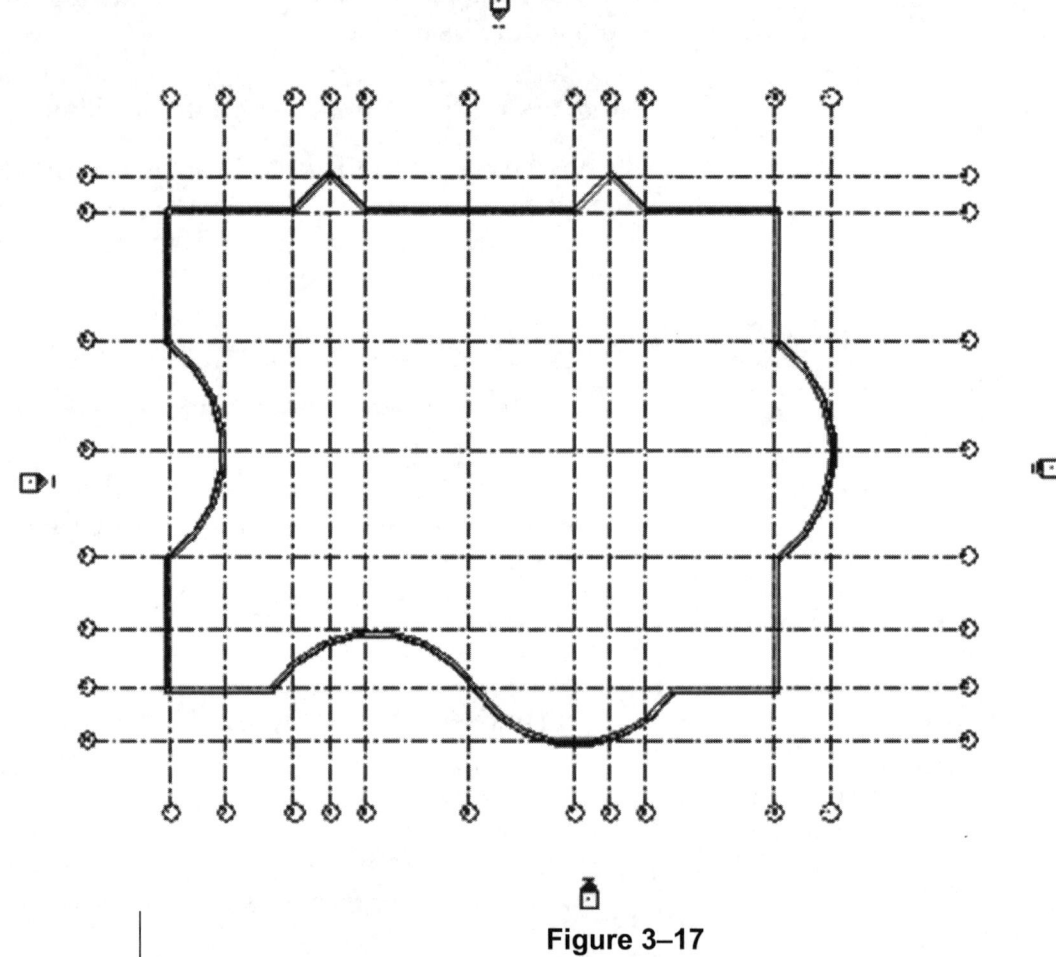

Figure 3–17

1. Start a new project based on the default imperial structural template by going to the *File* tab, expanding ▭ (New), and clicking ▭ (Project), or by pressing <Ctrl>+<N>. The file automatically opens in the **Structural Plans: Level 2** view.

2. In the *Insert* tab>Link panel, click ▭ (Link Revit).

3. In the Import/Link RVT dialog box, navigate to your practice files *Linked Revit Models* folder and select the file **Arch-Suites.rvt**. Ensure that the *Positioning* is set to **Auto - Internal Origin to Internal Origin** and click **Open**.

4. Select the linked model in the view (only grid lines display) and in the *Modify | RVT Links* tab>Modify panel, click

   (Pin). This will ensure that the linked model will not be accidentally moved in the view.

5. Adjust the building elevation markers so that they are around the link, as shown in Figure 3–18.

Only the grid lines are currently displayed because the view is set to display structural elements only.

Figure 3–18

6. Click in an empty space in the view and zoom to fit the view. (Hint: Type **ZF**.)

7. In Properties, change the *Discipline* to **Coordination**, as shown in Figure 3–19.

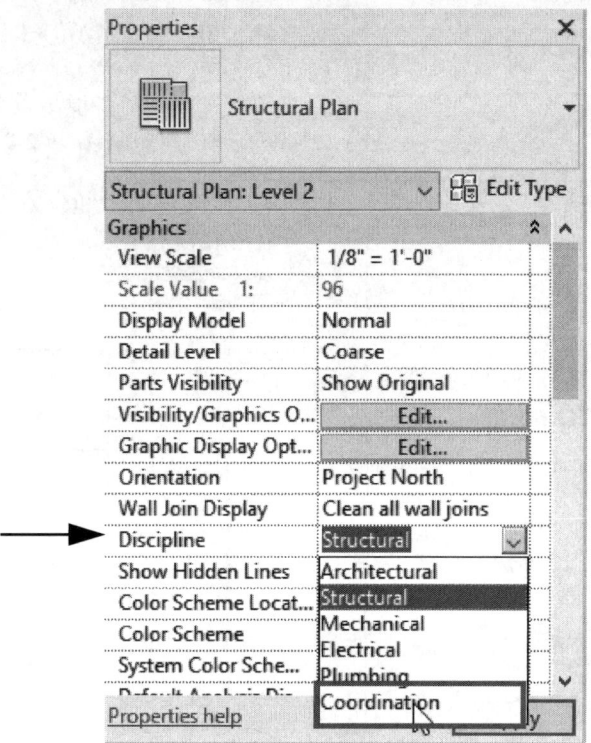

Figure 3–19

8. Click **Apply**. The architectural walls now display.

9. Save the project in your practice files folder as **Structural-Suites-<your initials>.rvt** and close the file.

Starting Structural Projects

3.3 Setting Up Levels

Levels define stories and other vertical heights, as shown in Figure 3–20. The default structural template includes two levels, but you can define as many levels in a project as required. Levels can be placed or moved below the elevation 0'-0" (using a negative value, as shown with T.O. Footing in Figure 3–20) or above 0'-0" (using a positive value).

Floor levels are frequently set by the architect and need to be copied and monitored into the structural model. You can also draw levels directly in a project, as required.

Figure 3–20

- You must be in an elevation or section view to define levels.

- Once you constrain an element to a level, it moves with the level when the level is changed.

How To: Create Levels

1. Open an elevation or section view.
2. In the *Structure* tab>Datum panel, click (Level), or type **LL**.
3. In the Type Selector, set the Level Head type, if needed.
4. In the Options Bar, select or clear **Make Plan View** as needed. You can also click **Plan View Types...** to select the types of views to create when you place the level.
5. In the *Modify | Place Level* tab>Draw panel, click:

   - (Line) to draw a level.

   - (Pick Lines) to select an element using an offset.

   Be careful when using **Pick Lines** that you do not place levels on top of each other or other elements by mistake.

6. Continue adding levels as needed.

- Level names are automatically incremented as you place them. This automatic numbering is most effective when you use names such as Floor 1, Floor 2, etc. (as opposed to First Floor, Second Floor, etc.). This also makes it easier to find the view in the Project Browser.

- A fast way to create multiple levels is to use the (Pick Lines) option using an offset. In the Options Bar, specify an *Offset,* select an existing level, and then pick above or below to place the new level, as shown in Figure 3–21.

You specify above or below the offset by hovering the mouse on the needed side.

Figure 3–21

- When using the (Line) option, alignments and temporary dimensions help you place the line correctly, as shown in Figure 3–22.

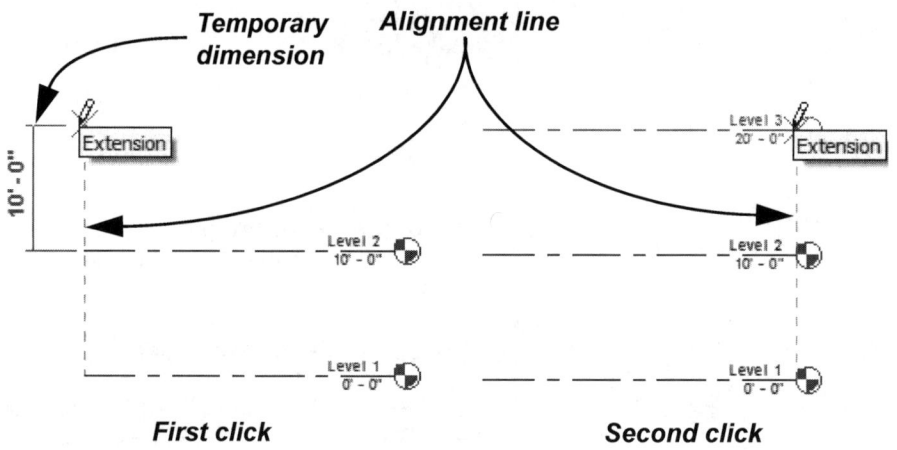

Figure 3–22

- Sketch each level line in the same direction (from left to right or from right to left) to keep the graphics of the level consistent.

- You can also use (Copy) to duplicate level lines. The level names are incremented but a plan view is not created. These are called reference levels.

- Levels display in the default 3D view. They can be modified and copied, but cannot be created in this view.

- Levels can be hidden in any view.

Modifying Levels

You can change levels using standard controls and temporary dimensions, as shown in Figure 3–23. You can make changes to the name and height of the level by selecting the individual items in the view or changing them in Properties. You can also change the name of the level in the Project Browser, but not the height.

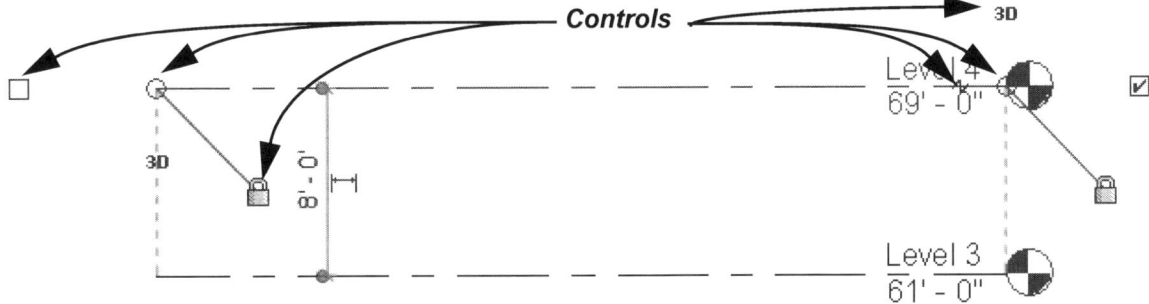

Figure 3–23

- ☑ ☐ (Hide / Show Bubble) displays on either end of the level line and toggles the level head symbol and level information on or off.

- 2D 3D (Switch to 3d / 2d extents) controls whether any movement or adjustment to the level line is reflected in other views (3D) or only affects the current view (2D).

- (Modify the level by dragging its model end) at each end of the line enables you to drag the level head to a new location.

- 🔒 🔓 (Create or remove a length or alignment constraint) controls whether the level is locked in alignment with the other levels. If it is locked and the level line is stretched, all of the other level lines stretch as well. If it is unlocked, the level line stretches independent of the other levels.

- Click (Add Elbow) to add a jog to the level line, as shown in Figure 3–24. Drag the shape handles to new locations as needed. This is a view-specific change.

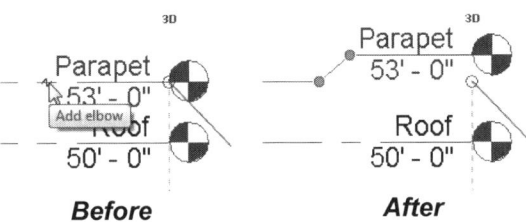

Before　　　**After**

Figure 3–24

- To change the level name or elevation, double-click on the information next to the level head, or select the level and modify the *Name* or *Elevation* fields in Properties, as shown in Figure 3–25.

Figure 3–25

- When you rename a level, an alert box opens, prompting you to rename the corresponding views, as shown in Figure 3–26.

Figure 3–26

- The view is also renamed in the Project Browser.

Starting Structural Projects

- If you delete a level, the views related to that level are also deleted. A warning displays, as shown in Figure 3–27.

Figure 3–27

Hint: Propagating Datum Extents

Datum elements, such as levels and column grids, might not always display as expected in a view. If this is the case, select the levels or grid lines in a view in which they are displayed and in the *Modify* contextual tab>Datum panel, click (Propagate Extents). In the Propagate datum extents dialog box (shown in Figure 3–28), select the views to project the levels or grid lines to.

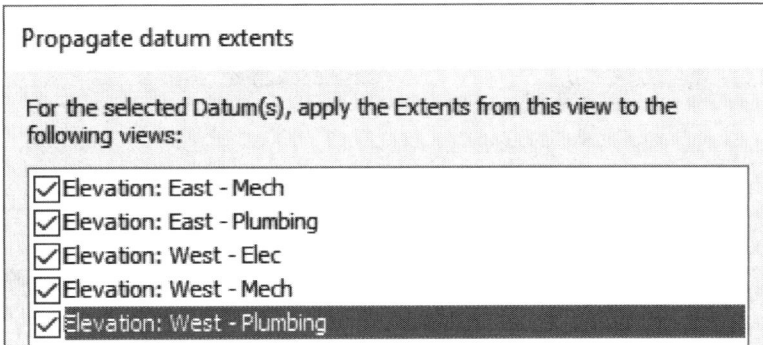

Figure 3–28

- (Propagate Extents) is particularly useful to make levels and grid lines display the same in all views.

Creating Plan Views

By default, when you place a level, plan views for that level are automatically created. If **Make Plan View** was toggled off when adding the level, or if the level was copied, you can create plan views to match the levels.

- Level heads with views are blue and level heads without views are black, as shown in Figure 3–29.

Typically, you do not need to create plan views for levels that specify data, such as the top of a foundation wall or the truss bearing height.

Figure 3–29

How To: Create Plan Views

1. In the *View* tab>Create panel, expand (Plan Views) and select the type of plan view you want to create, as shown on the left in Figure 3–30.
2. In the New Plan dialog box (shown on the right in Figure 3–30), select the levels for which you want to create plan views.

Hold <Ctrl> or <Shift> to select more than one level.

Figure 3–30

3. Click **OK**.

- When **Do not duplicate existing views** is selected, views without the selected plan type display in the list.

3.4 Copying and Monitoring Elements

Once a linked architectural model is in place, the next step is to copy and/or monitor elements that you need from the linked file into the structural project. These elements most often include grid lines, levels, columns, walls, and floors. You cannot copy monitor beams or braces. A monitoring system keeps track of the copied elements and prompts for updates if something is changed. In the example shown in Figure 3–31, grid lines have been linked from an architectural model, and the ⌁ (Monitor) icon indicates the elements are being monitored.

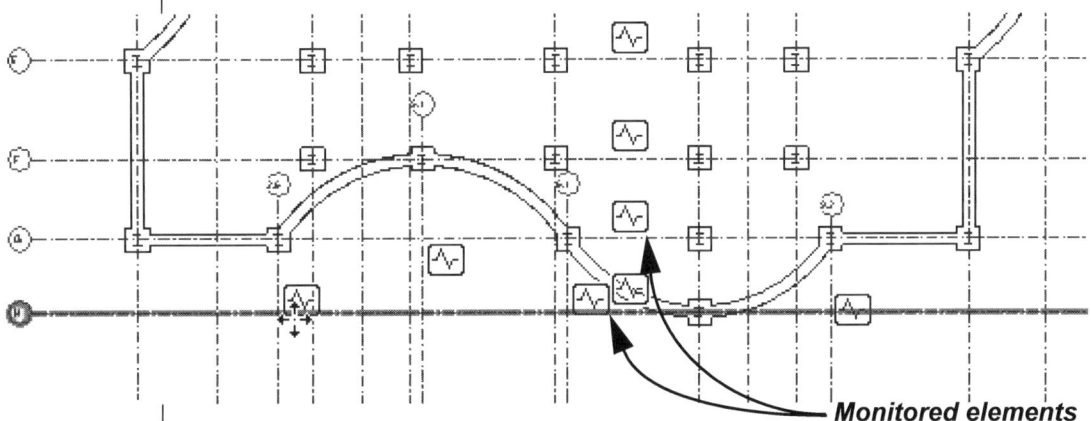

Figure 3–31

Before you start the Copy/Monitor command, you can specify options for levels, grid lines, columns, walls, and floors. You can choose to copy or monitor from the current project or from a linked Revit model. Use **Select Link** to monitor a linked file's elements if they could potentially be moved and affect your system.

- **Copy** copies the selected element from the linked model to the current model or host model, then monitors the element for any changes that may happen in the linked model.

- **Monitor** compares two elements of the same type against each other, either from a linked model to the current project (as shown in Figure 3–32) or within the current project.

Figure 3–32

Copy/Monitor Settings

You can specify copy/monitor options for the specific element types before starting the copy/monitor process. These options only apply to elements selected after the options have been modified.

In the *Copy/Monitor* tab>Tools panel, click 🔧 (Options). In the Copy/Monitor Options dialog box, select the tab for the type of element that you want to copy: *Levels*, *Grids*, *Columns*, *Walls*, or *Floors*, as shown in Figure 3–33.

Tabs display for the categories that exist in the linked project.

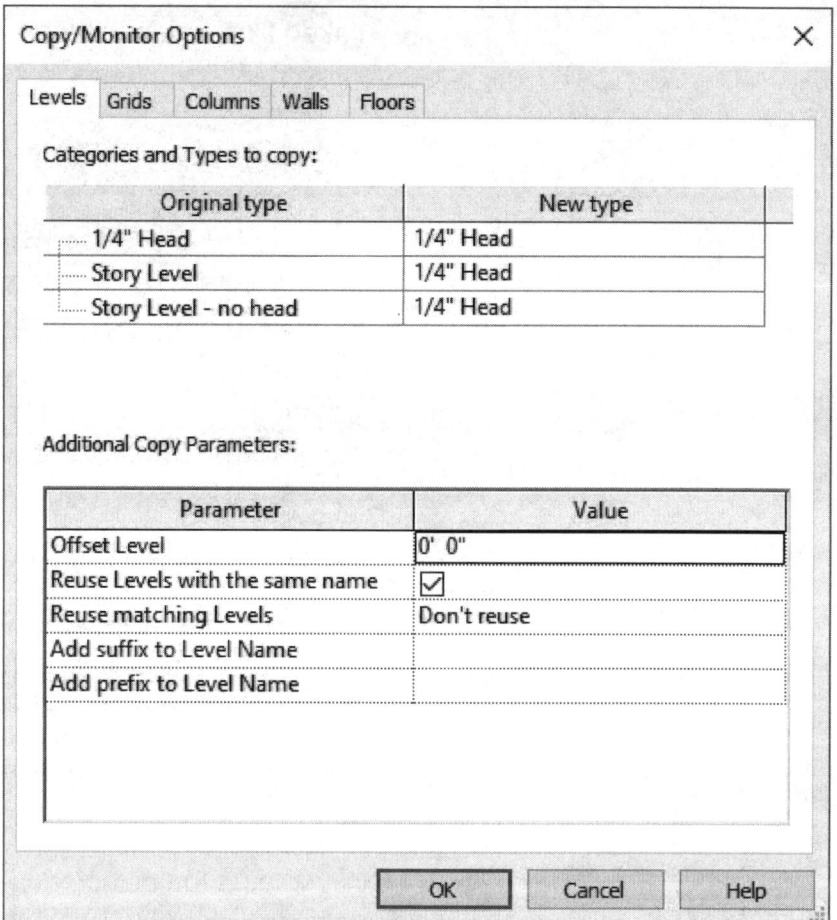

Figure 3–33

Additional Copy Parameters

Offset Level	Specify a level offset for a copied level.
Reuse Levels with the same name	If the current model has a level with the same name as a level in the linked model, you can select this option so a new level is not created. If the linked model's level is at a different height, then the level in the current model will change to match it.
Reuse matching Levels	**Don't reuse:** When selected, if the current model has a level at the same elevation as the linked model, it will still copy the level from the linked model. **Reuse if Elements Match Exactly:** When selected, if the current model and linked model have a level at the same elevation, the level in the linked model is not copied. **Reuse if within offset:** When selected, if the current model has a level within the offset level parameter's elevation, the linked model's level is not copied.
Add suffix to Level Name	Specify a suffix to add to the name of a copied level.
Add prefix to Level Name	Specify a prefix to add to the name of a copied level.
Split Columns by Levels	If copying columns from a linked model extends through multiple levels, selecting this option will break the continuous column into individual columns that stop and start at level lines.
Location line to align	Specify the copied wall's location line to match that of the structural walls.
Copy windows/ doors/openings	When selected, the openings of windows and doors are copied over from the linked model.
Copy openings/ inserts	When selected, if any floors copied from linked models have openings or hosted inserts, the openings/inserts will also copy over as well.

How To: Copy and Monitor Elements from a Linked File

1. In the *Collaborate* tab>Coordinate panel, expand (Copy/Monitor) and click (Select Link).

2. Select the link.

3. In the *Copy/Monitor* tab>Tools panel, click (Copy) or (Monitor).

4. If copying from the linked file, select each element that you want to copy. Alternatively, use the **Multiple** option:
   - In the Options Bar, select **Multiple**, as shown in Figure 3–34.

   Figure 3–34

   - Hold <Ctrl> and select the elements that you want to copy into your model individually, or use a pick and drag window around multiple elements.
   - In the Options Bar, click **Finish**.

   If monitoring elements in the current project with elements in the linked model, first select the element in the current project and then select the element in the linked model.

5. Click ✓ (Finish) to end the session of Copy/Monitor.

Warnings about duplicated or renamed types might display.

How To: Copy and Monitor Elements in the Current Project

1. In the *Collaborate* tab>Coordinate panel, expand (Copy/Monitor) and click (Use Current Project).

2. In the *Copy/Monitor* tab>Tools panel, click (Copy) or (Monitor).

3. Select the two elements you want to monitor.
4. Repeat the process for any additional elements.

5. Click ✓ (Finish) to end the command.

- The elements do not have to be at the same elevation or location for the software to monitor them.

Practice 3c Copy and Monitor Elements

Practice Objective

- Copy and monitor elements from the linked model into the current project.

In this practice, you will monitor an existing level and copy additional levels from a linked architectural model into the current structural project, as shown in Figure 3–35.

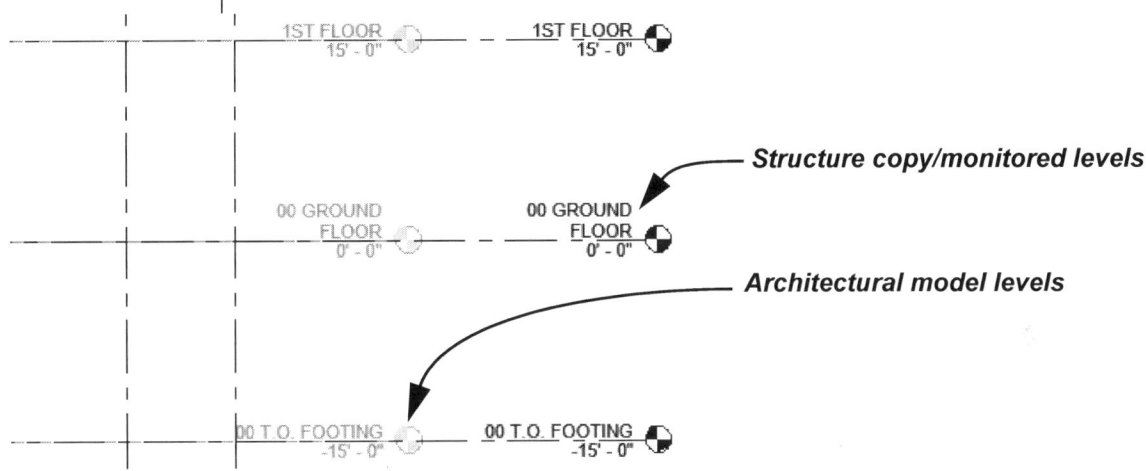

Figure 3–35

Task 1 - Monitor elements in the active project with elements in the linked model.

1. Open **Structural-Monitor.rvt** from the practice files folder.
   - If the linked file needs to be reloaded, in the Manage Links dialog box, click **Reload From**. Navigate to the practice files folder, select **Arch-Suites.rvt**, and click **Open**.

2. In the Project Browser, expand the **Elevations (Building Elevation)** node and open the **South** view.

3. Select the link. There are two existing levels in the current project and a large number of levels in the linked model, as shown in Figure 3–36.

Link levels

Existing levels

Figure 3–36

4. Right-click on the link and select **Override Graphics in View>By Category**. In the View-Specific Category Graphics dialog box, select **Halftone** and click **OK**.

5. Click (Modify).

6. Delete **Level 2**. A warning dialog box opens, as shown in Figure 3–37. Click **OK** to delete the corresponding views as they are not required in this project.

A later step creates new levels that are automatically named based on the linked model's levels.

Figure 3–37

7. Select the host project's **Level 1**. Use controls to drag the level line to the far right so it is longer than the level lines in the linked model. Use zoom and pan as needed.

8. Click on the level name and rename the level to **00 GROUND FLOOR**, as shown in Figure 3–38.

Figure 3–38

9. When prompted, click **Yes** to rename the associated views.

10. In the Project Browser, the former **Level 1** view has been renamed **00 GROUND FLOOR**, as shown in Figure 3–39.

Figure 3–39

11. In the Project Browser, right-click on the other two Level 1 views and rename them **00 GROUND FLOOR - Analytical** and **00 GROUND FLOOR - Coordination**.

12. If you opened one or more of the structural plan views, close them and return to the South elevation view. (Hint: In the Quick Access Toolbar, click (Close Inactive Windows).

13. Save the project.

Task 2 - Copy and monitor levels.

1. In the *Collaborate* tab>Coordinate panel, expand (Copy/Monitor) and click (Select Link).

2. Select the architectural linked model.

3. In the *Copy/Monitor* tab>Tools panel, click (Monitor).

4. Select level **00 GROUND FLOOR** in the host project and then select the corresponding level in the linked model. The level is now monitored. You will see the monitor icon when you select the levels, as shown in Figure 3–40.

   - You might need to zoom out to display the monitor icon.

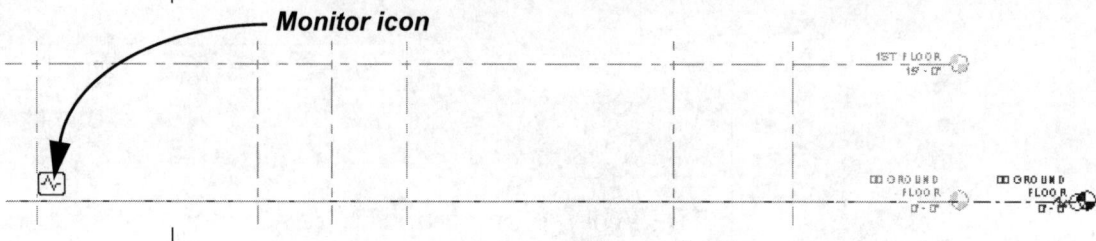

Figure 3–40

5. In the *Copy/Monitor* tab>Tools panel, click (Options).

6. In the Copy/Monitor Options dialog box, select the *Levels* tab. Change *Reuse matching Levels* to **Reuse if Elements match exactly**, as shown in Figure 3–41.

Parameter	Value
Offset Level	0' 0"
Reuse Levels with the same name	☑
Reuse matching Levels	Reuse if Elements match exactly
Add suffix to Level Name	Don't reuse
Add prefix to Level Name	Reuse if Elements match exactly
	Reuse if within offset

Figure 3–41

7. Click **OK**.

8. In the *Copy/Monitor* tab>Tools panel, click (Copy).

9. Select level **T.O. FOOTING**. Close the warning message about copies of the grid head being renamed. A replica of the level in the linked model is copied into the current project, as shown in Figure 3–42.

Figure 3–42

Starting Structural Projects

10. In the *Copy/Monitor* tab>Tools panel, click (Options).

11. In the Copy/Monitor Options dialog box, select the *Levels* tab. Set the *Offset Level* to (negative) **-0'-5"** and set the value for *Add prefix to Level Name* to **TOS-**, as shown in Figure 3–43.

Parameter	Value
Offset Level	-0' 5"
Reuse Levels with the same name	✓
Reuse matching Levels	Reuse if Elements match exactly
Add suffix to Level Name	
Add prefix to Level Name	TOS-

Figure 3–43

12. Click **OK**.

13. In the *Copy/Monitor* tab>Tools panel, click (Copy).

14. Select each of the levels for the 1st through 14th floors. (Monitor) displays at each level line as it is placed.

15. In the Copy/Monitor panel, click (Finish).

16. New levels with the prefix TOS- are copied into the current project at **5"** below the level in the linked model, as shown in Figure 3–44.

Align the level head symbols so that you can see both the current and linked levels on each end.

Figure 3–44

17. Zoom to fit the view (type **ZF**) and save the project.

Task 3 - Set up views.

1. In the Project Browser, note that the floor plans of the new levels do not display, as shown in Figure 3–45.

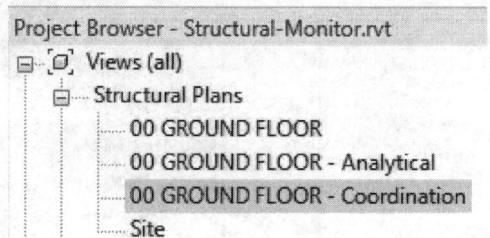

Figure 3–45

2. In the *View* tab>Create panel, expand ▭ (Plan Views) and click ▭ (Structural Plan).

3. In the New Structural Plan dialog box, select all of the levels, as shown in Figure 3–46, and click **OK**.

4. The new views display in the Project Browser, as shown in Figure 3–47. **TOS-14 ROOF** (the last plan created) is automatically opened.

Figure 3–46

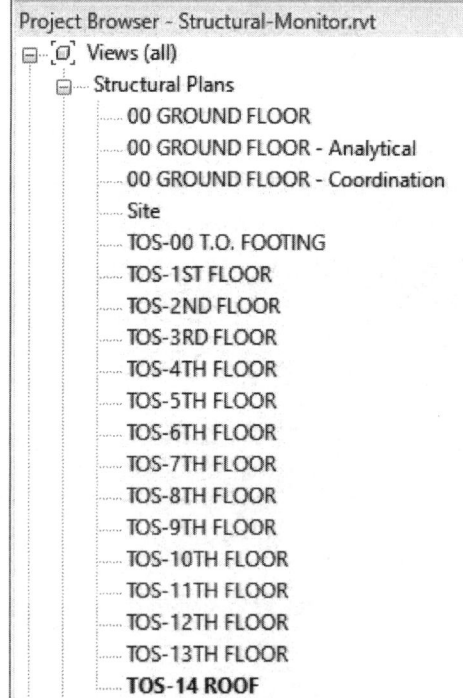

Figure 3–47

5. Open the **Elevations (Building Elevation): South** view.

6. Save and close the project.

Starting Structural Projects

3.5 Coordinating Linked Models

Monitoring elements identifies changes in the data as well as changes in placement. For example, if you move a grid line, a Coordination Monitor alert displays, as shown in Figure 3–48. You can run a Coordination Review to correct or accept these changes.

Figure 3–48

- If you open a project with a linked file that contains elements that have been modified and monitored, the Warning shown in Figure 3–49 displays.

Figure 3–49

- Warnings do not prevent you from making a change, but alert you that the element is monitored and needs further coordination.

- If you no longer want an element to be monitored, select it and in the associated *Modify* tab>Monitor panel, click (Stop Monitoring).

How To: Run a Coordination Review

1. In the *Collaborate* tab>Coordinate panel, expand (Coordination Review) and click (Use Current Project) or (Select Link). The Coordination Review dialog box lists any conflicts detected, as shown in Figure 3–50.
   - If there are no conflicts, the *Message* area is empty.

Figure 3–50

2. Use the Group by: drop-down list to group the information by **Status**, **Category**, and **Rule** in a variety of different ways. This is important if you have many elements to review.

3. Select an *Action* for each conflict related to the elements involved, as shown in Figure 3–51.

Figure 3–51

- **Postpone:** Do nothing, but leave it to be handled later.
- **Reject:** Do not accept the change. The change needs to be made in the other model.
- **Accept difference:** Make no change to the monitored element in the current project, but accept the change (such as a distance between the elements) in the monitor status.
- **Rename/Modify/Move:** Apply the change to the monitored element.
- Other options display when special cases occur. See the Autodesk Revit help documentation for more information.

4. To add a comment, click **Add comment** in the column to the right. This enables you to make a note about the change, such as the date of the modification.
5. Select the element names or click **Show** to display any items in conflict. Clicking **Show** changes the view to center the elements in your screen. Selecting the name does not change the view.
6. Click **Create Report** to create an HTML report that you can share with other users, as shown in Figure 3–52.

Revit Coordination Report

In host project

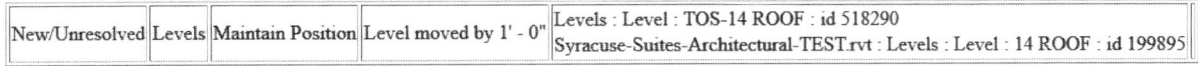

Figure 3–52

Hint: Troubleshooting

When working with various elements, warnings (such as the one shown in Figure 3–53) display when something is wrong, but you can keep on working. In many cases, you can close the dialog box and fix the issue or wait and do it later.

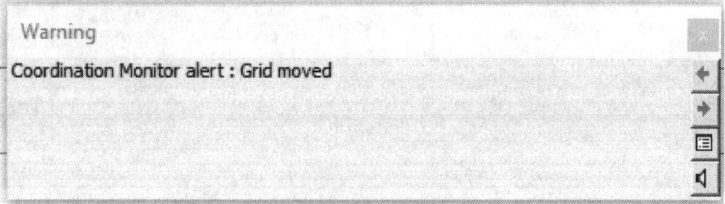

Figure 3–53

Sometimes Errors display where you must take action. These force you to stop and fix the situation.

When you select an element for which there has been a warning, ⚠ (Show Related Warnings) displays in the ribbon. It opens a dialog box in which you can review the warning(s) related to the selected element. You can also display a list of all of the warnings in the project by clicking (Review Warnings) in the *Manage* tab>Inquiry panel.

Practice 3d Coordinate Linked Models

Practice Objectives

- Make a modification to an architectural model.
- Run a Coordination Review.

In this practice, you will make a modification to the architectural model, and then open the structural project, which notifies you of the change. You will then run a Coordination Review and update the structural project to match the change in the architectural model, as shown in Figure 3–54.

Figure 3–54

Task 1 - Modify the architectural model.

1. Close the previous practice's project if you have not already done so. You cannot open a linked file with it open.

2. Open **Arch-Suites.rvt** from the practice files *Linked Revit Models* folder. This is the file that is linked into the structural project.

3. In the Project Browser, open the **Elevations (Building Elevation): SOUTH ELEVATION** view.

4. Zoom in on the upper levels of the building.

5. Double-click on the number below **14 ROOF** and change the height to **210'-0"**, as shown in Figure 3–55.

Figure 3–55

6. Save and close the model.

Task 2 - Coordinate the architectural and structural models.

1. Open **Structural-Coordinate.rvt** from the practice files folder.

2. A warning dialog box displays with a warning that the linked file needs a Coordination Review, as shown in Figure 3–56.

Figure 3–56

3. Click **OK**.

4. Select the linked model and in the *Modify RVT Links* tab> Monitor panel, click (Coordination Review).

5. In the Coordination Review dialog box, expand the **Level moved** node. In the *Action* column, expand the drop-down list and select **Move Level 'TOS-14 ROOF'**, as shown in Figure 3–57.

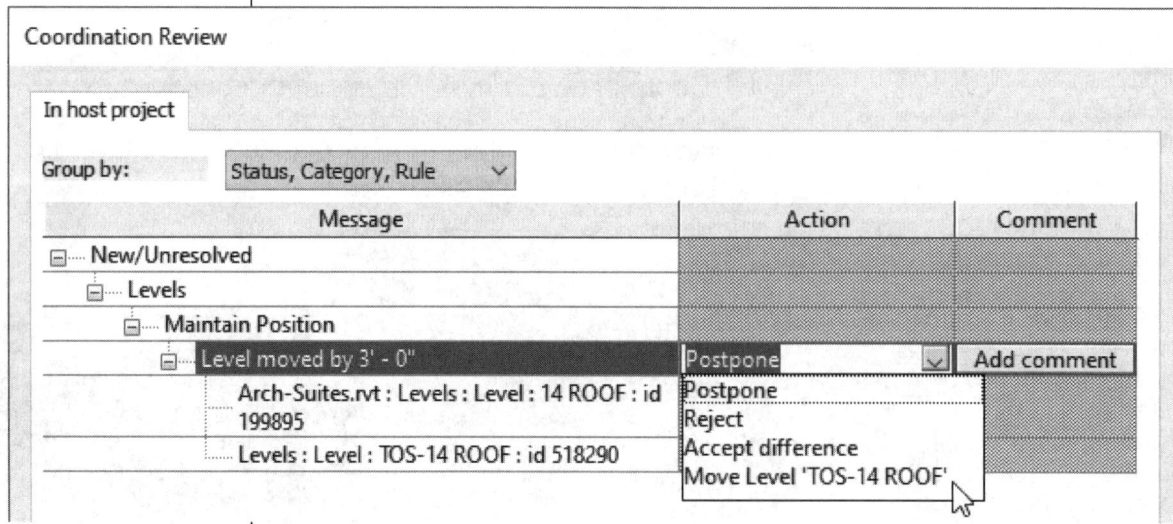

Figure 3–57

6. Click **OK**. The levels now reflect the change in both the linked model and the current model, as shown in Figure 3–58.

Figure 3–58

7. Click (Modify).

8. Zoom out to see the entire elevation.

9. Save and close the project.

Chapter Review Questions

1. When you import a CAD file into the Autodesk Revit software, as shown in Figure 3–59, it comes in as lines and text.

   Figure 3–59

   a. True
   b. False

2. Imported CAD files cannot be reloaded in the Manage Links dialog box.

   a. True
   b. False

3. To modify linked CAD files, which dialog box do you need to open?

   a. Type Properties
   b. Link CAD
   c. Manage Links
   d. Insert from File

4. What type of view do you need to be in to add a level to your project?

   a. Any non-plan view.
   b. As this is done using a dialog box, the view does not matter.
   c. Any view except for 3D.
   d. Any section or elevation view.

5. Which of the following elements can be copied and monitored? (Select all that apply.)
    a. Grid lines
    b. Levels
    c. Beams
    d. Braces

6. On which of the following element types can a Coordination Review with the host project be performed?
    a. CAD link
    b. CAD import
    c. Revit link
    d. Revit import

7. When linking an architectural model, you need to select the linked model and click (Pin) to keep the linked model from moving.
    a. True
    b. False

8. How many times can one project file be linked into another project?
    a. Once
    b. It is limited by the size of the link.
    c. As many as you want.

Command Summary

Button	Command	Location
General Tools		
	Level	• **Ribbon:** *Architecture* tab>Datum panel • **Shortcut:** LL
	Override By Category	• **Ribbon:** *Modify* tab>View panel, expand Override Graphics in View • **Shortcut Menu:** Override Graphics in View>By Category...
	Override By Element	• **Ribbon:** *Modify* tab>View panel, expand Override Graphics in View • **Shortcut Menu:** Override Graphics in View>By Element...
	Pin	• **Ribbon:** *Modify* tab>Modify Panel
Linked Revit and CAD Files		
	Coordination Review	• **Ribbon:** *Collaborate* tab>Coordinate panel
	Copy (from linked file)	• **Ribbon:** *Copy/Monitor* tab>Tools panel
	Copy/Monitor> Select Link	• **Ribbon:** *Collaborate* tab>Coordinate panel, expand Copy/Monitor
	Copy/Monitor> Use Current Project	• **Ribbon:** *Collaborate* tab>Coordinate panel, expand Copy/Monitor
	Import CAD	• **Ribbon:** *Insert* tab>Import panel
	Link CAD	• **Ribbon:** *Insert* tab>Link panel
	Link Revit	• **Ribbon:** *Insert* tab>Link panel
	Manage Links	• **Ribbon:** *Manage* tab>Manage Projects panel or *Insert* tab>Link panel
	Monitor	• **Ribbon:** *Copy/Monitor* tab>Tools panel
	Options (Copy/Monitor)	• **Ribbon:** *Copy/Monitor* tab>Tools panel

Chapter 4

Working with Views

Views are the cornerstone of working with Autodesk® Revit® models as they enable you to see the model in both 2D and 3D. As you are working, you can duplicate and change views to display different information based on the same view of the model. Callouts, elevations, and sections are especially important views for construction documents.

Learning Objectives in This Chapter

- Change the way elements display in different views to display required information and set views for construction documents.
- Duplicate views so that you can modify the display as you are creating a model.
- Duplicate views so that you can set the display for construction documents.
- Create callout views of parts of plans, sections, or elevations for detailing.
- Add building and interior elevations that can be used to demonstrate how a building will be built.
- Create building and wall sections to help you create the model and to include in construction documents.
- Create 3D section views using selection boxes and Orient to View.

4.1 Modifying the View Display

Views are powerful tools that enable you to create multiple versions of a model without having to recreate building elements. For example, you can have views that are specifically used for working on the model, while other views are annotated and used for construction documents. Different disciplines can have different views that show only the features they require, as shown in Figure 4–1. The properties of one view can be independent of the properties in other views.

Architectural

Structural

Figure 4–1

The view display can be modified in the following locations:

- View Control Bar
- Properties
- Shortcut menu
- Visibility/Graphic Overrides dialog box

View Control Bar

The most basic properties of a view are accessed using the View Control Bar (shown in Figure 4–2). These include the *Scale*, *Detail Level*, and *Visual Style* options. Additional options include temporary overrides and other advanced settings.

Figure 4–2

Working with Views

- The *Detail Level* controls whether you see the compound structure of elements (**Coarse**) or full scale elements (**Medium** and **Fine**), as shown in Figure 4–3. For example, Fine detail will look similar to Medium detail but will show the columns' fillets.

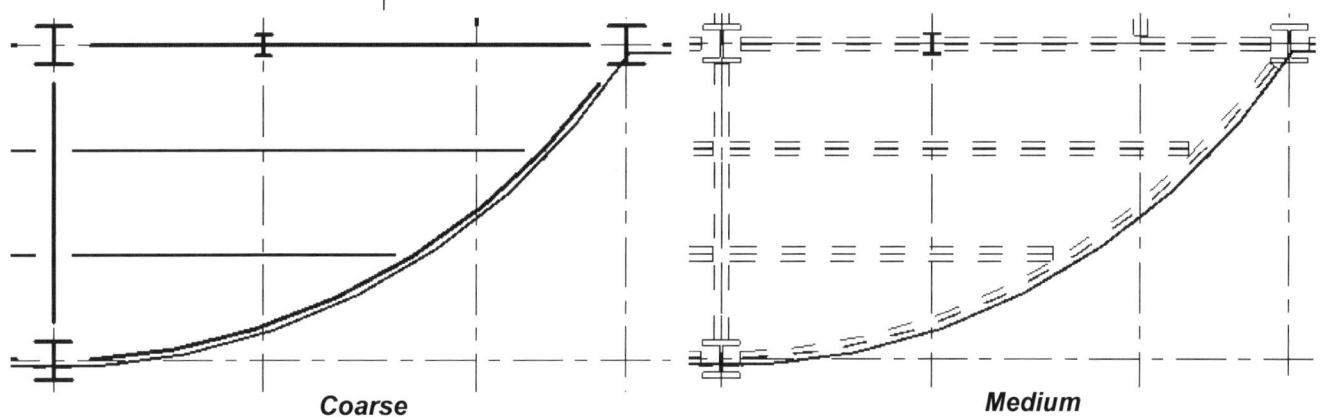

Coarse   Medium

Figure 4–3

View Properties

You can modify how a view displays by modifying the view's properties, as shown in Figure 4–4. These properties include *Underlays* and *View Range*, as well as many others. The *Discipline* of a view can also be set here.

The options in Properties vary according to the type of view. A plan view has different properties than a 3D view.

Figure 4–4

Setting an Underlay

Setting an *Underlay* is helpful if you need to display elements on a different level, such as the basement plan shown with an underlay of the first floor plan in Figure 4–5. You can then use the elements to trace over or even copy to the current level of the view.

Underlays are only available in floor plan and ceiling plan views.

Figure 4–5

In Properties in the *Underlay* section, specify the *Range: Base Level* and the *Range: Top Level*. You can also set the *Underlay Orientation* to **Look down** or **Look up**, as shown in Figure 4–6.

Underlay	
Range: Base Level	Floor 2
Range: Top Level	Floor 3
Underlay Orientation	Look down

Figure 4–6

- To prevent moving elements in the underlay by mistake, in the Select panel, expand the panel title and clear **Select underlay elements**. You can also toggle this on/off using (Select Underlay Elements) in the Status Bar.

Setting the View Range

The View Range controls the cut planes that control the visibility of plan views, as shown in the Sample View Range key in Figure 4–7. Elements outside the cut planes do not display unless you include an underlay.

Working with Views

Figure 4–7

How To: Set the View Range

1. In Properties, in the *Extents* section beside *View Range*, select **Edit…**, or type **VR**.
2. In the View Range dialog box (shown in Figure 4–8), modify the levels and offsets for the *Primary Range* and *View Depth*.
   - Click **<<Show** to display the Sample View Range key.

Figure 4–8

3. Click **OK**.

- If the settings used cannot be represented graphically, a warning displays, stating the inconsistency.

- A Reflected Ceiling Plan (RCP) is created, as if the ceiling is reflected by a mirror on the floor, so that the ceiling is the same orientation as the floor plan. The cutline is placed just below the ceiling to ensure that any windows and doors below do not display.

Setting the Discipline of a View

You can use a discipline in a view to display discipline-specific elements and to organize the Project Browser. When you duplicate or create a view, if it is not in the expected grouping in the Project Browser, you need to change its *Discipline* in Properties, as shown in Figure 4–9. For example, you can separate the Structural plans from the Architectural plans, as shown in Figure 4–10.

Figure 4–9

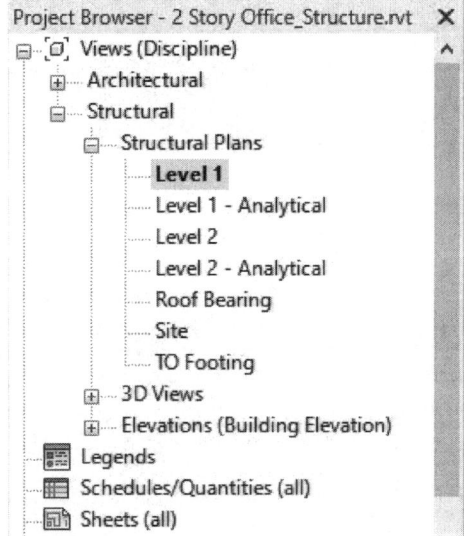

Figure 4–10

Hiding and Overriding Graphics

Two common ways to customize a view are to:

- Hide individual elements or categories.

- Modify how graphics display for elements or categories (e.g., altering line weight, color, or pattern).

An element is an individual item, such as one wall in a view, while a category includes all instances of a selected element, such as all walls in a view.

Working with Views

For example, you can gray out all of the foundation elements by modifying the category in a structural plan, as shown in Figure 4–11.

Figure 4–11

How To: Hide Elements or Categories in a View

1. Select the elements or categories you want to hide.
2. Right-click and select **Hide in View>Elements** or **Hide in View>Category**, as shown in Figure 4–12.
3. The elements or categories are hidden in the current view only.

*A quick way to hide entire categories is to select an element(s) and type **VH**.*

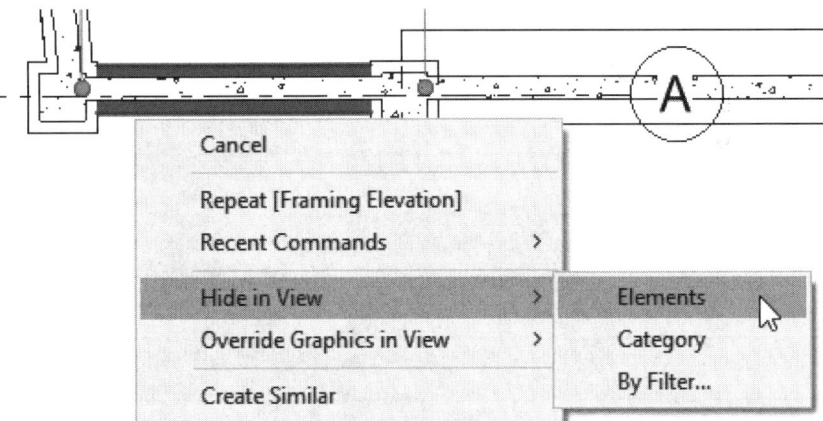

Figure 4–12

How To: Override Graphics of Elements or Categories in a View

1. Select the element(s) you want to modify.
2. Right-click and select **Override Graphics in View>By Element** or **By Category**. The View-Specific Element (or Category) Graphics dialog box opens, as shown in Figure 4–13.

The exact options in the dialog box vary depending on the type of elements selected.

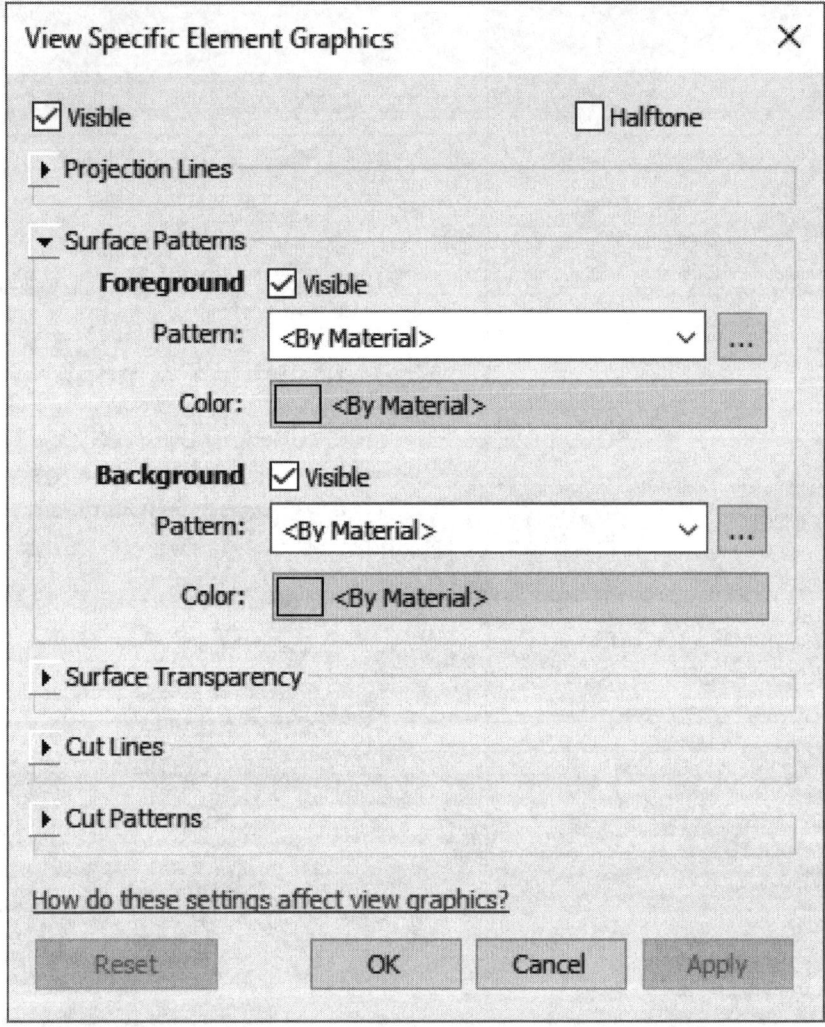

Figure 4–13

3. Select the changes you want to make and click **OK**.

View-Specific Options

- Clearing the **Visible** option is the same as hiding the elements or categories.

- Selecting the **Halftone** option grays out the elements or categories.

- The options for *Projection Lines* and *Cut Lines* include **Weight**, **Color**, and **Pattern**. The options for *Surface Patterns* and *Cut Patterns* include **Visibility**, **Pattern**, and **Color** for the Foreground and Background, as shown in Figure 4–13.

- **Surface Transparency** can be set by moving the slider bar, as shown in Figure 4–14.

Figure 4–14

- The View-Specific Category Graphics dialog box includes **Open the Visibility Graphics dialog...**, which opens the full dialog box of options.

The Visibility/Graphic Overrides Dialog Box

The options in the Visibility/Graphic Overrides dialog box (shown in Figure 4–15) control how every category and sub-category of elements is displayed per view. You can toggle categories on and off, override the *Projection/Surface* and *Cut* information, set categories to **Halftone**, and change the *Detail Level*.

Figure 4–15

To open the Visibility/Graphic Overrides dialog box, type **VV** or **VG**. It is also available in Properties: in the *Graphics* section, beside *Visibility/Graphic Overrides*, click **Edit...**.

- The Visibility/Graphic Overrides are divided into *Model*, *Annotation*, *Analytical Model*, *Imported*, and *Filters* categories.

- Other categories might be available if specific data has been included in the project, including *Design Options*, *Linked Files*, and *Worksets*.

Working with Views

- To limit the number of categories showing in the dialog box, select a discipline from the Filter list: drop-down list, as shown in Figure 4–16

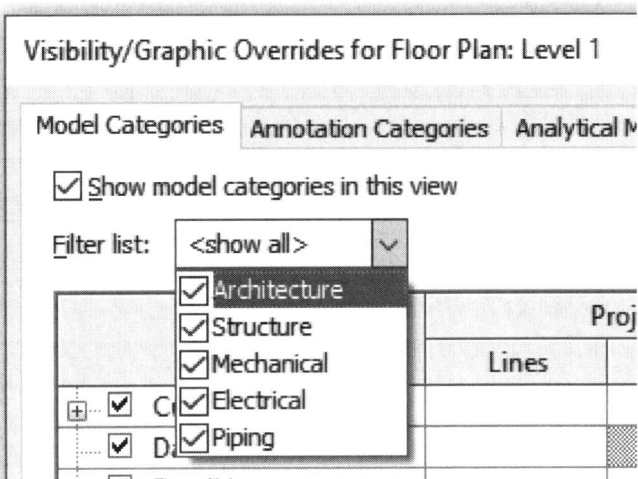

Figure 4–16

- To help you select categories, use the **All**, **None**, and **Invert** buttons. The **Expand All** button displays all of the sub-categories.

Temporarily Hide/Isolate

You might want to temporarily remove elements from a view, modify the project, and then restore the elements. Instead of completely toggling the elements off, you can temporarily hide them.

Select the elements you want to hide (make invisible) or isolate (keep displayed while all other elements are hidden) and click (Temporary Hide/Isolate). Select the method you want to use, as shown in Figure 4–17.

Figure 4–17

The elements or category are hidden or isolated. A cyan border displays around the view with a note in the upper-left corner, as shown in Figure 4–18. It indicates that the view contains temporarily hidden or isolated elements.

Figure 4–18

- Click (Temporary Hide/Isolate) again and select **Reset Temporary Hide/Isolate** to restore the elements to the view.

- If you want to permanently hide the elements in the view, select **Apply Hide/Isolate to View**.

- Elements that are temporarily hidden in a view are not hidden when the view is printed.

Restoring Hidden Elements or Categories

If you have hidden categories, you can display them using the Visibility/Graphic Overrides dialog box. However, to display hidden elements, you must temporarily reveal the elements first.

How To: Restore Hidden Elements or Categories

1. In the View Control Bar, click (Reveal Hidden Elements). The border and all hidden elements are displayed in magenta, while visible elements in the view are grayed out, as shown in Figure 4–19.

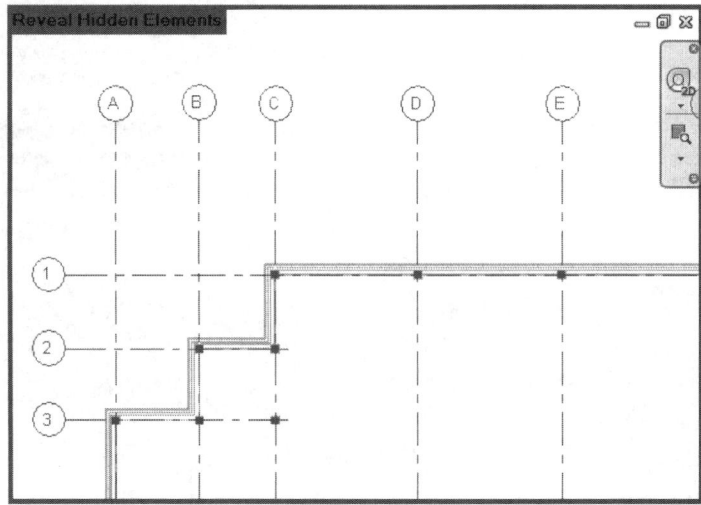

Figure 4–19

Working with Views

2. Select the hidden elements you want to restore, right-click, and select **Unhide in View>Elements** or **Unhide in View>Category**. Alternatively, in the *Modify* contextual tab>Reveal Hidden Elements panel, click (Unhide Element) or (Unhide Category).

- When you are finished, in the View Control Bar, click (Close Reveal Hidden Elements), or in the *Modify* contextual tab>Reveal Hidden Elements panel, click (Toggle Reveal Hidden Elements Mode).

Using View Templates

A powerful way to use views effectively is to set up a view and then save it as a view template. You can apply view templates to views individually or through Properties. Setting the view template using Properties helps to ensure that you do not accidentally modify the view while interacting with it.

How To: Create a View Template from a View

1. Set up a view, as needed.
2. In the Project Browser, right-click on the view and select **Create View Template from View**.
3. In the New View Template dialog box, type in a name and click **OK**.
4. The new view template is listed in the View Templates dialog box. Make any modifications needed in the *View Properties* section.
5. Click **OK**.

How To: Specify a View Template for a View

1. In the Project Browser, select the view or views to which you want to apply a view template.
2. In Properties, scroll down to the *Identity Data* section and click the button beside *View Template*.
    - Alternatively, right-click on the view and select **Apply Template Properties...**.

3. In the Apply View Template dialog box, select the view template from the list, as shown in Figure 4–20.

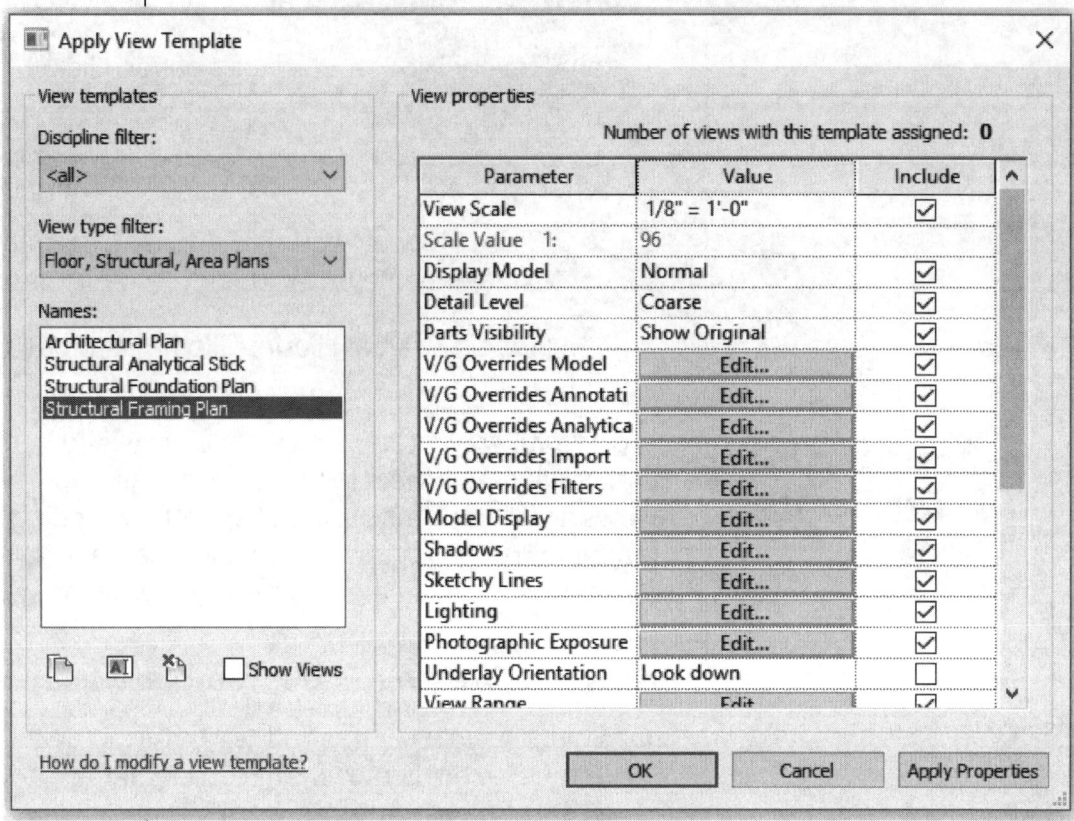

Figure 4–20

4. Click **OK**.

- In the View Control Bar, you can use ▦ (Temporary View Properties) to temporarily apply a view template to a view.

Project Browser Organization

When starting a project using the supplied Revit templates, the Project Browser displays the default organization for the tabs as **all** (as shown in Figure 4–21). You can customize how the views are displayed in the Project Browser by changing the browser organization for each of the tabs: *Views*, *Sheets*, or *Schedules*.

Working with Views

Figure 4–21

How To: Change How the Project Browser Displays Views

1. In the Project Browser, right-click on **Views (all)** and select **Browser Organization...**, as shown in Figure 4–22.

Figure 4–22

2. In the Browser Organization dialog box, select **Type/Discipline**, as shown in Figure 4–23.

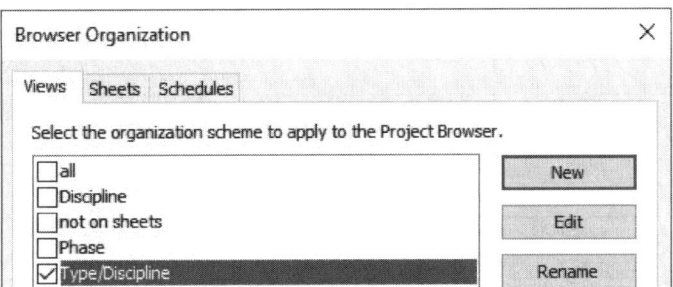

Figure 4–23

3. The Project Browser updates to sort by view type (e.g., Floor Plans, Ceiling Plans, etc.), then by discipline. Figure 4–24 shows the difference between the two browser organization types.

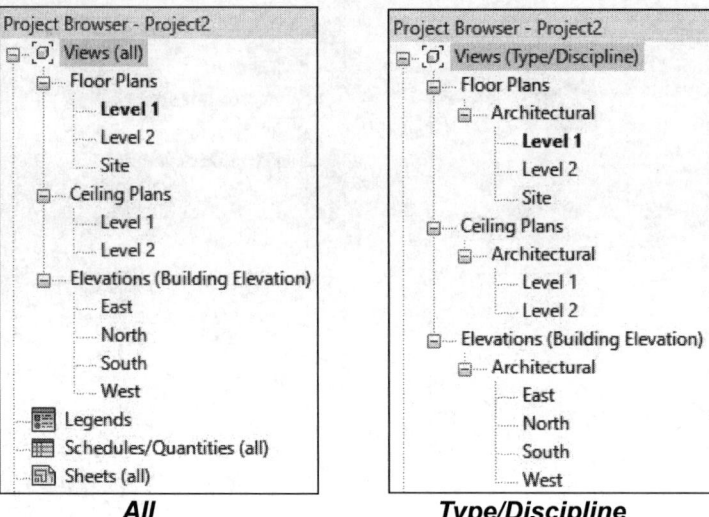

All *Type/Discipline*

Figure 4–24

4.2 Duplicating Views

Once you have created a model, you do not have to recreate the elements at different scales or copy them so that they can be used on more than one sheet. Instead, you can duplicate the required views and modify the views to suit your needs.

Duplication Types

Duplicate creates a copy of the view that only includes the building elements and view properties, as shown in Figure 4–25. Annotation and detailing are not copied into the new view. Building model elements automatically change in all views, but view-specific changes made to the new view are not reflected in the original view.

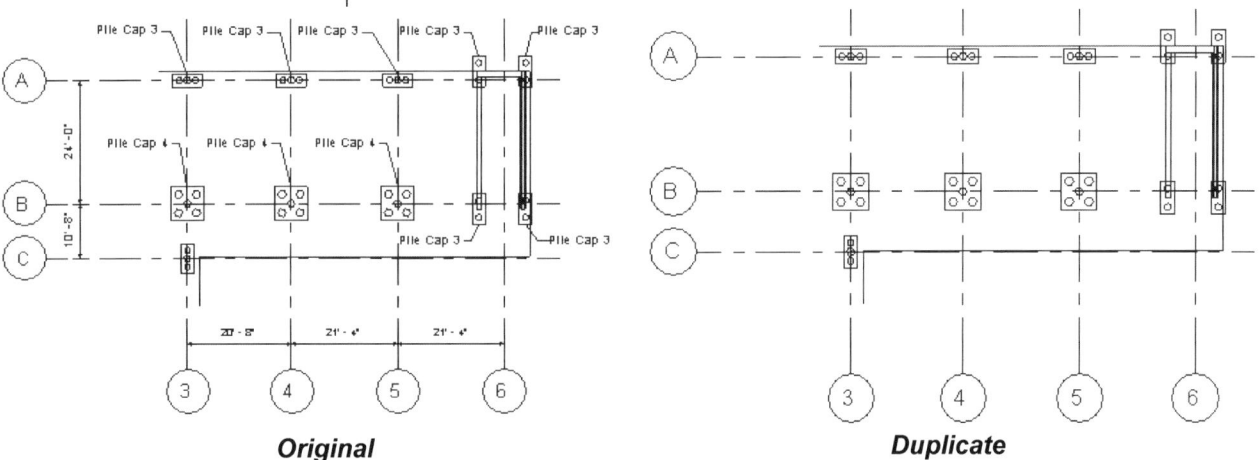

Original   *Duplicate*

Figure 4–25

Duplicate with Detailing creates a copy of the view and includes all annotation and detail elements (such as tags), as shown in Figure 4–26. Any annotation or view-specific elements created in the new view are not reflected in the original view.

Original   *Duplicate with Detailing*

Figure 4–26

Duplicate as a Dependent creates a copy of the view and links it to the original (parent) view, as shown in the Project Browser in Figure 4–27. View-specific changes made to the overall view, such as changing the *Scale*, are also reflected in the dependent (child) views and vice-versa.

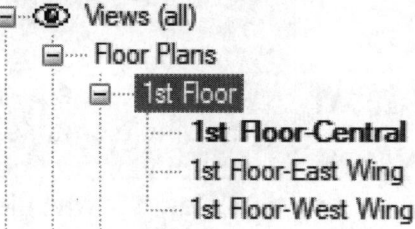

Figure 4–27

- Use dependent views when the building model is so large that you need to split the building onto separate sheets, while ensuring that the views are all the same scale.

- If you want to separate a dependent view from the original view, right-click on the dependent view and select **Convert to independent view**.

How To: Create Duplicate Views

1. Open the view you want to duplicate.
2. In the *View* tab>Create panel, expand **Duplicate View** and select the type of duplicate view you want to create, as shown in Figure 4–28.

Most types of views can be duplicated.

Figure 4–28

- Alternatively, you can right-click on a view in the Project Browser and select the type of duplicate that you want to use, as shown in Figure 4–29.

Figure 4–29

- To rename a view, slowly click twice on the view name so the text highlights, as shown in Figure 4–30, then enter a new name. You can also right-click on a view name and select **Rename...**, or press <F2>.

Figure 4–30

Practice 4a

Duplicate Views and Set the View Display

Practice Objectives

- Duplicate and rename views.
- Change the view template.

In this practice, you will create an analytical view by duplicating a view and then applying an analytical view template that sets the view display, as shown in Figure 4–31.

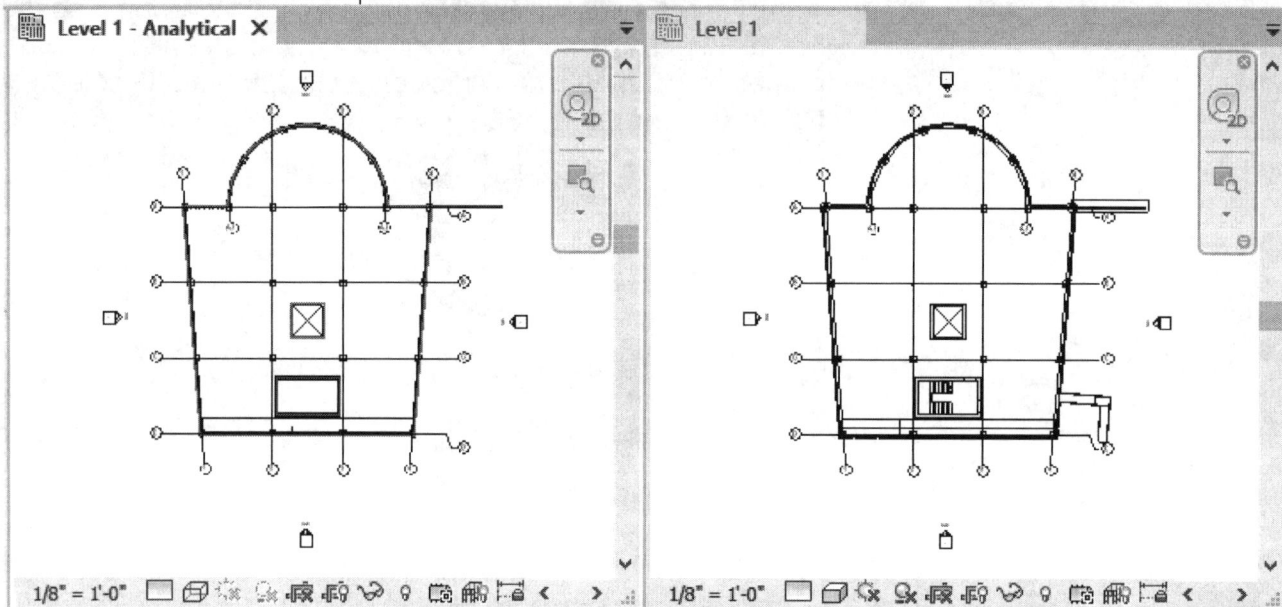

Figure 4–31

1. Open **Structural-Views.rvt** from the practice files folder, then open the **Structural Plans: Level 2** and **Structural Plans: Level 2 - Analytical** views to see the difference between the two views.

2. Close both of the **Level 2** views.

3. Right-click on **Level 1** and select **Duplicate View> Duplicate**.

4. In the Project Browser, rename the copy as **Level 1 - Analytical**.

5. Verify that only the two **Level 1** views are open and tile them. (Hint: Type **WT**.)

6. Zoom each view so that you can see the entire building. (Hint: Type **ZA**.)

7. Note that both of the views are the same, as shown in Figure 4–32.

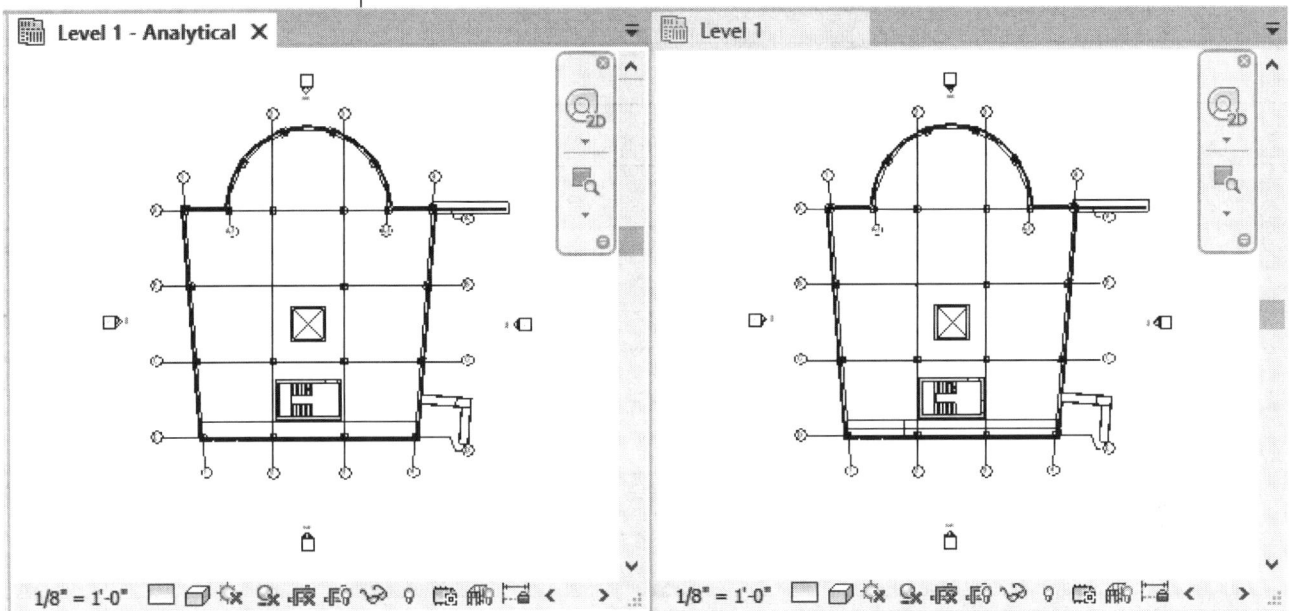

Figure 4–32

8. In the Project Browser, select the new **Level 1 - Analytical** view. Right-click and select **Apply Template Properties...**.

9. In the Apply View Template dialog box, in the *Names* area, select **Structural Analytical Stick** and click **OK**.

10. Zoom in on the view to see the analytical indicators, as shown in Figure 4–33.

Figure 4–33

11. Close the analytical view.

12. Save and close the project.

4.3 Adding Callout Views

Callouts are details of plan, elevation, or section views. When you place a callout in a view, as shown in Figure 4–34, it automatically creates a new view clipped to the boundary of the callout, as shown in Figure 4–35. You can create rectangular or sketched callout boundaries.

Callout in a view *Callout view*

Figure 4–34 **Figure 4–35**

- Callout views are saved in the same node in the Project Browser as the original view. For example, the callout view of a floor plan is placed within the Floor Plans node.

- To open the callout view, double-click on its name in the Project Browser or on the callout head (verify that the callout bubble itself is not selected before you double-click on it).

How To: Create a Rectangular Callout

1. In the *View* tab>Create panel, click (Callout).
2. Select points for two opposite corners to define the callout box around the area you want to detail.
3. Select the callout and use the shape handles to modify the location of the bubble and any other edges that might need to be changed.
4. In the Project Browser, you can rename the callout view.

How To: Create a Sketched Callout

1. In the *View* tab>Create panel, expand (Callout) and click (Sketch).
2. Sketch the shape of the callout using the tools in the *Modify | Edit Profile* tab>Draw panel, as shown in Figure 4–36.

Figure 4–36

3. Click (Finish) to complete the boundary.
4. Select the callout bubble and use the shape handles to modify the location of the bubble and any other edges that might need to be changed.
5. In the Project Browser, you can rename the callout view.

Modifying Callouts

Callouts are cropped versions of the original view. When you modify them, you are changing the crop region of the view.

Working with Views

- You can select the Drag Head grip of the callout bubble (as shown in Figure 4–37) to move the callout head to a different location. You can modify the leader landing by dragging the grip at the landing.

Figure 4–37

- If you change the size of the callout in the original view, it automatically updates the callout view and vice-versa.

- Callouts can be reshaped. Select the callout or crop region and in the *Modify | Floor Plan* tab>Mode panel, click (Edit Crop) and use the Draw tools to modify the sketch.

- If you want to return a sketched or modified callout or crop region to a rectangular configuration, click (Reset Crop).

- In a callout view, you can specify in Properties where the callout will show, in either **Intersecting Views** or just the **Parent View Only**, as shown in Figure 4–38.

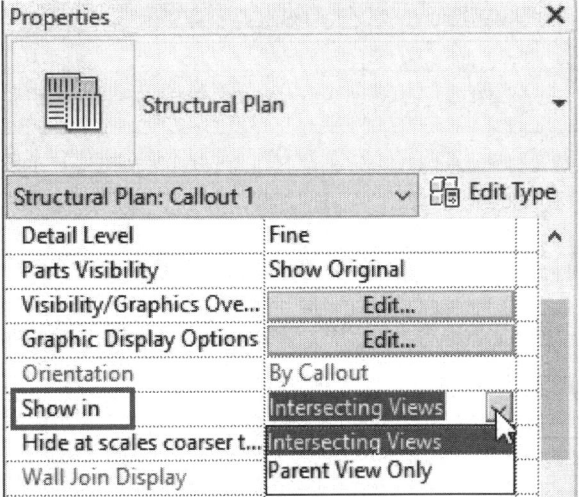

Figure 4–38

- Callout views can be preserved if the parent view is deleted. Open the callout view and, in Properties, set the *Parent View* to **<none>**, as shown in Figure 4–39.

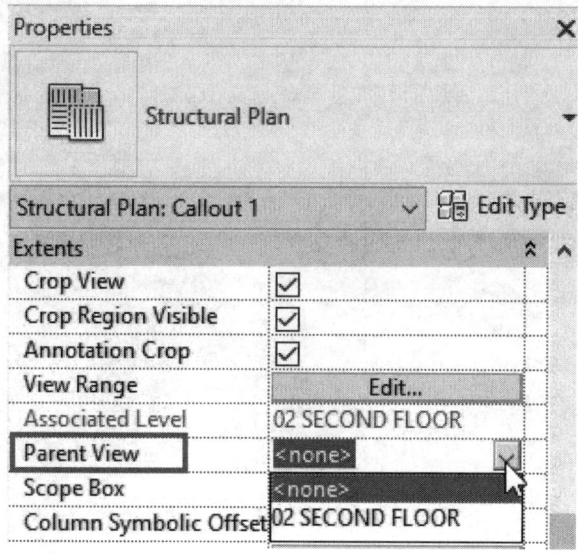

Figure 4–39

- If a parent view is deleted, a Dependent Callouts dialog box will appear, as shown in Figure 4–40, asking if you want to make the callout view that is associated with the deleted parent view an independent view or delete it.

*Click **Show details** to get more information about the associated callout view(s).*

Figure 4–40

- If a parent view is deleted, the callout view's *Show in* property defaults to **Intersecting Views** and is grayed out.

Working with Crop Regions

Plans, sections, elevations, and 3D views can all be modified by changing how much of the model is displayed in a view. One way to do this is to set the model crop region. If there are dimensions, tags, or text near the crop region, you can also use the annotation crop region to include these, as shown in Figure 4–41.

Figure 4–41

Zoom out if you do not see the crop region when you set it to be displayed.

- To display the crop region, in the View Control Bar, click (Show Crop Region). Alternatively, in Properties in the *Extents* section, select **Crop Region Visible**. **Annotation Crop** is also available in this section.

- It is best practice to hide a crop region before placing a view on a sheet. In the View Control Bar, click (Hide Crop Region).

- Resize the crop region using the ● control on each side of the region.

- Click the (Break Line) control to split the view into two regions, horizontally or vertically. Each part of the view can then be modified in size to display what is needed and be moved independently.

Breaking the crop region is typically used with sections or details.

- The annotation crop region crops any annotation outside of the crop region and any annotations that it touches. If the model crop region crops an element that is tagged, the tag or annotation will automatically be cropped as well. You can turn on Annotation Crop and resize the crop region closer to the model crop region using the grip controls or by using the Crop Region Size dialog box, as shown in Figure 4–42. In the *Modify | Floor Plan* tab>Crop panel, click (Size Crop) to open the dialog box.

Figure 4–42

Plan Regions

When you have a plan view with multiple levels of floors or ceilings, you can create plan regions that enable you to set a different view range for part of a view, as shown in Figure 4–43 for a set of clerestory windows.

Figure 4–43

Working with Views

How To: Create Plan Regions

1. In a plan view, in the *View* tab>Create panel, expand (Plan Views) and select (Plan Region).
2. In the *Modify | Create Plan Region Boundary* tab>Draw panel, select a draw tool and create the boundary for the plan region.
   - The boundary must be closed and cannot overlap other plan region boundaries, but the boundaries can be side by side.
3. Click (Finish Edit Mode).
4. In the *Modify | Plan Region* tab>Region panel, click (View Range).
5. In the View Range dialog box, specify the offsets for the plan region and click **OK**. The plan region is applied to the selected area.

- Plan regions can be copied to the clipboard and then pasted into other plan views.

- You can use shape handles to resize plan region boundaries without having to edit the boundary.

- If a plan region is above a door, the door swing displays but the door opening does not display, as shown in Figure 4–44.

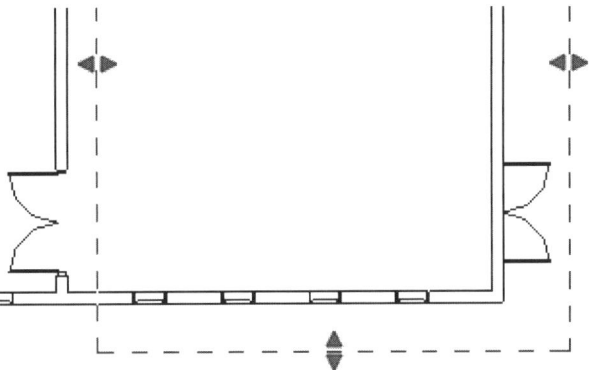

Figure 4–44

- Plan regions can be toggled on and off in the Visibility/ Graphic Overrides dialog box on the *Annotation Categories* tab. If they are displayed, the plan regions are not included when printing and exporting.

Hint: Depth Clipping and Far Clipping

Depth Clipping (shown in Figure 4–45) is a viewing option that sets how sloped walls are displayed if the *View Range* of a plan is set to a limited view.

Far Clipping (shown in Figure 4–46) is available for section and elevation views.

Figure 4–45 Figure 4–46

- An additional graphic display option enables you to specify *Depth Cueing*, so that items that are in the distance will be made lighter.

Practice 4b

Add Callout Views

Practice Objective

- Create callouts.

In this practice, you will create a callout view of the elevator pit walls, as shown in Figure 4–47.

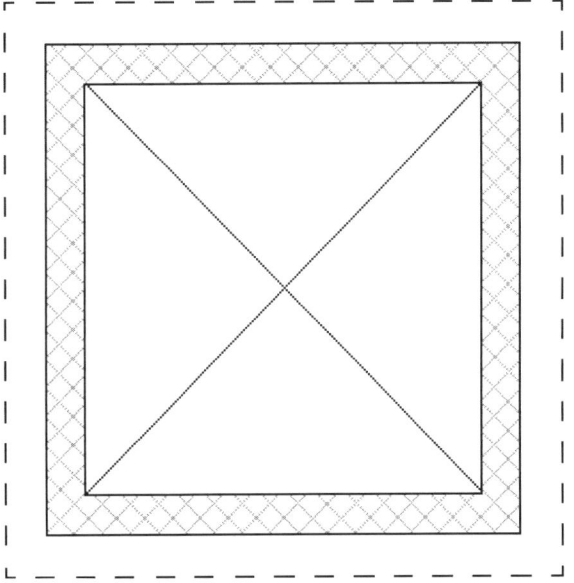

Figure 4–47

1. Open **Structural-Callouts.rvt** from the practice files folder.

2. Ensure that you are in the **Structural Plans: Level 1** view.

3. In the View Control Bar, check the *Scale* and *Detail Level* of the view, as shown in Figure 4–48.

Figure 4–48

4. In the *View* tab>Create panel, click (Callout).

5. Draw a callout around the elevator pit walls, as shown in Figure 4–49. Move the callout head as needed.

Figure 4–49

6. In the Project Browser, in the *Structural Plans* area, rename *Level 1 - Callout* as **Elevator Pit Enlarged Plan**.

7. Open the view to display the callout.

8. In the View Control Bar, set the *Scale* to **1/4"=1'-0"** and the *Detail Level* to **Fine**.

9. In the View Control Bar, click (Hide Crop Region).

10. Return to the **Level 1** view.

11. Save and close the project.

4.4 Creating Elevations and Sections

Elevations and sections are critical elements of construction documents and can assist you as you are working on a model. Any changes made in one of these views (such as the section in Figure 4–50) changes the entire model, and any changes made to the project model are also displayed in the elevations and sections.

Figure 4–50

- In the Project Browser, elevations are separated by elevation type and sections are separated by section type, as shown in Figure 4–51.

Figure 4–51

- To open an elevation or section view, double-click on the marker arrow or on its name in the Project Browser.

- To give the elevation or section a new name, in the Project Browser, slowly click twice on the name or right-click on it and select **Rename...**.

Elevations

Elevations are *face-on* views of the interiors and exteriors of a building. Four exterior elevation views are defined in the default template: **North**, **South**, **East**, and **West**. You can create additional building elevation views at other angles or framing elevation views, as shown in Figure 4–52.

Figure 4–52

- Elevation markers must be placed in plan views.

- A framing elevation is set up to only capture framing elements that are behind other model elements in an elevation of a building.
    - By default, the framing elevation snaps and sets the extents along the grid lines by using **Attach to Grid** in the Options Bar.

- The most common use for a framing elevation is to generate braced frames and shear wall elevations.

- When you add an elevation or section to a sheet, the detail and sheet number are automatically added to the view title and elevation/section marker.

How To: Create an Elevation

1. In the *View* tab>Create panel, expand (Elevation) and click (Elevation).
2. In the Type Selector, select the elevation type. Two types come with the templates: **Building Elevation** and **Interior Elevation**.
3. Move the cursor near one of the walls that defines the elevation. The marker follows the angle of the wall.
4. Click to place the marker.

The software remembers the last elevation type used, so you can click the top button if you want to use the same elevation command.

Working with Views

- The length, width, and height of an elevation are defined by the walls and ceiling/floor at which the elevation marker is pointing.

- When creating interior elevations, ensure that the floor or ceiling above is in place before creating the elevation or you will need to modify the elevation crop region so that the elevation markers do not show on all floors.

How To: Create Framing Elevations

1. Open a plan view.

2. In the *View* tab>Create panel, expand (Elevation) and click (Framing Elevation).

3. Hover the cursor over a grid line to display an elevation marker, as shown in Figure 4–53. Click to place the marker.

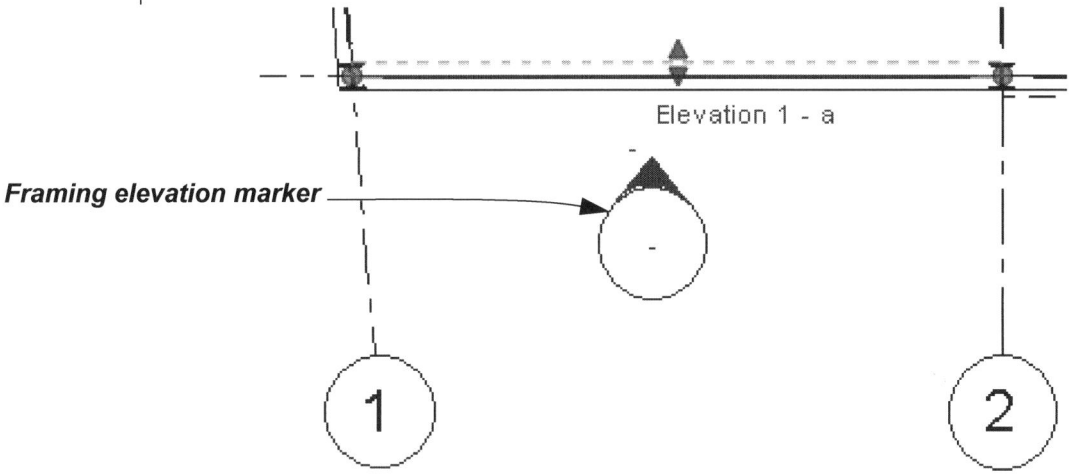

Figure 4–53

4. Click (Modify) and select the marker. The extents focus on the bracing bay only. You can use the round segment handles to expand the length of the elevation, as needed.

Framing elevations are listed in the Project Browser in the Elevations (Framing Elevation) area.

Sections

Sections are slices through a model. You can create a section through an entire building or through one wall for a detail. Sections can be created in plan, elevation, and other section views. You can flip, resize, or split a section. Figure 4–54 shows all of the components of a section marker.

Figure 4–54

- Sections can be created in plan, elevation, and other section views.

How To: Create a Section

1. In the *View* tab>Create panel or in the Quick Access Toolbar, click (Section).

2. In the Type Selector, select **Section: Building Section** or **Section: Wall Section**. If you want a section in a drafting view, select **Detail View: Detail**.
3. In the view, select a point where you want to locate the crop region and section marker.
4. Select the second or end point that defines the section.
5. The shape controls display. You can flip the arrow and change the size of the cutting plane, as well as the location of the bubble and flag.

- When placing a section you can snap to other elements in the model as the start and end points of the section line. You can also use the Align command to reorient a section line to an element such as an angled wall.

- Section lines can also be used as an alignment object and can be snapped to when placing other geometry.

Modifying Elevations and Sections

There are two parts to modifying elevations and sections:

- To modify the markers (as shown in Figure 4–55), use the controls to change the length and depth of elevations and sections. There are other specific type options as well.

Figure 4–55

- To modify the view (as shown in Figure 4–56), use the controls to modify the size or create view breaks.

Figure 4–56

Modifying Elevation Markers

When you modify elevation markers, you can specify the length and depth of the clip plane, as shown in Figure 4–57.

- Select the arrowhead of the elevation marker (not the circle portion) to display the clip plane.

- Drag the round shape handles to lengthen or shorten the elevation.

- Adjust the ▲▼ (Drag) controls to modify the depth of the elevation.

To display additional interior elevations from one marker, select the circle portion (not the arrowhead) and place a checkmark in the Show Arrow box in the directions that you want to display, as shown in Figure 4–57.

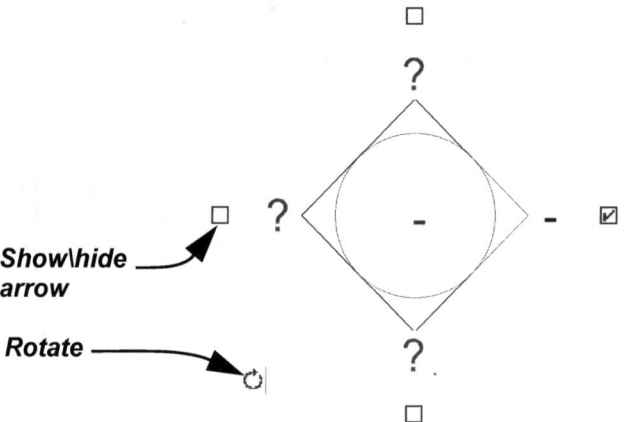

Figure 4–57

- Use the ↻ (Rotate) control to angle the marker (e.g., for a room with angled walls).

Modifying Section Markers

When you modify section markers, various shape handles and controls enable you to modify a section, as shown in Figure 4–58.

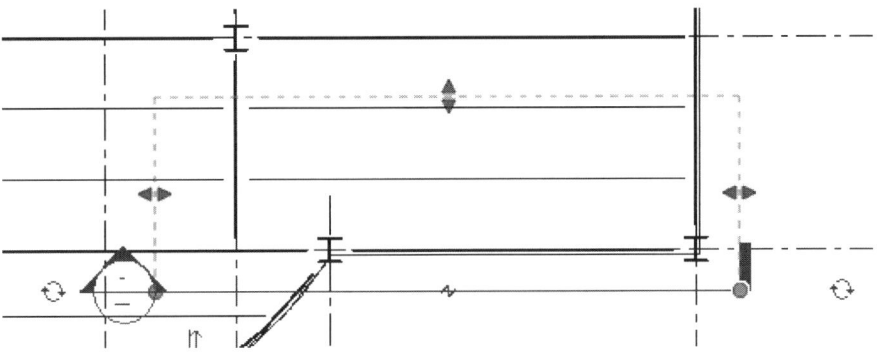

Figure 4–58

- Adjust the ⇕ (Drag) controls to change the length and depth of the cut plane.

- Drag the segment handle controls at either end of the section line to change the location of the arrow or flag without changing the cut boundary.

- Click ⇆ (Flip Section) to change the direction of the arrowhead, which also flips the entire section.

- Click ↻ (Cycle Section Head/Tail) to switch between an arrowhead, flag, or nothing on each end of the section.

- Click ⤲ (Gaps in Segments) to create an opening in section lines, as shown in Figure 4–59. Select it again to restore the full section cut.

Figure 4–59

How To: Add a Jog to a Section Line

1. Select the section line you want to modify.
2. In the *Modify | Views* tab>Section panel, click (Split Segment).
3. Select the point along the section line where you want to create the split, as shown in Figure 4–60.
4. Specify the location of the split line, as shown in Figure 4–61.

Figure 4–60   Figure 4–61

- If you need to adjust the location of any segment on the section line, modify it and drag the shape handles along each segment of the line, as shown in Figure 4–62.

Figure 4–62

- To bring a split section line back into place, use the shape handle to drag the jogged line until it is at the same level with the rest of the line.

Working with Views

> **Hint: Using Thin Lines**
>
> Revit automatically applies line weights to views, as shown for a section in Figure 4–63. If a line weight seems heavy or obscures elements, you can toggle off the line weights. In the Quick Access Toolbar or in the *View* tab>Graphics panel, click ![icon] (Thin Lines), or type **TL**. The lines display with the same weight, as shown in Figure 4–64.
>
>
>
> *Thin Lines off* *Thin Lines on*
> Figure 4–63   Figure 4–64
>
> - The **Thin Line** setting is remembered until you change it, even if you shut down and restart the software.

3D Section Views

There are two ways you can create section views of your 3D model: creating a selection box, as shown in Figure 4–65, and orienting to a view. Both of these are very helpful as you are working and also can be used in construction documents and presentations.

Figure 4–65

© 2021, ASCENT - Center for Technical Knowledge®   4–41

How To: Create a Selection Box

1. In a 3D view, select the elements you want to isolate. In the example shown in Figure 4–65, the front wall was selected.
2. In the *Modify* tab>View panel, click (Selection Box), or type **BX**.
3. The view is limited to a box around the selected item(s).
4. Use the controls of the section box to modify the size of the box to show exactly what you want.

- To toggle off a section box and restore the full model, in the view's Properties, in the *Extents* section, clear the checkmark from **Section Box**.

How To: Orient a 3D View to a View

1. Open a 3D view.
2. Right-click on the ViewCube and select **Orient to View>Floor Plans**, **Elevations**, **Sections**, or **3D Views**, as shown in Figure 4–66, and select the view from the list.

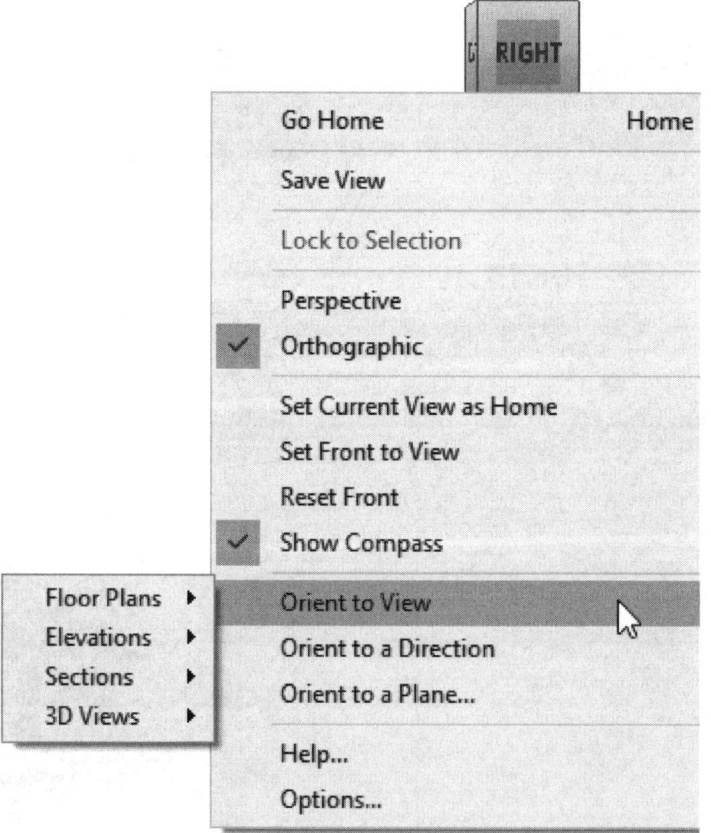

Figure 4–66

3. The view displays, as shown in the partial floor plan view of a stair in Figure 4–67. Use the 3D view rotation tools to navigate around the 3D model, as shown in Figure 4–68.

Figure 4–67

Figure 4–68

- **Orient to a Direction** allows you to rotate the view to a specific direction, as shown in Figure 4–69. This is similar to using the orientation planes of the ViewCube.

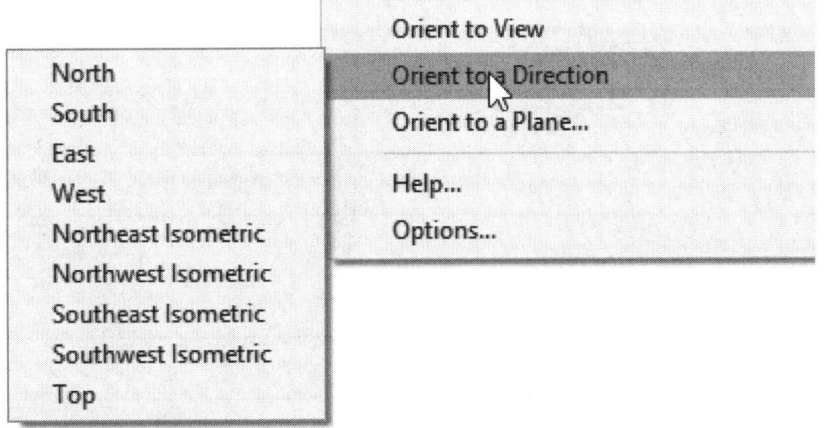

Figure 4–69

- **Orient to a Plane...** opens the Select Orientation Plane dialog box and allows you to specify a level, grid line, or named reference plane, or pick a plane or a line, as shown in Figure 4–70. The view is not cut at the plane but oriented in that direction.

Figure 4–70

Practice 4c Create Elevations and Sections

Practice Objectives

- Add building sections and wall sections.
- Add a framing elevation.

In this practice, you will add a building section and a wall section to an existing project. You will also add a framing elevation, as shown in Figure 4–71.

Figure 4–71

Task 1 - Create sections.

1. Open **Structural-Sections.rvt** from the practice files folder.

2. In the Project Browser, open the **Structural Plans: Level 1** view.

3. In the *View* tab>Create panel or in the Quick Access Toolbar, click (Section).

4. Place a vertical section offset slightly from the middle, between grid lines **2** and **3**. Change the width of the section using the shape controls, as shown in Figure 4–72.

Figure 4–72

5. In the Project Browser, expand *Sections (Building Section)*. Right-click on the new section and rename it **Building Section A**, as shown in Figure 4–73.

Figure 4–73

6. Open the new section by double-clicking on its name in the Project Browser. The entire building displays, as shown in Figure 4–74. Note that the view varies based on exactly where you placed the section.

Figure 4–74

7. Select the crop region and use the controls to shorten the section so that the curved walls to the left do not display, as shown in Figure 4–75.

Figure 4–75

8. Return to the Level 1 view. The boundary of the section has changed, as shown on the left in Figure 4–76. Use the segment control to move the section marker's head down, as shown on the right in Figure 4–76.

Figure 4–76

9. Start the **Section** command again.

10. In the Type Selector, select **Section: Wall Section**.

11. Draw a short section through the wall shown in Figure 4–77. Modify the section boundary so that it does not touch anything other than the wall.

Figure 4–77

12. In the Project Browser, expand *Sections (Wall Section)* and rename the section **Foundation Section**.

13. Open the new section view.

14. In the View Control Bar, change the *Scale* to **1/2"=1'-0"**.

15. By default, the section expands the entire height of the project. Use the controls to resize the section so that only the foundation displays, as shown in Figure 4–78.

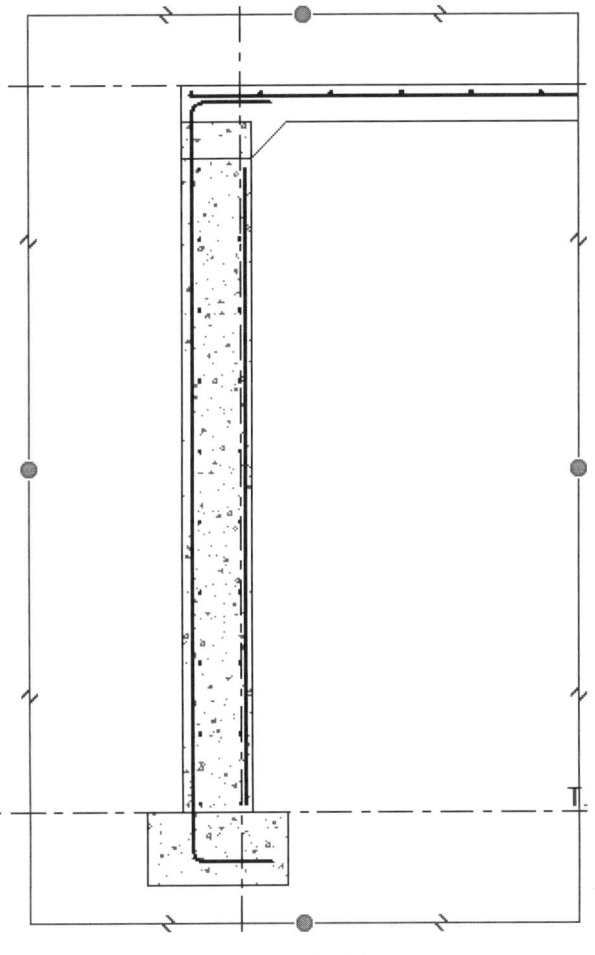

Figure 4–78

16. Save the project.

Task 2 - Add a framing elevation.

1. Open the **Structural Plans: Level 1** view.

2. Zoom in on the south wall of the building between grid intersections **D2** and **D3**.

3. In the *View* tab>Create panel, expand (Elevation) and click (Framing Elevation).

4. Hover the cursor over grid line **D**, as shown in Figure 4–79. Pick a point when the framing elevation marker displays on the outside of the building.

Figure 4–79

5. In the Project Browser, in the *Elevations (Framing Elevation)* area, rename the view as **Typical Bracing**.

6. Click on the arrowhead of the elevation marker to show the boundary. Using the controls, lengthen the elevation boundary so that it is just on each side of the columns, as shown in Figure 4–80.

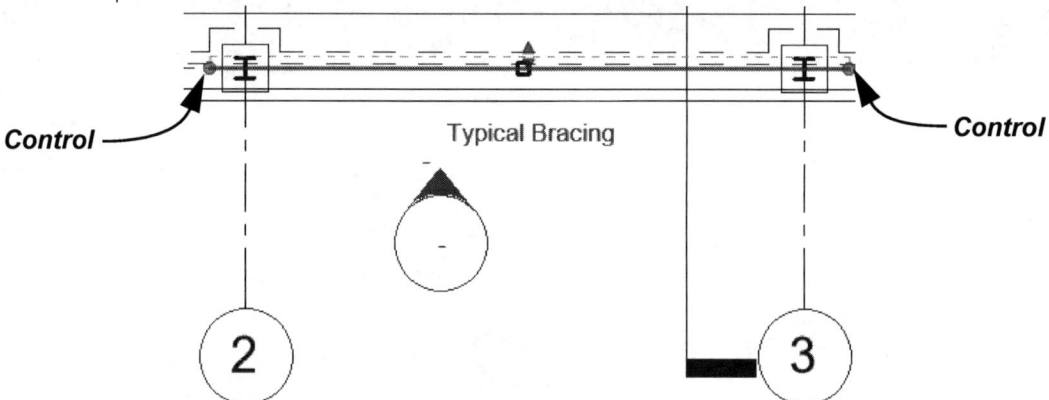

Figure 4–80

7. Open the framing elevation and in the View Control Bar, change the *Detail Level* to ▨ (Fine).

8. Modify the size of the elevation to only display the bracing, as shown in Figure 4–81.

Figure 4–81

9. Return to the **Structural Plans: Level 1** view.

10. Zoom out to display the entire building.

11. In the Quick Access Toolbar, click (Close Hidden Windows).

12. Save and close the project.

Chapter Review Questions

1. Which of the following commands creates a view that results in an independent view displaying the same model geometry and containing a copy of the annotation?

    a. Duplicate

    b. Duplicate with Detailing

    c. Duplicate as a Dependent

2. Which of the following is true about the Visibility/Graphic Overrides dialog box?

    a. Changes made in the dialog box only affect the current view.

    b. It can only be used to toggle categories on and off.

    c. It can be used to toggle individual elements on and off.

    d. It can be used to change the color of individual elements.

3. What is the purpose of creating a callout?

    a. To create a boundary around part of the model that needs revising, similar to a revision cloud.

    b. To create a view of part of the model for export to the AutoCAD® software for further detailing.

    c. To create a view of part of the model that is linked to the main view from which it is taken.

    d. To create a 2D view of part of the model.

4. You placed dimensions in a view but only some of them display, as shown on the left in Figure 4–82. You were expecting the view to display as shown on the right in Figure 4–83. What do you need to modify to see the missing dimensions?

Figure 4–82 Figure 4–83

   a. Dimension Settings
   b. Dimension Type
   c. Visibility/Graphic Overrides
   d. Annotation Crop Region

5. How do you create a jog in a building section, such as that shown in Figure 4–84?

Figure 4–84

a. Use the **Split Element** tool in the *Modify* tab>Modify panel.

b. Select the building section and then click **Split Segment** in the contextual tab.

c. Select the building section and click the blue control in the middle of the section line.

d. Draw two separate sections, and use the **Section Jog** tool to combine them into a jogged section.

Command Summary

Button	Command	Location
Views		
	Elevation	• **Ribbon:** *View* tab>Create panel> expand Elevation
	Callout: Rectangle	• **Ribbon:** *View* tab>Create panel> expand Callout
	Callout: Sketch	• **Ribbon:** *View* tab>Create panel> expand Callout
	Duplicate	• **Ribbon:** *View* tab>Create panel> expand Duplicate View • **Right-click:** (*on a view in the Project Browser*) expand Duplicate View
	Duplicate as Dependent	• **Ribbon:** *View* tab>Create panel> expand Duplicate View • **Right-click:** (*on a view in the Project Browser*) expand Duplicate View
	Duplicate with Detailing	• **Ribbon:** *View* tab>Create panel> expand Duplicate View • **Right-click:** (*on a view in the Project Browser*) Duplicate View
	Plan Region	• **Ribbon:** *View* tab>Create panel> expand Plan Views
	Section	• **Ribbon:** *View* tab>Create panel • **Quick Access Toolbar**
	Split Segment	• **Ribbon:** (*when the elevation or section marker is selected*) *Modify	Views* tab> Section panel
Crop Views		
	Crop View	• **View Control Bar** • **View Properties:** Crop View (*check*)
	Do Not Crop View	• **View Control Bar** • **View Properties:** Crop View (*clear*)
	Edit Crop	• **Ribbon:** (*when the crop region of a callout, elevation, or section view is selected*) *Modify	Views* tab>Mode panel
	Hide Crop Region	• **View Control Bar** • **View Properties:** Crop Region Visible (*clear*)

		Reset Crop	• **Ribbon:** *(when the crop region of a callout, elevation or section view is selected)* *Modify	Views* tab>Mode panel
		Show Crop Region	• **View Control Bar** • **View Properties:** Crop Region Visible (*check*)
		Size Crop	• **Ribbon:** *(when the crop region of a callout, elevation or section view is selected)* *Modify	Views* tab>Mode panel
View Display			
		Hide in View	• **Ribbon:** *Modify* tab>View Graphics panel>Hide>Elements *or* By Category • **Right-click:** *(when an element is selected)* Hide in View>Elements *or* Category
		Override Graphics in View	• **Ribbon:** *Modify* tab>View Graphics panel>Hide>Elements *or* By Category • **Right-click:** *(when an element is selected)* Override Graphics in View>By Element *or* By Category • **Shortcut:** *(category only)* VV or VG
		Plan Region	• **Ribbon:** *View* tab>Create panel> expand Plan Views
		Selection Box	• **Ribbon:** *Modify* tab>View panel • **Shortcut:** BX
		Reveal Hidden Elements	• **View Control Bar**
		Temporary Hide/Isolate	• **View Control Bar**
		Temporary View Properties	• **View Control Bar**

Chapter 5

Grids and Structural Columns

Grids are annotation elements that display in most views, including plan, ceiling, section, and elevation views. They help organize your design when developing a layout and describe the pattern and location for structural columns. Grids can be multi-segmented, arcs, or straight lines, and they can be hidden in the view if needed.

Learning Objectives in This Chapter

- Add grids to provide the location for structural columns.
- Add structural columns to the project as the first design consideration.

5.1 Adding Grid Lines

The grid indicates how to space the bays of a building and where to place columns, as shown in Figure 5–1. Any changes to the grid influences the elements that are referenced to them.

Figure 5–1

- Each line or arc in a grid is a separate entity and can be placed, moved, and modified individually.

- Grids cannot be drawn in a 3D view, but grids can be displayed in a 3D view, perspective view, or 3D view with a selection box, and when you click on a grid, the surface contour displays.

If you are upgrading a model to the 2022 version, you will need to turn on the grids.

How To: Create a Grid

1. In the *Structure* tab>Datum panel, click (Grid), or type **GR**.
2. In Properties, use the Type Selector to select the grid type, which will control the size of the bubble and the line style.
3. In the *Modify | Place Grid* tab>Draw panel (shown in Figure 5–2), select the draw method you want to use.

Figure 5–2

4. In the Options Bar, set the *Offset* if needed.
5. Start drawing grid lines.

Grids and Structural Columns

- Grid lines can be sketched at any angle, but you should ensure that all parallel grid lines are drawn in the same direction (e.g., from left to right or from bottom to top).

- When using the Multi-Segment tool, shown in Figure 5–3, sketch the line and click ✓ (Finish Edit Mode) to complete it.

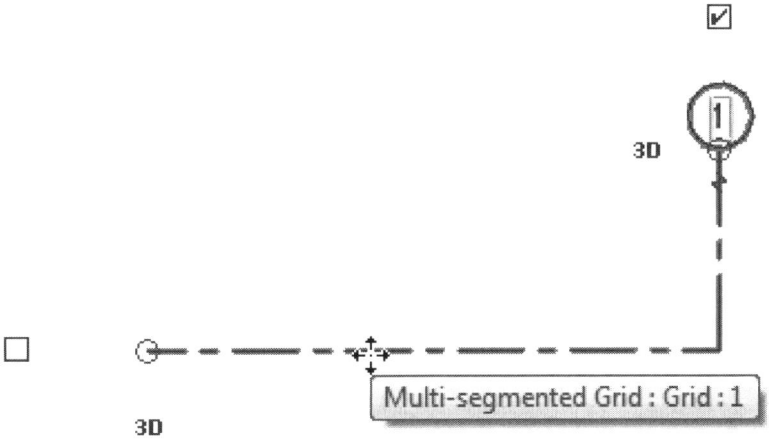

Figure 5–3

How To: Show Grids in 3D

1. Open a 3D or perspective view and press <Esc> twice to verify nothing is selected.
2. In Properties, click **Edit...** next to *Show Grids*, as shown in Figure 5–4.

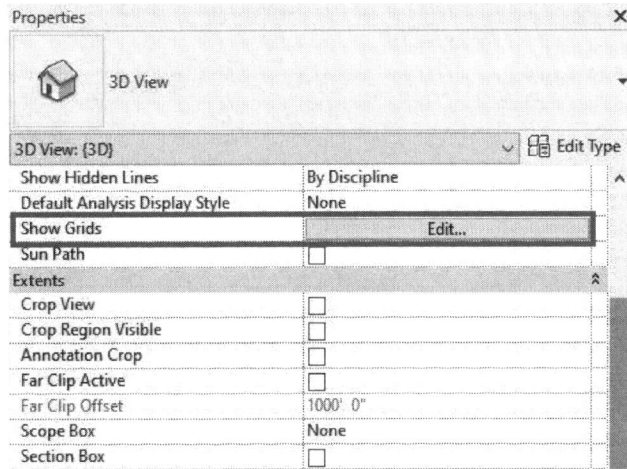

Figure 5–4

3. In the Show Grids dialog box, select the level(s) that you want the grids to display at in the 3D view, as shown in Figure 5–5.

Figure 5–5

4. Click **OK**.
5. (Optional) To display the grids on the bottom of a section box, in Properties, verify that **Section Box** is selected and click **Edit...** next to *Show Grids*.
6. In the Show Grids dialog box, select only the **Project Grids On Section Box** option, as shown in Figure 5–6, and click **OK**.

Figure 5–6

Modifying Grid Lines

Grid lines are very similar to level lines. You can modify grid lines using controls, alignments, and temporary dimensions in the view (as shown in Figure 5–7). You can change the bubble type using the Type Selector.

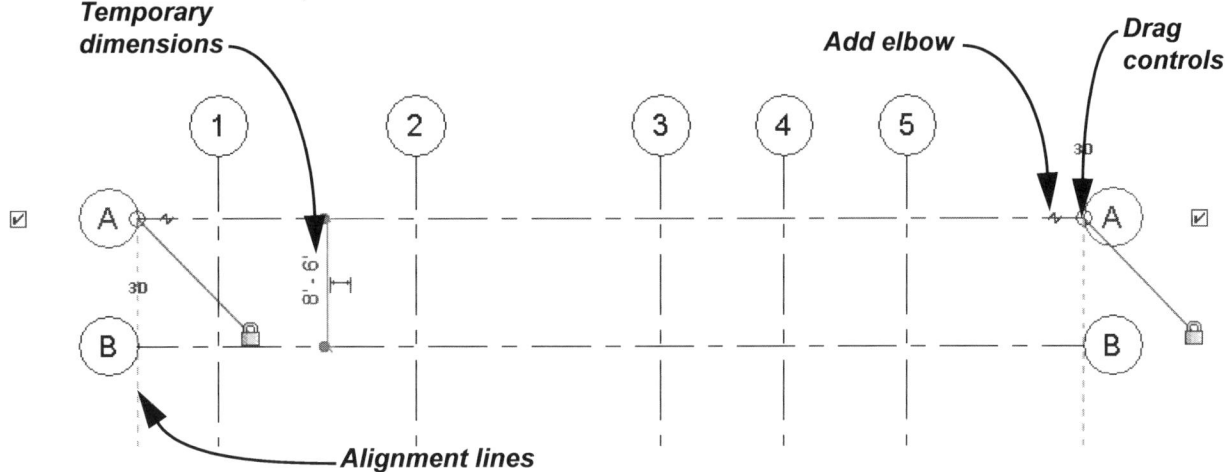

Figure 5–7

- Grid numbers can be numbers, letters, or a combination of the two. To modify a grid number, double-click on the number in the bubble and type the new letter/number. You can also change the grid number by entering a new *Name* in Properties.

- Grid numbers increment automatically.

Hint: Propagating Datum Extents

If column grids do not display in a view, this might be due to adding a level after the grid lines were added. To display the grid lines in plan views, select the grid lines in a view in which they are displayed. In the *Modify | Grids* tab>Datum panel, click (Propagate Extents). In the Propagate datum extents dialog box (shown in Figure 5–8), select the views to project the grid lines to.

Figure 5–8

- This also works for levels.

- (Propagate Extents) is particularly useful to make grid lines display the same in all views.

- In a 3D view, you can modify the grid line name and adjust the grid line and grid distance.
    - Click the ⌖ (Drag the extents of the grid in the model) control to lengthen the grid line.
    - Modify the temporary dimension (as shown in Figure 5–9) to change the grid line's distance from another grid line.

Figure 5–9

- Change the grid line name by selecting the bubble and typing in a new name; alternatively, the name can be changed in Properties.

Practice 5a

Add Grid Lines

Practice Objectives

- Copy and monitor grid lines from a linked architectural model.
- Add additional grid lines.

In this practice, you will copy and monitor grid lines from a linked architectural model. You will then add additional grid lines where curved walls need extra support, as shown in Figure 5–10.

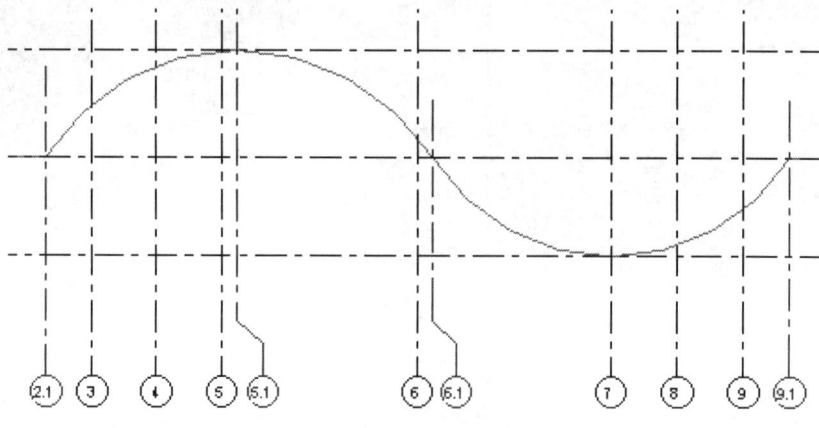

Figure 5–10

Task 1 - Copy and monitor grid lines.

1. Open **Structural-Grids.rvt** from the practice files folder.

2. Open the **Structural Plans: 00 GROUND FLOOR** view.

3. Start the **Copy/Monitor** command and select the linked model.

4. In the *Copy/Monitor* tab>Tools panel, click (Copy).

5. In the Options Bar, select **Multiple**.

For information on how to use a crossing window to select multiple elements, see 2.2 Editing Elements.

6. Select all of the grid lines. You can select them one by one (hold <Ctrl> as you do so) or select them all at once using a crossing window.

7. In the Options Bar, click **Finish**.

8. In the *Copy/Monitor* tab>Copy/Monitor panel, click (Finish).

9. Close the warning dialog box.

10. When selecting one or all of the grid lines, the ⌇ (Monitor) icon displays at each grid line, as shown in Figure 5–11.

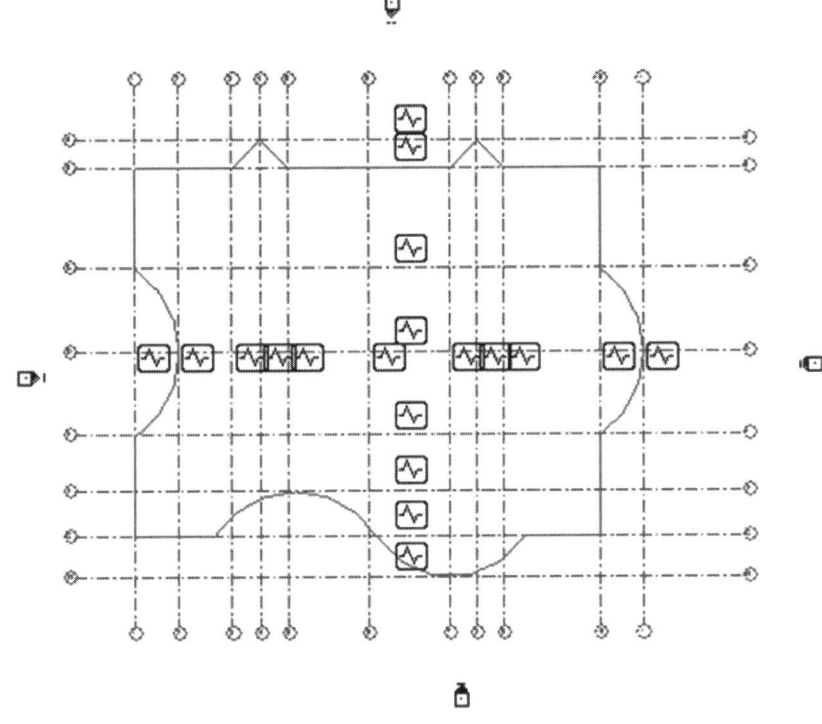

Figure 5–11

11. Navigate through the different floor plans. The grid lines have populated throughout each floor plan, as shown in Figure 5–12.

Figure 5–12

12. Open the **Structural Plans: 00 GROUND FLOOR** view.

13. Save the project.

Task 2 - Add grid lines at arc points.

1. In the **Structural Plans: 00 GROUND FLOOR** view, zoom in on the south side of the floor plan, where the green outline shows two curves (curtain wall locations). Additional grid lines need to be placed at the midpoints and end points of the arcs to support the curtain wall.

2. In the *Structure* tab>Datum panel, click (Grid). In the *Modify | Place Grid* tab>Draw panel, verify that (Line) is selected.

3. Select the end point of the arc on grid line **G** between grid lines **2** and **3** and draw the vertical grid line, as shown in Figure 5–13.

Figure 5–13

- Draw the grid line until the blue alignment line displays, as shown above in Figure 5–13. This ensures the new bubbles stay locked in line with the other bubbles.

4. Once the grid line is in place, rename it to **2.1**, as shown in Figure 5–14. At the top end of the grid line, clear the checkmark above the bubble to toggle it off. Then, stretch the grid line up to the north end.

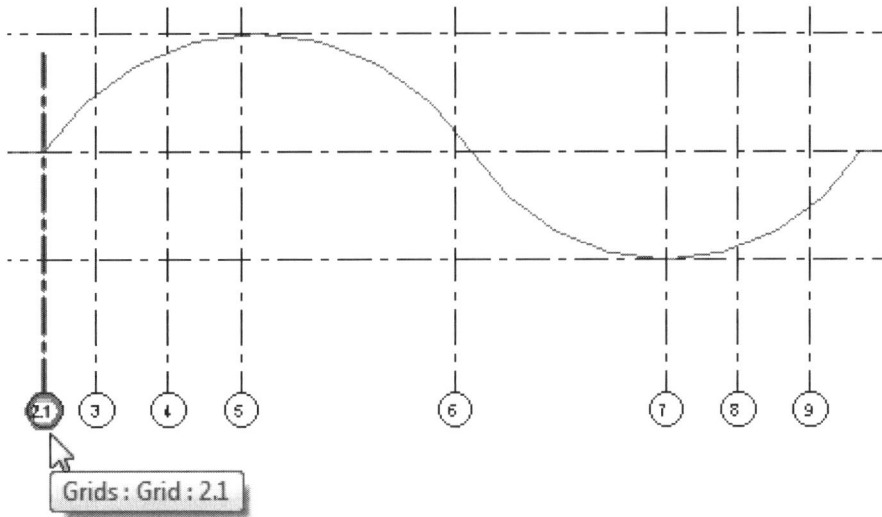

Figure 5–14

5. Draw another vertical grid line at the midpoint of the same arc, as shown in Figure 5–15. Rename the grid line to **5.1**. Use (Add Elbow) to modify the bubble location.

Figure 5–15

6. Add grid lines to the end points of the second arc, as shown in Figure 5–16. When you are finished, there should be four new grid lines: **2.1**, **5.1**, **6.1**, and **9.1**.

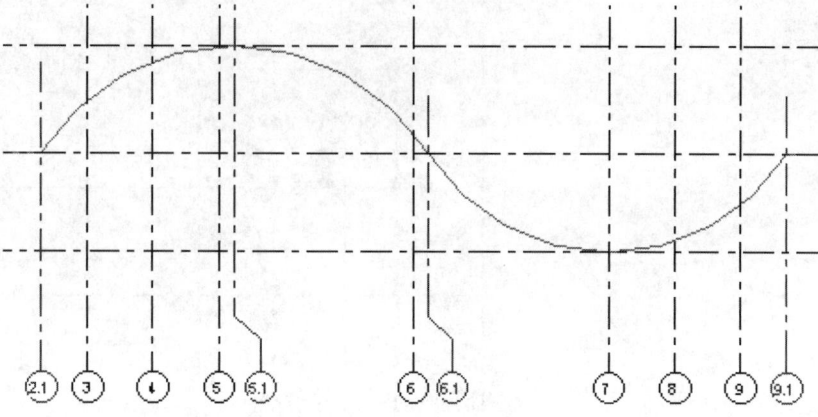

Figure 5–16

7. Clear the top bubbles and adjust the top ends of the grid lines to align them.

8. Click (Modify).

9. Zoom out to see the full layout.

10. Save and close the model.

5.2 Loading Components

To optimize project size and improve performance, by default, the Revit project templates are not fully loaded with all Revit families. However, you can load more families with multi-options from the Autodesk Revit Library or the Autodesk website. You can also load your company's custom families or families from other manufacturers that you may have available in your local device.

- You can also copy a component to the clipboard in one project and past it into a different project.

How To: Load a Component Family

1. In the *Insert* tab>Load from Library panel, click (Load Family).
2. In the Load Family dialog box, locate the folder that contains the family or families you want to load and select them, as shown in Figure 5–17. To load more than one family at a time, hold <Ctrl> while selecting.

- If the Load family dialog box does not default to the Revit Library folder, click on **Imperial Library** in the Places panel.

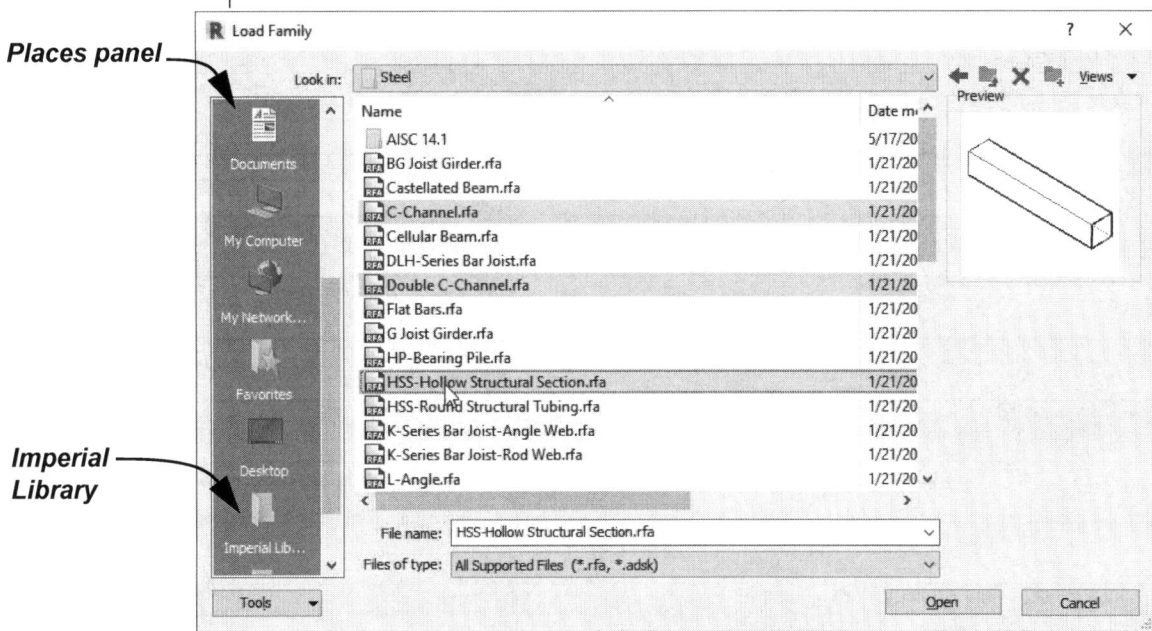

Figure 5–17

- The program remembers the last used folder.
3. Click **Open**.

- If a family has multiple types that you can select from, the Specify Types dialog box will appear, as shown in Figure 5–18. Select the type(s) you want to load and click **OK**.

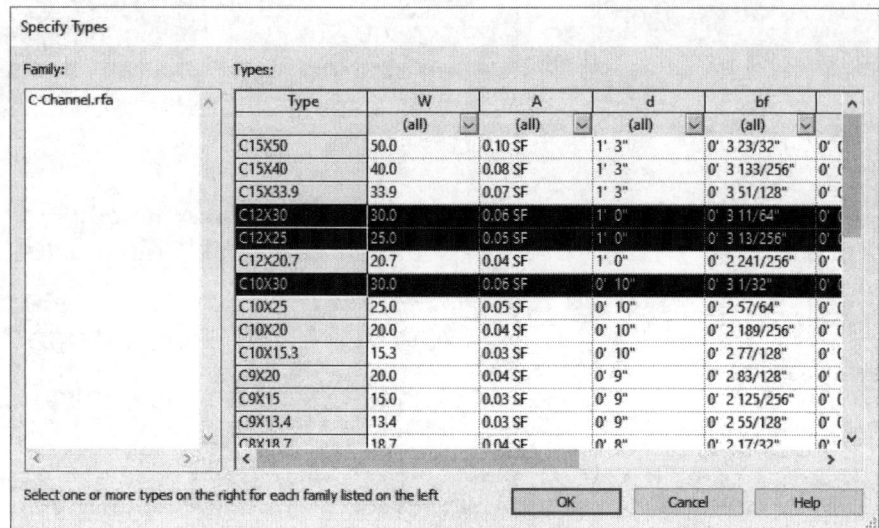

Figure 5–18

4. Once the family (or families) is loaded, in the Type Selector, select the type you want to use, as shown in Figure 5–19.

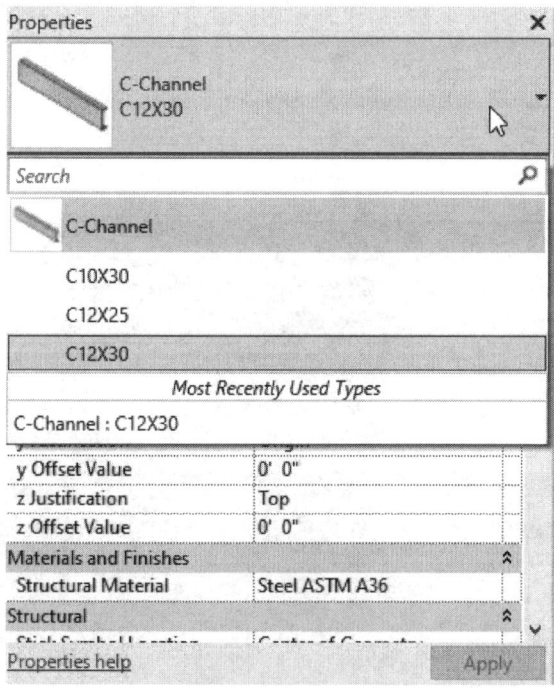

Figure 5–19

> **Hint: Loading Freestanding Components**
>
> Certain types of freestanding components, such as structural connectors, details, symbols, and mounting parts, can be loaded while using the (Place a Component) command.
>
> 1. In the *Structure* tab>Mode panel, click (Place a Component).
> 2. In the *Modify | Place Component tab*>Mode panel, click (Load Family).
> 3. In the Load Family dialog box, locate the folder that contains the family or families you want to load and select them.

How To: Load Autodesk Content

1. From the *Insert* tab>Load from Library, click (Load Autodesk Family).
2. In the Load Autodesk Family dialog box, filter your search by typing in what kind of family you are looking for, or click on a category in the Browse section, as shown in Figure 5–20.

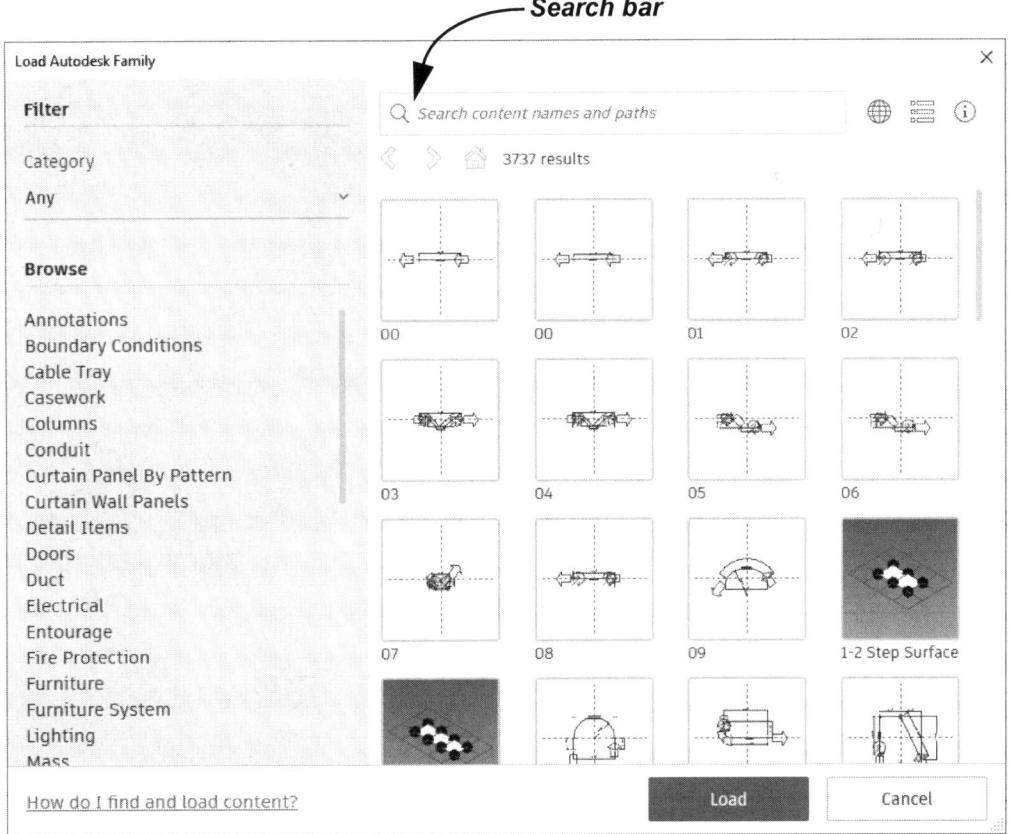

Figure 5–20

3. Click **Load** to load the family into your project.

5.3 Placing Structural Columns

Adding columns to a structural model is a straightforward process. Revit has a deep library containing standard steel structural shapes and concrete structural shapes, as shown in Figure 5–21. The software also keeps analytical data stored for each column that can be read by analytical software programs (such as Robot Structural Analysis, ETABS, RISA, and RAM). Structural columns can be placed on the grid line, on the grid intersection, or outside of the grids.

Figure 5–21

- Structural columns can be copied and monitored from linked files.

- Structural columns can be vertical or slanted, placed at grids or at columns, and tagged upon placement. Additionally, you can modify structural column settings from the Options Bar and Properties.

How To: Place Structural Columns

Structural Column is always the default.

1. In the *Structure* tab>Structure panel, click (Column).
2. In the Type Selector, select a column type.

3. In the Options Bar (shown in Figure 5–22), set the following information:

Figure 5–22

- *Depth* or *Height*: Architects typically draw columns from the bottom up.
- *Level/Unconnected:* Specify a level or select **Unconnected**. If you select **Unconnected**, assign a distance.
- *Rotate after placement*: Enables you to place the column and then graphically select a rotation angle.
- *Room bounding*: (Concrete only) The column can be used to define the boundary of a room for area and volume calculations.

4. To place individual columns, click at the required location. Columns automatically snap to grid lines and walls.

   To place multiple columns, in the *Modify | Place Structural Column* tab>Multiple panel, select one of the following:

   - (At Columns) places a structural column at the center of selected architectural columns. Select the architectural columns where you want the columns to be placed and then click (Finish).
   - (At Grids) places structural columns at intersecting grid lines. Select the grid lines where you want the columns to be placed and then click (Finish).
   - For information on working with slanted columns, see *B.2 Placing Slanted Structural Columns*.

Use (Filter) to help you select only the architectural columns or grids for these options.

Modifying Columns

When you select a column, you can change its type by selecting a different one in the Type Selector. You can also change a variety of constraints and other options in Properties (as shown in Figure 5–23) and attach columns to other elements so that they move with the elements.

The location of columns on grid lines are included in the properties of the column. If the column is not on a grid line, it displays the distance from the closest grid intersection.

Figure 5–23

- Verify that **Moves With Grids** is toggled on. This ensures that when a grid line is moved, the columns connected to it move as well. This toggle is normally on by default, but it is good practice to check its status.

- When changing the top and base levels and offsets, you should make these changes in a logical order, as having a zero or negative height column results in an error message.

How To: Attach Columns to Other Elements

1. Select a column or group of columns.
2. In the *Modify | Structural Columns* tab>Modify Column panel, click (Attach Top/Base).
3. In the Options Bar, set *Attach Column* to **Top** or **Base** and set the *Attachment Style* (as shown in Figure 5–24), *Attachment Justification*, and *Offset From Attachment*.

Attaching columns to other objects associates or constrains certain parameters, such as height.

Grids and Structural Columns

Figure 5–24

4. Select the floor, roof, footing, beam, reference plane, or level to which you want the column(s) attached.

- If you want to detach a column that has been attached, select the column and click ▭ (Detach Top/Base).

- You can use the **Attach Top/Base** command to attach structural columns to isolated foundations and footings. If the foundation height changes, the length of the column changes with it.

Loading Structural Content

When you are placing columns but the required structural column family or type is not listed, you can load additional families and add family types (sizes) from the Revit Library. This is true for all the structural component families, as shown in Figure 5–25.

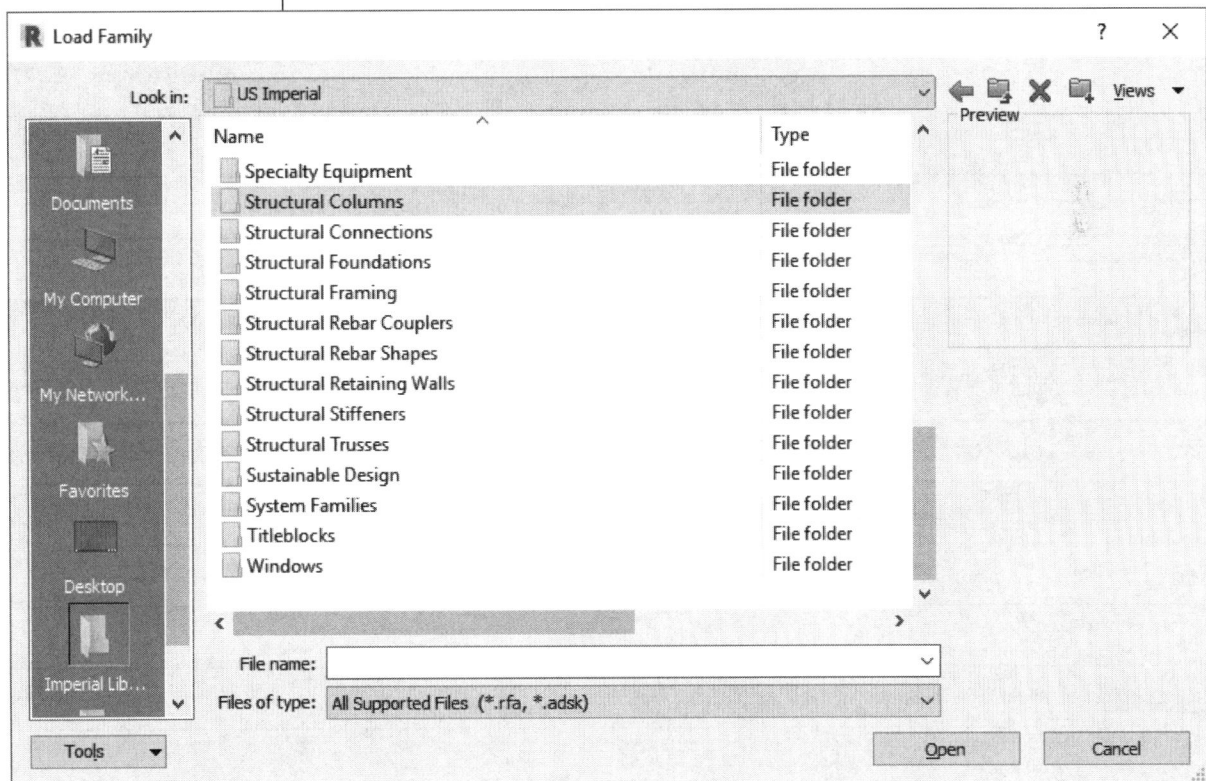

Figure 5–25

How To: Load Structural Column Types

1. Start the **Structural Column** command.
2. In the *Modify | Place Structural Column* tab>Mode panel, click ![icon] (Load Family).
3. In the Load Family dialog box, open the folder that contains the column families. In the default Revit Library, this is the *Structural Columns* folder, as shown in Figure 5–26. Select the column material folder and then select the individual column type you want to use.

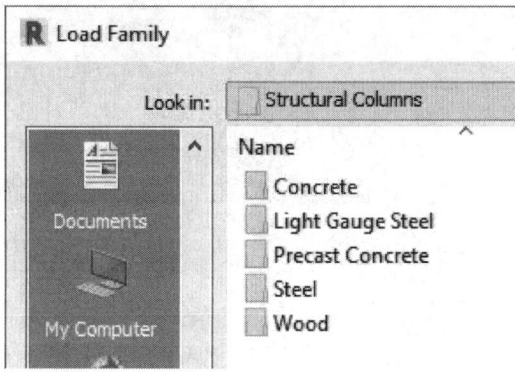

Figure 5–26

Hold <Ctrl> to select multiple families.

4. Navigate to the column family type that you want to use and click **Open**.
5. In the Specify Types dialog box (shown in Figure 5–27), select a column size in the list and click **OK**.

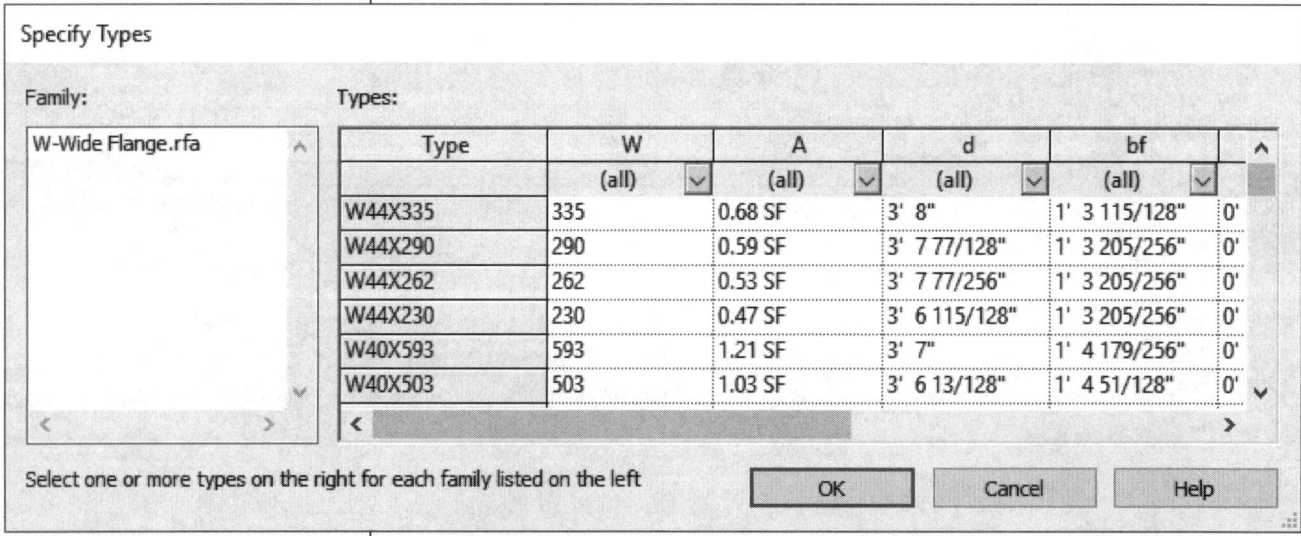

Figure 5–27

- If the Family Already Exists dialog box opens, as shown in Figure 5–28, select **Overwrite the existing version** or select **Overwrite the existing version and its parameter values**.

Grids and Structural Columns

*If you select **Overwrite the existing version and its parameter values**, any changes that you have made to any related families in the model are removed.*

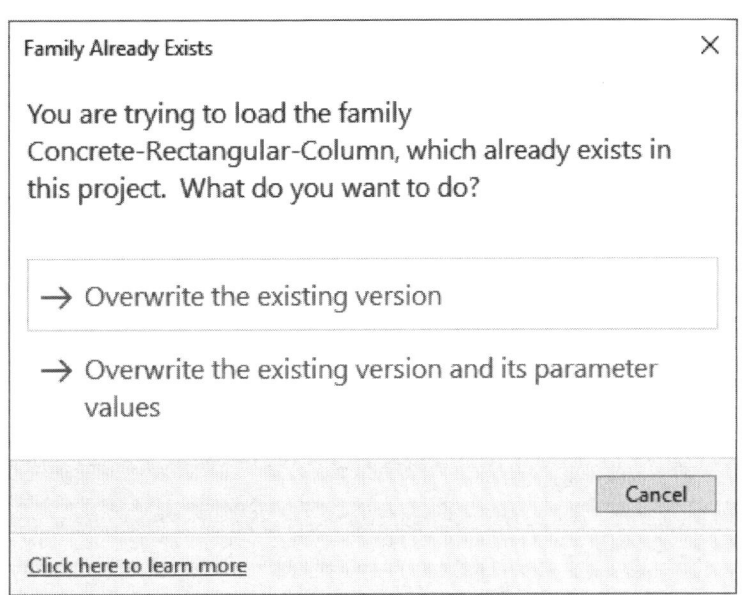

Figure 5–28

Hint: Family Library Location

If you need to load an out-of-the-box family, you can easily return to the default Revit family folder location by clicking on the Imperial Library folder icon in the Places panel within the Load Family dialog box, as shown in Figure 5–29.

Figure 5–29

Purging Unused Elements

You can remove unused elements from a project, including individual component types, as shown in Figure 5–30.

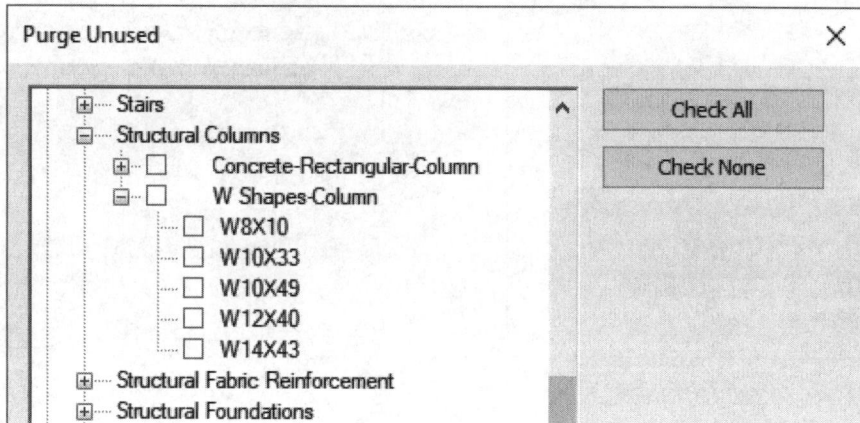

Figure 5–30

- Some elements are nested in other elements and it might require several rounds of purging the project to remove them.

How To: Purge Unused Elements

1. In the *Manage* tab>Settings panel, click (Purge Unused).
2. In the Purge Unused dialog box, click **Check None** and select the elements you want to purge.
3. Click **OK**.

Purging unused components not only helps simplify the component list, but also reduces the project file size.

Practice 5b | Place Structural Columns

Practice Objective

- Place columns on grids.

In this practice, you will place columns at the grid intersections. The completed practice is shown in 3D in Figure 5–31.

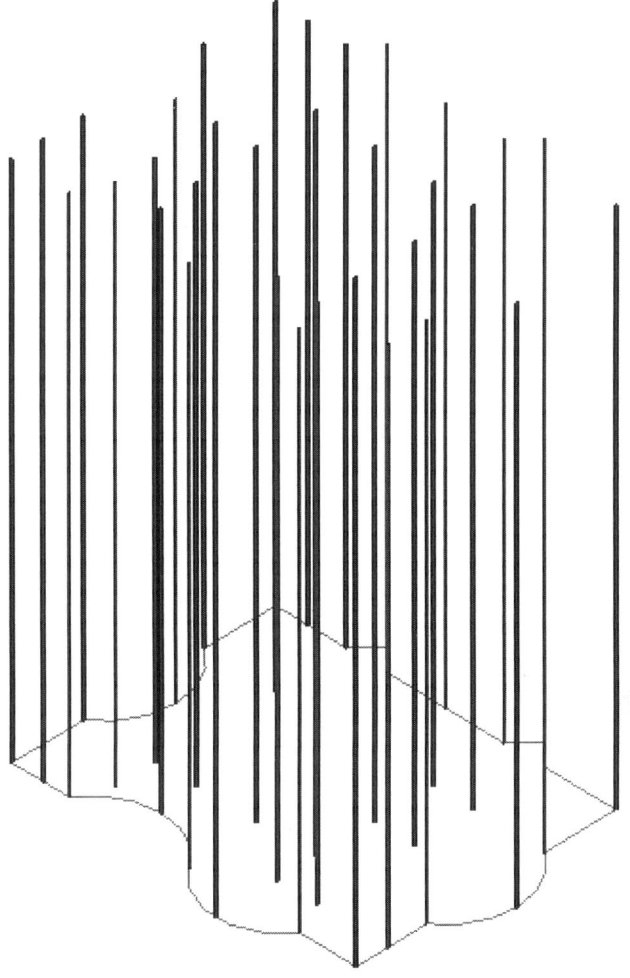

Figure 5–31

1. Open **Structural-Columns.rvt** from the practice files folder.

2. Ensure that you are in the **Structural Plans: 00 GROUND FLOOR** view.

3. In the *Structure* tab>Structure panel, click (Structural Column).

4. In the Type Selector, select **W-Wide flange-Column: W10x33**.

5. In the Options Bar, change *Depth* to **Height** and set the *Height* to **Level TOS-14 Roof**.

6. Place columns at the locations shown in Figure 5–32. (In some cases, it might be faster to place columns at the grid intersections and then delete any extra columns.)

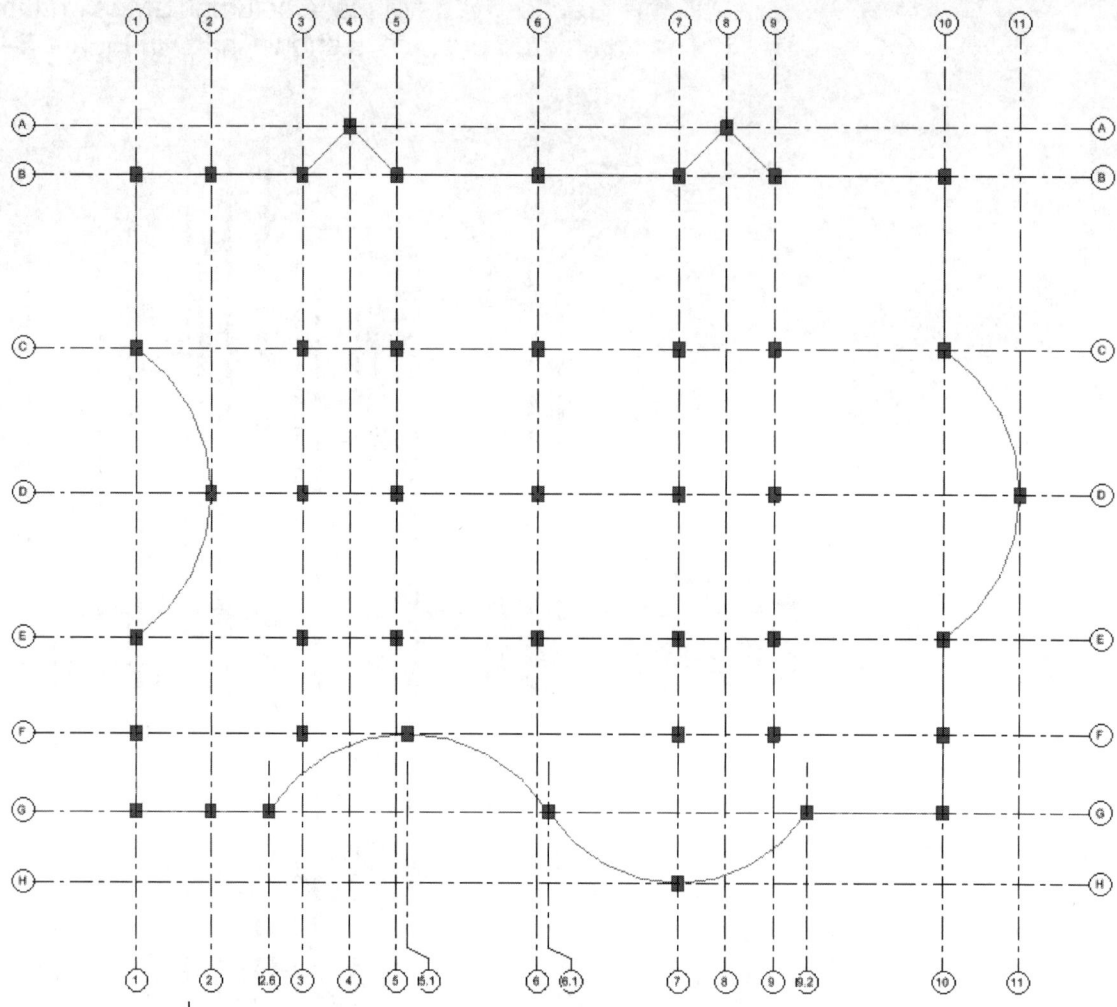

Figure 5–32

7. Open the **Default 3D** view to display the full height of the columns.

8. Save and close the project.

Chapter Review Questions

1. How do you line up grid lines that might be different lengths?
   a. Select the grid line and drag its model end to line up with the other grid lines.
   b. Use **Trim/Extend Multiple Elements** to line them up with a common reference line.
   c. Select the grid line, right-click, and select **Auto-Align**.
   d. In Properties, change the *Length* and then use **Move** to get them into position.

2. Structural columns can only be placed on grids.
   a. True
   b. False

3. How do you add additional column families to use in a project?
   a. Import them.
   b. Copy and paste them from another file.
   c. Draw them in the project.
   d. Load them from the Revit Library.

4. Grids can be displayed in a 3D view.
   a. True
   b. False

5. In order for structural columns to move with grids, what needs to be selected when placing the column?
   a. From the ribbon, select **At Grids**.
   b. Set the Top Constraint to grids.
   c. Columns always move with grids no matter what type.
   d. In Properties, select **Moves With Grids**.

Command Summary

Button	Command	Location
Columns and Grids		
	At Columns	• **Ribbon:** *Modify	Place Structural Column* tab>Multiple panel
	At Grids	• **Ribbon:** *Modify	Place Structural Column* tab>Multiple panel
	Grid	• **Ribbon:** *Structure* tab>Datum panel • **Shortcut:** GR
	Structural Column	• **Ribbon:** *Structure* tab>Structural panel • **Shortcut:** CL
	Vertical Column	• **Ribbon:** *Modify	Place Structural Column* tab>Placement panel
Tools		
	Attach Top/Base	• **Ribbon:** *Modify	Structural Column* tab>Modify Column panel
	Detach Top/Base	• **Ribbon:** *Modify	Structural Column* tab>Modify Column panel

Chapter 6

Foundations

Structural foundations are created using concrete walls, columns, and footings. Autodesk® Revit® includes standard tools for creating walls and columns in several different materials, as well as specific tools for adding footings.

Learning Objectives in This Chapter

- Create walls that can be used in foundations.
- Add bearing and retaining wall footings under the walls.
- Create column types to be used as piers and pilasters.
- Place isolated footings under the columns.

6.1 Modeling Walls

Walls in the Autodesk Revit software are more than just two lines on a plan. They are complete 3D elements that store detailed information, including height, thickness, and materials. This means they are useful in both 2D and 3D views. Structural walls (as shown in Figure 6–1) are bearing walls that can act as exterior, foundation, retaining, and shaft walls.

- Walls are a system family and are predefined in the Revit template file. They cannot be loaded in from an external location or saved out to a external location.

- Walls can be customized to suit your company needs, if necessary.

- Walls are not automatically reinforced. You must apply reinforcement as separate elements.

Figure 6–1

There are three broad categories of walls:

- *Basic walls:* Compound walls that contain one or more layers (e.g., blocks, air space, bricks, etc.).

- *Curtain walls:* Non-bearing walls made of glass with mullions.

- *Stacked walls:* Includes one wall type above another wall type, such as a brick wall over a concrete wall.

Wall Cross-Section

- The *Cross-Section* for the basic wall category can be modified to be **Vertical**, **Slanted**, or **Tapered**, as shown in Figure 6–2.

Figure 6–2

Vertical Wall

All walls are drawn by default as vertical walls and are at a 0° vertical when compared to a slanted wall type.

Note: If you change a wall's cross-section to **Tapered** and adjust the settings for the tapered wall, you will see only the tapered wall types displayed in the Type Selector. If you need to draw a vertical or slanted wall after the tapered wall is drawn, you will need to set the cross-section back to **Vertical** or **Slanted** so that you can see all the wall types in the Type Selector.

Slanted Wall

You can draw a slanted wall type and specify the **Angle From Vertical** degree value in Properties. The slant degree needs to be between -90° and 90°. You can also change a vertically drawn wall to a slanted wall type. If there are any doors, door openings, or windows added to the wall, you will need to select those objects and specify their *Orientation* in Properties. The direction to which the wall has been drawn (right to left or left to right) will determine the direction the angle will go. Figure 6–3 shows that when drawing from left to right, the wall slant will go in the negative direction, and when drawing from right to left, the slant wall goes in the positive direction.

Figure 6–3

- You cannot slant a wall that has the analytical turned on. You have to disable this first before changing the properties of the wall to slanted.

- Slanted walls can be modified in a plan, 3D, section, or perspective view.

- You can create a slanted wall with curved, circle, arc, polygon, or elliptical paths.

- If the angle is not going in the correct direction, you can add or remove the - (minus) symbol in front of the degree value in Properties.

Tapered Wall

You can create a tapered wall from any wall type except walls with sweeps and reveals. You must first edit the structure of the wall to set the variable thickness for the available wall layers. If not, you are prompted to set this before drawing the wall, as shown in Figure 6–4.

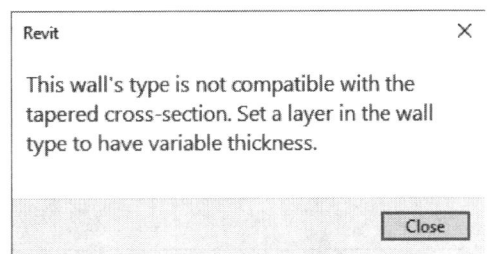

Figure 6–4

- To set the default angles of the tapered wall, in Type Properties, you can set the default exterior and interior angles.

- If you have multiple instances of the same tapered wall type, you can select a tapered wall and, in Properties, override the angles by selecting the **Override Type Properties** option and setting the *Exterior Angle* and *Interior Angle*, as shown in Figure 6–5.

Cross-Section	Tapered
Override Type Properties	✓
Exterior Angle	5.00°
Interior Angle	0.00°

Figure 6–5

- Curtain walls and stacked wall types cannot be tapered.

While some walls are made of only one material, such as poured concrete, other walls can be made of multiple layers, such as block, air space, and brick all in one wall type. These compound walls can have different justifications, as shown in Figure 6–6.

Figure 6–6

The core is typically the structural part of the wall.

How To: Model a Wall

1. In the *Structure* tab>Structure panel, click (Wall: Structural).
   - Architectural walls (which are created with the **Wall: Architectural** command) are typically non-bearing walls, such as curtain walls and partitions. They do not display when the view *Discipline* is set to **Structural**.
2. In the Type Selector, select a wall type, as shown in Figure 6–7.
   - You can use the Search box to quickly find specific types of walls.

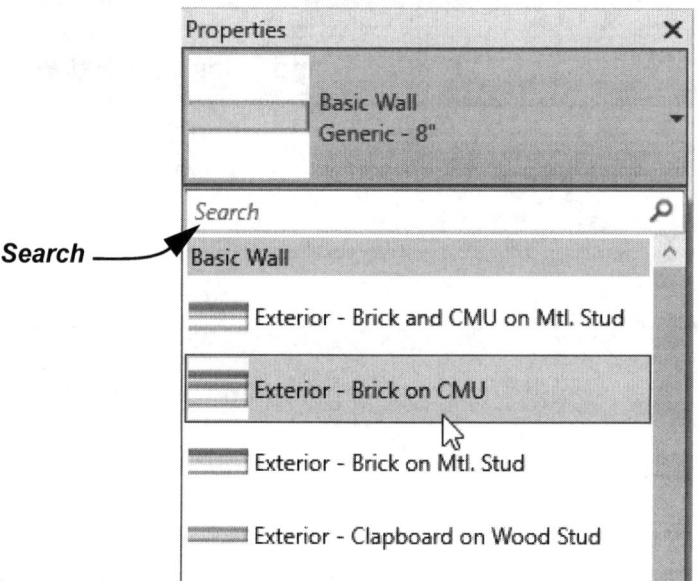

Figure 6–7

3. In Properties, set the *Cross-Section* to **Vertical**, **Slanted**, or **Tapered**, depending on the wall you need to create, as shown in Figure 6–8. Specify the Properties and Type Properties as needed. If this is not set at the beginning of drawing a wall, the last *Cross-Section* used will be the default.

Foundations

Figure 6–8

- If you set the *Cross-Section* to **Slanted**, you are able to set the *Angle From Vertical* degree, as shown in Figure 6–9.

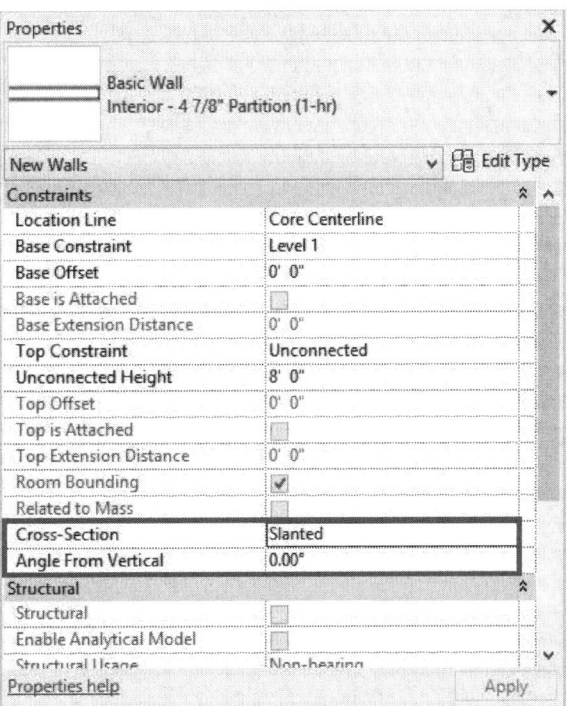

Figure 6–9

- If you set the *Cross-Section* to **Tapered**, you will get a warning about the wall type. You must first edit the structure of the wall before setting the *Cross-Section* to **Tapered**.

    - With the wall type selected, click **Edit Type** in Properties.
    - Click **Edit...** next to *Structure*.
    - In the Edit Assembly dialog box, select the option in the *Variable* column (as shown in Figure 6–10) for the layer that you want tapered.

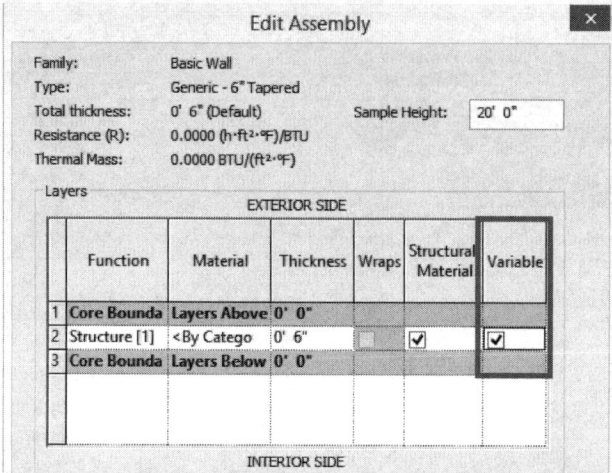

Figure 6–10

    - Click **OK**.
    - In the Type Properties dialog box, you will now have the ability to set the *Cross Section Properties*, as shown in Figure 6–11.

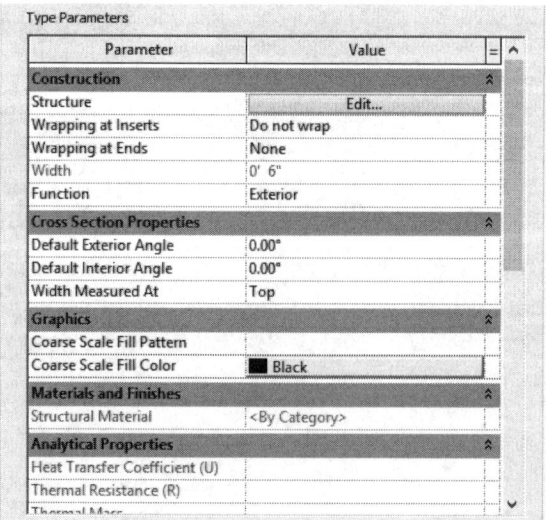

Figure 6–11

4. In the Options Bar (shown in Figure 6–12), specify the following information about the wall before you start drawing:

    - *Depth:* Set the depth of a wall either to **Unconnected** (with a specified distance) or to a level. This command can also be set to *Height*.
    - *Location Line:* Set the justification of the wall using the options shown in Figure 6–12.
    - *Chain:* Enables you to draw multiple connected walls.
    - *Offset:* Enables you to enter the distance at which a new wall is created from an existing element.
    - *Radius:* Adds a curve of a specified radius to connected walls as you draw.
    - *Join Status:* Choose between **Allow**, which permits automatic wall joins, and **Disallow**, which prohibits the walls from cleaning up when they touch other walls.

Figure 6–12

5. In the *Modify | Place Wall* tab>Draw panel (shown in Figure 6–13), select one of the options to create the wall.

Figure 6–13

- Use alignment lines, temporary dimensions, and snaps to place the walls.
- As you are sketching, you can press <Spacebar> to flip the orientation of compound walls.
- When using the **Chain** option, press <Esc> once to finish the string of walls and remain in the Wall command or press <Esc> twice to get out of the Wall command completely. Hint: Pressing <Esc> works similarly on other commands.

Modifying Walls

There are several methods of modifying walls. You can change the type of wall using the Type Selector, modify the Properties, use controls and shape handles to modify the length and wall orientation, and use temporary and permanent dimensions to change the location or length of a wall in 2D and 3D views, as shown in Figure 6–14. Additional tools enable you to modify wall joins, edit the profile of a wall, and add wall openings.

Figure 6–14

Modifying Slanted and Tapered Walls

Modifying a slanted or tapered wall is similar to modifying a vertical wall type with the exception of modifying the angle.

- When modifying a slanted wall type, you have the ability to modify the Drag Wall Slant grip or modify the temporary dimension in a 3D, section, elevation, or isometric view, as shown in Figure 6–15.

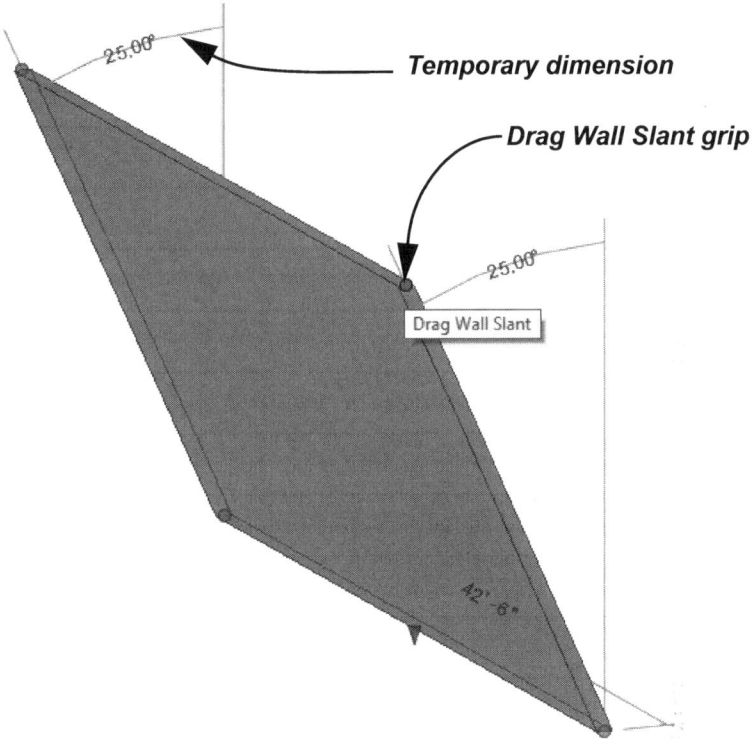

Figure 6–15

- When modifying a tapered wall, you have the ability to modify the Drag Wall Exterior Face Slant and Drag Wall Interior Face Slant grips or modify the temporary dimension in a 3D, section, elevation, or isometric view, as shown in Figure 6–16.

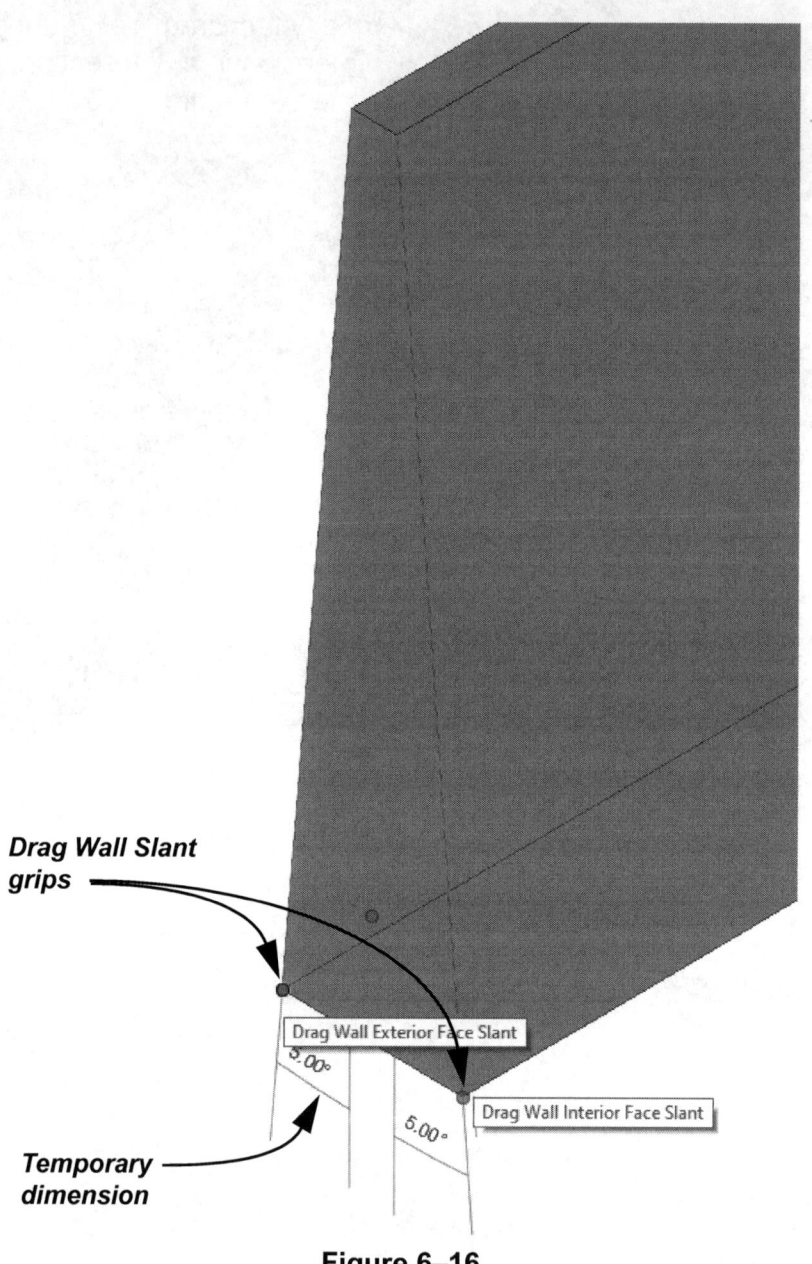

Figure 6–16

Foundations

- To display the hatching in the walls in plan views, in the View Control Bar, set the *Detail Level* to **Medium** or **Fine**, as shown in Figure 6–17.

Figure 6–17

Wall Joins

The software automatically joins walls with common materials when they come together at an intersection, as shown on the left in Figure 6–18. However, there are times when you do not want the walls to clean up, such as when one fire-rated wall butts into another or when a wall touches a column surround, as shown on the right in Figure 6–18.

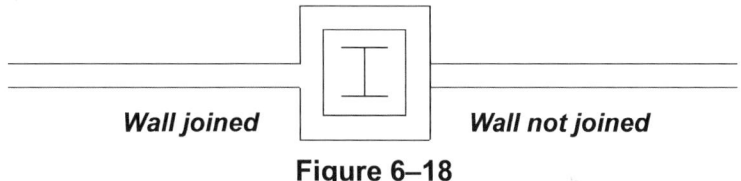

Figure 6–18

- While you are creating walls, change the *Join Status* to **Disallow** in the Options Bar.

- If a wall is already placed, select the wall, right-click on the Drag Wall End control at the end of the wall, and select **Disallow Join**, as shown on the left in Figure 6–19. Once the end is not joined, you can drag it to the appropriate location, as shown on the right in Figure 6–19.

Figure 6–19

To rejoin the walls, click (Allow Join) or right-click on the end control and select **Allow Join**. Manually drag the wall back to where you want it to touch the target wall.

- For more information about wall joins, see *B.3 Editing Wall Joins*.

Wall Openings

You can add openings in walls that are not windows or doors by using the **Wall Opening** tool. This creates rectangular openings for both straight and curved walls, as shown in Figure 6–20.

Figure 6–20

How To: Add Wall Openings

1. Open a plan, elevation, section, or 3D view.
2. In the *Architecture* tab>Openings panel, click (Wall Opening).
3. Select the wall.
4. Pick two points on the diagonal to determine the opening size if in an elevation, section, or 3D view. If you are in a plan view, you need to pick the start and stop points for the wall opening.

- You can use temporary dimensions to size the opening while in the command and both temporary dimensions and shape handles to modify the opening when it is selected, as shown in Figure 6–21.

Foundations

Figure 6–21

6.2 Adding Wall Footings

Wall footings for bearing and retaining are hosted by the walls. Once a footing is in place, you can add reinforcement, as shown in Figure 6–22. With the advantages of having a true foundation in place, you can accurately tag and schedule the footings.

Figure 6–22

- You can apply two types of continuous footing systems, as shown in Figure 6–23. You must have walls in your model to add a footing system.
    - **Retaining footings:** A footing with one side offset to accommodate additional lateral loads and reinforcement
    - **Bearing footings:** A footing with an equal distance on either side of the bearing wall.

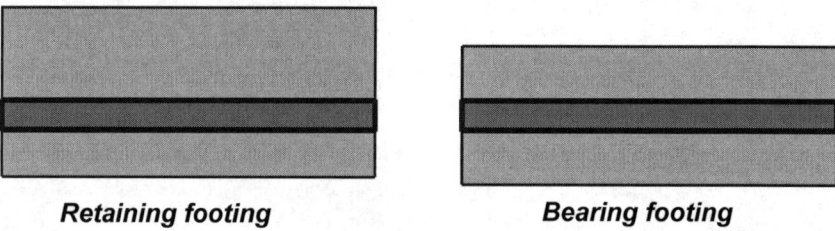

Figure 6–23

How To: Place a Bearing or Retaining Footing

1. Create walls or use existing ones.
    - A wall must be in place to add a bearing or retaining footing.

Wall foundations can also be placed in 3D, section, and elevation views.

Foundations

2. Open a foundation plan and set it up so that the walls are displayed and you can select them.
3. In the *Structure* tab>Foundation panel, click (Wall) to start the **Structural Foundations: Wall** command, or type **FT**.
4. In the Type Selector, select a type, as shown in Figure 6–24.

Figure 6–24

5. Select a wall. The footing is placed beneath the wall, as shown in Figure 6–25.

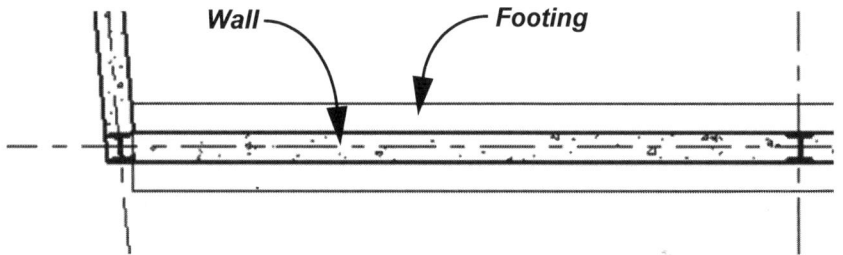

Figure 6–25

- To select multiple walls, hover over one wall and then press <Tab> to select all connected walls. Alternatively, in the *Modify | Place Wall Foundation* tab>Multiple panel, click (Select Multiple). Select the walls using any selection method and click (Finish) to place the footings.

- You can flip retaining footings using the Flip control, as shown in Figure 6–26.

Figure 6–26

How To: Create a Footing Type

1. Select an existing foundation wall element or start the **Structural Foundation: Wall** command.
2. In the Type Selector, select a type similar to the type that you want to create. In Properties, click ⊞ (Edit Type).
3. In the Type Properties dialog box, click **Duplicate**.
4. In the Name dialog box, type a new name for the element and click **OK**.
5. Make any changes to the type properties as needed, as shown in Figure 6–27.

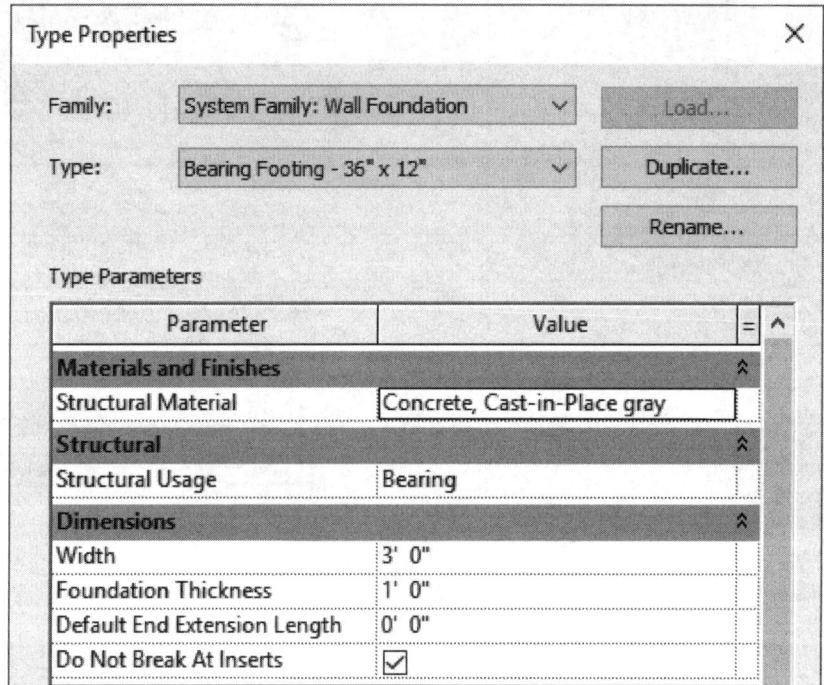

Figure 6–27

6. Click **OK** to close the dialog box.

Wall Profiles and Footings

Footings are appended to the bottom of a wall, which means that any change to the base of the host wall influences the footing. This occurs for lateral movement and horizontal movement. For the example shown in Figure 6–28, when the wall profile changes based on a sloped site (as shown on the left), the footing breaks and follows the modified profile (as shown on the right). This is accomplished by editing the profile of the foundation wall.

Foundations

Wall profile in process   *Completed wall with footing*

Figure 6–28

How To: Edit the Profile of a Wall

1. Open an elevation or section view in which you can see the face of the wall that you want to edit.
2. Select the wall (by highlighting the wall boundary).
   - Note: You cannot edit a tapered wall's profile.
3. In the *Modify | Walls* tab>Mode panel, click (Edit Profile). The wall is outlined in magenta indicating the profile of the wall.
4. In the *Modify | Walls>Edit Profile* tab>Draw panel, use the tools to modify the profile sketch of the wall, as shown on the top in Figure 6–29.
5. Once the profile is complete, click (Finish Edit Mode). The footing now follows the new profile, as shown on the bottom in Figure 6–29.

The sketch must form a continuous loop. Verify that the lines are clean without any gaps or overlaps. Use any of the tools in the Modify panel to clean up the sketch.

Figure 6–29

- After you adjust the sketch, you can add isolated footings to create the appropriate shape.

Hint: Materials

When you are creating some types, such a wall footings, one option is to set the *Structural Material*. In Type Properties, in the *Materials and Finishes* section, click in the *Value* column and then click (Browse), as shown in Figure 6–30.

Figure 6–30

In the Material Browser (shown in Figure 6–31), specify the material you want to use and click **OK**.

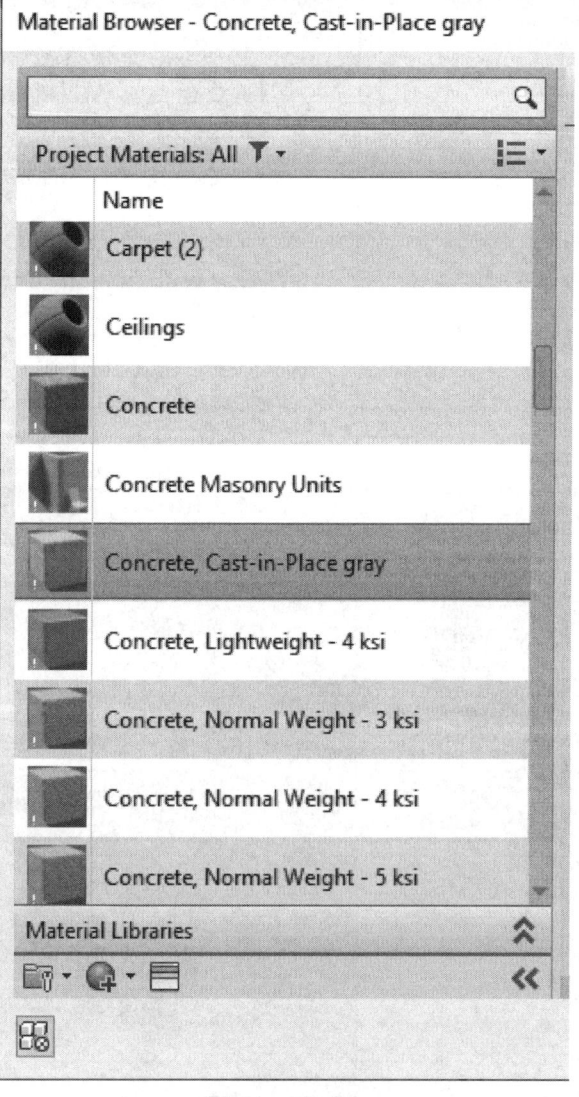

Figure 6–31

Foundations

Practice 6a | Model Walls and Wall Footings

Practice Objectives

- Place structural walls.
- Create and apply wall footings.

In this practice, you will model the perimeter foundation walls, as shown in Figure 6–32.

Figure 6–32

Task 1 - Add walls.

1. Open **Structural-Walls.rvt** from the practice files folder.

2. Open the **Structural Plan: 00 GROUND FLOOR** view. (The green lines are the outline of the building.)

3. In the *Structure* tab>Structure panel, click (Wall: Structural).

4. In the Type Selector, select **Basic Wall: Exterior - 8" Concrete**.

5. In the Options Bar, set the *Depth* to **T.O. FOOTING** and ensure that the *Location Line* is set to **Wall Centerline** and that **Chain** is selected.

© 2021, ASCENT - Center for Technical Knowledge®   6–21

6. In the *Modify | Place Structural Wall* tab>Draw panel, click (Line).

7. Select the start point by snapping to the **G1** grid intersection, as shown in Figure 6–33.

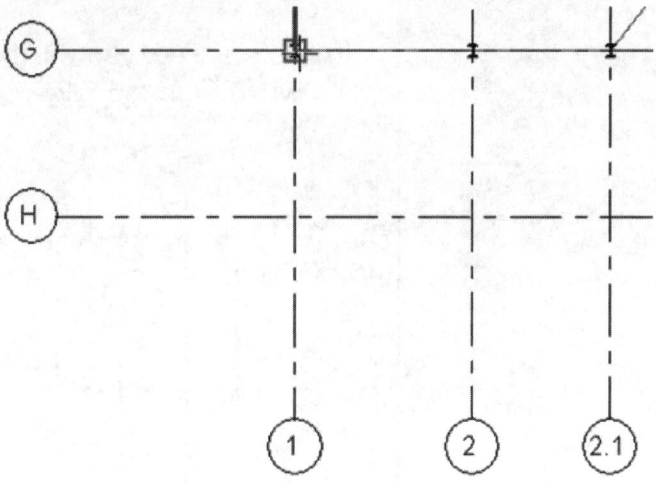

Figure 6–33

8. Draw the wall up to the **E1** grid intersection.

9. In the Draw panel, click (Start-End-Radius Arc). Select the second point at the **C1** grid intersection and then the third point anywhere along the green arc to specify the radius of the arc, as shown in Figure 6–34.

Figure 6–34

10. Click (Line) again and select the **B1** grid intersection.

11. Following the green outline, continue drawing walls all the way around the perimeter, as shown in Figure 6–35.

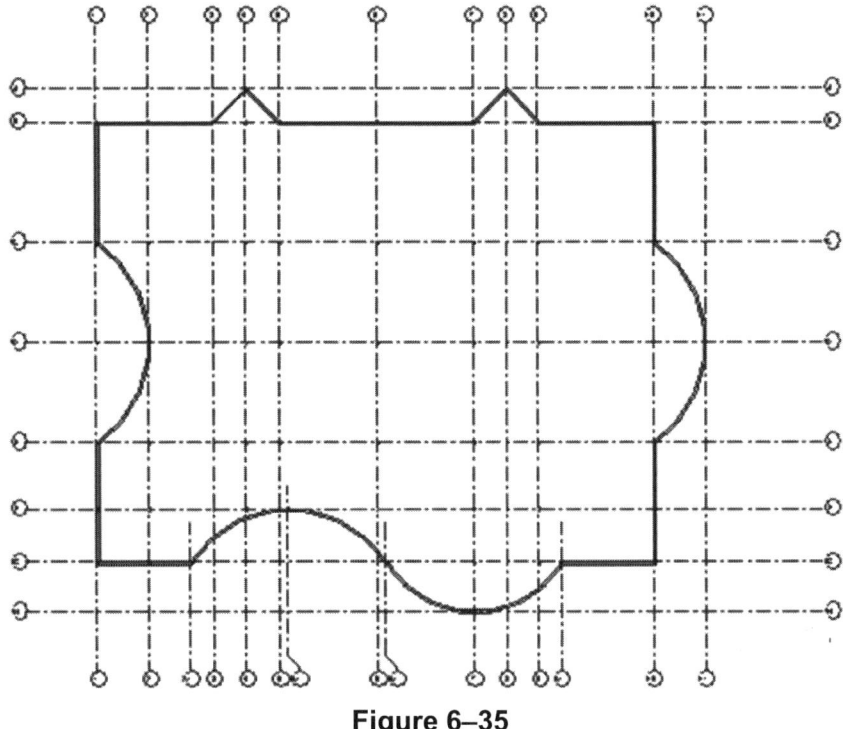

Figure 6–35

12. Click (Modify).

13. Save the project.

Task 2 - Create and apply wall footings.

1. Open the **Structural Plans: 000 FOUNDATION PLAN** view.

2. In the *Structure* tab>Foundation panel, click (Structural Foundation: Wall), or type **FT**.

3. Make sure the Type Selector is set to **Wall Foundation: Bearing Footing - 36" x 12"**. In Properties, click (Edit Type).

4. In the Type Properties dialog box, click **Duplicate...**.

5. In the Name dialog box, type **Bearing Footing – 24" x 12"** and click **OK**.

6. In the Type Properties dialog box, under *Dimensions*, set the *Width* to **2'-0"**, as shown in Figure 6–36.

Figure 6–36

7. Click **OK**.

8. You are still in the **Wall Foundation** command. In the Type Selector, ensure that the new **Wall Foundation: Bearing Footing - 24" x 12"** is selected, as shown in Figure 6–37.

Figure 6–37

9. Hover the cursor over one of the existing walls and press <Tab> to highlight the entire wall system. Click to select the walls. The footing is placed under the entire structure.

10. If you do not see the new wall foundation elements, you might be in an area of the view where they are not visible. Open the **Structural Plans: 000 FOUNDATION PLAN** view.

11. Click (Modify).

12. In the Quick Access Toolbar, click (Default 3D View) to go to a 3D view. Verify that the footing is placed correctly, as shown in part in Figure 6–38. Change the visual style as needed.

Figure 6–38

13. Save and close the project.

6.3 Creating Piers and Pilasters

The Autodesk Revit software does not have specific categories for piers and pilasters. If you need to create these elements, the best method is to use concrete columns, as shown in Figure 6–39. You can then analyze them as part of the foundation system and independently schedule them from the main column schedule. A concrete column also automatically embeds itself into a concrete wall.

Concrete column

Figure 6–39

- Poured concrete columns can be created in many sizes. For typical rectangular, square, and round columns, it is easy to create custom sizes.

How To: Create a Custom Column Size

1. Open a plan view.

2. In the *Structure* tab>Structure panel, click (Column).

3. In the Type Selector, select an existing column family type similar to the one you want to create, such as **Concrete-Rectangular-Column**.

4. In Properties, click (Edit Type).

5. In the Type Properties dialog box, click **Duplicate**.

6. In the Name dialog box, type a name, as shown in Figure 6–40. Click **OK**.

Figure 6–40

7. Modify the dimensions as required. Enter the required values for *b* (base) and *h* (height), as shown in Figure 6–41.

Figure 6–41

8. Click **OK**.

- The new pier column can be placed at the base of the existing steel columns, as shown in Figure 6–42.

Figure 6–42

Practice 6b Create Piers and Pilasters

Practice Objectives

- Create a new column type.
- Add columns.

In this practice, you will create a new column type and place piers and pilasters (types of columns). The resulting model is shown in Figure 6–43.

The steel columns have been hidden in this view for clarity.

Figure 6–43

Task 1 - Create a new column type.

1. Open **Structural-Foundations.rvt** from the practice files folder.

2. Open the **Structural Plans: 000 FOUNDATION PLAN** view.

3. In the *Structure* tab>Structure panel, click (Column), or type **CL**.

4. In the Type Selector, select one of the **Concrete-Rectangular-Column** types.

5. In Properties, click (Edit Type).

6. In the Type Properties dialog box, click **Duplicate**.

7. Rename the column to **24 x 24**. The family name, **Concrete-Rectangular-Column**, is automatically applied to the name. Click **OK**.

8. In the Type Properties dialog box, change the dimensions for both *b* (base) and *h* (height) to **2'-0"**, as shown in Figure 6–44.

Figure 6–44

9. Click **OK**.

10. Click (Modify).

Task 2 - Place piers and pilasters.

1. Select one of the steel columns. In the View Control Bar, expand (Temporary Hide/Isolate) and click **Isolate Category**, as shown in Figure 6–45. Only the columns display.

Figure 6–45

2. In the *Structure* tab>Structure panel, click (Column), or type **CL**.

3. Ensure that **Concrete-Rectangular-Column: 24 x 24** is selected in the Type Selector.

*This is one method that can help you place the columns. You can also use **At Grids** and delete the columns that you do not need.*

4. In the Options Bar, set *Depth* to **T.O. Footing**.

5. Place a concrete column at each existing steel column. Some of the columns will look odd (as shown in Figure 6–46) because they are connected to the concrete foundation walls that have been hidden in the view.

Figure 6–46

6. When you finish placing the concrete columns, in the View Control Bar, expand (Temporary Hide/Isolate) and select **Reset Temporary Hide/Isolate**.

7. In the Quick Access Toolbar, click (Default 3D View) and view the new column placement.

8. Save and close the project.

6.4 Adding Isolated Footings

Footings for columns (shown in Figure 6–47) are placed using the **Structural Foundation: Isolated** command. When you select a column, the footing automatically attaches to the bottom of the column. This is true even when the bottom of the column is on a lower level than the view you are working in.

Figure 6–47

How To: Place an Isolated Footing

1. Open a plan view, such as a **T.O. Footing** structural floor plan.
2. In the *Structure* tab>Foundation panel, click (Isolated) to start the **Structural Foundation: Isolated** command.
3. In the Type Selector, select a footing type.
4. In the view, click to place the individual footing, as shown in Figure 6–48.
   - If needed, press <Spacebar> to rotate the isolated footings after they are placed.

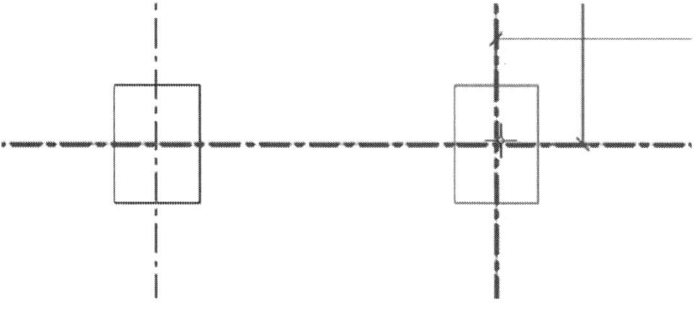

Figure 6–48

- To add more than one footing at a time, in the *Modify | Place Isolated Foundation* tab>Multiple panel, select (At Grids) or (At Columns) and select the grids or columns.
- If needed, press <Spacebar> to rotate the isolated footings after they are placed.
- If the material of the wall footing and the material of the isolated footing are the same, they automatically join, as shown in Figure 6–49.

Figure 6–49

Hint: Foundation Element Properties

Some of the element properties are automatically generated from the location and size of the element in the model and are grayed out, for example *Host*, *Elevation at Top*, and *Elevation at Bottom* as shown in Figure 6–50. These can be used in tags and schedules.

Figure 6–50

Foundations

Working with Custom Families

Sometimes you need to work with a custom family that has parameters that you can manipulate to fit a specific situation. For example, to add the step footings shown in Figure 6–51, you need to insert an angled isolated footing and modify it to fit the exact size and location.

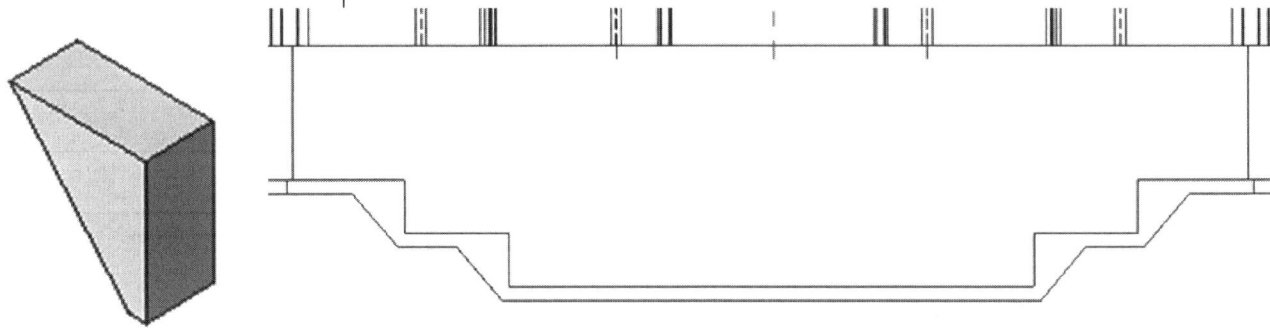

Figure 6–51

How To: Load, Insert, and Modify a Custom Footing

1. Open a plan view.
2. In the *Structure* tab>Foundation panel, click (Isolated).
3. In the *Modify | Place Isolated Foundation* tab>Mode panel, click (Load Family).
4. In the Load Family dialog box, find the structural foundation family that you want to use and click **Open**.
5. Place the footing in the plan view. It might not be in the right place, but you can modify it in a section or elevation view.
6. Open an elevation or section view.
7. Move the footing to the correct location. As long as it is in line with another footing, it automatically cleans up, as shown in Figure 6–52.

Figure 6–52

- Use ⬜ (Align) to align the isolated footing with the footing already in the model. When it is aligned, select the lock, as shown in Figure 6–53. This ensures that if the elevation of the footing wall changes, the step footing will also adjust appropriately.

Figure 6–53

- Some custom families have sizing options in either Properties (per instance) or in the Type Properties (as shown in Figure 6–54) so that you can create additional types in various sizes as needed in the project.

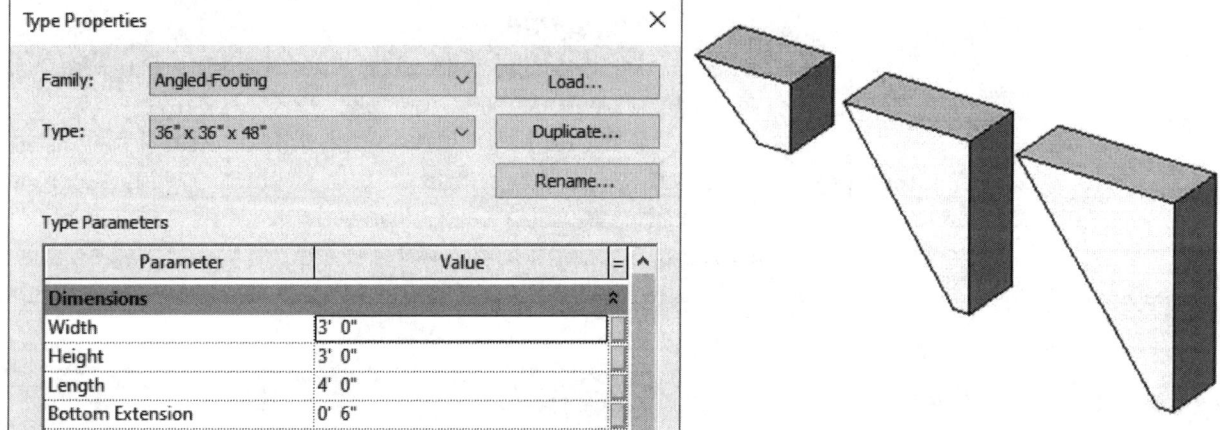

Figure 6–54

Practice 6c | Add Isolated Footings

Practice Objectives

- Place isolated footings.
- Modify a wall profile and add stepped footings.

In this practice, you will create a new footing type and place isolated footings, as shown in Figure 6–55. You will also create a series of stepped footings by modifying a wall profile and adding custom footings.

The steel columns have been hidden in this view for clarity.

Figure 6–55

Task 1 - Place isolated footings.

1. Open **Structural-Footings.rvt** from the practice files folder.

2. Open the **Structural Plans: T.O. FOOTING** view.

3. In the *Structure* tab>Foundation panel, click (Isolated).

4. In Properties, click (Edit Type).

5. Duplicate the type and name it **36"x36"x12"**.

6. In the Type Properties dialog box, set the following, as shown in Figure 6–56:
   - *Width*: **3'-0"**
   - *Length*: **3'-0"**
   - *Thickness*: **1'-0"**

Figure 6–56

7. Click **OK**.

8. Zoom in to the column at the **B1** grid intersection and place the isolated footing. The isolated footing and wall footing automatically join together, as shown in Figure 6–57.

Before *After*

Figure 6–57

9. In the *Modify | Place Isolated Foundation* tab>Multiple panel, click (At Columns). Use a pick window to select all of the columns and click (Finish).

10. Reopen the default 3D view.

The steel columns were hidden in this figure for clarity.

11. There should be an isolated footing under each pier and pilaster, as shown in Figure 6–58.

Figure 6–58

12. Save the project.

Task 2 - Modify the profile of a wall and add stepped footings.

1. Open the **Elevations (Building Elevation): North** view.

2. Zoom in on the left end of the foundation wall and select the wall located between grid lines **10** and **9**, as shown in Figure 6–59.

   Hint: You can turn on (Crop View) and (Show Crop Region) to show less in this view and make it easier to see the grid lines.

Figure 6–59

3. In the *Modify | Walls* tab>Mode panel, click (Edit Profile).

4. Use the Draw and Modify tools to add the stepped profile shown in Figure 6–60. The dimensions are for information only.

    - Make sure to remove the bottom of the wall's constraint by clicking on the lock or by moving the line and clicking **Remove Constraints** in the Error - cannot be ignored dialog box that appears.

Figure 6–60

5. Click (Finish Edit Mode).

6. The wall profile is modified along with the footings, as shown in Figure 6–61.

Foundations

Figure 6–61

7. Open the **Structural Plans: T.O. Footing** view and zoom in on the corner of the **B10** grid intersection. You should be able to see lines that show the steps of the footing below.

8. In the *Structure* tab>Foundation panel, click (Isolated).

9. In the *Modify | Place Isolated Foundation* tab>Mode panel, click (Load Family).

10. In the Load Family dialog box, navigate to the practice files *Custom Families* folder and select **Angled-Footing.rfa**. Click **Open**.

11. In the Type Selector, select **Angled-Footing: 24" x 24" x 36"**.

12. Place three footings along the wall, similar to those shown in Figure 6–62.

The exact location does not matter at this time.

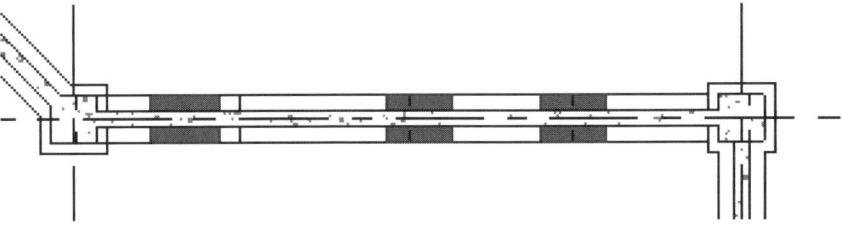

Figure 6–62

13. Return to the **North** elevation view. The three footings are still on the level where they were placed, as shown in Figure 6–63.

Figure 6–63

14. In the *Modify* tab>Modify panel, click (Align), or type **AL**.

15. Align each angled footing to the wall footings, as shown in Figure 6–64.

Figure 6–64

16. View the new footings in 3D, as shown in Figure 6–65.

Figure 6–65

17. (Optional) Modify the nearby wall, columns, and footings to match up with the new stepped footings.

18. Save and close the project.

Chapter Review Questions

1. Which of the following are ways that you can create walls in a project? (Select all that apply.)

   a. Draw Lines

   b. Pick Lines

   c. Insert Lines

   d. Pick Face

2. Which command do you use to insert a pier or a pilaster such as those shown in Figure 6–66?

   Figure 6–66

   a. **Structural Foundation**

   b. **Isolated Foundation**

   c. **Structural Column**

   d. **Isolated Column**

3. How do you create additional column sizes for column types already in the project?

   a. In Properties, duplicate an existing type and change the sizes.

   b. Start a new Autodesk Revit project and draw it there.

   c. Import additional sizes from another project.

   d. In the Revit Library, load additional sizes from other families.

4. Which element is the host for an isolated footing?

   a. Column

   b. Wall

   c. Slab

   d. Floor

5. The (Structural Foundation: Wall) command requires a host wall to already be in place.

   a. True

   b. False

6. Which command do you use to add a custom footing type under a wall such as the ones shown in Figure 6–67?

Figure 6–67

   a. **Component**

   b. **Structural Foundation: Isolated**

   c. **Structural Foundation: Wall**

   d. **Component: Structural Foundation**

Command Summary

Button	Command	Location
	Structural Foundation: Wall	• **Ribbon:** *Structure* tab>Foundation panel
	Structural Foundation: Isolated	• **Ribbon:** *Structure* tab>Foundation panel
	Wall: Structural	• **Ribbon:** *Structure* tab>Structure panel

Chapter 7

Structural Framing

The skeleton of a building is its structural framing. Together, elements such as columns, beams, bracing, and trusses give buildings the stability they need. While the basic process of adding these elements to the project is simple, you also need to complete more complex tasks, such as manipulating connections (by setting bearing offsets, cantilevers, cut backs, and justifications), applying beam coping, and editing beam joins.

Learning Objectives in This Chapter

- Sketch individual beams for girders connecting columns and structural walls.
- Create beam systems of multiple similar sized beams spaced at equal intervals to speed up adding joists.
- Add bracing to support the integrity of other framing members.
- Make changes to framing members so that the connections fit the exact situation.
- Add trusses to support long spans of open space.

7.1 Modeling Structural Framing

The Autodesk® Revit® software enables you to frame a building with wood, concrete, and steel framing and bracing, such as the steel example shown in Figure 7–1. You can add individual beams, as well as beam systems and bracing elements.

Figure 7–1

- Framing types include **Concrete**, **Light Gauge Steel**, **Precast Concrete**, **Steel**, and **Wood**.

- In views set to a **Coarse** detail level, the software assigns a line weight to the structural members based on their structural usage. For example, a girder displays in a heavier line weight than a joist, while a purlin displays with a dashed line, as shown in Figure 7–2.

Figure 7–2

Structural Framing

How To: Add Beams

1. In the *Structure* tab>Structure panel, click (Beam).
2. In the Type Selector, select a beam type.
3. In the Options Bar, specify the options, as shown in Figure 7–3 and described below.

Figure 7–3

- *Placement Plane:* Defaults to the current level if you are in a plan view but can be modified to other levels.

- *Structural Usage:* Select a type (as shown in Figure 7–3), or accept the default of **<Automatic>**.

- *3D Snapping:* Select this if you want to draw a beam from one point to another at different heights.

- *Chain:* Select this if you want to draw a series of beams in a row.

  - To stay in the command and start another chain, press <Esc> once.

4. For automatic tagging, in the *Modify | Place Beam* tab>Tag panel, click (Tag on Placement).
5. In the *Modify | Place Beam* tab>Draw panel, use the Draw tools to draw the beams.

How To: Add Multiple Beams on Grid Lines

1. Start the **Beam** command and specify the type and other options, as outlined above.

2. In the *Modify | Place Beam* tab>Multiple panel, click (On Grids).

3. Select the grid lines where you want to place the beams. A beam is placed between each grid intersection, as shown in Figure 7–4. Hold <Ctrl> to select more than one grid line, or use a selection window to select multiple grid lines at one time. Columns must be in place in order to add multiple beams at the same time.

Figure 7–4

4. In the *Modify | Place Beam>On Grid Line* tab>Multiple panel, click (Finish).

- Sometimes this can be the quickest way to add beams. If you need to use various sizes of beams, when you are finished, select those beams and make any changes in the Type Selector.

Beam Systems

Beam systems are layouts of parallel beams within a structural quadrant giving the structure added support, as shown in Figure 7–5. Typically used in joist layouts, beam systems can be set up to use either a fixed distance or number of beams.

- Beam systems can be created automatically with sufficient bounding elements (other beams). You can also sketch the boundary for a beam system.

- To use the automatic beam system, you need to have framing in the model already.

Structural Framing

Figure 7–5

How To: Add Automatic Beam Systems

1. In the *Structure* tab>Structure panel, click (Beam System), or type **BS**.
2. In the *Modify | Place Structural Beam System* tab>Beam System panel, click (Automatic Beam System).
   - If you do not have framing in the level, you are directed to the *Modify | Create Beam System Boundary* tab, where you will need to create your bay boundary.
3. When (Tag on Placement) is selected, in the Options Bar, set the *Tag Style* (as shown in Figure 7–6).
   - **Framing:** Tags each individual member.
   - **System:** Places one tag for the entire framing system.

Figure 7–6

4. In the Options Bar (shown in Figure 7–7), set the *Beam Type*, *Justification*, and *Layout Rule*.

Figure 7–7

- The *Layout Rule* options include **Clear Spacing**, **Fixed Distance**, **Fixed Number**, and **Maximum Spacing**. Set the required distance or number.
- Make changes in Properties or in the Options Bar as needed to establish the required beam system.

5. Move the cursor over an existing beam until the guide lines display in the correct area and direction, as shown vertically and horizontally in Figure 7–8. This can also identify angled lines.

Figure 7–8

6. Select the existing beam to place the system.
7. Repeat this step in other bays, as needed.

- The beam system is one uniform group. You can change the beam type and spacing in the Options Bar or in Properties.

- If a grid line is moved, the beams automatically space themselves. If the bay increases beyond the minimum spacing, a beam is added. If the bay shrinks below the allowable spacing, a beam is removed.

- If you need to change the system to individual beams, in the *Modify | Structural Beam Systems* tab>Beam System panel, click (Remove Beam System). The individual beams remain but are no longer grouped together.

How To: Sketch a Beam System

1. In the *Structure* tab>Structure panel, click ▯ (Beam System).
2. In the *Modify | Place Structural Beam System* tab>Beam System panel, click ▯ (Sketch Beam System).
3. In the *Modify | Create Beam System Boundary* tab>Draw panel, click ▯ (Pick Supports) or use one of the other drawing tools. The first beam that you select will be the beam direction.
4. To modify the beam direction, from the Draw panel, click ▯ (Beam Direction) and select one of the sketch lines that you want the system to run parallel to, as shown on the top horizontal beam in Figure 7–9.

Figure 7–9

5. Clean up all of the corners so that there are no overlaps or gaps.
6. In the *Modify | Create Beam System Boundary* tab>Mode panel, click ▯ (Finish Edit Mode).
7. Make changes in Properties or in the Options Bar as needed to establish the required beam system.

- To include an opening in a beam system, select the beam system and in the *Modify | Structural Beam Systems* tab>Mode panel, click ▯ (Edit Boundary). From the Draw panel, select ▯ (Boundary Line) and draw another opening inside the original sketched boundary.

Adding Bracing

Braces automatically attach to other structural elements, such as beams, columns, and walls. They recognize typical snap points, such as the end point of a column and the middle of a beam, as shown in Figure 7–10.

Figure 7–10

- Bracing can be added in plan view or, more typically, in a framing elevation view.

How To: Add Bracing

1. Create and open a framing elevation.
2. In the *Structure* tab>Structure panel, click ⊠ (Brace).
3. In the Type Selector, select a brace type.
4. Pick two points for the end points of the brace.

   - Work from the centerline of all of the framing members so that the analytical line extends into the adjacent framing, even though the graphical member stops at the edge of the column or beam, as shown in Figure 7–11.

Figure 7–11

Cross Bracing Settings

In plan view, cross bracing needs to be displayed graphically, usually by hidden lines. The software has a separate setting that controls cross bracing as viewed in a plan. This setting enables you to display bracing above, below, or both. You can set the bracing to be displayed as parallel lines or as a line at an angle, as shown in Figure 7–12.

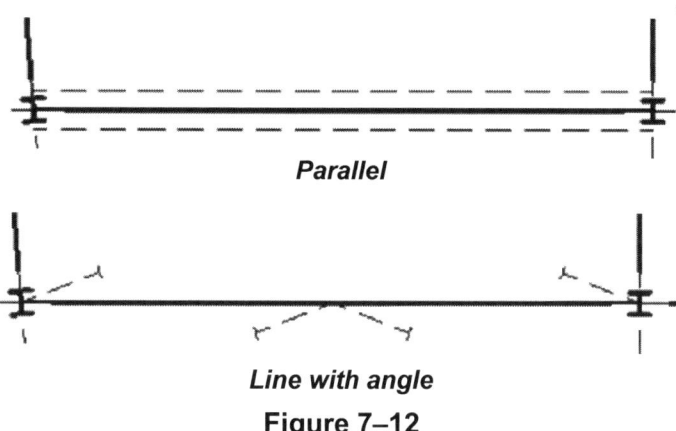

Parallel

Line with angle

Figure 7–12

- In the *Manage* tab>Settings panel, expand (Structural Settings) and click (Structural Settings). In the Structural Settings dialog box, in the *Symbolic Representation Settings* tab, select the **Brace Symbols** options, as shown in Figure 7–13.

Figure 7–13

Hint: Copying Elements to Multiple Levels

Instead of drawing the same elements on each level, you can copy them to the clipboard and then paste them aligned to the other levels.

1. Select the required elements.
2. In the *Modify* contextual tab>Clipboard panel, click (Copy to Clipboard).
3. In the *Modify* tab>Clipboard panel, expand (Paste) and click (Aligned to Selected Levels).
4. In the Select Levels dialog box (shown in Figure 7–14), select the levels to which you want to copy the elements.

Figure 7–14

5. Click **OK**.

- This command is for copying model elements only. If you want to include tags or other annotations, use **Paste>Aligned to Selected Views**.

Practice 7a

Model Structural Framing

Practice Objectives

- Place beams and beam systems.
- Copy framing to additional levels.
- Create a framing elevation.
- Add bracing.

In this practice, you will add framing for one floor of a building (as shown in Figure 7–15), and then copy and paste the framing to the levels above. You will then add bracing to one part of the structure.

This graphic is modified for clarity.

Figure 7–15

Task 1 - Place perimeter beams.

In this task, you will add framing between each column (and in some cases, between beams), as shown in Figure 7–16.

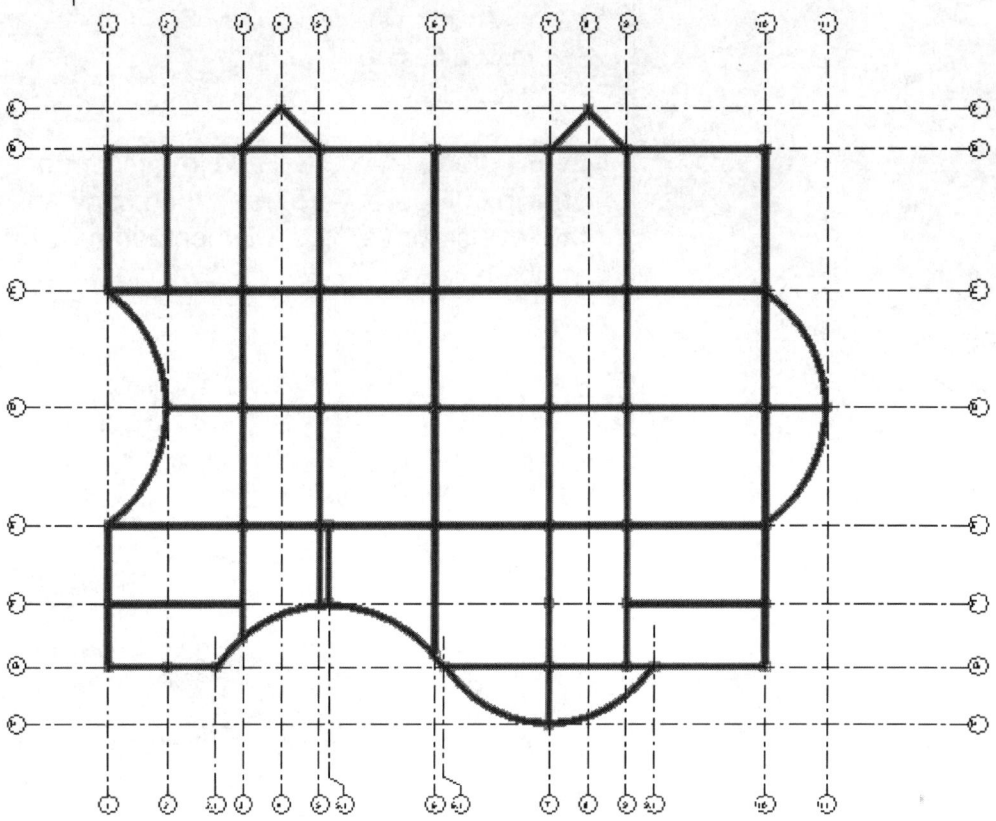

Figure 7–16

1. Open **Structural-Beams.rvt** from the practice files folder.

2. Open the **Structural Plans: TOS-1ST FLOOR** view.

3. In Properties, in the *Underlay* section, set the *Range: Base Level* to **T.O. FOOTING** so that you can see the outline of the building.

4. In the View Control Bar, set the *Detail Level* to (Medium).

5. In the *Structure* tab>Structure panel, click (Beam).

6. In the Type Selector, select **W-Wide-Flange: W14x30**.

7. Use the following techniques to place the beams:

   - If you use (At Grids), ensure that you select the correct grid lines. Delete beams that are not used.

- If you are sketching the beams, in the Options Bar, select **Chain** to keep the sketching active between picks. Press <Esc> once to end the chain but remain in the command.
- To place the curved beams, use either (Pick Lines) or the (Start-End-Radius Arc) tool.

8. Use (Split Element) to break each curved beam into two beams at the midpoint.

9. Select the curved beams and in Properties, in the *Structural* section, change the *Structural Usage* to **Girder**, if needed.

10. Click (Modify).

11. Save the project.

Task 2 - Create beam systems.

1. In the *Structure* tab>Structure panel, click (Beam System).

2. In the *Modify | Place Structural Beam System* tab, verify that (Automatic Beam System) is selected.

3. In the Tag panel, click (Tag on Placement) to toggle it off, if needed.

4. In the Options Bar, set the following:
   - *Beam Type:* **W12x26**
   - *Layout Rule:* **Maximum Spacing** of **6'-0"**

5. Click inside each bay, ensuring that the beams are running in a west-east direction. Exclude the bays on the corners of the east end shown in Figure 7–17.

This graphic has been modified for clarity.

Figure 7–17

6. Use (Sketch Beam System) for any bays that cannot be applied automatically.
   - In Properties, in the *Identity Data* section, set *Tag new members in view* to **None**.

7. Once all of the framing is in place, end the command.

8. Save the project.

Task 3 - Copy the framing to the other levels.

1. Select everything on the first floor except the grid lines.

2. In the Status Bar, click (Filter).

3. In the Filter dialog box, clear the **Structural Columns** category, as shown in Figure 7–18. If elements other than framing are displayed, clear those categories as well.

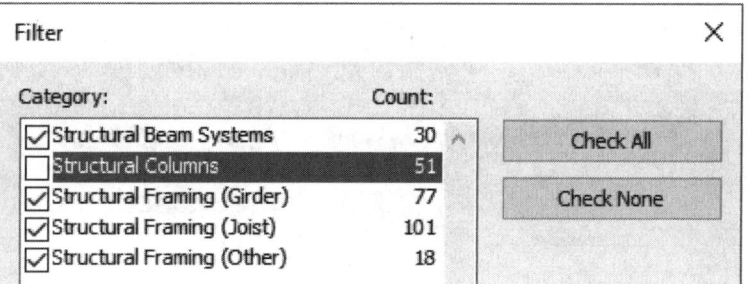

Figure 7–18

4. Click **OK**.

5. In the *Modify | Multi-Select* tab>Clipboard panel, click (Copy to Clipboard).

6. In the Clipboard panel, expand (Paste) and click (Aligned to Selected Levels).

7. In the Select Levels dialog box, select **TOS-2ND FLOOR** to **TOS-13TH FLOOR**, as shown in Figure 7–19. (Hint: Hold <Ctrl> or <Shift> to select multiple levels.)

Structural Framing

Figure 7–19

8. Click **OK**. This will take some time to process.

9. Open the **Structural Plans: TOS-13TH FLOOR** view.

10. Only the girder beams of each bay are required on the roof level. With a crossing window, select everything and filter out everything but **Structural Framing (Girder)**.

11. Press <Ctrl>+<C> (the **Copy to Clipboard** shortcut).

12. In the Clipboard panel, expand (Paste) and click (Aligned to Selected Levels).

13. In the Select Levels dialog box, select **TOS-14 ROOF** and click **OK**.

14. Open the **TOS-14 Roof** view and set the *Detail Level* to **Medium** so you can see the girder placement.

15. Open a 3D view to see the full model, as shown in Figure 7–20.

*This graphic is shown at the Coarse detail level with **Show Analytical Model** on for clarity.*

Figure 7–20

16. Save the project.

Task 4 - Create a framing elevation.

1. Open the **TOS-1st FLOOR** structural plan view.

2. In the *View* tab>Create panel, expand (Elevation) and click (Framing Elevation).

3. Select the beam between grid intersections **B1** and **C1**, as shown in Figure 7–21.

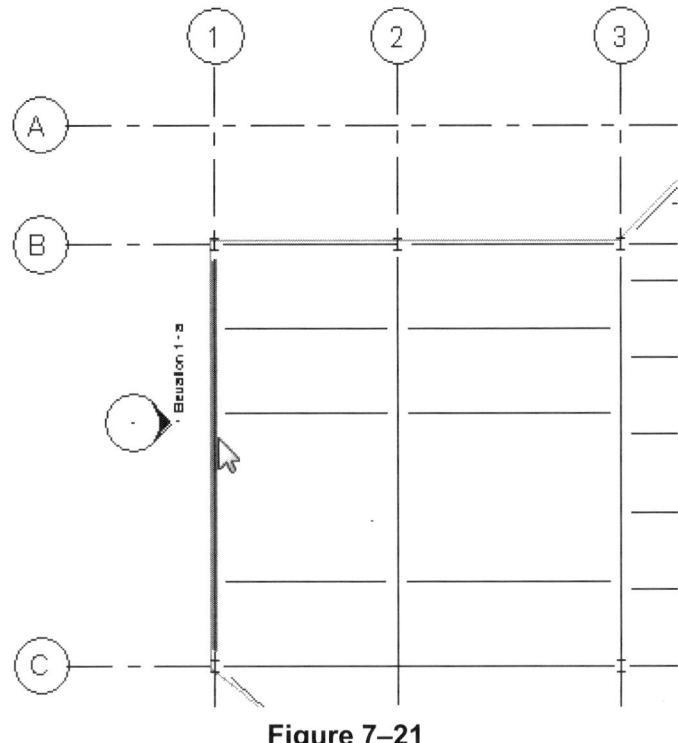

Figure 7–21

4. In the Project Browser, expand *Elevations (Framing Elevation)* and rename Elevation 1 – a as **West Bracing**.

5. Open the framing elevation.

6. Modify the crop region to display the columns.

7. In the View Control Bar, set the *Detail Level* to ▦ (Fine).

8. Zoom in to display the **00 GROUND FLOOR** and **TOS-1ST FLOOR** level heads.

9. Save the project.

Task 5 - Add bracing.

1. In the *Structure* tab>Structure panel, click ▨ (Brace).

2. In the Type Selector, select **HSS Square: HSS6X6X1/2**.

3. Draw from the centerline of the base of the column on the left to the midpoint of the beam located on **TOS-1ST FLOOR**, as shown in Figure 7–22. Repeat this step on the other side.

Figure 7–22

*Note that the entrance level is listed as **Ground Floor**. This is typical in some Canadian and British naming schemes.*

4. Click (Modify) and select the two new braces.

5. Copy the braces to the clipboard and use **Paste>Aligned to Selected Levels** to place them on each of the levels from **TOS-1ST FLOOR** to **TOS-13TH FLOOR**. Exclude the **00 GROUND FLOOR**, **T.O.FOOTING**, and **TOS-14 ROOF** levels.

6. In the West Bracing elevation, pan up to the top level.

7. Select the top two braces and drag the circular control to the midpoint of the beam above it, as shown in Figure 7–23.

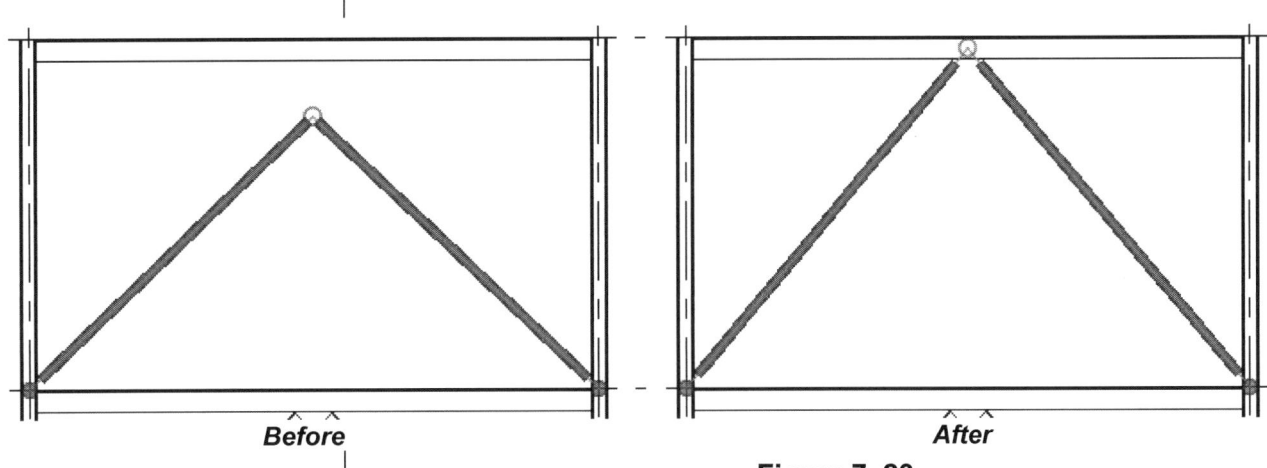

Figure 7–23

8. Click (Modify).

9. Zoom out to see the entire framing elevation.

10. Save and close the project.

7.2 Modifying Structural Framing

The default connections of columns, beams, and braces might need to be modified to suit specific situations, such as when the beams are offset from their associated level or cantilevered beyond a framing member. Modifications can be made by using graphical controls and shape handles, the Properties palette, or special tools found on the *Modify | Structural Framing* tab, as shown in Figure 7–24.

Figure 7–24

- The *Detail Level* of a view impacts the way in which framing members display, as shown in Figure 7–25. Some editing tools only work in a Medium or Fine detail view.

Coarse detail level

Medium detail level

Figure 7–25

- For a visual reference, you can use either location lines (shown in Figure 7–26) or analytical lines (shown in Figure 7–27).
  - To show location lines, in the Visibility/Graphic Overrides dialog box>*Model Categories* tab, expand **Structural Framing** and then select **Location Line**.
  - To toggle the display of analytical lines, in the View Control Bar, click (Show/Hide Analytical Model).

Figure 7–26

Figure 7–27

- When you draw framing members, the start/end orientation is based on the first and second points picked. In some modification instances, it is important to know the start point versus the end point. In the analytical model, the start point is green and the end point is red, as shown in Figure 7–28.

Figure 7–28

- To flip the start and end points:
  - In a plan view, click the **Flip Structure Framing ends** icon, as shown in Figure 7–29.
  - In a 3D view, right-click on the member and select **Flip Structural Framing ends**.

Figure 7–29

Sloping and Offsetting Beams

Beams can be modified to slope or offset from the level where they are placed. This can be done by first unpinning the beam, selecting it, and clicking the (Prevent or allow change of element position) icon in the view, and then using the *Start/End Level Offset* control (as shown in Figure 7–30) or modifying *Start/End Level Offset* in Properties (as shown in Figure 7–31).

Figure 7–30

Figure 7–31

- Setting the offset at only one end slopes the beam, as shown in Figure 7–32.

Sloped beams

Figure 7–32

- The *Cross-Section Rotation* option in Properties rotates the beam along its axis at the angle specified.

- Setting the *Start/End Level Offset* the same at each end raises or lowers the entire beam. For example, when wide flange beams are supporting open web steel joists (as shown in Figure 7–33), you need to offset that increment based on the specific joist's seat.

Structural Framing

Figure 7–33

> **Hint: Using 3D Snapping**
>
> When you draw beams, you can toggle on **3D Snapping** from the Options Bar. This allows you to snap to other beams or structural walls of different heights.
>
> You can also use 3D Snapping when placing beam systems using the Automatic Beam System tool. When you toggle on 3D Snapping, you have an additional option, which is **Walls Define Slope**. When selected, this option allows you to use walls to define the slop of your beam system.
>
> On the left in Figure 7–34, the **3D Snapping** and **Walls Define Slope** options are selected, while on the right they are not.
>
>
>
> Figure 7–34

Adding Beam Cantilevers and Cutbacks

Use this method to extend joists for a fascia system or in any situation in which a roof or slab extends past the main structure.

It is common to need a joist extension that cantilevers a bearing member. In the example shown in Figure 7–35, the joist seat needs to extend past the beam it bears on to frame into a cantilevered ridge beam. By modifying the individual joists, you can extend either end to meet the requirements.

Figure 7–35

To cantilever or cutback a beam that is joined to other structural elements, use the shape handles to drag it to a new location, or set the *Start* or *End Join Cutback* in Properties, as shown in Figure 7–36.

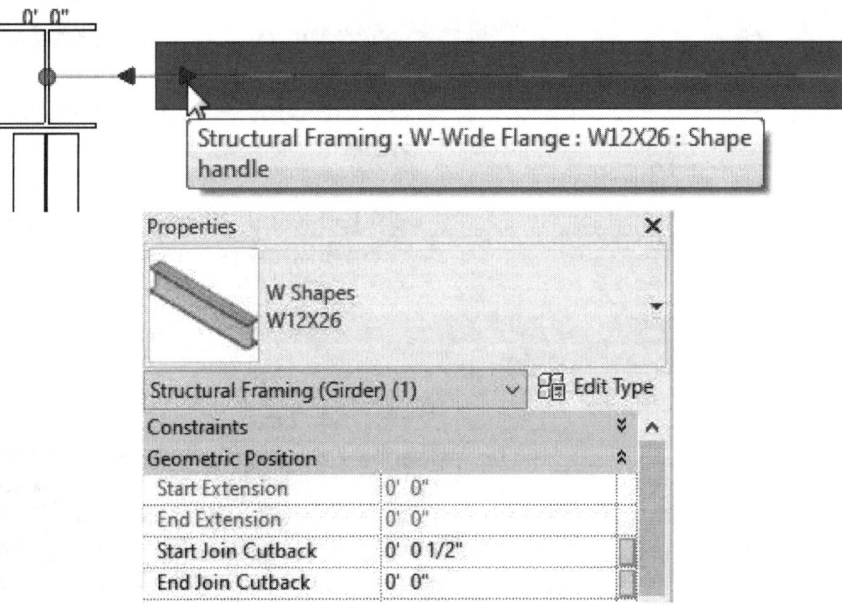

Figure 7–36

To cantilever a beam when the beam is not joined to other elements, you can use the **Drag Structural Framing Component End** shape handle (as shown in Figure 7–37), or set the *Start* or *End Extension* in Properties.

Structural Framing

Figure 7–37

- When modifying beams, you first need to unpin the individual beam you want to work with. Select it and click the

  (Prevent or allow change of element position) icon.

> **Hint: Structural Connections and Fabrication**
>
> Over 150 standard structural connections can be added to framing joins to share in-depth information about the join with the contractor and fabricator. You can also add fabrication elements, such as plates, bolts, and welds, and modify plates and other steel elements using copes and other cuts. These tools, which are beyond the scope of this learning guide, are found on the *Steel* tab, as shown in Figure 7–38.
>
>
>
> Figure 7–38

Changing the Cutback

Modifying the join connection of structural framing can be done by changing the cutback from the connected element. For example, the default cutback of the column shown in Figure 7–39 is the bounding box of the column, not the vertical support. You can change the reference to a more appropriate part of the framing.

You can select more than one element to adjust as long as they are connected to the same reference.

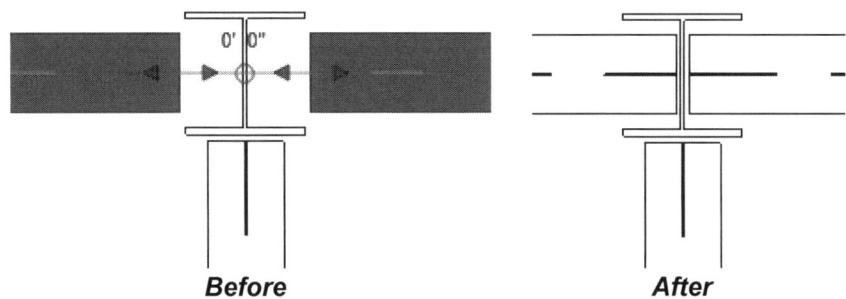

Figure 7–39

- You can change the reference in plan and 3D views if the *Display Level* is set to **Medium** or **Fine**.

> **Hint: Bounding Boxes**
>
> An element bounding box is an invisible rectangular box around the element that defines a single element and how it reacts to other elements. Figure 7–40 shows the bounding box for a column in dashed lines.
>
>
>
> Figure 7–40

How To: Adjust the Cutback of Structural Framing

1. Select the structural framing member you want to modify.
2. In the *Modify | Structural Framing* tab>Join Tools panel, click (Change Reference).
3. Select the reference point for alignment, as shown on the left in Figure 7–41. This can be another beam, a structural column, or a structural wall.

Before **After**

Figure 7–41

- The end of the member lengthens to the new reference location (it does not move the beam), as shown on the right in Figure 7–41.

4. In Properties, modify the *Start Join Cutback* or *End Join Cutback* distance, as needed.

- To return the beam end to its default setback position, click ⤺ (Change Reference) again and select the bounding box (dashed lines) of the other element.

Changing Justifications

Modifying the location of a framing element can be done by modifying the justification. You can set the horizontal (y) and vertical (z) justification points to one of nine different points, such as **Origin Left** (as shown in Figure 7–42). The location line remains in place, with the framing element moved to the new justification. You can also change the offset from the justification point in either the **y** (left to right) or **z** (top to bottom) directions. Both of these options can be modified either graphically or in Properties.

Figure 7–42

How To: Set the Justification of Framing Elements Graphically

1. Select the beam you want to modify.
2. In the *Modify | Structural Framing* tab>Justification panel, click ✥ (Justification Points), or type **JP**.

3. Select the justification points you want to use, as shown in Figure 7–43.

Figure 7–43

- The location line does not change, but the framing element repositions to the selected justification point.

- You can also modify the justification points using the *y Justification* and *z Justification* parameters in Properties, as shown in Figure 7–44.

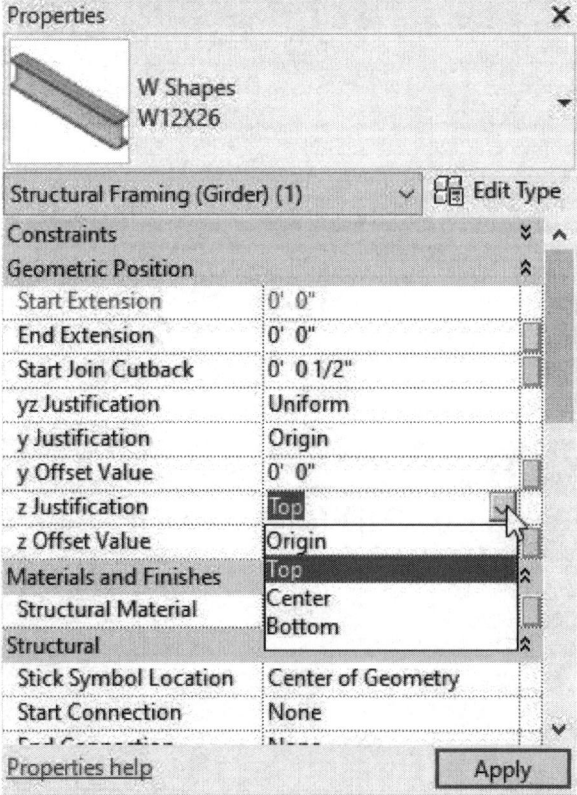

Figure 7–44

Structural Framing

How To: Change the Justification Offset Graphically

1. Select the structural framing element.
2. In the *Modify | Structural Framing* tab>Justification panel:
   - Modify the horizontal offset and distance by clicking ⌐ (y Offset), or type **JY**.
   - Modify the vertical offset and distance by clicking ⌐ (z Offset), or type **JZ**.
3. Select the offset start point and then the offset end point.

- You can also modify the offset values in Properties by using the *y Offset Value* and *z Offset Value* parameters.

- You can set the *yz Justification* (shown in Figure 7–45) to the following:
  - **Uniform:** The same justification offset is applied to both ends.
  - **Independent:** The justification offset can be different for each end.

  When the *yz Justification* is selected, you can set the *Start y* (or *Start z*) *Offset Value* and the *End y* (or *End z*) *Offset Value* in Properties.

Figure 7–45

> **Hint: Viewing Justifications**
>
> At the Coarse detail level, when you select the beam, the justification line is displayed, as shown in Figure 7–46.
>
>
>
> Figure 7–46
>
> When working in the Medium (or Fine) detail level, along with toggling on the location line in Visibility/Graphic Overrides, it can help to display the analytical model, as shown in
>
> Figure 7–47. In the View Control Bar, click (Show Analytical Model).
>
>
>
> Figure 7–47

Attaching a Column to a Beam

The columns that support the cantilever can be attached to the bottom of the framing member, as shown in Figure 7–48. This removes the need to estimate the actual bearing depth of the framing member and ensures that the column always remains connected to the beam.

Figure 7–48

Structural Framing

How To: Attach a Column to the Bottom of a Beam

1. Select a column.
2. In the *Modify | Structural Columns* tab>Modify Column panel, click (Attach Top/Base).
3. In the Options Bar, set the options as needed. If you need to add a bearing plate, set the *Offset from Attachment* value.
4. Select the beam that the column will attach to.

- You can also use this command to attach the base of a beam to structural footings. When the footing moves in height, the length of the column resizes to match.

Applying Beam Coping

When one beam connects with another beam, you might need to modify the connection. In the example shown in Figure 7–49, the lower joist-bearing beam runs into the perimeter beam. This is a coping situation.

Figure 7–49

How To: Cope Beams

1. Open a 3D, section, or detail view.
2. Zoom in to a beam-to-beam (or beam-to-column) connection.
3. In the *Modify* tab>Geometry panel, expand (Cope) and select (Apply Coping).
4. Select the beam to be coped first, followed by the column/beam from which to cut. The cope is then completed.
   - You can change the coping distance by selecting the beam and changing the *Coping Distance* value in Properties.

Editing Beam Joins

When you add beams to a project, there is a default layout to the beam joins. However, you might need to override the joins. You can do this by adjusting how the beams frame into each other, as shown in Figure 7–50.

Figure 7–50

How To: Edit Beam Joins

1. In the *Modify* tab>Geometry panel, click (Beam/Column Joins). The work area switches to sketch mode.
   - Only the beams and/or columns that can be changed are highlighted.
   - You cannot use this tool on beams that are attached to vertical columns.
2. In the Options Bar, specify the types of beams that you want to work with, as shown in Figure 7–51.

Figure 7–51

3. Click the **Change Beam Status** control to toggle the join, as shown in Figure 7–52.

Figure 7–52

Structural Framing

4. Click (Beam/Column Joins) again or click (Modify) to end the command.

   - If you are mitering a corner, you can lock the miter, as shown in Figure 7–53.

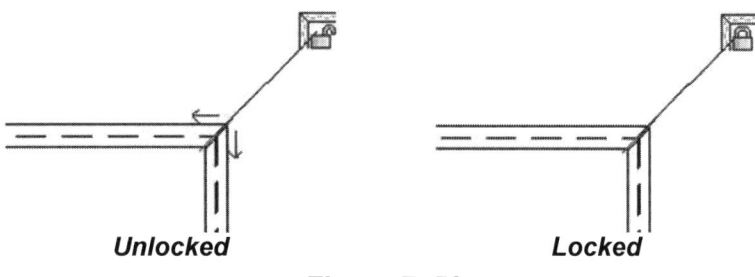

Unlocked   Locked

Figure 7–53

Hint: Join Status

You can modify the *Join Status* of structural frames to position framing that butts against a wall or other beams. Right-click on the join control (the circle), select **Disallow Join** (as shown on the left in Figure 7–54), and make the required modifications. Click **Allow Join** to rejoin the elements.

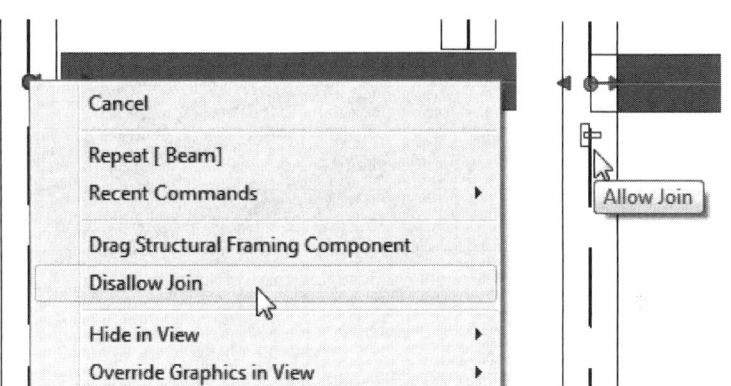

Figure 7–54

- *Join Status* is a field that can be used in schedules. You can modify the join status in the schedule and it will update in the model.

Practice 7b   Modify Structural Framing

Practice Objectives

- Modify beam level offsets.
- Add beam systems.

In this practice, you will modify beam level offsets for correct joist bearing and add beam systems using the automatic method where you can. Then, you will sketch beam systems in areas where they cannot be automatically placed, as shown in Figure 7–55.

Figure 7–55

Task 1 - Modify beam level offsets.

1. Open **Structural-Framing.rvt** from the practice files folder.
2. Open the **Structural Plans: TOS-14 ROOF** view.
3. Hide the grid lines.

Structural Framing

If you selected bracing elements, you need to filter them out.

4. For this level, you need to lower the beams of each bay. Select all of the beams running in the north-south direction for the joist bearing, including the arc beams, as shown in Figure 7–56.

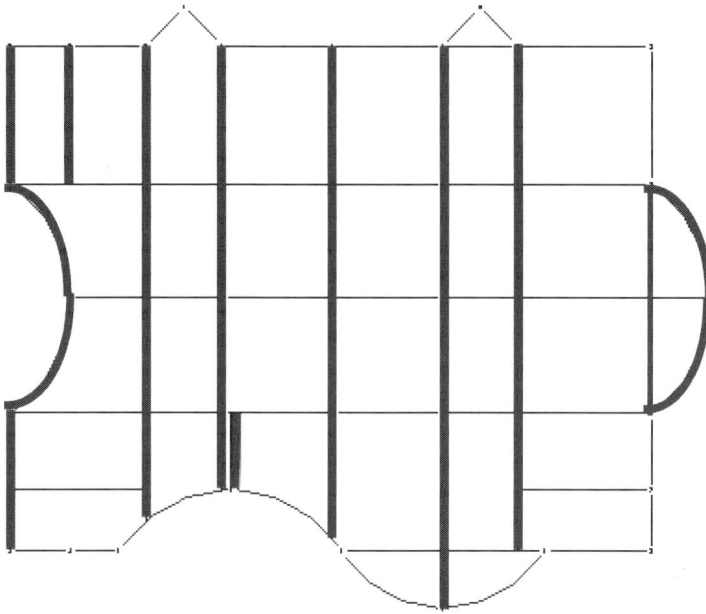

Figure 7–56

5. In Properties, change both the *Start Level Offset* and *End Level Offset* to (negative) **-2-1/2"**.

6. Click **Apply**.

7. Open a 3D view and zoom in on one of the top floor intersections. The north-south girders should be displayed below the east-west girders, as shown in Figure 7–57.

Figure 7–57

8. Save the project.

Task 2 - Add beam systems.

1. Switch to the **Structural Plans: TOS-14 ROOF** view.

2. In the *Insert* tab>Load from Library panel, click (Load Family).

3. In the Load Family dialog box, navigate to the practice files *Custom Families* folder and select **K-Series Bar Joist-Rod Web.rfa**, then click **Open**.

4. In the Specify Types dialog box, select **16K7** from the list and click **OK**.

5. In the *Structure* tab>Structure panel, click (Beam System). In the Options Bar, set the following parameters:
   - *Beam Type:* **16K7**
   - *Layout Rule:* **Maximum Spacing**
   - *Maximum Spacing:* **6'-0"**

6. Use (Automatic Beam System) to fill in as many bays as possible, as shown in Figure 7–58.

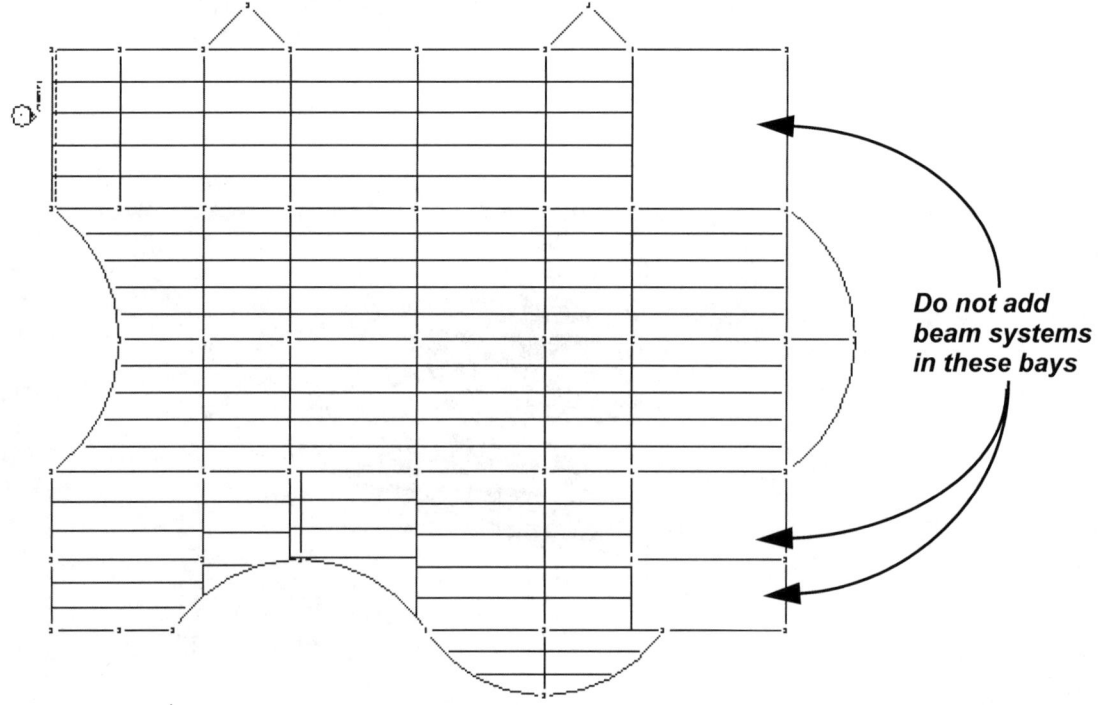

Figure 7–58

- If the error shown in Figure 7–59 opens, the space for the joist might be too small to be created by the **Beam System** command. Click **Delete Type**. You can add a beam separately, as needed.

These errors occur so you are aware of potential problems, and they should be addressed. They are an important part of using the BIM model process.

Figure 7–59

- If you end up with areas where the automatic method does not work (such as the example shown in Figure 7–60), switch to (Sketch Beam System). When sketching beam systems, in Properties, in the *Identity Data* section, change *Tag new members in view* to **None**.

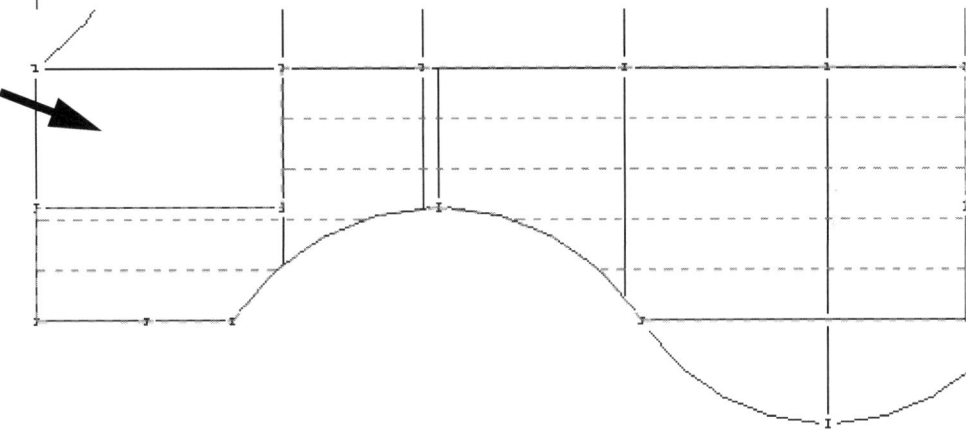

Figure 7–60

7. Click (Modify).

8. Switch to the 3D view to see the newly placed joists.

9. Save and close the project.

7.3 Adding Trusses

A truss can be added to a project using the same basic method as placing a beam. Trusses are typically composed of one or more triangular sections, as shown in Figure 7–61. These sections are constructed with structural members whose ends are connected at joints, which are referred to as nodes. As various forces act on these nodes, the triangular shape provides structural stability to prevent bending.

Figure 7–61

The elements of a truss are:

- the lower horizontal member, called the **bottom chord**;
- the upper horizontal member, called the **top chord**; and
- the series of structural framing elements that stabilize the truss, called the **Web**.

The top and bottom chords fulfill the same function as a beam's top and bottom flanges. The web takes the place of the beam's continuous plate.

How To: Add Trusses

1. In the *Structure* tab>Structure panel, click (Structural Trusses).
2. In the Type Selector, select the type of truss you want to use.

    - Click (Load Family) and navigate to the *Structural Trusses* folder in the Revit Library to add families to the project.

3. In the *Modify | Place Truss* tab>Draw panel, click (Line) or (Pick Lines) and add the trusses to the project.

Attaching Trusses to Roofs

Trusses can be attached to roofs or floor slabs. They can also follow the slope of the roof and automatically extend to fit, as shown in Figure 7–62.

Figure 7–62

How To: Attach Trusses to Roofs

1. In the *Modify | Structural Trusses* tab>Modify Truss panel, click (Attach Top/Bottom).
2. In the Options Bar, set *Attach Trusses* to **Top** or **Bottom**.
3. Select the roof or floor element. The truss attaches to the element and follows the angle or slope, as shown in Figure 7–63.

Figure 7–63

- The top chord must be one continuous line in the family. If it is broken into segments, attaching it might not work properly.

- Verify that the bottom chord is specified as the bearing chord in the element properties of the truss. This ensures that the roof loads are carried throughout the truss appropriately.

- If the roof/floor slab does not cover the length of the truss, an error message opens and you might have to detach the truss.

Setting Framing Types in Trusses

When truss families are created, they can include structural framing members for the chords and webs. However, they often just use default members. Therefore, you need to specify the precise framing types you want to use in the project.

In the Type Properties dialog box, select the *Structural Framing Type* from a list of families loaded into the project, as shown in Figure 7–64. This should be set for the **Top Chords**, **Vertical Webs**, **Diagonal Webs**, and **Bottom Chords**.

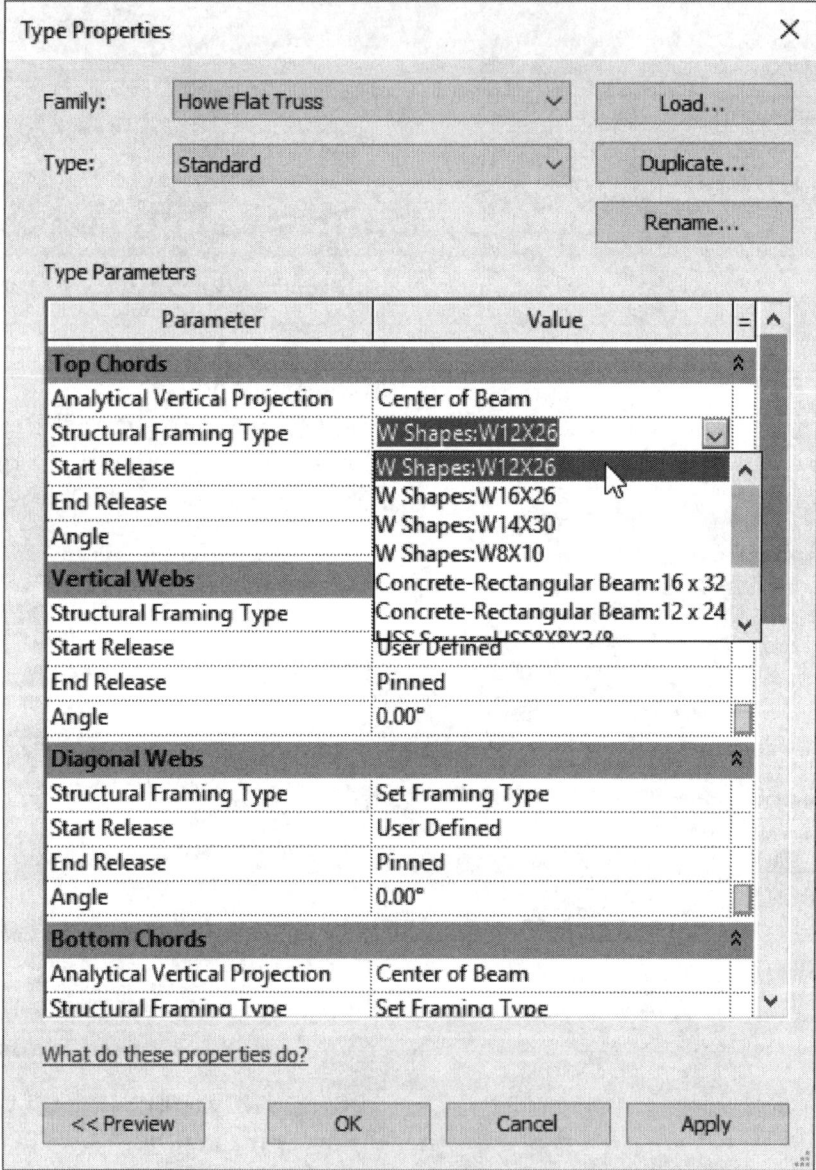

Figure 7–64

- To select an entire truss, ensure that the dashed lines are displayed, as shown on the left in Figure 7–65. To select one element of the truss, press <Tab> until the element that you want to select is highlighted, as shown on the right in Figure 7–65.

Figure 7–65

- Individual truss members are pinned to the truss framework. If you want to modify one of these, you need to click

  (Prevent or allow change of element position) to unpin only that member.

- You can rotate trusses and specify if the chords rotate with the truss. In Properties, type in a *Rotation Angle* and select or clear *Rotate Chords With Truss*, as shown in Figure 7–66.

Chords not rotated   Chords rotated

Figure 7–66

Practice 7c Add Trusses

Practice Objectives

- Set up a truss type.
- Add trusses to a project.
- Attach trusses to a roof.

In this practice, you will set up a truss using specific structural framing types for the chords and webs. You will then draw a truss and array it across an open span. Finally, you will attach the trusses to an existing roof element, as shown in Figure 7–67.

Figure 7–67

Task 1 - Set up a truss type.

1. Open **Structural-Trusses.rvt** from the practice files folder.

2. In the *Structure* tab>Structure panel, click (Truss).

3. In the Type Selector, select **Howe Flat Truss: Standard**. In Properties, click (Edit Type).

4. In the Type Properties dialog box, click **Duplicate**.

5. In the Name dialog box, type **Skylight** and click **OK**.

6. In the Type Properties dialog box, set the following properties, as shown in Figure 7–68:
   - **Top Cords** and **Bottom Chords:**
     Set the *Structural Framing Type* to **LL-Double Angle:2L6X4X5/8LLBB**.
   - **Vertical Webs** and **Diagonal Webs:**
     Set the *Structural Framing Type* to **LL-Double Angle:2L3X2-1/2X1/2LLBB**.

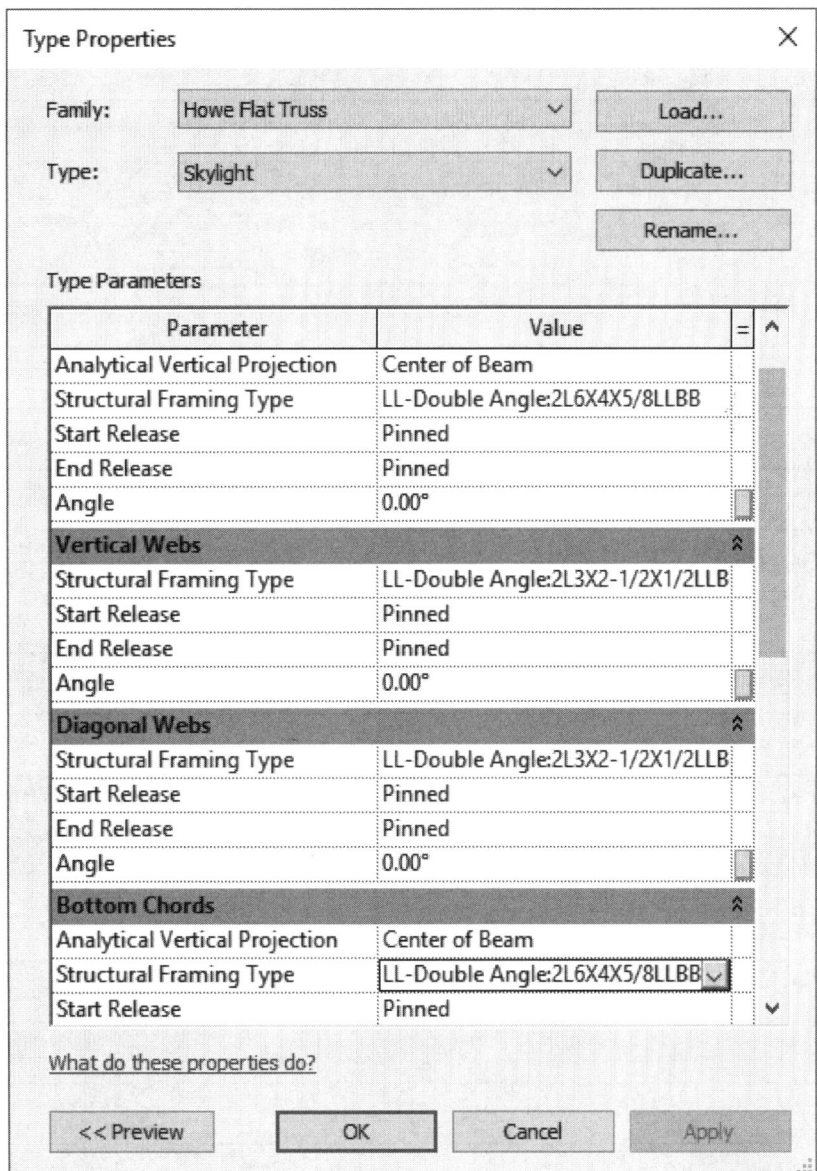

Figure 7–68

7. Click **OK**.

8. Save the project.

Task 2 - Add trusses.

1. Open the **Structural Plans: TOS-14 ROOF** view. Some of the structural framing has been removed in this plan to make way for a large skylight, as shown in Figure 7–69.

Figure 7–69

2. Start the (Truss) command.

3. In the Type Selector, verify that the **Howe Flat Truss: Skylight** is selected.

4. In Properties, set the *Bearing Chord* to **Bottom** and the *Truss Height* to **4'-0"**.

5. Draw the first truss between grid intersections **C5** and **C7**, as shown in Figure 7–70.

Structural Framing

Image has been cropped for clarification.

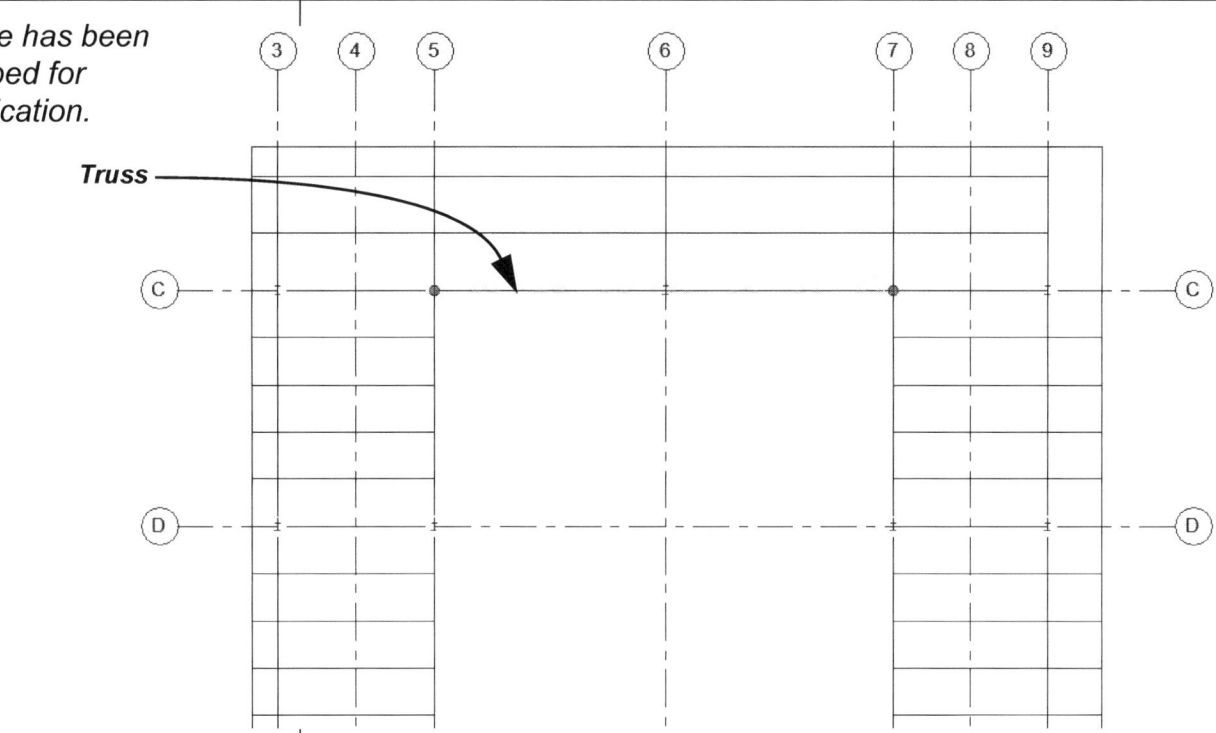

Figure 7–70

6. Click (Modify) and select the new truss.

7. In the *Modify | Structural Trusses* tab>Modify panel, click (Array).

8. In the Options Bar:

    - Select (Linear).
    - Uncheck **Group And Associate**.
    - Set *Number* to **15**.
    - Set *Move To:* to **Last**.

9. To specify the length of the array, click on grid line **C** and then on grid line **E**.

10. Click (Modify).

11. Open the **3D Views: Roof and Skylight** view and rotate the view to display the trusses, as shown in Figure 7–71.

Figure 7–71

12. Save the project.

Task 3 - Attach the trusses to a roof.

1. Open the Visibility/Graphic Overrides dialog box and toggle on **Roofs**. An existing roof (referencing the location of the skylight) displays.

2. In the Quick Access Toolbar, click (Close Inactive Windows) so that only the 3D view displays.

3. Open the **Elevations (Building Elevations): East** and **South** views.

4. Type **WT** to tile the three views and **ZA** so that they are all zoomed out fully.

5. Zoom in on the skylight roof in the two elevation views, similar to that shown in Figure 7–72.

Figure 7–72

6. In the **Elevation: East** view, select one truss, then right-click and select **Select all Instances>In Entire Project**.

7. In the *Modify |Structural Trusses* tab>Modify Truss panel, click (Attach Top/Bottom) and verify in the Options Bar that *Attach Trusses* is set to **Top**.

8. Select the roof. Allow time for it all to process until the trusses expand to touch the roof, as shown in Figure 7–73.

Figure 7–73

9. Make the **3D View: Roof and Skylight** view active and type **TW** to return to the tabbed view.

10. Save and close the project.

Chapter Review Questions

1. When placing a beam from the Options Bar, which of the following is NOT an option?

   a. Structural Usage
   b. Placement Plane
   c. 3D Snapping
   d. At Columns

2. Which of the following describes a beam system?

   a. Parallel beams grouped together after they are placed.
   b. Parallel beams placed at the same time.
   c. All beams in a bay grouped together after they are placed.
   d. All beams in a bay placed at the same time.

3. In a plan view, which of the following changes the display to show the stick symbol for beams, as shown in Figure 7–74?

   Figure 7–74

   a. Detail Level: Coarse
   b. Detail Level: Medium
   c. Visual Style: Wireframe
   d. Visual Style: Hidden

4. How do you create sloped beams such as those shown in Figure 7–75?

Figure 7–75

a. Specify the *Slope* before you start drawing the beam.

b. Specify the *Start/End Level Offset* before you start drawing the beam.

c. Change the *Slope* after you have drawn the beam.

d. Change the *Start/End Level Offset* after you have drawn the beam.

5. Where do you assign the structural member types and sizes for the components of a truss, such as that shown in Figure 7–76? (Select all that apply.)

Figure 7–76

a. In Family Types
b. In Properties
c. In Type Properties
d. In the Options Bar

Command Summary

Button	Command	Location
Clipboard		
	Copy to Clipboard	• **Ribbon:** *Modify* tab>Clipboard panel • **Shortcut:** <Ctrl>+C
	Paste	• **Ribbon:** *Modify* tab>Clipboard panel • **Shortcut:** <Ctrl>+<V>
	(Paste) Aligned to Selected Levels	• **Ribbon:** *Modify* tab>Clipboard panel
	(Paste) Aligned to Selected View	• **Ribbon:** *Modify* tab>Clipboard panel
Structural Framing Elements		
	Beam	• **Ribbon:** *Structure* tab>Structure panel
	Beam System	• **Ribbon:** *Structure* tab>Structure panel
	Brace	• **Ribbon:** *Structure* tab>Structure panel • **Shortcut:** BR
	Structural Trusses	• **Ribbon:** *Structure* tab>Structure panel
Structural Framing Modification		
	Apply Coping	• **Ribbon:** *Modify* tab>Geometry panel, expand Cope
	Attach Top/Base	• **Ribbon:** *Modify	Structural Columns* tab>Modify Column panel
	Attach Top/Bottom	• **Ribbon:** *Modify	Structural Trusses* tab>Modify Truss panel
	Beam/Column Joins	• **Ribbon:** *Modify* tab>Geometry panel
	Change Reference	• **Ribbon:** *Modify	Structural Framing* tab>Join Tools panel
	Connection	• **Ribbon:** *Structure* tab>Connection panel
	Detach Top/Base	• **Ribbon:** *Modify	Structural Columns* tab>Modify Column panel
	Detach Top/Bottom	• **Ribbon:** *Modify	Structural Trusses* tab>Modify Truss panel

		Justification Points	• **Ribbon:** *Modify	Structural Framing* tab>Justification panel • **Shortcut:** JP
		Offset	• **Ribbon:** *Modify	Structural Framing* tab>Justification panel
		y Offset	• **Ribbon:** *Modify	Structural Framing* tab>Justification panel • **Shortcut:** JY
		z Offset	• **Ribbon:** *Modify	Structural Framing* tab>Justification panel • **Shortcut:** JZ

Chapter 8

Adding Structural Slabs

Structural slabs can be used for foundation slabs (slab on grade), floors, and roofs. Slab edges can be added to foundation slabs and floors to provide additional stability. For multi-story buildings, you can cut holes in the slabs, either individually or by creating a shaft that passes through several slabs.

Learning Objectives in This Chapter

- Create slabs for foundations, structural floors, and roofs.
- Add slab edges for stability along each side of the slab.
- Create shaft openings that pass through multiple levels for elevators and stairwells.

8.1 Modeling Structural Slabs

Floors, some roofs, and foundation slabs (shown in Figure 8–1) are created by sketching a boundary and then applying options such as span direction and slope. After you create a structural slab, you can add and modify the slab thickness and edges.

The term slab in this topic applies to structural foundation slabs, floors, and roofs.

Figure 8–1

How To: Place a Structural Slab for Foundations or Floors

1. In the *Structure* tab>Foundation panel, click (Slab), or in the *Structure* tab>Structure panel, click (Floor: Structural), or type **SB**.
2. In the Type Selector, select the slab or floor type you want to use.
3. In Properties, you can adjust *Constraints* and *Structural* values.
4. In the Options Bar, you can set an offset that places the sketched line at a distance offset from a selected wall or another sketched line.
5. The **Extend into wall (to core)** option is also available in the Options Bar. Use this if you want the slab to cut into the wall. For example, the slab would cut through the gypsum wall board and the air space but would stop at a core layer, such as CMU.
6. In the *Modify | Create Floor Boundary* tab>Draw panel, use one of the following options to create a closed boundary:

   - Use the Draw tools, such as (Line) or (Pick Lines) when the slab is not defined by walls or other structural elements.

- Use (Pick Walls) when walls define the perimeter.
- Use (Pick Supports) and select structural walls or beams if support beams have already been placed in the project.

7. Click (Span Direction) to modify the direction for floor spans. The first pick or line drawn is automatically the boundary line and is displayed with the span direction symbol, as shown in Figure 8–2.

8. (Flip) switches the inside/outside status of the boundary location if you have a wall selected, as shown in Figure 8–2.

Figure 8–2

- If you select one of the boundary sketches, you can also set **Cantilevers** for *Concrete* or *Steel*, as shown in Figure 8–3.

Figure 8–3

- Each line that defines the perimeter of the slab has its own set of properties. This is because different sides of the building can have different slab edge conditions. Setting a cantilever can control the detail, as shown in Figure 8–4.

Figure 8–4

- If you specify a cantilever, such as the example shown in Figure 8–5, both the magenta line for the sketch and the black line for the actual slab edge display. This affects how the decking is terminated.

Figure 8–5

- This does not add a pour stop or edge angle. You can do so after you finish the sketch.

- To create an opening inside the sketch, create a separate closed loop inside the first sketch, as shown in Figure 8–6.

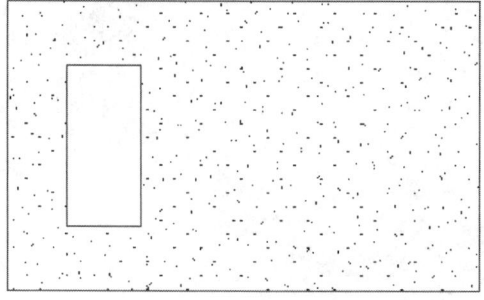

Figure 8–6

Adding Structural Slabs

9. In the *Modify | Create Floor Boundary* tab>Mode panel, click (Finish Edit Mode).

- If you create a floor on an upper level, an alert box displays asking if you want the walls below to be attached to the underside of the floor and its level. If you have a variety of wall heights, it is better to click **No** and attach the walls separately.

- Another alert box might open referencing joining geometry between the floor/roof and walls. You can automatically join the geometry now or later.

- If the *Visual Style* is set to (Hidden Line), the slab hides any lines that are underneath it, usually displaying as a dashed line, as shown in Figure 8–7.

Figure 8–7

How To: Place a Roof Slab

Structural floor elements are occasionally used in place of roof elements.

1. In the *Architecture* tab>Build panel, expand (Roof) and click (Roof by Footprint)
2. In the Type Selector, select the roof type you want to use.
3. In the *Modify | Create Roof Footprint* tab>Draw panel, use the Draw tools to create a closed boundary, such as (Line), (Pick Lines), or (Pick Walls) when walls define the perimeter.
4. In the Options Bar, set the slope and overhang options. For a flat roof, clear the **Defines slope** option and set *Overhang* to **0**, as shown in Figure 8–8.

Figure 8–8

5. Click (Finish Edit Mode).

Modifying Slabs

You can change a slab to a different type in the Type Selector. In Properties, you can modify parameters including the *Height Offset From Level*, as shown for a structural floor in Figure 8–9. When you have a slab selected, you can also edit the boundaries.

The slab type controls the thickness of a slab.

For information on slab types, see B.4 Creating Slab Types.

Figure 8–9

How To: Modify the Slab Boundaries

1. Select a slab. You might need to hover your cursor over an element near the slab and press <Tab> until the type displays in the Status Bar or in a tooltip, as shown in Figure 8–10.

Figure 8–10

> **Hint: Selecting Slab Faces**
>
> If it is difficult to select the slab edges, toggle on 🗔 (Select elements by face). This enables you to select the slab face in addition to the edges. This is also helpful to use when selecting walls in elevation or section views.

2. In the *Modify* contextual tab>Mode panel, click 🗒 (Edit Boundary). You are placed in sketch mode.

3. Modify the sketch lines by using the Draw tools, controls, and other modify tools.
   - Double-click on a slab to move directly to editing the boundary.
   - When modifying a slab, you can add an opening by drawing a closed loop within the slab boundaries.
   - Sketches can be edited in plan and 3D views, but not in elevations. If you try to edit a sketch in an elevation view, you are prompted to select another view for editing.

4. Click ✓ (Finish Edit Mode).
   - You can modify the Foundation Span Direction symbol (shown in Figure 8–11) after a slab has been placed by selecting it, clicking (Align Perpendicular) in the *Modify | Foundation Span Direction Symbol* tab, and selecting the slab edge, grid line, or beam edge to realign the span direction. This is useful if you are placing metal decking.

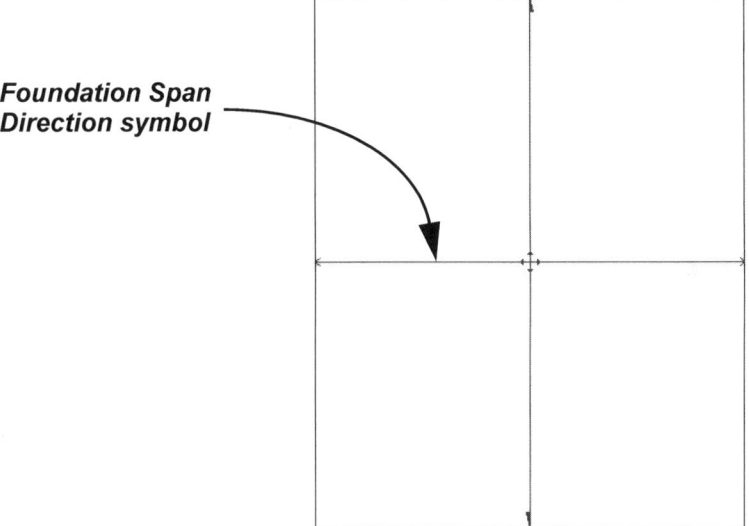

Figure 8–11

Slab Edges

Cutting a section through the objects you want to join helps to display them more clearly.

You can add elements to a foundation slab or structural floor for a haunched or thickened slab edge, as shown in Figure 8–12. Once the slab edge is in place, it needs to be joined to the slab or structural floor.

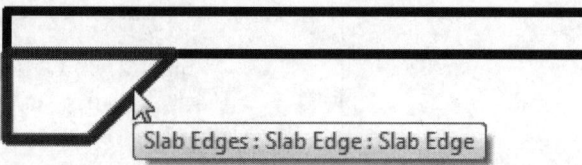

Figure 8–12

- Slab edges cannot be applied to roof elements.

How To: Place a Slab Edge

1. Open a 3D view showing the slab.
2. In the *Structure* tab>Foundation panel, expand (Slab), or in the *Structure* tab>Structure panel, expand (Floor) and click (Floor: Slab Edge).
3. In the Type Selector, select the slab edge type.
4. Select the edges of the slab or floor where you want to apply the slab edge, as shown in Figure 8–13. You can press <Tab> to highlight and select all sides of the slab.

Figure 8–13

Joining Geometry

If the material is not exactly the same, a thin line still separates the elements.

Join Geometry is a versatile command used to clean up intersections. The elements remain separate, but the intersections are cleaned up. It can be used with many types of elements, including slabs, floors, walls, and roofs. A typical use is to connect slab edges with the slab, as shown in the section views in Figure 8–14.

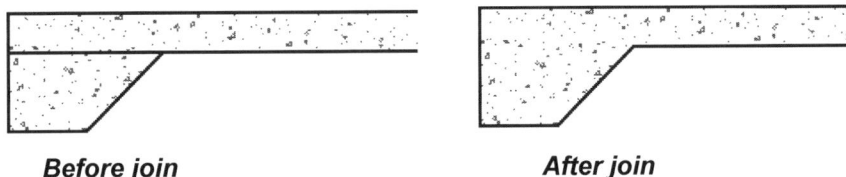

Before join   **After join**

Figure 8–14

- Joining geometry makes two separate elements display as one, but they can still be modified individually after being joined.

How To: Join Geometry

1. In the *Modify* tab>Geometry panel, expand (Join) and click (Join Geometry).
2. For the first pick, you will select the element you want to join to another. For the second pick, you will select the element to be joined to.

- If you toggle on the **Multiple Join** option in the Options Bar, you can select several elements to join to the first selection.

- To remove the join, expand (Join), click (Unjoin Geometry), and select the elements to unjoin.

Practice 8a   Model Structural Slabs

Practice Objectives

- Add a slab with an edge.
- Add structural floors.

In this practice, you will create slab foundations at the base of elevator shafts and add a slab edge to them. You will also create a floor slab and then copy and modify the type to create the rest of the floors and roof deck, as shown in Figure 8–15.

Figure 8–15

- This practice file contains additional wall elements.

Task 1 - Add slab foundations for elevator shafts.

1. Open **Structure-Slab.rvt** from the practice files folder.

2. Open the **Structural Plans: T.O. FOOTING** view.

3. Zoom in to the lower-right corner of the building to the elevator shaft between grid intersections **E9** and **F10**, where the section marker is.

Adding Structural Slabs

4. In the *Structure* tab>Foundation panel, click (Slab).

5. In the Type Selector, select **Foundation Slab: 12" Foundation Slab.**

6. In the Options Bar, set the *Offset* to **2'-0"**, and in the *Modify | Create Floor Boundary* tab>Draw panel, click (Pick Walls).

7. Click on each wall to create a boundary line, as shown in Figure 8–16.

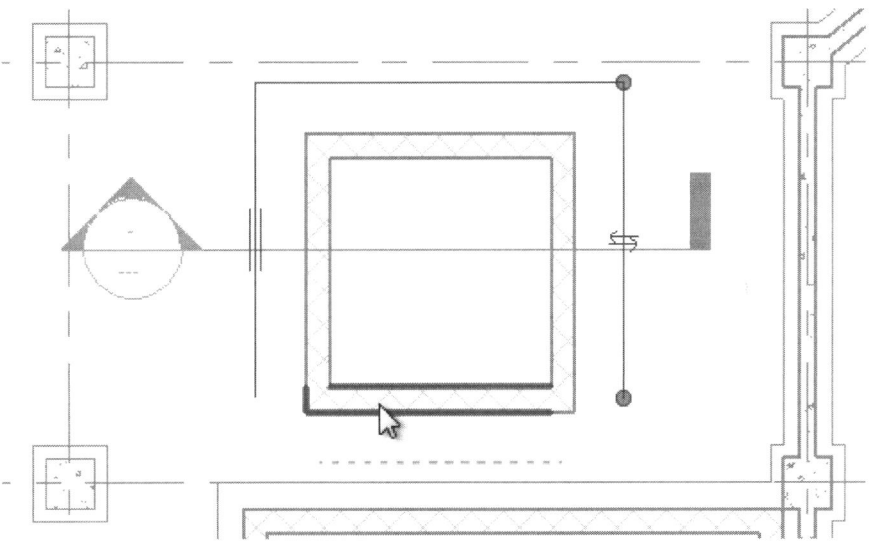

Figure 8–16

8. Click (Finish Edit Mode).

9. Click (Modify) and select the **Foundation Span Direction** symbol, which is automatically added when you finish the sketch. Open the Visibility/Graphic Overrides dialog box (type **VG** or **VV**) and on the *Annotation Categories* tab, turn off **Span Direction Symbol**. Alternatively, you can delete the symbol in this view (it can be added again in a working document view).

10. Save the project.

Task 2 - Add a slab edge to the slab.

1. Open the default 3D view.

2. In the View Control Bar, click (Hide Analytical Model).

    - Once complete, the icon displays as and the tooltip displays **Show Analytical Model**.

3. Select at least one beam, beam system, column, and wall. in the View Control Bar, expand (Temporary Hide/Isolate) and select **Hide Category**. Hide any other elements that might be in the way of seeing just the slabs, such as rebar.

4. In the View Control Bar, set the *Visual Style* to (Consistent Colors).

5. Use the ViewCube to rotate the model so you are viewing the bottom of the slab, as shown in Figure 8–17. (Hint: In the ViewCube, click the corner at the intersection of the **FRONT**, **RIGHT**, and **BOTTOM** planes.)

Figure 8–17

6. Zoom in on the slab.

7. In the *Structure* tab>Foundation panel, expand (Slab) and click (Floor: Slab Edge).

Adding Structural Slabs

If you add a slab edge in a plan view, the software selects the top edge of the slab rather than the bottom.

8. Select the four bottom edges of the slab, as shown in Figure 8–18. Rotate the view as required to see each edge.

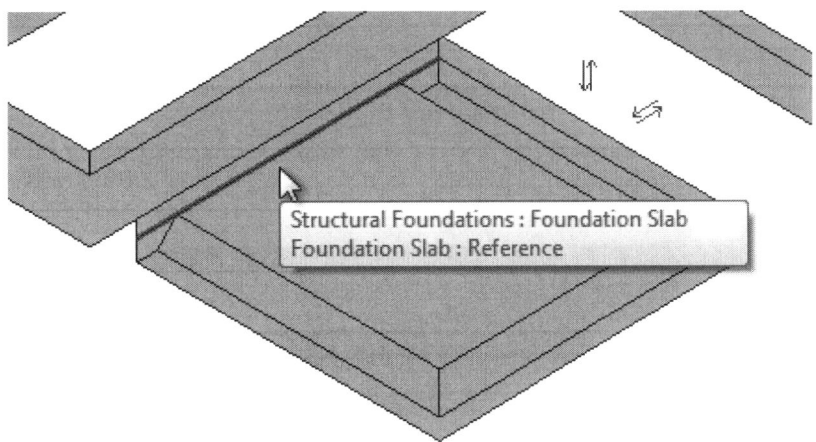

Figure 8–18

9. Click (Modify).

10. Reorient the view and select **Reset Temporary Hide/Isolate**.

11. Switch back to the **Structural Plans: T.O. FOOTING** view and double-click on the section heads arrow to open the section of the slab. The geometry should look similar to that shown in Figure 8–19.

Figure 8–19

12. In the *Modify* tab>Geometry panel, click (Join). Select the foundation and then the thickened slab edge. You only need to select one segment of the edge as it is one element.

13. Return to the **Structural Plans: T.O. FOOTING** view.

Image has been cropped for clarification.

14. Select the slab and copy it to the elevator shaft located between grid intersections **B9** and **C10**, as shown in Figure 8–20.

Figure 8–20

15. Click in an empty area in the view to clear the selection.
16. Save the project.

Task 3 - Add a structural floor to the ground floor level.

1. Open the **Structural Plans: 00 GROUND FLOOR** view.

2. In the *Structure* tab>Structure panel, click (Floor: Structural).

3. In the Type Selector, select **Floor: 6" Concrete**. In Properties, set the *Height Offset From Level* to **0'-0"**.

4. In the *Modify | Create Floor Boundary* tab>Draw panel, click (Pick Walls).

5. In the Options Bar, set the *Offset* to **0** and clear the checkmark from **Extend into wall (to core)**.

6. Hover over one of the perimeter walls and press <Tab> until all walls are highlighted, then click to select all of the walls, as shown in Figure 8–21. Ensure the cursor is on the outside of the wall, as shown in Figure 8–22. Click to accept the selection.

Figure 8–21 **Figure 8–22**

- If you selected the inside of the walls, use the Flip control to relocate the sketch lines to the outside of the walls.

7. In the Mode panel, click (Finish Edit Mode).

8. Click **Attach** in the Attaching to floor dialog box to attach walls that go up to this floor's level to its bottom.

9. Click in an empty area in the view to clear the selection.

10. Zoom out and save the project.

Task 4 - Add floor slabs to the rest of the floors.

1. Open the default 3D view and select the slab.

2. In the *Modify | Floors* tab>Clipboard panel, click (Copy to Clipboard).

3. In the same panel, expand (Paste) and click (Aligned to Selected Levels).

4. In the Select Levels dialog box, select **TOS-1ST FLOOR** and click **OK**.

5. The new slab is highlighted on level **TOS-1ST FLOOR**, as shown in Figure 8–23. In the Type Selector, change the floor type to **Floor: 3" LW Concrete on 2" Metal Deck**.

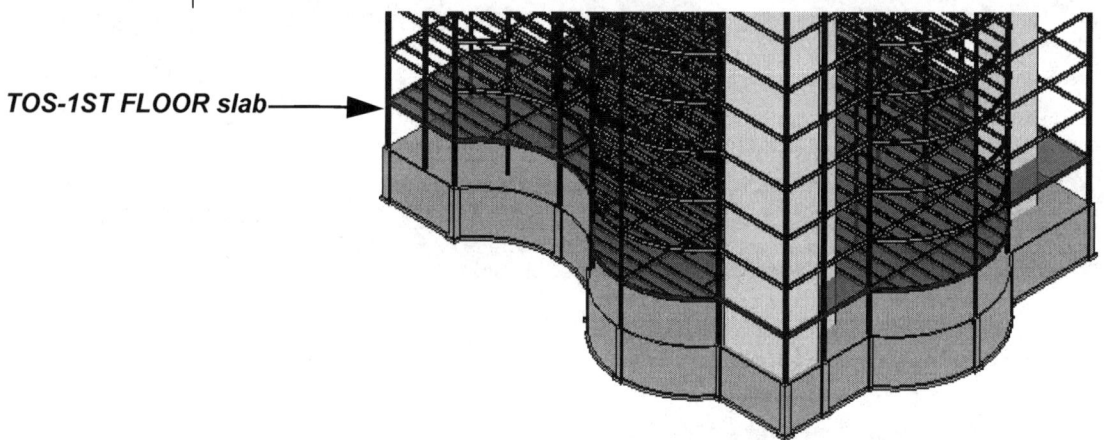

Figure 8–23

6. In Properties, under *Constraints*, change the *Height Offset From Level* to **5"** to leave room for the steel structure below the slab. Click **Apply**.

7. Using **Copy to the Clipboard** and **Paste Aligned to Selected Levels**, copy the metal deck floor to the rest of the floors, from **TOS-2ND FLOOR** up to **TOS-14 ROOF**.

8. Zoom out to see the entire building. The top slab is still selected, as shown on the right in Figure 8–24. In the Type Selector, change the type to **Floor: 1 1/2" Metal Roof Deck**, and in Properties, change the *Height Offset From Level* to **0'-1 1/2"**, as shown on the left in Figure 8–24.

Figure 8–24

9. Click in an empty area in the view to clear the selection.
10. Save the project.

Task 5 - Add a slab edge to the ground floor.

Slab edges are copied with the slab. Since a slab edge is not required on the upper floors, add the slab edge after copying the slab.

1. Zoom in on the ground floor slab.

2. Change the *Visual Style* to 🗔 (Wireframe).

3. In the *Structure* tab>Foundation panel, expand 🗀 (Slab) and click 🗀 (Floor: Slab Edge).

4. Hover over the bottom edge of the ground floor slab and press <Tab> to select the entire chain of lines.

5. Click to place the slab edge. It is placed around the entire edge of the slab, as shown in Figure 8–25.

Figure 8–25

6. Click (Modify).

7. Zoom out (Hint: Type **ZE**) to see the overall 3D view of the model, and return the *Visual Style* to (Consistent Colors).

8. Save and close the project.

8.2 Creating Shaft Openings

Shaft openings are designed to create a void through multiple levels in the structure, cutting through only floors/slabs, roofs, and ceilings. Structural components like beams, walls, and framing can pass through the opening, as shown in Figure 8–26. If the geometry of the shaft opening changes or moves on one level, it automatically updates on all levels.

Figure 8–26

How To: Create a Shaft Opening

1. In the *Structure* tab>Opening panel, click (Shaft Opening).
2. In the *Modify | Create Shaft Opening Sketch* tab>Draw panel, click (Boundary Line) and draw a line to define the opening.
3. In the Draw panel, click (Symbolic Line) and add lines that show the opening symbol in plan view.
4. In Properties, set the following:
   - *Base and Top Constraint*
   - *Base and Top Offset* or *Unconnected Height*

5. In the Options Bar, set the *Offset* and select **Chain**, if needed.

6. Click ✓ (Finish Edit Mode) to create the opening.

   - When using ▶ (Pick Walls) or other drawing tools to define the perimeter of the opening, you can select the Flip control to flip the lines to the outside, as shown in Figure 8–27.

Figure 8–27

   - A shaft opening element can include symbolic lines that repeat on each level, displaying the shaft in a plan view.

7. A shaft is a separate element from the floor, roof, ceiling, or wall, and can be deleted without selecting a host element.

Adding Structural Slabs

Practice 8b Create Shaft Openings

Practice Objective

- Create shaft openings.

In this practice, you will add shaft openings in the two elevator shafts and the stairwell, as shown in Figure 8–28.

Figure 8–28

Task 1 - Add shaft openings.

1. Open **Structural-Shafts.rvt** from the practice files folder.

2. Open the **Structural Plans: T.O. FOOTING** view. Zoom in on the stairwell between grid intersections **F9.1** and **G10**, in the lower-right corner.

3. In the *Structure* tab>Opening panel, click (Shaft).

4. In the *Modify | Create Shaft Opening Sketch* tab>Draw panel, ensure that (Boundary Line) is highlighted and click (Pick Walls).

5. Verify that in the Options Bar, the *Offset* is **0'-0"** and **Extend into wall (to core)** is unchecked.

6. Select the exterior face of the masonry walls around the stairwell (select one wall and press <Tab> to select the chain of walls). If needed, select the Flip control to flip the lines to the exterior side of the walls, as shown in Figure 8–29.

Figure 8–29

7. In the *Draw* panel, click (Symbolic Line).

8. Using (Line), draw an **X** in the opening, as shown in Figure 8–30.

Figure 8–30

9. In the Mode panel, click (Finish Edit Mode).

10. Repeat the procedure for the two elevator shafts. Ensure that the shaft openings are aligned with the outside faces of the shaft walls.

11. Zoom to fit the view and save the project.

Task 2 - Modify the shaft properties.

1. Create a building section through the three shafts, limiting the width of the section so that it does not display the entire building.

2. Open the section view. The shafts do not display, but you can hover over one of them near the base of the footing and select it. The shaft only extends through one set of floors, as shown in Figure 8–31.

Figure 8–31

3. Hold <Ctrl> and select the other two shafts.

4. In Properties, set the following parameters:

    - *Base Constraint:* **T.O. FOOTING**
    - *Base Offset:* **1"**
    - *Top Constraint:* **Up to level: TOS-14TH ROOF**
    - *Top Offset:* (negative) **-1'-3"**

5. Zoom out to see that the shafts now expand from the top of the footing to just below the roof.

    - Note: Setting the base and top offset prevents the void from cutting the foundation and roof.

6. Click in an empty space in the view to clear the selection.

7. Save and close the project.

Chapter Review Questions

1. When creating a slab, which of the following Draw tools used to create a boundary automatically updates the slab boundary if the other elements are changed? (Select all that apply.)

   a. (Line)

   b. (Pick Lines)

   c. (Pick Walls)

   d. (Pick Supports)

2. Foundation slabs often have slab edges, as shown in a section in Figure 8–32. Which of the following is true of slab edges?

   Figure 8–32

   a. They come in automatically when you draw the slab.

   b. You can add them by selecting **Slab Edge** in the Options Bar.

   c. You need to add them with the separate **Slab Edge** command.

   d. You can add them by modifying the Type Properties of the slab.

3. Which of the following elements cannot be cut by a shaft opening, such as those shown in Figure 8–33?

Figure 8–33

   a. Roofs
   b. Floors
   c. Ceilings
   d. Beams

4. Which tool would you use to set or modify the direction of metal decking in a structural floor?

   a. Boundary Line
   b. Slope Arrow
   c. Span Direction
   d. Pick Supports

Command Summary

Button	Command	Location
	Align Perpendicular	• **Ribbon:** *Modify	Foundation Span Direction Symbol* tab
	Floor: Slab Edge	• **Ribbon:** *Structure* tab>Foundation panel, expand Slab
	Floor: Structural	• **Ribbon:** *Structure* tab>Structure panel, expand Floor • **Shortcut:** SB
	Roof by Footprint	• **Ribbon:** *Architecture* tab>Build panel, expand Roof
	Shaft	• **Ribbon:** *Structure* tab>Opening panel
	Structural Foundation: Slab	• **Ribbon:** *Structure* tab>Foundation panel, expand Slab

Chapter 9

Structural Reinforcement

Adding reinforcement is an important part of the process when designing concrete structures. One of the primary methods of adding reinforcement is rebar, which comes in many possible sizes and shapes. You can add rebar types individually, in an area, along a path, and using fabric reinforcement sheets.

Learning Objectives in This Chapter

- Examine the types of elements that can have reinforcement added to them.
- Set the reinforcement settings.
- Place existing rebar shapes and sketch custom shapes for single or multi-planar rebar.
- Modify rebar by using controls, properties, and other modification tools.
- Add a rebar coupler and modify coupler ends.
- Place area and path reinforcement in walls or floors.
- Add fabric reinforcement.

9.1 Structural Reinforcement

The Autodesk® Revit® software provides tools for modeling reinforcement in concrete and structural elements, as shown in Figure 9–1. Rebar components are attached to host elements, such as concrete or precast concrete beams, columns, or foundations.

Walls, structural floors, and slab edges can also be valid hosts as long as they have a structural usage and contain a concrete layer.

Figure 9–1

You can place reinforcements using the following element types:

• Structural Framing	• Structural Columns
• Structural Foundations	• Walls
• Structural Floors	• Structural Connections
• Foundation Slabs	• Wall Foundations
• Slab Edges	• Imported concrete elements from SAT files or InfraWorks

- Rebar can be placed in free-form concrete elements, such as curved columns and slabs.

Structural Reinforcement

Before you add rebar to a project, there are two groups of settings you can establish.

- *Rebar Cover Settings* control the acceptable distance from the element's face, so that when you add rebar to a host you are limited to that setting.
- *Reinforcement Settings* indicate the reinforcement elements display and how to annotate the reinforcement using custom symbols and tags.

Setting the Rebar Cover Depth

Rebar cover settings can differ depending on the project's soil or regional conditions and other issues. Although the software has default settings, they can be changed or additional cover settings can be created when required. As you place reinforcement, the cover depth displays with dashed lines as shown in Figure 9–2.

Cover depth

Figure 9–2

- Each structural element has preset cover settings. You can customize the settings by element or by the individual faces in an element.

How To: Add a Rebar Cover Setting

1. In the *Structure* tab, expand the Reinforcement panel title and click 🗐 (Rebar Cover Settings).
2. In the Rebar Cover Settings dialog box, click **Add** to create a new cover setting, or select an existing setting and click **Duplicate**.

3. A new setting is added as shown in Figure 9–3. Rename the Description for the purpose of the setting and set the *Setting* clearance.

Figure 9–3

4. Click **OK**.

How To: Edit the Rebar Cover

1. In the *Structure* tab>Reinforcement panel, click (Cover).
2. From the Options Bar, select (Pick Elements) or (Pick Faces).
3. Select an element or the face of an element.
4. In the Options Bar, select the cover settings for this specific object as shown in Figure 9–4.

Figure 9–4

Structural Reinforcement

- For more options, click ⬚ (Browse) to open the Rebar Cover Settings dialog box in which you can add a new cover restraint.

- Cover settings can also be modified in Properties when a rebar host element is selected, as shown in Figure 9–5. This only modifies the selected element.

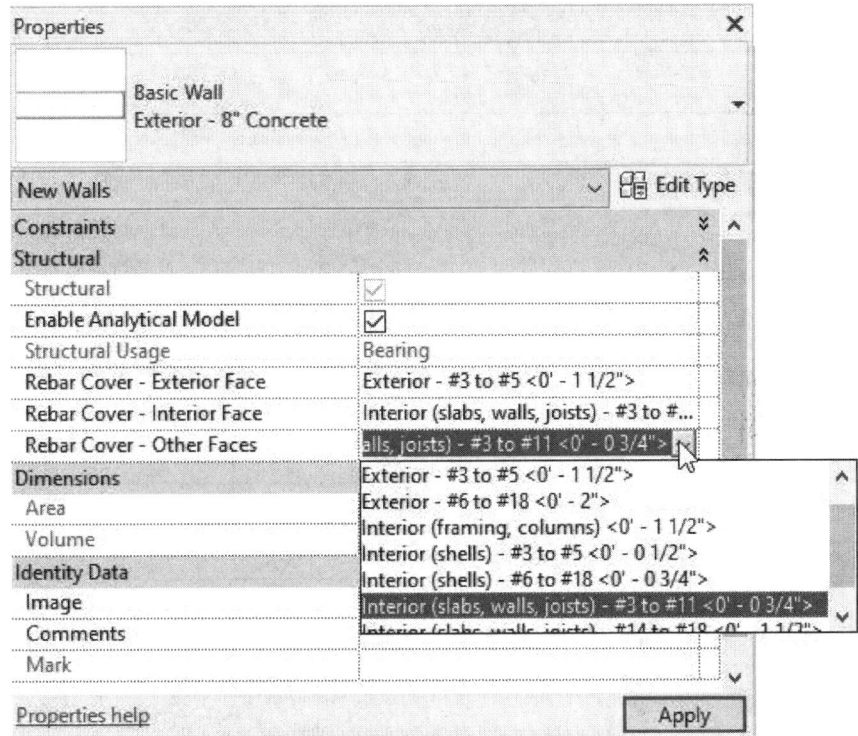

Figure 9–5

Reinforcement Settings

Using Reinforcement Settings, you can specify the structural rebar hosting of area/path reinforcement and annotate the area/path reinforcement region using custom symbols and tags.

- In the *Structure* tab> Reinforcement panel, expand the panel title and click 🔧 (Reinforcement Settings).

General Pane

In the *General* pane, as shown in Figure 9–6, you can determine how area and path reinforcements work in their host elements of floors and walls as well as if hooks are included in rebar shapes. Both of these are on by default in new projects. If you are using couplers to define end treatments then select **Include end treatments in Rebar Shape definition**. This option is off by default.

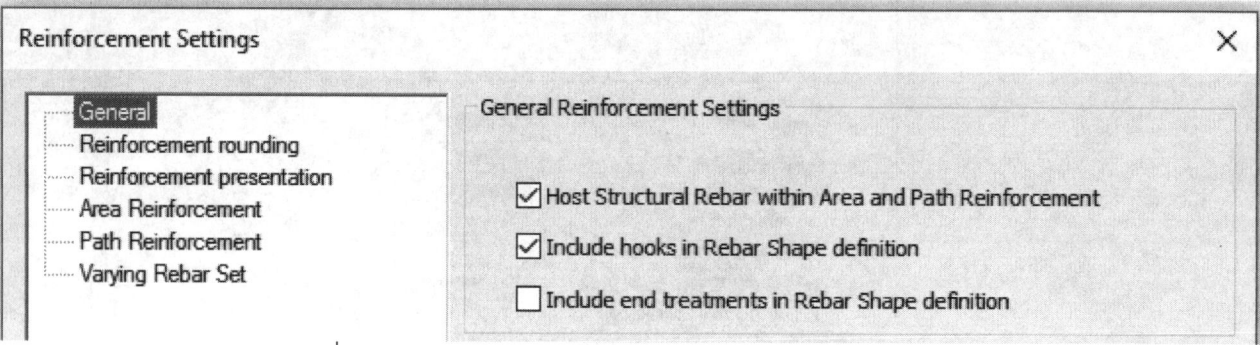

Figure 9–6

- These options must be set before you place any rebar in a project.

- The first time you place rebar an alert box displays noting which settings are selected as shown in Figure 9–7.

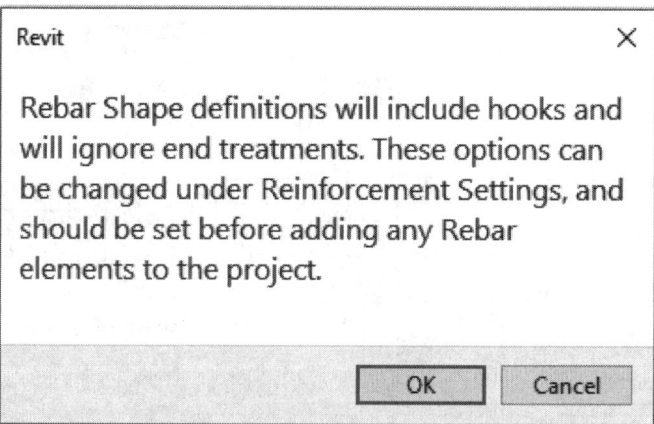

Figure 9–7

When **Host Structural Rebar with Area and Path Reinforcement** is selected, the structural rebar elements display in the floor or wall, as shown on the left in Figure 9–8. When this option is cleared, the structural rebar elements do not display in the floor or wall, as shown on the right in Figure 9–8, but you can annotate the area/path reinforcement region using custom symbols and tags.

Structural Reinforcement

Rebar hosted

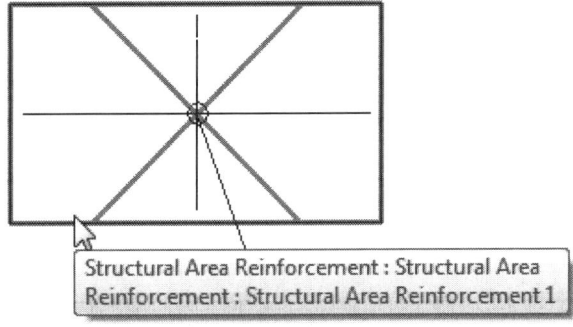
Rebar not hosted

Figure 9–8

When **Include hooks in Rebar Shape definition** is selected, any added hooks are included in standard rebar shapes. This minimizes the number of custom shapes in a project. When this option is cleared, adding hooks to a shape creates additional shapes.

Reinforcement Rounding Pane

In the *Reinforcement rounding* pane (shown in Figure 9–9), you can specify and set up the rounding method (i.e., Nearest, Up, or Down), and the amount of rounding for Structural Rebar and Structural Fabric Reinforcement. This overrides Project Units rounding for these elements.

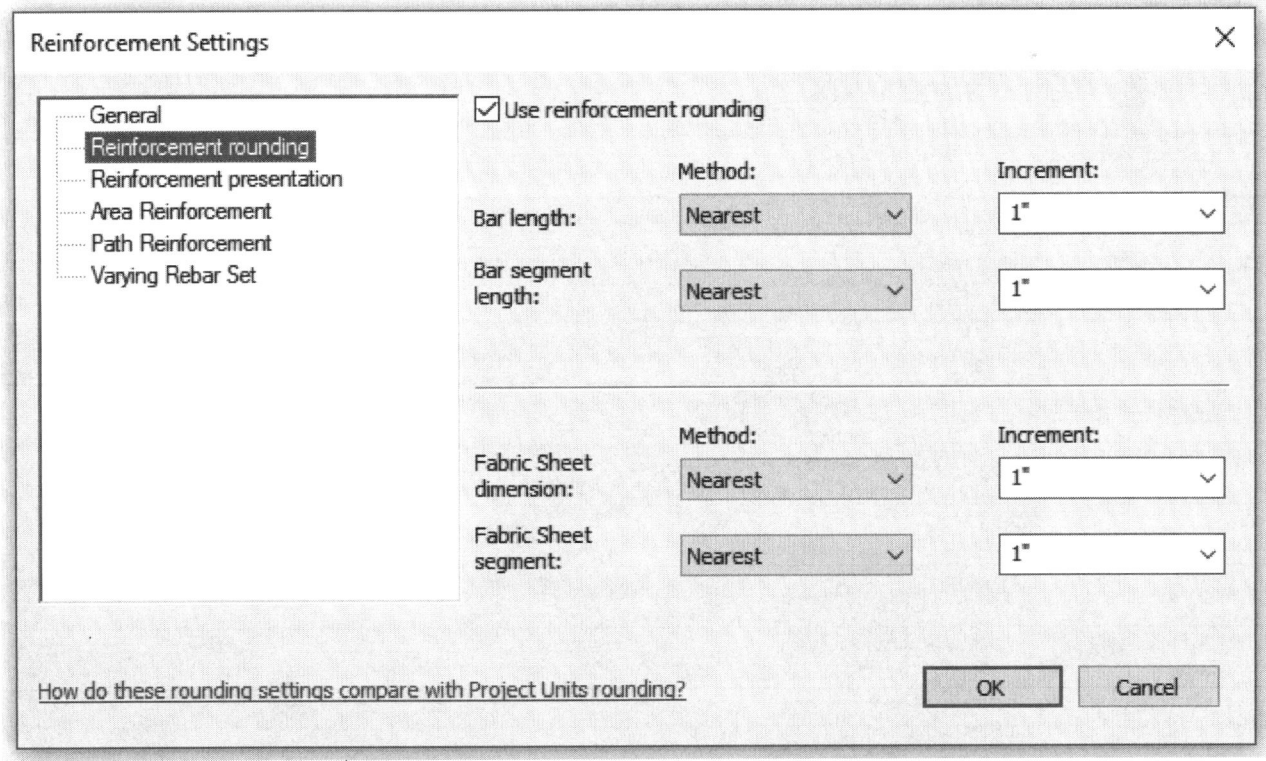

Figure 9–9

Reinforcement Presentation Pane

In the *Reinforcement presentation* pane you can specify how Rebar Sets display in views and sections, as shown in Figure 9–10.

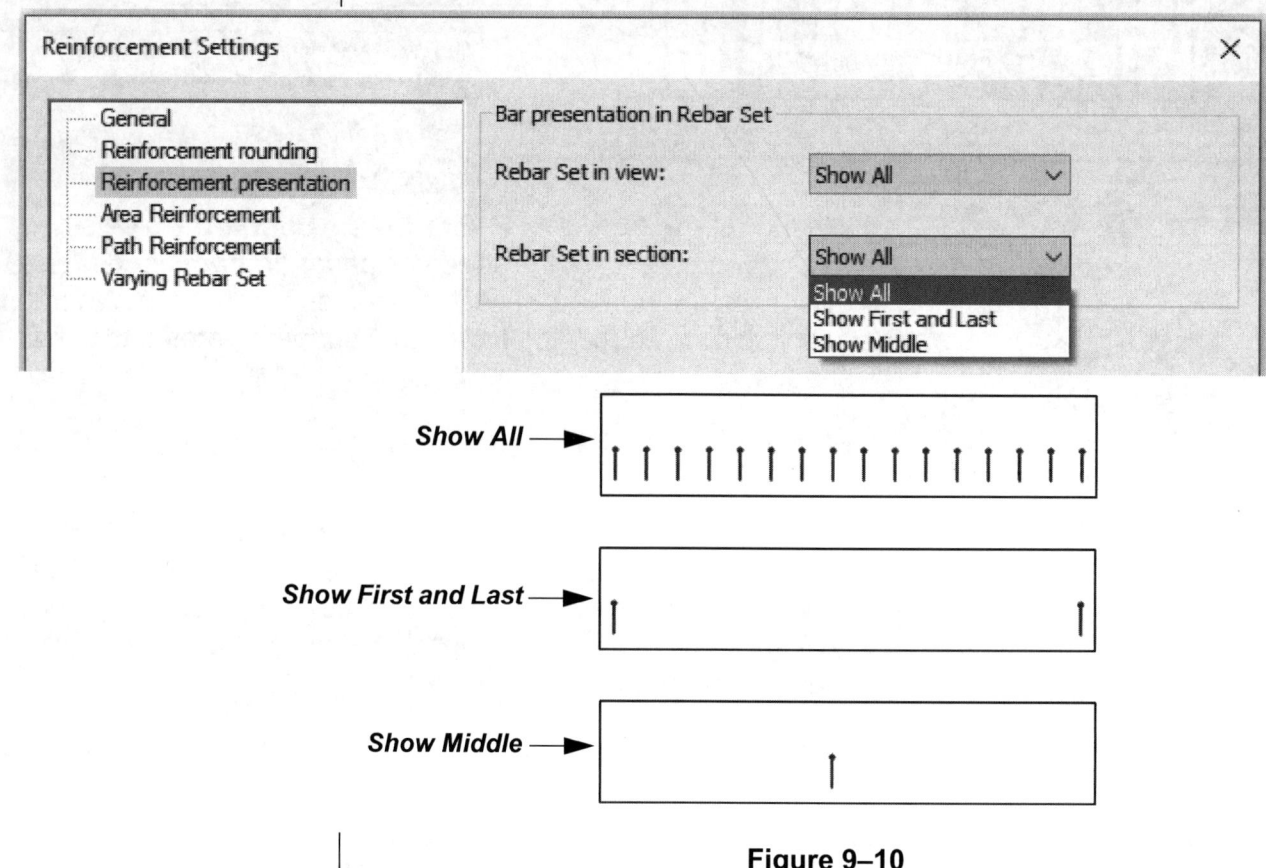

Figure 9–10

Structural Reinforcement

Area and Path Reinforcement Panes

In the *Area Reinforcement* or *Path Reinforcement* panes, specify the values (abbreviations) used in tags. For example, for **Area Reinforcements**, you might want to change the *Value* for Slab Top - Major Direction and Slab Top - Minor Direction to **Slab Top**, as shown in Figure 9–11.

Figure 9–11

Varying Rebar Set

In the Varying Rebar Set pane (shown in Figure 9–12), you can specify the numbering method for the rebar set of different lengths.

Figure 9–12

- **Number bars Individually:** Each rebar in the set is assigned a different number, though similar rebar will be matched throughout the project.

- **Number bars as a whole:** Each rebar in the set is assigned the same number with additional suffix numbers.

Rebar Visibility

By default, rebar automatically displays in section views, but not in other views. If you want to display rebar in other views, such as the 3D view shown in Figure 9–13, set the **View Visibility States** of the rebar.

Figure 9–13

How To: Set the Rebar Visibility

1. In a section view, select the rebar in a structural element.
2. In Properties, in the *Graphics* area, beside *View Visibility States*, click **Edit...**.
3. In the Rebar Element View Visibility States dialog box, as shown in Figure 9–14, you can set where and in which views to display the reinforcement in your model.

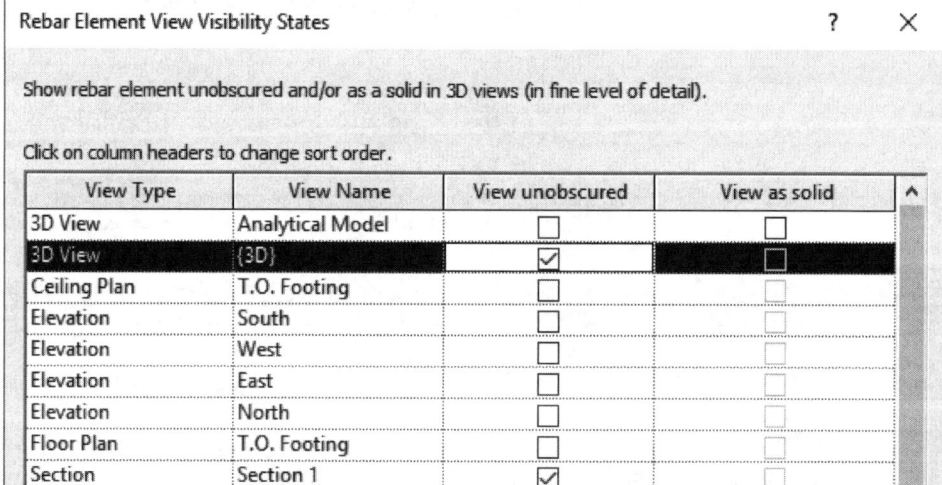

Figure 9–14

Hint: Structural Precast for Revit Add-In

To take your Autodesk Revit model to the next level, you can use the Autodesk Structural Precast Extension for Revit add-in. This tool enables you to create complex assemblies required for construction, automatically create shop drawings, and generate CAM files.

9.2 Adding Rebar

As you start reinforcing structural walls, columns, slabs, and framing, you can add rebar shapes directly into the host elements individually or as a rebar set. You can place existing rebar shapes either parallel to the work plane (or cover) or perpendicular to the cover. You can also draw a custom sketch (as shown in Figure 9–15) and model freeform rebar.

Figure 9–15

You typically work in a wall section as you place the rebar, but rebar can be added in any 2D view. You can sketch rebar and add free-form rebar in 3D views.

- The Rebar tools are available in the *Structure* tab> Reinforcement panel.
    - When a structural host element is selected first, you can start the rebar tool from the *Modify | Structural* contextual tab>Reinforcement panel as shown in Figure 9–16.

Figure 9–16

When working with rebar sizes, you can set the *Model Bar Diameter* in the rebar's Type Properties so it includes the ribbing of the rebar, as shown in Figure 9–17.

Figure 9–17

- The view you are in (e.g., 3D, section, plan, or elevation) will determine which options you see on the ribbon. When you start the **Rebar** command in a section, elevation, or plan view, the contextual *Modify | Place Rebar* tab displays, as shown on the top in Figure 9–18. If in a 3D view, the *Modify | Place Free Form Rebar* contextual tab displays, as shown on the bottom in Figure 9–18.

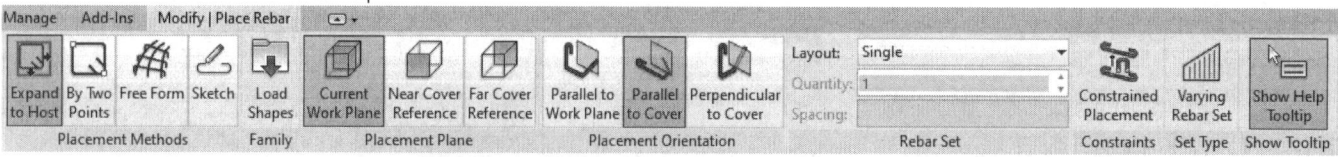
Contextual tab when placing rebar in a plan or section view

Contextual tab when placing rebar in a 3D view

Figure 9–18

Structural Reinforcement

Placement Methods

To reinforce your structural model elements, you can add rebar either by placing predefined rebar shapes or sketching custom rebar.

![]	Expand to Host	Allows you to place an instance of a rebar shape to fill and expand to the space allowed by the concrete host.
![]	By Two Points	Place an instance of rebar using two pick points to define the size and rebar shape.
![]	Free Form	Place free-form rebar on irregularly shaped concrete hosts and specify the distribution type and rebar set.
![]	Sketch	Using the draw tools, draw a free-form rebar shape within a concrete surface in 2D or 3D views.

- If you select **Expand to Host** or **By Two Points**, you can toggle (Show Help Tooltip) on or off. When on, this option adds a tooltip to the end of the cursor, as shown in Figure 9–19, indicating what can be done to the rebar while it is being placed. For instance, pressing <Spacebar> will rotate or flip the rebar.

Figure 9–19

Placement Plane

The placement plane that is selected defines the plane the rebar will be placed at in the host. This can either be a work plane or a plane in relationship to the cover.

![]	Current Work Plane	Places rebar on the active work plane in the view.
![]	Near Cover Reference	Places rebar on the closest cover reference parallel to the view.
![]	Far Cover Reference	Places rebar on the farthest cover reference parallel to the view.

Hint: Rebar Ribbon Options

- Depending on the size and shape of your screen you may not see the information in the panels. Click on the arrow at the bottom of the panel to display the full panel, as shown in Figure 9–20.

Figure 9–20

Placement Orientation

When placing rebar using either the **Expand to Host** or **By Two Points** method, the placement orientation options will display differently on the contextual tab. Setting the orientation defines how the rebar will align based off of the current work plane and the host that the rebar will be placed on. The placement orientation options are described in the table below.

	Parallel to Work Plane	Places rebar parallel to the established work plane and in the cover references.
	Parallel to Cover	Places rebar parallel to the nearest cover reference and perpendicular to the work plane.
	Perpendicular to Cover	Places rebar perpendicular to the work plane and perpendicular to the nearest cover reference.
	Perpendicular Segment	Places a single rebar segment perpendicular to the work plane.
	Horizontal	Places rebar perpendicular and horizontally to the current view's work plane.
	Vertical	Places rebar perpendicular and vertically to the current view's work plane.

Structural Reinforcement

How To: Place Rebar

1. Verify the reinforcement settings are set up. In the *Structure* tab>Reinforcement panel, expand the panel title and click (Reinforcement Settings).

2. In the *Structure* tab>Reinforcement panel, click (Rebar).

3. In the *Modify | Place Rebar* tab>Placement Methods panel, select a placement method.

   - Alternatively you can select a rebar host element, and from the contextual tab>Reinforcement panel, click (Rebar).

4. In the Options Bar or Rebar Shape Browser, select a rebar shape, as shown in Figure 9–21. You can also select the rebar type from the Type Selector.

   - If the Rebar Shape Browser does not display, in the Options Bar, click the (Browse) button.

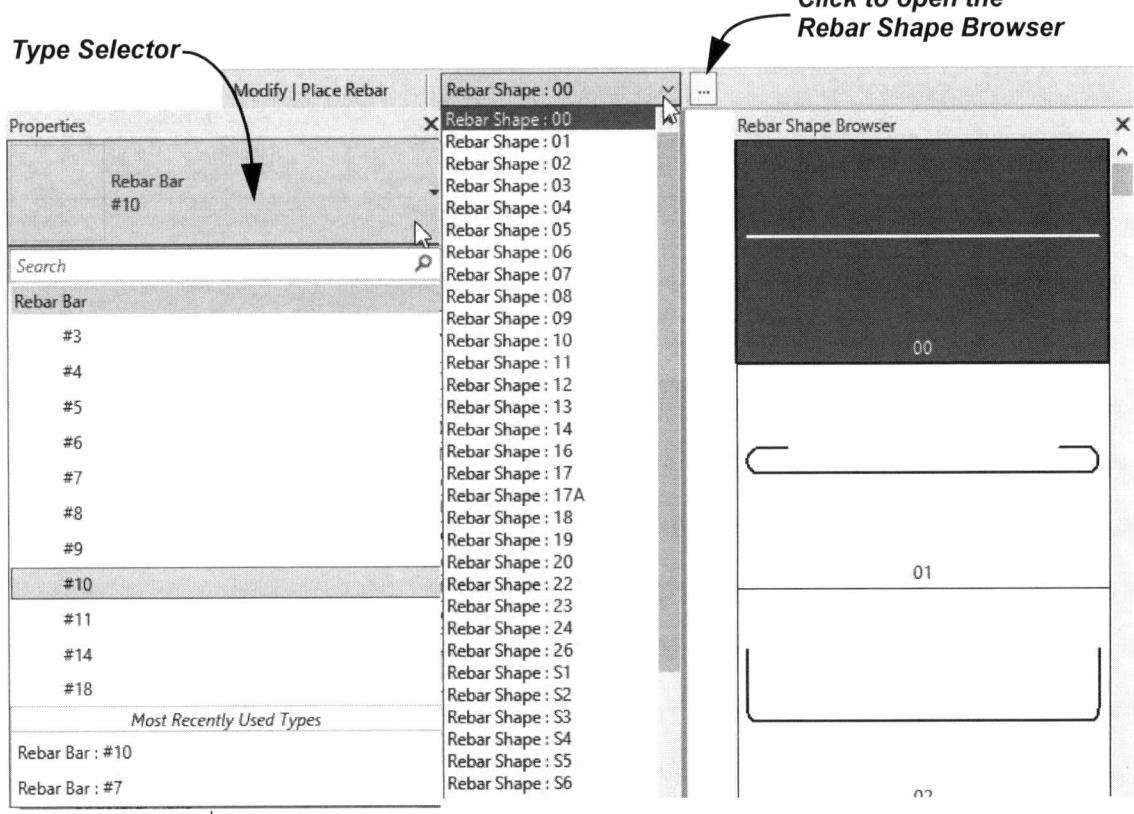

Figure 9–21

- In the *Modify | Place Rebar* tab>Family panel, click (Load Shapes) to load additional rebar family types.

5. In the *Modify | Place Rebar* tab>Placement Plane panel select the placement location.
6. In the *Modify | Place Rebar* tab>Placement Orientation panel, select the parallel or perpendicular placement orientation.
7. In the *Modify | Place Rebar* tab>Rebar Set panel (shown in Figure 9–22), or in the *Rebar Set* area of Properties (shown in Figure 9–23), specify the *Layout Rule* and then set up the corresponding *Quantity* and *Spacing* as required. The *Layout Rule* options are:

    - **Single**
    - **Fixed Number**
    - **Maximum Space**
    - **Number with Spacing**
    - **Minimum Clear Spacing**

Figure 9–22

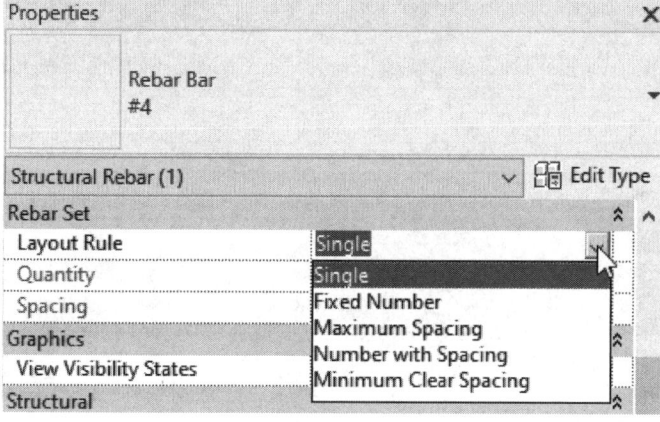

Figure 9–23

8. Hover the cursor over the element that you want to reinforce as shown in Figure 9–24. Click to place it when it is in the required position.

Figure 9–24

- The green dashed lines indicate the maximum cover settings of the host element.
- Press <Spacebar> to flip or rotate the rebar element before or after it is placed.

Structural Reinforcement

- Press <Shift> to place the rebar parallel to any host face.
- For the single session of Revit, your rebar selections on the *Modify | Place Rebar* tab are remembered the next time the Rebar command is started.
- For more information on rebar types, see *B.5 Creating Rebar Types*.

Constraining Rebar to Other Rebar

To help you place rebar more precisely, you can constrain rebar to nearby shapes. When you move the original rebar, all the constrained elements move as well, as shown in Figure 9–25.

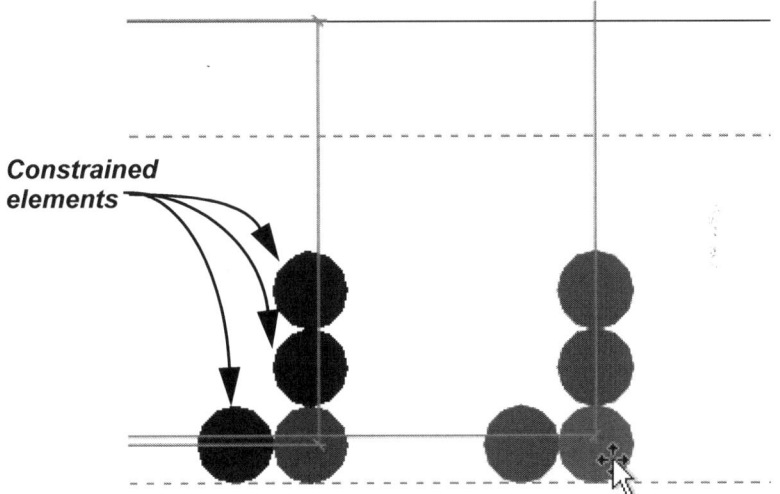

Figure 9–25

- In the *Modify | Place Rebar* tab> Rebar Constraints panel, click (Constrained Placement). Then, move the cursor close to the other rebar and click when you see it snap to the preferred constraint.

- Once the rebar is placed, you can select it and use the temporary dimensions to change the location. This breaks the constraint.

  - This tool only works when placing single rebar.

Sketching Rebar Shapes

At times, the standard rebar shapes are not exactly what is required. In these cases, you can sketch a new shape as shown in Figure 9–26.

Figure 9–26

- When sketching rebar, you are not restricted to the rebar cover settings.

How To: Place a Rebar Shape by Sketch

1. In the *Structure* tab>Reinforcement panel, click (Rebar).
2. In the *Modify | Place Rebar* tab>Placement Methods panel, click (Sketch).
3. Select the host for the rebar (unless it is already selected).
4. To draw the sketch, use the tools in the *Modify | Create Rebar Sketch* tab>Draw panel, as shown in Figure 9–27.

Figure 9–27

5. Click (Finish Edit Mode).

- The new Rebar Shape displays in the Shape Browser. To change the shape name, in the Project Browser, expand the *Families>Structural Rebar>Rebar Shape* node, right-click on the shape name and select **Rename**.

Multi-planar Rebar

When you are sketching rebar you can also create multi-planar reinforcement. The rebar shape is sketched in 2D and then duplicated and connected by a segment, as shown in Figure 9–28.

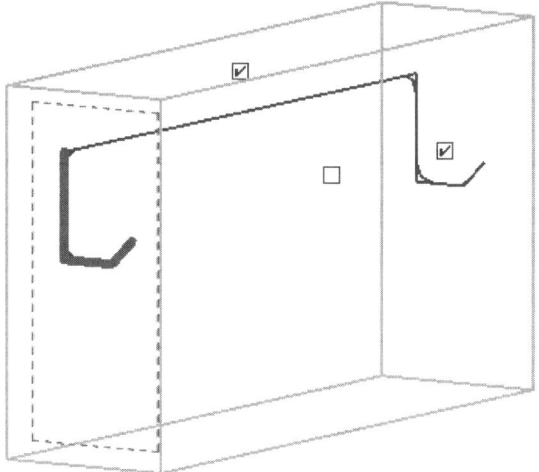

Figure 9–28

How To: Sketch Multi-planar Rebar

1. Start the **Rebar** command with the **Sketch** option.
2. Select the host if not already selected.
3. In the *Modify | Create Rebar Sketch* tab>Reinforcement panel, click ⌐ (Multi-planar).

4. Draw the rebar sketch in the 2D view. It automatically displays in any open 3D views, as shown in Figure 9–29.

5. Select the appropriate checkboxes on the sketch.

Figure 9–29

6. From the Type Selector, select the Rebar bar size, then set other parameters in Properties, as needed.

7. Click ✓ (Finish Edit Mode). The rebar is added to the length of the element as shown in Figure 9–30.

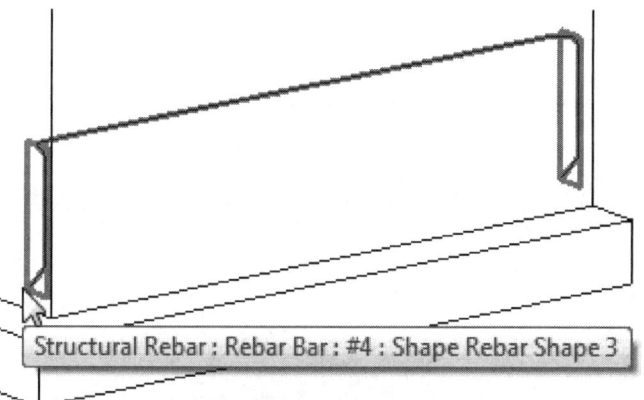

Figure 9–30

- You can modify the multi-planar rebar shape using the drag controls, as shown in Figure 9–31. Alternatively, in the *Modify | Structural Rebar* tab>Mode panel, click (Edit Sketch).

For information about modifying detail views, see B.6 Editing Plan and Section Profiles.

Figure 9–31

Free-Form Rebar

You can add free-form rebar when you need rebar to follow complex concrete structures, as shown in Figure 9–32. These elements are frequently created using model in place or family tools.

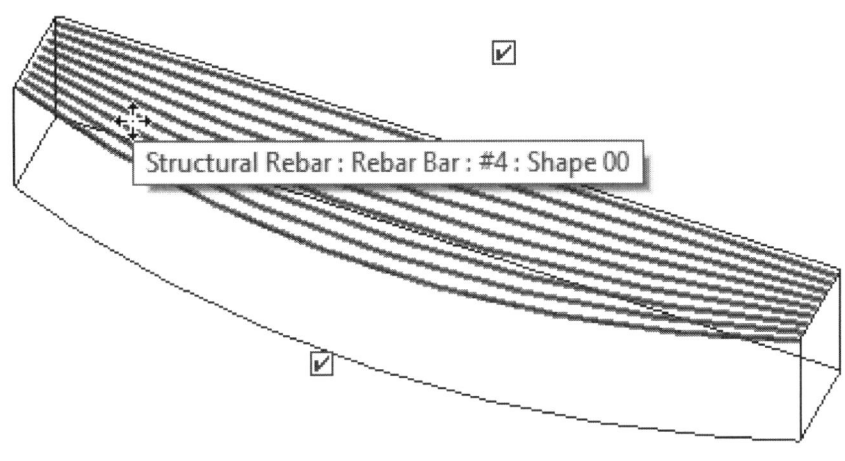

Figure 9–32

How To: Place Free-Form Rebar

1. In the *Structure* tab>Reinforcement panel, click (Rebar).
2. In the *Modify | Place Rebar* tab>Placement Methods panel, click (Free Form).
   - The *Modify | Place Free Form Rebar* tab displays with (Surface Distribution) selected.
3. In the Type Selector, select the Rebar type.

If you are in a 3D view, the Free Form rebar tool is automatically selected.

4. In the Rebar Set panel, specify the *Layout*, *Number*, and *Spacing*, as needed.
5. Toggle (Select Multiple) off for simple surfaces or on for more complex surfaces, as needed.
6. Select the host surface(s), start surface(s), and end surface(s), as shown for a simple surface in Figure 9–33.

Select Host   **Select Start Surface**   **Select End Surface**

Figure 9–33

7. Press <Esc> to finish the selections. The rebar displays as shown in Figure 9–34 with a Rebar Set specified.

Figure 9–34

- If you are selecting multiple faces you can press <Spacebar> between sets of selections and press <Enter> to finish.

- You can add rebar to model-in-place stairs and ramps which frequently need free-form rebar.

Applying a Rebar Set is covered in 9.3 Modifying Rebar.

9.3 Modifying Rebar

You can make additional changes to the rebar once it is placed. For example, select the rebar and use the shape handles to move it into place, as shown in Figure 9–35. Rebar that is perpendicular to the work plane also has temporary dimensions.

Figure 9–35

- To quickly select multiple instances of related rebar, select one, right-click, and select **Select All Rebar in Host**.

- You can use other modify tools to place rebar, such as **Move**, **Copy**, and **Mirror**.

When you select existing rebar in a model a number of tools display in the *Modify | Structural Rebar* tab, as shown in Figure 9–36. You can create or modify rebar sets, pick a new host for the rebar, edit the constraints of the rebar, edit or remove individual bars within a set, apply rebar couplers, and specify a variable length rebar set type.

Figure 9–36

- When the rebar that is placed in a view is interfering with another element, you can edit the rebar set and either modify or remove rebar from a set.

	Modify Bars	Modify the selected rebar by using the **Move**, **Rotate**, or **Align** tools. You can also select to remove the selected rebar.
	Show Removed	Shows any rebar that was removed from the selected rebar set.
	Remove Bar	Remove selected rebar from the rebar set.
	Reset Position	Reset a rebar's position if it was moved, rotated, or aligned out of its original place.
	Reset All	Reset moved or removed rebar.

- Rebar couplers can be added to the end or between lengths of rebar. When couplers are added, the rebar dimensions are altered.

Rebar Set Visibility

In a view, when you select a rebar set, you can specify how that set displays. The default presentation style is set in the Reinforcement Settings dialog box, but you can change each rebar set individually.

Select a rebar set and in the *Modify | Structural Rebar* tab> Presentation panel, choose the presentation style, as shown in Figure 9–37.

Figure 9–37

- You can also choose to display each end of a rebar set using checkboxes, as shown in Figure 9–38.

Figure 9–38

How To: Pick a New Host

1. To change the element that supports rebar. Select the rebar and, in the *Modify | Structural Rebar* tab>Host panel, click (Pick New Host).
2. Select the new host element.

For example, in Figure 9–39, the rebar is hosted by the wall on the left and by the slab on the right. You can see the difference in the constraints.

Figure 9–39

> **Hint: Thin Lines**
>
> If you have trouble viewing the reinforcement because of the thickness of the lines (as shown on the left in Figure 9–40), you can change the view to display as thin line weight, as shown on the right in Figure 9–40. In the Quick Access Toolbar, click ▤ (Thin Lines) to toggle back and forth between the two view types.
>
>
>
> Figure 9–40
>
> - The look of rebar in a view is also controlled by the Detail Level. **Coarse** displays 1-line representation, while **Medium** and **Fine** displays the actual size of the rebar.

How To: Edit Rebar Constraints

1. To graphically override the nearby constraints, select the rebar you want to modify.
2. In the *Modify | Structural Rebar* tab>Rebar Constraints panel, click (Edit Constraints). The element and reference are highlighted in orange.
3. Using the temporary dimension, type in a new distance, as shown in Figure 9–41.

Figure 9–41

4. Click (Finish).

Structural Reinforcement

- If additional constraint references are available, they are highlighted in blue. Click on the blue reference to switch to that dimension.

- You can edit rebar constraints in 3D views.

How To: Edit or Remove Bars

1. In a view, select a rebar or rebar set.
2. In the *Modify | Structural Rebar* tab>Customization panel, select (Edit Bars).
3. In the *Modify | Modify* tab>Mode panel, select (Modify Bars).
4. Select one or more rebar that you want to modify and do one of the following to modify the selected rebar:
   - From the *Modify | Structural Rebar* tab>Modify panel, select the **Move**, **Rotate** or **Align** tool to modify the selected rebar.
   - Select (Remove Bar) to remove the selected bar(s).
   - If you have accidentally repositioned or removed rebar, select (Reset Position) or (Reset All).
5. Click (Finish).
   - Select (Show Removed) to temporarily see the removed rebar.

How To: Add Varying Rebar Sets

1. To have rebar follow the angle of a host element, set up the rebar following standard processes as shown for a wall in Figure 9–42. Varying rebar sets can be placed in curved and free-form elements.

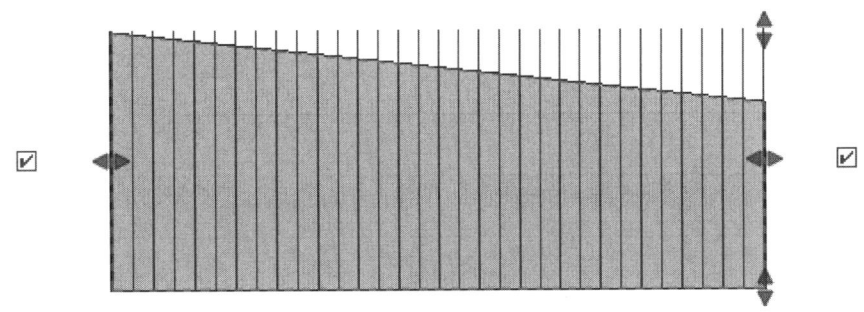

Figure 9–42

2. In the *Modify | Structural Rebar* tab> Rebar Set Type panel, click (Varying Rebar Set). The rebar now follows the edge as shown in Figure 9–43. This tool is an on/off toggle.

Figure 9–43

3. Use the arrow-like shape handles to resize the rebar to fit the element if needed, as shown in Figure 9–44.

Figure 9–44

3D Rebar Shapes

For standees reinforcing rebar in footings or slabs, you can model 3D rebar shapes by placing rebar, then rotating the hook's start and/or end and, if needed, adjusting the hook length by instance with the rebar properties. The hook rotation and length can also be modified with existing rebar in the model, as shown in Figure 9–45.

Structural Reinforcement

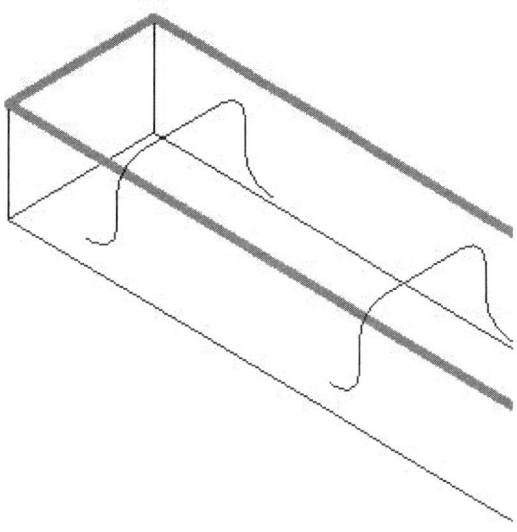

Figure 9–45

- For existing rebar, select it and adjust the *Hook At Start/Hook At End* and *Hook Rotation At Start/Hook Rotation At End* settings within Properties, as shown in Figure 9–46. These settings are available to modify before adding free-form and sketched rebar in a 2D or 3D view.

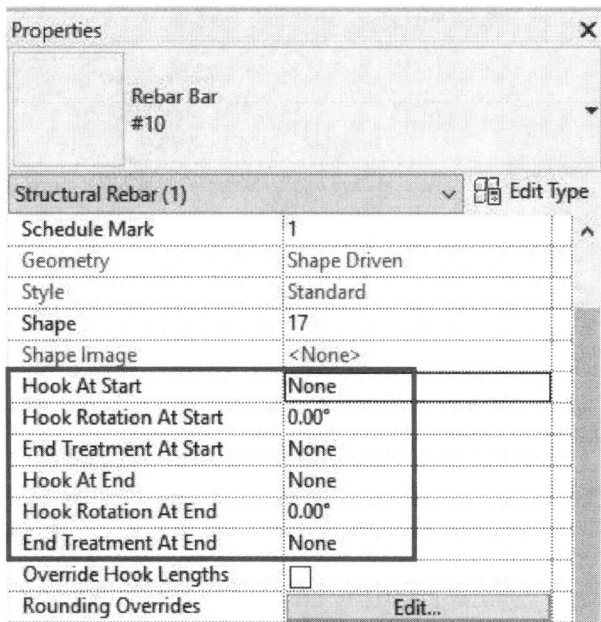

Figure 9–46

- Upon placing rebar, you can modify the hook lengths by checking the box to **Override Hook Lengths** and then changing them within the *Dimensions* area within Properties, as shown in Figure 9–47.

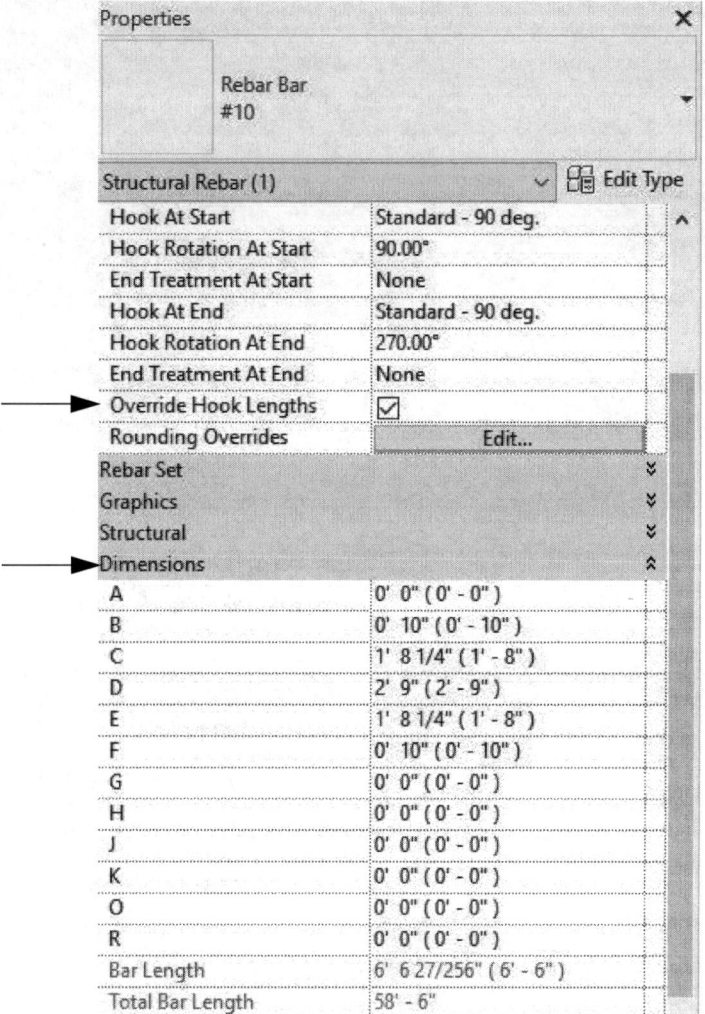

Figure 9–47

- You can press <Spacebar> to rotate the rebar before or after placing it.

How To: Rotate Hooks and Adjust Hook Length

1. Select an existing rebar or rebar set.
2. In Properties, specify the *Hook At Start/Hook At End* and *Hook Rotation At Start/Hook Rotation At End*.
3. To adjust the hook's length, check the box next to **Override Hook Lengths** and adjust the length values in the *Dimensions* area in Properties.

Rebar Coupler

- If you are adding rebar in 2D or 3D using the Free Form or Sketch placement methods, you can specify the rotation before you place the rebar.

A rebar coupler joins adjacent or spliced rebar together so they behave as one continuous length of reinforcement, as shown on the top in Figure 9–48. Rebar couplers will populate across a rebar set or can be placed on individual bars. You can also add headed anchors or cap the end of rebar instances or sets, as shown on the bottom in Figure 9–48. For curved walls, concrete tanks, or tunnels, you can connect tangent arc rebar with couplers.

Figure 9–48

- When couplers are added to rebar, the end treatment of the rebar adjusts within its properties to threaded.

- Couplers can be moved along the length of the rebar and the bars will adjust.

- Couplers can be added to groups and assemblies and be tagged and scheduled.

- You can add an end treatment to rebar without using a coupler.

Coupler Tolerance

- Rebar ends need to have a tolerance of 10 bar diameters or an offset no more than 3 bar diameters from each other to be connected by a coupler.

- If you need to join to arc bars, the centers need to be in the same position.

How To: Add a Rebar Coupler to Join Two Rebar

1. From the *Structure* tab>Reinforcement panel, click (Rebar Coupler). Alternatively, you can select a rebar and from the *Modify |Structural Rebar* tab, click (Insert Coupler).
2. If no couplers are loaded, you are prompted to load one. If you need to load a different coupler, you can stay in the command and switch to the *Insert* tab>Load from Library panel and click (Load Family).
3. From the Type Selector, select the coupler type needed.
4. From the *Modify | Insert Rebar Coupler* tab>Placement Options panel, select (Place between Two Bars).
5. Select the first rebar and then the second rebar to place the coupler.

How To: Add a Coupler to the End of a Bar

1. From the *Structure* tab>Reinforcement panel, click (Rebar Coupler). Alternatively, you can select a rebar and from the *Modify |Structural Rebar* tab, click (Insert Coupler).
2. If no couplers are loaded, you are prompted to load one. If you need to load a different coupler, you can stay in the command and switch to the *Insert* tab>Load from Library panel and click (Load Family).
3. From the Type Selector, select the coupler type needed.
4. From the *Modify | Insert Rebar Coupler* tab>Placement Options panel, select (Place on Bar End).
5. Select the end of the bar that you want to add the coupler end to.

Practice 9a

Add Rebar

Practice Objectives

- Add individual rebar elements.
- Create a repeating layout of rebar.
- Sketch a rebar design.

In this practice, you will add individual rebar to a wall in a foundation section using premade shapes, and then modify the exact location and size using controls. You will then change the layout to create rebar sets. You will also sketch a new rebar shape, as shown in Figure 9–49.

Figure 9–49

Task 1 - Add rebar.

1. Open **Structural-Rebar.rvt** from the practice files folder.

2. Open the **Sections (Wall Section): Typical Foundation Wall Section** view.

3. Zoom in on the footing.

4. In the *Structure* tab>Reinforcement panel, click (Rebar). If an alert about Hooks included in Rebar Shapes comes up, click **OK**.

5. In Properties, in the Type Selector, select **Rebar Bar: #4**.

6. In the *Modify | Place Rebar* tab>Placement Methods panel, select (Expand to Host).

7. In the *Modify | Place Rebar* tab>Placement Plane panel, verify that (Current Work Plane) is selected.

8. In the *Modify | Place Rebar* tab>Placement Orientation panel, click (Parallel to Work Plane).

9. In the Rebar Shape Browser, select **Rebar Shape: 17A**.

10. Add the rebar shape to the footing, as shown in Figure 9–50.

The rebar shape fits exactly within the preset constraints.

Figure 9–50

11. Press <Esc> after the rebar is placed and then select the rebar.

12. Use the handles and controls to modify the shape so that it extends into the wall, as shown in Figure 9–51.

- You can also modify the *B* and *C* rebar dimensions in Properties in the *Dimensions* section.

Structural Reinforcement

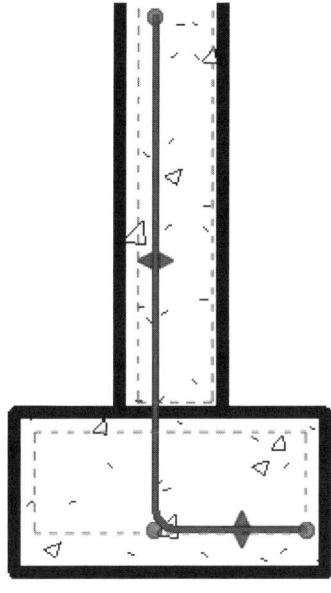

Figure 9–51

13. In the *Structure* tab>Reinforcement panel, click (Rebar).

14. In Properties, in the Type Selector, select **Rebar Bar: #4**.

15. In the *Modify | Place Rebar* tab>Placement Methods panel, select (Expand to Host).

16. In the *Modify | Place Rebar* tab>Placement Orientation panel, click (Perpendicular to Cover).

17. In the Rebar Set panel, change the *Layout* to **Fixed Number** and the *Quantity* to **3**.

18. Add **Rebar Shape: 00** to the bottom left face of the footing. Three rebar are placed, as shown in Figure 9–52.

Figure 9–52

19. Click (Modify). Select and move the L-shaped rebar above the three Rebar Shape: 00 of the continuous footing, as shown in Figure 9–53.

Figure 9–53

20. With the L-shaped rebar still selected, in the *Modify | Structural Rebar* tab>Rebar Set panel, change the *Layout* to **Maximum Spacing** and *Spacing* to **1'-0"**, as shown in Figure 9–54.

Figure 9–54

21. Click (Modify).

22. In the *Structure* tab>Reinforcement panel, click (Rebar).

23. In Properties, in the Type Selector, select **Rebar Bar: #4**.

24. In the *Modify | Place Rebar* tab>Placement Methods panel, select (By Two Points).

25. In the *Modify | Place Rebar* tab>Placement Plane panel, verify that (Current Work Plane) is selected.

26. In the *Modify | Place Rebar* tab>Placement Orientation panel, click (Parallel to Work Plane).

27. In the Rebar Shape Browser, select **Rebar Shape: 17**.

Structural Reinforcement

28. Select the bottom right corner as the first pick point, as shown in Figure 9–55. Click above the far right rebar, as shown in Figure 9–56. Add the rebar shape to the footing below the three straight rebar.

Figure 9–55

Figure 9–56

29. Press <Esc> after the rebar is placed and then select the rebar.

30. Use the handles and controls to modify the shape so that it extends into the wall, as shown in Figure 9–57.

Figure 9–57

31. Click (Modify).

32. Select the new rebar and set the following in the *Modify | Structural Rebar* tab>Rebar Set panel:

- *Layout:* **Maximum Spacing**
- *Spacing:* **0'-10"**

33. Click in an empty area in the view to clear the selection.

34. Save the project.

Task 2 - Sketch individual rebar.

1. Pan up to the slab and slab edge.
2. In the *Structure* tab>Reinforcement panel, click (Rebar).
3. In the *Modify | Place Rebar* tab>Placement Methods panel, click (Sketch).
4. In the Status Bar, the software prompts you to pick a host for the rebar. Select the wall.
   - Although most of this rebar is outside the wall, selecting the wall ensures that the rebar is only along this specific wall. If you had selected the slab, the rebar would have spaced themselves the entire span of the slab or other side of the building, regardless of the wall underneath them.
5. Use the **Draw** tools to sketch a rebar similar to the one shown in Figure 9–58.

Figure 9–58

6. In the *Modify | Create Rebar Sketch* tab>Mode panel, click (Finish Edit Mode). A rebar is created with the new Rebar Shape in the Rebar Browser, as shown in Figure 9–59.

The picture might vary depending on how you drew the shape.

Figure 9–59

Structural Reinforcement

7. Click (Modify) and select the new rebar. Use the controls on the ends and the shape handles on the midpoint of the bar to make small adjustments.

8. In the Rebar Set panel, set *Layout* to **Maximum Spacing** and *Spacing* to **1'-0"**.

9. Save the project.

Task 3 - Create a 3D section view.

1. In the Quick Access Toolbar, click (Default 3D View).

2. Right-click on the ViewCube and select **Orient to View> Sections>Section: Typical Foundation Wall Section**.

3. Rotate the view and hide the section box, as shown in Figure 9–60.

Figure 9–60

4. In the Project Browser, in the 3D Views node, rename the view to **3D Foundation**.

5. Window around everything and select it. You can see the rebar. Using (Filter) select only the Structural Rebar.

6. In Properties, next to *View Visibility States,* click **Edit...**.

7. In the Rebar Element View Visibility States dialog box, beside the **3D Foundation** view name, select **View unobscured** and **View as solid** and click **OK**.

8. The rebar sets now display in the view.

9. In the View Control Bar, set the *Detail Level* to (Fine).

10. Save the project.

Task 4 - Add 3D hooks.

1. Open the **Sections (Wall Section) Typical Foundation Wall Section** view and select **Rebar Shape: 17A**.

2. In Properties (as shown on the left in Figure 9–61), set the value for *Hook At Start* to **Standard - 90 deg.**, select **Override Hook Lengths**, and set the *Dimensions A* value to **0'-4"**. The rebar should now look like the image on the right in Figure 9–61.

Figure 9–61

3. Save and close the project.

9.4 Reinforcing Walls, Floors, and Slabs

Instead of adding individual rebar to large surfaces, there are three types of reinforcement that can be used with walls, floors, and slabs.

- Area Reinforcement places evenly spaced rebar in structural walls and floors according to a boundary you specify, as shown on the wall in Figure 9–62.

- Path Reinforcement enables you to specify reinforcing that bends from the slab into the bearing wall, as shown on the floor in Figure 9–62.

- Fabric Reinforcement places sheets of reinforcing wires within a boundary you specify.

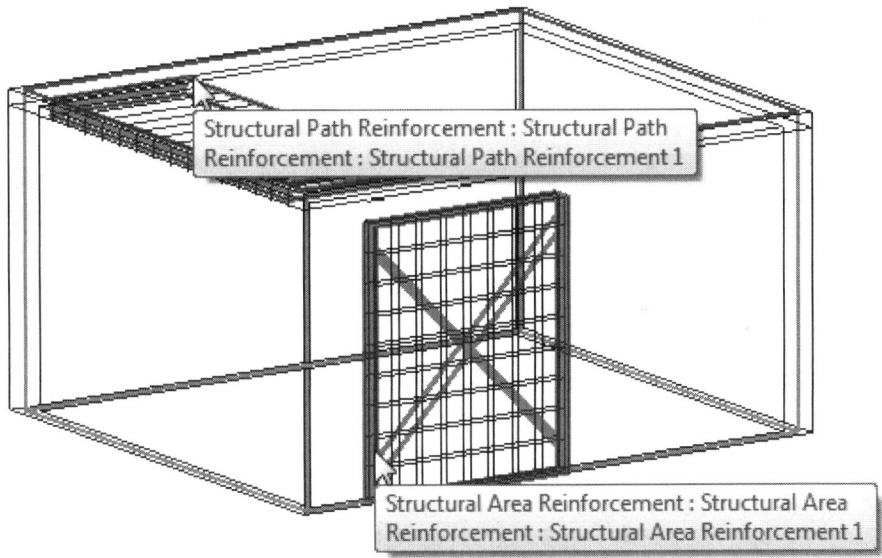

Figure 9–62

Hint: Structural Precast for Revit

You can create complex precast assemblies using additional reinforcement tools found in the Autodesk Structural Precast Extension for Revit.

Area Reinforcement

When creating an **Area Reinforcement**, you sketch a boundary, as shown in Figure 9–63, and then set up the spacing and layers in Properties. Using area reinforcement, you can place up to four layers of reinforcement in a large area like foundation slabs, floors, walls, and other structural concrete hosts. Area reinforcement can be placed in 3D, plan, elevation, or section views depending on the element you are reinforcing.

Figure 9–63

- To avoid conflict with other elements in the model, individual rebar within an area reinforcement can be modified or removed.

How To: Add Area Reinforcement

1. In the *Structure* tab>Reinforcement panel, click ▦ (Area) and select a structural floor or a wall.
2. If an element is already selected, in the *Modify* contextual tab>Reinforcement panel, click ▦ (Area).
   - Area reinforcement can be added to architectural walls and floors.
3. In Properties, modify the parameters as needed for the exterior and interior major and minor direction and spacing.
4. Click **Apply**.

Note that locking sketches to elements increases the size of the model. You should only do this if it is more efficient in the long run.

5. In the *Modify | Create Reinforcement Boundary* tab>Draw panel, click (Pick Lines) or one of the other draw tools.
   - If you are using **Pick Lines**, you can lock the lines to the elements you pick. When you select an edge a padlock symbol displays. Select it to lock the area reinforcement boundary to the wall or slab edge perimeter so that any changes made to the wall or slab automatically update the area reinforcement as well.
   - If you select **Lock** in the Options Bar, each sketch line is locked to the selected edge. This only works with **Pick Lines**.
   - The boundary must be a closed loop without any overlapping lines. Use the **Modify** tools if needed.

6. Click (Finish Edit Mode). The reinforcement displays either as just the symbol, as shown in Figure 9–64, or displays the rebar depending on how the view is set.

Figure 9–64

- When drawing the boundary, the first line you select displays a set of double lines indicating the major direction, as shown in Figure 9–65. To change it, in the *Modify | Structural Area Reinforcement>Edit Boundary* tab>Draw panel, click (Major Direction) and select or draw the edge that defines the direction for the major bars.

Figure 9–65

> **Hint: Displaying Area and Path Reinforcement**
>
> When you first place area or path reinforcement, a box displays at the boundary of the elements. By default, the rebar does not display, but it can be displayed when the Visual Style is set to ▭ (Wireframe) or if you modify the View Visibility State of the rebar element in Properties, as shown in Figure 9–66.
>
> *Area Reinforcement not displayed*
>
> *Area Reinforcement displayed*
>
> Figure 9–66

How To: Edit or Remove Rebar in Area Reinforcements

1. In a view, select an area reinforcement.
2. In the *Modify | Structural Rebar* tab>Customization panel, select (Edit Bars).
3. In the *Modify | Modify* tab>Mode panel, select (Modify Bars).
4. Select one or more rebar that you want to modify and do one of the following to modify the selected rebar:
   - From the *Modify | Structural Rebar* tab>Modify panel, select the **Move**, **Rotate** or **Align** tools to modify the selected rebar.
   - Select (Remove Bar) to remove the selected bar(s).
   - If you have accidentally repositioned or removed rebar, select (Reset Position) or (Reset All).
5. Click (Finish).
   - Select (Show Removed) to temporarily see the removed rebar.

Path Reinforcement

In some cases, additional reinforcement is required along the length of some edges to prevent curling and other issues. Path Reinforcement creates reinforcing that bends from the slab into the bearing wall, but is only extended into the slab at a specified distance, as shown in Figure 9–67. This is also handy for the foundation design of pre-engineered metal structures, where the pilasters and other elements need to be pinned back to the slab.

Figure 9–67

- To avoid conflict with other elements in the model, individual rebar within a path reinforcement can be modified or removed.

How To: Add Path Reinforcement

1. In the *Structure* tab>Reinforcement panel, click (Path Reinforcement).
2. Select the structural floor or wall.
3. In the *Modify | Create Reinforcement Path* tab>Draw panel, use the Draw tools to place a single line specifying an open path, as shown in Figure 9–68.

Figure 9–68

4. Click (Flip) as required, to set the placement of the path.

5. In Properties, as shown in Figure 9–69, modify the parameters as needed.

Figure 9–69

6. In the Mode panel, click ![checkmark] (Finish Edit Mode). The Reinforcement is added as shown in Figure 9–70.

Figure 9–70

How To: Edit or Remove Rebar in Path Reinforcements

1. In a view, select a path reinforcement.
2. In the *Modify | Structural Rebar* tab>Customization panel, select (Edit Bars).
3. In the *Modify | Modify* tab>Mode panel, select (Modify Bars).
4. Select one or more rebar that you want to modify and do one of the following to modify the selected rebar:
   - From the *Modify | Structural Rebar* tab>Modify panel, select the **Move**, **Rotate** or **Align** tools to modify the selected rebar.
   - Select (Remove Bar) to remove the selected bar(s).
   - If you have accidentally repositioned or removed rebar, select (Reset Position) or (Reset All).
5. Click (Finish).
   - Select (Show Removed) to temporarily see the removed rebar.

Fabric Reinforcement

The Structural Fabric Area tool sketches the boundary of a fabric area to populate with fabric sheets, as shown in Figure 9–71. Fabric reinforcement is made up of two element types, Fabric Wire and Fabric Sheets. The Fabric Wire is used to define the reinforcing wire which is used to create the Fabric Sheets. You can also add individual fabric sheets.

Figure 9–71

- Fabric reinforcement can be hosted in structural floors, foundation slabs, and structural walls.
- If there are no fabric reinforcement symbols or tags loaded, you are prompted with the opportunity to load one, as shown in Figure 9–72.

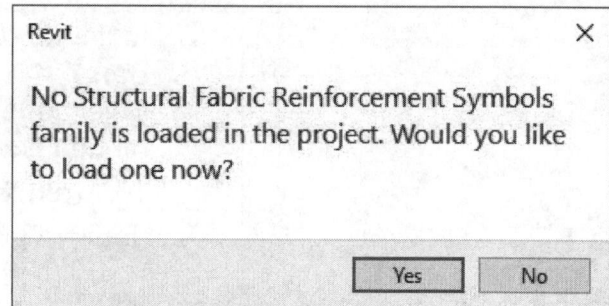

Figure 9–72

How To: Add a Single Fabric Sheet

1. In the *Structure* tab>Reinforcement panel (or if you have already selected an element, in the *Modify* contextual tab), click (Fabric Sheet).
2. In the Type Selector specify the type of sheet you want to use.
3. In Properties specify the *Location* (**Top** or **Bottom**), and other settings.
4. Click to place the sheet where you want it. (It must be in a concrete host, such as a wall, floor, or foundation slab.)
5. The command remains active and you can place additional sheets, as shown in Figure 9–73.

Figure 9–73

6. Click (Modify) to end the command.

Structural Reinforcement

How To: Add a Bent Fabric Sheet

1. Open a view perpendicular to the work plane, such as a section.
2. Start the (Fabric Sheet) command.
3. In the *Modify | Place Fabric Sheet* tab> Mode panel, click (Bend Sketch)
4. Select the host for the bent fabric sheet.
5. Using the tools in the *Modify | Create Bend Profile* tab, sketch a profile such as the one shown in Figure 9–74.

Figure 9–74

6. Click (Finish). The fabric sheet is bent following the sketch, as shown in Figure 9–75.

Figure 9–75

How To: Add Fabric Area Reinforcement

1. In the *Structure* tab>Reinforcement panel (or in the *Modify* contextual tab if you have already selected an element), click (Fabric Area).

2. Select the structural wall, floor, or slab if you did not select it already.
3. In the *Modify | Create Fabric Boundary* tab>Draw panel, use the Draw tools to define the closed boundary.

   - Use (Pick lines) and lock the boundary to the host element so that it automatically updates if the host is changed.
   - The set of double lines indicates the major direction. To change it, in the *Modify | Create Fabric Boundary* tab> Draw panel, click (Major Direction) and select one of the other lines to set the direction of the reinforcement.

4. The preview graphics displays the full size of the sheets as delivered to the construction site, as shown in Figure 9–76. Use the checkboxes and Properties to obtain the needed fabric sheet layout.

- The checkboxes at each edge determine the start point of the Fabric sheet layout and its direction. The start point is defined by at least two selected checkboxes on the rectangular edges, as shown in Figure 9–76. Select additional checkboxes to determine the fabric sheet alignment.

Figure 9–76

5. In Properties, as shown in Figure 9–77, modify the parameters as required for the *Fabric Sheet, Location, Lap Splice Position, Major* and *Minor lap Splice Length*, etc.

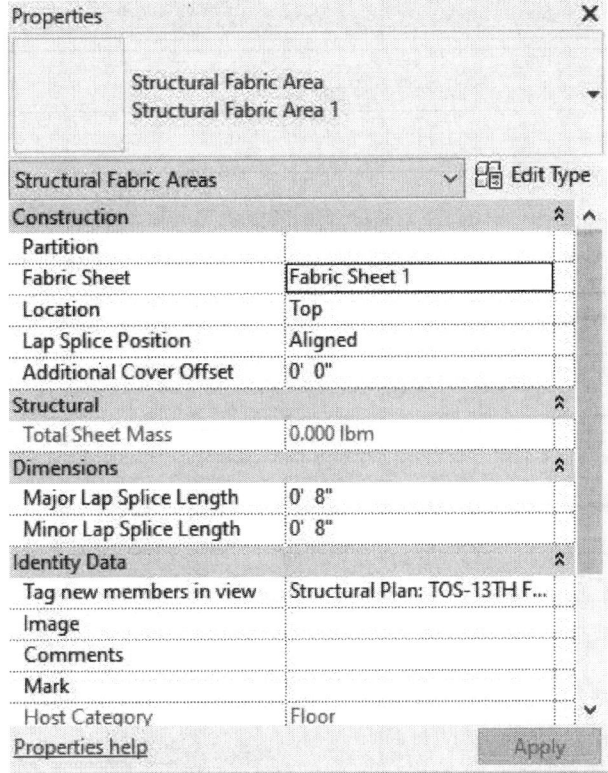

Figure 9–77

6. Click ✓ (Finish Edit Mode) and the fabric reinforcement is added to the element with the specified overlaps, as shown in Figure 9–78.

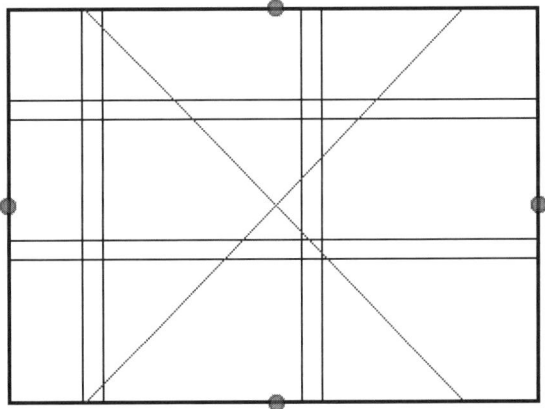

Figure 9–78

- If you want to change the way the fabric sheets overlap, modify the *Lap Splice Position* in Properties. For example, the sheets shown in Figure 9–79 are set to **Major Half-way Stagger**. The *Major* and *Minor Lap Splice Lengths* can also be modified.

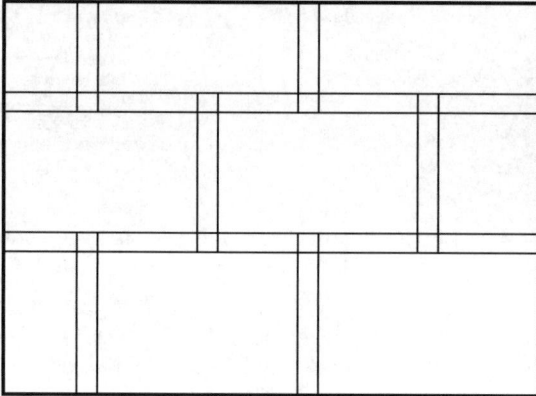

Figure 9–79

- To place symbols and tags automatically, in Properties, under *Identity Data*, select a view from the Tag new members in view drop-down list, as shown in Figure 9–80.

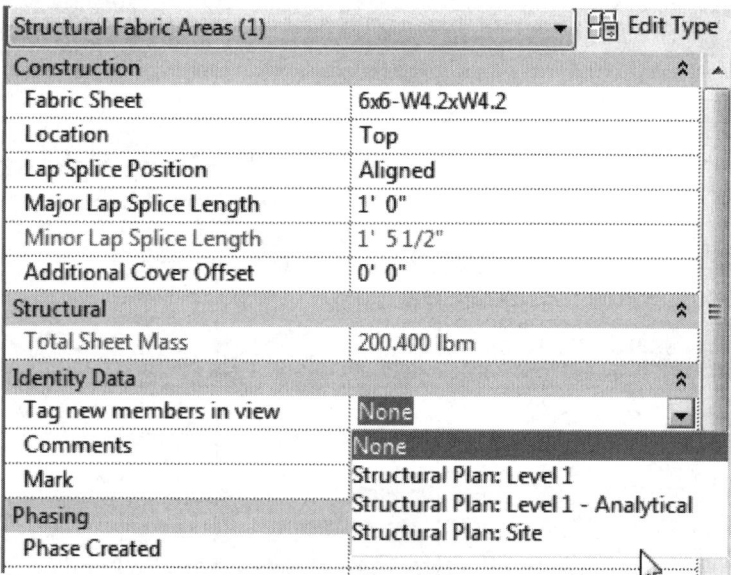

Figure 9–80

- Only views that are parallel to the placement plane are listed in the drop-down list. Using this parameter also defines the view to place new symbols and tags if the fabric area changes size during regeneration.

Modifying Area, Path, and Fabric Reinforcement

As with most elements in Autodesk Revit software, there are a variety of ways to modify area, path, and fabric reinforcement, including editing the boundary or path, using shape handles, and changing the properties, as shown in Figure 9–81. You can also delete entire systems or break the systems down into individual rebar elements or sheets.

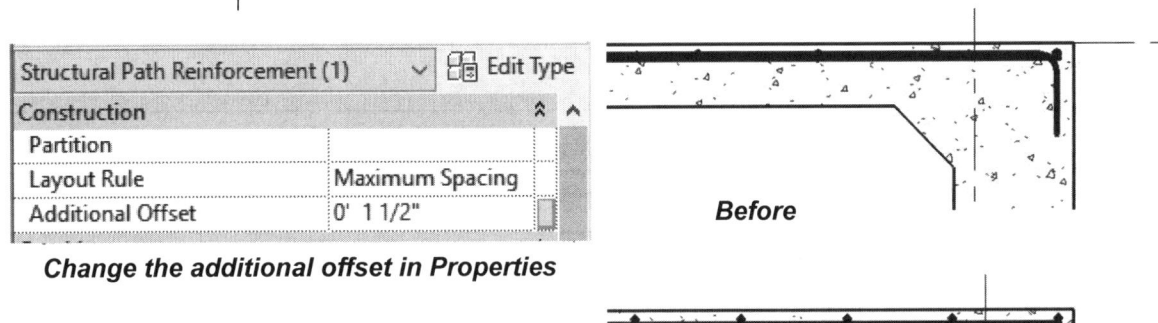

Figure 9–81

- To quickly select multiple instances of related rebar or fabric, select one, right-click and select **Select All Rebar in Host** or **Select All Fabric in Host**.

- When you select the area, path, or fabric area reinforcement you can adjust the boundary by stretching the shape handles, as shown in Figure 9–82.

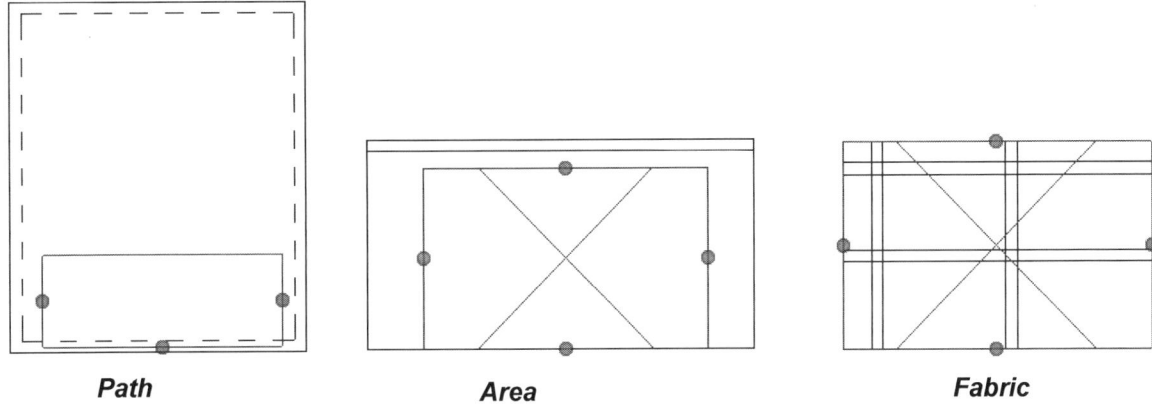

Figure 9–82

- When you have the reinforcement selected you can use the related (Edit) tool found in the Mode panel. This opens the sketch mode where you can use the draw tools to change the boundary or path.

- If you want to remove the reinforcement completely, ensure that you select the boundary of the system and then delete it.

- If you want to keep the individual rebar elements but remove the system, click ▦ (Remove Area System), ⬚ (Remove Path System), or ▨ (Remove Fabric System) in the respective *Modify* tabs.

- When you remove a fabric system it deletes the boundary and leaves the full size of all of the sheets, as shown on the right in Figure 9–83.

 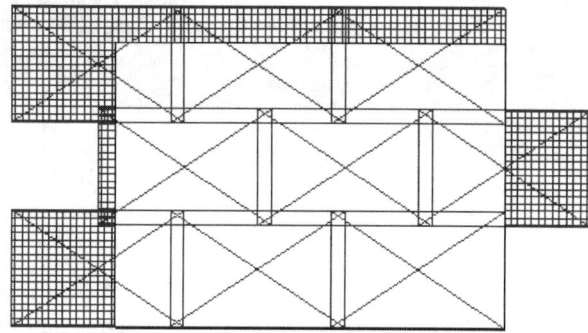

Fabric system before **Fabric system after**

Figure 9–83

- When the area or path system is removed, the individual bars create standard joins to the hosting elements. In some cases this can cause these bars to shift slightly. This is much more evident if Stirrup/Tie bars are in close proximity to the hosted bars.

- When the system is removed, the associated tags, symbols, and dimensions are also removed.

- It can help to view reinforcement in a section view. For example, in path reinforcement you can check the hook direction and modify it with the **Toggle Hook Orientation** control, as shown in Figure 9–84.

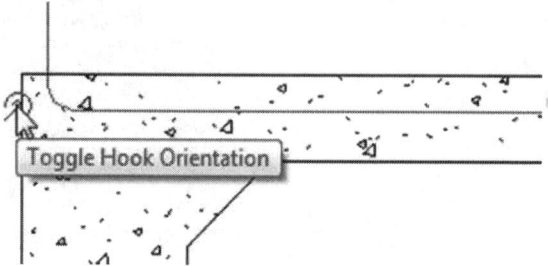

Figure 9–84

- You can also modify the other hook information in Properties. For example, you can change the **Primary Bar-Start Hook Type** as shown in Figure 9–85.

Figure 9–85

Practice 9b Reinforce Structural Elements

Practice Objective

- Add area, path, and fabric reinforcement.

In this practice, you will apply area and path reinforcement to a slab. You will also add area reinforcement to a wall and fabric reinforcement, as shown in Figure 9–86.

Area reinforcement
Path reinforcement
Fabric area reinforcement
Fabric sheet reinforcement

Figure 9–86

Task 1 - Apply area reinforcement.

1. Open **Structural-Reinforcing.rvt** from the practice files folder.

2. In the **Structural Plans: 00 GROUND FLOOR** view, change the *Visual Style* to (Hidden Line).

3. Select the structural floor by clicking on an edge. You can use <Tab> to cycle through elements.

4. In the View Control Bar, expand (Temporary Hide/Isolate) and select **Isolate Element**. This makes it easier for you to work specifically with the slab outline only.

5. In the *Modify | Floors* tab>Reinforcement panel, click (Area Reinforcement) and select the floor.

Structural Reinforcement

6. In Properties, under *Layers*, clear the **Bottom Major Direction** and **Bottom Minor Direction** parameters.

7. In the *Modify | Create Reinforcement Boundary* tab>Draw panel, click (Pick Lines).

8. In the Options Bar, select **Lock**. This ensures that, if the floor slab is modified, the boundary of the area reinforcement will update to match.

9. Select the outside edges of the slab and the outlines of the elevator and stairwell. To quickly select the outlines, hover over one line and press <Tab> so that all the connected lines highlight.

    - Verify that the magenta sketch lines do not overlap, do not have any gaps, and form a closed loop on the outside and around each opening.

10. In the *Modify | Create Reinforcement Boundary* tab>Draw panel, click (Major Direction) and select a horizontal line.

11. In the Mode panel, click (Finish Edit Mode). The area reinforcement symbol and tag display as shown in Figure 9–87.

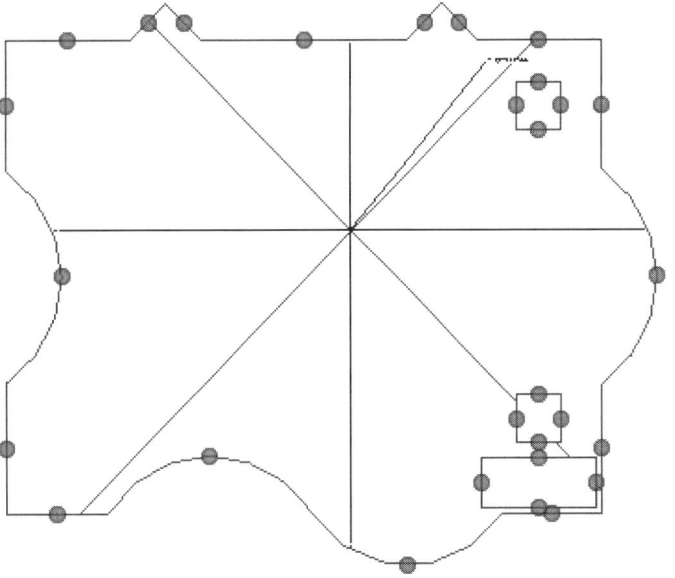

Figure 9–87

12. With the area reinforcement element still selected, in Properties, next to *View Visibility States*, click **Edit...**.

13. In the Rebar Element View Visibility States dialog box, for *Structural Plan: 00 GROUND FLOOR*, select **View unobscured,** as shown in Figure 9–88. Click **OK**.

Figure 9–88

14. Press <Esc> so that the area reinforcement is not selected. Then highlight the elements. Each rebar displays individually, as shown in Figure 9–89.

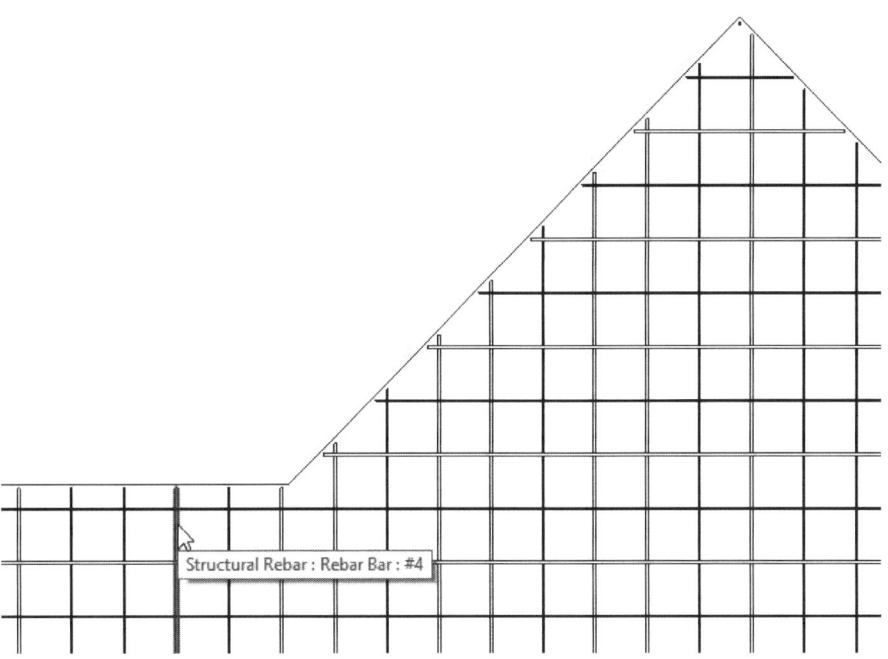

Figure 9–89

15. Select one of the rebar elements and review its properties. Most of the parameters are automatically assigned by the area reinforcement element but you can change the *Schedule Mark* and *View Visibility States*.

16. Select the entire area reinforcement element. Edit *View Visibility States* and clear the **View unobscured** for the *Structural Plan: 00 GROUND FLOOR* view and click **OK**. The view displays just the outline.

17. Open the **Sections (Wall Section): Typical Foundation Wall Section** view. The area reinforcement displays in the section as shown in Figure 9–90. The rebar and area reinforcement elements can be selected separately.

Figure 9–90

18. Save the project.

Task 2 - Apply path reinforcement.

1. Switch back to the **Structural Plans: 00 GROUND FLOOR** view with only the floor displaying.

2. In the *Structure* tab>Reinforcement panel, click (Path) and select the floor.

3. In Properties, set the *Additional Offset* to **1-1/2"** and the *Primary Bar - Shape* to **Rebar Shape 1**, as shown in Figure 9–91. Ensure that the *Alternating Bars* is toggled off.

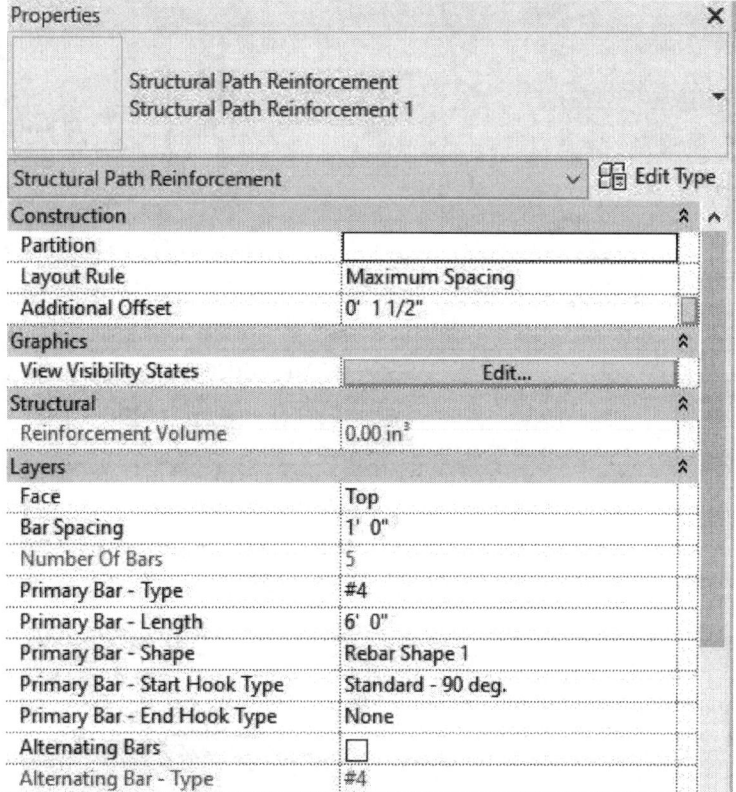

Figure 9–91

4. Using the tools in the Draw panel, draw a single line path along the north wall. Flip the path reinforcement, if needed, so that it is set to the inside, as shown in Figure 9–92.

Figure 9–92

Structural Reinforcement

5. In the Mode panel, click ✓ (Finish Edit Mode).

6. In the View Control Bar, click 🕶 (Temporary Hide/Isolate) and select **Reset Temporary Hide Isolate**.

7. Open the **Sections (Wall Section): Typical Foundation Wall Section** view. The path reinforcement displays in the section as shown in Figure 9–93.

Figure 9–93

8. Save the project.

Task 3 - Reinforce walls.

1. In the **Typical Foundation Wall Section** view, select the wall.

2. Open the **Elevations (Building Elevation): North** view and zoom in on the selected foundation wall. Do not isolate the element because you need to see the other elements to draw the correct boundary.

3. In the *Modify | Walls* tab>Reinforcement panel, click ▦ (Area).

4. Draw the boundary between the piers excluding the slab and set the *Major Direction* to the vertical sketch line to the left, as shown in Figure 9–94. Use the **Trim** command to clean up the corners. Remember that there cannot be any gaps or overlapping lines.

Figure 9–94

5. In Properties, ensure that both the *Interior* and *Exterior Major* and *Minor* spacing is set to **1'-0"**.

6. In the Mode panel, click ✓ (Finish Edit Mode).

7. The new area reinforcement is added, as shown in Figure 9–95.

Figure 9–95

8. Save the project.

Structural Reinforcement

Task 4 - Fabric area and sheet reinforcement.

1. Open **Elevations (Building Elevation): West** view.

2. Zoom in to the lower right corner of the building and select the wall as shown in Figure 9–96.

Figure 9–96

3. In the *Modify | Walls* tab>Reinforcement panel, click (Fabric Area).

4. When prompted, do not load the Structural Fabric Reinforcement Symbols or Tags by clicking **No**.

5. Use the (Rectangle) Draw tool and draw the boundary shown in Figure 9–97. The sheets extend beyond the boundary.

The boundary is highlighted for clarification.

Figure 9–97

6. Select all of the checkboxes so that the ending edges are set up, as shown in Figure 9–98.

Figure 9–98

7. Click ✓ (Finish Edit Mode).

8. The fabric sheets display. You can modify the fabric sheet origins to change the fit, if needed.

9. Select the same wall and in the *Modify | Walls* tab> Reinforcement panel, click 📄 (Fabric Sheet).

10. When prompted, do not load the Structural Fabric Reinforcement Tags by clicking **No**.

11. Add individual fabric sheets to the wall area to the right of the previous fabric area reinforcement, as shown in Figure 9–99. You can press <Spacebar> to rotate the sheets as you place them.

Figure 9–99

12. Open a 3D view and rotate it to display the area where the fabric reinforcement is added, as shown in Figure 9–100.

Figure 9–100

13. Select the fabric sheet and area and, in Properties, click **Edit** next to *View Visibility States*. Select **View unobscured** for the 3D view you are currently in, as shown in Figure 9–101.

Figure 9–101

14. Save and close the project.

Chapter Review Questions

1. Which of the following elements can have reinforcement added to it? (Select all that apply.)

    a. Structural walls

    b. Non-structural walls

    c. Foundation walls

    d. Partition walls

2. The settings in the Rebar Cover Settings dialog box, as shown in Figure 9–102, are contained in the host that is being reinforced.

Figure 9–102

    a. True

    b. False

3. How do you load additional reinforcement into your model if it is not already available? (Select all that apply.)

    a. In the Rebar Shape Browser, right-click and select **Load**.

    b. In the *Modify | Place Rebar* tab>Family panel, select **Load Shapes**.

    c. In the *Insert* tab>Load from Library panel, select **Load Family**.

    d. In the Project Browser, in the Families>Structural Rebar section, right-click and select **Load Shapes**.

4. How do you add multiple evenly spaced instances of rebar such as that shown in Figure 9–103?

Figure 9–103

   a. Modify the Layout Rule.
   b. Use the **Array** command.
   c. Edit the Constraints.
   d. Change the **Quantity** option.

5. After sketching a custom rebar shape, as shown in Figure 9–104, where do you assign the name?

Figure 9–104

   a. Right-click on the rebar and select **Rename**.
   b. After finishing the sketch type it in the Name dialog box that comes up.
   c. In Properties, beside the Shape parameter.
   d. In the Project Browser, under Structural Rebar>Rebar Shape.

6. In which type of elements can you add structural area reinforcement as shown in Figure 9–105? (Select all that apply.)

Figure 9–105

   a. Foundation slabs
   b. Structural floors
   c. Structural walls
   d. Wall Foundations

7. To display reinforcement in a 3D view, as shown in Figure 9–106, where do you make the modification?

Figure 9–106

   a. The Visibility/Graphic Overrides dialog box.
   b. The View Visibility State in the rebar properties.
   c. The 3D View Properties in the view properties.
   d. The Visual Style of the view.

Command Summary

Button	Command	Location
Rebar Set Presentation Tools		
	Select	• **Ribbon:** In a plan view with a rebar set selected, *Modify	Structural Rebar* tab> Presentation panel
	Show All	• **Ribbon:** In a plan view with a rebar set selected, *Modify	Structural Rebar* tab> Presentation panel
	Show First and Last	• **Ribbon:** In a plan view with a rebar set selected, *Modify	Structural Rebar* tab> Presentation panel
	Show Middle	• **Ribbon:** In a plan view with a rebar set selected, *Modify	Structural Rebar* tab> Presentation panel
Reinforcement Elements		
	Area	• **Ribbon:** *Structure* tab> Reinforcement panel or with a concrete structural member selected *Modify	contextual* tab>Reinforcement panel
	Fabric Area	• **Ribbon:** *Structure* tab> Reinforcement panel or with a concrete structural member selected *Modify	contextual* tab>Reinforcement panel
	Fabric Sheet	• **Ribbon:** *Structure* tab> Reinforcement panel or with a concrete structural member selected *Modify	contextual* tab>Reinforcement panel
	Free Form Rebar	• **Ribbon:** *Modify	Place Rebar* tab > Placement Methods.
	Path	• **Ribbon:** *Structure* tab> Reinforcement panel or with a concrete structural member selected *Modify	contextual* tab>Reinforcement panel
	Rebar	• **Ribbon:** *Structure* tab> Reinforcement panel or with a concrete structural member selected *Modify	contextual* tab>Reinforcement panel
Reinforcement Tools		
	Cover	• **Ribbon:** *Structure* tab> Reinforcement panel
	Edit Constraints	• **Ribbon:** *Modify	Structural Rebar* tab> Rebar Constraints panel
	Constrained Placement	• **Ribbon:** *Modify	Structural Rebar* tab> Rebar Constraints panel

	Multi-planar	• **Ribbon:** *Modify	Create Rebar Sketch* tab>Reinforcement panel
	Parallel to Work Plane	• **Ribbon:** *Modify	Place Rebar* tab> Placement Orientation panel
	Parallel to Cover	• **Ribbon:** *Modify	Place Rebar* tab> Placement Orientation panel
	Perpendicular to Cover	• **Ribbon:** *Modify	Place Rebar* tab> Placement Orientation panel
	Pick New Host	• **Ribbon:** *Modify	Structural Rebar* tab> Host panel
	Rebar Cover Settings	• **Ribbon:** *Structure* tab> Reinforcement panel
	Reinforcement Settings	• **Ribbon:** *Structure* tab> Reinforcement panel
	Remove Fabric System	• **Ribbon:** with a structural fabric area selected *Modify	contextual* tab> Reinforcement panel
	Sketch Rebar	• **Ribbon:** *Modify	Place Rebar* tab> Placement Methods panel

Chapter 10

Structural Analysis

Once all of the framing, foundations, and slabs are in place, you can test the model to ensure that it will stand up to the loads that will be placed upon the building. To do this in the Autodesk® Revit® software, you use the analytical model.

Learning Objectives in This Chapter

- Prepare a model for analysis.
- Display analytical model elements in a view.
- Make adjustments to the structural analytical model elements.
- Set boundary conditions with information about the surrounding environment.
- Add area loads, line loads, and point loads.

10.1 Preparing Projects for Structural Analysis

Although the Autodesk Revit software does not perform the actual calculations, it can provide all of the information required for analysis. In the program, you can set up and create structural settings (such as load cases), create analytical views, adjust analytical elements, and add point loads, line loads, and area loads using analytical views, as shown in Figure 10–1.

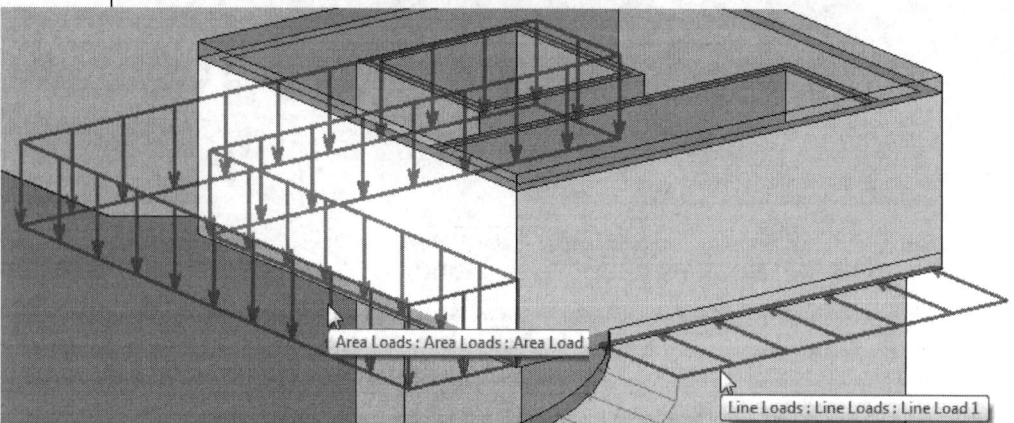

Figure 10–1

- To have a fully integrated BIM analysis workflow, you can use the Structural Analysis Toolkit for Autodesk Revit, which extends the analysis to the Autodesk Robot™ Structural Analysis Professional software or other third-party solutions. This is available with a subscription to the Autodesk Architecture, Engineering, and Construction collection.

- Once the loads are in place, the model is exported to your analysis software. After the calculations have been performed, the model is imported back into the Autodesk Revit software.

- During this process, the model does not physically move. This procedure is a flow of data. You do not have to worry about finding an insertion point or ensuring that the model is lined up correctly.

- The actual steps of exporting to and importing from analysis programs depend on the program that you have selected. Some install an add-on to the Autodesk Revit software and others have you export a specific file format.

Check your analytical software to ensure that it accepts loads from the Autodesk Revit software.

Structural Settings

The first step in preparing the analytical model is to review the structural settings in the Autodesk Revit software. The Structural Settings dialog box (shown in Figure 10–2) has five tabs containing information for *Symbolic Representation Settings*, *Load Cases*, *Load Combinations*, *Analytical Mode Settings*, and *Boundary Conditions Settings*.

Figure 10–2

- To open the Structural Settings dialog box, in the *Manage* tab>Settings panel, expand (Structural Settings) and select (Structural Settings), or in the *Structure* tab>Structure panel's title, click (Structural Settings) in the lower-right corner.

- The Structural Settings dialog box includes all of the structural settings, not just the analytical settings. The *Symbolic Representation Settings* tab (shown in Figure 10–2, above) contains options that are mainly used for the graphical model and the common defaults.

Load Cases

The *Load Cases* tab (shown in Figure 10–3) enables you to display and modify existing Autodesk Revit load cases and create new ones to suit the code and analysis software with which you are working. For example, you might need a specific load case for an extra large mechanical rooftop unit or a special sub-category (or nature), such as Residential or Offices for the *Live Loads* category.

- You can also open this dialog box using the ribbon. In the *Analyze* tab>Analytical Model panel, click (Load Cases).

Structural Analysis

Figure 10–3

- Before you place loads in the model, it is good practice to establish all of the required loads in this dialog box.

How To: Create Load Cases

1. In the Structural Settings dialog box>*Load Cases* tab, select a load case from the list and click **Duplicate**.
2. A new case is added to the list. Type a new *Name* and select the *Nature* and *Category* from the lists.

- The new load case can be used as an area load and be physically placed in the model.

- To create a new load nature, click in the *Load Natures* table and click **Add**. Type a new *Name* for the load nature.

- When you create a new load case or nature, it can be exported as a load into the analysis software you are using.

Load Combinations

In Autodesk Revit, you can create load combinations (as shown in Figure 10–4) by using a formula based on existing loads. You can assign gravity, lateral, or a combination of the two. You can build the load combination and then physically apply it to the model.

- You can also open this dialog box using the ribbon. In the *Analyze* tab>Analytical Model panel, click (Load Combinations).

Figure 10–4

Structural Analysis

How To: Create Load Combinations

1. In the Structural Settings dialog box>*Load Combinations* tab, in the top-right corner of the *Load Combination* area, click **Add**.
2. Enter a name for the new load combination in the *Name* field, such as the example shown in Figure 10–5.

Figure 10–5

3. To create the formula, verify that the new load combination is selected.
4. In the *Edit Selected Formula* area, click **Add** to add the number of cases you want to use.
5. In the *Case or Combination* column, select from the drop-down list.
6. In the *Factor* column, specify the intensity of the case applied, as shown in Figure 10–6.

Figure 10–6

7. In the *Load Combination Usage* area, click **Add**, enter a *Name*, and select the **Set** option (as shown in Figure 10–7) so that it applies to the current load combination.

    - The *Load Combination Usage* is a descriptive field. Keep this naming convention as consistent with your analysis software as possible.

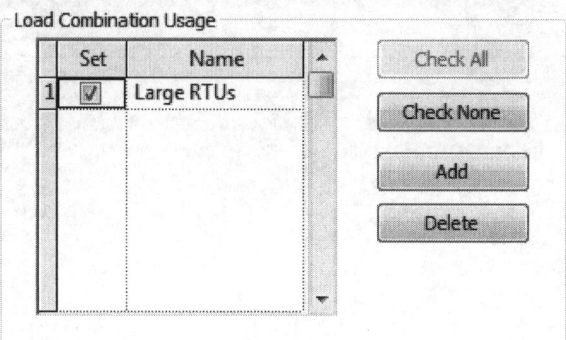

Figure 10–7

8. Back in the *Load Combination* area, select the *Type* from the drop-down list:
    - **Combination:** Provides information for a single combination.
    - **Envelope:** Provides the maximum and minimum results for a group of load combinations.
9. Select the *State* from the drop-down list:
    - **Serviceability:** Categorizes the load based on an expected force (such as wind and gravity) and natural loads (such as snow and even deflection).
    - **Ultimate:** Tests the load against unexpected forces and the overall stability of the structure when pushed to an ultimate state.
10. Click **OK** to close the dialog box. The new load combination is available for use.

Analytical Model Settings

The *Analytical Model Settings* tab (shown in Figure 10–8) is used to check the structural stability of your model as you design. You can customize when warning dialog boxes open if a structural item is placed incorrectly in the model.

- You can also open this dialog box using the ribbon. In the *Analyze* tab>Analytical Model Tools panel's title, click
    - (Analytical Model Settings).

Structural Analysis

Figure 10–8

In the *Automatic Checks* area, select which relationships you want to check as structural elements are placed in the project. The options are **Member Supports** and **Analytical / Physical Model Consistency**.

- These automatic checks can become cumbersome as you design; therefore, these options are rarely used early in the project where many structural members are unsupported. For example, if **Member Supports** is selected and you place a structural column without a bearing footing or pier, a warning prompts you about the structural deficiency.

The *Tolerances* area (shown in Figure 10–9) enables you to adjust the maximum distances permitted when you use the automatic check options.

Figure 10–9

> **Hint: Reviewing Design Issues**
>
> Instead of running automatic checks as you are designing a project, you can wait to review and check for issues later.
>
> - In the *Manage* tab>Inquiry panel, click (Review Warnings). This opens a dialog box containing a list of all of the warnings for the entire model.
>
> - There are two tools in the *Analyze* tab>Analytical Model Tools panel: (Check Supports) and (Consistency Checks). These tools produce warnings based on settings in this dialog box so that you know where to make potential adjustments.

- In the *Member Supports Check* area, specify if you want to enable checks for **Circular references** either during automatic checks or when you run one of the analysis checking tools.

- In the *Analytical/Physical Model Consistency Check* area, specify the options you want to check either during automatic checks or when you run one of the analysis checking tools.

- In the *Analytical Model Visibility* area, select **Differentiate ends of linear analytical models** if you want to see different colors for the start and end of analytical elements, as shown in Figure 10–10.

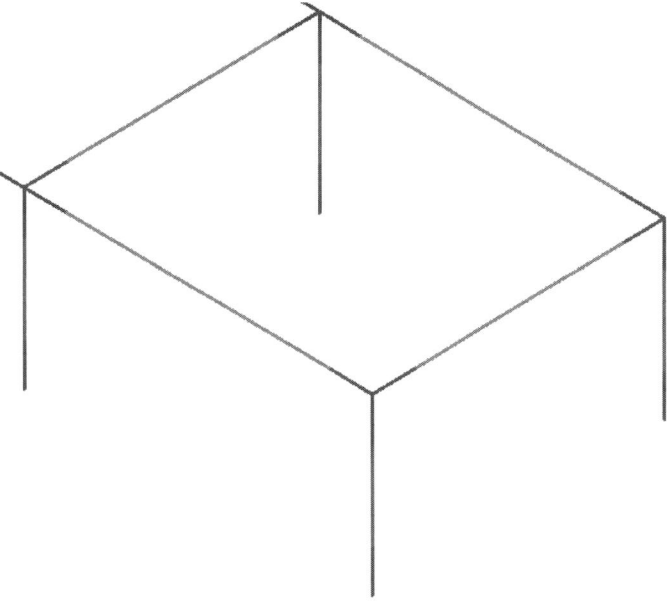

Figure 10–10

Boundary Conditions Settings

Boundary Conditions Settings are applicable if you are defining a condition in which other forces are assumed to support a structural element. A typical boundary condition would be supporting the earth underneath a footing (as shown in Figure 10–11) or a slab on grade. As you place a boundary condition in the model, these settings define its appearance.

Figure 10–11

- There are four definable boundary conditions for the family symbol: *Fixed*, *Pinned*, *Roller*, and *User Defined*, as shown in Figure 10–12.

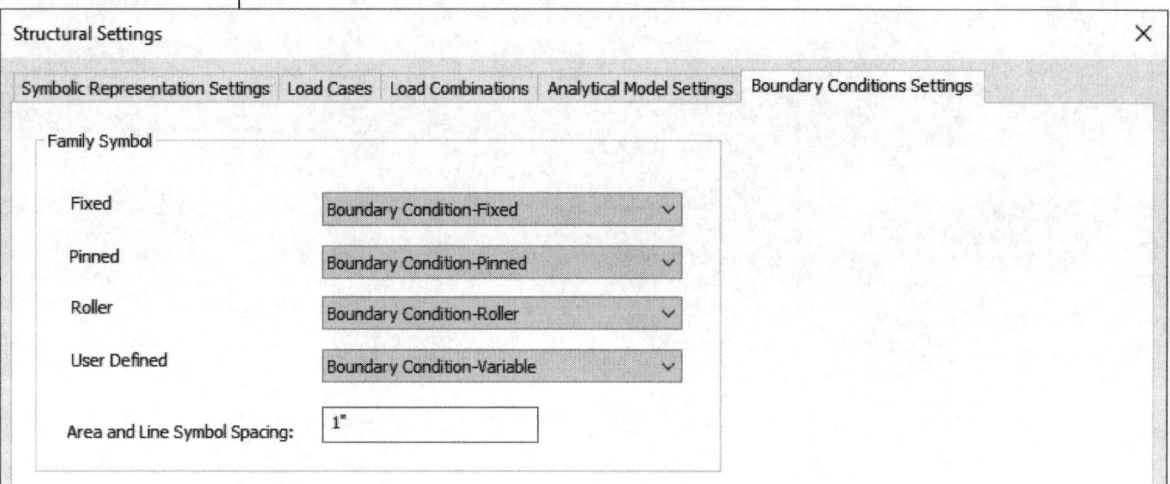

Figure 10–12

- You can also open this dialog box using the ribbon. In the *Analyze* tab>Analytical Model panel's title, click (Boundary Condition Settings).

- In general, you should maintain the same family symbol with the condition to avoid confusion.

10.2 Viewing Analytical Models

As structural components are placed into the model, an analytical representation equivalent to the components is added as well. The default structural project template includes structural plan analytical views for Level 1 and Level 2, as well as a 3D analytical view. These views do not contain additional information, but instead display the model elements differently. Figure 10–13 shows the visual difference between an analytical model (on the left) and a physical model (on the right).

Figure 10–13

- In the View Control Bar, you can toggle between (Hide Analytical Model) and (Show Analytical Model) in any view.

- To select the analytical element, use <Tab> to cycle through the options. You can also hide the physical element.

- To establish a view as an analytical view, you can apply a view template to it. In the Project Browser, right-click on the view name and select **Apply Template Properties**. Select the appropriate analytical view template from the list, as shown in Figure 10–14.

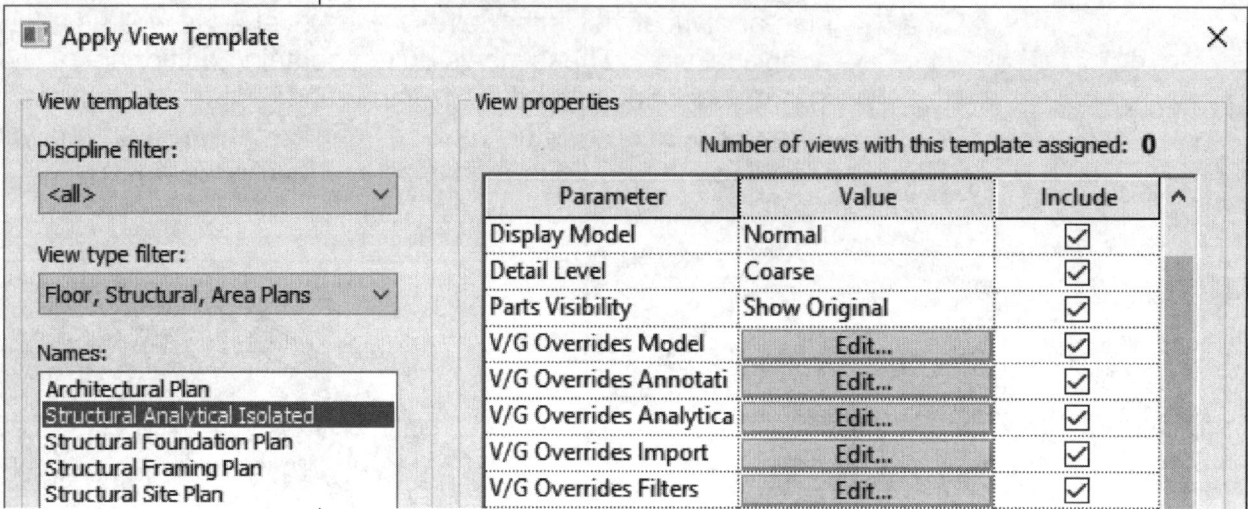

Figure 10–14

- Your company template might provide other options.

- View templates can be copied from one project to another using **Transfer Project Standards**.

- You can temporarily override view properties to see the analytical elements or other view template setups. In the View Control Bar, expand (Temporary View Properties) and select a view template, as shown in Figure 10–15. If no recent templates display, select **Temporarily Apply Template Properties...** and in the dialog box, select the view template you want to use.

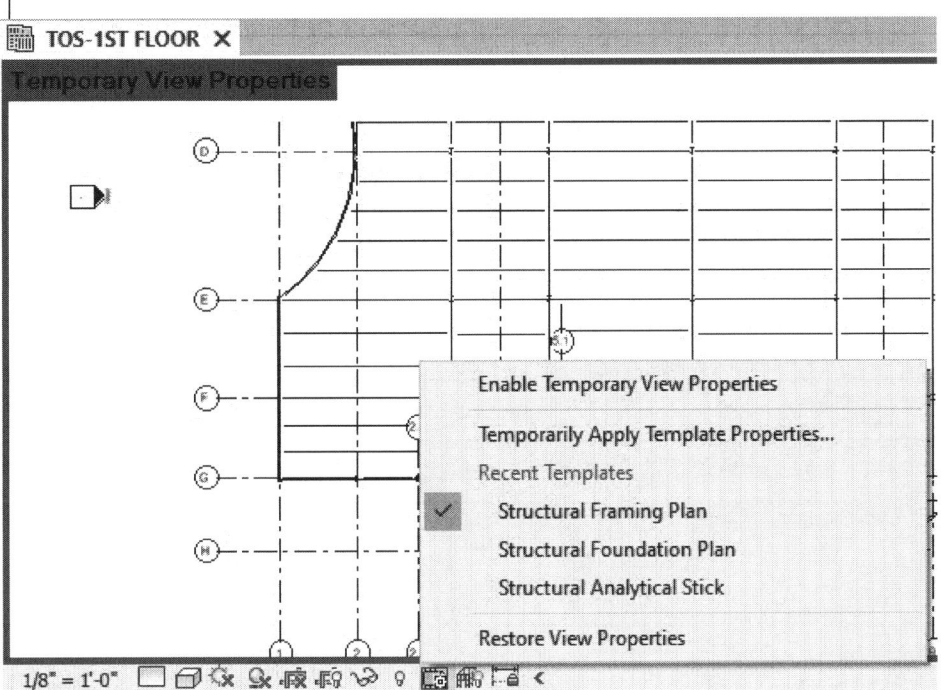

Figure 10–15

- To toggle off the temporary view properties, in the View Control Bar, expand (Temporary View Properties) and select **Restore View Properties**.

Graphic Overrides for Analytical Model Categories

The Autodesk Revit software uses different colors to indicate the different types of analytical lines. For example, the analytical lines for beams display in orange, columns display in blue, braces display in light mossy green (as shown in Figure 10–16), structural walls display in cyan, and structural floors display in brown. The appearance of elements in the analytical model are set globally in Object Styles.

Figure 10–16

- The appearance and visibility of analytical elements can be overridden in a specific view using the Visibility/Graphic Overrides dialog box, as shown in Figure 10–17.

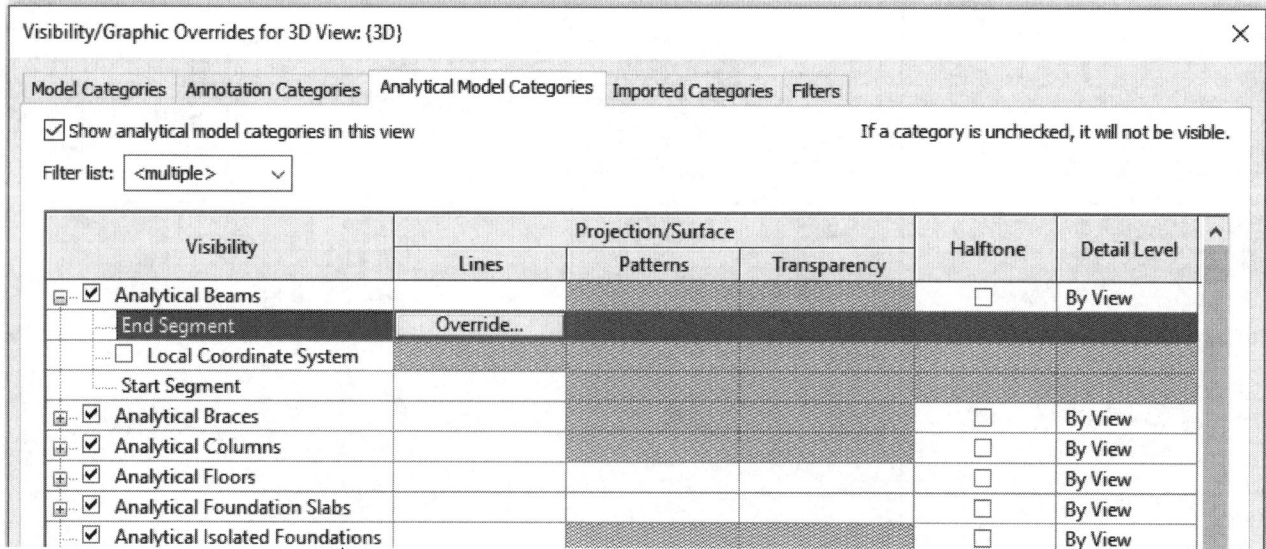

Figure 10–17

Structural Analysis

- You can override the default colors in the Visibility/Graphic Overrides dialog box by expanding the category (such as *Analytical Beams*, shown in Figure 10–17) and selecting a color for the *End Segment* or *Start Segment*.

- To see the different colors for the end segment and start segment of analytical elements (as shown for a brace in Figure 10–18), in the Structural Settings dialog box> *Analytical Model Settings* tab, select **Differentiate ends of linear analytical elements**.

Figure 10–18

Displaying the Local Coordinate System

To display the local coordinate system (LCS) widget, expand the category (such as *Analytical Beams*, as shown previously in Figure 10–17) and select **Local Coordinate System**.

- The widget shows the X-axis (red), Y-axis (green), and Z-axis (blue) of the LCS, as shown in Figure 10–19 for a beam. It displays on straight and curved beams and walls.

Coarse detail level *Medium/Fine detail level*

Figure 10–19

- Analytical beams (shown in Figure 10–19), braces, and columns are oriented with the X-axis from the beginning to the end of the element. The Y-axis is the horizontal strong axis, and the Z-axis is the vertical weak axis.

- Elements that host the LCS include analytical beams, braces, columns, floors, foundation slabs, and walls.

- Analytical walls (as shown on the left in Figure 10–20) are oriented with the X-axis in the vertical orientation, the Y-axis perpendicular to the X-axis, and the Z-axis from the interior to the exterior face.

- Analytical floors and slabs (as shown on the right in Figure 10–20) are oriented with the X-axis following the span direction, the Y-axis perpendicular to the X-axis, and the Z-axis perpendicular to the top surface.

Analytical walls   *Analytical floors*

Figure 10–20

Practice 10a Analytical Settings and Views

Practice Objectives

- Create analytical views and view the analytical model.
- Create load cases and load combinations.

In this practice, you will create analytical views for a foundation and a roof plan. You will then modify analytical settings to show the start and end of beams and display this in a 3D view. You will also add a load case and a load combination to the structural settings for a project, as shown in Figure 10–21. The items set here work in conjunction with the next practice, which involves placing loads into the model.

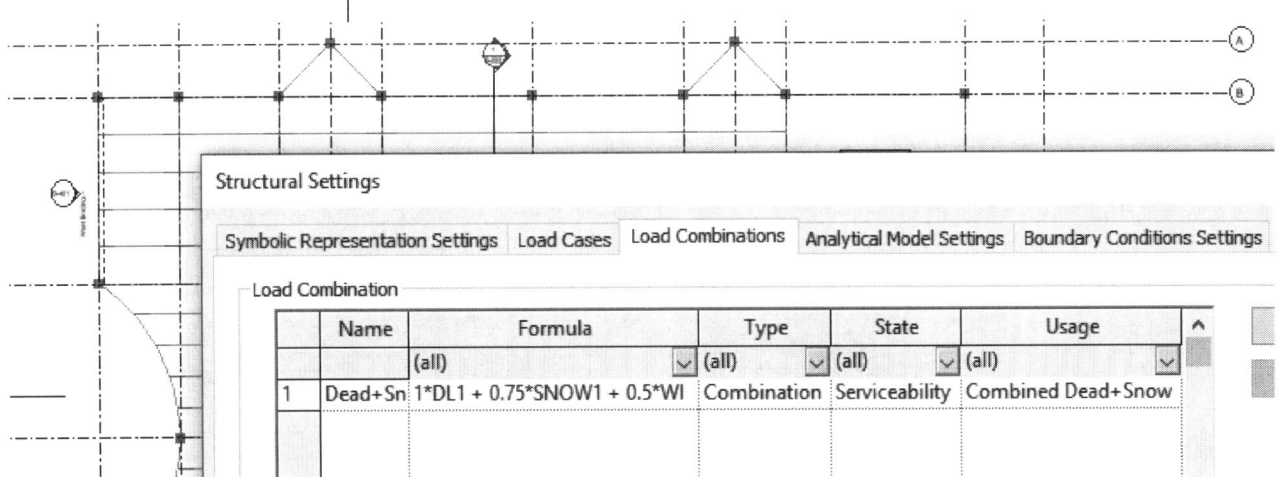

Figure 10–21

Task 1 - Create analytical views.

1. Open **Structural-Settings.rvt** from the practice files folder.

2. In the Project Browser, right-click on **Structural Plans: T.O. FOOTING** and select **Duplicate View>Duplicate With Detailing**.

3. Rename the new view **T.O. FOOTING – Analytical**.

4. In the Project Browser, right-click on the new view and select **Apply Template Properties...**.

5. In the Names area, select **Structural Analytical Stick** and click **OK**.

6. Zoom in on the plan to display the analytical view, as shown in Figure 10–22.

Figure 10–22

7. Duplicate the **Structural Plans: TOS-14 ROOF** view and rename it **TOS-14 ROOF - Analytical**. Apply the **Structural Analytical Stick** template to it as well.

8. Save the project.

Task 2 - Viewing analytical models.

1. Open the 3D Views>**View 1- Analytical** view.

2. In the View Control Bar, expand (Temporary View Properties) and select **Temporarily Apply Template Properties**.

3. In the Temporarily Apply Template Properties dialog box, select **Structural Analytical Isolated-3D** and click **OK**. Only the analytical elements display, as shown in Figure 10–23.

Structural Analysis

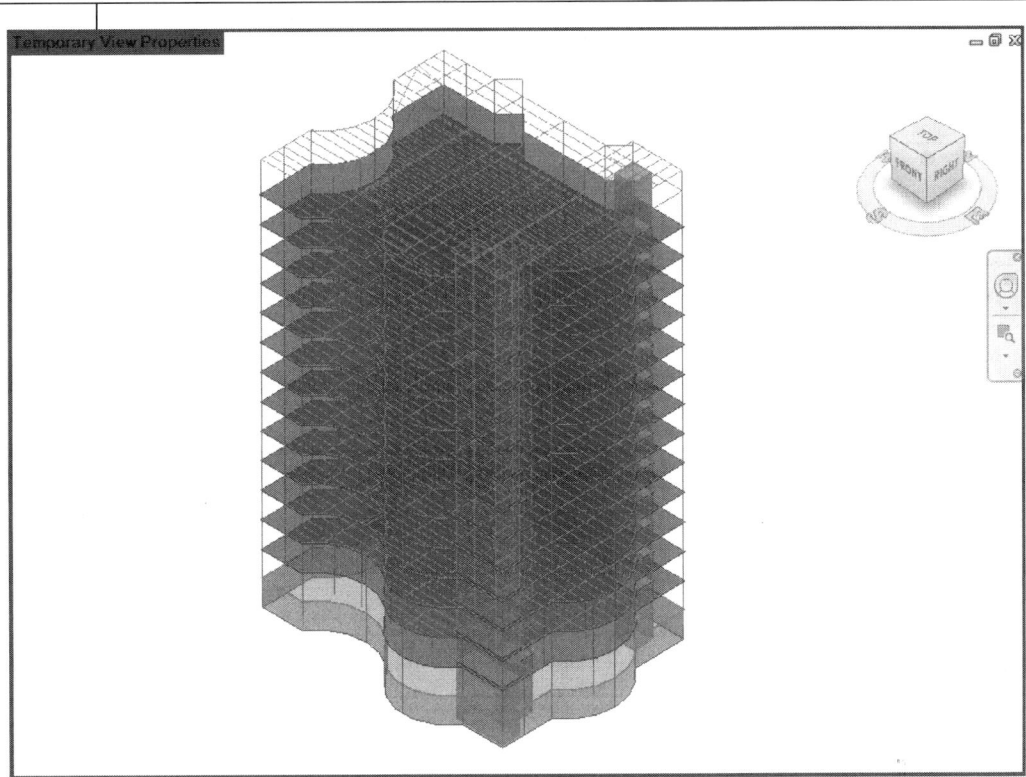

Figure 10–23

4. Zoom in to an intersection of columns and beams.

5. In the *Structure* tab>Structure panel's title, click ⁕ (Structural Settings).

6. In the Structural Settings dialog box, select the *Analytical Model Settings* tab.

7. At the bottom of the dialog box, select **Differentiate ends of linear analytical models** and click **OK**.

8. The beam start and end colors now display, as shown in Figure 10–24.

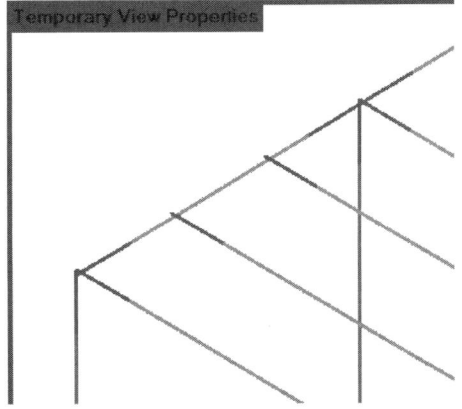

Figure 10–24

9. Open the Visibility/Graphic Overrides dialog box.

The Structural Settings dialog box automatically opens to the Load Cases tab because of the way you selected to open it.

10. In the *Analytical Model Categories* tab, expand *Analytical Beams,* select **Local Coordinate System**, and click **OK**.

11. The LCS widget displays on the beams.

12. Save the project.

Task 3 - Create load cases and load combinations.

1. In the *Analyze* tab>Analytical Model panel, click (Load Cases).

2. In the Structural Settings dialog box>*Load Cases* tab, in the *Load Cases* area, select the *Name* **SNOW1**.

3. Click **Duplicate**.

4. Click in the new load case **SNOW1 (1)** and rename it as **DRIFT**. By duplicating it, the *Nature* and *Category* are already set to **Snow** and **Snow Loads**, as shown in Figure 10–25.

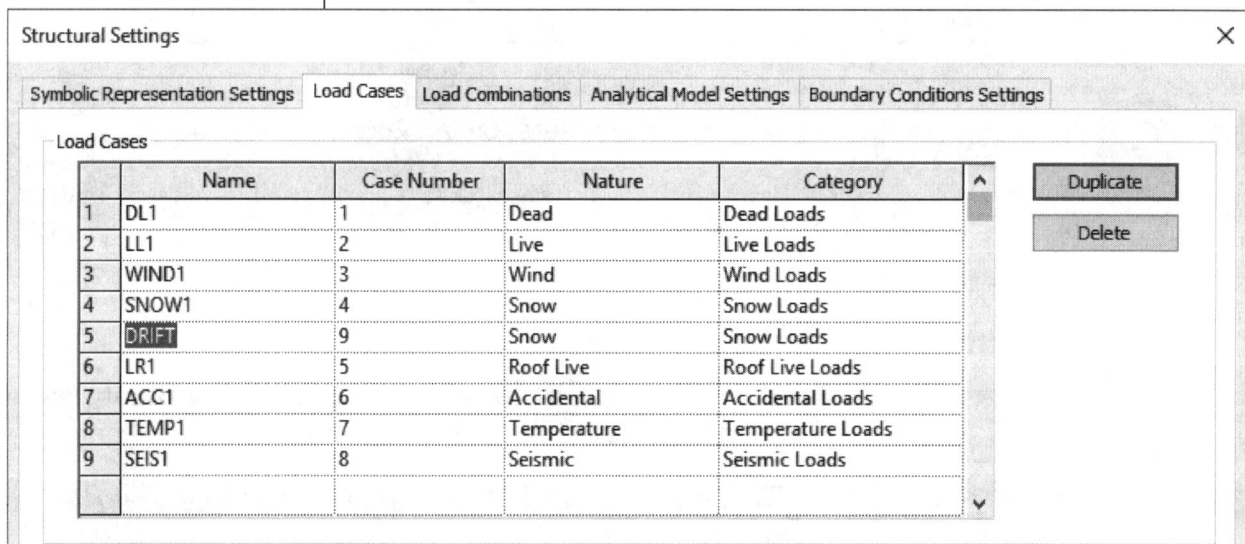

Figure 10–25

5. Switch to the *Load Combinations* tab.

6. In the *Load Combination* area, click **Add**. Name the combination **Dead+Snow+Wind**, as shown in Figure 10–26.

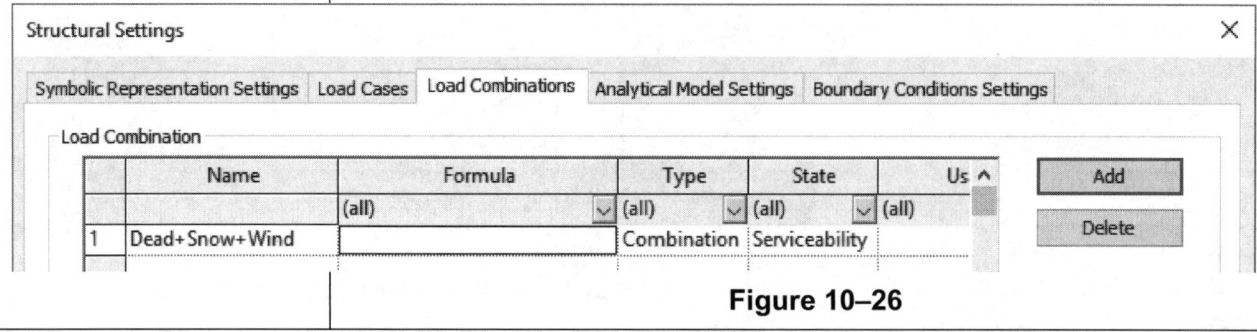

Figure 10–26

7. Select the new name.

8. In the lower-left corner, in the *Edit Selected Formula* area, click **Add** three times. Set up the *Factor* and *Case or Combination* for each row, as follows:

	Factor	Case or Combination
1	1.000000	DL1
2	0.750000	SNOW1
3	0.500000	WIND1

- The *Edit Selected Formula* area should appear as shown in Figure 10–27.

Figure 10–27

- This also displays in the *Formula* area for the load combination.

9. In the lower-right corner, in the *Load Combination Usage* area, click **Add**. Set the *Name* to **Combined Dead+Snow+Wind** and select the **Set** option, as shown in Figure 10–28.

Figure 10–28

10. In the Structural Settings dialog box, click **OK**.

11. Save and close the project.

10.3 Adjusting Analytical Models

You are keeping track of two aspects of the model as you build and use the settings that control the behavior and relationship between the physical and analytical models. As you model a structure, it is recommended that you study how your model is designed analytically (as shown in Figure 10–29), as well as physically. Taking the time to set up and adjust a model for analysis is beneficial when you need to export the model to an analysis software package.

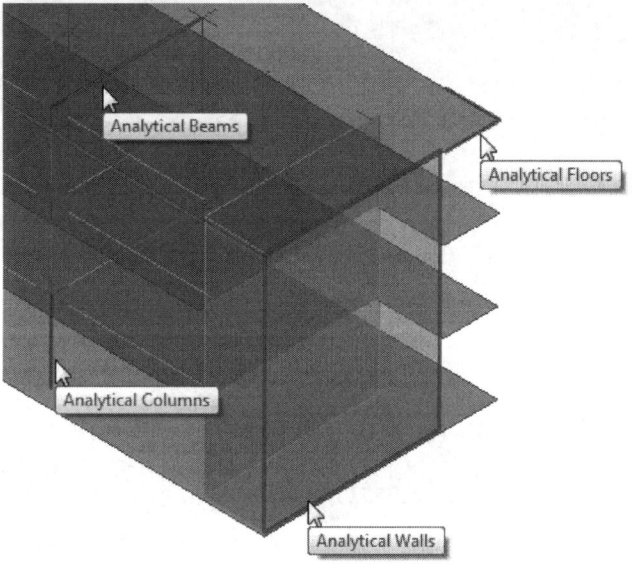

Figure 10–29

- If you do not want to include an analytical element in your analysis, you can temporarily disassociate the analytical from the physical model elements. Select the analytical element. In the *Modify | Analytical Element* tab>Analytical Model panel, click (Disable Analytical). When you want to display it again, select the physical model element and in Properties, select **Enable Analytical Model**, as shown in Figure 10–30.

Figure 10–30

Analytical Justifications

To understand what you can change, it helps to have an understanding of the standard justifications for analytical elements. Typically, the analytical lines of a structural element extend to connect it with the supporting structural element's analytical lines. For example, framing lines extend to columns and joists extend to beams, even if these are not at the same elevation.

Columns, Beams, and Braces

- By default, the analytical line element for beams and braces displays at the top of the physical framing members, while the analytical line for columns is centered on the column. This can be changed in the properties of the analytical elements.

- In cases where a beam is attached to columns and supported by braces, the analytical line might stay at the reference level even if the beam is offset below that level.

- Bracing, where the framing is at an angle, is analyzed at a chord centerline that extends into the members it is laterally supporting. The problem occurs when the physical model stops and the analytical plane keeps extending. This starts to influence the analytical model and can force unwanted inconsistencies.

Foundation Slabs and Structural Floors

- If a slab is placed in the model, the default analytical positioning occurs at the top outside edge of the slab system. If the same slab is placed bearing on walls below, the analytical plane adjusts to align with the analytical plane settings in the bearing wall. The slab analytical plane also adjusts to be at the bottom of the slab.

Walls and Footings

- The analytical walls have similar properties to framing in that the analytical model can be dependent on its host-related physical geometry or can be configured to extend to other members regardless of its host's offset from level.

- When a new wall is drawn on top of a foundation wall with the inside face flush (as shown on the left in Figure 10–31), in a 3D analytical view, the analytical plane is aligned with the analytical plane of the bearing wall (as shown on the right in Figure 10–31), although the physical centerlines of these walls do not line up.

Figure 10–31

Analytical Properties

Each type of analytical element includes properties for structural analysis. The element's connection to the model, analytical properties, and analytical alignment are shown for an analytical column in Figure 10–32.

Press <Tab> to cycle through the elements and select the analytical element, or in Properties, expand the element type and select the analytical element.

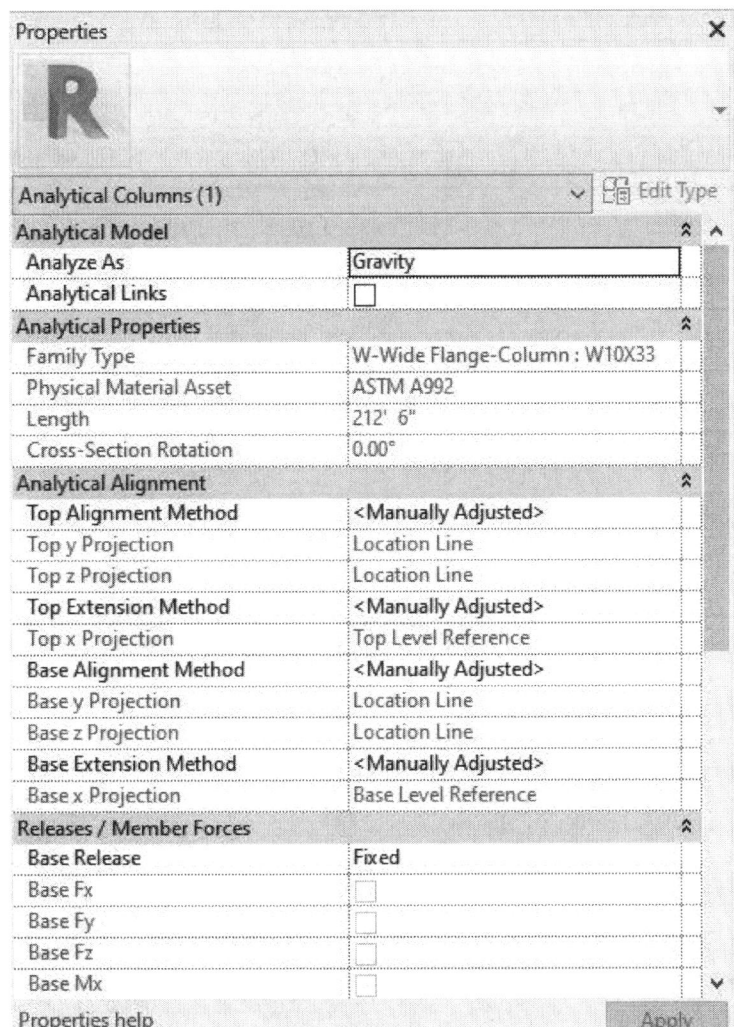

Figure 10–32

Changing Analytical Alignments in Properties

Although setting analytical alignments to **Auto-detect** works well, you sometimes require the projection be set to a specific location in the element. For example, a column can extend beyond a slab to represent a true graphical appearance of column splicing. However, analytically it should be set to the level. This is the required location for analysis when exporting the analytical model.

How To: Change the Analytical Alignment

1. Select the analytical element that you want to modify.
2. In Properties, in the *Analytical Alignment* section, expand the *Alignment* or *Extension Method* for the part of the element that you want to modify and change it to **Projection**, as shown in Figure 10–33.

Figure 10–33

3. Once the method has been set to **Projection**, you can modify the projections using the drop-down lists.

- *Extensions* (vertical) can be set to the levels or top or bottom of the element, while *Alignments* (horizontal) can be set to the justifications of the elements or along a grid line.

- If the analytical projection is beyond an acceptable difference between the physical model and the analytical model, a warning dialog box opens. Some clearance is to be expected, but should be within reason. You can set the tolerances for the analytical representations model in the Structural Settings dialog box>*Analytical Model Settings* tab.

Manually Adjusting the Analytical Model

The **Analytical Adjust** tool enables you to directly manipulate the nodes of beams and columns. It opens the Edit Analytical Model panel and toggles on nodes at the ends of beams and columns, as shown in Figure 10–34. You can select nodes and move them individually, either by dragging the node itself or using the 3D control to move the node along specific axes or planes. The tool panel also has a tool to facilitate the adjustment of analytical walls.

Structural Analysis

Figure 10–34

How To: Make Manual Adjustments to the Analytical Model

1. In the *Analyze* tab>Analytical Model Tools panel, click (Adjust).
2. Select the node that you want to modify.
3. Drag the node or use the 3D control to change the location. Press <Spacebar> to toggle the coordinate system of the 3D control between world coordinates and relative coordinates.
4. Repeat with other nodes, as needed.
5. In the floating Edit Analytical Model panel, click (Finish).

- (Wall Adjustment) enables you to modify the analytical walls in relation to other analytical walls.

- If you want to return to the default alignment methods used with **Auto-detect**, click (Reset). This removes any adjustments made manually or with projection.

Openings

An analytical model with openings in wall and floor structures can be simplified by specifying that specific openings should be excluded from analysis.

How To: Include or Exclude Openings in the Analytical Model

1. In the *Analyze* tab>Analytical Model Tools panel, click (Adjust).
2. In the Edit Analytical Model floating panel, click (Openings).
3. Checkboxes display in all of the openings, as shown on the left in Figure 10–35. Clear the box for any openings that you want excluded from the analytical model. The analytical surface color fills the opening, as shown on the right in Figure 10–35.

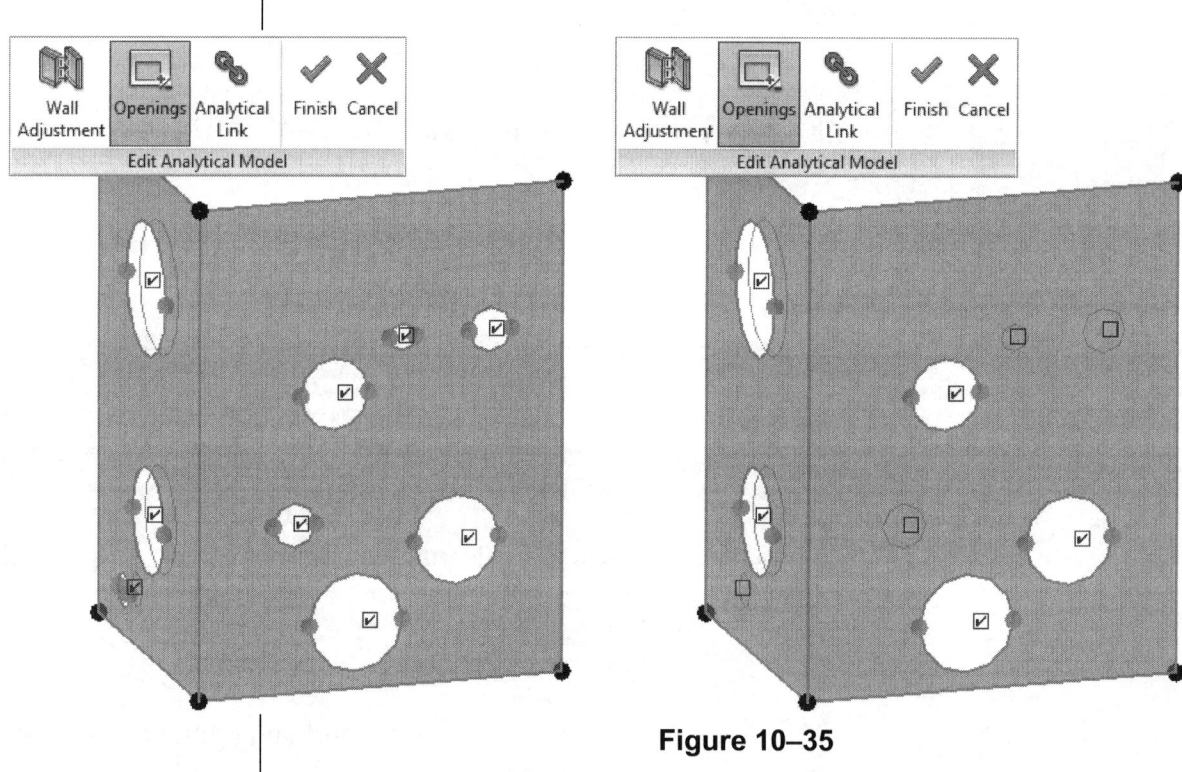

Figure 10–35

4. Click (Finish).

- The physical wall has all of its openings as before, but some of the openings do not display in the analytical model, as shown in Figure 10–36.

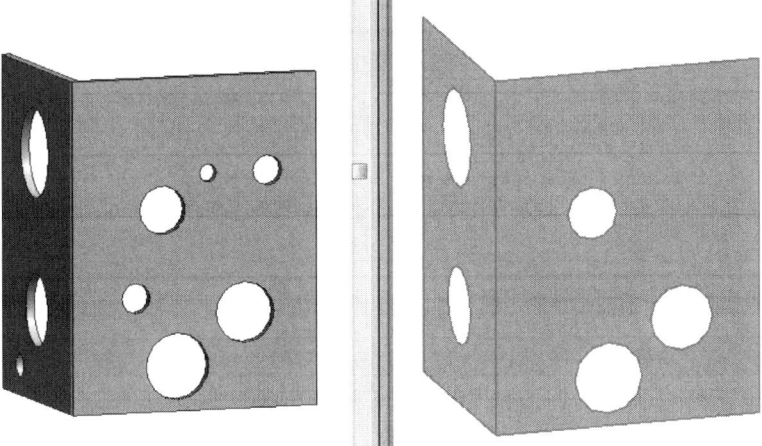

Figure 10–36

Creating Analytical Links

The Autodesk Revit software enables you to manually create analytical links between analytical nodes, which do not have a connection based on a physical structural element at the same location, as seen in Figure 10–37.

Figure 10–37

- Analytical links can be created in any direction, including vertical.

- The physical model is disregarded when calculating the tolerance for analytical links.

- The tolerance is not calculated along an axis, but as a distance in 3D space.

How To: Create Analytical Links

1. In the *Analyze* tab>Analytical Model Tools panel, click (Adjust).
2. In the Edit Analytical Model floating panel, click (Analytical Link).
3. Select the two analytical nodes between which you need a link, as shown on the left in Figure 10–38. The Autodesk Revit software draws a link between the two nodes, as shown on the right in Figure 10–38.

Analytical nodes   **Link between nodes**

Figure 10–38

4. Click (Finish).

- The rigidity of the links can be set in the Type Properties dialog box. The appearance of the link line is based on the *Analytical Link* category in Object Styles or Visibility/Graphic Overrides.

10.4 Placing Loads

As you continue to prepare your model to be analyzed, you can add loads to the building. These include boundary conditions with information about the surrounding environment, area loads (as shown in Figure 10–39), line loads, and point loads.

Figure 10–39

Boundary Conditions

A boundary condition defines the support conditions of the surrounding environment, such as the footing bearing on earth. Although you physically do not have topography, this setting sends the data to your analysis application, indicating that a natural bearing surface is not physically defined in the model. For example, the analytical wall foundation lines around the building are selected, as shown in Figure 10–40.

Figure 10–40

How To: Add a Boundary Condition

1. Open a structural plan or 3D analytical view.
2. In the *Analyze* tab>Analytical Model panel, click (Boundary Conditions).
3. In the *Modify | Place Boundary Conditions* tab>Boundary Conditions panel, click (Point), (Line), or (Area) depending on the condition being added.

	Point conditions define the support of the end or join of structural framing elements, such as an isolated footing, column, or beam. The available *States* for a point condition are **Fixed**, **Pinned**, **Roller**, and **User**.
	Line conditions define the support of a linear structural framing element, such as a structural wall or linear footing. The available *States* for a line condition are **Fixed**, **Pinned**, and **User**.
	Area conditions define the support for a structural floor or a foundation slab. The available *States* for an area condition are **Pinned** and **User**.

4. In the Options Bar (or Properties), select the *State,* as shown in Figure 10–41.

Figure 10–41

- When you select **User**, you need to modify the X, Y, and Z *Translation in* and *Rotation about* options in Properties. Area conditions do not have *Rotation about* options.

5. In Properties, specify the *Orient to* option. This can be set to **Project** or **Host Local Coordinate System**.
6. Select the appropriate point, line, or area boundary.
7. Ensure that the boundary symbol is attached to the correct analytical line. It helps to be in a 3D analytical view to display this because it can indicate where potential problems are located, as shown in Figure 10–42.

To fix the problem, in Properties, set the Base Extension of the analytical column so that it touches the foundation. The point boundary condition moves with the analytical column.

Figure 10–42

Adding Loads

Once you have placed the boundary conditions, you can create the same three kinds of load placements: **Point Load**, **Line Load** (as shown in Figure 10–43), and **Area Load**. These are used by the analysis software to size the structural members.

Figure 10–43

For each of the three types of loads, you can place them in a model independently by clicking on the screen or selecting a host. This results in six different options for placing a load, as shown in Figure 10–44.

Figure 10–44

For example, if you have a snow load, you can place it into the model as an area load hosted by the roof. If you want to add a drifting snow load, you would sketch the area load, as shown in Figure 10–45. Placing independent loads requires more work than using hosts, but you still need to assign load cases and set the orientation in either method.

Figure 10–45

- Before placing loads, set up any load cases you might need.

  In the *Analyze* tab>Analytical Model panel, click (Load Cases), or open the Structural Settings dialog box and select the *Load Cases* tab.

Load Types

	Point Load: Set the *Placement Plane* in the Options Bar before selecting the location for the point.
	Line Load: Draw the line load using the tools in the Draw panel. In the Options Bar, set the *Placement Plane* and whether you want to **Chain** the lines as you draw.
	Area Load: Draw the area load using the tools in the Draw panel. In the Options Bar, set the **Chain** and **Offset** options, as needed. You can also create a sloped area load using (Reference Point) in the Tools panel. You can select **Projected Load** in Properties for the load intensity to be projected along the sloped projection.
	Hosted Point Load: Select an analytical point to host the load. Analytical points are at the ends of structural elements.
	Hosted Line Load: Select an analytical element. The load is assigned along the entire linear edge.
	Hosted Area Load: Select an analytical element. The load is assigned all around the analytical element, such as a slab or wall.

Structural Analysis

How To: Add Loads

1. Open an analytical view, such as a 3D analytical view.
2. In the *Analyze* tab>Analytical Model panel, click (Loads).
3. In the *Modify | Place Loads* tab>Load panel, select the type of load you want to use.
4. For non-hosted loads, in the Options Bar, specify the *Placement Plane*. This can be any datum element, including grid lines, levels, and reference planes.
5. In Properties, modify the parameters as needed.
   - *Load Case:* Applies the load case to the load that is added to the model.
   - *Nature:* Shows the user-friendly name for the load setup in the *Load Cases* tab of the Structural Settings dialog box.
   - *Orient to:* Specifies the coordinate system for the orientation of the load.
   - *Fx, Fy, Fz:* Indicates the direction from which the load is coming.
   - *Mx, My, Mz:* Indicates the moment around the axis.
6. For non-hosted loads, click the point or use the Draw panel tools to sketch the line or area boundary. When drawing an area load, click (Finish Edit Mode) to complete the boundary and place the load.

   For hosted loads, select the host. Figure 10–46 shows a load displayed for a hosted load on an analytical slab.

If you placed boundary conditions, they might be displayed. You can hide these conditions as needed.

Figure 10–46

Coordinate System Orientation Options

- **Project:** Uses the global coordinate system (X-, Y-, Z-axis) of the project.

- **Work Plane:** Uses the current work plane as the coordinate system. (This only works with non-hosted loads.)

- **Host Local Coordinate System:** Uses the LCS of the selected host. (This only works with hosted loads.)

Setting the Direction

You can change the direction of a line load by changing the force direction. In the example shown in Figure 10–47, a line load is placed on a host beam. Then, in Properties, the *Fx1*, *Fy1*, and *Fz1* parameters are set to modify the direction.

Figure 10–47

Structural Analysis

Practice 10b

Place Loads

Practice Objectives

- Place boundary conditions.
- Place area loads and line loads.

In this practice, you will add boundary conditions around linear and isolated footings, and place line loads and area loads (as shown in Figure 10–48) on a roof.

Figure 10–48

Task 1 - Place boundary conditions.

1. Open **Structural-Loads.rvt** from the practice files folder.

2. Open the **Structural Plans: T.O. FOOTING - Analytical** view.

3. Zoom in on the lower-left corner of the building.

4. Select one of the cyan analytical wall elements (press <Tab> to cycle through options). Hold <Ctrl> and select one of the foundation walls, as shown in Figure 10–49.

Figure 10–49

5. In the View Control Bar, expand (Temporary Hide/Isolate) and select **Hide Category**. All of the foundation walls and their associated analytical walls are temporarily hidden and the dark green analytical lines for the foundation are displayed, as shown in Figure 10–50.

Figure 10–50

You want to put the boundary conditions on the analytical footings and not on the foundation wall.

6. In the *Analyze* tab>Analytical Model panel, click (Boundary Conditions).

7. In the *Place Boundary Conditions* tab>Boundary Conditions panel, click (Line).

8. In the Options Bar, set the *State* to **Fixed**.

9. Select the analytical wall foundations that define the center of the footings to place the boundary conditions, as shown in Figure 10–51. Continue around the entire perimeter of the building.

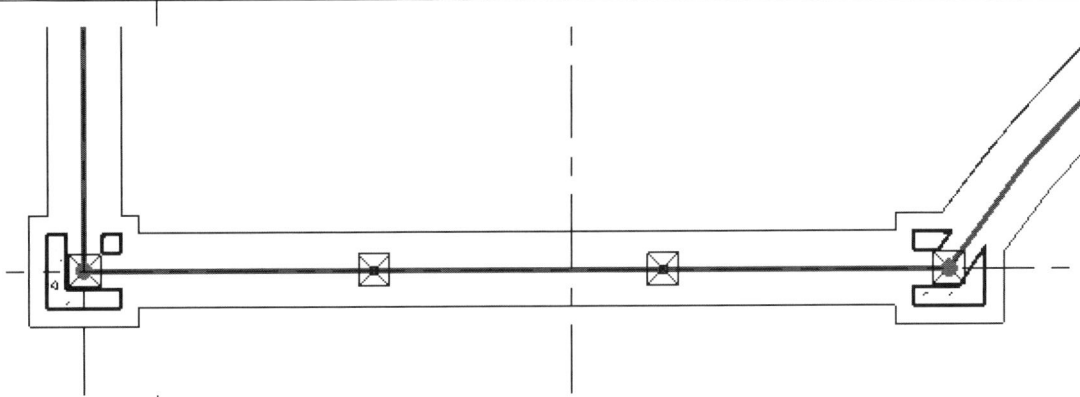

Figure 10–51

10. Open the **3D Views: View 1 - Analytical** view.

11. Rotate the view to display the bottom of the building.

12. Window around the bottom of the building and then filter out everything except **Analytical Columns**, as shown in Figure 10–52. Click **OK**.

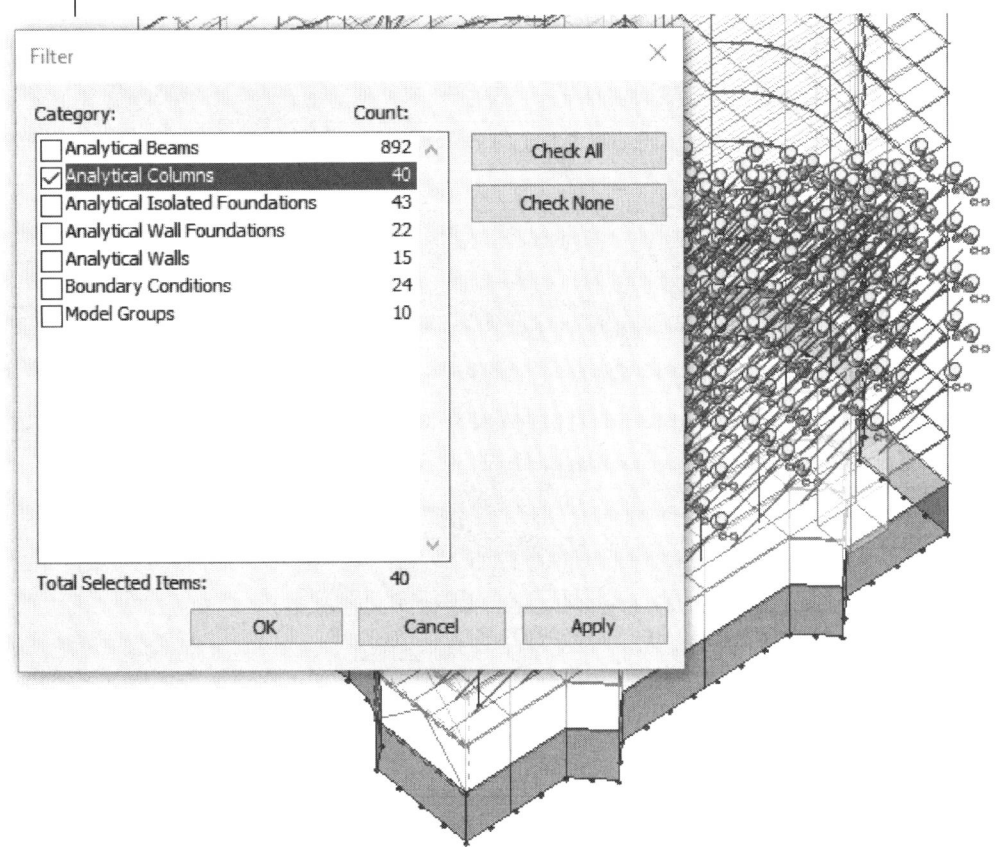

Figure 10–52

13. In the View Control Bar, expand *Temporary Hide/Isolate* and select **Isolate Element**. Note that only the selected columns display, and you can apply boundary conditions to them more easily.

14. In the *Analyze* tab>Analytical Model panel, click (Boundary Conditions).

15. In the *Modify | Place Boundary Conditions* tab>Boundary Conditions panel, click (Point).

16. In the Options Bar, set the *State* to **Fixed**.

17. Click on the bottom of each of the isolated footings on which the piers bear weight.

18. Zoom in as needed to select the dots at the bottom of the blue analytical column for each of the analytical isolated footings, as shown in Figure 10–53.

Figure 10–53

19. Click (Modify).

20. Reset **Temporary Hide/Isolate**.

21. Save the project.

Task 2 - Place area loads.

1. Open the **Structural Plans: TOS-14 ROOF - Analytical** view.

2. Select one of the structural framing tags and type **VH** to hide all of them in the view.

3. Zoom in on the upper-right area between grid intersections **A8** and **C10**, which is the penthouse area, as shown in Figure 10–54.

Figure 10–54

4. In the *Analyze* tab>Analytical Model panel, click (Loads).

5. In the *Place Loads* tab>Loads panel, click (Area Load).

6. In Properties, in the *Structural Analysis* section, set the *Load Case* to **DRIFT (9)** and the *Orient to* to **Work Plane**, and verify that *Fz1* is set to (negative) **-0.1000**, as shown in Figure 10–55.

Figure 10–55

7. Draw a sketch of the drift region around the penthouse area and offset **8'-0"** from grid line **C**, as shown in Figure 10–56.

   - Use Trim to ensure the boundary line forms a complete, closed loop.

Figure 10–56

8. You will repeat adding an area load around the penthouse on the other side between grid intersections **E8** and **G10**, as shown in Figure 10–57. (You can sketch more than one area in a session, but they each must be closed sketches.)

Figure 10–57

9. In the Mode panel, click ✓ (Finish Edit Mode).

10. The model displays as shown in Figure 10–58.

Figure 10–58

11. Save the project.

Task 3 - Place line loads.

1. Continue working in the **Structural Plans: TOS-14 ROOF - Analytical** view.

2. Zoom and pan to display the south edge of the building.

3. In the *Analyze* tab>Analytical Model panel, click (Loads).

4. In the *Modify | Place Loads* tab>Loads panel, click (Hosted Line Load).

5. In Properties, within the *Structural Analysis* section, set the *Load Case* to **WIND1 (3)**. In the *Forces* section, set *Fy1* to **0.500 kip/ft** and set *Fz1* to **0.00kip/ft**, as shown in Figure 10–59.

Figure 10–59

6. Select the analytical beam lines on the south edge of the building, as shown in Figure 10–60.

Figure 10–60

7. Click ▸ (Modify) to end the command.

8. Return to the 3D analytical view and rotate it so you can see the loads on the roof.

9. Save and close the project.

Chapter Review Questions

For the first four questions, match the graphics in Figure 10–61 to the correct description of each view.

Figure 10–61

1. Medium/fine level of detail set in the View Control Bar.
    a. Figure A
    b. Figure B
    c. Figure C
    d. Figure D

2. Boundary conditions added to the model.
    a. Figure A
    b. Figure B
    c. Figure C
    d. Figure D

3. Coarse level of detail set in the View Control Bar.
    a. Figure A
    b. Figure B
    c. Figure C
    d. Figure D

4. Analytical isolated view template applied.
    a. Figure A
    b. Figure B
    c. Figure C
    d. Figure D

5. If you are having a hard time selecting an analytical element in a view, which of the following is a short-term method that would help?
    a. Set the *Detail Level* to **Coarse**.
    b. Use **Temporary Hide/Isolate**.
    c. Apply a Temporary View Properties override.
    d. Toggle off non-analytical elements in Visibility/Graphic Overrides.

6. Figure 10–62 is an example of which structural setting?

	Name	Formula	
		(all)	(a
1	Dead+Snow+Wind	1*DL1 + 0.75*SNOW1 + 0.5*WIND1	C

Figure 10–62

    a. Load Cases
    b. Load Combinations
    c. Boundary Conditions
    d. Analytical Settings

7. Boundary conditions include information about the surrounding environment, not physical loads on the structure.
    a. True
    b. False

8. Which of the following is NOT a type of load that can be accessed using the **Loads** command, as shown in Figure 10–63?

   Figure 10–63

   a. Point
   b. Area
   c. Node
   d. Line

9. Which of the following enable you to make manual adjustments to the analytical model without changing the physical model? (Select all that apply.)

   a. In the *Analyze* tab, select the **Analytical Adjust** command.
   b. In an analytical view, select the analytical line and use the **Move** command in the *Modify* tab.
   c. In Properties, select the *Start level* and *End level offset*.
   d. In an analytical view, select an analytical line and change its properties.

Command Summary

Button	Command	Location
Adjusting Analytical Models		
	Adjust	• **Ribbon**: *Analyze* tab>Analytical Model Tools panel • **Shortcut**: AA
	Analytical Link	• **Floating panel**: Edit Analytical Model
	Reset	• **Ribbon**: *Analyze* tab>Analytical Model Tools panel • **Shortcut**: RA
	Supports	• **Ribbon**: *Analyze* tab>Analytical Model Tools panel
	Consistency	• **Ribbon**: *Analyze* tab>Analytical Model Tools panel
	Disable Analytical	• **Ribbon**: *Modify	Analytical Element* tab>Analytical Model panel
	Openings	• **Floating panel**: Edit Analytical Model
	Show/Hide Analytical Model	• **View Control Bar**
	Temporary View Properties	• **View Control Bar**
	Wall Adjustments	• **Floating panel**: Edit Analytical Model
Boundary Conditions		
	Area (Boundary Conditions)	• **Ribbon**: *Modify	Place Boundary Conditions* tab>Boundary Conditions panel
	Boundary Conditions	• **Ribbon**: *Analyze* tab>Analytical Model panel
	Boundary Conditions Settings	• **Ribbon**: *Analyze* tab>Analytical Model panel's title
	Point (Boundary Conditions)	• **Ribbon**: *Modify	Place Boundary Conditions* tab>Boundary Conditions panel

Loads		
	Area Load	• **Ribbon**: *Modify	Place Loads* tab> Loads panel
	Hosted Area Load	• **Ribbon**: *Modify	Place Loads* tab> Loads panel
	Hosted Line Load	• **Ribbon**: *Modify	Place Loads* tab> Loads panel
	Hosted Point Load	• **Ribbon**: *Modify	Place Loads* tab> Loads panel
	Line Load	• **Ribbon**: *Modify	Place Loads* tab> Loads panel
	Loads	• **Ribbon**: *Analyze* tab>Analytical Model panel
	Point Load	• **Ribbon**: *Modify	Place Loads* tab> Loads panel
Structural Settings		
	Analytical Model Settings	• **Ribbon**: *Analyze* tab>Analytical Model Tools panel's title
	Load Cases (Settings)	• **Ribbon**: *Analyze* tab>Analytical Model panel
	Load Combinations (Settings)	• **Ribbon**: *Analyze* tab>Analytical Model panel
or	Structural Settings	• **Ribbon**: *Manage* tab>Settings panel or • **Ribbon**: *Structure* tab>Structure panel's title

Chapter 11

Creating Construction Documents

The accurate creation of construction documents in the Autodesk® Revit® software ensures that the design is correctly communicated to downstream users. Construction documents are created primarily in special views called sheets. Selecting title blocks, assigning title block information, placing views, and printing the sheets are essential steps in the construction documentation process.

Learning Objectives in This Chapter

- Add sheets with title blocks and views of a project.
- Enter the title block information for individual sheets and for an entire project.
- Place and organize views on sheets.
- Print sheets using the default Print dialog box.

11.1 Setting Up Sheets

While you are modeling a project, the foundations of the working drawings are already in progress. Any view (such as a floor plan, section, callout, or schedule) can be placed on a sheet, as shown in Figure 11–1.

Figure 11–1

- Company templates can be created with standard sheets using the company (or project) title block and related views already placed on the sheet.

- The sheet size is based on the selected title block family.

- Sheets are listed in the *Sheets* area in the Project Browser.

- Most information on sheets is included in the views. You can add general notes and other non-model elements directly to the sheet, though it is better to add them using drafting views or legends, as these can be placed on multiple sheets.

Creating Construction Documents

How To: Set Up Sheets

1. In the Project Browser, right-click on the *Sheets* area header and select **New Sheet...**, or in the *View* tab>Sheet Composition panel, click (Sheet).
2. In the New Sheet dialog box, select a title block from the list, as shown in Figure 11–2. Alternatively, if there is a list of placeholder sheets, select one or more from the list.

*Click **Load...** to load a sheet from the Revit Library.*

Hold <Ctrl> to select multiple placeholder sheets.

Figure 11–2

3. Click **OK**. A new sheet is created using the selected title block.
4. Fill out the information in the title block, as needed.
5. Add views to the sheet.

- When you create sheets, the next sheet is incremented numerically.

- Slowly click twice on the sheet name to change the name and number in the Sheet Title dialog box.

- When you change the *Sheet Name* and/or *Number* in the title block, it automatically changes the name and number of the sheet in the Project Browser.

- The plot stamp on the side of the sheet automatically updates according to the current date and time. The format of the display uses the regional settings of your computer.

- The *Scale* is automatically entered when a view is inserted onto a sheet. If a sheet has multiple views with different scales, the scale displays as **As Indicated.**

Sheet (Title Block) Properties

Each new sheet includes a title block. You can change the title block information in Properties, as shown in Figure 11–3, or by selecting any blue label you want to edit (*Sheet Name*, *Sheet Number*, *Drawn by*, etc.), as shown in Figure 11–4.

Figure 11–3

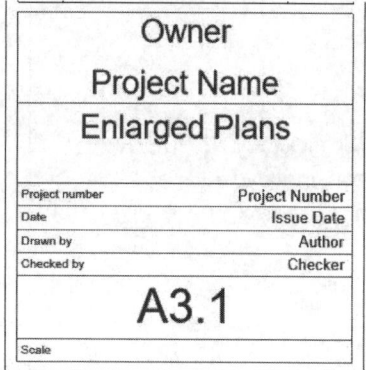

Figure 11–4

Properties that apply to all sheets can be entered in the Project Information dialog box (as shown in Figure 11–5). In the *Manage* tab>Settings panel, click (Project Information).

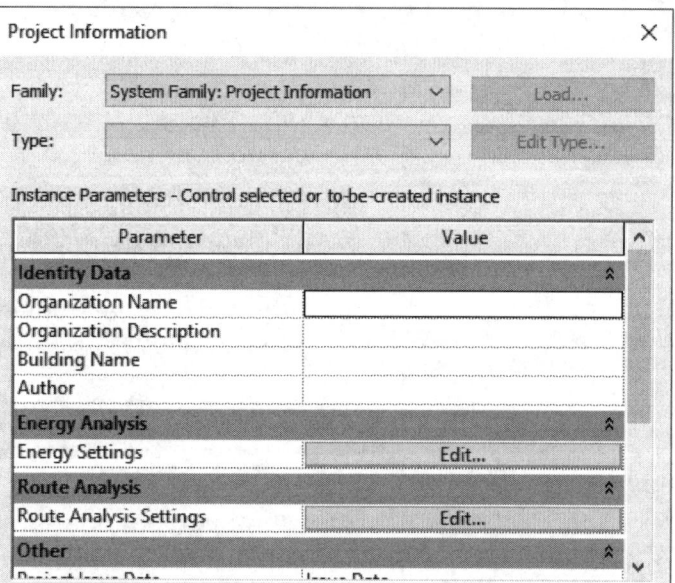

Figure 11–5

11.2 Placing and Modifying Views on Sheets

The process of adding views to a sheet is simple. Drag and drop a view from the Project Browser onto the sheet. The new view on the sheet is displayed at the scale specified in the original view. The view title displays the name, number, and scale of the view, as shown in Figure 11–6.

Figure 11–6

How To: Place Views on Sheets

Alignment lines from existing views display to help you place additional views.

1. Set up the view as you want it to display on the sheet, including the scale and visibility of elements.
2. Create or open the sheet where you want to place the view.
3. Select the view in the Project Browser, and drag and drop it onto the sheet.
4. The center of the view is attached to the cursor. Click to place it on the sheet.

Placing Views on Sheets

- Views can only be placed on a sheet once. However, you can duplicate the view and place that copy on a sheet.
- Views on a sheet are associative. They automatically update to reflect changes to the project.
- Each view on a sheet is listed under the sheet name in the Project Browser, as shown in Figure 11–7.

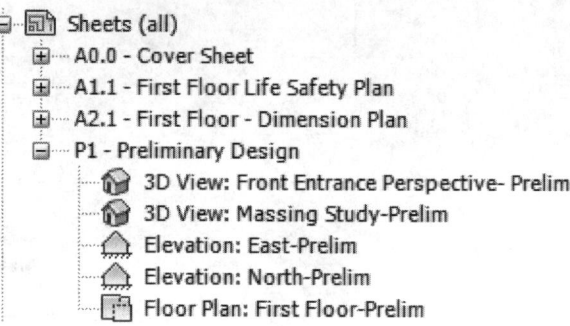

Figure 11–7

- You can also use two other methods to place views on sheets:

    - In the Project Browser, right-click on the sheet name and select **Add View...**.
    - In the *View* tab>Sheet Composition panel, click (Place View).

    Then, in the Views dialog box (shown in Figure 11–8), select the view you want to use and click **Add View to Sheet.**

This method lists only those views which have not yet been placed on a sheet.

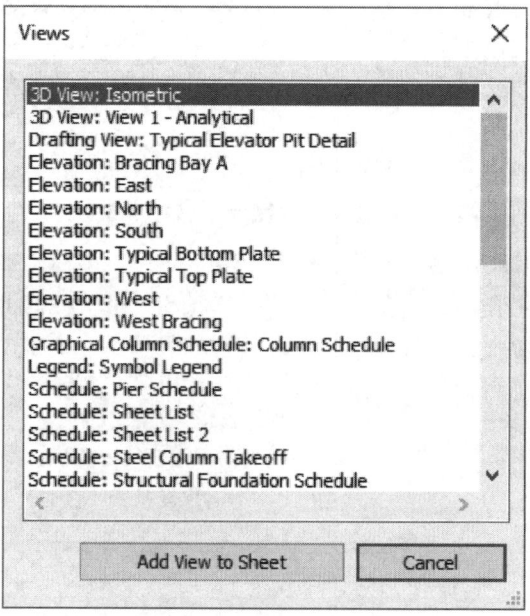

Figure 11–8

- To remove a view from a sheet, select it and press <Delete>. Alternatively, in the Project Browser, expand the individual sheet information to show the views, right-click on the view name, and select **Remove From Sheet**.

> **Hint: Setting Up the Project Browser**
>
> To view and change the Project Browser's type, select the top level node of the Project Browser (which is set to *Views (all)* by default) and select the type you want to use from the Type Selector. For example, you can set the Project Browser to only display views that are not on sheets, as shown in Figure 11–9.
>
>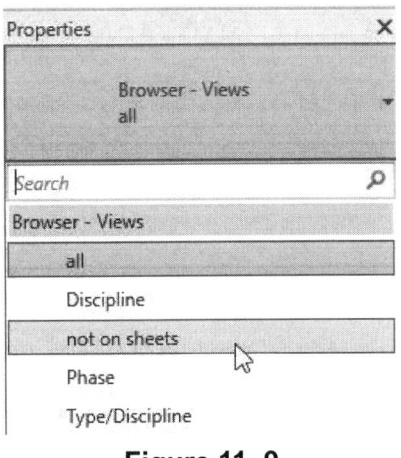
>
> Figure 11–9

Moving Views and View Titles

*You can also use the **Move** command or the arrow keys to move a view.*

- To move a view on a sheet, select the edge of the view and drag it to a new location. The view title moves with the view.

- To move only the view title, select only the view title and drag it to the new location.

- To modify the length of the line under the title name, select the edge of the view and drag the controls, as shown in Figure 11–10.

Figure 11–10

- To change the title of a view on a sheet without changing its name in the Project Browser, in Properties, in the *Identity Data* section, type a new title for the *Title on Sheet* parameter, as shown in Figure 11–11.

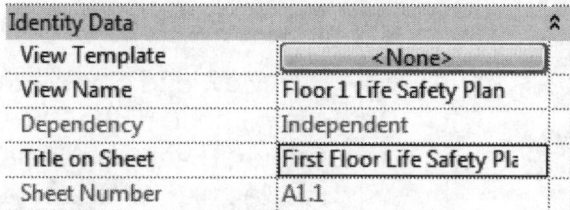

Figure 11–11

Rotating Views

- When creating a vertical sheet, you can rotate the view on the sheet by 90 degrees. Select the view and set the direction of rotation in the Rotation on Sheet drop-down list in the Options Bar, as shown in Figure 11–12.

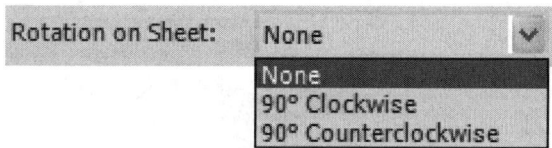

Figure 11–12

- To rotate a view to an angle other than 90 degrees, open the view, toggle on and select the crop region, and use the **Rotate** command to change the angle.

Working Inside Views

To make small changes to a view while working on a sheet:

- Double-click *inside* the view to activate it.
- Double-click *outside* the view to deactivate it.

Only elements in the viewport are available for modification. The rest of the sheet is grayed out, as shown in Figure 11–13.

Only use this method for small changes. Significant changes should be made directly in the view.

Figure 11–13

- You can activate and deactivate views by right-clicking on the edge of the view or by using the tools found in the *Modify | Viewports* and *Views* tab>Sheet Composition panel.

- Changes you make to elements when a view is activated also display in the original view.

- If you are unsure which sheet a view is on, right-click on the view in the Project Browser and select **Open Sheet**. This item is grayed out if the view has not been placed on a sheet and is not available for schedules and legends, which can be placed on more than one sheet.

Resizing Views on Sheets

Each view displays the extents of the model or the elements contained in the crop region. If the view does not fit on a sheet (as shown in Figure 11–14), you might need to crop the view or move the elevation markers closer to the building.

If the extents of the view change dramatically based on a scale change or a crop region, it is easier to delete the view on the sheet and drag it over again.

Figure 11–14

- For information about laying out views on sheets using guide grids, see *B.7 Working with Guide Grids on Sheets*.

- For information about working with revisions in views and on sheets, see *B.8 Revision Tracking*.

How To: Add an Image to a Sheet

Company logos and renderings saved to image files (such as .JPG and .PNG) can be added directly on a sheet or in a view.

1. In the *Insert* tab>Import panel, click (Image).
2. In the Import Image dialog box, select and open the image file. The extents of the image display, as shown in Figure 11–15.

Figure 11–15

3. Place the image where you want it.
4. The image is displayed. Pick one of the grips and extend it to modify the size of the image.

- In Properties, you can adjust the height and width and also set the *Draw Layer* to either **Background** or **Foreground**, as shown in Figure 11–16.

Dimensions	
Width	1' 5 185/256"
Height	1' 1 41/64"
Horizontal Scale	1.000000
Vertical Scale	1.000000
Lock Proportions	✓
Other	
Draw Layer	Background

Figure 11–16

- You can select more than one image at a time and move them as a group to the background or foreground.

- In the *Modify | Raster Images* tab (as shown in Figure 11–17), you can access the Arrange options and the **Manage Images** command.

Figure 11–17

Practice 11a Create Construction Documents

Practice Objectives

- Set up project properties.
- Create sheets individually.
- Place views on sheets.

In this practice, you will complete project information, create a cover sheet, and add views to the sheet. You will then create a foundation plan sheet, as shown in Figure 11–18, and as many other sheets as time permits, modifying the scales as required.

Figure 11–18

Task 1 - Complete the project information.

1. Open **Structural-Sheets.rvt** from the practice files folder.

2. In the *Manage* tab>Setting panel, click (Project Information).

Creating Construction Documents

These properties are used across the entire sheet set and do not need to be entered on each sheet.

3. In the Project Properties dialog box, in the *Other* section, set the following parameters (or use your own information based on your company standards):

   - *Project Issue Date:* current date
   - *Project Status:* **Design Development**
   - *Client Name:* **ASCENT Structural Properties**
   - *Project Address:* (click **...**) **Enter any address**
   - *Project Name:* **Structural Suites**
   - *Project Number:* **1234-567**

4. Click **OK**.

5. Save the project.

Task 2 - Create a cover sheet.

1. In the Project Browser, right-click on *Sheets (all)* and select **New Sheet**, as shown in Figure 11–19. Alternatively, in the *View* tab>Sheet Composition panel, click (New Sheet).

Some sheets already exist in the project.

Figure 11–19

2. In the New Sheet dialog box, in the *Select Titleblocks* area, select **ASCENT_Cover Sheet: 30x42 Horizontal** and click **OK**.

3. In the Project Browser, in the *Sheets* area, right-click on the new sheet and select **Rename**.

4. In the Sheet Title dialog box, set *Number* to **S-000** and *Name* to **Cover Sheet**, as shown in Figure 11–20. Click **OK**.

Figure 11–20

5. Zoom back out to display the whole sheet.

6. In the *Insert* tab>Import panel, click (Import Image).

7. In the Import Image dialog box, navigate to the practice files *Images* folder and select **Structural Suite Perspective.png**. Click **Open**.

8. Your cursor will have an X shape (indicating the size of your image). Click to place the image on the sheet.

9. Click (Modify).

10. In the *Legends* category, add the Symbol Legend to the sheet, as shown in Figure 11–21.

Figure 11–21

11. Select the edge of the viewport. In the Type Selector, select **Viewport: No Title**.

12. Save the project.

Task 3 - Create additional sheets.

1. In the *View* tab>Sheet Composition panel, click 🗋 (Sheet).

2. In the New Sheet dialog box, select the title block **ASCENT_30x42: 30x42 Horizontal** and click **OK**.

3. In the Project Browser, right-click on **S-001 – Unnamed** and rename it as **S-201: FOUNDATION PLAN**, as shown in Figure 11–22.

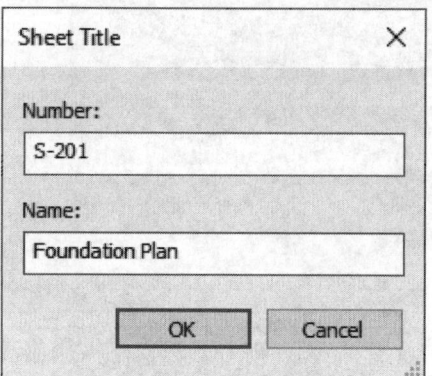

Figure 11–22

4. Click **OK**.

5. In the Project Browser, find the **T.O. FOOTING** structural plan view and drag it onto the sheet, centering it in the view, as shown in Figure 11–23.

Figure 11–23

6. Several sheets already exist in the project. Place the **Structural Plans: 00 GROUND FLOOR PLAN** view on the sheet **S-202-Ground Floor Plan.**

7. Zoom in to see the title of the view. It displays as **00 GROUND FLOOR PLAN**, as shown in Figure 11–24.

00 GROUND FLOOR PLAN
1/8" = 1'-0"

Figure 11–24

8. In the Project Browser, select the view. In Properties, scroll down to the *Identity Data* section and change the *Title on Sheet* to **GROUND FLOOR - STRUCTURAL PLAN**, as shown in Figure 11–25.

Identity Data	
View Template	<None>
View Name	00 GROUND FLOOR PLAN
Dependency	Independent
Title on Sheet	GROUND FLOOR - STRUCTURAL PLAN
Sheet Number	S-202
Sheet Name	Ground Floor Plan

Figure 11–25

9. Click **Apply**. The title changes on the sheet, as shown in Figure 11–26.

GROUND FLOOR - STRUCTURAL PLAN
1/8" = 1'-0"

Figure 11–26

10. (Optional) Add views to the other sheets.

    - If any views do not fit on the sheet, change the scale.

11. When section or elevation views have been added to sheets, open views with the markers on them and note that all of the tags are filled out, as shown in Figure 11–27. This enables you to verify whether the tags point to the sheets correctly. If a tag does not display detail and sheet numbers, the view has not been dragged onto a sheet.

Figure 11–27

12. Save and close the project.

11.3 Printing Sheets

With the **Print** command, you can print individual sheets or a list of selected sheets. You can also print an individual view or a portion of a view for check prints or presentations. To open the Print dialog box (shown in Figure 11–28), in the *File* tab, click (Print), or press <Ctrl>+P.

Figure 11–28

Printing Options

The Print dialog box is divided into the following areas: *Printer, File, Print Range, Options,* and *Settings*. Modify them as needed to produce the plot you want.

- **Printing Tips** opens Autodesk WikiHelp online, in which you can find help with troubleshooting printing issues.

- **Preview** opens a preview of the print output so that you can see what is going to be printed.

Printer

Select from the list of available printers, as shown in Figure 11–29. Click **Properties...** to adjust the properties of the selected printer. The options vary according to the printer. Select the **Print to file** option to print to a file rather than directly to a printer. You can create .PLT or .PRN files.

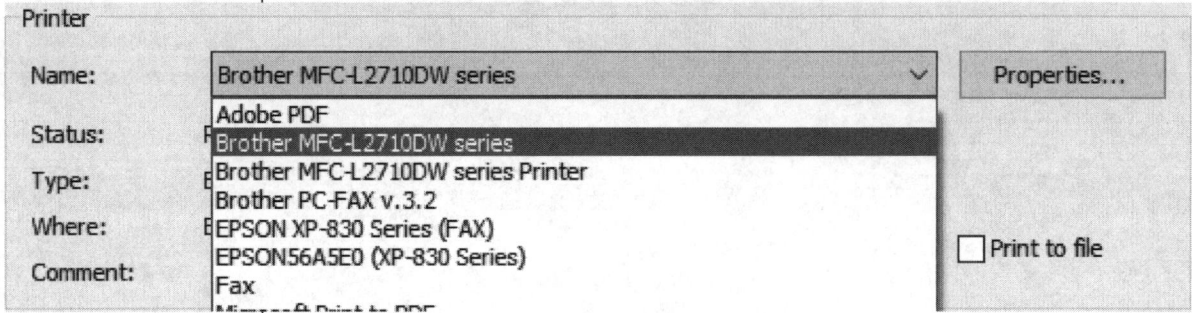

Figure 11–29

- You must have a PDF print driver installed on your system to print to PDF, or you can export views and sheets to PDF.

File

The *File* area is only available if the **Print to file** option has been selected in the *Printer* area or if you are printing to an electronic-only type of printer. You can create one file or multiple files depending on the type of printer you are using, as shown in Figure 11–30. Click **Browse...** to select the file location and name.

Figure 11–30

Print Range

The *Print Range* area enables you to print individual views/sheets or sets of views/sheets, as shown in Figure 11–31.

Figure 11–31

- **Current window:** Prints the entire current sheet or view you have open.

- **Visible portion of current window:** Prints only what is displayed in the current sheet or view.

- **Selected views/sheets:** Prints multiple views or sheets. Click **Select...** to open the View/Sheet Set dialog box to choose what to include in the print set. You can save these sets by name so that you can more easily print the same group again.

Options

If your printer supports multiple copies, you can specify the number in the *Options* area, as shown in Figure 11–32. You can also reverse the print order or collate your prints. These options are also available in the printer properties.

Figure 11–32

Settings

Click **Setup...** to open the Print Setup dialog box, as shown in Figure 11–33. Here, you can specify the *Orientation* and *Zoom* settings, among others. You can also save these settings by name.

Figure 11–33

- In the *Options* area, specify the types of elements you want to print or not print. Unless specified, all of the elements in a view or sheet print.

- Sheets should always be printed with **Zoom** set to **100%** size unless you are creating a quick markup set that does not need to be exact.

Export Views and Sheets to PDF

If you do not have a PDF driver to use in the Print dialog box, you can export your views or sheets to PDF.

How To: Export Views and Sheets to PDF

1. In the *File* tab, select (Export)> (PDF).
2. In the PDF Export dialog box (shown in Figure 11–34), enter a file name and the location you would like the PDF to be exported to and set any other settings, as needed.
    - The PDF Export settings are similar to those found in the Revit Print dialog box.

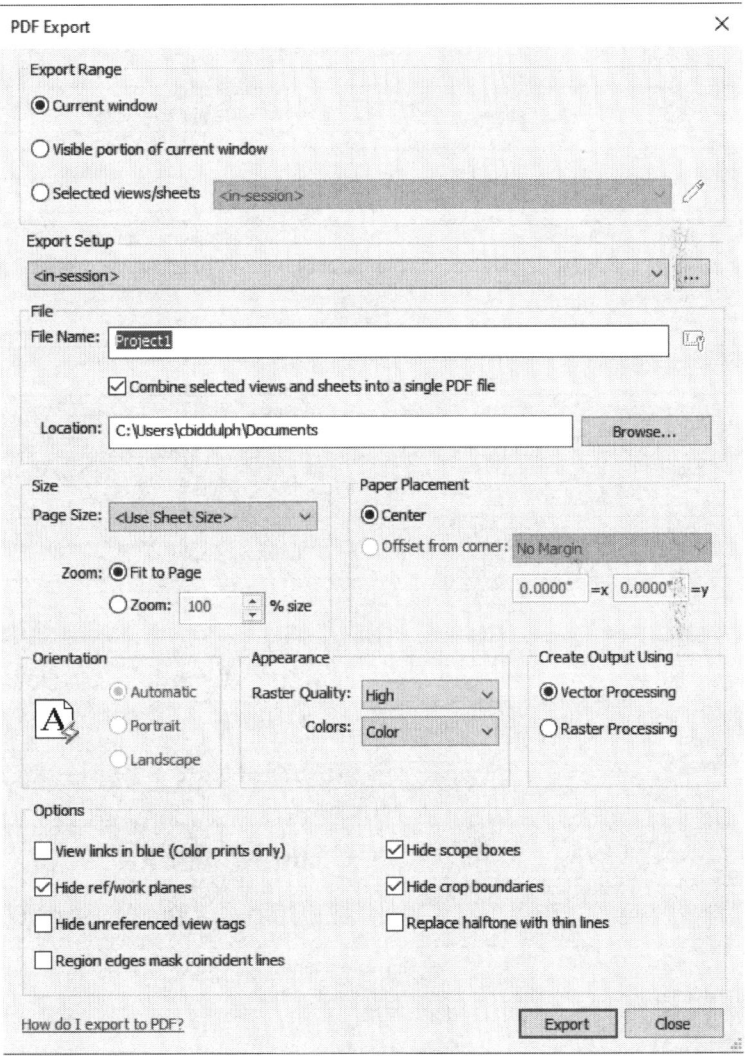

Figure 11–34

3. Click **Export**.

Chapter Review Questions

1. How do you specify the size of a sheet?
   a. In the Sheet Properties, specify the **Sheet Size**.
   b. In the Options Bar, specify the **Sheet Size**.
   c. In the New Sheet dialog box, select a title block to control the sheet size.
   d. In the Sheet view, right-click and select **Sheet Size**.

2. How is the title block information filled in, as shown in Figure 11–35? (Select all that apply.)

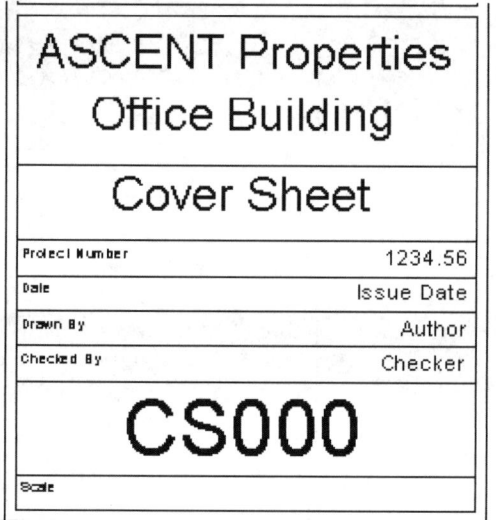

Figure 11–35

   a. Select the title block and select the label that you want to change.
   b. Select the title block and modify it in Properties.
   c. Right-click on the sheet in the Project Browser and select **Information**.
   d. Some of the information is filled in automatically.

3. On how many sheets can you place a plan view?
   a. 1
   b. 2-5
   c. 6+
   d. As many as you want

4. How do you set up a view on a sheet that only displays part of a floor plan, as shown in Figure 11–36?

Figure 11–36

   a. Drag and drop the view to the sheet and use the crop region to modify it.

   b. Activate the view and rescale it.

   c. Create a callout view displaying the part that you want to use and place the callout view on the sheet.

   d. Open the view in the Project Browser and change the *View Scale*.

Command Summary

Button	Command	Location
	Activate View	• **Ribbon:** (*select the view*) *Modify | Viewports* tab>Viewport panel • **Double-click:** *(in viewport)* • **Right-click:** (*on view*) Activate View
	Deactivate View	• **Ribbon:** *View* tab>Sheet Composition panel>expand Viewports • **Double-click:** *(on sheet)* • **Right-click:** (*on view*) Deactivate View
	Place View	• **Ribbon:** *View* tab>Sheet Composition panel
	Print	• **Ribbon:** *File* tab
	Sheet	• **Ribbon:** *View* tab>Sheet Composition panel

Chapter 12

Annotating Construction Documents

When you create construction documents, annotations are required to show the design intent. Annotations such as dimensions and text can be added to views at any time during the creation of a project. Detail lines and symbols can also be added to views as you create the working drawing sheets, while legends can be created to provide a place to document any symbols that are used in a project.

Learning Objectives in This Chapter

- Add dimensions to the model as a part of the working drawings.
- Add text to a view and use leaders to create notes pointing to a specific part of the model.
- Create text types using different fonts and sizes to suit your company standards.
- Draw detail lines to further enhance the documentation view.
- Add tags and view-specific annotation symbols for added clarity.
- Create legend views and populate them with symbols of elements in the project.

12.1 Working with Dimensions

You can create permanent dimensions using aligned, linear, angular, radial, diameter, and arc length dimensions. These can be individual or a string of dimensions, as shown in Figure 12–1. With aligned dimensions, you can also dimension entire walls with openings, grid lines, and intersecting walls. With structural plates and webbing, you can dimension to the center of a plate or webbing for a more detailed communication.

Figure 12–1

- Dimensions referencing model elements must be added to the model in a view. You can dimension on sheets, but only to items added directly on the sheets.

- Dimensions are available in the *Annotate* tab>Dimension panel (as shown in Figure 12–2) and the *Modify* tab>Measure panel.

Figure 12–2

(Aligned) is also located in the Quick Access Toolbar.

How To: Add Aligned Dimensions with Options

1. Start the (Aligned) command or type **DI**.
2. In the Type Selector, select a dimension style.

3. In the Options Bar, select the location line of the wall to dimension from, as shown in Figure 12–3.
   - This option can be changed as you add dimensions.

Figure 12–3

4. In the Options Bar, select your preference from the Pick drop-down list:
   - **Individual References:** Select the elements in order (as shown in Figure 12–4) and then click in an empty space to position the dimension string.

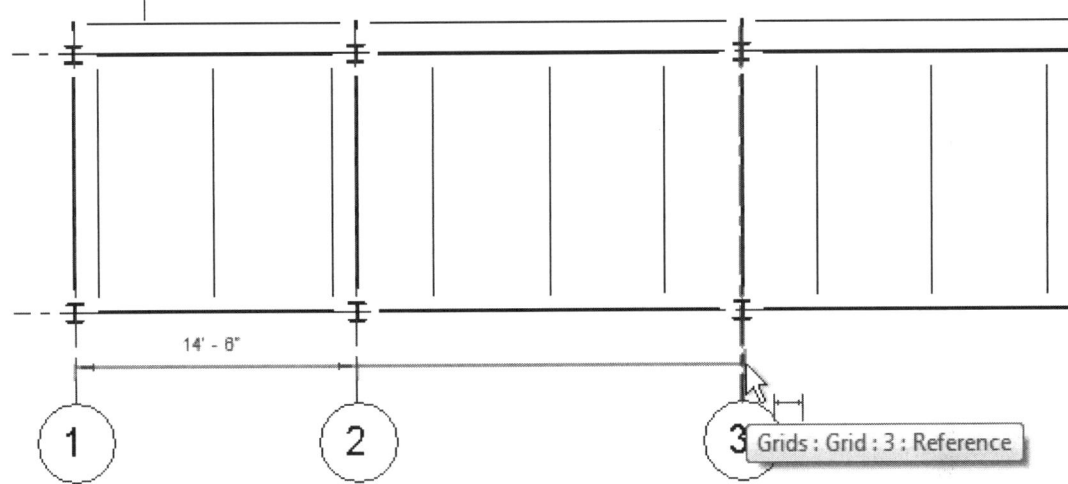

Figure 12–4

   - **Entire Walls:** Select the wall you want to dimension and then click the cursor to position the dimension string, as shown in Figure 12–5.

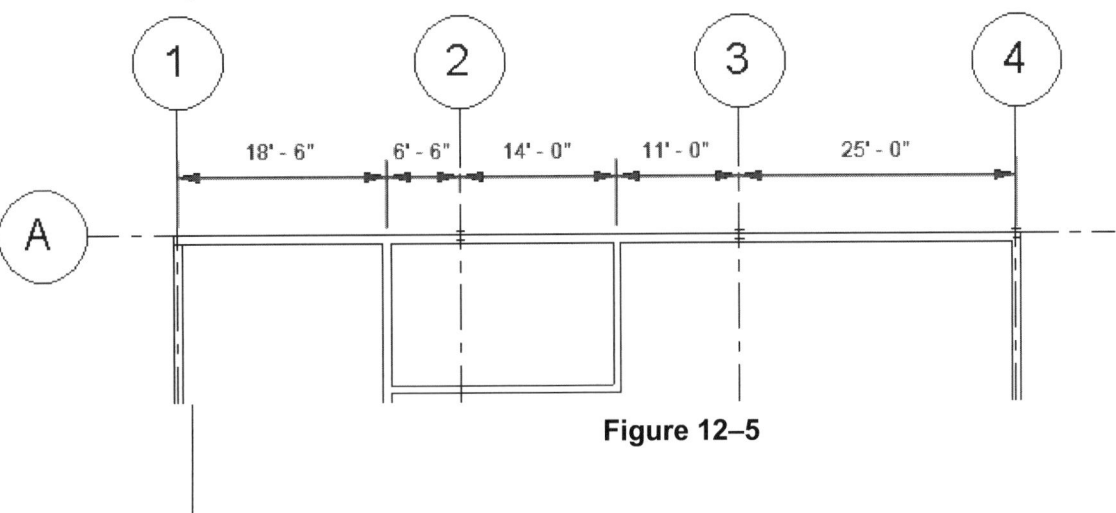

Figure 12–5

- When dimensioning entire walls you can specify how you want *Openings*, *Intersecting Walls*, and *Intersecting Grids* to be treated by the dimension string. In the Options Bar, click **Options**. In the Auto Dimension Options dialog box (shown in Figure 12–6), select the references you want to have automatically dimensioned.

*If the **Entire Wall** option is selected without additional options, it places an overall wall dimension.*

Figure 12–6

How To: Add Other Types of Dimensions

1. In the *Annotate* tab>Dimension panel, select a dimension method.

*When the **Dimension** command is active, the dimension methods are also accessible in the Modify | Place Dimensions*

	Aligned	Most commonly used dimension type. Select individual elements or entire walls to dimension.
	Linear	Used when you need to specify certain points on elements.
	Angular	Used to dimension the angle between two elements.
	Radial	Used to dimension the radius of circular elements.
	Diameter	Used to dimension the diameter of circular elements.
	Arc Length	Used to dimension the length of the arc of circular elements.

2. In the Type Selector, select the dimension type.
3. Follow the prompts for the selected method.

Modifying Dimensions

When you move elements that are dimensioned, the dimensions automatically update. You can also modify dimensions by selecting a dimension or dimension string and making changes, as shown in Figure 12–7.

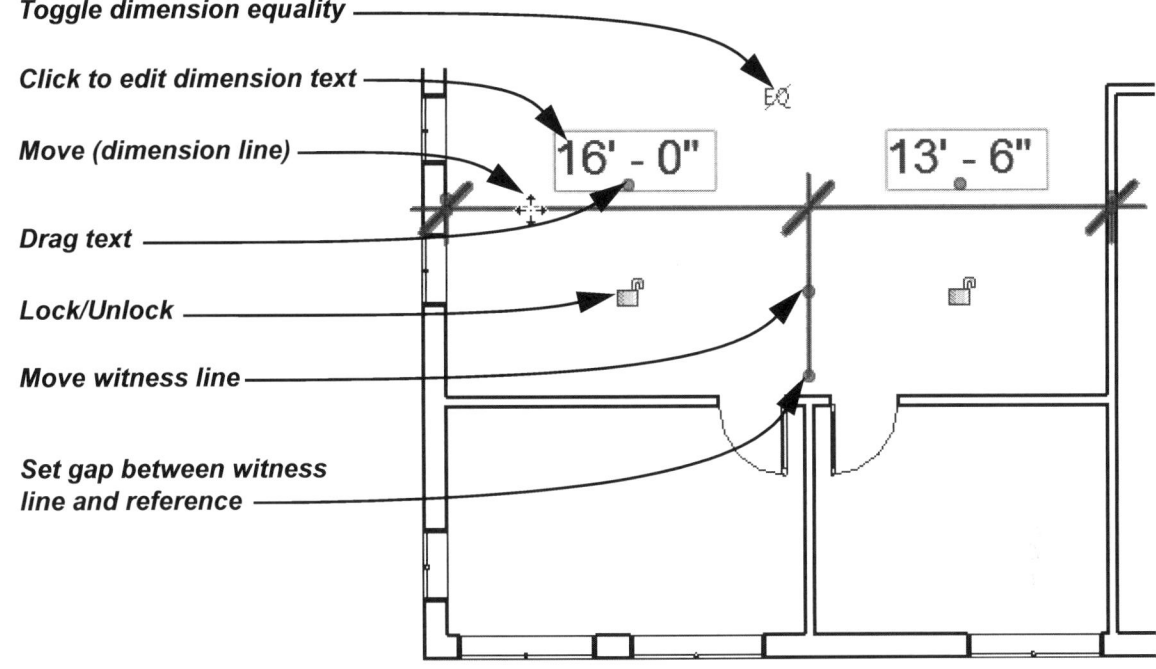

Toggle dimension equality
Click to edit dimension text
Move (dimension line)
Drag text
Lock/Unlock
Move witness line
Set gap between witness line and reference

Figure 12–7

- To move the dimension text, select the **Drag text** control under the text and drag it to a new location. It automatically creates a leader from the dimension line if you drag it away. The style of the leader (arc or line) depends on the dimension style.

- To move the dimension line (the line parallel to the element being dimensioned) simply drag the line to a new location or select the dimension and drag the (Drag to new position) control.

- To change the gap between the witness line and the element being dimensioned, drag the control at the end of the witness line.

- To move the witness line (the line perpendicular to the element being dimensioned) to a different element or face of a wall, use the **Move Witness Line** control in the middle of the witness line. While moving the witness line, you can hover your cursor over an element or component and press <Tab> repeatedly to cycle through the various options. You can also drag this control to move the witness line to a different element, or right-click on the control and select **Move Witness Line**.

Adding and Deleting Dimensions in a String

- To add a witness line to a string of dimensions, select the dimension and, in the *Modify | Dimensions* tab>Witness Lines panel, click (Edit Witness Lines). Select the element(s) you want to add to the dimension. Click in an empty space in the view to finish.

- To delete a witness line, drag the **Move Witness Line** control to a nearby witness line element. Alternatively, you can hover the cursor over the control, right-click, and select **Delete Witness Line**.

- To delete one dimension in a string and break the string into two separate dimensions, select the string, hover your cursor over the dimension that you want to delete, and press <Tab>. When it highlights (as shown on top in Figure 12–8), pick it and press <Delete>. The selected dimension is deleted and the dimension string is separated into two elements as shown on the bottom in Figure 12–8.

Figure 12–8

Modifying the Dimension Text

Because the Autodesk® Revit® software is parametric, changing the dimension text without changing the elements dimensioned would cause problems throughout the project. These issues could cause problems beyond the model if you use the project model to estimate materials or work with other disciplines.

Annotating Construction Documents

You can append the existing dimension text with prefixes and suffixes (as shown in Figure 12–9), which can help you in renovation projects.

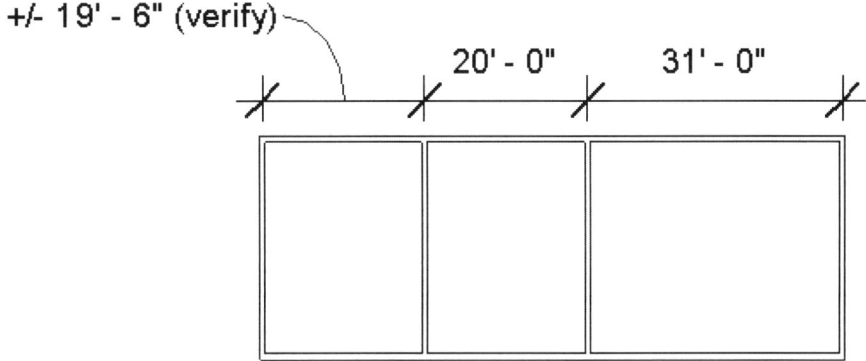

Figure 12–9

Double-click on the dimension text to open the Dimension Text dialog box, as shown in Figure 12–10, and make modifications as needed.

Figure 12–10

If you find that you are always modifying dimensions manually, you can create a type-driven dimension style by duplicating the dimension style and specifying a set prefix and suffix within the type parameters, as shown in Figure 12–11.

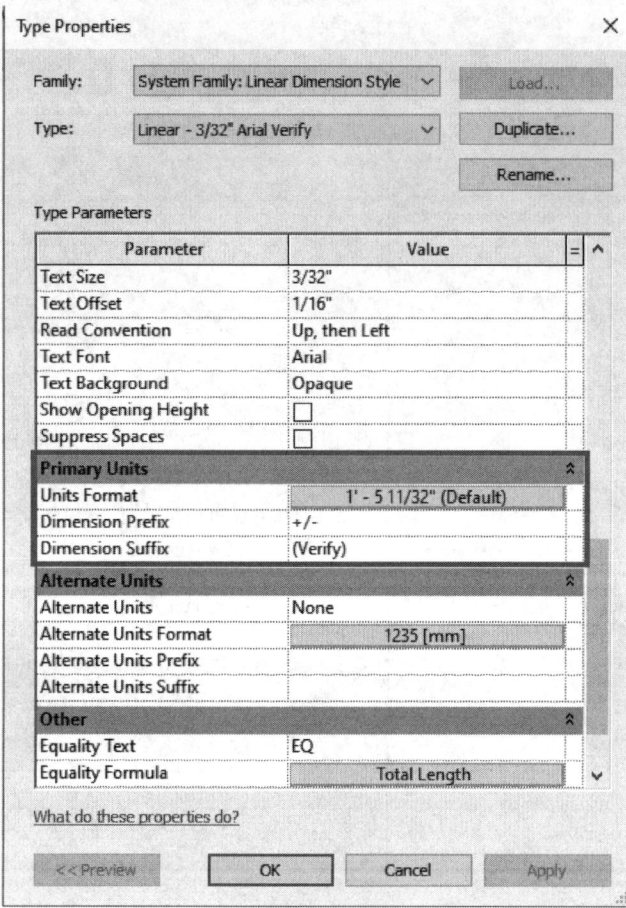

Figure 12–11

This eliminates the need to manually modify the dimension every time you need to add a prefix or suffix.

Setting Constraints

The three types of constraints that work with dimensions are locks and equal settings, as shown in Figure 12–12, as well as labels.

Figure 12–12

Locking Dimensions

When you lock a dimension, the value is set and you cannot make a change between it and the referenced elements. If it is unlocked, you can move it and change its value.

Note that when you use this and move an element, any elements that are locked to the dimension also move.

Setting Dimensions Equal

For a string of dimensions, select the **EQ** symbol to constrain the elements to be at an equal distance apart. This actually moves the elements that are dimensioned.

- The equality text display can be changed in Properties, as shown in Figure 12–13. The style for each of the display types is set in the dimension type.

Figure 12–13

Labeling Dimensions

If you have a distance that needs to be repeated multiple times, such as the *Wall to Window* label shown in Figure 12–14, or one where you want to use a formula based on another dimension, you can create and apply a global parameter, also called a label, to the dimension.

Figure 12–14

- To apply an existing label to a dimension, select the dimension and in the *Modify | Dimension* tab>Label Dimension panel, select the label in the drop-down list, as shown in Figure 12–15.

Figure 12–15

Annotating Construction Documents

How To: Create a Label

1. Select a dimension.
2. In the *Modify | Dimension* tab>Label Dimension panel, click (Create Parameter)
3. In the Global Parameter Properties dialog box type in a *Name* as shown in Figure 12–16 and click **OK**.

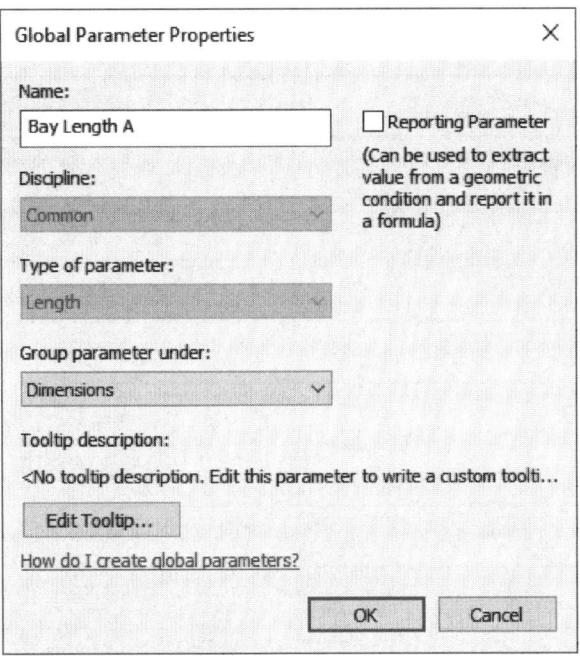

Figure 12–16

4. The label is applied to the dimension.

How To: Edit the Label Information

1. Select a labeled dimension.
2. Click (Global Parameters), as shown in Figure 12–17.

Figure 12–17

3. In the Global Parameters dialog box, in the *Value* column, type the new distance, as shown in Figure 12–18.

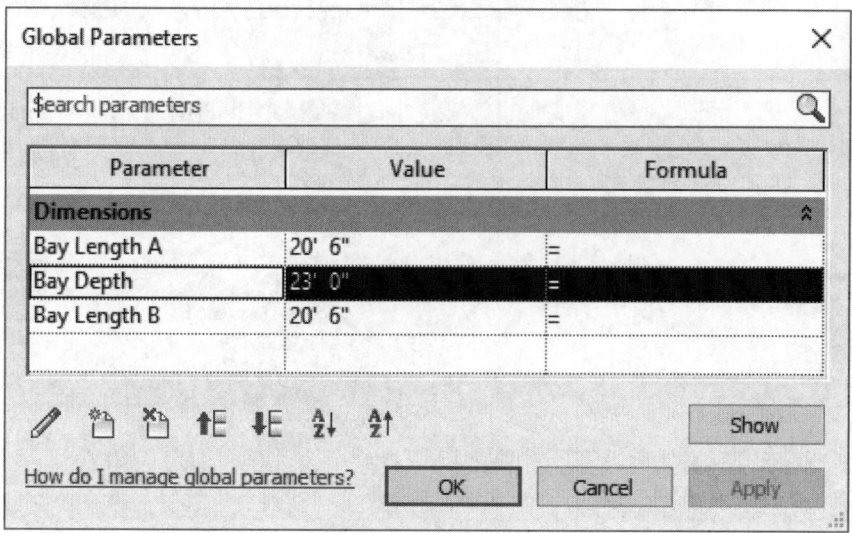

Figure 12–18

4. Click **OK**. The selected dimension and any other dimensions using the same label are updated.

- You can also edit, create, and delete Global Parameters in this dialog box.

Working with Constraints

To find out which elements have constraints applied to them, in the View Control Bar, click (Reveal Constraints). Constraints display as shown in Figure 12–19.

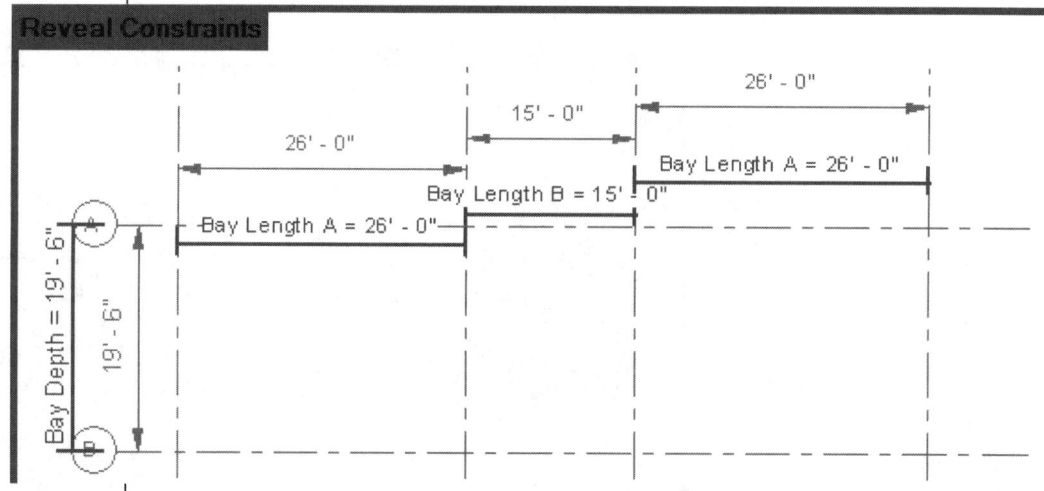

Figure 12–19

- If you try to move the element beyond the appropriate constrains, a warning dialog box displays, as shown in Figure 12–20.

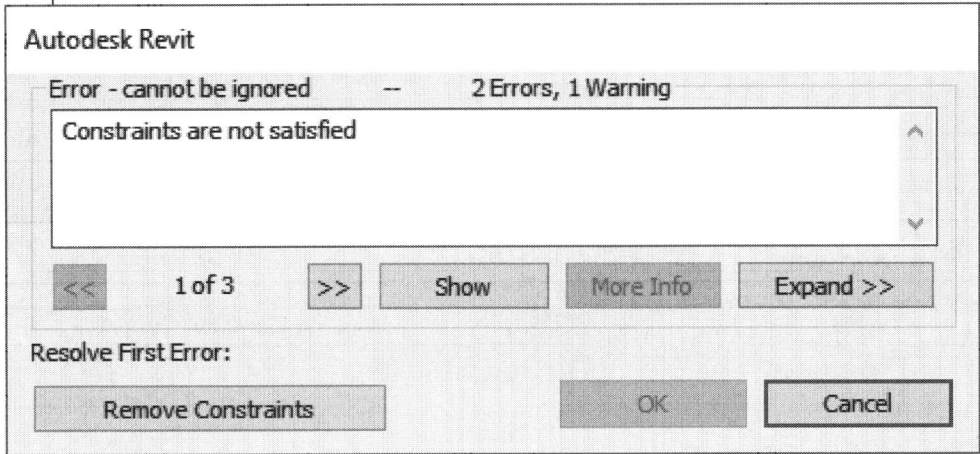

Figure 12–20

- If you delete dimensions that are constrained, a warning dialog box displays, as shown in Figure 12–21. Click **OK** to retain the constraint or **Unconstrain** to remove the constraint.

Figure 12–21

Spot Slope on Ramps

You can add a spot slope to a straight or curved ramp. Spot slopes can be added in a plan (as shown in Figure 12–22), section, elevation, or 3D view.

Figure 12–22

Multi-Rebar Annotation

These annotations only work with rebar created using the multi-rebar layout. This does not work with structural area, path, or fabric reinforcement.

How To: Add a Spot Slope

1. Zoom in to a ramp in the model.
2. In the *Annotate* tab>Dimensions panel, select ◹ (Spot Slope).
3. Click on the ramp surface to place the spot slope.

The dimension-like Multi-Rebar Annotation tool dimensions and tags multiple rebar elements based on the parameters from the referenced elements, as shown in Figure 12–23.

Figure 12–23

- There are two different types: aligned (annotations display parallel to the tagged rebar) and linear (annotations are aligned to the horizontal or vertical axis of the view).

- There must be at least two rebar elements in a set for the multiple-rebar dimensions to work.

- Multi-Rebar Annotation can be used with curved and angled rebar sets.

Annotating Construction Documents

How To: Add Multi-Rebar Annotation

1. In the *Annotate* tab>Tag panel, expand (Multi-Rebar Annotation) and select (Aligned Multi-Rebar Annotation) or (Linear Multi-Rebar Annotation).
2. In the Type Selector, select the annotation type you want to use.
3. Select the element to tag.
4. Select the edge of the concrete, as required.
5. Click to place the dimension string.
6. Click to place the line off the dimension string
7. Click to place the tag (text).
- The dimensions and tags can be modified separately. After you select one of the elements, in the *Modify | Multi-Rebar Annotations* tab>Edit panel, click (Select Tag) or (Select Dimension). Then modify the elements using controls, as shown for a tag in Figure 12–24.

Figure 12–24

- Editing the dimension uses the same controls as other dimension strings.

- The dimensions of the Multi-Rebar Annotation change automatically in relation to the Rebar Presentation style. For example, in Figure 12–25, ☐ (Show First and Last) is shown on the left and ▦ (Show All) on the right. This graphic uses the **Structural Rebar Section** Multi-Rebar Annotations type.

Figure 12–25

Practice 12a Work with Dimensions

Practice Objectives

- Add a string of dimensions.
- Dimension using the **Entire Walls** option.
- Edit the witness lines of dimensions.

In this practice, you will annotate a structural plan by adding Aligned dimensions for grid line locations and Radial dimensions for curved beams, as shown in Figure 12–26. You will also add text notes to a plan and detail view, and multi-rebar annotation to an elevation callout.

Figure 12–26

Task 1 - Duplicate a view and create a typical dimension type.

1. Open **Structural-Dimensions.rvt** from the practice files folder.

2. In the Project Browser, right-click on the **Structural Plans: TOS-1ST FLOOR** view and select **Duplicate View> Duplicate**.

3. Rename the new view to **TOS-1ST FLOOR - Dimensioned**.
4. In the View Control Bar, change the *Scale* to **1/16" = 1'-0"**.
5. Start the **Dimension** command.
6. In Type Properties, duplicate the **Arrow - 3/32" Arial** dimension style and call it **3/32" Arial (TYP)**.
7. In the *Primary Units* section, enter **(TYP)** next to *Dimensions Suffix* and click **OK**.
8. Click (Modify).
9. Save the project.

Task 2 - Place dimensions.

1. Still in the **TOS-1ST FLOOR - Dimensioned** plan, in the *Annotate* tab>Dimension panel or Quick Access Toolbar, click (Aligned).
2. In the Type Selector, select **3/32" Arial (TYP)**.
3. Dimension the elevator walls on the north side of the building, as shown in Figure 12–27.

Figure 12–27

4. Stay in the Dimension command. In the Type Selector, change the dimension style to **Arrow - 3/32" Arial**.

5. Zoom out or pan so you can see grid lines **1** and **11**.

6. Dimension from grid line **1** to grid line **11** and then click out to the right of grid line **11** to create one overall dimension, as shown across the top in Figure 12–28.

7. You are still in the Dimension command. Select grid line **1** and continue selecting the other grid lines in sequence without stopping until you select grid line **11**. When you get to the end, click to the right of the string to place the dimensions, as shown below the overall dimension in Figure 12–28.

Figure 12–28

8. Add an overall dimension vertically from grid line **A** to grid line **H**. and another single dimension from grid line **A** to grid line **H**. Modify the location of the grid markers as needed.

9. In the *Modify | Place Dimension* tab>Dimension panel, click (Radial) and add radial dimensions to the four circular bays, as shown for one of them in Figure 12–29.

If there is overlapping text, select the text and move it to an open area where it can be read.

Figure 12–29

10. Save the project.

Task 3 - Add multi-rebar annotation.

1. Open the **Elevations (Building Elevation): North** view.

2. Zoom in on the foundation wall between grid lines **5** and **7** where you see the area reinforcement tag, as shown in Figure 12–30.

3. In the *View* tab>Create panel, click (Callout) and in the Type Selector select **Detail**. Draw the callout as shown in Figure 12–30.

    - When you use the **Detail** callout type, it automatically displays the rebar. If you use the **Elevation** type, you need to modify the **View Visibility State** of the rebar for that view.

Figure 12–30

4. In the Project Browser, In the **Detail Views (Detail)** node, rename the new view to **Foundation Rebar Elevation** and open it.

5. Move the level head away from the crop region for clarity.

6. In the *Annotate* tab>Tag panel, expand (Multi-Rebar) and select (Aligned Multi-Rebar Annotation).

7. Select the top rebar set and place the annotation above it. Every instance in the rebar set is automatically dimensioned, as shown in Figure 12–31.

Figure 12–31

8. Click ▸ (Modify) and select the rebar set.

9. In the *Modify | Structural Rebar* tab>Presentation panel, click ☐ (Show First and Last).

10. The dimensions are modified to fit the presentation style, as shown in Figure 12–32.

Figure 12–32

11. Save and close the project.

12.2 Working with Text

The **Text** command enables you to add notes to views or sheets, such as the detail shown in Figure 12–33. The same command is used to create text with or without leaders.

Figure 12–33

The text height is automatically set by the text type in conjunction with the scale of the view (as shown in Figure 12–34, using the same size text type at two different scales). Text types display at the specified height, both in the views and on the sheet.

Figure 12–34

Annotating Construction Documents

How To: Add Text

1. In the Quick Access Toolbar or *Annotate* tab>Text panel, click **A** (Text).
2. In the Type Selector, set the text type.
3. In the *Modify | Place Text* tab>Leader panel, select the method you want to use: **A** (No Leader), **←A** (One Segment), **⤺A** (Two Segments), or **⤾A** (Curved).
4. In the Alignment panel, set the overall justification for the text and leader, as shown in Figure 12–35.

The text type sets the font and height of the text.

Figure 12–35

5. Select the location for the leader and text.
   - If **No leader** is selected, select the start point for the text and begin typing.
   - If using a leader, the first point places the arrow and you then select points for the leader. The text starts at the last leader point.
   - To set a word wrapping distance, click and drag the circle grip controls to set the start and end points of the text.
6. Type the required text. In the *Edit Text* tab, specify additional options for the font and paragraph, as shown in Figure 12–36.

Use alignment lines to help you align the text with other text elements.

Figure 12–36

7. In the Edit Text tab>Edit Text panel, click **X** (Close) or click outside the text box to complete the text element.
   - Pressing <Enter> after a line of text starts a new line of text in the same text window.

How To: Add Text Symbols

1. Start the **Text** command and click to place the text.
2. As you are typing text and need to insert a symbol, right-click and select **Symbols** from the shortcut menu. Select from the list of commonly used symbols, as shown in Figure 12–37.

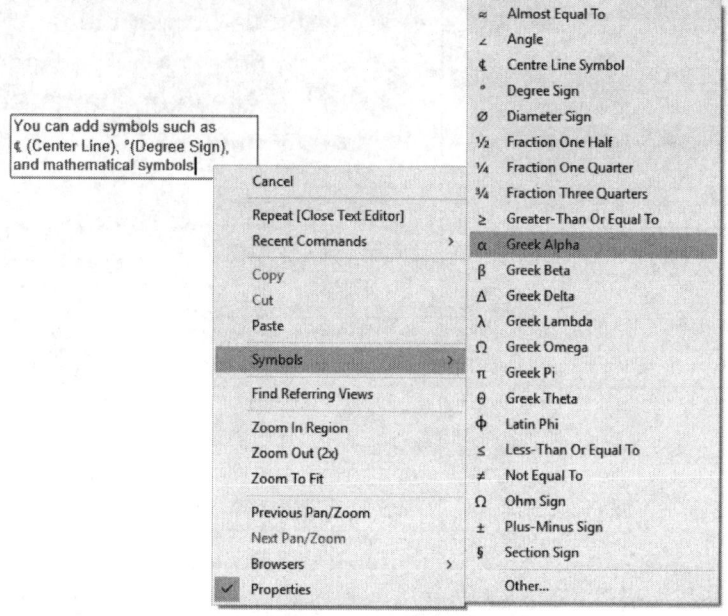

Figure 12–37

3. If the symbol you need is not listed, click **Other**.
4. In the Character Map dialog box, click on a symbol and click **Select**, as shown in Figure 12–38.

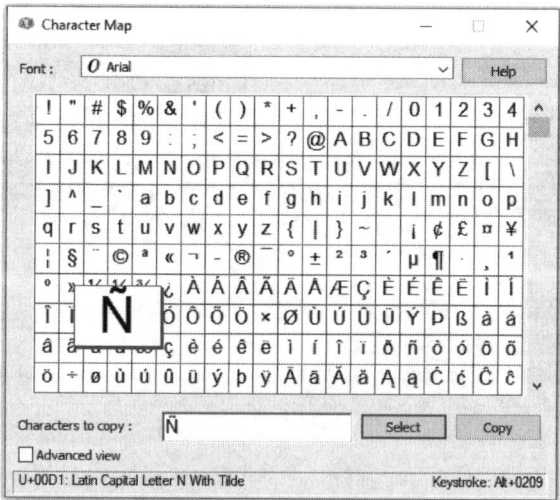

Figure 12–38

5. Click **Copy** to copy the character to the clipboard and paste it into the text box.

- The Font in the Character Map should match the font used by the text type. You do not want to use a different font for symbols.

Editing Text

Editing text notes takes place at two levels:

- Modifying the text note, which includes the **Leader** and **Paragraph** styles.

- Editing the text, which includes changes to individual letters, word, and paragraphs in the text note.

Modifying the Text Note

Click once on the text note to modify the text box and leaders using controls, as shown in Figure 12–39, or using the tools in the *Modify | Text Notes* tab.

Figure 12–39

How To: Add a Leader to Text Notes

1. Select the text note.
2. In the *Modify | Text Notes* tab>Leader panel, select the direction and justification for the new leader, as shown in Figure 12–40.
3. The leader is applied, as shown in Figure 12–41. Use the drag controls to place the arrow as needed.

Figure 12–40

Figure 12–41

- You can remove leaders by clicking ⥿A (Remove Last Leader).

Editing the Text

The *Edit Text* tab enables you to make various customizations. These include modifying the font of selected words as well as creating bulleted and numbered lists, as shown in Figure 12–42.

<u>**General Notes**</u>
1. Notify designer of intention to start construction at least 10 days prior to start of site work.
2. Installer shall provide the following:
   - 24-hour notice of start of construction
   - Inspection of bottom of bed or covering required by state inspector
   - All environmental management inspection sheets must be emailed to designer's office within 24 hours of inspection.

Figure 12–42

- You can **Cut**, **Copy**, and **Paste** text using the clipboard. For example, you can copy text from a document and then paste it into the text editor in Revit.

- To help you see the text better as you are modifying it, in the *Edit Text* tab, expand the Edit Text panel, and select one or both of the options, as shown in Figure 12–43.

Figure 12–43

Annotating Construction Documents

How To: Modify the Font

1. Select Individual letters or words.
2. Click on the font modification you want to include:

B (Bold)	X_2 (Subscript)
I (Italic)	X^2 (Superscript)
U (Underline)	ªA (All Caps)

- When pasting text from a document outside of Autodesk Revit, font modifications (e.g, Bold, Italic, etc.) are retained.

How To: Create Lists

1. In Edit Text mode, place the cursor in the line where you want to add to a list.
2. In the *Edit Text* tab>Paragraph panel, click the type of list you want to create:

(Bullets)	(Uppercase Letters)
(Numbers)	(Lowercase Letters)

The indent distance is set up by the Text Type Tab Size.

3. As you type, press <Enter> and the next line in the list is incremented.
4. To include sub-lists, at the beginning of the next line, click (Increase Indent). This indents the line and applies the next level of lists, as shown in Figure 12–44.

Figure 12–44

- You can change the type of list after you have applied the first increment. For example, you might want to use a list of bullets instead of letters, as shown in Figure 12–45.

5. Click 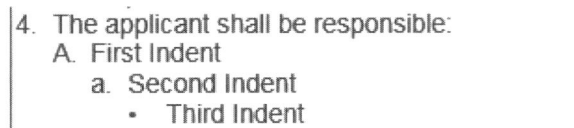 (Decrease Indent) to return to the previous list style.

- Press <Shift>+<Enter> to create a blank line in a numbered list.

- To create columns or other separate text boxes that build on a numbering system (as shown in Figure 12–45), create the second text box and list. Then, place the cursor on one of the lines and in the Paragraph panel, click (Increment List Value) until the list matches the next number in the sequence.

Figure 12–45

6. Click (Decrement List Value) to move back a number.

> **Hint: Model Text**
>
> Model text is different from annotation text. It is designed to create full-size text on the model itself. For example, you would use model text to create a sign on a door, as shown in Figure 12–46. One model text type is included with the default template. You can create other types as needed.
>
>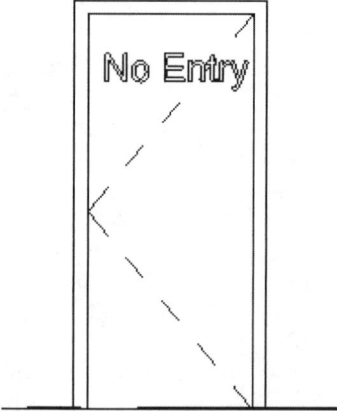
>
> Figure 12–46
>
> - Model text can be viewed in all views.
> - Model text is added from the *Architecture* tab>Model panel by clicking (Model Text).

Annotating Construction Documents

Spell Checking

The Spelling dialog box displays any misspelled words in context and provides several options for changing them, as shown in Figure 12–47.

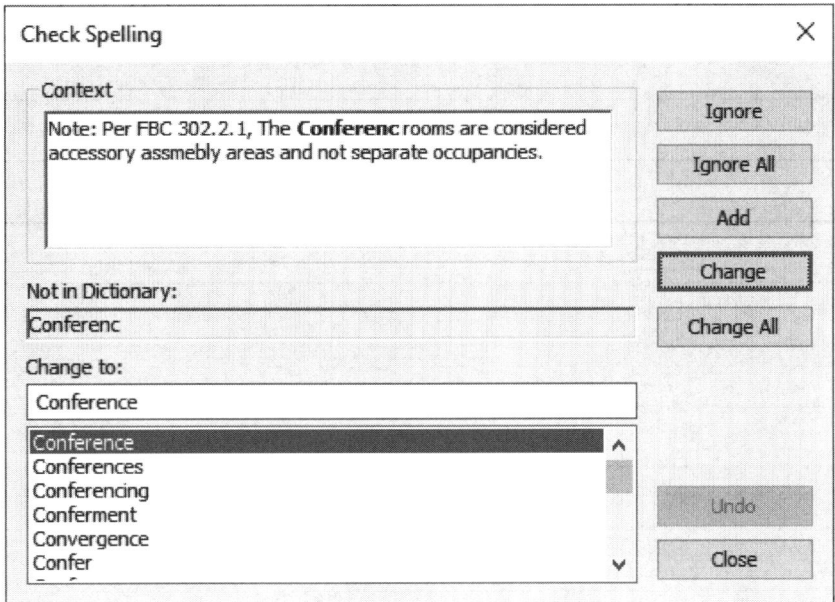

Figure 12–47

- Revit does not have active spell checking. It will only spell check when the command is activated.

- To spell check all text in a view, in the *Annotate* tab>Text panel, click ABC✓ (Spelling) or press <F7>. As with other spell checkers, you can **Ignore**, **Add**, or **Change** the word.

- You can also check the spelling in selected text. With text selected, in the *Modify | Text Notes* tab>Tools panel, click ABC✓ (Check Spelling).

Creating Text Types

If you need new text types with a different text size or font (such as for a title or hand-lettering), you can create new ones, as shown in Figure 12–48. It is recommended that you create these in a project template so they are available in future projects.

General Notes

1. This project consists of furnishing and installing...

Figure 12–48

- You can copy and paste text types from one project to another or use **Transfer Project Standards**.

How To: Create Text Types

1. In the *Annotate* tab>Text panel, click (Text Types).
2. In the Type Properties dialog box, click **Duplicate**.
3. In the Name dialog box, type a new name and click **OK**.
4. Modify the text parameters, as needed. The parameters are shown in Figure 12–49.

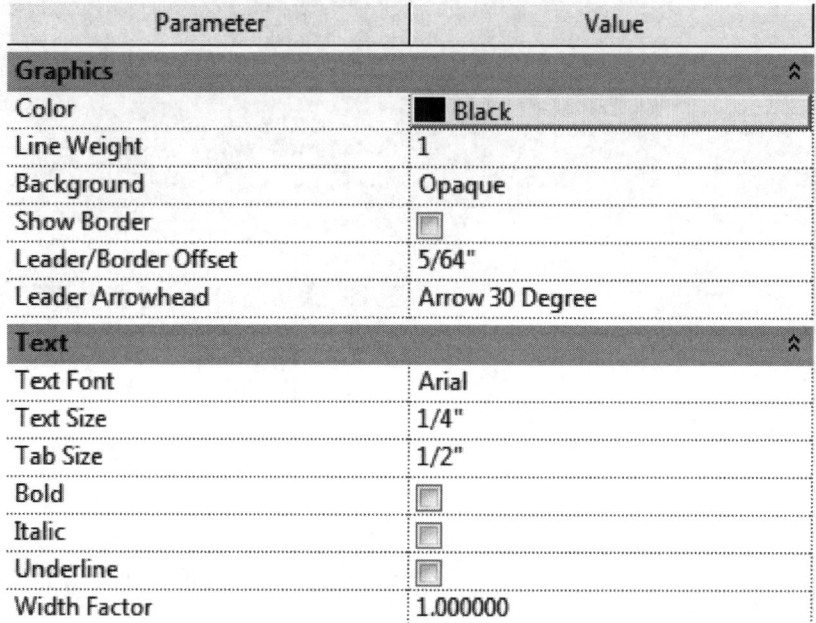

Figure 12–49

- The *Background* parameter can be set to **Opaque** or **Transparent**. An opaque background includes a masking region that hides lines or elements behind the text.
- In the *Text* area, the *Width Factor* parameter controls the width of the lettering, but does not affect the height. A width factor greater than **1** spreads the text out and a width factor less than **1** compresses it.
- The **Show Border** parameter, when selected, includes a rectangle around the text.

5. Click **OK** to close the Type Properties dialog box.

Practice 12b Work with Text

Practice Objectives

- Add text notes.
- Modify text with lists.

In this practice, you will add text into a structural plan view and a framing elevation, as shown in Figure 12–50. You will then copy in a text note and create a numbered list.

Figure 12–50

Task 1 - Create text types.

1. Open the project **Structural-Text.rvt** from the practice files folder.

2. In the *Annotate* tab>Text panel, click **A** (Text).

3. In Properties, click (Edit Type).

4. In the Type Properties dialog box, duplicate an existing text type and create new types, as follows:

	1/8" Arial Narrow	1/8" Arial Narrow Italic
Text Font	Arial Narrow	Arial Narrow
Text Size	1/8"	1/8"
Tab Size	1/4"	1/4"
Width Factor	0.9	0.9
Italic	No	Yes

5. Click **OK** to save the settings and close the dialog box.

6. Click **OK**.

7. Save the project.

Task 2 - Add text to a structural plan view.

1. Open the **Structural Plans: TOS-1ST FLOOR - Dimensioned** view.

2. Zoom in on the upper-left corner of the plan.

3. In the *Annotate* tab>Text panel, click **A** (Text).

4. In the Type Selector, select **Text: 3/32" Arial**.

5. In the *Modify | Place text* tab>Leader panel, click (Two Segments).

6. Select the first point so that the text points to the slab edge. This is what you are going to label. Select the second point any distance away from the first point.

7. Type **Slab Edge** (in Title case) and click (Modify).

8. Position the text as needed.

9. Double click on the text so that the *Edit Text* tab opens.

10. Highlight all of the letters and in the *Edit Text* tab>Font panel, click (All Caps). The text updates as shown in Figure 12–51. Close the *Edit Text* tab.

Do you use uppercase letters for your notes? It is not important anymore because of the clarity of typed in text. Check your office standards.

Figure 12–51

11. Click in an empty space in the view to clear the selected text.

12. Zoom out to fit the view.

13. Save the project.

Task 3 - Add text to a framing elevation.

1. Open the **Elevations (Framing Elevation): Typical Top Plate** view.

2. Modify the location of the level markers so that they do not overlap the view.

3. Add the text leaders **3/4" THICK PLATE** and **5" CONCRETE SLAB**, as shown in Figure 12–52.

Figure 12–52

4. Save the project.

Task 4 - Add General Notes and create lists.

1. Open the **S-000 - COVER SHEET** view.

2. Zoom in on the area with the Symbol Legend.

3. Start the **Text** command and in the *Modify | Place Text* tab> Leader panel, click **A** (No Leader).

4. In the Type Selector, select **Text: 1/4" Arial**.

5. Click and drag to place a box similar to Figure 12–53.

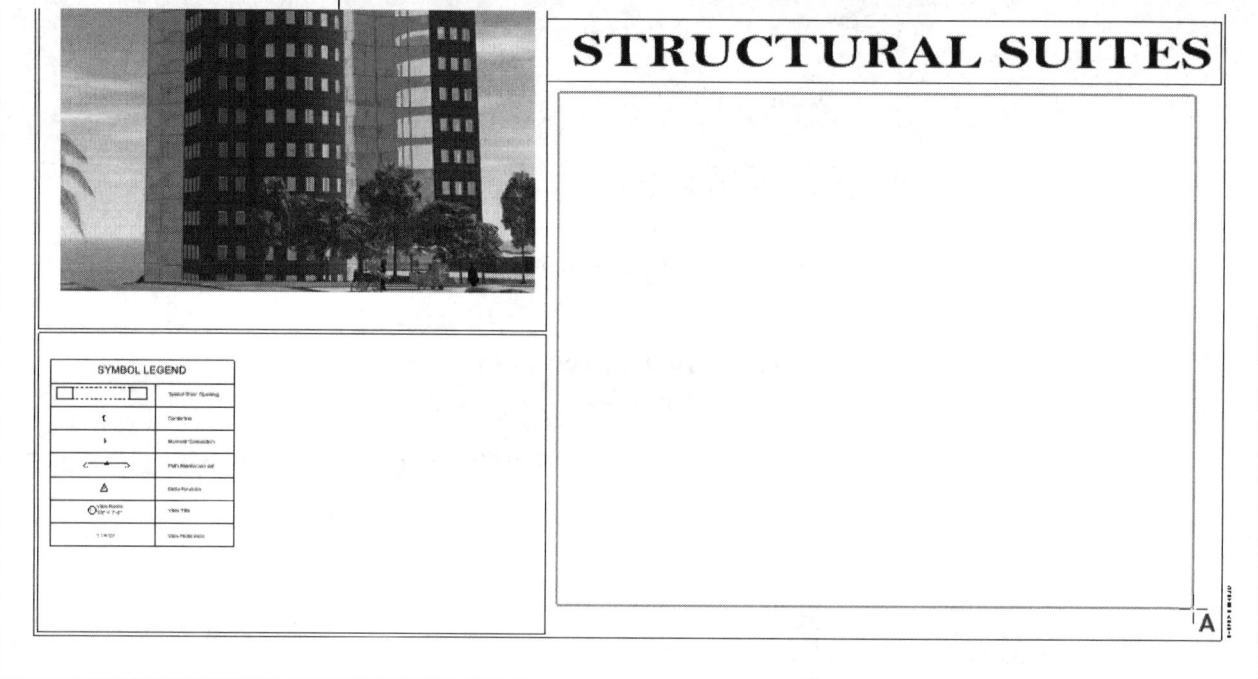

Figure 12–53

6. From the practice files *Documents* folder, open **Structural Steel Notes.docx** or **Structural Steel Notes.txt** in Microsoft Word or another text editor.

7. Select all of the text and copy it to the clipboard (type <Ctrl>+C).

Annotating Construction Documents

8. Return to Autodesk Revit and in the *Edit Text* tab>Clipboard panel, click (Paste). The text is added as shown in Figure 12–54.

Structural Steel Notes

A. CODES AND SPECIFICATIONS
ABC BUILDING CODE, 2010.
ASCE 7-05, MINIMUM DESIGN LOADS FOR BUILDINGS AND OTHER STRUCTURES.
ACI 301-05 SPECIFICATIONS FOR STRUCTURAL CONCRETE FOR BUILDINGS AS MODIFIED BY THE CONSTRUCTION DOCUMENTS.
AISC 303-05 CODE OF STANDARD PRACTICE FOR STEEL BUILDINGS AND BRIDGES AS MODIFIED BY THE CONSTRUCTION DOCUMENTS.
ANSI/AWS D1.1 STRUCTURAL WELDING CODE - STEEL

B. FOUNDATIONS
THE FOUNDATION DESIGN IS BASED UPON THE RECOMMEDATIONS INCLUDED IN THE REPORT OF GEOTECHNICAL EXPLORATION PREPARED BY H.C. NUTTING, DATED MAY 17, 2011.
FOUNDATION ELEVATIONS SHOWN ARE ESTIMATED AND ARE FOR BIDDING PURPOSES ONLY.
ACTUAL ELEVATIONS MAY VARY TO SUIT SUBSURFACE SOIL CONDITIONS
COLUMN SPREAD FOOTINGS ARE DESIGNED FOR A MAXIMUM BEARING PRESSURE OF 3000 PSF.
BASEMENT WALL FOOTING MAXIMUM BEARING PRESSURE 2500 PSF. NON-BASEMENT WALL FOOTINGS MAXIMUM BEARING PRESSURE 2000 PSF. SOILS UNSUITABLE FOR SUPPORTING FOUNDATIONS SHALL BE REMOVED AS DIRECTED BY THE GEOTECHNICAL ENGINEER, AND BACKFILLED TO DESIGN BEARING ELEVATION WITH LEAN CONCRETE.
ALL BEARING SURFACES SHALL BE UNDISTURBED, LEVEL (WITHIN 1 IN 12), AND SHALL BE APPROVED BY THE GEOTECHNICAL ENGINEER PRIOR TO PLACING CONCRETE.
UNLESS APPROVED OTHERWISE BY THE GEOTECHNICAL ENGINEER AND THE STRUCTURAL ENGINEER, ALL FOOTINGS ARE TO BE POURED NEAT (WITHOUT SIDE FORMS). WHERE EARTH CUTS WILL NOT STAND, SIDES SHALL BE FORMED, SUBJECT TO ENGINEERS' APPROVAL.
SET COLUMN DOWELS AND ANCHOR RODS WITH TEMPLATE PRIOR TO CONCRETING.

C. CONCRETE
CONCRETE STRENGTHS:
    FOOTINGS AND GRADE BEAMS: 3000 PSI
    EXTERIOR CONCRETE EXPOSED TO WEATHER: 4500 PSI AE
    TYPICAL CONCRETE UNLESS NOTED OTHERWISE: 4000 PSI
    INTERIOR CONCRETE SLABS ON METAL DECK: 4000 PSI NORMAL WEIGHT
    BACKFILL (LEAN) CONCRETE: 1000 PSI
PROVIDE 3/4" BEVELS AT CORNERS OF ALL EXPOSED COLUMNS, EDGES OF EXPOSED BEAMS AND SLABS, AND TOP EDGES AND CORNERS OF EXPOSED WALLS.
MAXIMUM LENGTH OF WALL POUR BETWEEN CONSTRUCTION JOINTS SHALL NOT EXCEED 120 FEET.
MAXIMUM LENGTH OF SLAB POURS BETWEEN CONSTRUCTION JOINTS SHALL NOT EXCEED 120 FEET. MAXIMUM AREA OF SLAB POURS NOT TO EXCEED 10,000 SF.
JOINTS NOT INDICATED ON STRUCTURAL DRAWINGS ARE NOT PERMITTED UNLESS APPROVED BY STRUCTURAL ENGINEER.
PLACE NO OPENINGS, SLEEVES, INSERTS, ETC., IN CONCRETE WORK UNLESS CRITERIA INDICATED ON STRUCTURAL DRAWINGS IS MET, OR IS APPROVED IN WRITING BY THE STRUCTURAL ENGINEER.
CONCRETE CONSTRUCTION TOLERANCES ARE AS SHOWN IN THE PROJECT SPECIFICATIONS.

Figure 12–54

9. Zoom in and modify the text so it resembles that in Figure 12–55.

   - Select the **Notes** heading and click ᵃÂ (All Caps).
   - Set the **A. B.** and **C.** headings to **B** (Bold).
   - Select each group of text and click (List: Numbers).
   - Change the indented list to (List: Uppercase Letters).

   STRUCTURAL STEEL NOTES

   A. CODES AND SPECIFICATIONS
   1. ABC BUILDING CODE, 2010.
   2. ASCE 7-05, MINIMUM DESIGN LOADS FOR BUILDINGS AND OTHER STRUCTURES.
   3. ACI 301-05 SPECIFICATIONS FOR STRUCTURAL CONCRETE FOR BUILDINGS AS MODIFIED BY THE CONSTRUCTION DOCUMENTS.
   4. AISC 303-05 CODE OF STANDARD PRACTICE FOR STEEL BUILDINGS AND BRIDGES AS MODIFIED BY THE CONSTRUCTION DOCUMENTS.
   5. ANSI/AWS D1.1 STRUCTURAL WELDING CODE - STEEL

   B. FOUNDATIONS
   1. THE FOUNDATION DESIGN IS BASED UPON THE RECOMMEDATIONS INCLUDED IN THE REPORT OF GEOTECHNICAL EXPLORATION PREPARED BY H.C. NUTTING, DATED MAY 17, 2011.
   2. FOUNDATION ELEVATIONS SHOWN ARE ESTIMATED AND ARE FOR BIDDING PURPOSES ONLY. ACTUAL ELEVATIONS MAY VARY TO SUIT SUBSURFACE SOIL CONDITIONS
   3. COLUMN SPREAD FOOTINGS ARE DESIGNED FOR A MAXIMUM BEARING PRESSURE OF 3000 PSF. BASEMENT WALL FOOTING MAXIMUM BEARING PRESSURE 2500 PSF. NON-BASEMENT WALL FOOTINGS MAXIMUM BEARING PRESSURE 2000 PSF. SOILS UNSUITABLE FOR SUPPORTING FOUNDATIONS SHALL BE REMOVED AS DIRECTED BY THE GEOTECHNICAL ENGINEER, AND BACKFILLED TO DESIGN BEARING ELEVATION WITH LEAN CONCRETE.
   4. ALL BEARING SURFACES SHALL BE UNDISTURBED, LEVEL (WITHIN 1 IN 12), AND SHALL BE APPROVED BY THE GEOTECHNICAL ENGINEER PRIOR TO PLACING CONCRETE.
   5. UNLESS APPROVED OTHERWISE BY THE GEOTECHNICAL ENGINEER AND THE STRUCTURAL ENGINEER, ALL FOOTINGS ARE TO BE POURED NEAT (WITHOUT SIDE FORMS). WHERE EARTH CUTS WILL NOT STAND, SIDES SHALL BE FORMED, SUBJECT TO ENGINEERS' APPROVAL.
   6. SET COLUMN DOWELS AND ANCHOR RODS WITH TEMPLATE PRIOR TO CONCRETING.

   C. CONCRETE
   1. CONCRETE STRENGTHS:
      A. FOOTINGS AND GRADE BEAMS: 3000 PSI
      B. EXTERIOR CONCRETE EXPOSED TO WEATHER: 4500 PSI AE
      C. TYPICAL CONCRETE UNLESS NOTED OTHERWISE: 4000 PSI
      D. INTERIOR CONCRETE SLABS ON METAL DECK: 4000 PSI NORMAL WEIGHT
      E. BACKFILL (LEAN) CONCRETE: 1000 PSI
   2. PROVIDE 3/4" BEVELS AT CORNERS OF ALL EXPOSED COLUMNS, EDGES OF EXPOSED BEAMS AND SLABS, AND TOP EDGES AND CORNERS OF EXPOSED WALLS.
   3. MAXIMUM LENGTH OF WALL POUR BETWEEN CONSTRUCTION JOINTS SHALL NOT EXCEED 120 FEET. MAXIMUM LENGTH OF SLAB POURS BETWEEN CONSTRUCTION JOINTS SHALL NOT EXCEED 120 FEET. MAXIMUM AREA OF SLAB POURS NOT TO EXCEED 10,000 SF.
   4. JOINTS NOT INDICATED ON STRUCTURAL DRAWINGS ARE NOT PERMITTED UNLESS APPROVED BY STRUCTURAL ENGINEER.
   5. PLACE NO OPENINGS, SLEEVES, INSERTS, ETC., IN CONCRETE WORK UNLESS CRITERIA INDICATED ON STRUCTURAL DRAWINGS IS MET, OR IS APPROVED IN WRITING BY THE STRUCTURAL ENGINEER.
   6. CONCRETE CONSTRUCTION TOLERANCES ARE AS SHOWN IN THE PROJECT SPECIFICATIONS.

   Figure 12–55

10. Zoom out to see the full sheet.

11. Save and close the project.

Annotating Construction Documents

12.3 Adding Tags

Tags identify elements that are listed in schedules. Door and window tags are inserted automatically if you use the **Tag on Placement** option when inserting the door or window or other elements. You can also add them later to specific views as needed. Many other types of tags are available in the Autodesk® Revit® software, such as structural column tags and structural framing tags, as shown in Figure 12–56.

Additional tags are stored in the Revit Library in the Annotations folder.

Figure 12–56

- The **Tag by Category** command works for most elements, except for a few that have separate commands.

- Tags can be letters, numbers, or a combination of the two.

You can place three types of tags, as follows:

- (Tag by Category): Tags according to the category of the element. It places door tags on doors and wall tags on walls.

- (Multi-Category): Tags elements belonging to multiple categories. The tags display information from parameters that they have in common.

- (Material Tag): Tags that display the type of material. They are typically used in detailing.

How To: Add Tags

1. In the *Annotate* tab>Tag panel, click (Tag by Category), (Multi-Category), or (Material Tag) depending on the type of tag you want to place.

2. In the Options Bar, set the options as needed, as shown in Figure 12–57.

Figure 12–57

In the Load Family dialog box, if you are not routed to the Revit families folder location, click on Imperial Library in the Places panel.

3. Select the element you want to tag. If a tag for the selected element is not loaded, you are prompted to load it from the Revit Library.

Tag Options

- In the Options Bar, you can set tag options for leaders and tag rotation, as shown in Figure 12–58. You can also press <Spacebar> to toggle the rotation while placing or modifying the tag.

Figure 12–58

- Tag orientation can be set to one of the following:

    - **Horizontal:** Tag stays horizontal (0°) to the element it is tagging.

    - **Vertical:** Forces the tag to stay vertical (90°) to the element it is tagging no matter what.

    - **Model:** Tag rotates freely from the element, similar to room tags.

- Leaders can have an **Attached End** or a **Free End**, as shown in Figure 12–59. The attached end must be connected to the element being tagged. A free end has an additional drag control where the leader touches the element.

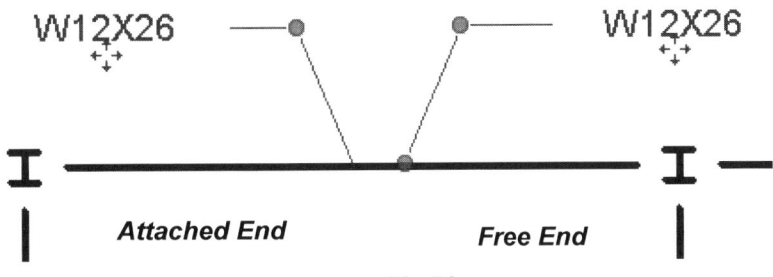

Figure 12–59

- If you change between **Attached End** and **Free End**, the tag does not move and the leader does not change location.

- The **Length** option specifies the length of the leader in plotting units. It is grayed out if **Leader** is not selected or if a **Free End** leader is defined.

- If a tag is not loaded a warning dialog box opens as shown in Figure 12–60. Click **Yes** to open the Load Family dialog box in which you can select the appropriate tag.

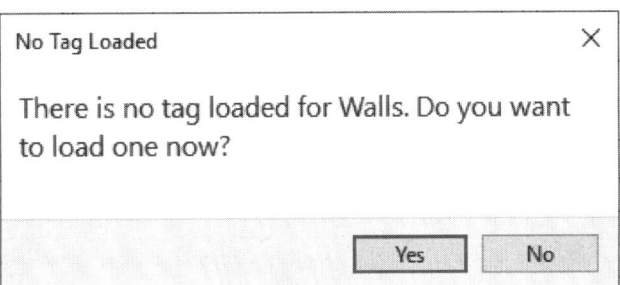

Figure 12–60

- Tags can be pinned to they stay in place if you move the element that is tagged. This is primarily used when tags have leaders, as shown in Figure 12–61.

Figure 12–61

Multi-Leader Tags

If you have elements that need to be tagged that are in close proximity to one another, you can tag one element and then select other similar elements. This adds more leader lines from the elements to the tag like the windows shown in Figure 12–62. When selecting the tag, you can see how many host elements it is tagging in Properties (as shown on the left in Figure 12–62).

You cannot select elements that are of different categories, like beams and columns. You can only select similar elements to share a tag.

Figure 12–62

If you select, for instance, both structural framing joists and girders that are different sizes, you will get a <varies> tag because they are different sizes, as shown in Figure 12–63.

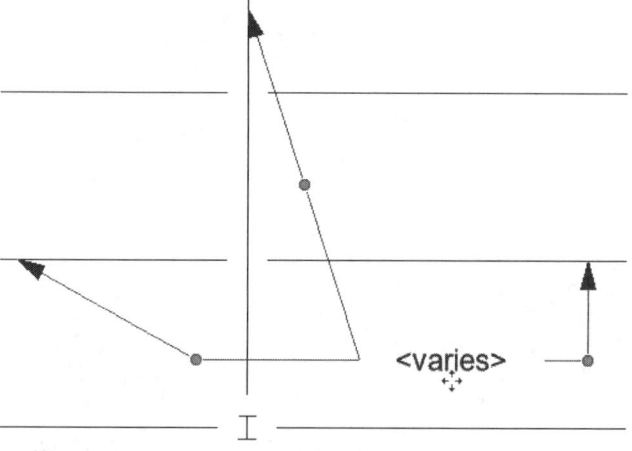

Figure 12–63

Annotating Construction Documents

How To: Add a Multi-Leader Tag

1. Start the **Tag by Category** command.
2. Set the required options in the Options Bar.
3. Tag one element in the model.
4. Verify **Add/Remove Host** is on, as shown in Figure 12–64.

Figure 12–64

5. Select the other similar elements to add to the tag.
6. Alternatively, if you have a tag already placed in the model and you want to add elements to the tag, select the tag and in the contextual tab, select (Add/Remove Host), then select the other elements.
7. A leader line will be added for each element you select.

How To: Remove Elements from a Multi-Leader Tag

1. To remove an element from the tag, select the tag, then select (Add/Remove Host) in the ribbon.
2. Select the element in the model. The leader line is removed.

How To: Tag All

1. In the *Annotate* tab>Tag panel, click (Tag All).
2. In the Tag All Not Tagged dialog box (shown in Figure 12–65), select the checkbox beside one or more categories to tag. Selecting the checkbox beside the Category title selects all of the tags.

*To tag only some elements, select them before starting this command. In the Tag All Not Tagged dialog box, select **Only selected objects in current view**.*

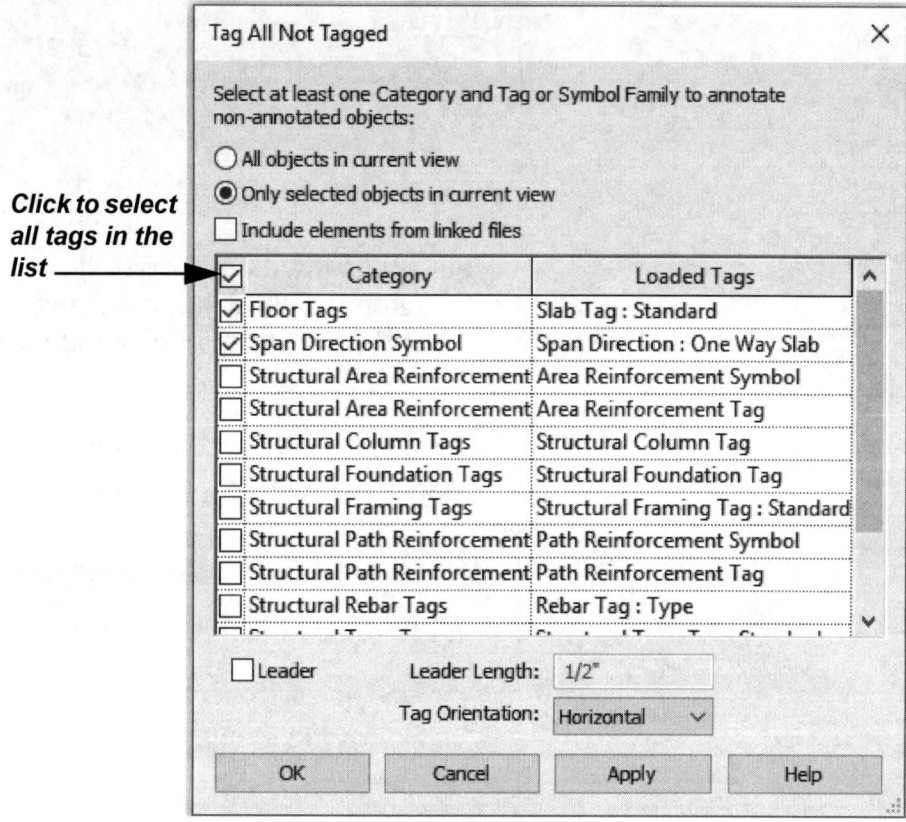

Figure 12–65

3. Set the *Leader* and *Tag Orientation* as needed.
4. Click **Apply** to apply the tags and stay in the dialog box. Click **OK** to apply the tags and close the dialog box.

- When you select a tag, the properties of that tag display. To display the properties of the tagged element, in the *Modify* contextual tab>Host panel, click (Select Host).

Annotating Construction Documents

How To: Load Tags

1. In the *Annotate* tab, expand the Tag panel and click (Loaded Tags And Symbols) or, when a Tag command is active, in the Options Bar click **Tags...**
2. In the Loaded Tags And Symbols dialog box (shown in Figure 12–66), click **Load Family...**.

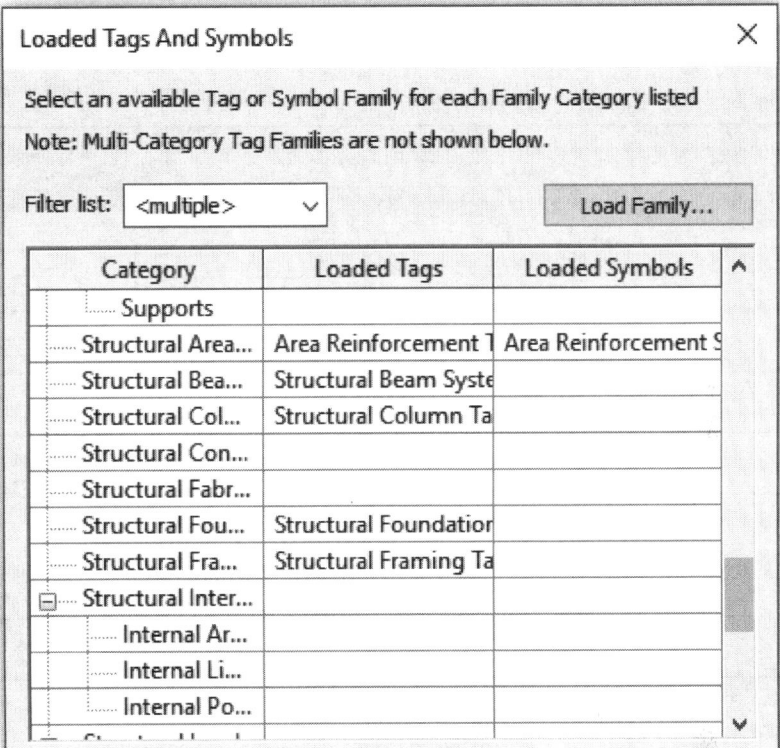

Figure 12–66

3. In the Load Family dialog box, navigate to the appropriate *Annotations* folder in the Revit Library, select the tag(s) needed, and click **Open**.
4. The tag is added to the category in the dialog box. Click **OK**.

Instance vs. Type-Based Tags

Some elements are tagged in a numbered sequence, with each instance of the element having a separate tag number. Other elements (such as trusses and walls) are tagged by type. Changing the information in one tag changes all instances of that element.

- To modify the number of an instance tag (such as a door or room), slowly click twice directly on the number in the tag and modify it, or, you can modify the *Mark* property. Only that one instance updates.

- To modify the number of a type tag, you can slowly click twice directly on the number in the tag and modify it. Alternatively, you can select the element and in the *Modify* contextual tab> Host panel, click (Select Host), then in Properties, click (Edit Type). In the Type Properties dialog box, in the *Identity Data* area, modify the *Type Mark*, as shown in Figure 12–67. All instances of this element then update.

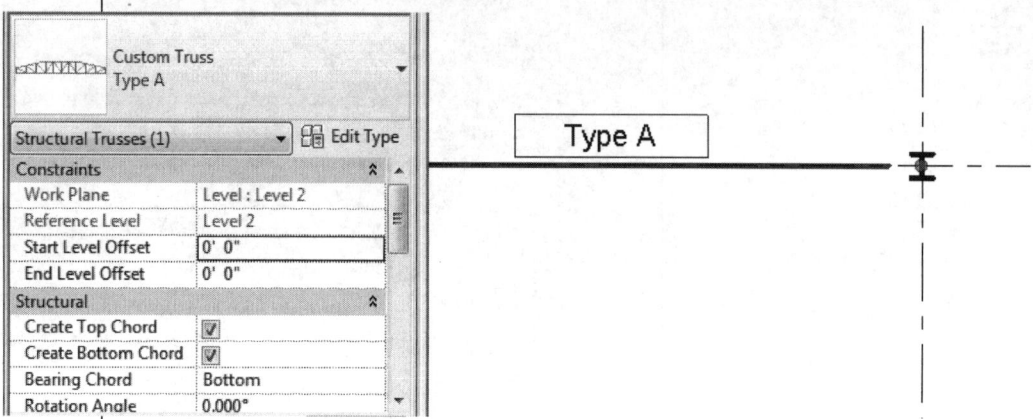

Figure 12–67

- When you change a type tag, an alert box opens to warn you that changing a type parameter affects other elements, as shown in Figure 12–68. If you want the tag to modify all elements of this type, click **Yes**.

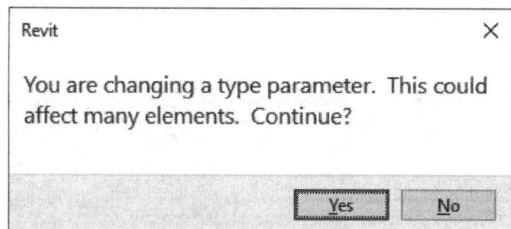

Figure 12–68

- If a tag displays with a question mark, it means that no information has been assigned to that parameter yet.

Annotating Construction Documents

> **Hint: Tagging Elements in Detail Views**
>
> When you tag elements in a cropped view, the tag is placed at the default location of the element and might not display in the callout. In the View Control Bar, click (Do not Crop). Tag the elements, and then move the new tags in the crop window, as shown in Figure 12–69. Click (Crop View) to return to the area of the callout view.
>
>
>
> **Figure 12–69**

Tagging in 3D Views

You can add tags to isometric 3D views, as shown in Figure 12–70, as long as the views are locked first.

Figure 12–70

- Dimensions can be added to isometric 3D views whether they are locked or not. Proceed with caution when selecting the items to dimension to ensure that the witness lines and text orient is snapping to and extending in the correct direction as intended.
- Locked views can be used with perspective views. This enables you to create the view as you want it and then save it from being modified.

How To: Lock a 3D View

1. Open a 3D view and set it up as you want it to display.
2. In the View Control Bar, click (Unlocked 3D View) and click (Save Orientation and Lock View).
   - If you are using the default 3D view and it has not been saved, you are prompted to name and save the view first.
   - You can modify the orientation of the view by clicking (Locked 3D View) and clicking (Unlock View). This also removes any tags you have applied.
3. To return to the previous locked view, click (Unlocked 3D View) and click (Restore Orientation and Lock View).

Beam Annotations

The Beam Annotation tools enable you to place beam tags, annotations, and spot elevations to all elements in a view, as shown in Figure 12–71.

14' - 7"	W12X26	14' - 7"	14
	14' - 7"		
14' - 7"	W12X26	14' - 7"	14
	14' - 7"		
14' - 7"	W12X26	14' - 7"	14
	14' - 7"		

Figure 12–71

- Beam annotations can be put at the end points and midpoints on either side of beams. You can also specify different annotations for level beams and sloped beams.

Annotating Construction Documents

- To limit the number of beams that are annotated, select them first and then start the command. Otherwise, all of the beams in a view are annotated.

- Beams in linked files can be included.

- You can replace existing annotations or leave them in place without duplicating them.

- You can define values for steel connection parameters, including releases and member forces. These values can be used by the designer, fabricator, and analysis applications. They are available for use in schedules and annotations.

How To: Place Beam Annotations

1. In the *Annotate* tab>Tag panel, click (Beam Annotations).
2. In the Beam Annotations dialog box, as shown in Figure 12–72, specify the locations of the annotation at which you want them to display on each beam.

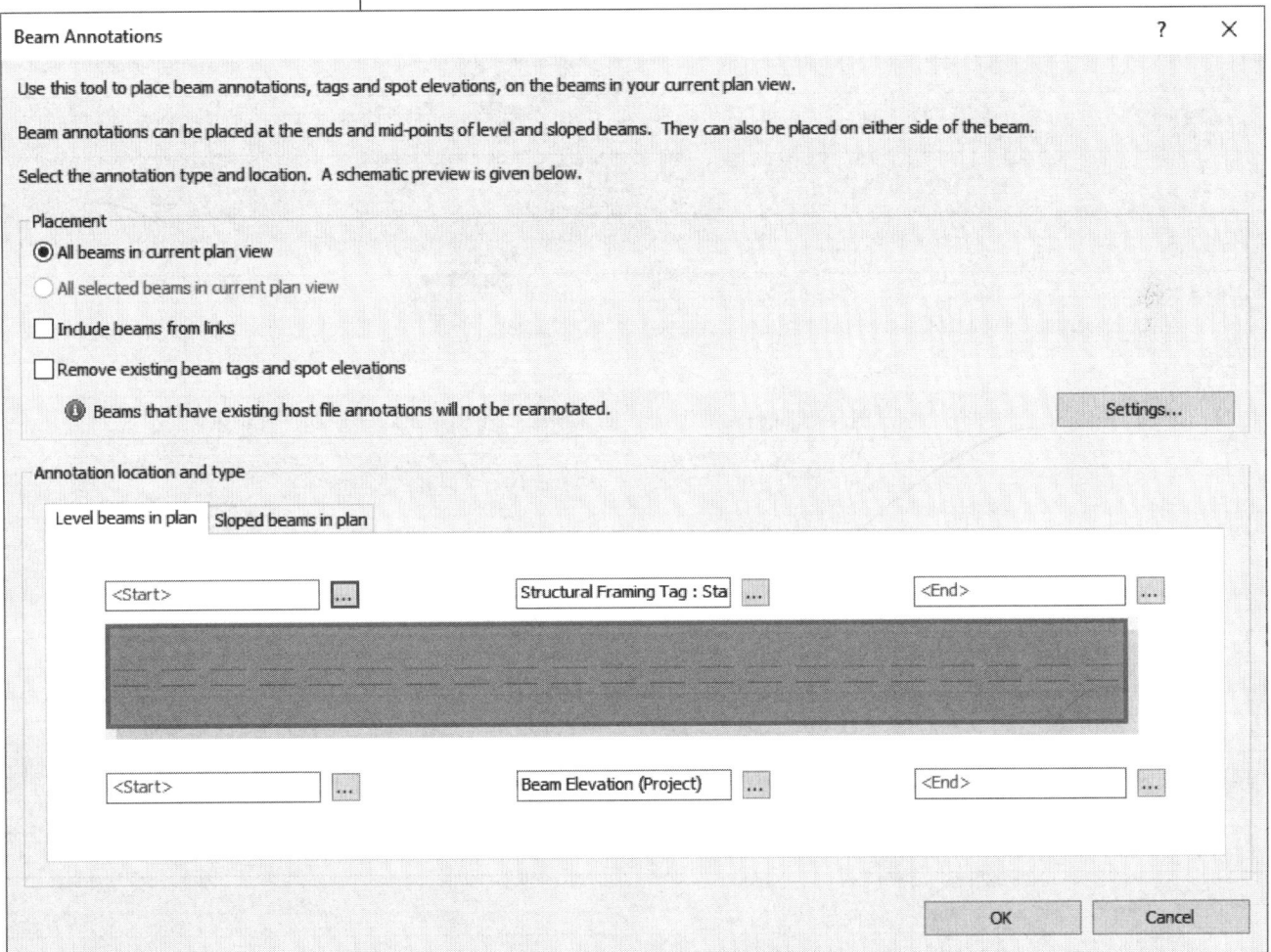

Figure 12–72

3. To change the type of annotation at various locations, click ▭ (Browse) next to the edit box to open the Select Annotation Type dialog box. In the *Select Element to Place* area, specify an option, such as the **Spot Elevation** shown in Figure 12–73. The option you select modifies the information you can specify.

Figure 12–73

4. Specify the options in the dialog box and click **OK**.

5. Click **OK** to place the beam annotations.

12.4 Adding Detail Lines and Symbols

While annotating views for construction documents, you might need to add detail lines and symbols to clarify the design intent or show information. Several symbols, such as the **Span Direction Symbol** (shown in Figure 12–74), are specific to structural projects.

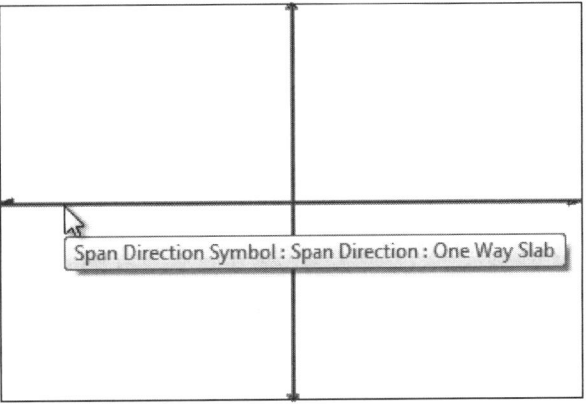

Figure 12–74

- Detail lines and symbols are view-specific, which means that they only display in the view in which they were created.

How To: Draw Detail Lines

1. In the *Annotation* tab>Detail panel, click (Detail Line).
2. In the *Modify | Place Detail Lines* tab>Line Style panel, select the type of line you want to use, as shown in Figure 12–75.

Figure 12–75

3. Use the tools in the Draw panel to create the detail lines.

Using Symbols

Many of the annotations used in working drawings are frequently repeated. Several of them have been saved as symbols in the Autodesk Revit software, such as the North Arrow, Center Line, and Graphic Scale annotations as shown in Figure 12–76.

Figure 12–76

- Symbols are 2D elements that only display in views placed, while components can be in 3D and display in many views.

- You can also create or load custom annotation symbols.

How To: Place a Symbol

1. In the *Annotate* tab>Symbol panel, click (Symbol).
2. In the Type Selector, select the symbol you want to use.
3. In the *Modify | Place Symbol* tab>Mode panel, click (Load Family) if you want to load other symbols.
4. In the Options Bar, as shown in Figure 12–77, set the *Number of Leaders* and select **Rotate after placement** if you want to rotate the symbol as you insert it.

Figure 12–77

5. Place the symbol in the view. Rotate it if you selected the **Rotate after placement** option. If you specified leaders, use the controls to move them into place.

- For information about adding tags to dependent views see, *B.10 Importing and Exporting Schedules*.

Structural Specific Symbols

Several types of structural elements use symbols or symbols and tags together. If the associated symbols are not applied when you create the element, you can add them later. They are found in the *Annotate* tab>Symbol panel, as shown in Figure 12–78.

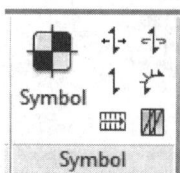

Figure 12–78

Annotating Construction Documents

- You can also use the **Tag All Not Tagged** command to add symbols to a view.

How To: Add Reinforcement Symbols

1. In the *Annotate* tab>Symbol panel, click the type of symbol you want to use:

    - (Beam System Symbol)
    - (Span Direction Symbol)
    - (Area Reinforcement Symbol)
    - (Path Reinforcement Symbol)
    - (Fabric Reinforcement Symbol)

2. Select the related reinforcement element (not the individual rebar).
3. Select a location for the symbol. The symbol expands to fit the extents of the beam system, as shown for **Path Reinforcement** in Figure 12–79.

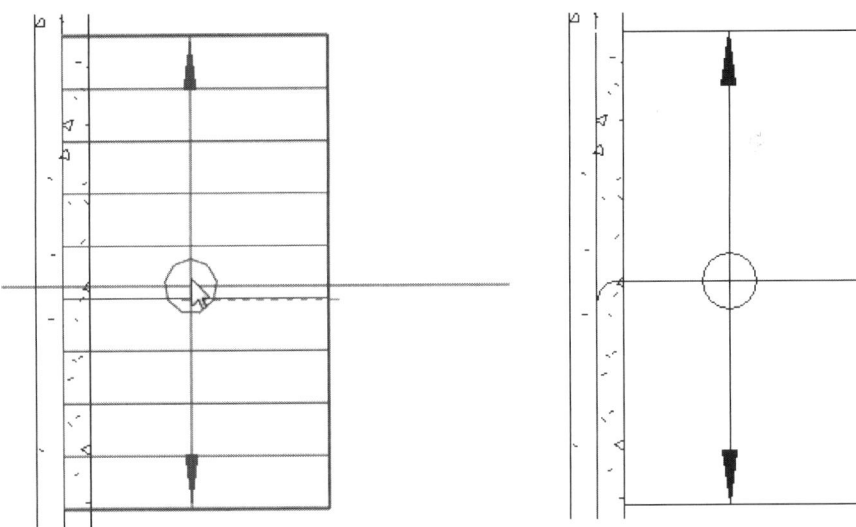

Figure 12–79

4. You can continue selecting similar elements and placing the symbol.
5. When you are finished, click (Modify) or press <Esc> to end the command.

- To add a tag to the reinforcement elements, use the (Tag by Category) command.

Changing the Span Direction of Floors and Slabs

By default, span direction symbols are added when you create a structural floor or foundation slab. They can be used to change the span direction of the floor or slab without having to edit the sketch. You can modify the floor span direction symbol once it is in the view through the Type Selector, as shown in Figure 12–80. (Note that Foundation Span Direction Symbols do not have these choices.)

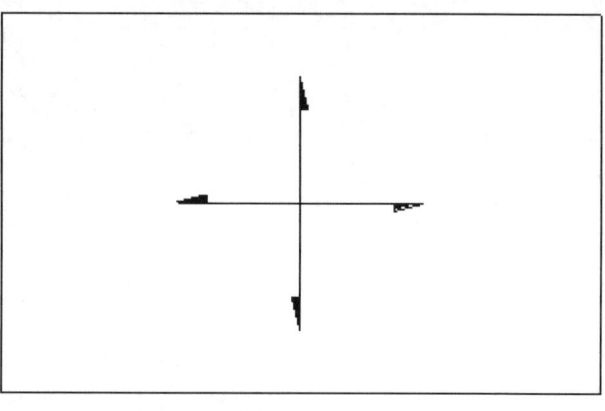

Figure 12–80

How To: Change the Span Direction

1. Select the Span Direction symbol.
2. In the *Modify | Span Direction Symbol* tab>Align Symbol panel, click (Align Perpendicular).
3. Select the side of the slab that you want the span to be perpendicular to.
4. The Span Direction Symbol changes direction, as shown in Figure 12–81.

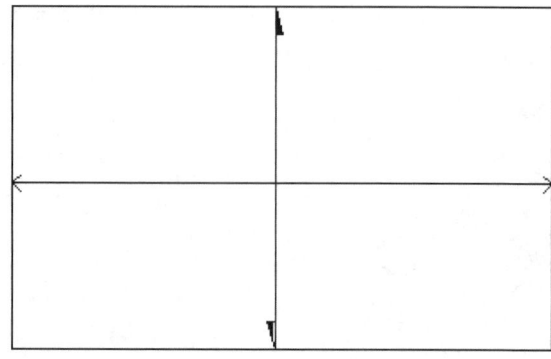

Figure 12–81

Annotating Construction Documents

Beam System Symbols vs. Framing Tags

Beam Systems can be annotated by either tagging each individual beam, or by using a beam system symbol, as shown in Figure 12–82. When placing a beam system, you can select (Tag on Placement), and in the Options Bar, set the *Tag Style* to either **Framing** or **System**. The *Framing* option tags each beam in the system, while the *System* option applies a beam system symbol.

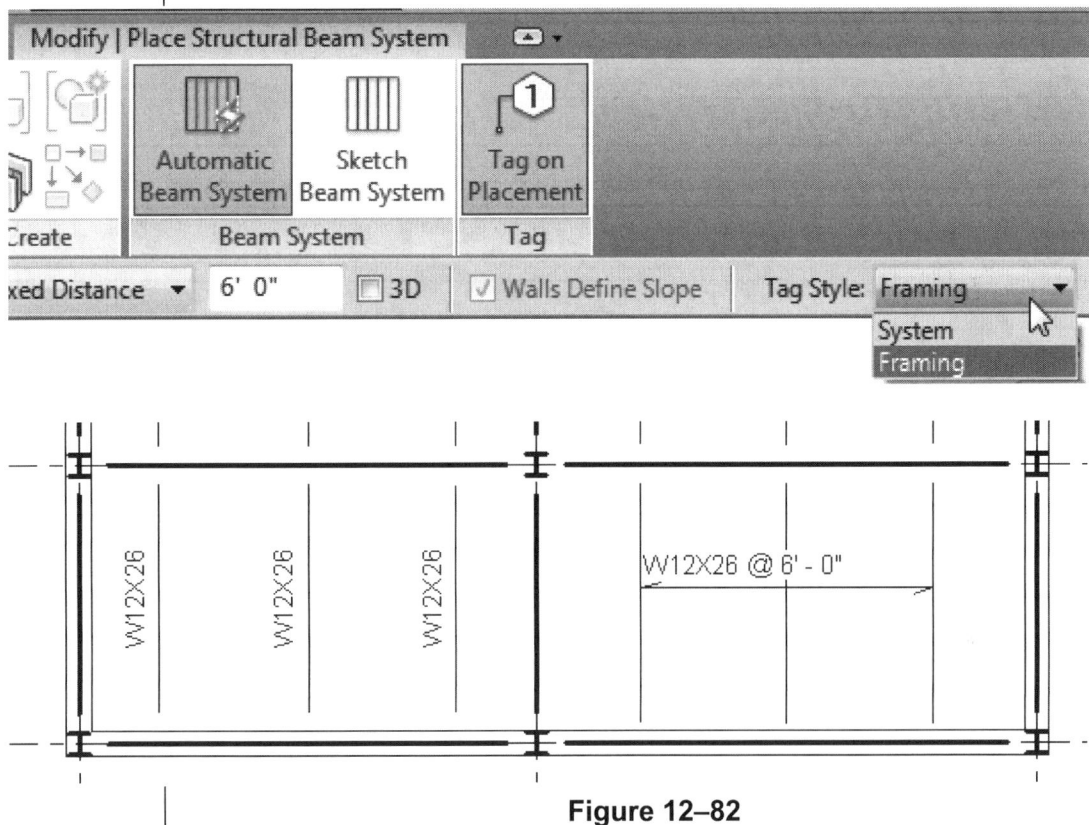

Figure 12–82

- To add the individual framing tags later, use the (Tag by Category) command. To add a Beam System Symbol use the (Beam System Symbol) command.

Practice 12c Add Tags and Symbols

Practice Objectives

- Add tags.
- Place beam system symbols.

In this practice, you will tag some framing elements using the **Tag by Category** command and the **Beam System Symbol**. You will then use **Tag All Not Tagged** to tag the rest of the framing elements. You will then add the rest of the beam system symbols, as shown in Figure 12–83.

Figure 12–83

Task 1 - Tag framing elements using Tag by Category and Beam System Symbol.

1. Open **Structural-Tags.rvt** from the practice files folder.

2. Create a duplicate of the **Structural Plans: TOS-1ST FLOOR** view and name it **TOS-1ST FLOOR - Framing**.

3. In the *Annotate* tab>Tag panel, click (Tag by Category).

4. In the Options Bar, ensure that **Leader** is not selected.

5. Tag several of the outside beams, as shown in Figure 12–84.

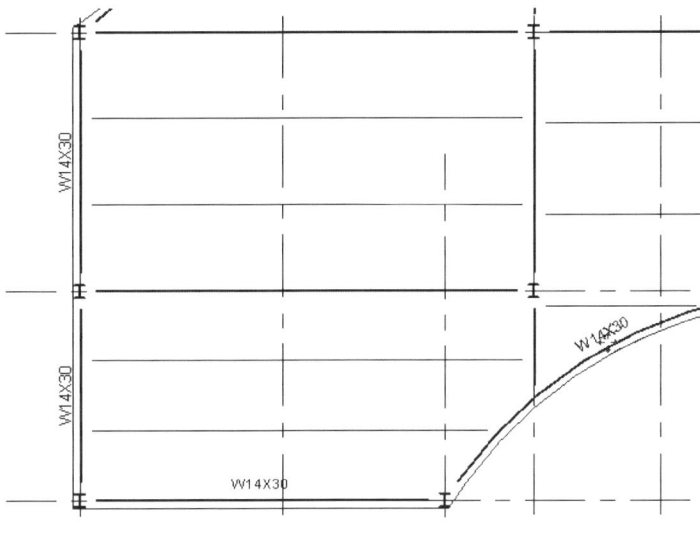

Figure 12–84

6. While still in the command, hover the cursor over the inside beams. Note that you can tag each beam separately.

7. Click (Modify)

8. In the *Annotate* tab>Symbol panel, click (Beam).

9. Click on a beam system and then click to place the location of the symbol. It automatically fits to the correct size of the beam system, as shown in Figure 12–85.

Figure 12–85

10. Save the project.

Task 2 - Tag framing elements that are not tagged.

1. Continue working in the **TOS-1ST FLOOR - Framing** view.

2. In the *Annotate* tab>Tag panel, click (Tag All).

3. In the Tagged All Not Tagged dialog box, ensure that **All objects in current view** is selected.

4. Browse to the *Structural Framing* category and select **Structural Framing Tag: Standard**, as shown in Figure 12–86. Click **OK**.

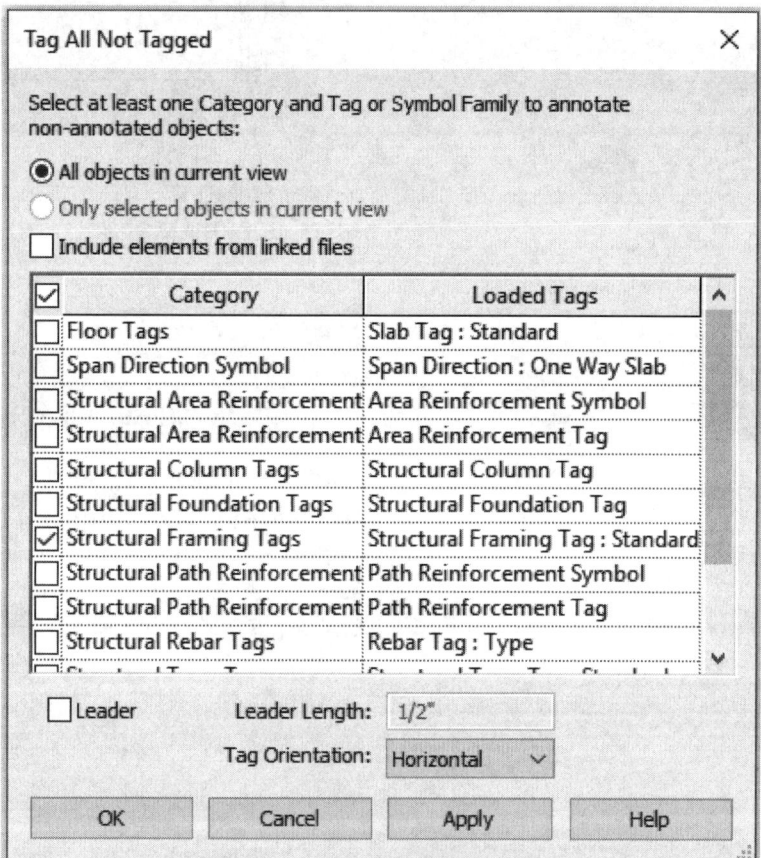

Figure 12–86

5. This tags all of the structural framing elements, including each one of the beams in the beam systems.

6. Undo the tagging.

7. Select one of the beam system joist beams in the framing system.

Annotating Construction Documents

8. Right-click and select **Select All Instances>Visible in View**. All of the joists that are the same are selected, as shown in Figure 12–87.

Figure 12–87

9. In the View Control Bar, select (Temporary Hide/Isolate) and then select **Hide Element**. (Do not hide the category as you still want to be able to tag the rest of the beams.

10. Run the (Tag All) command again, selecting the same structural framing tag.

11. This time only the non-joist beams are tagged.

12. In the View Control Bar, select (Temporary Hide/Isolate) and then select **Reset Temporary Hide/Isolate**. The beam system joists display once again.

13. The Beam System Symbol is not available in **Tag All Not Tagged**, therefore you need to use the (Beam System Symbol) command to tag the rest of these. Use the alignment lines to help you place the symbols relative to other nearby symbols.

14. Zoom to fit the view.

15. If you have time, you can apply the various reinforcement symbols to other views as applicable.

16. Save the project.

12.5 Creating Legends

A legend is a separate view that can be placed on multiple sheets. Legends can be used to hold installation notes that need to be placed on a sheet with each floor plan, key plans, or any 2D items that need to be repeated. You can also create and list the symbols that are used in your project, and provide explanatory notes next to the, as shown in Figure 12–88.

*The elements in this figure are inserted using the **Symbol** command rather that the **Legend Component** or **Detail Component** commands.*

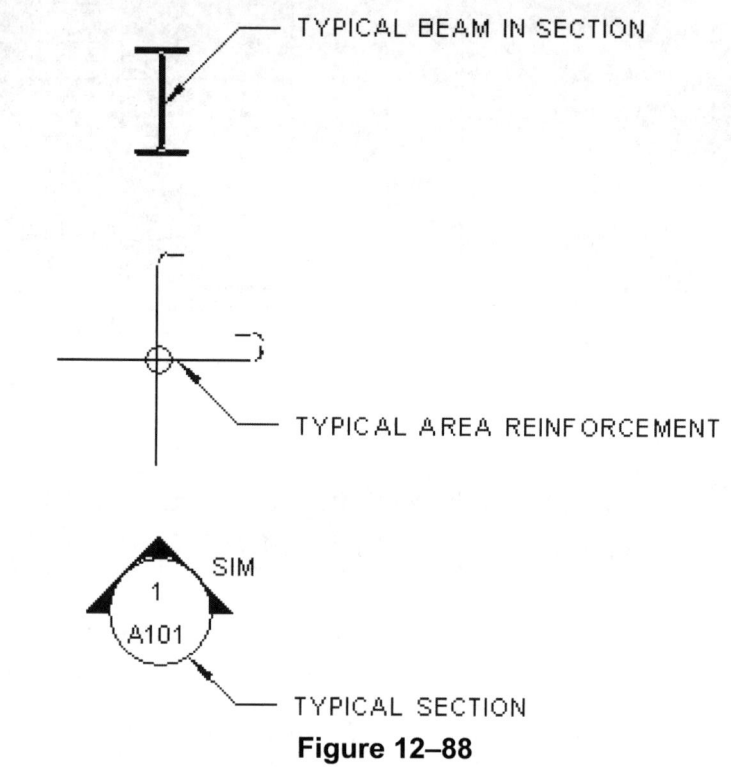

Figure 12–88

- You use (Detail Lines) and (Text) to create the table and explanatory notes. Once you have a legend view, you can use commands, such as (Legend Component), (Detail Component), and (Symbol), to place elements in the view.

- Unlike other views, legend views can be attached to more than one sheet.

- You can set a legend's scale in the View Control Bar.

- Elements in legends can be dimensioned.

Annotating Construction Documents

How To: Create a Legend

1. In the *View* tab>Create panel, expand (Legends) and click (Legend) or in the Project Browser, right-click on the *Legends* area title and select **New Legend**.
2. In the New Legend View dialog box, enter a name and select a scale for the legend, as shown in Figure 12–89, and click **OK**.

Figure 12–89

3. Place the components in the view first, and then sketch the outline of the table when you know the sizes. Use **Ref Planes** to line up the components.

How To: Use Legend Components

1. In the *Annotate* tab>Detail panel, expand (Component) and click (Legend Component).
2. In the Options Bar, select the *Family* type that you want to use, as shown in Figure 12–90.

    - This list contains all of the elements in a project that can be used in a legend.

Figure 12–90

3. Select the *View* of the element that you want to use. For example, you might want to display the section of the floors, as shown in Figure 12–91.

Figure 12–91

4. For section elements (such as walls, floors, and roofs), type a distance for the *Host Length*.

- Elements that are full size, such as columns or footings come in at their full size.

- Legends are views that can be placed on multiple sheets. You can use Copy to the Clipboard and Paste to copy legends from sheet to sheet.

Practice 12d Create Legends

Practice Objective

- Create legends using legend components and text.

In this practice, you will add a legend and populate it with legend components, symbols, associated text, and detail lines (as shown in Figure 12–92), as well as create a key plan for use on multiple sheets.

Figure 12–92

Task 1 - Add a symbol legend.

1. Open **Structural-Legends.rvt** from the practice files folder.

2. In the *View* tab>Create panel, expand ▦ (Legends) and click ▦ (Legend).

3. In the New Legend View dialog box, set the *Name* to **Typical Symbols Legend** and set the *Scale* to **3/4" = 1'-0"**, as shown in Figure 12–93.

Figure 12–93

4. Click **OK**.

5. In the *Annotate* tab>Detail panel, expand (Component) and click (Legend Component).

6. In the Options Bar, set the following, as shown in Figure 12–94:

   - *Family*: **Floors: Floor: 3" LW Concrete on 2" Composite Metal Deck**
   - *View*: **Section**
   - *Host Length*: **4'-0"**

Figure 12–94

7. Click to place the floor legend component in the view.

8. Add the text **TYPICAL UPPER LEVEL FLOOR** close to legend, as shown in Figure 12–95. Adjust the text size from the Type Selector as needed.

 TYPICAL UPPER LEVEL FLOOR

Figure 12–95

9. Add several other legend components such as a wall in plan view, a column in section view, and add titles beside them.

10. In the *Annotate* tab>Symbol panel, click (Symbol).

11. In the Type Selector, select **Centerline**. Place it below at the bottom of the symbol legend and add the text **CENTER OF LINE DESIGNATION** next to it.

12. Add another symbol, **Connection - Moment - Filled** and label it **MOMENT CONNECTION**.

13. Add several more elements and label them, as shown in Figure 12–96.

14. In the *Annotate* tab>Detail panel, click (Detail Line). Select a Line Style and use (Rectangle) and/or (Line) in the Draw panel to draw a frame around the symbols and text as shown in Figure 12–96, and then at the top of the legend, add the text note **SYMBOL LEGEND** as a title.

Your legend will vary according to the symbols you selected to add.

Figure 12–96

15. Save the project.

Task 2 - Create a key plan legend.

1. Open the **Structural Plans: 00 GROUND FLOOR Plan** view.

2. Select just the **Foundation Slab 6" Foundation Slab** and temporarily isolate the elements. This displays the outline of the building.

3. In the *Annotate* tab>Detail panel, click (Detail Line).

4. In the *Modify | Place Detail Lines* tab>Line Styles panel, select the *Line Style*: **Wide Lines**.

5. In the Draw panel, click (Pick Lines).

6. Select the lines of the slab all of the way around to establish the key plan outline.

7. Click (Modify) to clear the selection of the lines.

8. Select all of the detail lines. (Hint: use Filter.)

9. In the *Modify Lines* tab>Clipboard panel, click (Cut to Clipboard). You can also press <Ctrl> + X.

10. In the *View* tab>Create panel, expand (Legends) and click (Legend).

11. Give the legend a *Name* and *Scale* as shown in Figure 12–97.

Figure 12–97

12. Click **OK**.

13. Press <Ctrl>+V and then click to place the elements.

14. In the *Modify | Detail Groups* tab>Edit Pasted panel, click (Finish).

15. Modify the outline as required to create a useful key plan, as shown in Figure 12–98.

    - Use **Detail Lines** to divide the outline.
    - Use **Text** to add information. Create a new text size so it is large enough to see.

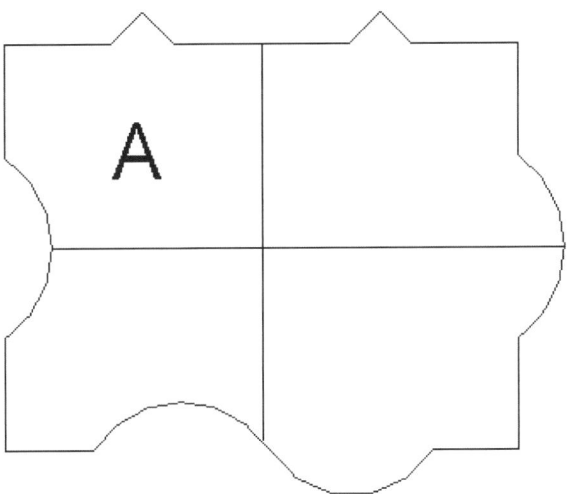

Figure 12–98

*It is important to use the **Duplicate with Detailing** option as **Detail Lines** and **Text** are detail elements.*

16. In the Project Browser, in the *Legends* area, select the **Key Plan Area A** legend view. Right-click and select **Duplicate> Duplicate with Detailing**. This creates a copy of the key plan that you can modify as shown in Figure 12–99.

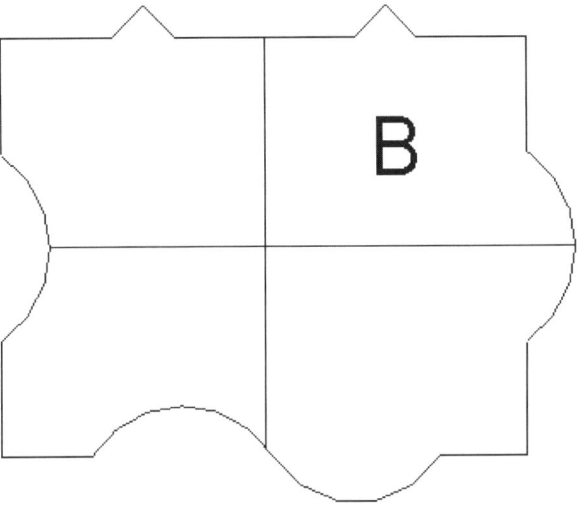

Figure 12–99

17. Save and close the project.

Chapter Review Questions

1. When a grid line is moved (as shown in Figure 12–100), how do you update the dimension?

    Figure 12–100

    a. Edit the dimension and move it over.

    b. Select the dimension and then click **Update** in the Options Bar.

    c. The dimension automatically updates.

    d. Delete the existing dimension and add a new one.

2. How do you create new text styles?

    a. Using the **Text Styles** command.

    b. Duplicate an existing type.

    c. They must be included in a template.

    d. Using the **Format Styles** command.

3. When you edit text, how many leaders can be added using the leader tools shown in Figure 12–101?

Figure 12–101

    a. One

    b. One on each end of the text.

    c. As many as you want at each end of the text.

4. Detail Lines created in one view also display in the related view.

    a. True

    b. False

5. Which of the following describes the difference between a symbol and a component?

    a. Symbols are 3D and only display in one view. Components are 2D and display in many views.

    b. Symbols are 2D and only display in one view. Components are 3D and display in many views.

    c. Symbols are 2D and display in many views. Components are 3D and only display in one view.

    d. Symbols are 3D and display in many views. Components are 2D and only display in one view.

6. When creating a Legend, which of the following elements cannot be added?

    a. Legend Components

    b. Tags

    c. Rooms

    d. Symbols

Command Summary

Button	Command	Location
Dimensions and Text		
	Aligned (Dimension)	• **Ribbon:** *Annotate* tab>Dimension panel or *Modify* tab>Measure panel, expanded drop-down list • **Quick Access Toolbar** • **Shortcut:** DI
	Angular (Dimension)	• **Ribbon:** *Annotate* tab>Dimension panel or *Modify* tab>Measure panel, expanded drop-down list
	Arc Length (Dimension)	• **Ribbon:** *Annotate* tab>Dimension panel or *Modify* tab>Measure panel, expanded drop-down list
	Diameter (Dimension)	• **Ribbon:** *Annotate* tab>Dimension panel or *Modify* tab>Measure panel, expanded drop-down list
	Linear (Dimension)	• **Ribbon:** *Annotate* tab>Dimension panel or *Modify* tab>Measure panel, expanded drop-down list
	Radial (Dimension)	• **Ribbon:** *Annotate* tab>Dimension panel or *Modify* tab>Measure panel, expanded drop-down list
	Text	• **Ribbon:** *Annotate* tab>Text panel • **Shortcut:** TX
Additional Annotation Tools		
	Detail Component	• **Ribbon:** *Annotate* tab>Detail panel
	Detail Line	• **Ribbon:** *Annotate* tab>Detail panel • **Shortcut:** DL
	Symbol	• **Ribbon:** *Annotate* tab>Symbol panel
	Area Reinforcement Symbol	• **Ribbon:** *Annotate* tab>Symbol panel
	Beam System Symbol)	• **Ribbon:** *Annotate* tab>Symbol panel
	Fabric Reinforcement Symbol	• **Ribbon:** *Annotate* tab>Symbol panel
	Path Reinforcement Symbol	• **Ribbon:** *Annotate* tab>Symbol panel

	Span Direction Symbol	• **Ribbon:** *Annotate* tab>Symbol panel
	Tag by Category	• **Ribbon:** *Annotate* tab>Tag panel
	Multi-Category	• **Ribbon:** *Annotate* tab>Tag panel
	Material Tag	• **Ribbon:** *Annotate* tab>Tag panel
	Tag All	• **Ribbon:** *Annotate* tab>Tag panel
	Loaded Tags And Symbols	• **Ribbon:** *Annotate* tab>expanded Tag panel
	Beam Annotations	• **Ribbon:** *Annotate* tab>Tag panel
Legends		
	Legend (View)	• **Ribbon:** *View* tab>Create panel> expand Legends
	Legend Component	• **Ribbon:** *Annotate* tab>Detail panel> expand Component

Chapter 13

Creating Details

Creating details is a critical part of the design process, as it is the step where you specify the exact information that is required to build a construction project. The elements that you can add to a model include detail components, detail lines, text, tags, symbols, and filled regions for patterning. Details can be created from views in the model, but you can also add 2D details in separate views.

Learning Objectives in This Chapter

- Create drafting views where you can add 2D details.
- Add detail components that show the typical elements in a detail.
- Annotate details using detail lines, text, tags, symbols, and patterns that define materials.

13.1 Setting Up Detail Views

Most of the work you do in the Autodesk® Revit® software is exclusively with *smart* elements that interconnect and work together in the model. However, the software does not automatically display how elements should be built to fit together. For this, you need to create detail drawings, as shown in Figure 13–1.

Details are created either in 2D drafting views, or in callouts from plan, elevation, or section views.

Figure 13–1

How To: Create a Drafting View

1. In the *View* tab>Create panel, click (Drafting View).
2. In the New Drafting View dialog box, enter a *Name* and set a *Scale*, as shown in Figure 13–2.

Drafting views are listed in their own section in the Project Browser.

Figure 13–2

3. Click **OK**. A blank view is created with space in which you can sketch the detail.

Creating Details

How To: Create a Detail View from Model Elements

1. Start the **Section** or **Callout** command.
2. In the Type Selector, select the **Detail View: Detail** type.
   - The marker indicates that it is a detail, as shown for a section in Figure 13–3.

Callouts also have a Detail View type that can be used in the same way.

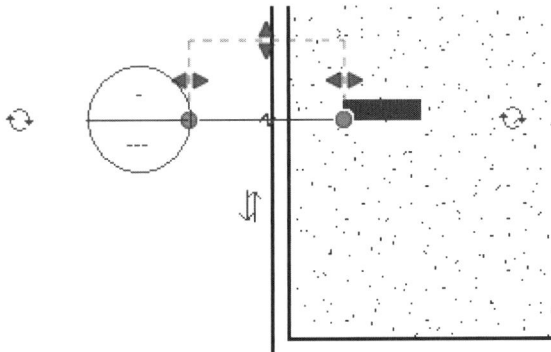

Figure 13–3

3. Place the section or a callout of the area you want to use for the detail.
4. Open the new detail. Use the tools to sketch on top of or add to the building elements.
5. Change the detail level to see more or less of the element materials.

- Because you are working with smart elements, a detail of the model is a true representation. When the building elements change, the detail changes as well, as shown in Figure 13–4.

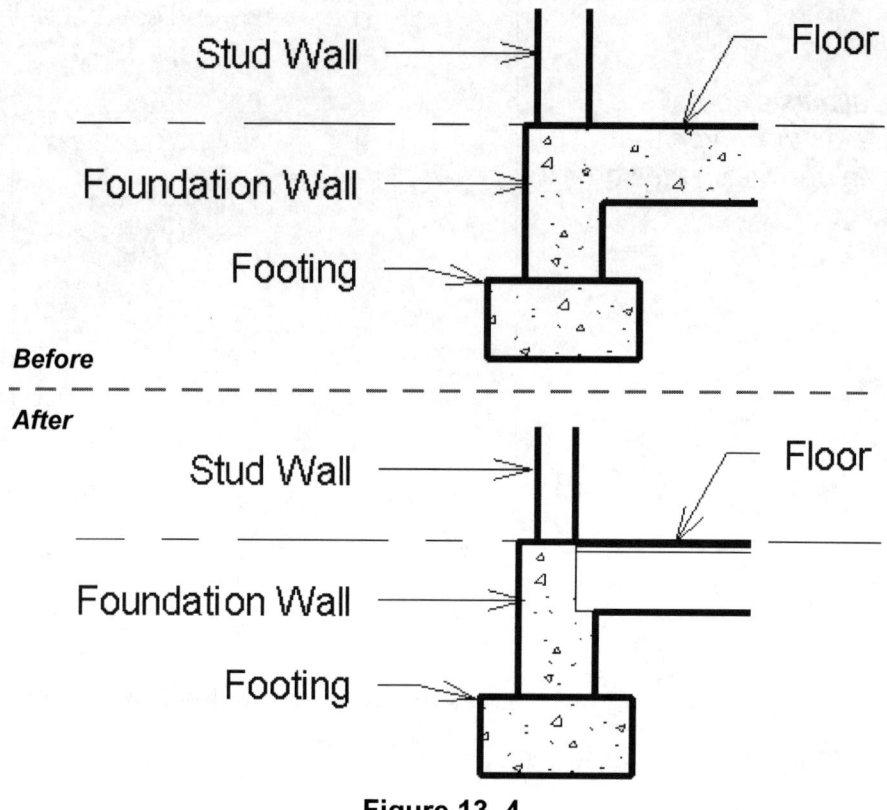

Figure 13–4

- You can create detail elements on top of the model and then toggle the model off so that it does not show in the detail view. In Properties, in the *Graphics* section, change *Display Model* to **Do not display**. You can also set the model to **Halftone**, as shown in Figure 13–5.

Figure 13–5

Referencing a Drafting View

Once you have created a drafting view, you can reference it in another view (such as a callout, elevation, or section view), as shown in Figure 13–6. For example, in a section view, you might want to reference an existing roof detail. You can reference drafting views, sections, elevations, and callouts.

Figure 13–6

- You can use the search feature to limit the information displayed.

How To: Reference a Drafting View

1. Open the view in which you want to place the reference.
2. Start the **Section**, **Callout**, or **Elevation** command.
3. In the *Modify* contextual tab>Reference panel, select **Reference Other View**.
4. In the drop-down list, select **<New Drafting View>** or an existing drafting view.
5. Place the view marker.
6. When you place the associated drafting view on a sheet, the marker in this view updates with the appropriate information.

- If you select **<New Drafting View>** from the drop-down list, a new view is created in the *Drafting Views (Detail)* area in the Project Browser. You can rename it as needed. The new view does not include any model elements.

- When you create a detail based on a section, elevation, or callout, you do not need to link it to a drafting view.

- You can change a referenced view to a different view. Select the view marker and in the ribbon, select the new view from the list.

Saving Drafting Views

To create a library of standard details, save the non-model specific drafting views to your server. They can then be imported into a project and modified to suit. They are saved as .RVT files.

Drafting views can be saved in two ways:

- Save an individual drafting view to a new file.
- Save all of the drafting views as a group in one new file.

How To: Save One Drafting View to a File

1. In the Project Browser, right-click on the drafting view you want to save and select **Save to New File...**, as shown in Figure 13–7.

Figure 13–7

2. In the Save As dialog box, specify a name and location for the file and click **Save**.

How To: Save a Group of Drafting Views to a File

You can save sheets, drafting views, model views (floor plans), schedules, and reports.

1. In the *File* tab, expand (Save As), expand (Library), and then click (View).
2. In the Save Views dialog box, in the *Views:* pane, expand the list and select **Show drafting views only**.
3. Select the drafting views that you want to save, as shown in Figure 13–8.

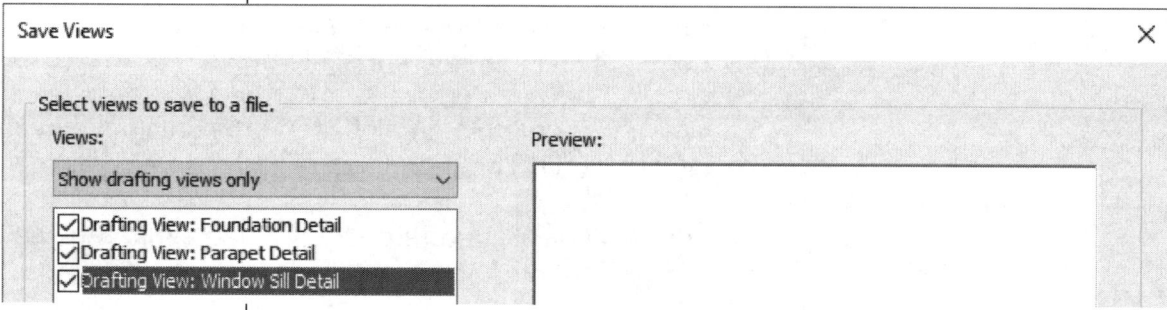

Figure 13–8

4. Click **OK**.
5. In the Save As dialog box, specify a name and location for the file and click **Save**.

Creating Details

How To: Use a Saved Drafting View in Another Project

1. Open the project to which you want to add the drafting view.
2. In the *Insert* tab>Import panel, expand (Insert from File) and click (Insert Views from File).
3. In the Open dialog box, select the project in which you saved the detail and click **Open**.
4. In the Insert Views dialog box, limit the types of views to **Show drafting views only**, as shown in Figure 13–9.

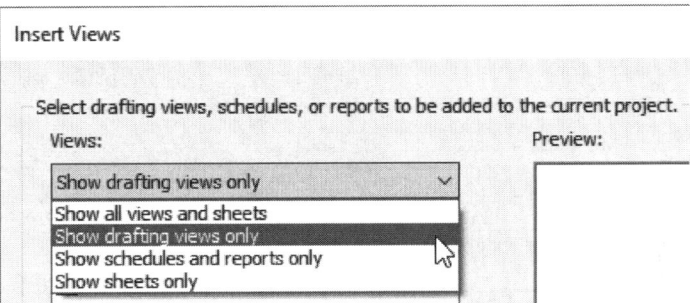

Figure 13–9

5. Select the view(s) that you want to insert and click **OK**.

> **Hint: Importing Details from Other CAD Software**
>
> You might already have a set of standard details created in a different CAD program, such as the AutoCAD® software. You can reuse the details in the Autodesk Revit software by importing them into a temporary project. Once you have imported the detail, it helps to clean it up and save it as a view before bringing it into your active project.
>
> 1. In a new project, create a drafting view and make it active.
> 2. In the *Insert* tab>Import panel, click (Import CAD).
> 3. In the Import CAD dialog box, select the file to import. Most of the default values are what you need. You might want to change the *Layer/Level colors* to **Black and White**.
> 4. Click **Open**.
>
> - If you want to modify the detail, select the imported data. In the *Modify | [filename]* tab>Import Instance panel, expand (Explode) and click (Partial Explode) or (Full Explode). Click (Delete Layers) before you explode the detail. A full explode greatly increases the file size.
>
> - Modify the detail using the tools in the Modify panel. Change all the text and line styles to Autodesk Revit-specific elements.

Creating Details

13.2 Adding Detail Components

Autodesk Revit elements, such as the casework section shown in Figure 13–10, typically require additional information to ensure that they are constructed correctly. To create details such as the one shown in Figure 13–11, you add detail components, detail lines, and various annotation elements.

Section
Figure 13–10

Detail built on section
Figure 13–11

- Detail elements are not directly connected to the model, even if model elements display in the view.
- If you want to draw detail lines in 3D, use **Model Line**. Detail Line is grayed out when you are in a 3D view or perspective view.

Detail Components

Detail components are families made of 2D and annotation elements. Over 500 detail components organized by CSI format are found in the *Detail Items* folder of the Revit Library, as shown in Figure 13–12.

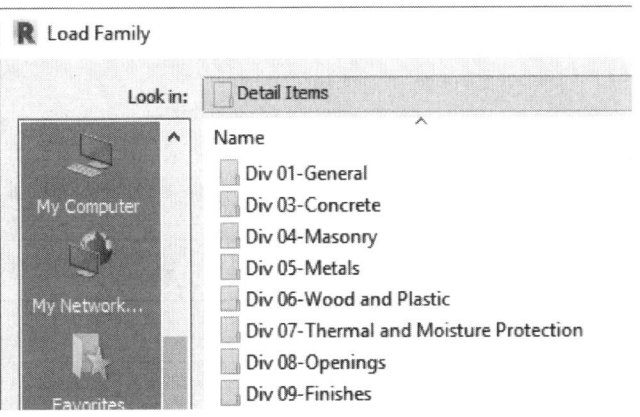
Figure 13–12

For more information on how to load detail items using the Load Autodesk Family dialog box, see 5.2 Loading Components.

- You can also access Detail Items from the Load Autodesk Family dialog box, as shown in Figure 13–13.

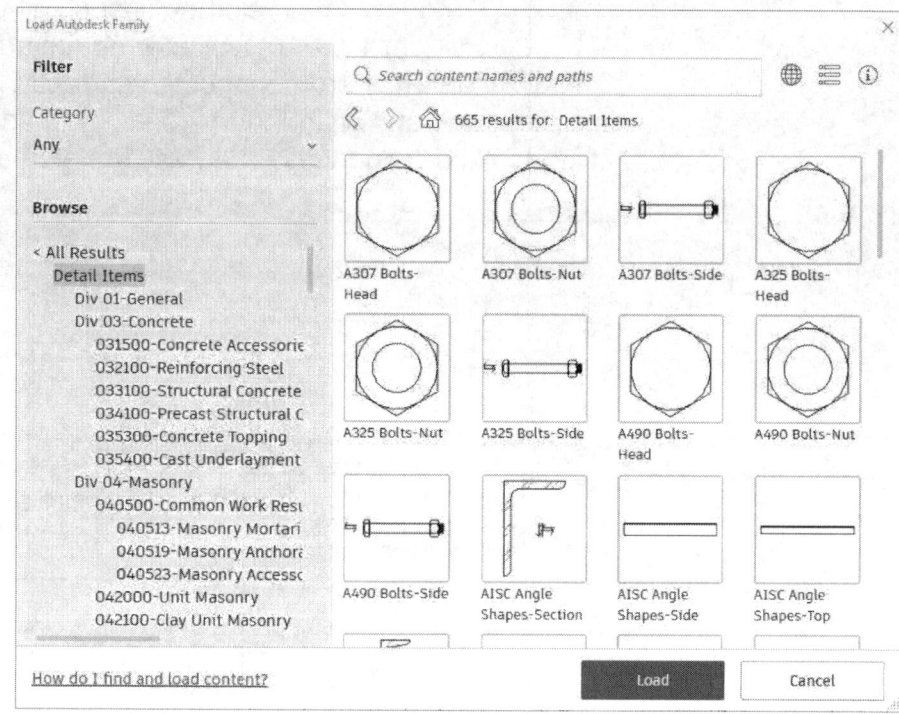

Figure 13–13

How To: Add a Detail Component

1. In the *Annotate* tab>Detail panel, expand (Component) and click (Detail Component).
2. In the Type Selector, select the detail component type. You can load additional types from the Revit Library.
3. Many detail components can be rotated as you insert them by pressing <Spacebar>. Alternatively, select **Rotate after placement** in the Options Bar, as shown in Figure 13–14.

Figure 13–14

4. Place the component in the view.

Adding Break Lines

The break line is a detail component found in the Revit Library's *Detail Items\Div 01-General* folder. It consists of a rectangular area (shown highlighted in Figure 13–15) that is used to block out elements behind it. You can modify the size of the area that is covered and change the size of the cut line using the controls.

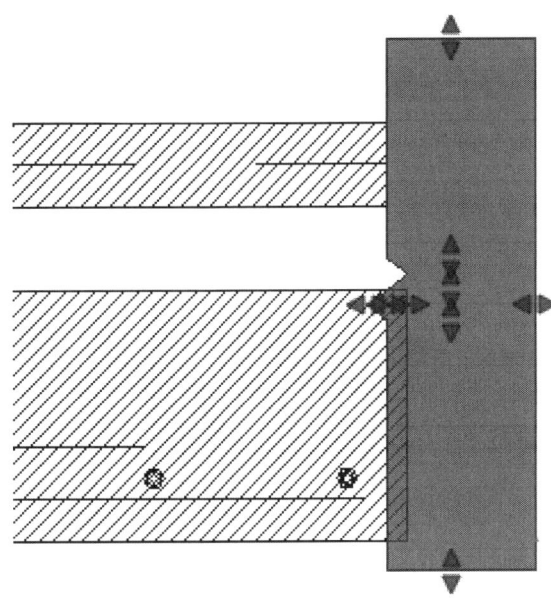

Figure 13–15

Hint: Working with the Draw Order of Details

When you select detail elements in a view, you can change the draw order of the elements in the *Modify | Detail Items* tab> Arrange panel. You can bring elements in front of other elements or place them behind elements, as shown in Figure 13–16.

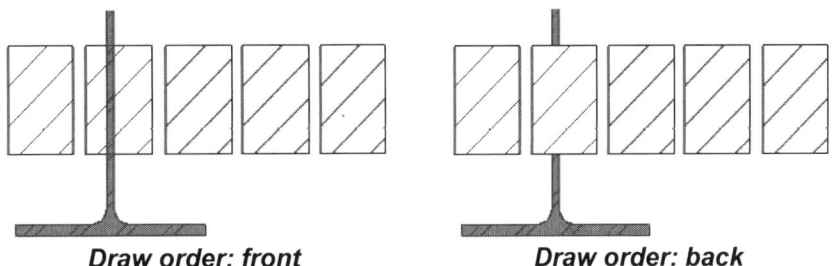

Draw order: front   *Draw order: back*

Figure 13–16

- (Bring to Front): Places element in front of all other elements.

- (Send to Back): Places element behind all other elements.

- (Bring Forward): Moves element one step to the front.

- (Send Backward): Moves element one step to the back.

- You can select multiple detail elements and change the draw order of all of them in one step. They keep the relative order of the original selection.

Repeating Details

Instead of having to insert a component multiple times (such as with a brick or concrete block), you can use (Repeating Detail Component) and create a string of components, as shown in Figure 13–17.

Figure 13–17

How To: Insert a Repeating Detail Component

1. In the *Annotate* tab>Detail panel, expand (Component) and click (Repeating Detail Component).
2. In the Type Selector, select the detail you want to use.
3. In the Draw panel, click (Line) or (Pick Lines).
4. In the Options Bar, type a value for the *Offset*, if needed.
5. The components repeat as required to fit the length of the sketched or selected line, as shown in Figure 13–18. You can lock the components to the line.

Figure 13–18

- For information on customizing repeating details, see *B.12 Creating a Repeating Detail*.

13.3 Annotating Details

After you have added components and sketched detail lines, you need to add annotations to the detail view. You can place text notes and dimensions, as shown in Figure 13–19, as well as symbols and tags. Filled regions are used to add hatching.

Figure 13–19

Creating Filled Regions

Many elements include material information that displays in plan and section views, while other elements need more details to be added. For example, the concrete wall shown in Figure 13–20 includes material information, while the earth to the left of the wall needs to be added using the **Filled Region** command.

Figure 13–20

The patterns used in details are *drafting patterns*. They are scaled to the view scale and update if you modify it. You can also add full-size *model patterns*, such as a Flemish Bond brick pattern, to the surface of some elements.

How To: Add a Filled Region

1. In the *Annotate* tab>Detail panel, expand (Region) and click (Filled Region).
2. Create a closed boundary using the Draw tools.
3. In the Line Style panel, select the line style for the outside edge of the boundary. If you do not want the boundary to display, select the **<Invisible lines>** style.
4. In the Type Selector, select the fill type, as shown in Figure 13–21.

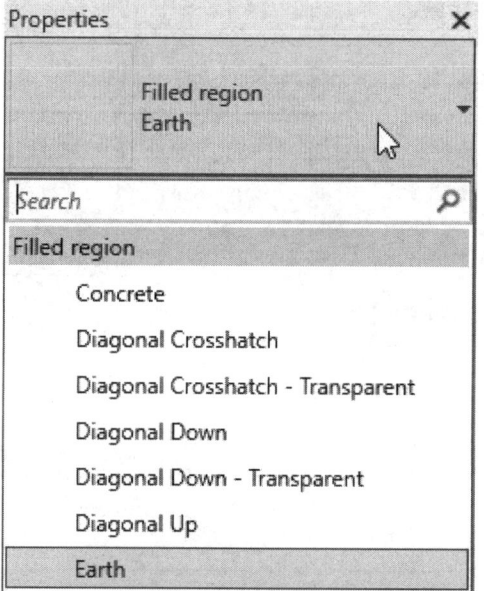

Figure 13–21

5. Click (Finish Edit Mode).

- You can modify a region by changing the fill type in the Type Selector or by editing the sketch.

- Double-click on the edge of the filled region to edit the sketch.

    If you have the Selection option set to (Select elements by face), you can select the pattern.

Hint: Creating a Filled Region Pattern Type

You can create a custom pattern by duplicating and editing an existing pattern type.

1. Select an existing region or create a boundary.
2. In Properties, click 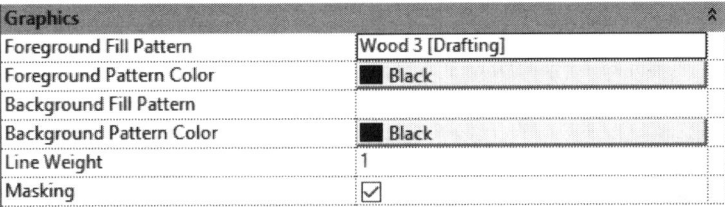 (Edit Type).
3. In the Type Properties dialog box, click **Duplicate** and name the new pattern.
4. Select the *Foreground/ Background Fill Pattern* and *Color* and specify the *Line Weight* and *Masking*, as shown in Figure 13–22.

Figure 13–22

5. Click **OK**.

- You can select from two types of fill patterns: **Drafting**, as shown in Figure 13–23, and **Model**. Drafting fill patterns scale to the view scale factor. Model fill patterns display full scale on the model.

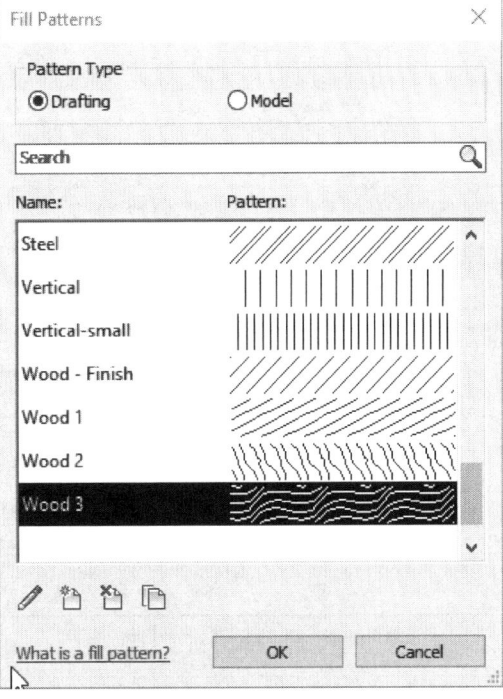

Figure 13–23

Adding Detail Tags

Besides adding text to a detail, you can tag detail components using (Tag By Category). The tag name is set in the Type Parameters for that component, as shown in Figure 13–24. This means that if you have more than one copy of the component in your project, you do not have to rename it each time you place its tag.

*The **Detail Item Tag.rfa** tag is located in the Annotations folder in the Revit Library.*

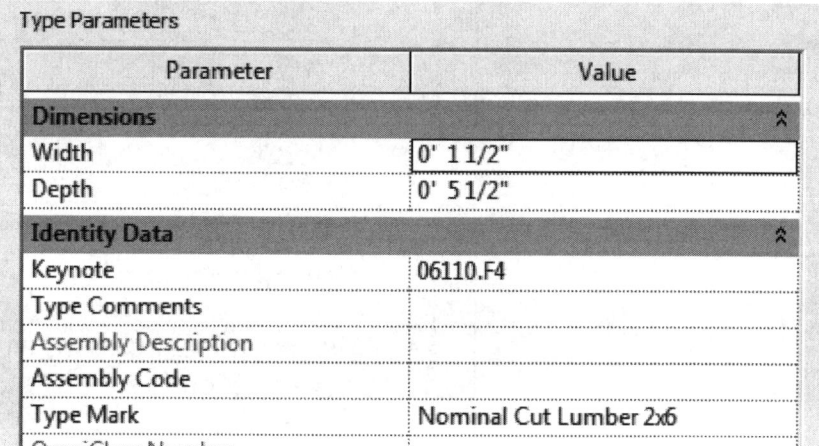

Figure 13–24

Hint: Multiple Dimension Options

If you are creating details that show one element with multiple dimension values, as shown in Figure 13–25, you can easily modify the dimension text.

Figure 13–25

Select the dimension and then the dimension text. The Dimension Text dialog box opens. You can replace the text, as shown in Figure 13–26, or add text fields above or below, as well as a prefix or suffix.

Figure 13–26

- This also works with Equality Text Labels.

Linework

To emphasize a particular line or change the look of a line in elevations and other views, modify the lines with the **Linework** command. Changes made to lines with the Linework command are view-specific, applying only to the view in which you make them.

- The Linework command can be used on project edges of model elements, cut edges of model elements, edges in imported CAD files, and edges in linked Autodesk Revit models.

- You cannot use the Linework command to change the line style of annotation lines like a dimension line or leader line.

How To: Adjust Linework

1. In the *Modify* tab>View panel, click (Linework), or type the shortcut **LW**.
2. In the *Modify | Linework* tab>Line Style panel, select the line style you want to use from the list.
3. Move the cursor and highlight the line you want to change. You can use <Tab> to toggle through the lines as needed.
4. Click on the line to change it to the new line style.
5. Click on other lines as needed or click (Modify) to end the command

- If the line is too long or short, you can modify the length using the controls at the end of the line.

Practice 13a

Create a Detail Based on a Section Callout

Practice Objectives

- Create a detail based on a section.
- Add filled regions, detail components, and annotations.

In this practice, you will create an enlarged detail based on a section, modify line weights, create filled regions, and add detail components and annotations, as shown in Figure 13–27.

Figure 13–27

Task 1 - Create an enlarged detail.

1. Open **Structural-Detailing.rvt** from the practice files folder.

2. Open the **Sections (Building Section): North-South Section** view.

3. Zoom in on the intersection of the **TOS-1ST FLOOR** level and grid line **B** (on the left). Adjust the crop region.

4. In the *View* tab>Create panel, click ⌀ (Callout).

5. Create a callout as shown in Figure 13–28, then double-click on the callout head to open it.

Figure 13–28

Set the Detail Level to ▩ (Fine), if needed.

6. In the View Control Bar, set the *Scale* to **3/4"=1'-0"**.

7. Select the **TOS-1ST FLOOR** level datum and use the **Hide Bubble** control to hide the bubble on the right.

8. Hide the linked .RVT file in this view.

9. Zoom in close to the intersection to display the line thicknesses. The slab and beam section cut lines are too heavy.

10. Select the slab. Right-click and select **Override Graphics in View>By Element...**.

11. In the View-Specific Element Graphics dialog box, change the *Cut Lines Weight* to **2**, as shown in Figure 13–29.

Figure 13–29

12. Click **OK**.

13. Select the beam that is cut in section and change the *Cut Lines Weight* to **3**.

14. Save the project.

Task 2 - Create filled regions to display an architectural floor.

1. In the *Annotate* tab>Detail panel, click (Filled Region).

2. In the Type Selector, select **Filled Region: Solid Black.**

3. Click (Edit Type).

4. In the Type Properties dialog box, click **Duplicate...** and create a new type named **Solid Gray**.

5. In the Type Parameters, change the *Color* to a light gray.

6. Click **OK** to return to the sketch.

7. In the *Modify | Create Filled Region Boundary* tab>Draw panel, use the drawing tools to create a **1"** thick boundary above the floor slab, as shown in Figure 13–30.

Figure 13–30

8. Click (Finish Edit Mode) in the Mode panel. The region representing an architectural floor displays, as shown in Figure 13–31.

Figure 13–31

Task 3 - Add detail components.

1. In the *Annotate* tab>Detail panel, click (Detail Component).

2. In the *Modify | Place Detail Component* tab>Mode panel, click (Load Family).

3. Browse to the practice files *Custom Families* folder. Press <Ctrl> to select both **L-Angle-Bolted Connection-Elevation.rfa** and **L-Angle-Bolted Connection-Section.rfa**, then click **Open**.

4. In the Type Selector, select **L-Angle-Bolted Connection-Elevation: L3x3x1/4"**.

5. Click (Edit Type).

6. In the Type Properties dialog box, change the *Number Of Bolts* to **3**. Click **OK**.

7. Place the component at the intersection of the midpoint on the beam in elevation and the column it frames into, as shown in Figure 13–32.

Figure 13–32

8. Repeat the procedure. This time place the **L-Angle-Bolted Connection-Section** on the sectioned beam. After it is placed, select it and stretch the ◀▶ grips to be tight around the member, as shown in Figure 13–33.

To make it easier to see, toggle on (Thin Lines) in the Quick Access Toolbar.

Figure 13–33

9. Click (Modify).
10. Save the project.

Task 4 - Add repeating detail components.

1. In the *Annotate* tab>Detail panel, expand (Component) and click (Repeating Detail Component).

2. In the Type Selector, select **Repeating Detail: CMU**.

3. In the Options Bar, set the *Offset* to **0'-3-13/16"** (or **=7-5/8" / 2**). (Hint: You can type formulas wherever a number can be added.)

4. Select the bottom midpoint of the **W14x30** section and draw a line down to display at least 2 CMU blocks, as shown in Figure 13–34.

Figure 13–34

5. Select the new CMU wall, and in the *Modify | Detail Items* tab>Arrange panel, click (Send to Back).

6. Click (Move) to move the entire CMU wall down **1"** to create space for a bearing plate for the beam.

7. Click (Modify).

8. Save the project.

Task 5 - Annotate the detail.

For more information on loading families, see 5.2 Loading Components.

1. In the *Annotate* tab>Detail panel, click (Detail Component). Click (Load Family) to add a break line.

2. Browse to the Revit Library's *Detail Items>Div 01-General* folder and open the file **Break Line.rfa**.

3. Add break lines to the top, bottom, and right side of the detail, as shown in Figure 13–35. Press <Spacebar> to rotate the break line, as needed.

Figure 13–35

Modify the crop region so that excess elements do not display on the outside of the break lines.

4. Leave plenty of room for annotations by making the annotation crop region larger.

5. In the *Annotate* tab>Text panel, click (Text).

6. Add notes to complete the detail, as shown in Figure 13–36.

Figure 13–36

7. In the View Control Bar, click (Hide Crop Region).
8. Save and close the project.

Practice 13b

Create a Bracing Detail

Practice Objective

- Create callouts and add tags and details lines.

In this practice, you will create a callout of a framing elevation and add tags and a detail of a top plate, as shown in Figure 13–37.

Figure 13–37

Task 1 - Create a bracing detail.

1. Open **Structural-Detailing.rvt** from the practice files folder.

2. Open the **Elevations (Framing Elevation): West Bracing** view.

3. In the *View* tab>Create panel, click (Callout).

4. In the Type Selector, select **Elevation: Framing Elevation**.

5. Draw the callout around the entire bay between the 1st and 2nd floors, as shown in Figure 13–38.

Figure 13–38

6. In the Project Browser, in the *Elevations (Framing Elevation)* area, rename the callout as **Bracing Bay A**.

7. Open the callout.

8. Set the *Scale* to **1/4"=1'-0"**, if it is not already set.

9. Add tags to the braces.

10. Save the project.

Task 2 - Create a detail of a callout.

1. Create another callout of the area where the top plate should be added.

2. Open it and set the *Scale* to **3/4"=1'-0"**.

3. In the Type Selector, set the type to **Elevation: Framing Elevation**.

4. In the Project Browser, rename the callout **Typical Top Plate**.

5. In the View Control Bar, click (Do Not Crop View).

6. Use (Tag by Category) without a leader and tag the bracing. It shows outside of the cropped area, so you need to move the tags into the crop area, as shown in Figure 13–39.

7. In the View Control Bar, click (Crop View) to reapply the cropping.

8. In the *Annotate* tab>Detail panel, click (Detail Line).

9. In the *Modify | Place Detail Lines* tab>Line Styles panel, select **Thin Lines**. Use the **Line** command to draw and represent a gusset plate, as shown in Figure 13–39.

Figure 13–39

10. If time permits create, annotate, and detail a typical bottom plate.

11. Save and close the project.

Practice 13c — Additional Details

Practice Objective

- Create and annotate details.

In this practice, you will create two structural details.

Use the project **Structural-Detailing.rvt** from the practice files folder for these details.

Task 1 - Create a foundation detail.

Create a new drafting view and draw the detail shown in Figure 13–40 using the various sketching tools and structural detail components.

Figure 13–40

- Use the **Invisible lines** line type when you draw the lines for the fill boundary. The curved lines are made with splines.

- Create the Earth pattern type by duplicating an existing type and assigning a new drafting pattern to it.

Task 2 - Create a typical elevator pit detail.

Create a new drafting view and draw the detail shown in Figure 13–41 using the various sketching tools, annotation elements, and filled regions.

Figure 13–41

Add concrete filled regions as shown in Figure 13–42.

Figure 13–42

Chapter Review Questions

1. Which of the following are ways in which you can create a detail? (Select all that apply.)

    a. Make a callout of a section and sketch over it.

    b. Draw all of the elements from scratch.

    c. Import a CAD detail and modify or sketch over it.

    d. Insert an existing drafting view from another file.

2. In which type of view (access shown in Figure 13–43) can you NOT add detail lines?

    Figure 13–43

    a. Plans

    b. Elevations

    c. 3D Views

    d. Legends

3. How are detail components different from building components?

    a. There is no difference.

    b. Detail components are made of 2D lines and annotations only.

    c. Detail components are made of building elements, but only display in detail views.

    d. Detail components are made of 2D and 3D elements.

4. Which of the following statements is true when you sketch detail lines?

    a. Always the same width.

    b. Vary in width according to the view.

    c. Display in all views associated with the detail.

    d. Display only in the view in which they were created.

5. Which command do you use to add a pattern (such as concrete or earth, as shown in Figure 13–44) to part of a detail?

Figure 13–44

a. Region
b. Filled Region
c. Masking Region
d. Pattern Region

Command Summary

Button	Command	Location
CAD Import Tools		
	Delete Layers	• **Ribbon:** *Modify	<imported filename>* tab>Import Instance panel
	Full Explode	• **Ribbon:** *Modify	<imported filename>* tab>Import Instance panel>expand Explode
	Import CAD	• **Ribbon:** *Insert* tab>Import panel
	Partial Explode	• **Ribbon:** *Modify	<imported filename>* tab>Import Instance panel>expand Explode
Detail Tools		
	Detail Component	• **Ribbon:** *Annotate* tab>Detail panel> expand Component
	Detail Line	• **Ribbon:** *Annotate* tab>Detail panel
	Insulation	• **Ribbon:** *Annotate* tab>Detail panel
	Filled Region	• **Ribbon:** *Annotate* tab>Detail panel
	Repeating Detail Component	• **Ribbon:** *Annotate* tab>Detail panel> expand Component
View Tools		
	Bring Forward	• **Ribbon:** *Modify	Detail Items* tab> Arrange panel
	Bring to Front	• **Ribbon:** *Modify	Detail Items* tab> Arrange panel
	Drafting View	• **Ribbon:** *View* tab>Create panel
	Insert from File: Insert Views from File	• **Ribbon:** *Insert* tab>Import panel> expand Insert from File
	Send Backward	• **Ribbon:** *Modify	Detail Items* tab> Arrange panel
	Send to Back	• **Ribbon:** *Modify	Detail Items* tab> Arrange panel

Chapter 14

Scheduling

Schedules are used to gather information stored in the various elements in the project and present them in a table format. In Autodesk® Revit®, you can create schedules specifically for structural projects, such as footing schedules, material takeoff schedules, and graphical column schedules. These schedules can then be added to sheets to create construction documentation.

Learning Objectives in This Chapter

- Understand schedules and their use in structural projects.
- Create and modify graphical column schedules that show the number, location, and height of columns.
- Modify schedule content, including the instance and type properties of related elements.
- Add schedules to sheets to create construction documents.

14.1 Structural Schedules

The Autodesk Revit software enables you to quickly create accurate schedules that can otherwise be time-consuming and difficult to maintain accurately throughout the lifecycle of a project. When you add model elements to a project, the schedule automatically updates to include the elements. For example, If columns are in the model, they are also in the schedule. If columns move, change size or length, or are deleted, the schedule updates to accurately reflect these changes.

There are two types of schedules used specifically with columns: graphical column schedules (as shown in Figure 14–1) and material takeoff schedules. Other schedules can be created as required for a project.

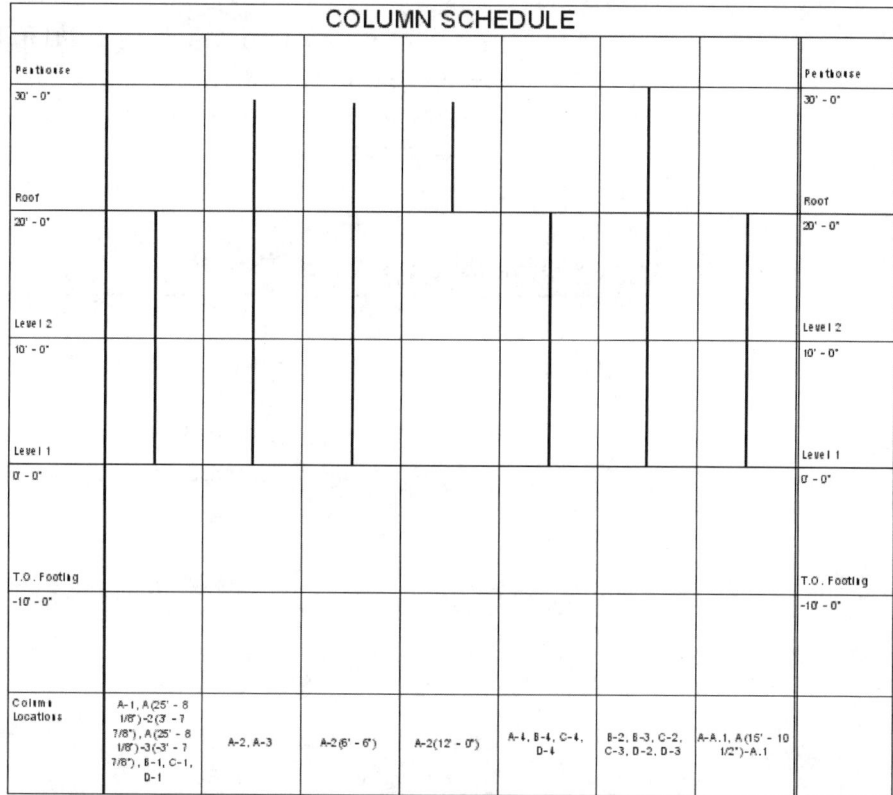

Figure 14–1

- Schedules can be created in templates so that they can be reused in multiple projects.

- You are not required to have actual elements in the model when you are creating schedules. You can schedule information that model elements contain.

- All properties that are stored in the model elements, as well as those specified by the user, can be added to schedules.

14.2 Graphical Column Schedules

Graphical column schedules are commonly displayed at the end of a set of construction documents. The schedule identifies the type of column, the floors to which the column extends, column locations, and the group to which similar columns belong, as shown in a closeup view in Figure 14–2.

Figure 14–2

How To: Create a Graphical Column Schedule

1. In the *View* tab>Create panel, expand (Schedules) and click (Graphical Column Schedule), or in the Project Browser, right-click on the Schedule/Quantities node and select **New Graphical Column Schedule...**.
   - A warning dialog box might open stating *Some columns in Graphical Column Schedule exceed the segment's upper/lower bounds. You can add levels or adjust the view parameters.*, which you can ignore. This can be fixed later.

Graphical column schedules are located in the Project Browser under Graphical Column Schedules (not under Schedule/Quantities like most other schedules).

2. A column schedule is created using the columns already placed in the project, as shown in Figure 14–3.

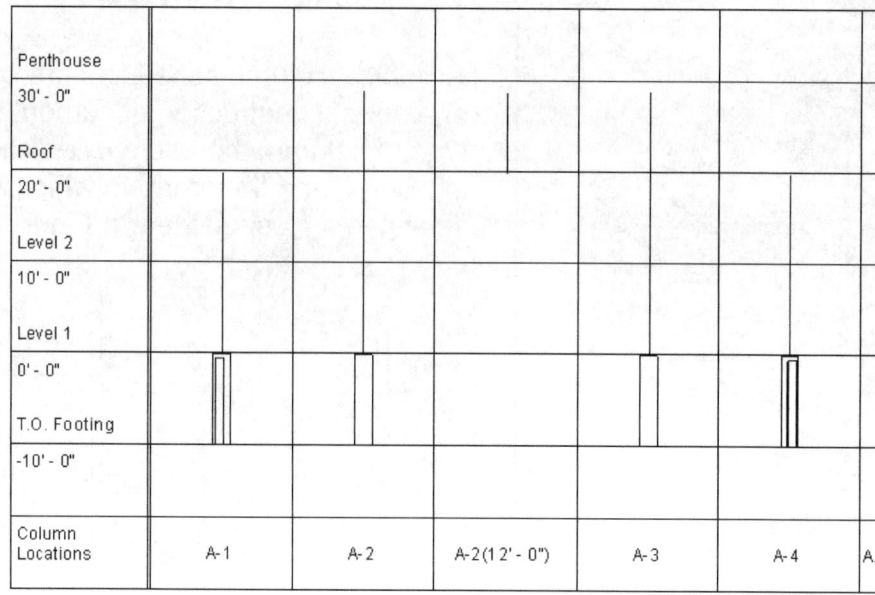

Figure 14–3

Modifying Graphical Column Schedules

Once you have a graphical column schedule in your project, you can adjust the properties, as shown in Figure 14–4. You can format the schedule and display the information to suit your particular requirements.

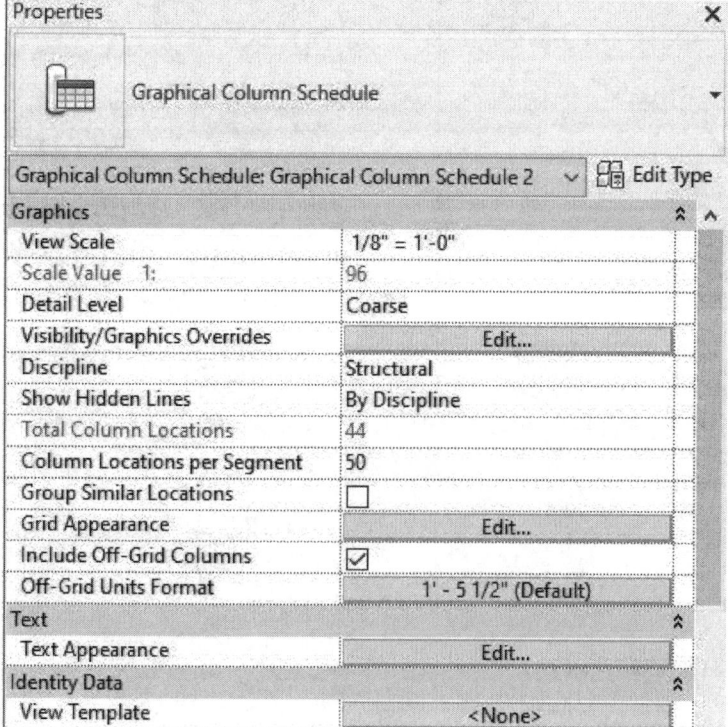

Figure 14–4

Scheduling

- **Group Similar Locations:** Modifies the column layout to only display one type of each column and then lists the applicable column locations for each type.

- **Grid Appearance:** Opens the Graphical Column Schedule Properties dialog box with the *Grid Appearance* tab selected, as shown in Figure 14–5, with options on how to display the grid lines.

Figure 14–5

- **Include Off-Grid Columns** and **Off-Grid Units Format:** Groups the column with the column designation and adds the offset dimension in the box below the column.

- **Text Appearance:** Opens the Graphical Column Schedule Properties dialog box with the *Text Appearance* tab selected, as shown in Figure 14–6. This is where you set up the font style, size, and options for the text in the schedule.

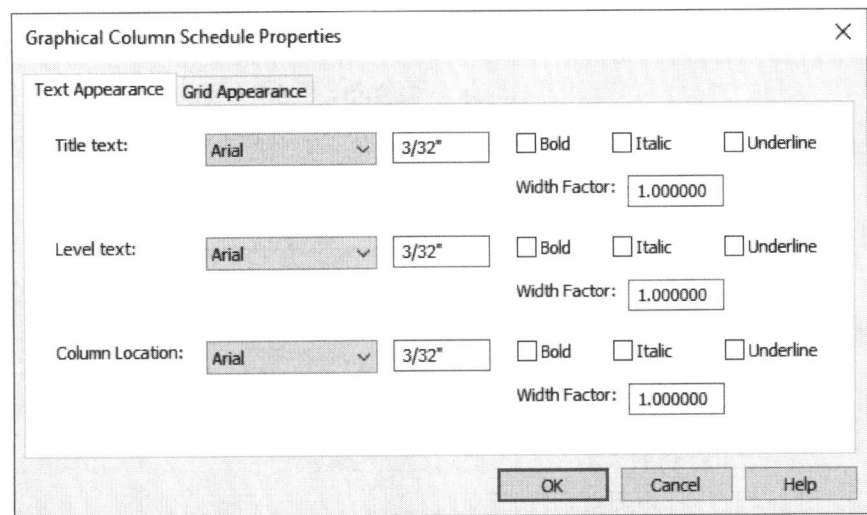

Figure 14–6

In the *Other* section, as shown in Figure 14–7, you can specify the columns, levels, and materials that are displayed.

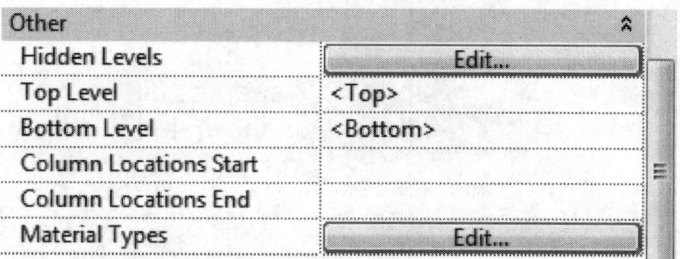

Figure 14–7

- **Hidden Levels:** Enables you to remove any arbitrary levels using the Levels Hidden in Graphical Column Schedules dialog box, as shown in Figure 14–8.

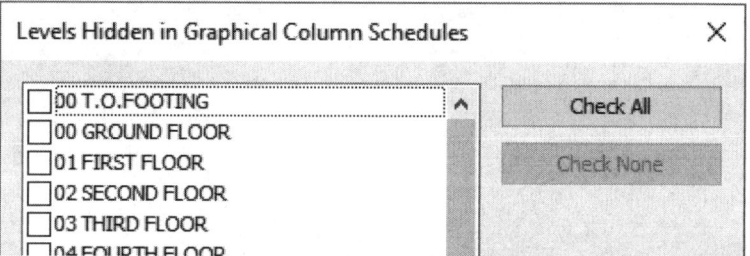

Figure 14–8

- **Top Level** and **Bottom Level:** Sets where the schedule displays the top and bottom levels. The default is normally used.

- **Column Locations Start** and **Column Locations End:** Enables you to specify the locations that are used to start and end the schedule. Sometimes the start is not logically going to be A1.

- **Material Type:** Enables you to create a filter of columns by materials. For example, if you only want the schedule to display steel columns, select that material in the Structural Material dialog box, as shown in Figure 14–9.

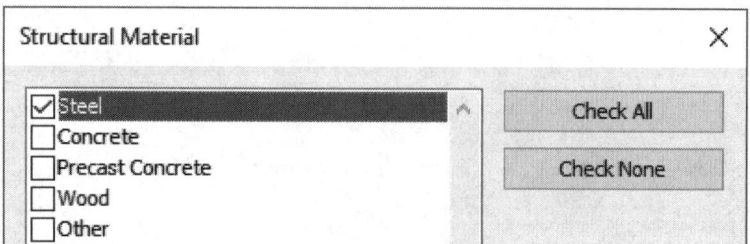

Figure 14–9

Practice 14a Create a Graphical Column Schedule

Practice Objective

- Create a graphical column schedule.

In this practice, you will create a graphical column schedule that shows only steel columns, as shown in part in Figure 14–10.

Figure 14–10

1. Open **Structural-Schedules.rvt** from the practice files folder.

2. In the *View* tab>Create panel, expand (Schedules) and click (Graphical Column Schedule). A graphical column schedule view displays.

3. In the Project Browser, expand the *Graphical Column Schedule* category and rename the new schedule to **Steel Column Schedule**.

4. In the View Control Bar, change the *Scale* to **3/32" = 1'-0"** and set the *Detail Level* to **Fine**.

5. In Properties, select the *Group Similar Locations* option. The schedule changes to display only one of each type of column.

6. Next to *Grid Appearance*, click **Edit...**.

7. In the Graphical Column Schedule Properties dialog box, in the *Grid Appearance* tab, set the following, as shown in Figure 14–11:

    - *Horizontal Widths>For Column Locations:* **2"**
    - *Vertical Heights>Below Bottom Level:* **2"**

Figure 14–11

8. Switch to the *Text Appearance* tab.

9. Ensure that the *Title text* font is **Arial**, increase the size to **1/4"**, and make the text **Bold**, as shown in Figure 14–12.

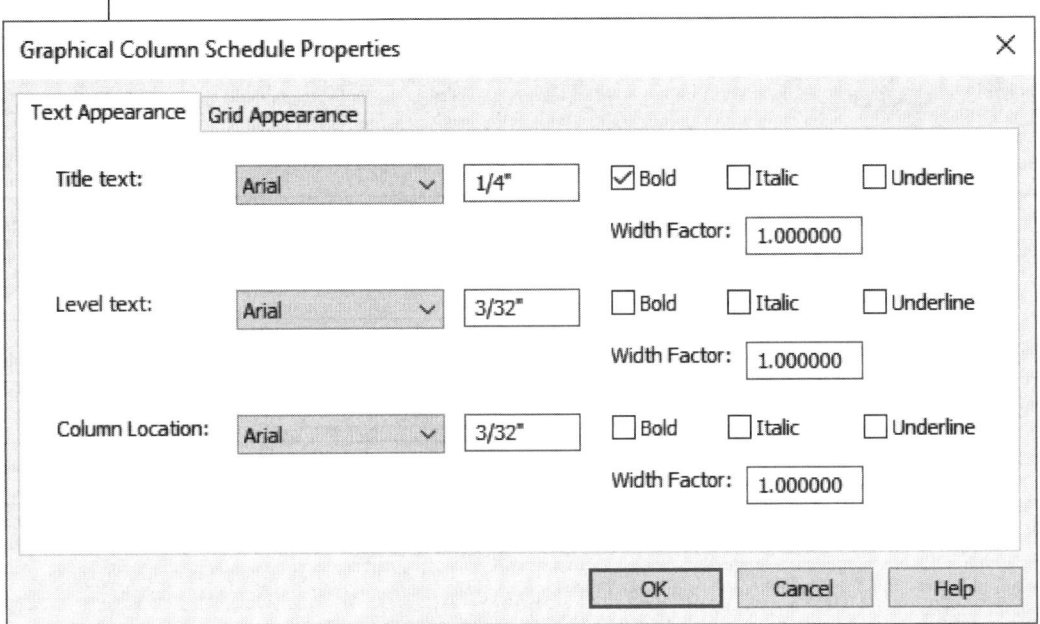

Figure 14–12

10. Click **OK**.

11. In the *Other* section, beside *Material Types,* click **Edit...**.

12. In the Structural Material dialog box, click **Check None** and then select only the **Steel** option, as shown in Figure 14–13.

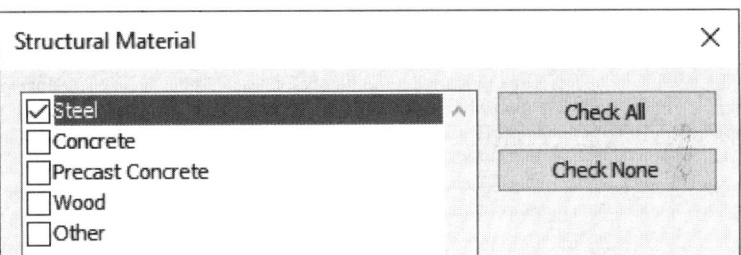

Figure 14–13

13. Click **OK**. The schedule is now limited to steel columns.

14. In Properties, in the *Identity Data* section, type **Steel Column Schedule** next to *Title*.

15. Save and close the project.

14.3 Working with Schedules

Schedules extract information from a project and display it in table form. Each schedule is stored as a separate view and can be placed on sheets, as shown in Figure 14–14. Any changes you make to the project elements that affect the schedules are automatically updated in both views and sheets.

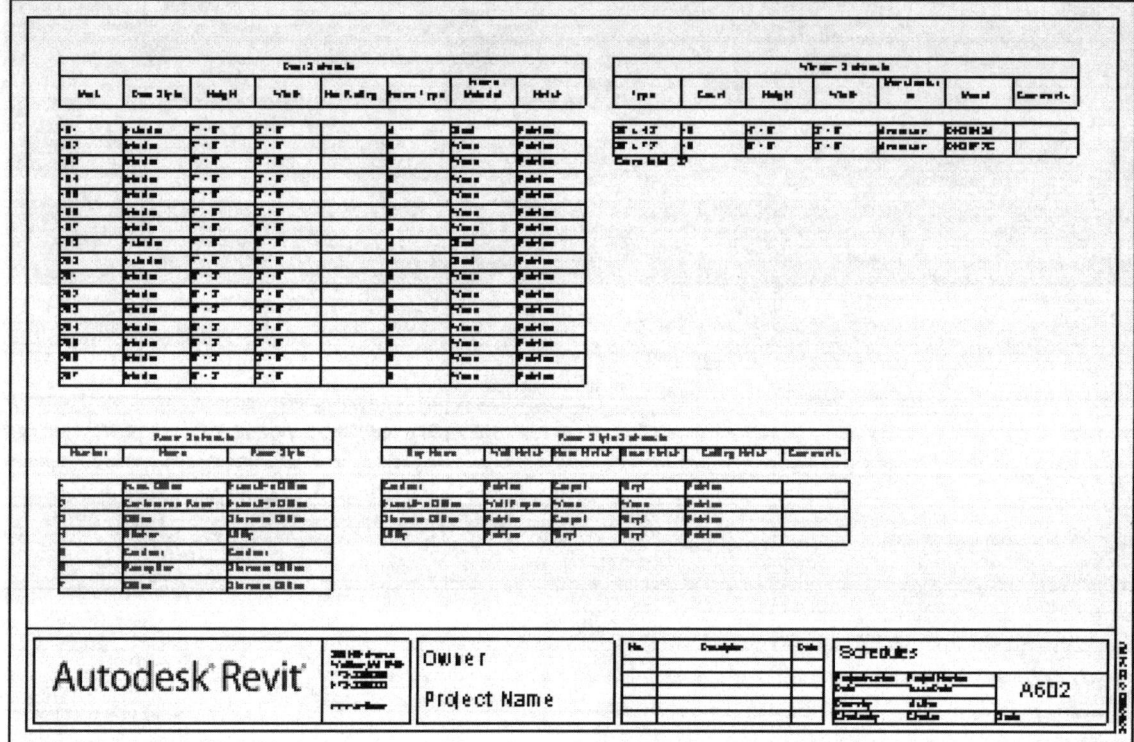

Figure 14–14

- The structural template (**Structural Analysis-Default.rte**) does not include any schedules. The **Construction-Default.rte**, **Residential-Default.rte**, and **Commercial-Default.rte** template files do include useful schedules.

How To: Work with Schedules

1. In the Project Browser, expand the *Schedules/Quantities* area (as shown in Figure 14–15) and double-click on the schedule you want to open.

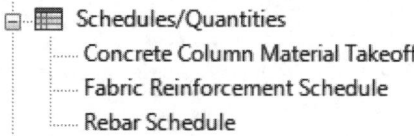

Figure 14–15

2. Schedules are automatically filled out with the information stored in the instance and type parameters of related elements that are added to the model.
3. Fill out additional information in either the schedule or Properties.
4. In the *Modify Schedule/Quantities* tab>Titles & Headers panel, you can select (Freeze Header) to keep the header row visible while you scroll through the schedule.
5. When selecting on a schedule's row, it will highlight in blue.
6. Drag and drop the schedule onto a sheet.

- You can zoom in to read small text in schedule views. Hold <Ctrl> and scroll using the mouse wheel, or press <Ctrl>+<+> to zoom in or <Ctrl>+<-> to zoom out.

Modifying Schedules

Information in schedules is bi-directional:

- If you make changes to elements, the schedule automatically updates.
- If you change information in the cells of the schedule, it automatically updates the elements in the project.

How To: Modify Schedule Cells

1. Open the schedule view.
2. Select the cell you want to change. Some cells have drop-down lists, as shown in Figure 14–16. Others have editable fields.

A	B	C	D	E
Family and Type	Major Direction Wir	Major Spacing	Minor Direction Wir	Minor Spacing
Fabric Sheet: 6	W4.2	0' - 6"	W4.2	0' - 6"
Fabric Sheet: 6	W4.0	0' - 6"	W4.2	0' - 6"
Fabric Sheet: 6	W4.2	0' - 6"	W4.2	0' - 6"
Fabric Sheet: 6	W4.4	0' - 6"	W4.2	0' - 6"
Fabric Sheet: 6	W4.7	0' - 6"	W4.2	0' - 6"
Fabric Sheet: 6	W7.5	0' - 6"	W4.2	0' - 6"
Fabric Sheet: 6	W8.1	0' - 6"	W4.2	0' - 6"
Fabric Sheet: 6	W8.3	0' - 6"	W4.2	0' - 6"
Fabric Sheet: 6	W4.2	0' - 6"	W4.2	0' - 6"
Fabric Sheet: 6	W4.2	0' - 6"	W4.2	0' - 6"

Figure 14–16

3. Add the new information. The change is reflected in the schedule, on the sheet, and in the elements of the project.

If you change a type property in the schedule, it applies to all elements of that type. If you change an instance property, it only applies to that one element.

- If you change a *Type Property*, an alert box opens, as shown in Figure 14–17.

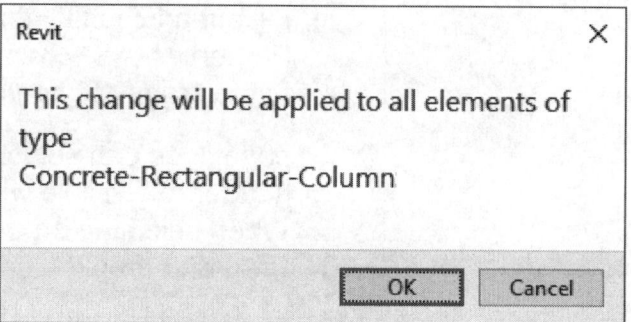

Figure 14–17

- When you select an element in a schedule, in the *Modify Schedule/Quantities* tab>Element panel, you can click (Highlight in Model). This opens a close-up view of the element with the Show Element(s) in View dialog box, as shown in Figure 14–18. Click **Show** to display more views of the element. Click **Close** to finish the command.

Figure 14–18

> **Hint: Customizing Schedules**
>
> Schedules are typically included in project templates, which are set up by the BIM manager or other advanced users. They can be complex to create as there are many options.
>
> - For more information about creating basic schedules, see *B.11 Creating Building Component Schedules*.
>
> - For more information on using schedule data outside of Autodesk Revit, see *B.10 Importing and Exporting Schedules*.
>
> - For more information about creating schedules, refer to the ASCENT guide *Autodesk Revit: BIM Management: Template and Family Creation*.

Scheduling

Modifying a Schedule on a Sheet

Once you have placed a schedule on a sheet, you can manipulate it to fit the information into the available space. Select the schedule to display the controls that enable you to modify it, as shown in Figure 14–19.

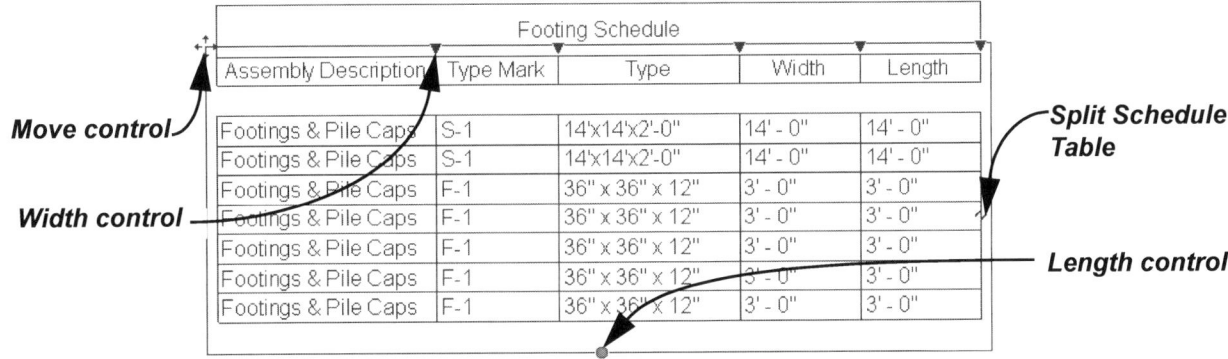

Figure 14–19

- The blue triangles modify the width of each column.

- The break mark splits the schedule into two parts.

- In a split schedule, you can use the arrows in the upper-left corner to move that portion of the schedule table. The control at the bottom of the first table changes the length of the table and impacts any connected splits, as shown in Figure 14–20.

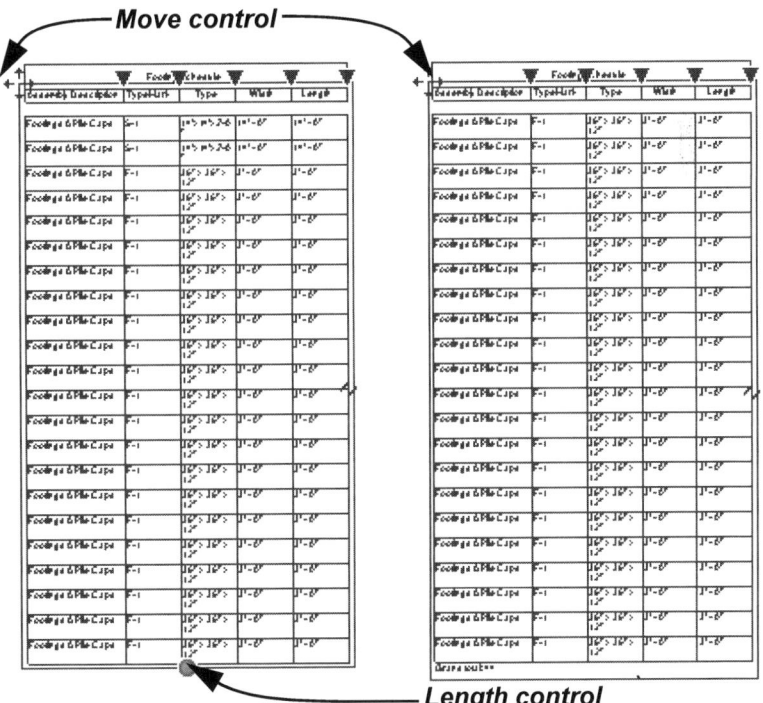

Figure 14–20

- To unsplit a schedule, drag the Move control from the side of the schedule that you want to unsplit back to the original column.

Split a Schedule Across Multiple Sheets

When a schedule becomes too long, you need to be able to split it and place it on multiple sheets. You can split a schedule evenly or by setting a custom height. When a schedule has been split, you can expand the **Schedules/Quantities (all)** node in the Project Browser to see the segments of the schedule, as shown in Figure 14–21.

Figure 14–21

If the split is not what you wanted, you can delete the segmented schedules from the Project Browser. Do not delete the main schedule.

How To: Split a Schedule and Place It on Multiple Sheets

1. Make additional sheets, if needed. In a schedule view, from the *Modify Schedule/Quantities* tab>Split panel, select (Split & Place).
2. In the Split Schedule and Place on Sheets dialog box, select the sheets that you want to distribute the split schedule to, as shown in Figure 14–22.

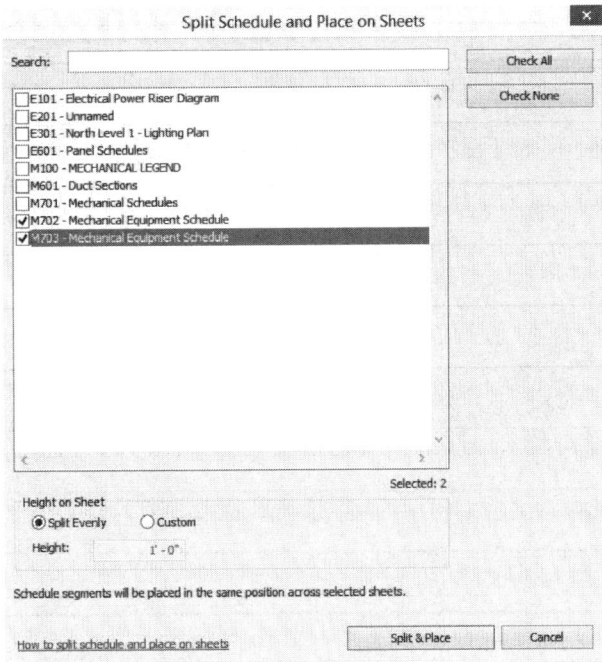

Figure 14–22

3. In the *Height on Sheet* section, select **Split Evenly** or **Custom**. If **Custom** is selected, specify a *Height*.
4. Click **Split & Place**.
5. The first sheet selected in the list opens and the first segment of the split schedule is attached to your cursor. Place it on the sheet.
6. If you selected multiple sheets in the Split Schedule and Place on Sheets dialog box, the rest of the segment schedule will automatically be placed exactly where you initially placed the first segment of the schedule.
7. Open each sheet and use the control grips to adjust the columns and stretch the schedule to fit the sheet, as needed.

How To: Remove Split Schedules

1. In the Project Browser, expand the schedule.
2. Select the segmented schedules and press <Delete>, or right-click and select **Delete**.

Practice 14b Work with Schedules

Practice Objectives

- Update schedule information.
- Add a schedule to a sheet.

In this practice, you will add *Type Mark* information to a structural elements schedule and the elements that are connected to that schedule. You will then place the schedule on a sheet and add elements in the project. The final information displays as shown in Figure 14–23.

Structural Elements Schedule		
Type Mark	Family and Type	Count
Structural Columns		
P-1	Concrete-Rectangular-Column: 24 x 24	43
	W-Wide Flange-Column: W8X10	2
	W-Wide Flange-Column: W10X33	41
Structural Foundations		
	Footing-Rectangular: 14'x14'x2'-0"	2
	Footing-Rectangular: 36" x 36" x 12"	43
	Foundation Slab: 6" Foundation Slab	1
W-1	Wall Foundation: Bearing Footing - 24" x 12"	17
W-2	Wall Foundation: Bearing Footing - 36" x 12"	4
Structural Framing		
	HSS-Hollow Structural Section: HSS6X6X.500	28
	K-Series Bar Joist-Rod Web: 14K6	16
	K-Series Bar Joist-Rod Web: 16K7	100
	W-Wide Flange: W12X26	1558
	W-Wide Flange: W14X30	1023

Figure 14–23

Task 1 - Review a schedule.

1. Open **Structural-Schedules.rvt** from the practice files folder.

2. In the Project Browser, expand the **Schedules/Quantities (all)** node. Note that four schedules have been added to this project.

3. Double-click on the **Footing Schedule** to open it.

4. Note that the Bearing Footing lengths are shown as <varies>, as shown in Figure 14–24, indicating that there is more than one length.

<Footing Schedule>			
A	B	C	D
Type Mark	Type	Width	Length
	6" Foundation Slab	180' - 11 1/2"	180' - 11 1/2"
	14"x14"x2'-0"	14' - 0"	14' - 0"
	36" x 36" x 12"	3' - 0"	3' - 0"
	Bearing Footing - 24" x 12"	2' - 0"	<varies>
	Bearing Footing - 36" x 12"	3' - 0"	<varies>
Grand total: 66			

Figure 14–24

5. In Properties, click **Edit...** next to *Sorting/Grouping*. In the Schedule Properties dialog box, select **Itemize every instance**.

6. Click **OK**.

7. The schedule now lists all the footing types and their lengths.

8. In the *Modify Schedule/Quantities* tab>Titles & Headers panel, select **Freeze Header**. This lets you scroll down a long schedule and still see the schedule column names.

9. Save the project.

Task 2 - Fill in schedules.

1. Open the **3D Views: 3D Foundation** view. This view only displays the foundation elements, including concrete piers, footings, walls, and wall footings.

2. Rotate the view so you can see the stair and elevator shaft openings, as shown in Figure 14–25.

Figure 14–25

3. Close any other open view tabs and projects.

4. Open the **Structural Elements Schedule**. The existing structural elements in the project populate the schedule, as shown in Figure 14–26. Expand the width of the columns, as needed, to read the content.

\<Structural Elements Schedule\>		
A	**B**	**C**
Type Mark	Family and Type	Count
Structural Columns		
P-1	Concrete-Rectangular-Column: 24 x 24	42
	W-Wide Flange-Column: W8X10	2
	W-Wide Flange-Column: W10X33	41
Structural Foundations		
	Footing-Rectangular: 14'x14'x2'-0"	2
	Footing-Rectangular: 36" x 36" x 12"	42
	Foundation Slab: 6" Foundation Slab	1
	Wall Foundation: Bearing Footing - 24" x 12"	17
	Wall Foundation: Bearing Footing - 36" x 12"	4
Structural Framing		
	HSS-Hollow Structural Section: HSS6X6X.500	28
	K-Series Bar Joist-Rod Web: 14K6	16
	K-Series Bar Joist-Rod Web: 16K7	100
	W-Wide Flange: W12X26	1558
	W-Wide Flange: W14X30	1023

Figure 14–26

Scheduling

5. Note that only the *Concrete* columns have a **Type Mark**.

6. In the *Type Mark* column beside **Wall Foundation: Bearing Footing - 24" x 12"**, type **W-1**.

7. The warning dialog box shown in Figure 14–27 displays because the element is a type parameter; therefore, you are alerted before you make any changes. Click **OK**.

Figure 14–27

8. Select **Wall Foundation: Bearing Footing - 36" x 12"**.

9. In the *Modify | Schedule/Quantities* tab>Element panel, click ▣ (Highlight in Model).

10. In the Show Element(s) in View dialog box, click **Show** until you see a foundation element displayed in the **3D Foundations** view, as shown in Figure 14–28. Click **Close**.

Figure 14–28

11. With the elements highlighted, in Properties, click ▣ (Edit Type).

12. In the Type Properties dialog box, in the *Identity Data* section, set the *Type Mark* to **W-2**.

13. Click **OK** to finish.

14. Return to the **Structural Elements Schedule** view, as shown in Figure 14–29. The *Type Mark* is now applied.

<Structural Elements Schedule>

A	B	C
Type Mark	Family and Type	Count
Structural Columns		
P-1	Concrete-Rectangular-Column: 24 x 24	42
	W-Wide Flange-Column: W8X10	2
	W-Wide Flange-Column: W10X33	41
Structural Foundations		
	Footing-Rectangular: 14'x14'x2'-0"	2
	Footing-Rectangular: 36" x 36" x 12"	42
	Foundation Slab: 6" Foundation Slab	1
W-1	Wall Foundation: Bearing Footing - 24" x 12"	17
W-2	Wall Foundation: Bearing Footing - 36" x 12"	4
Structural Framing		
	HSS-Hollow Structural Section: HSS6X6X.500	28
	K-Series Bar Joist-Rod Web: 14K6	16
	K-Series Bar Joist-Rod Web: 16K7	100
	W-Wide Flange: W12X26	1558
	W-Wide Flange: W14X30	1023

Figure 14–29

15. Open the other schedules and review the information.

16. Save the project.

Task 3 - Add schedules to a sheet.

1. In the Project Browser, open the sheet **S801 - Schedules**.

2. Drag and drop the **Structural Elements Schedule** view onto the sheet, as shown in Figure 14–30. Your schedule may look different then the one shown.

Structural Elements Schedule		
Type Mark	Family and Type	Count
Structural Columns		
P-1	Concrete-Rectangular-Column: 24 x 24	42
	W-Wide Flange-Column: W8X10	2
	W-Wide Flange-Column: W10X33	41
Structural Foundations		
	Footing-Rectangular: 14'x14'x2'-0"	2
	Footing-Rectangular: 36" x 36" x 12"	42
	Foundation Slab: 6" Foundation Slab	1
W-1	Wall Foundation: Bearing Footing - 24" x 12"	17
W-2	Wall Foundation: Bearing Footing - 36" x 12"	4
Structural Framing		
	HSS-Hollow Structural Section: HSS6X6X.500	28
	K-Series Bar Joist-Rod Web: 14K6	16
	K-Series Bar Joist-Rod Web: 16K7	100
	W-Wide Flange: W12X26	1558
	W-Wide Flange: W14X30	1024

Figure 14–30

3. Zoom in and use the arrows at the top of the schedule to modify the width of the columns to ensure that the titles display correctly.

4. In the schedule, note the number of concrete columns and their related footings.

5. Open the **Structural Plans: 00 T.O. Footing** view.

6. Zoom in and copy a concrete column and its footing to a nearby grid line location that does not have an existing column, similar to that shown in Figure 14–31.

Figure 14–31

7. Switch back to the sheet view. Note that the numbers in the schedule have automatically updated to include the new column.

8. Switch to the **Structural Elements Schedule** view. Note that these column numbers have also been updated.

9. Save and close the project.

Chapter Review Questions

1. What happens when you delete a column in the model?
    a. You must delete the column on the drawing sheet.
    b. You must delete the column from the schedule.
    c. The column is removed from the model, but not from the schedule.
    d. The column is removed from the model and the schedule.

2. How do you add a column to a graphical column schedule?
    a. Type the *Column Number* into the column schedule. The rest of the information is automatically updated.
    b. The column information is added automatically to the schedule when you add the column to the model.
    c. Select **Update** in the schedule view to add the column to the schedule.
    d. Draw the column in the graphical column schedule.

3. In a schedule, if you change type information (such as a **Type Mark**), all instances of that type update with the new information.
    a. True
    b. False

Command Summary

Button	Command	Location
	Freeze Headers	• **Ribbon:** *Modify Schedule/Quantities* tab> Titles & Headers panel
	Graphical Column Schedule	• **Ribbon:** *View* tab>Create panel>expand Schedules
	Highlight in Model	• **Ribbon:** *Modify Schedule/Quantities* tab> Element panel
	Split & Place	• **Ribbon:** *Modify Schedule/Quantities* tab> Split panel

Appendix A

Introduction to Worksharing

Autodesk® Revit® worksharing gives multiple team members connected on the same network the ability to co-author a single project model (one .RVT file). The appropriate team member creates a central model and worksets. Team members open and work in a local copy of the model that is linked back to the central model through saving and synchronizing. For more information about establishing and using worksets, refer to the ASCENT guide *Autodesk Revit: Collaboration Tools*.

Learning Objectives in This Appendix

- Review worksharing terminology and workflow.
- Learn about opening a local file to make changes to your part of a project.
- Review how to synchronize your local file with the central model, which contains changes from all the local files.

A.1 Introduction to Worksharing

A workshared project consists of one central model (also known as a central file) and individual models for each user known as local files, as shown in Figure A–1. Each team member will work in their local file and use a function called *synchronizing with central* to send and receive updates with the central model.

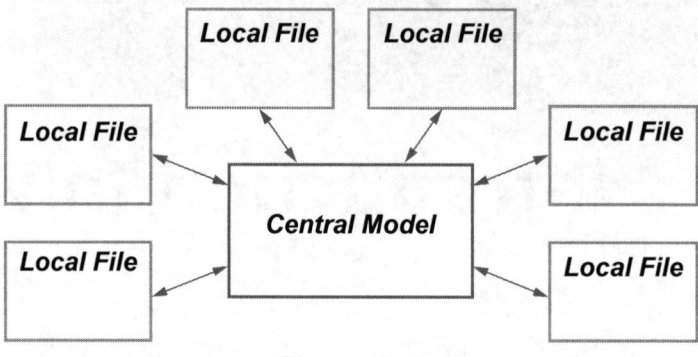

Figure A–1

- The **central model** is created by the BIM manager, project manager, or project lead and is stored on a server or in the cloud, enabling multiple users to access it.

- A **local file** is a copy of the central model that is stored on your computer.

- All local files are saved back to the central model, and updates to the central model are sent out to the local files. This way, all changes remain in one file, while the project, model, views, and sheets are automatically updated.

Worksharing Definitions

Worksharing: This is a functionality that, when enabled, allows multiple members of the team to access a project stored in one centralized location, which gives multiple users the ability to work on the same project simultaneously.

Workshared file: This is a project that has worksets enabled. If the project has no worksets enabled, it is called a *non-workshared file*.

Workset: This is a collection of elements that are related geometrically, parametrically, or by location within an overall project that are subdivided so they can be worked on while isolated from the rest of the model. When worksharing is enabled, worksets are automatically activated and the *Workset1* and *Shared Grids and Levels* worksets are added to the project by default.

Central model: Also called the central file, this is the main project file that is stored on a local network that all users can access. Using a central model is called *file-based worksharing*. The central model stores workset and element information in the project and is the file to which everyone saves and synchronizes their changes. The central model updates all the local files with the latest model information. This file should not be edited directly.

Local file: This is a copy of the central model that is saved to your local computer. This is the file that you modify and work in. As you work, you save the file locally and synchronize it with the central model.

Element borrowing: This refers to the process of modifying items in the project that are not part of the workset you have checked out. This either happens automatically (if no one else has checked out a workset) or specifically, when you request to have control of the elements (if someone else has a workset checked out).

Active workset: The workset that displays in the Status Bar is the active workset. Any new elements that are added will be placed on this workset. As you work, you will change the active workset accordingly.

Relinquish: This releases or returns a checked-out workset so that others can work on the elements within that workset. If you do not release or relinquish your checked-out worksets, other users will get a warning that they cannot edit the workset until you relinquish it, and they are given the option to request to borrow the workset. **Relinquish All Mine** allows you to relinquish worksets without synchronizing to the central model.

Reload Latest: This updates your local file without you needing to synchronize with the central model.

General Process of Using Worksets

1. Wait for the appropriate team member to enable worksharing, set up worksets, and create the central model.
2. Create a local file from the central model.
3. Work in your local file and select the worksets that you need to work on by verifying the active workset.
   - Work in your local model by adding, deleting, and modifying elements.
   - You may need to request to borrow elements in worksets that are currently checked out by other team members.

4. Save the local file as frequently as you would save any other project.
5. Synchronize the local file with the central model several times a day or as required by company policy or project status.
   - This reloads any changes from the central model to your local file and vice versa.
   - If the option to **Save Local File before and after synchronizing with central** is checked, your local file will be saved, but it is always recommended to save the local file yourself every time you synchronize to the central model.

How To: Create a Local File

1. In the *File* tab or Quick Access Toolbar, click (Open).
2. In the Open dialog box, navigate to the central model server location and select the central model. Do not work in this file. Select **Create New Local**, as shown in Figure A–2, and click **Open**.

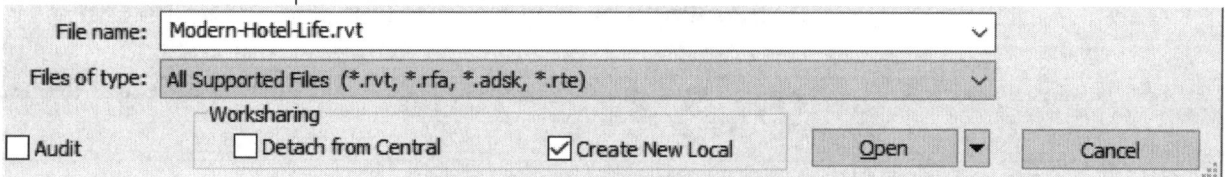

Figure A–2

3. A copy of the project is created. It will have the same name as the central model with your Autodesk Revit username added to the end.

Introduction to Worksharing

- If you are working with a recently used central model, it may display on the Home screen with the icon shown in Figure A–3. Clicking this file automatically creates a local copy of the model. The first time you use this option, a warning displays, as shown in Figure A–4.

Figure A–3

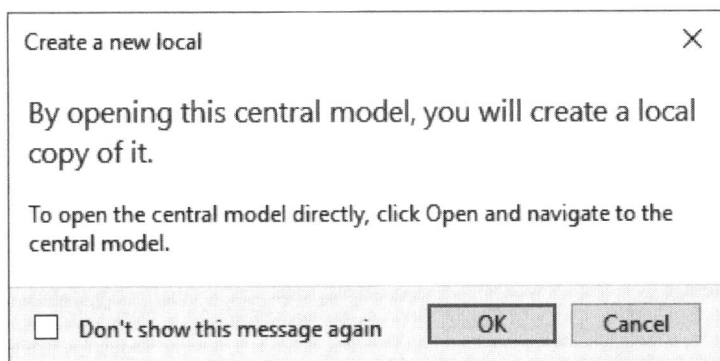

Figure A–4

4. You can save the file using the default name, or use

   ![] (Save As) and name the file according to your office's standard. It should include *Local* in the name to indicate that it is saved on your local computer, or that you are the only one working with that version of the file.

- Delete any old local files to ensure that you are working on the latest version.

How To: Work in a Workshared Project

1. Open your local file.
2. In the Status Bar, expand the Active Workset drop-down list and select a workset, as shown in Figure A–5. By setting the active workset, other people can work in the project but cannot edit elements that you add to the workset.

Figure A–5

3. Work on the project as needed.

Saving a Workshared Project

When you are working on a workshared project, you need to save the project locally and centrally.

- Save the local file frequently (every 15-30 minutes). In the Quick Access Toolbar, click 🖫 (Save) to save the local file just as you would any other project.

- Synchronize the local file with the central model periodically (every hour or two) or after you have made major changes to the project.

> **Hint: Set Up Notifications to Save and Synchronize**
>
> You can set up reminders to save and synchronize files to the central model in the Options dialog box, on the *General* tab, as shown in Figure A–6.
>
> **Figure A–6**

Synchronizing to the Central Model

There are two methods for synchronizing to the central model. In the Quick Access Toolbar or *Collaborate* tab>Synchronize panel, expand (Synchronize with Central) and click (Synchronize Now) or (Synchronize and Modify Settings). The last-used command is active if you click the top-level icon.

- **Synchronize Now:** Updates the central model and then the local file with any changes to the central model since the last synchronization without prompting you for any settings. It automatically relinquishes elements borrowed from any workset but retains worksets used by the current user.

- **Synchronize and Modify Settings:** Opens the Synchronize with Central dialog box, shown in Figure A–7, so you can set the options for relinquishing worksets and elements, add comments, and specify to save the file locally before and after synchronization.

Introduction to Worksharing

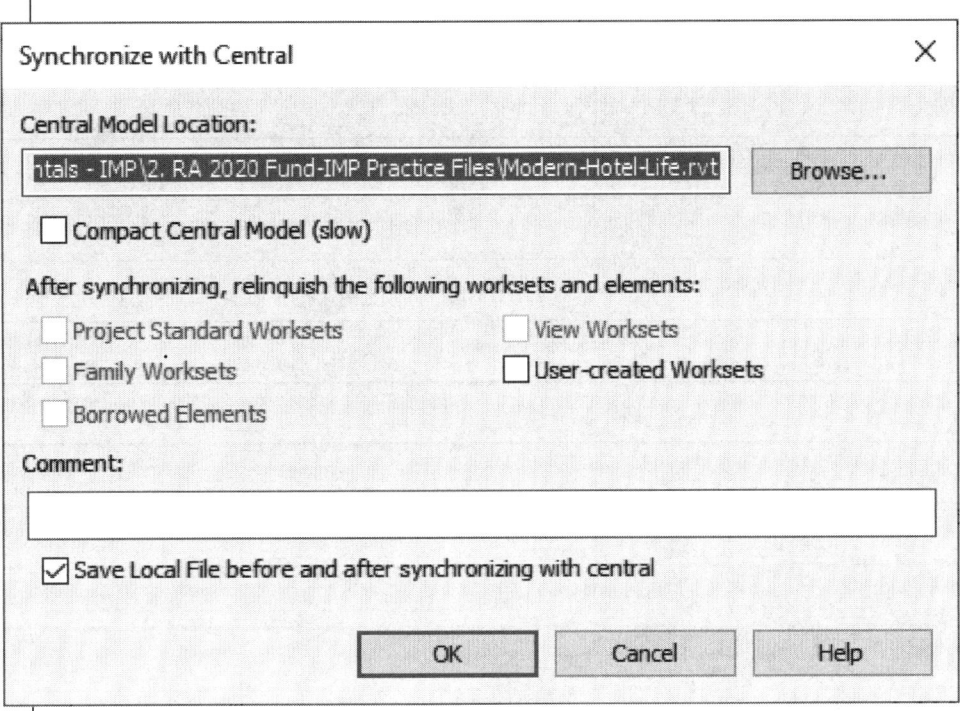

Figure A–7

- Always keep **Save Local File before and after synchronizing with central** checked to ensure your local copy is up to date with the latest changes from the central model.

- When you close a local file without saving to the central model, you are prompted to do so, as shown in Figure A–8.

Figure A–8

Command Summary

Button	Command	Location
🖫	Save	• **Quick Access Toolbar** • **File tab:** Save • **Shortcut:** <Ctrl>+<S>
	Synchronize and Modify Settings	• **Quick Access Toolbar** • **Ribbon:** *Collaborate* tab> Synchronize panel>expand Synchronize with Central
	Synchronize Now	• **Quick Access Toolbar** • **Ribbon:** *Collaborate* tab> Synchronize panel>expand Synchronize with Central

Appendix B

Additional Tools

There are many other tools available in the Autodesk® Revit® software that you can use when creating and using models. This appendix provides details about several tools and commands that are related to those covered in this guide.

Learning Objectives in This Appendix

- Save and use selection sets of multiple building elements.
- Add slanted structural columns.
- Edit wall joins.
- Create structural slab types for foundation slabs.
- Create rebar types.
- Edit plan and section profiles.
- Use guide grids to help place views on sheets.
- Add revision clouds, tags, and information.
- Annotate dependent views with matchlines and view references.
- Import and export schedules.
- Create basic building component schedules.
- Create repeating detail types.

B.1 Selection Sets

When multiple elements types are selected, you can save the selection set so that it can be reused. For example, a structural column and an architectural column need to move together. Instead of picking each element, create a selection set that you can quickly access, as shown in Figure B–1. You can also edit selection sets to add or remove elements from the set.

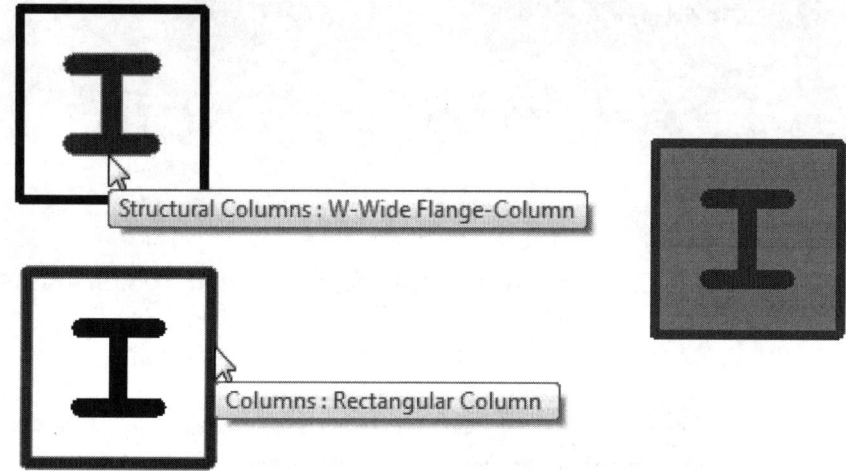

Figure B–1

- Selection sets are a filter of specific elements rather than types of elements.

How To: Save Selection Sets

1. Select the elements that you want to include in the selection set.
2. In the *Modify | Multi-Select* tab>Selection panel, click (Save).
3. In the Save Selection dialog box, type a name for the set, as shown in Figure B–2, and click **OK**.

Figure B–2

Additional Tools

How To: Retrieve Selection Sets

1. Select any other elements you might want to use. In the *Modify | Multi-Select* tab>Selection panel, click (Load). Alternatively, without any other selection, in the *Manage* tab>Selection panel, click (Load).
2. In the Retrieve Filters dialog box (shown in Figure B–3), select the set that you want to use and click **OK**.

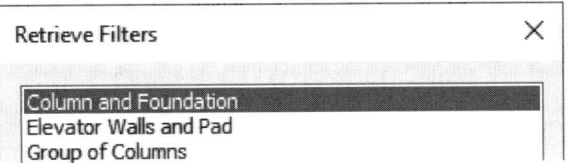

Figure B–3

3. The elements are selected and you can continue to select other elements or use the selection.

How To: Edit Selection Sets

1. If elements are selected, in the *Modify | Multi-Select* tab>Selection panel, click (Edit). Alternatively, without any selection, in the *Manage* tab>Selection panel, click (Edit).
2. In the Edit Filters dialog box (shown in Figure B–4), in the **Selection Filters** node, select the set that you want to edit and click **Edit...**.

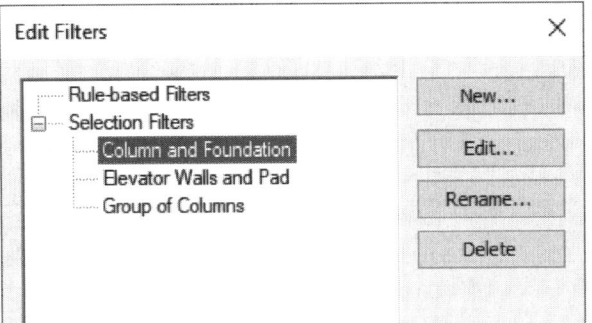

Figure B–4

- If you want to modify the name of the filter, click **Rename...**.

3. The selection set elements remain black while the rest of the elements are grayed out. The *Edit Selection Set* contextual tab displays as well, as shown in Figure B–5.

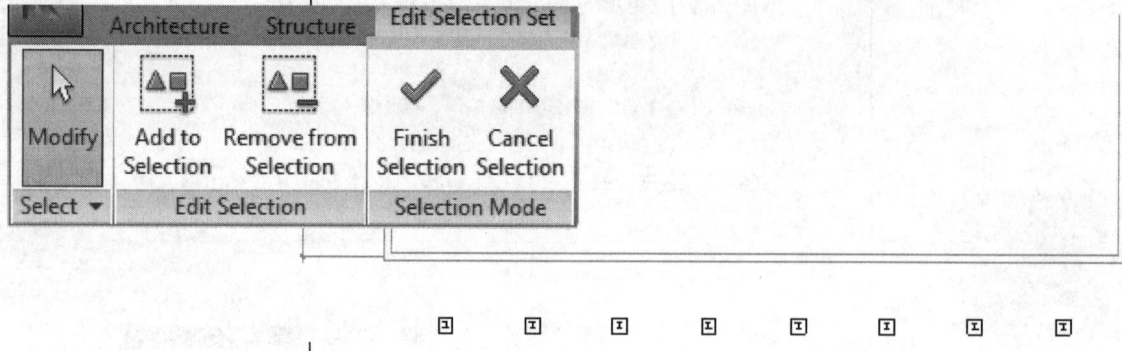

Figure B–5

4. Use (Add to Selection) to select additional elements for the set and (Remove from Selection) to delete elements from the set.

5. When you have finished editing, click (Finish Selection).

- In the Edit Filters dialog box, click **OK** to finish.

Additional Tools

B.2 Placing Slanted Structural Columns

In today's building designs, it is not uncommon to come across slanted (tilted) structural columns, as shown in Figure B–6. Slanted structural columns can be placed in plan views, elevations, sections, or 3D views.

Figure B–6

- Slanted columns are not included in graphical column schedules, but can be included in building component schedules based on structural columns.

How To: Place Slanted Structural Columns in Plan Views

1. In the *Structure* tab>Structure panel, click (Column).
2. In the Type Selector, select the required column type.
3. In the *Modify | Place Structural Column* tab>Placement panel, click (Slanted Column).
4. In the Options Bar, set the elevation for the *1st Click* and *2nd Click*, as shown in Figure B–7. You can also set the offsets from the elevation.

Figure B–7

5. Select a point for the *1st Click*.
6. For the *2nd Click* location (with the elevation set in the Options Bar), select a point on any required element or anywhere in the drawing area.

Working in 3D Views

The simplest way to place a slanted column in a 3D view is to set the **3D Snapping** option and then select two points anywhere along a structural element or on an endpoint, as shown on the left in Figure B–8.

In progress *Completed column*

Figure B–8

- The selection of structural elements defaults to the structural analysis line. This ensures that the slanted structural column is joined correctly for support and analysis.

Additional Tools

Working in Elevations or Sections

While placing a slanted structural column in an elevation or a section view, you want to set the work plane along a grid line or named reference plane. This can be done before or during the **Structural Column** command.

- In the Work Plane dialog box, select a work plane from the Name drop-down list, as shown in Figure B–9. Click **OK**.

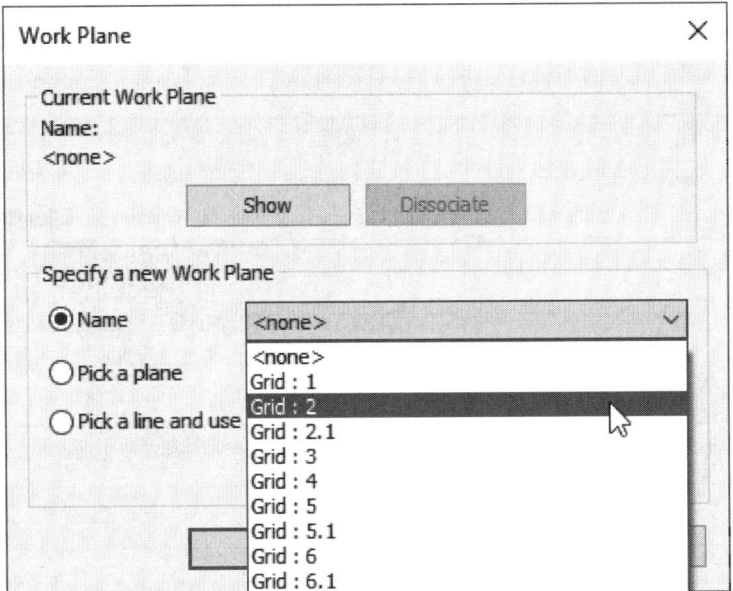

Figure B–9

Modifying Slanted Structural Columns

Several tools enable you to modify slanted structural columns:

- A slanted column can be adjusted along an attached beam and be able to cut the slanted column to an attached structural floor or slab.

- A slanted column can be cut horizontally, vertically, or perpendicularly, even when it is not attached to an element.

- Beam joins automatically adjust when resizing an existing slanted column.

B.3 Editing Wall Joins

Use **Edit Wall Joins** to modify the configuration of the intersections, as shown in Figure B–10. Do not use this command if you have complex wall joins; instead, modify the length of the wall in relation to the adjoining walls.

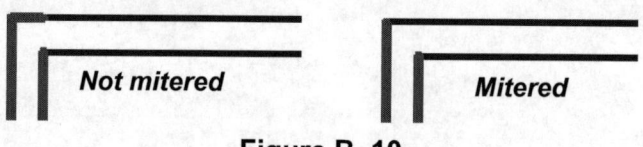

Figure B–10

How To: Modify the Configuration of a Wall Join

1. In the *Modify* tab>Geometry panel, click (Wall Joins).
2. Click on the wall join that you want to edit. There is a square box around the join. Hold <Ctrl> to select multiple joins.
3. In the Options Bar, the configuration options display, as shown in Figure B–11. Select the required option.

Figure B–11

- Select from three configurations: **Butt**, **Miter**, and **Square off**, as shown in Figure B–12.

Figure B–12

- Click **Previous** and **Next** to toggle the butt or squared-off corner configurations through the various intersection options.
- **Allow Join** automatically cleans up the join while **Disallow Join** breaks the connection.

4. The **Wall Joins** command remains active until you select another command.

Additional Tools

How To: Modify Display Options of Wall Joins

1. In the *Modify* tab>Geometry panel, click (Wall Joins).
2. Click on the wall join that you want to edit.
    - To modify multiple joins at the same time, draw a window around several wall intersections (as shown in Figure B–13), or hold <Ctrl> and pick additional intersections. A square box displays around each join.

Figure B–13

- The *Display* controls whether or not wall joins are displayed. The options are **Use View Setting** (set up in View Properties), **Clean Join**, and **Don't Clean Join**, as shown in Figure B–14.

Figure B–14

3. If you select the end of a wall that is not joined to another wall, you can change the option to **Allow Join** in the Options Bar, as shown in Figure B–15. Reselect the wall join to make the configurations available.

Figure B–15

B.4 Creating Slab Types

Several slab types are available in the template files that are included with the software, as shown in Figure B–16. You can also create additional slab types based on the provided types, as needed.

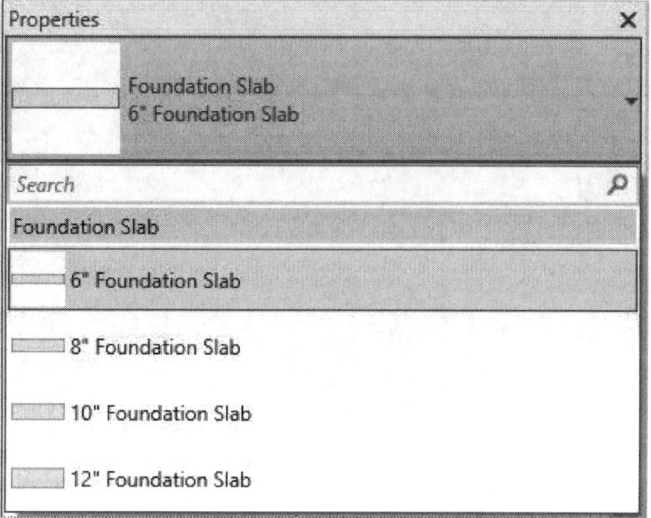

Figure B–16

- Reinforcement is placed in a slab in a separate function. Therefore, you are not required to add it to the slab type.

- The process of creating a structural floor or roof slab type is similar.

How To: Create a Slab Type

1. Start the **Structural Foundation: Slab** command or select an existing slab.
2. In the Type Selector, select a type similar to the one you want to create. In Properties, click ⊞ (Edit Type).
3. In the Type Properties dialog box, click **Duplicate...** and enter a name for the new type.
4. Next to the *Structure* parameter, click **Edit...**, as shown in Figure B–17.

Figure B–17

- You can also set up *Graphics*, *Identity Data*, and some *Analytical Properties* in the Type Properties dialog box.

5. In the Edit Assembly dialog box, as shown with the Preview pane open in Figure B–18, you can change the composition of the slab. When you are finished, click **OK** to close the Edit Assembly dialog box and to close Type Properties.

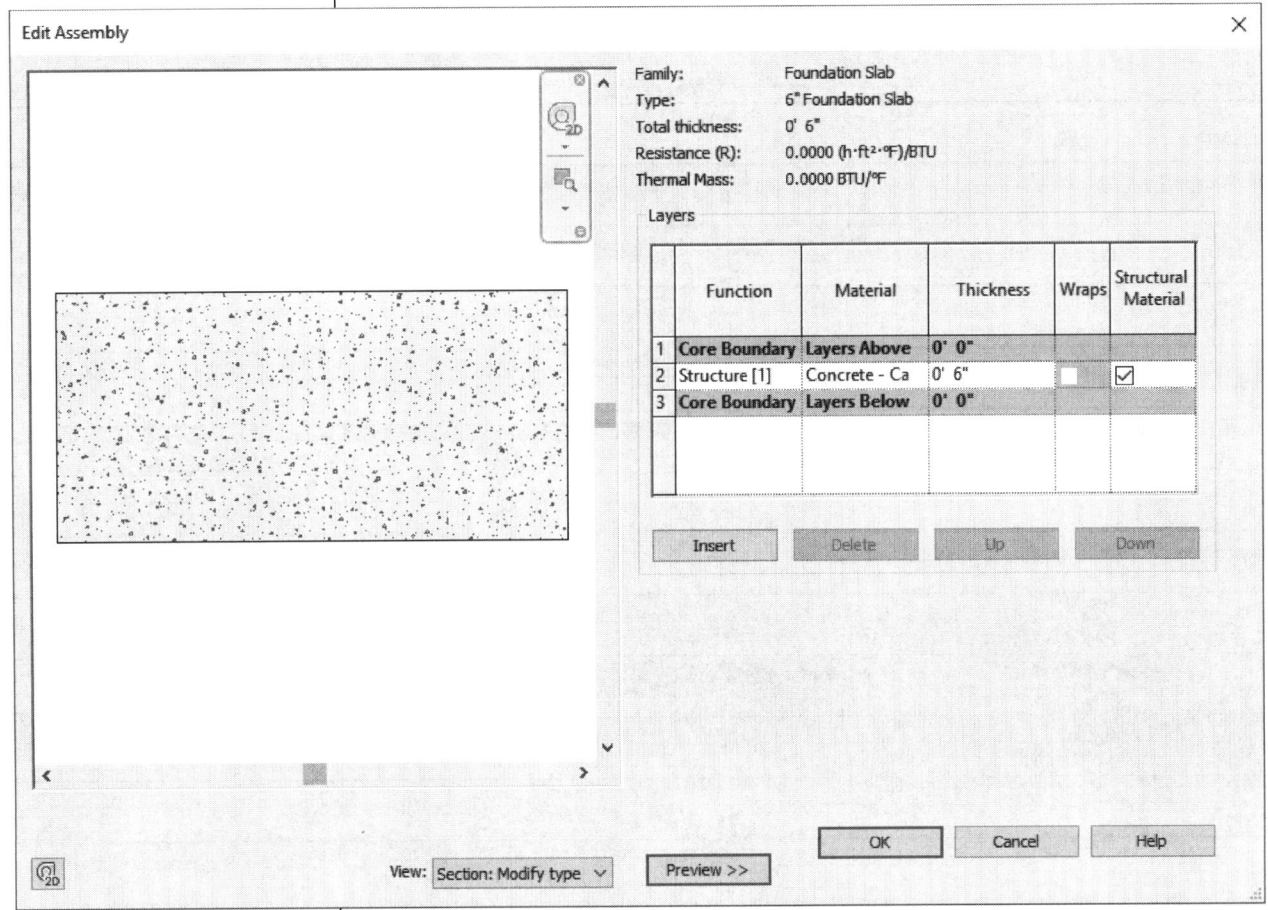

Figure B–18

- When you specify the layers for the compound element, you assign them a *Function*, *Material*, and *Thickness*.

- Use the buttons to insert additional layers and to rearrange them in the layer list. You can also delete layers from the list.

- Core boundaries separate the structural core of the slab assembly from non-structural layers above and below.

- Click **<<Preview** to display the layers of the slab in section. This tool is most useful when the slab is more complex.

B.5 Creating Rebar Types

You can create new rebar types. When a rebar element is selected, click ▦ (Edit Type) in Properties. In the Type Properties dialog box, duplicate an existing type and fill out the rest of the parameters, as shown in Figure B–19. Any changes made here impact all other instances of the Rebar Bar type.

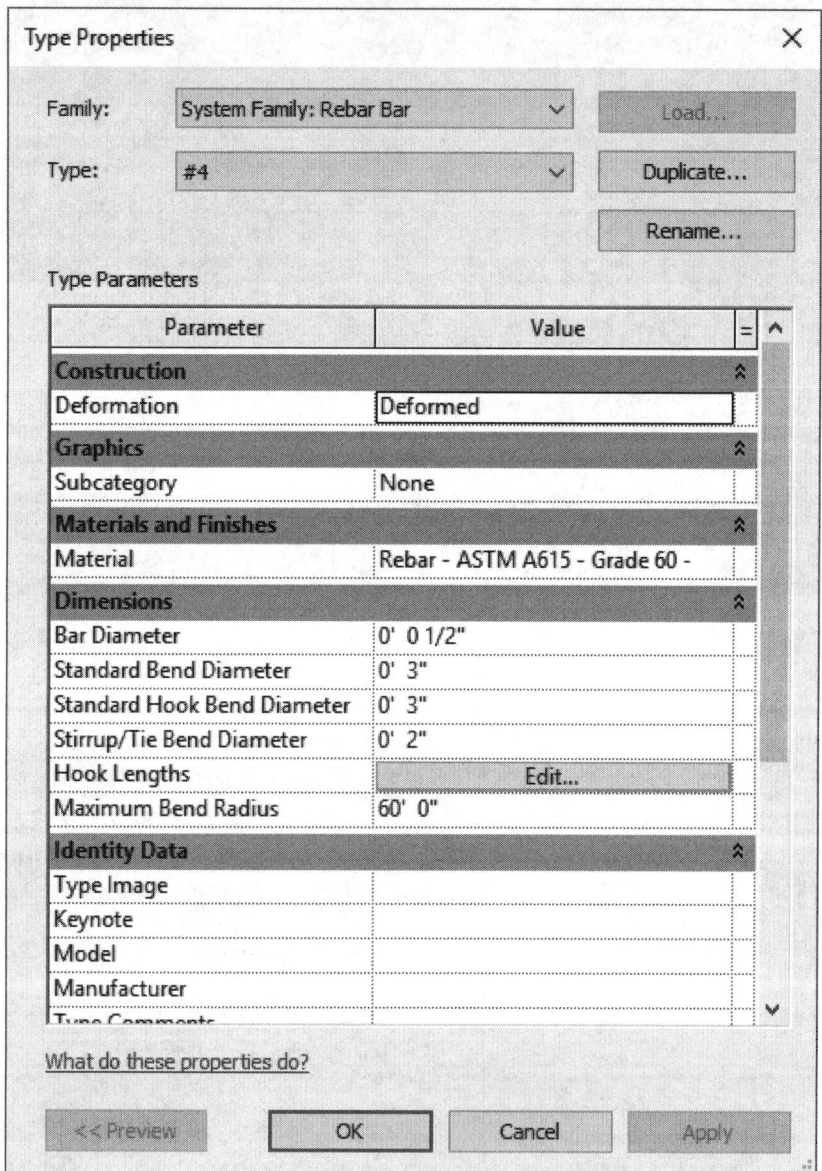

Figure B–19

- You can change the *Hook Lengths* parameter by clicking **Edit...** and using the Rebar Hook Lengths dialog box, as shown in Figure B–20. Options include *Hook Length*, *Tangent Length*, and *Offset Length*.

Additional Tools

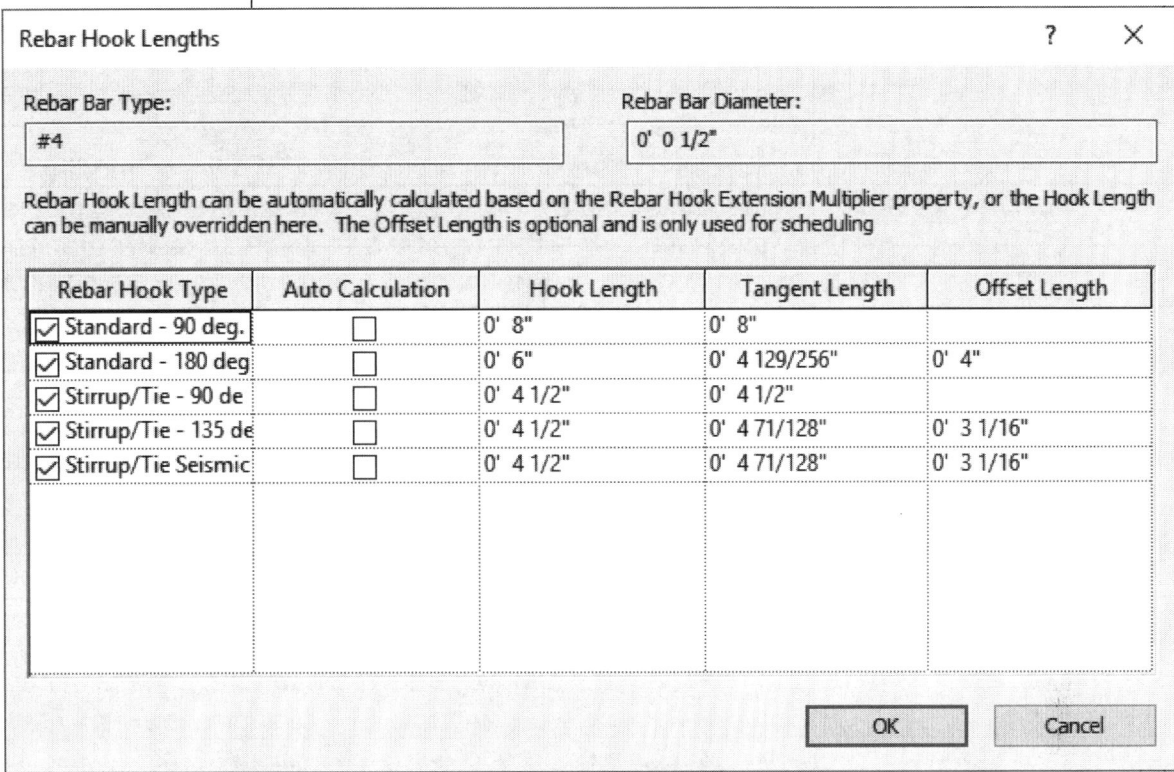

Figure B–20

Hint: Creating Rebar Hook Types

If you need to add rebar hook types, you can duplicate an existing type in the Project Browser, in the *Families>Structural Rebar* category.

Double-click on the new hook type. This opens the Type Properties in which you can modify the *Style*, *Hook Angle*, and *Extension Multiplier*, as shown in Figure B–21.

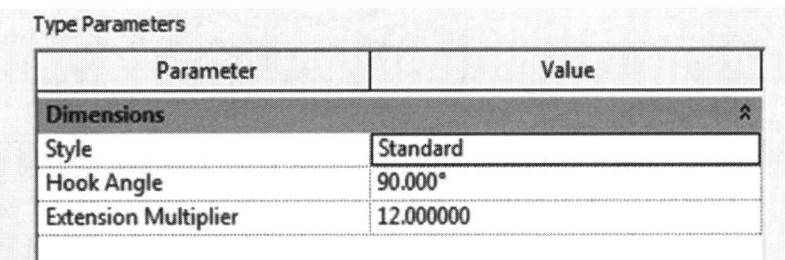

Figure B–21

The *Extension Multiplier* value is multiplied by the diameter of the bar and then adds the bend radius to the equation. Therefore, if the bar *Diameter* is **0.5"** and the *Multiplier* is **24**, the actual hook *Length* is **1'-0"**.

B.6 Editing Plan and Section Profiles

In plan and section details, you might need to modify portions of the cut to display the specific intersection of two faces, as shown in Figure B–22. This can be done using **Cut Profile.** The cut profile changes the shape of the elements at their cut plane, but does not modify their 3D information. The cut is only displayed in the view in which it is drawn.

Figure B–22

- If you are working on a compound face, such as a wall with several layers of information, change the *Detail Level* to **Medium** or **Fine** to display the fill patterns.

- You can modify the cut of walls, floors, and roofs.

How To: Use Cut Profile

1. In the *View* tab>Graphics panel, click (Cut Profile).
2. In the Options Bar, select to edit the **Face** or **Boundary between faces**, as shown in Figure B–23.

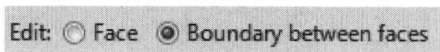

Figure B–23

3. Select the face or boundary that you want to edit.
4. In the *Modify | Create Cut Profile Sketch* tab>Draw panel, use the sketch tools to sketch a new profile, as shown in Figure B–24.

Figure B–24

5. Click (Finish Edit Mode).

- If a warning dialog box opens, verify that the lines start and end on the same boundary line and that they do not make a closed loop or cross over each other.

B.7 Working with Guide Grids on Sheets

You can use a guide grid to help you place views on a sheet, as shown in Figure B–25. Guide grids can be set up per sheet. You can also create different types with various grid line spacings.

When moving a view to a guide grid, only orthogonal datum elements (levels and grid lines) and reference planes snap to the guide grid.

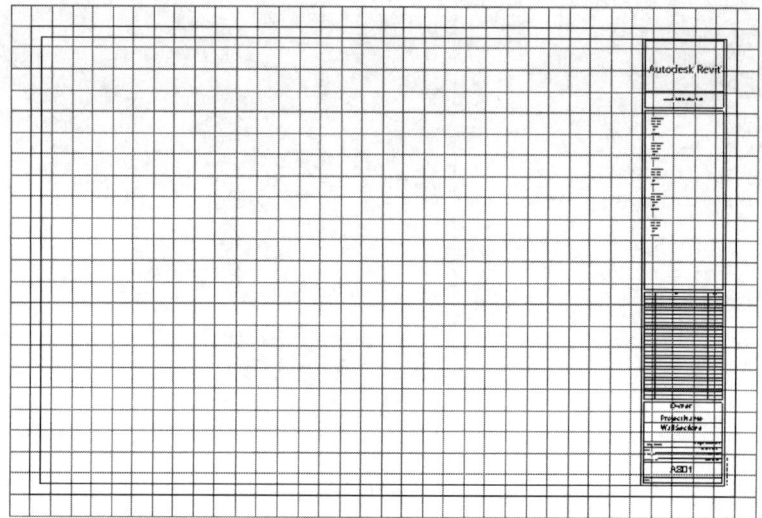

Figure B–25

- You can move guide grids and resize them using controls.

How To: Add a Guide Grid

1. When a sheet is open, in the *View* tab>Sheet Composition panel, click (Guide Grid).
2. In the Assign Guide Grid dialog box, select from existing guide grids (as shown in Figure B–26), or create a new one and give it a name.

Figure B–26

3. The guide grid displays using the specified sizing.

Additional Tools

How To: Modify Guide Grid Sizing

1. If you create a new guide grid, you need to update it to the correct size in Properties. Select the edge of the guide grid.
2. In Properties, set the *Guide Spacing*, as shown in Figure B–27.

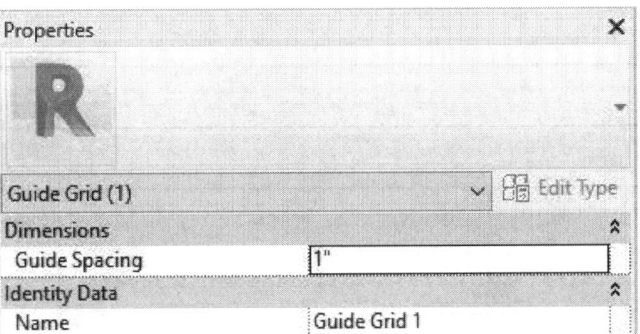

Figure B–27

B.8 Revision Tracking

When a set of working drawings has been put into production, you need to show where changes are made. Typically, these are shown on sheets using revision clouds and tags along with a revision schedule in the title block, as shown in Figure B–28. The revision information is set up in the Sheet Issues/Revisions dialog box.

Figure B–28

- More than one revision cloud can be associated with a revision number.

- The title blocks that come with the Autodesk Revit software already have a revision schedule inserted into the title area. It is recommended that you also add a revision schedule to your company title block.

- You have the ability to create multiple revision numbering sequences, and you can use Transfer Project Standards to transfer these custom revision settings and revision numbering sequences to other projects. (For more information on Transfer Project Standards, see the Revit Help documentation.)

How To: Add Revision Information to the Project

1. In the *View* tab>Sheet Composition panel, click (Sheet Issues/Revisions).
2. In the Sheet Issues/Revisions dialog box, set the type of *Numbering* you want to use.
3. Click **Add** to add a new revision.

4. Specify the *Date* and *Description* for the revision, as shown in Figure B–29.

Figure B–29

- Do not modify the *Issued*, *Issued by*, or *Issued to* columns. You should wait to issue revisions until you are ready to print the sheets.

5. Click **OK** when you have finished adding revisions.

- To remove a revision, select its *Sequence* number and click **Delete**.

Revision Options

- *Numbering:* Specify **Per Project** (the numbering sequence is used throughout the project) or **Per Sheet** (the number sequence is per sheet).

- *Row*: To reorganize the revisions, select a row and click **Move Up** and **Move Down**, or use **Merge Up** and **Merge Down** to combine the revisions into one.

- *Customize Numbering:* Click **Numbering...** to bring up the Numbering dialog box (shown in Figure B–30). You can edit the **Alphanumeric** or **Numeric** sequences or create custom sequences.

Figure B–30

- To create a new numbering sequence, click (New numbering sequence) to open the New Numbering Sequence dialog box. You can specify whether to create the new numbering sequence based off of a Numeric or Alphanumeric type, as well as specify any prefix or suffix, as shown in Figure B–31.

Additional Tools

Figure B–31

- *Arc length:* Specify the length of the arcs that form the revision cloud. It is an annotation element and is scaled according to the view scale.

How To: Add Revision Clouds and Tag

1. In the *Annotate* tab>Detail panel, click (Revision Cloud).
2. In the *Modify | Create Revision Cloud Sketch* tab>Draw panel, use the draw tools to create the cloud.
3. In Properties, select which *Revision* type to use, as shown in Figure B–32.

Figure B–32

4. Click ✓ (Finish Edit Mode).
5. To modify a revision cloud, select a revision cloud and in the Options Bar or Properties, expand the Revision drop-down list and select the revision, as shown in Figure B–33.

If the revision table has not be set up, you can do this at a later date.

Figure B–33

6. In the *Annotate* tab>Tag panel, click (Tag By Category).
7. Select the revision cloud to tag. A tooltip containing the revision number and revision from the cloud properties displays when you hover the cursor over the revision cloud, as shown in Figure B–34.

Figure B–34

- If the revision cloud tag is not loaded, load **Revision Tag.rfa** from the *Annotations* folder in the Revit Library.

- The *Revision Number* and *Date* are automatically assigned according to the specifications in the revision table.

- Double-click on the edge of revision cloud to switch to Edit Sketch mode and modify the size or location of the revision cloud arcs.

- You can create an open cloud (e.g., as a tree line), as shown in Figure B–35.

Figure B–35

Issuing Revisions

When you have completed the revisions and are ready to submit new documents to the field, you should first lock the revision for the record. This is called issuing the revision. An issued revision is noted in the tooltip of a revision cloud, as shown in Figure B–36.

Figure B–36

How To: Issue Revisions

1. In the *View* tab>Sheet Composition panel, click (Sheet Issues/Revisions).
2. In the Sheet Issues/Revisions dialog box, in the row for the revision that you are issuing, type a name in the *Issued to* and *Issued by* fields, as needed.
3. In the same row, select **Issued**.
4. Continue issuing any other revisions, as needed.
5. Click **OK** to finish.

- Once the **Issued** option is selected, you cannot modify that revision in the Revisions dialog box or by moving the revision cloud(s). The tooltip on the cloud(s) notes that it is **Issued**.

- You can unlock the revision by clearing the **Issued** option. Unlocking enables you to modify the revision after it has been locked.

B.9 Annotating Dependent Views

The **Duplicate as a Dependent** command creates a copy of the view and links it to the selected view. Changes made to the original view are also made in the dependent view and vice-versa. Use dependent views when the building model is so large that you are required to split it into separate sheets, as shown in Figure B–37.

Figure B–37

- Using one overall view with several dependent views makes it easier to see changes, such as to the *scale* or *detail level*.

- Dependent views display in the Project Browser under the top-level view, as shown in Figure B–38.

Additional Tools

Dependant views of 01 Mechanical Plan

Figure B–38

How To: Duplicate Dependent Views

1. Select the view you want to use as the top-level view.
2. Right-click and select **Duplicate View>Duplicate as a Dependent**.
3. Rename the dependent views as needed.
4. Modify the crop region of the dependent view to show the specified portion of the model.

- If you want to separate a dependent view from the original view, right-click on the dependent view and select **Convert to independent view**.

Annotating Views

Annotation crop regions and matchlines can be used in any type of view.

To clarify and annotate dependent views, use **matchlines** and **view references**, as shown in Figure B–39.

Figure B–39

- Sketch **matchlines** in the primary view to specify where dependent views separate. They display in all related views and extend through all levels of the project by default.

- **View references** are special tags that display the sheet location of the dependent views.

How To: Add Matchlines

1. In the *View* tab>Sheet Composition panel, click (Matchline).
2. In the Draw panel, click (Line) and draw the location of the matchline.
3. In the Matchline panel, click (Finish Edit Mode) when you are finished.

- To modify an existing matchline, select it and in the *Modify | Matchline* tab>Mode panel, click (Edit Sketch).

- To modify the color and linetype of matchlines, in the *Manage* tab>Settings panel, click (Object Styles). In the Object Styles dialog box that opens, on the *Annotation Objects* tab, you can make changes to matchline properties.

How To: Add View References

1. In the *View* tab>Sheet Composition panel or *Annotate* tab>Tag panel, click (View Reference).
2. In the *Modify | View Reference* tab>View Reference panel, specify the *View Type* and *Target View*, as shown in Figure B–40.

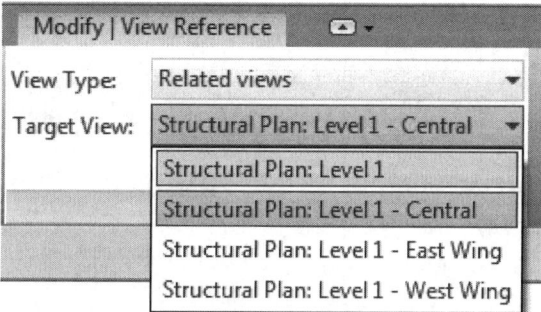

Figure B–40

3. Place the tag on the side of the matchline that corresponds to the target view.
4. Click (Modify) to clear the selection.
5. Repeat the process and place the tag on the other side of the matchline.

6. The tags display as empty dashes until the views are placed onto sheets. They then update to include the detail and sheet number, as shown in Figure B–41.

Before added to a sheet   After added to a sheet

Figure B–41

- Double-click on the view reference to open the associated view.

- If only a label named **REF** displays when you place a view reference, it means you need to load and update the tag. The **View Reference.rfa** tag is located in the *Annotations* folder of the Revit Library. Once you have the tag loaded, in the Type Selector, select one of the view references and, in Properties, click (Edit Type). Select the **View Reference** tag in the drop-down list, as shown in Figure B–42, and click **OK** to close the dialog box. The new tag displays.

Figure B–42

B.10 Importing and Exporting Schedules

Schedules are views and can be copied into your project from other projects. Only the formatting information is copied; the information about individually scheduled items is not included. That information is automatically added by the project the schedule is copied into. You can also export the schedule information to be used in spreadsheets.

How To: Import Schedules

1. In the *Insert* tab>Import panel, expand (Insert from File) and click (Insert Views from File).
2. In the Open dialog box, locate the project file containing the schedule you want to use.
3. Select the schedules you want to import, as shown in Figure B–43.

*If the referenced project contains many types of views, change Views: to **Show schedules and reports only**.*

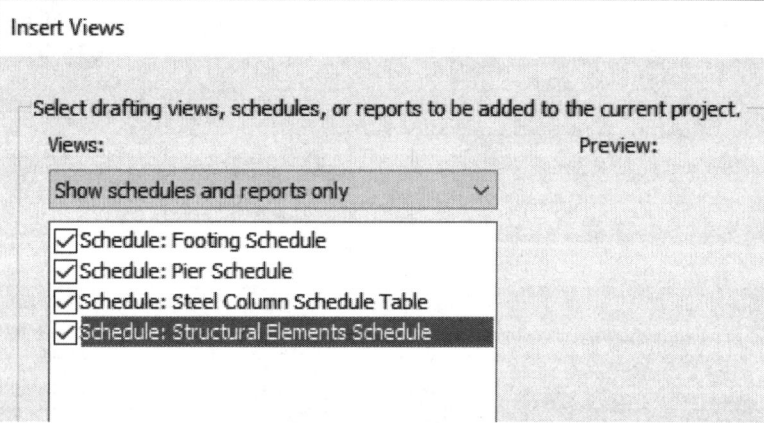

Figure B–43

4. Click **OK**.

How To: Export Schedule Information

1. Switch to the schedule view that you want to export.
2. In the *File* tab, click (Export)> (Reports)> (Schedule).
3. Select a location and name for the text file in the Export Schedule dialog box and click **Save**.

Additional Tools

4. In the Export Schedule dialog box, set the options in the *Schedule appearance* and *Output options* areas that best suit your spreadsheet software, as shown in Figure B–44.

Figure B–44

5. Click **OK**. A new text file is created that you can open in a spreadsheet, as shown in Figure B–45.

Figure B–45

B.11 Creating Building Component Schedules

A building component schedule is a table view of the type and instance parameters of a specific element. You can specify the parameters (fields) you want to include in the schedule. All of the parameters found in the type of element you are scheduling are available to use. For example, a concrete column schedule (as shown in Figure B–46) can include instance parameters that are automatically filled in (such as the **Height** and **Width**) and type parameters that might need to have the information assigned in the schedule or element type (such as the **Fire Rating** and **Frame**).

<Concrete Column Material Takeoff>

A	B	C	D	E	F
		Dimensions			
Type Mark	Count	Type	Length	Base Level	Material
A	6	12 x 18	10' - 0"	Level 1	Concrete, Cast-in-Place gray
B	6	18 x 24	12' - 0"	T.O. Footing	Concrete, Cast-in-Place gray
C	14	24 x 30	12' - 0"	T.O. Footing	Concrete, Cast-in-Place gray
Grand total: 26					

Figure B–46

How To: Create a Building Component Schedule

1. In the *View* tab>Create panel, expand ▦ (Schedules) and click ▦ (Schedule/Quantities), or in the Project Browser, right-click on the *Schedule/Quantities* node and select **New Schedule/Quantities**.

Additional Tools

In the Filter list drop-down list, you can specify the discipline(s) to show only the categories that you want to display.

2. In the New Schedule dialog box, select the type of schedule you want to create (e.g., Structural Columns) from the *Category* list, as shown in Figure B–47.

Figure B–47

3. Type a new *Name*, if the default does not suit.
4. Select **Schedule building components.**
5. Specify the *Phase*, as needed.
6. Click **OK**.
7. Fill out the information in the Schedule Properties dialog box. This includes the information in the *Fields*, *Filter*, *Sorting/Grouping*, *Formatting*, and *Appearance* tabs.
8. Once you have entered the schedule properties, click **OK**. A schedule report is created in its own view.

Schedule Properties – Fields Tab

In the *Fields* tab, you can select from a list of available fields and organize them in the order in which you want them to display in the schedule, as shown in Figure B–48. You can also sort the available fields by Parameter Type, Discipline, or Value Type, as shown in Figure B–48. If you are working in a workshared model, you can schedule worksets.

Figure B–48

Additional Tools

You can also double-click on a field to move it from the Available fields area to the Scheduled fields area or double-click on a field to remove it from the Scheduled Fields area.

How To: Fill Out the Fields Tab

1. In the *Available fields* area, select one or more fields you want to add to the schedule and click ⬅ (Add parameter(s)). The field(s) are placed in the *Scheduled fields (in order)* area.
2. Continue adding fields, as required.

   - Click ⬅ (Remove parameter(s)) to move a field from the *Scheduled fields* area back to the *Available fields* area.
   - Use ⬆ (Move parameter up) and ⬇ (Move parameter down) to change the order of the scheduled fields.

Other Fields Tab Options

Select available fields from	Enables you to select additional category fields for the specified schedule. The available list of fields depends on the original category of the schedule. Typically, they include room information.
Include elements in links	Includes elements that are in files linked to the current project, so that their elements can be included in the schedule.
(New parameter)	Adds a new field according to your specification. New fields can be placed by instance or by type.
f_x (Add Calculated parameter)	Enables you to create a field that uses a formula based on other fields.
(Combine parameters)	Enables you to combine two or more parameters in one column. You can put any fields together even if they are used in another column.
(Edit parameter)	Enables you to edit custom fields. This is grayed out if you select a standard field.
(Delete parameter)	Deletes selected custom fields. This is grayed out if you select a standard field.

Schedule Properties – Filter Tab

In the *Filter* tab, you can set up filters so that only elements meeting specific criteria are included in the schedule. For example, you might only want to show information for one level, as shown in Figure B–49. You can create filters for up to eight values. All values must be satisfied for the elements to display.

Figure B–49

- The parameter you want to use as a filter must be included in the schedule. You can hide the parameter once you have completed the schedule, if needed.

Filter by	Specifies the field to filter. Not all fields are available to be filtered.
Condition	Specifies the condition that must be met. This includes options such as **equal**, **not equal**, **greater than**, and **less than**.
Value	Specifies the value of the element to be filtered. You can select from a drop-down list of appropriate values. For example, if you set **Filter By** to **Level**, it displays the list of levels in the project.

Schedule Properties – Sorting/Grouping Tab

In the *Sorting/Grouping* tab, you can set how you want the information to be sorted, as shown in Figure B–50. For example, you can sort by **Mark** (number) and then **Type**.

Additional Tools

Figure B–50

Sort by	Enables you to select the field(s) you want to sort by. You can select up to four levels of sorting.
Ascending/ Descending	Sorts fields in **Ascending** or **Descending** order.
Header/ Footer	Enables you to group similar information and separate it by a **Header** with a title and/or a **Footer** with quantity information.
Blank line	Adds a blank line between groups.
Grand totals	Selects which totals to display for the entire schedule. You can specify a name to display in the schedule for the Grand total.
Itemize every instance	If selected, displays each instance of the element in the schedule. If not selected, displays only one instance of each type.

Schedule Properties – Formatting Tab

In the *Formatting* tab, you can control how the headers of each field display, as shown in Figure B–51.

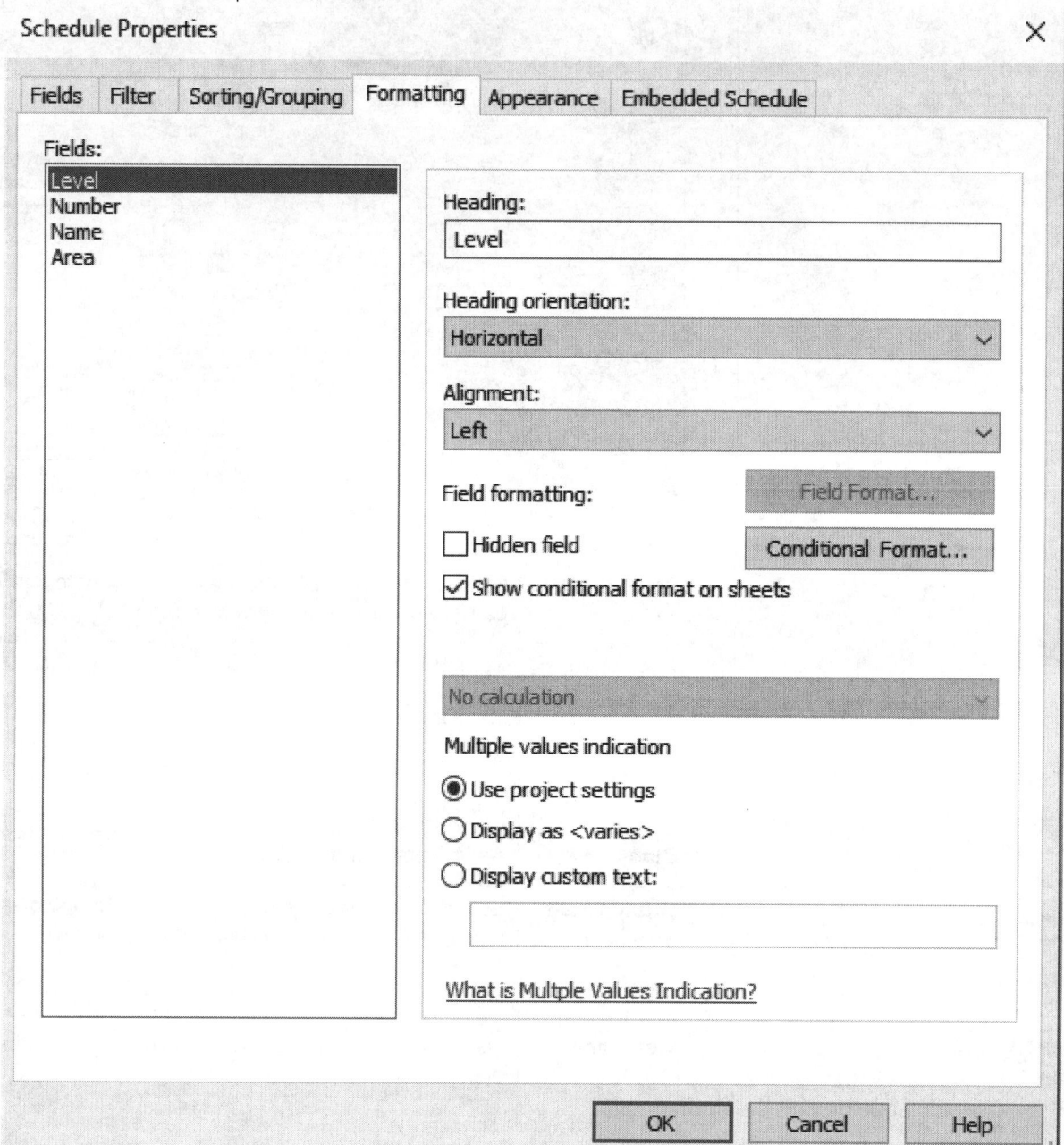

Figure B–51

Additional Tools

Fields	Enables you to select the field for which you want to modify the formatting.
Heading	Enables you to change the heading of the field if you want it to be different from the field name. For example, you might want to replace **Mark** (a generic name) with the more specific **Door Number** in a door schedule.
Heading orientation	Enables you to set the heading on sheets to **Horizontal** or **Vertical**. This does not impact the schedule view.
Alignment	Aligns the text in rows under the heading to be **Left**, **Right**, or **Center**.
Field Format...	Sets the units format for the length, area, volume, angle, or number field. By default, this is set to use the project settings.
Conditional Format...	Sets up the schedule to display visual feedback based on the conditions listed.
Hidden field	Enables you to hide a field. For example, you might want to use a field for sorting purposes, but not have it display in the schedule. You can also modify this option in the schedule view later.
Show conditional format on sheets	Select if you want the color code set up in the Conditional Format dialog box to display on sheets.
Calculation options	Select the type of calculation you want to use. All values in a field are: • **Standard** - Calculated separately. • **Calculate totals** - Added together. • **Calculate minimum** - Reviewed and only the smallest amount is displayed. • **Calculate maximum** - Reviewed and only the largest amount is displayed. • **Calculate minimum and maximum** - Reviewed and both the smallest and largest amounts are displayed. • This is often used with rebar sets.
Multiple values indication	When a schedule is not set to itemize every instance, select how the value needs to display.

Schedule Properties – Appearance Tab

In the *Appearance* tab, you can set the text style and grid line options for a schedule, as shown in Figure B–52.

Figure B–52

Grid lines	Displays lines between each instance listed and around the outside of the schedule. Select the style of lines from the drop-down list; this controls all lines for the schedule, unless modified.
Grid in headers/ footers/spacers	Extends the vertical grid lines between the columns.
Outline	Specify a different line type for the outline of the schedule.
Blank row before data	Select this option if you want a blank row to be displayed before the data begins in the schedule.
Stripe Rows	Select this option if you want to highlight alternating rows within the schedule to help differentiate the rows in large schedules.
Show Title/Show Headers	Select these options to include the text in the schedule.
Title text/Header text/Body text	Select the text style for the title, header, and body text.

Schedule Properties

Schedule views have properties including the *View Name*, *Phase*, and methods of returning to the Schedule Properties dialog box, as shown in Figure B–53. In the *Other* section, select the button next to the tab that you want to open in the Schedule Properties dialog box. In the dialog box, you can switch from tab to tab and make any required changes to the overall schedule.

Door schedule properties

Room schedule properties

Figure B–53

Material Takeoff Schedules

Material takeoff or count schedules (shown in Figure B–54) are used for material estimates and organization. This type of schedule can be added to a drawing sheet, but is typically intended for project quantities.

<Concrete Column Material Takeoff>

A	B	C	D	E	F
		Dimensions			
Type Mark	Count	Type	Length	Base Level	Material
A	6	12 x 18	10' - 0"	Level 1	Concrete, Cast-in-Place gray
B	6	18 x 24	12' - 0"	T.O. Footing	Concrete, Cast-in-Place gray
C	14	24 x 30	12' - 0"	T.O. Footing	Concrete, Cast-in-Place gray
Grand total: 26					

Figure B–54

- The procedure for creating material takeoff schedules is the same as building component schedules, except that it uses a different command. In the *View* tab>Create panel, expand ▦ (Schedules) and click 🚚 (Material Takeoff). Alternatively, in the Project Browser, right-click on the *Schedule/Quantities* node and select **New Material Takeoff**.

- The available fields include all of the material parameters, as shown in Figure B–55.

Figure B–55

B.12 Creating a Repeating Detail

Repeating detail components are very useful when working on complex details, such as those that include a brick wall. You can also create a repeating detail using any detail component, such as the glass block shown in Figure B–56.

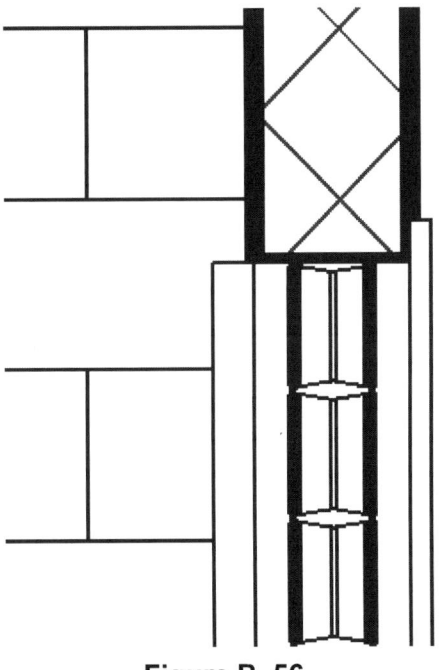

Figure B–56

How To: Create a Repeating Detail

1. Load the detail component that you want to use.
2. In the *Annotate* tab>Detail panel, expand (Component) and click (Repeating Detail Component).
3. In Properties, click (Edit Type).
4. In the Type Properties dialog box, click **Duplicate...**. Enter a name.
5. Set the *Detail* parameter. This is the component name.

6. Fill out the rest of the parameters, as shown in Figure B–57.

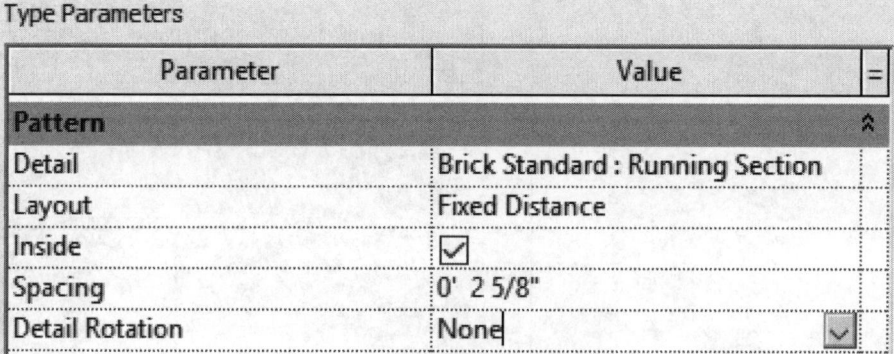

Figure B–57

7. Set the *Layout* to **Fill Available Space**, **Fixed Distance**, **Fixed Number**, or **Maximum Spacing**. Select the **Inside** option if you want all components to be within the specified distance or line. Leaving this option clear causes the first component to start before the first point.
8. Set the *Spacing* between components if you are using **Fixed Distance** or **Maximum Spacing**.
9. Set the *Detail Rotation* as required, and close the dialog box.

Command Summary

Button	Command	Location
Annotations		
	Matchline	• **Ribbon:** *View* tab>Sheet Composition panel
	View Reference	• **Ribbon:** *View* tab>Sheet Composition panel or *Annotate* tab>Tag panel
Slanted Columns		
	Structural Column	• **Ribbon:** *Structure* tab>Create Panel • **Shortcut:** CL
	Slanted Column	• **Ribbon:** *Modify	Place Structural Column*>Placement panel
Revisions		
	Revision Cloud	• **Ribbon:** *Annotate* tab>Detail panel
	Sheet Issues/ Revisions	• **Ribbon:** *Manage* tab>Settings panel> expand Additional Settings
Schedules		
	Schedule/ Quantities	• **Ribbon:** *View* tab>Create panel> expand Schedules • **Project Browser:** right-click on **Schedule/Quantities** node>New Schedule/Quantities...
	Insert Views from File	• **Ribbon:** *Insert* tab>expand Insert from File
n/a	Schedule (Export)	• **Ribbon:** *File* tab>expand Export> Reports>Schedule
Selection Sets		
	Edit Selection	• **Ribbon:** *Modify	Multi-Select*> Selection panel
	Load Selection	• **Ribbon:** *Modify	Multi-Select*> Selection panel
	Save Selection	• **Ribbon:** *Modify	Multi-Select*> Selection panel

Appendix C

Project - Concrete Structure

This appendix contains a practice project that can be used to gain additional hands-on experience with the topics and commands covered in this learning guide. This project is intended to be self-guided and does not include step-by-step information.

Project Objectives in This Appendix

- Start a new project and add datum elements (levels and grid lines) and concrete columns that establish the base of the concrete structure.
- Create the foundation elements of the building, including walls, wall foundations, and footings under the columns.
- Add beams and beam systems to complete the structural framework, and add floors.

C.1 Start a Structural Project

Practice Objectives

- Start a new project based on a template.
- Add levels and grid lines.
- Add structural columns.

In this practice, you will start a new project and add levels, grid lines, and concrete columns, as shown in Figure C–1.

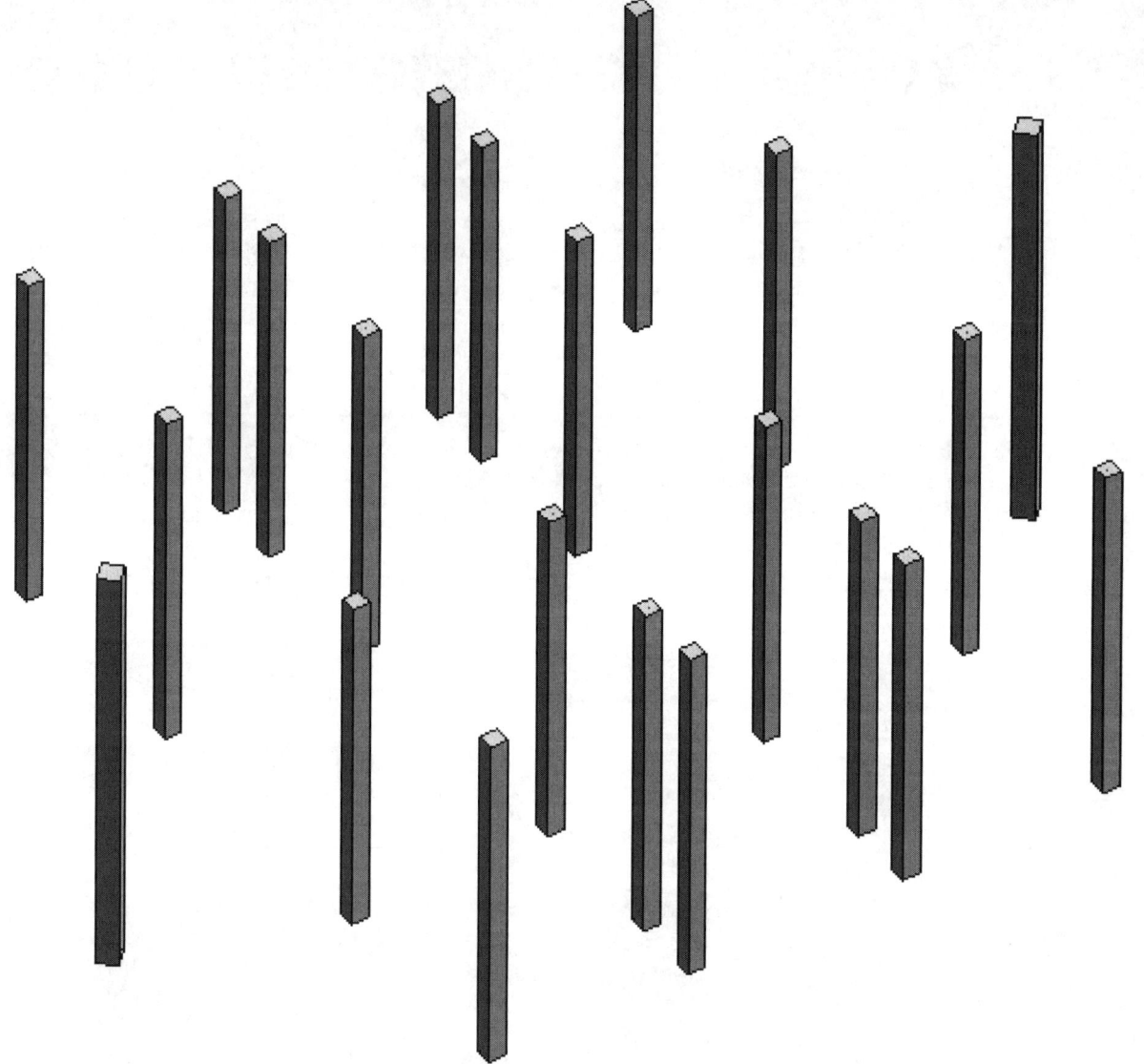

Figure C–1

Task 1 - Start a new project and add datum elements.

1. Start a new project based on the default **Structural Template**. Save the new project to your practice files folder as **Concrete Structure.rvt**.

2. Open the **Elevations (Building Elevation): South** view.

3. Add the levels shown in Figure C–2.

Ensure that you create plan views for each level. If you copy them, you need to add the plan views after finishing the levels.

```
─ ─ ─ ─ ─ ─ ─ ─ ─ ─ ─ ─ ─ ─ ─ ─  Roof
                                 30'-0"

─ ─ ─ ─ ─ ─ ─ ─ ─ ─ ─ ─ ─ ─ ─ ─  Level 3
                                 20'-0"

─ ─ ─ ─ ─ ─ ─ ─ ─ ─ ─ ─ ─ ─ ─ ─  Level 2
                                 10'-0"

─ ─ ─ ─ ─ ─ ─ ─ ─ ─ ─ ─ ─ ─ ─ ─  Level 1
                                 0'-0"

─ ─ ─ ─ ─ ─ ─ ─ ─ ─ ─ ─ ─ ─ ─ ─  T.O. Footing
                                 -10'-0"
```

Figure C–2

4. Open the **Structural Plans: Level 1** view.

5. Add the grid lines that are shown in Figure C–3. The dimensions are for information only.

Figure C–3

6. Save the project.

Task 2 - Add columns.

1. Open the **Structural Plans: Level 1** view.

2. Start the (Structural Column) command. Duplicate one of the **Concrete-Rectangular Columns** types and create a new 24 x 24 column type.

3. Add columns that go from the **T.O.Footing** level to the **Roof** level, as shown in Figure C–4.

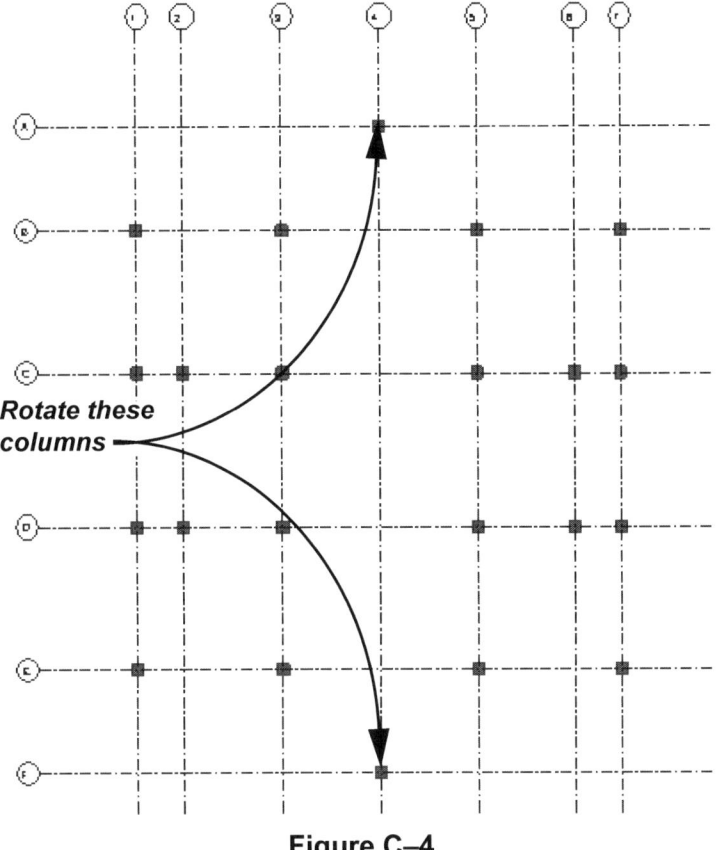

Figure C–4

4. Rotate the top and bottom columns 45 degrees.

5. Open a 3D view to view the columns.

6. Save and close the project.

C.2 Create Foundation Elements

Practice Objectives

- Add structural foundation walls.
- Add wall footings and isolated footings.

In this practice, you will add walls, foundation walls, and isolated foundations, as shown in Figure C–5.

Figure C–5

Project - Concrete Structure

Task 1 - Add walls.

1. Open **Xtra-Appx-1.rvt** from the practice files folder.

2. Open the **Structural Plans: Level 1** view.

3. Draw the walls shown in Figure C–6 using the following information:

    - *Type:* Basic Wall: **Foundation - 12" Concrete**
    - *Base Constraint:* **Level 1**
    - *Base Offset:* (negative) **-10'-0"**
    - *Top Constraint:* **Up to level: Level 1**
    - *Top Offset:* **0'-0"**

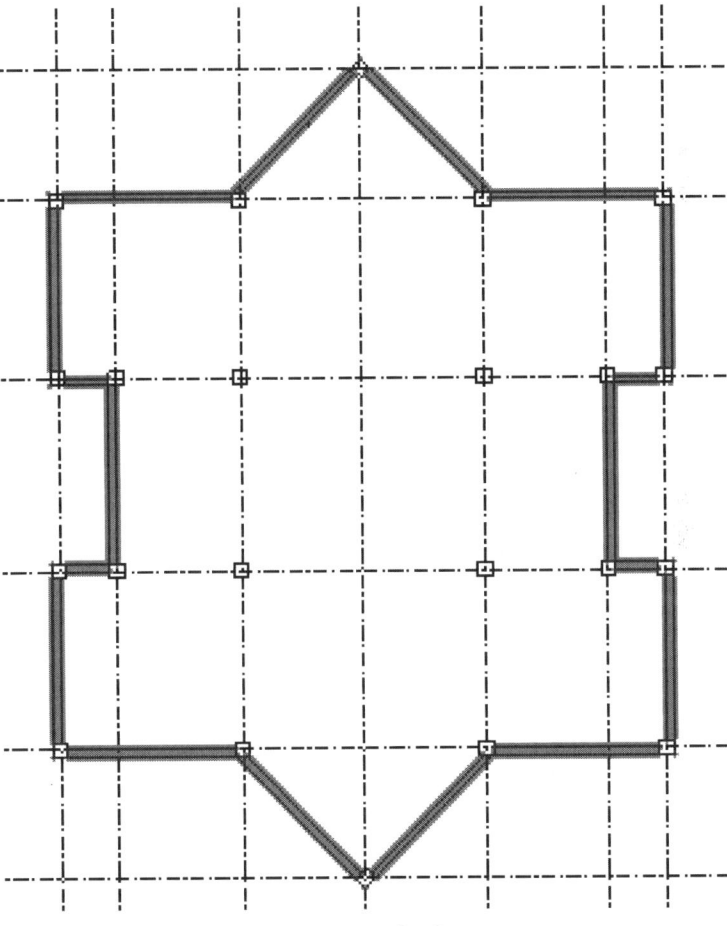

Figure C–6

- The outside edge of the walls are aligned to the outside of the columns.

4. Save the project.

Task 2 - Add foundations.

1. Open the **Structural Plans: T.O. Footing** view.

2. Add isolated footings under all of the columns. Create a new **Footing-Rectangular: 72" x 72" x 18"** in size.

3. Add wall footings under all of the walls. Create a new **Wall Foundation: Bearing Footing - 36" x 18"** in size. When you are finished, the plan should look like Figure C–7.

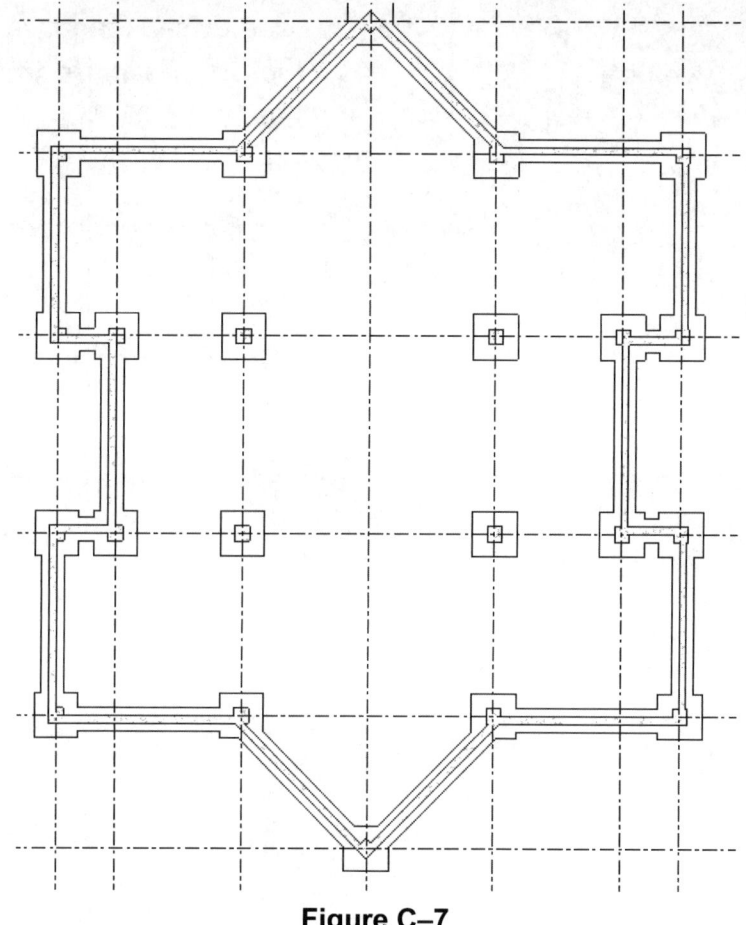

Figure C–7

4. Save and close the project.

C.3 Frame a Concrete Structure

Practice Objectives

- Add beams and beam systems.
- Add structural floors.

In this practice, you will frame the concrete structure shown in Figure C–8. You will add girders using individual beams and joists using beam systems. You will then copy and paste the structural elements to additional floors. Finally, you will add a floor and then copy it to the other levels.

Figure C–8

Task 1 - Add girders.

1. Open **Xtra-Appx-2.rvt** from the practice files folder.

2. On Level 1, add beams using the type **Concrete Rectangular Beam: 12x24**, as shown in Figure C–9.

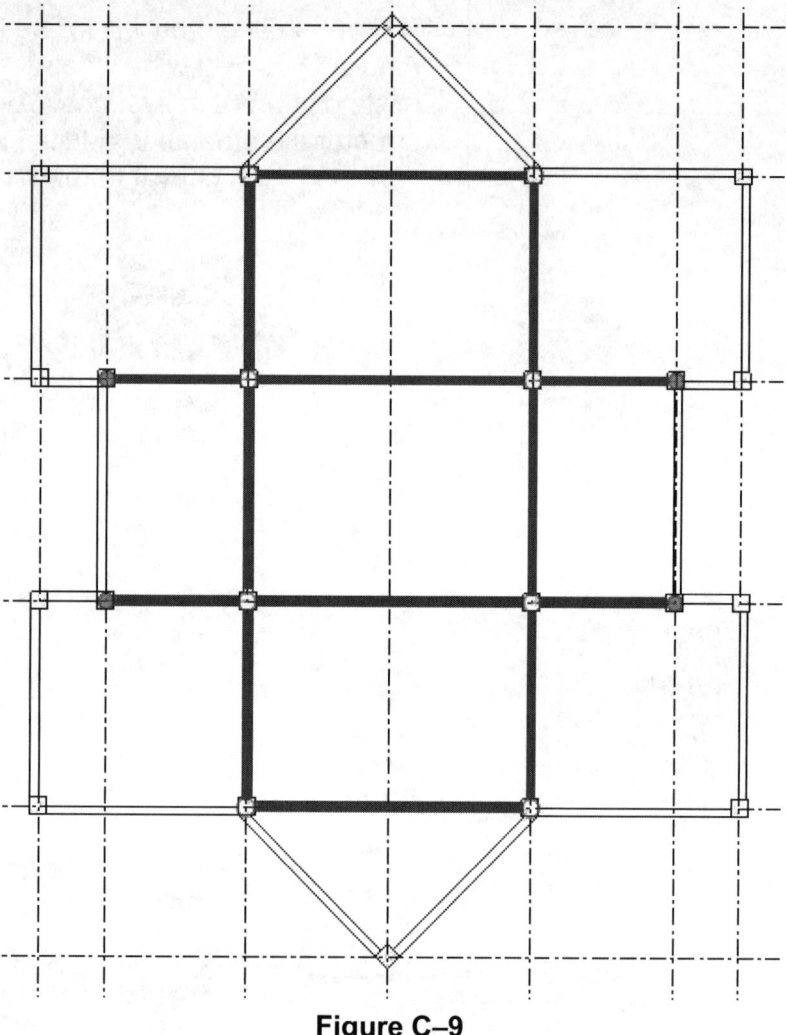

Figure C–9

3. Save the project.

Task 2 - Add joists using beam systems.

1. Load the **Pan Joist.rfa** family from the Revit Library> *Structural Framing>Concrete* folder.

2. Using the (Beam System) command and the following parameters, add the joists as shown in Figure C–10. Where you cannot use **Automatic Beam System**, sketch the beam system.

   - *Elevation:* **4-1/2"**
   - *Layout Rule:* **Maximum Spacing**
   - *Maximum Spacing:* **5'-0"**
   - *Beam Type:* **Pan Joist: 8 x 24**
   - *Tag on Placement:* **off**
   - *Tag new Members in view:* **None (for Sketched)**

Figure C–10

3. Save the project

Task 3 - Add beams and beam systems to the other floors.

1. Repeat the process of creating beams and beam systems on Level 2. All girders should be on center (as shown in Figure C–11) and, therefore, all of the beam systems can be placed automatically.

Figure C–11

- For the angled bays, it is easiest to add the beam system using one of the default directions, and then edit the boundary to change the beam direction.

2. Copy (using **Copy to the Clipboard** and **Paste Aligned**) all of the beams and beam systems from Level 2 to Level 3 and the Roof level.

    - Select only the **Structural Framing (Girder)** and **Structural Beam Systems**, not **Structural Framing (Joist)** as they are part of the beam system.

3. Open a 3D view. The copied beams and beam systems display as shown in Figure C–12.

Figure C–12

4. Save the project.

Task 4 - Adding floors.

1. In the **Level 1** view, add a structural floor using the **Floor: 6" Concrete** type with the *Height Offset From Level* set to **6"**. Select the outside face of the wall for the boundary and attach the walls to the floors.

2. Copy the floor to the other levels above the first floor.

3. The new floors display as shown in Figure C–13.

Figure C–13

4. Save and close the project.

Index

#

2022 Enhancement
   Create a dimension style with prefix and suffix **12-8**
   Export views and sheets to PDF **11-23**
   Grids in 3D view **5-2**
   Import FormIt files **3-2**
   Multiple values indication **B-37**
   Place rebar using Expand to Host **9-13**
   Place rebar using two pick points **9-13**
   Rebar settings remembered for single session of Revit **9-17**
   Remove callout parent view association **4-26**
   Schedule Worksets **B-32**
   Specify which views the callout will show in **4-25**
   Split a schedule **14-14**
   Spot Slope on Ramps **12-13**
   Tapered walls **6-4**
   Tooltip when placing rebar **9-13**
   Transfer custom revision settings **B-18**
   Type driven dimension style **12-8**

3D Views
   Default **1-32**
   Isometric **1-32**
   Locking **12-46**

A

Align command **2-41**
Aligned Multi-Rebar Annotation **12-15**
Alignment Lines **2-5**
Analysis Software **10-2**
Analytical Adjust **10-28**
Analytical Alignments **10-27**
Analytical Justifications **10-25**
Analytical Model Settings **10-8**
Analytical Properties **10-26**
Apply View Template **10-14**
Area Load **10-36**
Area Reinforcement
   Adding **9-42**
   Displaying **9-44**
   Modifying **9-53**
Array
   Linear **2-29**
   Modifying Groups **2-31**
   Radial **2-31**

B

Beam Systems **7-5**
   Automatic **7-5**
   Sketching **7-7**
Beams
   Adding **7-3**
   Adding Multiple **7-3**
   Annotations **12-47**
   Attaching a Column **7-30**
   Coping **7-31**
   Joins **7-32**
Bearing Footings **6-16**
BIM
   Building Information Modeling **1-2**
   Construction Documents **1-5**
   Workflow **1-3**
Bottom Chord **7-38**
Boundary Conditions **10-33**
   Settings **10-11**
Bracing
   Adding **7-8**
   Settings **7-9**
Break Lines **13-10**

C

CAD Files
   Link or Import **3-3**
Callout command **4-23**
Callout Views
   Modifying **4-27**
   Rectangular **4-23**
   Sketched **4-24**
Camera **1-33**
Check Supports **10-10**

Clipboard
    Copy to **2-25**
    Cut to **2-25**
Close Inactive Views **1-10**
Columns
    Create Custom Size **6-26**
    Slanted **B-5**
Consistency Checks **10-10**
Contextual Tabs **2-10**
Controls **2-10**
Coordination Review **3-36**
Copy **2-24**
    To Clipboard **2-25**
Copy/Monitor **3-27**
Copy/Monitor Settings **3-26**
Create
    Local Files **A-4**
    Text Types **12-29**
Cut Profile **B-14**
Cut to Clipboard **2-25**

D

Datum Elements **1-4**
Default 3D View command **1-32**
Delete **2-10**
Dependent Views **B-25**
Depth Clipping **4-30**
Detail Components **13-9**
    Repeating **13-12**
Detail Lines **12-49**
Details
    Annotating **13-13**
    Import **13-8**
    Tagging **13-16**
Dimensions
    Aligned **12-4**
    Angular **12-4**
    Arc Length **12-4**
    Constraints **12-9**
    Diameter **12-4**
    Feet and inches **2-6**
    Labeling **12-10**
    Linear **12-4**
    Modifying **12-5**
    Radial **12-4**
Disable Analytical **10-24**
Drafting Views
    Creating **13-2**
    Referencing **13-5**
    Saving **13-6**
Drag Elements on Selection **2-16**
Draw Order **13-11**
Draw Tools **2-2**
Drawing Aids **2-5**

Duplicate
    As Dependent **4-18**
    Detailing **4-17**
Duplicate views **4-17**

E

Edit Crop **4-25**
Edit Wall Joins command **B-8**
Elements
    Datum **1-4**
    Model **1-4**
    View-specific **1-5**
Elevations **4-34**
    Framing Elevations **4-35**
    Modifying **4-37**

F

Fabric Reinforcement
    Adding **9-47**
    Modifying **9-53**
Families
    Files (.rfa) **1-22**
Far Clipping **4-30**
File Tab **1-13**
File Types **1-22**
Filled Regions **13-14**
Filter **2-15**
Floors
    Slab Edge **8-8**
    Structural **8-2**
Footings
    Bearing **6-16**
    Retaining **6-16**
Foundation Wall **6-17**
Framing Elevations **4-35**

G

Global Parameters **12-11**
Graphical Column Schedule
    Creating **14-3**
Graphical Column Schedules
    Modifying **14-4**
Grids
    Creating **5-2**
    Modifying **5-5**
    Multi-Segment **5-3**

H

Hide
    Categories **4-7**
Hide Analytical Model **10-13**
Hide Elements **4-7**
Hide in View **4-7**
Hook Lengths **B-12**
Hosted Area Load **10-36**
Hosted Line Load **10-36**
Hosted Point Load **10-36**

I

Images **11-11**
Import
    Details **13-8**
    PDF **3-4**
Import CAD command **3-3**
Import Trible and SketchUp files **3-2**
Improved graphics in Realistic views **1-37**
InfoCenter **1-8**
Insert Views from File **B-28**
Instance Properties **1-15**
Interface **1-6**
Isolated Footings
    Placing **6-31**
Isometric Views **1-32**

J

Join/Unjoin Geometry **8-9**

K

Key Plan Legend **12-64**

L

Legend **12-58**
    Components **12-59**
    Create **12-59**
    Key Plan **12-64**
Levels
    Create **3-19**
    Modify **3-21**
Line Load **10-36**
Linear Elements **2-3**
Linear Multi-Rebar Annotation **12-15**
Linework **13-18**
Linework command **13-18**
Link
    Managing Links **3-14**
    PDF **3-4**
Link CAD command **3-3**
Link Revit command **3-12**
Linking vs. Importing **3-2**
Load Cases **10-4**
Load Combinations **10-6**
Load Family **5-21**, **6-33**
Loaded Tags And Symbols command **12-43**
Loads
    Adding **10-37**
    Area **10-35**, **10-36**
    Hosted Area **10-36**
    Hosted Line **10-36**
    Hosted Point **10-36**
    Line **10-36**
    Point **10-36**
    Setting the Direction **10-38**
Local Files
    Create **A-4**
Lock 3D Views **12-46**

M

Matchlines **B-26**
Mirror - Draw Axis **2-28**
Mirror - Pick Axis **2-28**
Model Elements **1-4**
Model Text **12-28**
Modify command **1-12**
Monitor **3-28**
Move **2-24**
Multi-planar Rebar **9-19**

N

Navigation Bar **1-12**
New Project **1-25**

O

Offset **2-46**
Open **1-23**
Options Bar **1-10**
Orient to a Direction **4-43**
Orient to a Plane **4-44**
Orient to View **4-42**
Overriding Graphics **4-8**

P

Pan **1-29**
Paste
    From Clipboard **2-25**
Path Reinforcement
    Adding **9-45**
    Displaying **9-44**
    Modifying **9-53**
Permanent Dimensions **2-6**
Perspective Views **1-33**
Pick a New Host **9-25**
Pick Tools **2-5**
Pin **2-26**
Pinned Elements **2-26**
Plan Regions **4-28**, **4-29**
Plan Views **3-24**
Point Load **10-36**
Print command **11-19**
Project Browser **1-17**
Propagating Datum Extents **3-23**, **5-6**
Properties **2-10**
Purge Unused **5-22**

Q

Quick Access Toolbar **1-8**

R

Rebar
   Constrained Placement **9-17**
   Creating Types **B-12**
   Edit Constraints **9-26**
   Element Types **9-2**
   Hook Types **B-13**
   Modifying **9-23**
   Multi-planar Rebar **9-19**
   Pick New Host **9-25**
   Place **9-15**
   Place By Sketch **9-18**
   Rebar Set Visibility **9-24**
   Rebar Sets **9-16**
   Set Visibility **9-10**
   Varying Rebar Sets **9-27**
Rebar Cover Settings
   Adding **9-3**
   Editing **9-4**
Rebar Sets **9-16**
Reference Plane command **2-8**
Reference Planes **2-8**
Reflected Ceiling Plan Views **3-24**
Reinforcement Settings **9-5**
Rename Views **1-32**
Rendering **1-37**
Repeating Detail Component **13-12**
Repeating Details **B-41**
Reports **1-4**
Reset Crop **4-25**
Retaining footings **6-16**
Reveal Hidden Elements **4-12**
Review Warnings **3-38**, **10-10**
Revision Tracking **B-18**
Revisions **B-23**
Ribbon **1-11**
Roof by Footprint **8-5**
Rooms
   Tags **12-41**
Rotate **2-26**

S

Saving **1-26**
Scale **2-29**
Schedule Properties
   Appearance Tab **B-38**
   Fields Tab **B-32**
   Filter Tab **B-34**
   Formatting Tab **B-36**
   Sorting/Grouping Tab **B-34**
Schedule/Quantities **B-30**
Schedules
   Building Component Schedule **B-30**
   Export **B-29**
   Import **B-28**
   Material Takeoff **B-39**
   Modifying Cells **14-11**
   On Sheets **14-13**
   Working with **14-10**
Sections **4-36**
   Add Jog **4-40**
   Modifying **4-37**
Select
   Drag elements **2-16**
   Elements **2-13**
   Links **2-16**
   Pinned elements **2-16**
   Select elements by face **2-16**
   Underlay elements **2-16**
Selection Box **4-42**
Selection Sets **B-2**
Shadows **1-34**
Shaft Opening **8-19**
Shape Handles **2-10**
Sheet Issues/Revisions **B-18**
Sheets
   Add **11-3**
   Guide Grids **B-16**
   Modifying Views **11-7**
   Placing Views **11-5**
Shortcut Keys **1-12**
Shortcut Menus **1-21**
Show Analytical Model **10-13**
Show Related Warnings **3-38**
Size Crop **4-28**
Slab
   Creating Types **B-10**
   Edges **8-8**
   Floor **8-2**
   Foundation **8-2**
   Roof **8-5**
Slanted Columns **B-5**
Slanted walls **6-2**
Snaps **2-6**
   Settings and Overrides **2-7**
Spelling **12-29**
Split
   Split Element **2-42**
   Split with Gap command **2-43**
Status Bar **1-21**
Stop Monitoring command **3-35**
Structural Columns
   Attach Top/Base **5-18**
   Loading **5-20**
   Modifying **5-18**
   Place At Columns **5-17**
   Place At Grids **5-17**
   Placing **5-16**
Structural Connections **7-25**, **7-26**
Structural Foundation
   Isolated **6-31**
   Wall **6-17**

Index

Structural Plan Views **3-24**
Structural Settings **7-9**, **10-3**
Structural Slabs **8-2**
Switch Windows **1-9**
Symbolic Representation Settings **10-4**
Symbols **12-50**

T

Tab Views **1-10**
Tags
    3D Views **12-45**
    Adding **12-38**
    By Category **12-37**
    Instance vs. Type **12-43**
    Loading **12-43**
    Material **12-37**
    Multi-Category **12-37**
    Tag All **12-42**
    Tag All Not Tagged **12-42**
Template Files (.RTE) **1-22**
Temporary Dimensions **2-6**, **2-10**
    Editing **2-12**
Temporary View Properties **10-14**
Text
    Adding **12-23**
    Create Types **12-29**
    Model **12-28**
    Symbols **12-24**
Thin Lines **4-41**, **9-26**
Tile Views **1-10**
Tooltips **1-11**
Top Chord **7-38**
Trim/Extend
    Multiple Elements **2-44**
    Single Element **2-44**
    To Corner **2-43**
Trusses
    Adding **7-38**
    Attach to Roofs **7-39**
    Bottom Chord **7-38**
    Top Chord **7-38**
    Type Properties **7-40**
    Web **7-38**
Type Properties **1-15**
Type Selector **1-16**, **2-10**

U

Unhide
    Category **4-13**
    Element **4-13**

V

Varying Rebar Sets **9-27**
View Control Bar **1-19**
View Range **4-5**
View References **B-26**
View Visibility States (Rebar) **9-10**
ViewCube **1-35**
Views **1-4**
    Camera **1-31**
    Default 3D View **1-31**
    Dependant **B-25**
    Duplicate View **4-18**
    Duplication Types **4-17**
    Plan Region **4-29**
    Renaming **1-32**
    Underlay **4-4**
View-Specific Elements **1-5**
Visibility/Graphics Overrides **4-10**
    Display Settings **3-15**
    Halftone **3-6**
Visual Styles **1-36**

W

Walls
    Edit Profile **6-19**
    Foundation **6-17**
    Modeling **6-6**
    Tapered walls **6-4**
    Wall Adjustment command **10-29**
Web **7-38**
Worksets **A-2**
    Saving Files **A-6**

Z

Zoom **1-29**